EXTREMES IN THE ARCHIPELAGO

V E R H A N D E L I N G E N
VAN HET KONINKLIJK INSTITUUT
VOOR TAAL-, LAND- EN VOLKENKUNDE

190

JEROEN TOUWEN

EXTREMES IN THE ARCHIPELAGO

Trade and economic development in the Outer Islands of Indonesia 1900-1942

2001
KITLV Press
Leiden

Published by:

KITLV Press
Koninklijk Instituut voor Taal-, Land- en Volkenkunde
(Royal Institute of Linguistics and Anthropology)
P.O. Box 9515
2300 RA Leiden
The Netherlands

Cover: Marque's grafische ontwerpen, Leiden

ISBN 90 6718 159 5

Printed in the Netherlands

Contents

List of maps, tables and figures

Maps

Tables

Figures

List of abbreviations

ADEK	Algemeen Delisch Emigratie Kantoor
ARA	Algemeen Rijksarchief (The Hague)
AVROS	Algemene Vereniging van Rubberplanters ter Oostkust van Sumatra
BB	Binnenlands Bestuur
Borsumij	Borneo-Sumatra Handel-Maatschappij
BPM	Bataafsche Petroleum-Maatschappij
BTW	Banka Tin Winning
CKS	Centraal Kantoor voor de Statistiek
DPV	Deli Planters Vereniging
DSM	Deli Spoorweg Maatschappij
IRRA	International Rubber Restriction Agreement
KIT	Koninklijk Instituut voor de Tropen
KNIL	Koninklijk Nederlandsch-Indisch Leger
Kol	Archief Ministerie van Koloniën 1901-1963 (ARA, Colonial Archive)
KPM	Koninklijke Paketvaart-Maatschappij
LVD	Landbouwvoorlichtingsdienst (Agricultural Extension Service)
MvO	Memorie van Overgave
NHM	Nederlandse Handel-Maatschappij
NIAM	Nederlandsch-Indische Aardolie-Maatschappij
NZG	Nederlandsch Zendelingen Genootschap
OBM	Oost-Borneo (Steenkool-) Maatschappij
PNI	Pendidikan Nasional Indonesia
PRV	Pontianak Rivier Vervoer
PVC	Producten Verkoop Centrale (Minahasa)
ZUSUMA	Zuid-Sumatra Landbouw- en Nijverheids Vereniging
VOC	Verenigde Oost-Indische Compagnie
VvS	Verslag van Subagent van de NHM (Report of NHM Subagent)
ZSS	Zuid-Sumatra Spoorweg

Glossary

benzoin	a resin, used for medicine and perfume
cintu	cargo clerk on a boat
copal-	a resin, used for varnish, shellac, and torches
copra	dried kernel of coconut
dacin	pair of scales
damar	a resin
gambir	plant producing an ingredient used in betel chewing, tanning, and dyeing
haji	one who has made the pilgrimage to Mecca
hulu	(lands on) upper course of the river (southern Sumatra)
ilir	(lands on) lower course of the river (southern Sumatra)
jaluran	harvested tobacco field (lit. strip of land)
klontong	Chinese peddlar
kongsi	Chinese cooperative community
ladang	unirrigated field
laukeh	veteran worker used for recruiting
lebak	lands in river bends inundated during rainy season (southern Sumatra)
marga	municipality (southern Sumatra)
panglong	timber industry
pasar	market
peranakan	Chinese born in Indonesia
picul	unit of weight equal to 61.7 kg
pinang	nuts of the areca palm, used in chewing betel
prahu	indigenous wooden boat
rakit	raft
rakit trade	trade of indigenous rubber transported by river raft
renah	naturally irrigated land along a river (southern Sumatra)
sawah	irrigated rice field
singkeh	newly arrived immigrant Chinese
talang	higher ground along a river (southern Sumatra)
toko	shop
tumpakan	small shed on a river raft, used in the rubber trade
uleëbalang	district head in East Aceh
warung	small shop

Note on spelling

Throughout this book I use standard Bahasa Indonesia spelling. This means that colonial names are spelled in the modern way: Djambi becomes Jambi, Benkoelen becomes Bengkulu, Tjepoe becomes Cepu, Pladjoe becomes Plaju. Province names refer to the colonial provinces (residencies). In Chapter II, I indicate in which present province these are located. I refer to the Dutch East Indies as Indonesia.

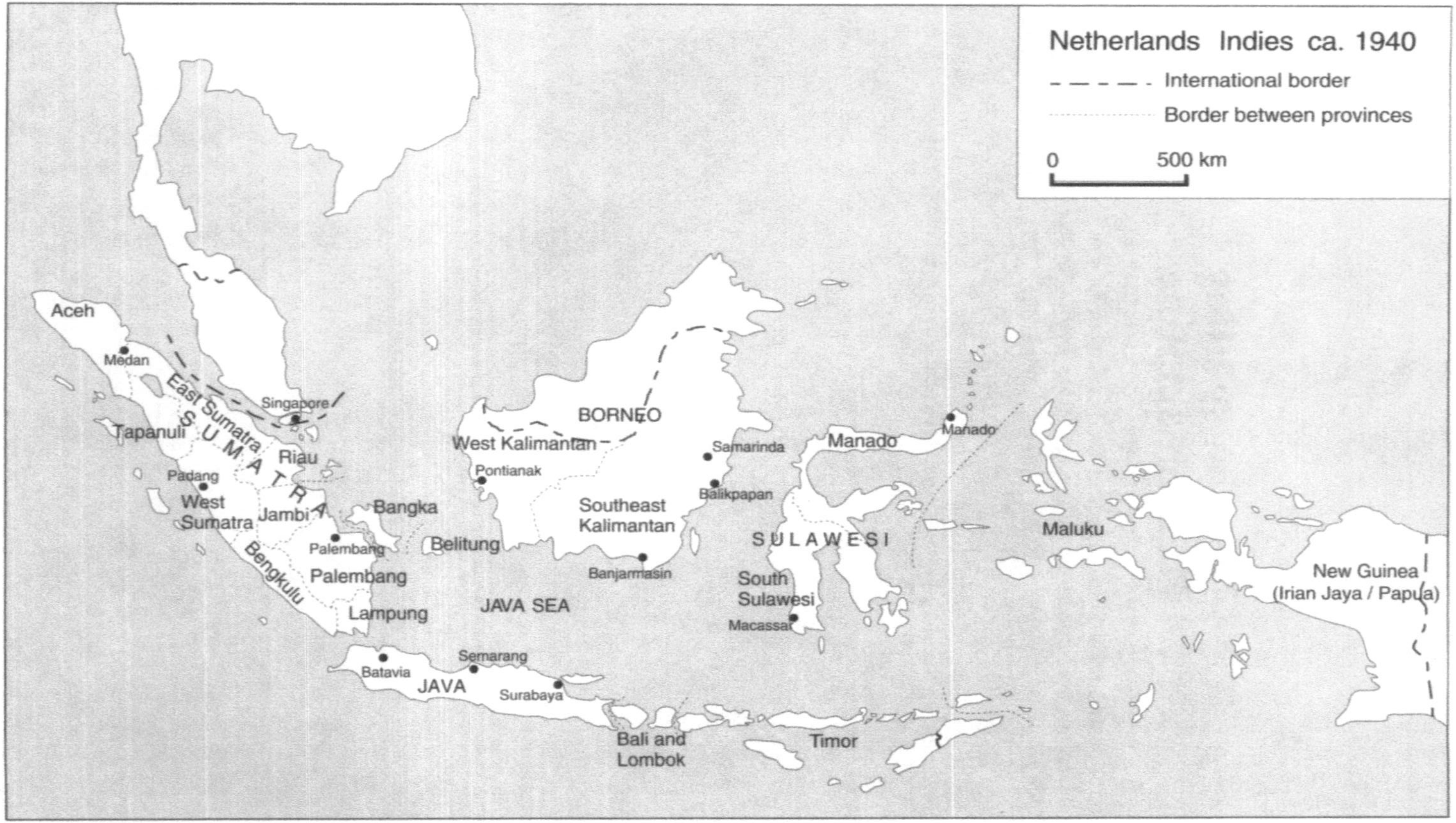

Map 1. The Netherlands Indies in 1940

Preface

To analyse in one book the enormous area covered by the Outer Islands of Indonesia may be seen as overly ambitious. So much of what has been written on the history of Indonesia, however, focuses almost exclusively on Java, leaving the surrounding islands largely unexamined. To fill this gap, I offer an economic analysis of the Outer Islands in the late colonial period. During this period, the Outer Islands formed a vast, productive, generally sparsely populated and fertile area, the setting of a wide range of dynamic economic developments. Although this book takes the dichotomy between Java and the Outer Islands as a starting point, I make a point of differentiating between the individual Outer Islands. This is done on the basis of trade – foreign and domestic – whereby the colonial provinces are grouped according to the type and volume of their trade.

One of the largest and most tumultuous economies of Southeast Asia, Indonesia nowadays attracts a lot of international attention. Indonesia values its history, and the interest of Indonesians in their history is booming. This book is intended to further the study of the diverse and dynamic economic history of late colonial times.

Many people assisted me in writing this book, either through their comments on earlier versions, or in many other ways. First of all I would like to thank Thomas Lindblad, to whom this book is undeniably indebted. Next, in no particular order, I would like to thank Doreen Arnoldus, Peter Boomgaard, Rajeswary Brown, Rita DeCoursey, Peter Doorn, Pierre van der Eng, Marjan Groen, Vincent Houben, Raimond Reijmers, Rosemary Robson-McKillop, Heather Sutherland, Thee Kian Wie, Arjen Taselaar, and the late Hille de Vries. I am of course responsible for all remaining errors.

This research was supported by the Netherlands Organization for Scientific Research (NWO), the Council for the Humanities.

CHAPTER I

Introduction

The dynamic economy of the Outer Islands

The 'conception' of an Asian tiger

Between roughly 1965 and 1997, Indonesia impressed the international community with its solid economic growth. During this period the Western world anxiously observed how Asia's star was rising in the world theatre, and although the financial crisis of 1997 tempered some of these expectations, Southeast Asia has become an important player in the world economy. Among the Southeast Asian economies, Indonesia has been securing its position, displaying a striking economic performance since the late 1960s. Average per capita growth has been well over 4 per cent per year since the inception of the New Order, and over 6 per cent from the mid-1980s to 1997. Indonesia has been regarded as a success compared to other poor and labour-abundant economies as well as to other countries rich in oil and minerals (*East Asian miracle* 1993; Booth 1992b; Hill 1992a:589-90, 1992b). There is no doubt that Indonesia continues to be dynamic and resourceful.

Recent scholarship has drawn a continuous line from early modern colonial encounters to colonial state formation and subsequent independence. Some scholars argue, for example, that the Indonesian economy experienced a period of stagnation between 1930 and 1965, and that this interval formed an intermission in a longer period of economic expansion. It is also argued that New Order policy in Indonesia between 1965 and 1997 bore a resemblance to the colonial regime, and that the emergence of a national economy in Indonesia benefited from colonial economic developments.[1] This is in sharp contrast to the predominantly negative evaluation of colonialism and the effects of the intervention of capitalist countries that prevailed in the 1960s and 1970s.[2] Recent views assess both the positive and negative characteristics of colonial

1 For example Anderson 1983; Booth 1988, 1998; Cribb 1994b; Dick 1996.

2 A survey and selected historiography of the dependency theories, and other theories of development, are given below.

systems and venture to draw parallels between fundamentally different regimes, comparing economic characteristics over longer periods of time.

When the focus is set on the late colonial economic development of Indonesia, during the years 1900-1942, several remarkable features stand out. Whereas Java had dominated the economy for many years, the main economic weight in terms of export earnings shifted during this period to the Outer Islands, where European entrepreneurs produced for export markets alongside Indonesian smallholders. Java suffered from population pressure and a scarcity of arable land, whereas the Outer Islands were thinly populated and had an abundance of land. Within a few decades, the Outer Islands displayed a growth potential that was phenomenal. The dramatic upsurge in exports, and the subsequent opening up of previously relatively isolated regions, was of great importance for post-war economic development, which relied heavily on Outer Islands exports of raw materials.

Research goal

This study focuses on the development of export trade and its economic effects in the Outer Islands during the late colonial period (1900-1942). The aim is to identify and explain differences in the economic development of the Outer Islands, concentrating on the way the various provinces were integrated into the world market.[3] In the study of economic development in the Outer Islands regional differentiation is important, because of the wide diversity in economic structure and factor endowments (land, labour, capital, entrepreneurship) between regions (resulting in different economic performance), and also in the degree of interaction: within the archipelago, with Southeast Asia, and with the wider world. Regional differentiation in the study of export growth necessitates a comparative approach. This means the macroeconomic analysis shifts to the trade performance of each province, examining the differences and similarities between provinces. My aim is to compare regions, to give a survey of comparative economic developments, and to analyse the effects of foreign trade. Such a study cannot be exhaustive in regional detail. However, regional characteristics will frequently be used to obtain insight into local patterns.

Other questions that will be dealt with are: How did European and indigenous entrepreneurship in export trade develop? What was the influence of

3 In the colonial administrative division, the Outer Islands were: eleven provinces in Sumatra (Aceh, Tapanuli, East Sumatra, West Sumatra, Riau, Jambi, Palembang, Bengkulu, and Lampung, and the two tin islands Bangka and Belitung); two provinces in Borneo (West Kalimantan, Southeast Kalimantan); and the 'Great East': Manado, South Sulawesi (*today:* Sulawesi Selatan, Tengah, and Tenggara), Bali, Timor and Dependencies (often referred to as Timor), and Maluku and New Guinea. See Map 1. Current names of provinces are given in Chapter II.

the Chinese intermediary trade? In what way did the maritime trading network in the archipelago contribute to the development of trade? What was the impact of the economic policies of the colonial government?

The next section of this introductory chapter describes the units of observation in this study, and the boundaries in space and time. The third section provides a survey of recent economic historiography on the Outer Islands. Next, the fourth section gives a theoretical framework, based on a review of the scholarship on economic growth and economic development in a colonial economy. The fifth section briefly introduces the archival sources that have been used for this study. The final section of this chapter provides a survey of the rest of the book.

Setting of this study

In the late nineteenth century the Outer Islands were largely unknown territories in a colony that had its centre in Java. While the Pax Neerlandica slowly expanded in the archipelago – with the conflicts in Aceh and Lombok drawing the particular attention of later historians – the presence of the colonizers was concentrated in a few harbours and military outposts, and considerable parts of the archipelago remained largely unknown. During the last decades of the nineteenth century, only East Sumatra had witnessed the settlement of increasing groups of pioneering entrepreneurs near Deli and Serdang, active in the cultivation of tobacco. Outside the Deli region, foreign exports from the Outer Islands were scarce. Between 1900 and about 1940 all this changed. New European agricultural estates were established not only in East Sumatra, but also in Palembang and Southeast Kalimantan. Oil and tin formed the basis of a rapid expansion of the mining sector. The indigenous population produced an increasing output of both more traditional export crops such as coffee and pepper, and new export crops such as rubber and copra. Four phases may be distinguished. The period 1900-1918 was one of gradual growth, whereas export revenues skyrocketed during the period 1919-1928. In 1929-1935 revenues fell when prices slumped, as the foreign markets for raw materials had become overstocked. The Depression of the 1930s led to several years of lower export revenues, estates cutting down on production, and governments slashing their budgets.[4] The final period, 1935-1942, showed a slow but steady recovery. During these years, trade regained its impetus and the government

4 Interesting in this regard is the view put forward by H.W. Dick that the major disruption in economic development was not the Second World War, but the year 1930, which marked a change from a period of expansion to a period of contraction. It also marked the end of an era of free trade (Dick 1993b; see also Dick 1996). This point is also made by W.J. O'Malley (1977:13).

strengthened its grip on the economic processes within the colony. After 1942, the economy of colonial Indonesia was disrupted by the Pacific War.[5]

Boundaries in time and space

The final four decades of colonial rule form a fascinating period for a study of the Outer Islands. Before 1870, apart from a certain measure of 'frontier imperialism', the Outer Islands were largely disregarded by official colonial policy, which concentrated on Java (Fasseur 1979). In a chronological perspective, the nineteenth century may thus be called 'the age of Java'. After the Cultivation System gradually began to be abolished starting from 1870, a 'liberal' period began during which an increasing number of pioneers ventured into the Outer Islands. But it was only after 1900 that the economic expansion of the Outer Islands gained momentum, which is clearly shown by the foreign export figures. Foreign exports from the Outer Islands increased within two decades from less than 100 million to more than 700 million guilders (Figures 1 and 20). Not only did the volume of exports expand dramatically, the character of exports also changed. This change had two aspects: the domination of Java in export production began to yield to the domination of the Outer Islands; and within the Outer Islands, indigenous export production constituted a gradually increasing share. On these grounds, it is possible to assert that after 1900 'the era of the Outer Islands' commenced.[6]

The Outer Islands comprised a vast area, including islands large and small, regions isolated and accessible, soils fertile and infertile. There were regions that were economically active and that underwent rapid change, and regions where the local economy seemed to be less flexibly disposed towards change. Several arguments can be given to motivate a study that concentrates on such a diverse area. Two common features apply to all the provinces: foreign exports of raw materials, and increasing economic integration within the archipelago. A comparative study of this kind is facilitated by the availability of archival data recorded by the colonial administration. Since both government reports and trade statistics were registered at the residency level, researchers have at their disposal sets of comparable data.[7] Of course, aggregate data should not tempt the researcher to assume that the unit of ob-

5 Although the Japanese invasion of the Netherlands Indies began on 10 January 1942, world trade had been seriously disrupted since 1940.

6 I focus on the growth of foreign trade. From a socio-cultural perspective, one may argue that the Western impact on Southeast Asian societies had been felt since 1800, when significant social changes became discernible. This is far more valid for Java and a few coastal regions in the Outer Islands than for the Outer Islands at large. Compare Van Niel 1990:113; Wertheim 1956.

7 In some cases, as in Sumatra, government officials were aware of the fact that internal borders could easily be crossed and that registration of trade flows within one province would not be exact. These caveats will be mentioned where necessary.

servation (in this case the province) experienced a homogeneous development. As in the use of national accounts, such data may obscure a rich diversity in local patterns of economic development.[8] Regional differences at a lower level than the province should not be disregarded. This is especially true in heterogeneous provinces such as East Sumatra or Riau. In the large residency of East Sumatra, most of the estates were concentrated in the small area of Deli. Several islands in the Riau Archipelago, where both European and Chinese companies were established, displayed more economic activity than mainland Indragiri, where indigenous entrepreneurship dominated the economy. Other examples of heterogeneity within a province are Manado, where the Minahasa region was a forerunner in education and Dutch influence, and Southeast Kalimantan, where Hulu Sungai, in the south, was much further developed than the northern interior regions. Other provinces, such as Jambi and West Kalimantan, seem to be more homogeneous, although even in these provinces a distinction should be made between coastal and mountainous areas.[9]

Regional characteristics may also exert influence beyond provincial borders. Minangkabau trading customs were not confined to West Sumatra but resulted in networks throughout southern Sumatra. In coastal Sumatra and Borneo, Malay traders operated very differently from inland Batak or Dayak peoples. Mountain products in the Barisan Mountains in Sumatra were transported to market places in neighbouring residencies, unnoticed by regional statistics. In contrast, for smaller islands such as Bangka, Belitung, Bali, Timor and Dependencies, and Maluku, as well as geographically well-defined regions such as Aceh, the provincial division coincides with most other aspects of colonial economic development. Local differences within the provinces will be dealt with whenever relevant, but they should not prevent a comparison at the provincial level.[10]

A new dualism?

One recurring theme in this book will be the parallel production lines of indigenous export agriculture and European estates. In a study of the Outer Islands it is essential to be aware of the vast economic extremes. There were two types of antipodes. One consists of the contrast between the individual provinces, some provinces being successful and others lagging behind. The

8 In fact, this refers to the assumption in classical economic theory that the Ricardean comparative advantage presupposes a homogeneous domestic economy.

9 As Sutherland says: 'Social, political and economic solidarities do not coincide necessarily with administrative or state boundaries' (Sutherland 1985:132).

10 Compare Hill and Weidemann 1989:4, who, in their study of post-1970 regional development, argue that even though 'sub-national units may reflect arbitrary geographic boundaries', the province can be used as a unit of analysis.

second contrast is in type of production: there was a fundamental difference between the low-capital, poor-quality, and small-scale export production of the smallholder, and the relatively capital-intensive European agricultural estates and mining companies. This second contrast has been referred to as economic dualism.

In addressing the issue of economic dualism, or rather, dualist economy, it would be impossible to overlook the concept of dualism as put forward by J.H. Boeke. In his concept of a dualist economy, Boeke typified the Eastern sector as 'stagnant', failing to act according to rational economic thought.[11] This characterization, we now know (and this was also known to agriculturalists in the field in the 1930s), is not true.[12] For many decades, scholars have been refuting Boeke's concept of a stagnant Eastern sector. It has been pointed out repeatedly that the indigenous sector in the economy did respond to market impulses. Accordingly, the reader should perceive my emphasis on indigenous or Asian economic dynamism as a necessary component in the re-evaluation of the forces of growth in the economy – more in line with Higgins's technological dualism (or 'bi-modal production') (Higgins 1984:66). In this study, 'economic dualism' is not used in the traditional sense of explanation. It merely serves as an ordering principle in the analysis of the eighteen Outer Provinces. In the following section on historiography, I will make a few additional remarks on the central position of the dualism debate in the writing of the economic history of colonial Indonesia.

Colonialism: good or bad?

To stress the beneficial effects of the colonial presence or the improvements in the national economy due to Dutch colonial government, without mentioning the negative effects of the intrusion of a Western power into an indigenous society, would be unjust. While some researchers believe that Dutch colonial rule was at least in some respects beneficial to the Netherlands Indies, others maintain that colonial rule negatively affected the development of the colonized countries, which should have taken place on their own strength and along their own path.[13] It cannot be denied that colonialism brought social disruption, economic exploitation, and human injustice. European ways in many cases seriously disrupted traditional customs. They interfered with the social structure, and they unsettled relationships between ruling classes (landowners) and peasants. Some examples of this have been

11 A good summary of the discussion on dualism is that by Wertheim (*Indonesian economics* 1961). One of the first extensive surveys of the weaknesses of dualism is Higgins 1956.

12 This point is stressed by Egbert de Vries, who was an official with the Agricultural Extension Service in Indonesia before the war (Van der Eng 1991:43).

13 See for example Van Doorn 1994:12-3; Breman 1987:3-22.

amply studied, for instance the arrival of European entrepreneurship in East Sumatra and the economic situation in Lombok, where the living conditions of the peasants definitely worsened as a consequence of the hardening attitude of indigenous landowners.[14] Another example is the modernization of the isolated Karo highlands in East Sumatra, where infrastructural developments released unforeseen economic potential in the cultivation of cash crops, but replaced the traditional outlook on life with modern economic thinking, and also replaced handicrafts in silver and gold with cheap foreign imports (Thee Kian Wie 1977; Burger 1975).

This study assumes that the development of versatile indigenous export production was a positive development. In principle, it should result in higher income per capita, and facilitate the development of the local economy in a broader sense. Later in this chapter, a definition will be given of 'development' which includes higher per capita consumption, better access to medical services and education, increasing human dignity, and increasing freedom of choice (Todaro 1992:487). I focus on economic development, and by doing so am prevented from analysing the cultural and socio-political effects of the development of foreign trade in any great depth. Nor will negative ecological consequences of monocultural cash-crop cultivation, however important, be studied in this book. In general, export production may give rise to a justifiable concern about many of these issues. While acknowledging this, it should be emphasized that in many Outer Islands, export growth also brought development and prosperity, most explicitly observed in additional ways of earning income (alongside traditional subsistence methods), and improved infrastructure. The section below on the theoretical background of this study will deal extensively with the debate on the impact of trade on growth and development.

Implications of terminology

In this study, I use the term 'indigenous' to indicate all 'Indonesians' living in colonial Indonesia.[15] This reflects the division by law of 1906, which distinguished three population groups: Europeans, indigenous Indonesians, and foreign Asians (called Foreign Orientals: mainly Chinese and Arabs, but also Indians and others) (Fasseur 1994:37, 40). People of Chinese or Arab origin, even if they had lived in the archipelago for generations, were not considered indigenous.[16] It should be noted that, for example, in Sumatra 'indigenous'

14 Van der Kraan 1980b:173-4. Compare Stoler 1985; Elson 1984; Van Niel 1990:119-20.

15 I prefer the term 'indigenous' because it would be grossly anachronistic to speak of 'Indonesians'. Note that those legally classified as Indo-Europeans did *not*, in most cases, belong to the 'indigenous' group.

16 After 1899, Japanese inhabitants fell under the category of 'Europeans' in regard to jurisdiction. After 1905, however, they were counted in the censuses as 'Foreign Orientals'. See Appendix A.

includes immigrant Javanese or Banjarese as well as native Batak, Minangkabau, and Malays. When the origin or cultural identity of these groups is relevant, it will be indicated. In the indigenous rubber production in East Sumatra, the Batak and Malay population, as well as Javanese ex-coolies who had settled in the region, are labelled indigenous producers. Similarly, coastal Malays in Bangka will be called indigenous, as will the original inhabitants of Bangka – whereas *peranakan* Chinese pepper smallholders will consistently be called Chinese.

Like the term 'Netherlands Indies', the term 'European' is used in this book in accordance with colonial convention. 'European' referred to those of West European or North American origin. As in the census of 1930, in which the population group 'Europeans' consisted of Europeans and Americans, European can be read as 'Western' (*Volkstelling* 1933). However, the term 'European' is preferred to 'Western' to avoid the paradigm 'Western versus Eastern', which suggests a difference in mentality that is not at issue here (Van Doorn 1994:17). Since the centre of gravity in colonial Indonesia had been in Java for centuries, it is understandable that the other islands in the archipelago were historically defined in terms of being outside Java, and thus called the Outer Islands or Outer Provinces ('Buitenbezittingen', 'Buitengewesten').[17]

In this study no specific attention is paid to gender. Within the peasant economy the household was the most important unit of production. The subsistence production of rice as well as many other crops lay predominantly in the hands of the women of the household. This was particularly so in the matrilineal Minangkabau society in West Sumatra, but was also the case in several other provinces. When I use the word peasant or smallholder, I leave aside the issue of whether in fact a male or female member of the household did the work; in most cases I merely refer to the indigenous household as opposed to the European or Chinese household. Indigenous income is often used to mean household income rather than individual income.

The modern economic historiography of the Outer Islands

In the historiography of colonial Indonesia the Outer Islands have received considerably less attention than Java.[18] With the dawning consciousness of

17 'Outer Provinces' or 'Outer Islands' (*Buitengewesten*) was the term used in all government reports, publications, statistics, and correspondence. In recent Indonesian and Australian historiography the latter translation tends to prevail. In some instances, 'Other Islands' is used, as in the series *Changing Economy in Indonesia* (Creutzberg 1975, 1976 and so on) and Van der Eng 1992. This is less exact and stresses the negative, Java-centred definition of the area. I will use 'Outer Provinces' when the emphasis is on the administrative classification.

18 As a general history of Indonesia, the most recent edition of Ricklefs's *A history of modern*

this oversight, many studies and articles have been published in recent years to bridge this gap. I will mention the most important of these studies, divided into four groups:

a. textbooks and conference proceedings on economic history;
b. studies on the Outer Islands as an entity;
c. studies dealing with individual regions; and
d. studies dealing with a specific aspect of the colonial economy.[19]

a. Textbooks and conference proceedings

Several older textbooks provide a thorough and valuable review of the economic history of colonial Indonesia.[20] Although they do not underestimate the economic role of the Outer Islands, specific information by province is scant. In the 1950s and 1960s the number of publications on colonial Indonesia declined. Then, in 1975, a textbook was published of which the manuscript had been written by D.H. Burger in 1955 (Burger 1975). The year 1975 marks the beginning of a new flow of publications on colonial Indonesia. Burger's book surveys the socio-economic history of Indonesia between 1870 and 1955, with emphasis on the institutional development of the economy and its effects on traditional economic institutions. Its treatment of the Outer Islands is typical of many textbooks: only 47 pages of the 250 pages of Part II, on the twentieth century, deal with the archipelago outside Java. The recent textbook by Anne Booth on the Indonesian economy in the nineteenth and twentieth centuries uses a macroeconomic framework and describes the economic history of Indonesia in a well-documented and sometimes provocative manner (Booth 1998).

Readers looking for a good review of the current social and economic historiography of colonial Indonesia may be referred to four recent volumes of conference proceedings, resulting from a joint effort by Indonesian, Australian, and Dutch scholars. The first one, *Economic Growth in Indonesia, 1820-1940*, appeared in 1989 (Maddison and Prince 1989). This volume is characterized by a quantitative-economic approach. The chapter by Thee Kian Wie in this volume is especially helpful on the Outer Islands. He argues that East Sumatra was not typical of the Outer Provinces since it represented an

Indonesia is very useful; pages 125-54 focus on the Outer Islands (Ricklefs 1993). It is interesting that several new textbooks on the general and political history of the Netherlands Indies have been published recently in the Netherlands (Van Goor 1994; Van den Doel 1996; De Jong 1998). The voluminous textbook by De Jong (in Dutch) includes economic aspects and recent debates (De Jong 1998).

19 Reviews of recent historiography are: Van der Eng 1996b; Lindblad 1990a, 1995; O'Malley 1990. Van Niel 1990 concentrates on the historiography of colonialism.

20 Gonggrijp 1938; Furnivall 1944; Broek 1942; Boeke 1946, 1953. A useful encyclopedia on agriculture in the Netherlands Indies is Van Hall and Van de Koppel 1946-50.

enclave economy in which all production factors – apart from the land itself – were imported from outside the region.[21]

In 1990, *Indonesian Economic History in the Dutch Colonial Era* was published, based on a conference in Australia in 1983 (Booth, O'Malley and Weidemann 1990). Of the fifteen chapters, those by Booth and Dick deserve particular mention. Both deal with the archipelago at large. In her valuable contribution, Booth gives a survey of the debate on trade, development, and economic growth. She is the first researcher to have analysed export-led expansion in late colonial Indonesia within the framework of modern economic growth theory. She examines various ideas about the benefits of export growth and the question of why export growth does not necessarily lead to economic development, thereby addressing the applicability to the Indonesian economy of concepts developed by economists (Ricardo, Hirschman, Baldwin, Lewis, Frank, Myint; see further below). Dick examines economic integration within the archipelago and is one of the first to study interregional trade flows. In his introduction, O'Malley presents a historiographical survey, drawing attention to the Java-centricity of much of the nineteenth and early twentieth century literature.

Another pooling of efforts by scholars from Indonesia, Australia, and the Netherlands resulted in a series of conferences in the early 1990s (Jakarta 1991, Canberra 1992, and Amsterdam 1994). Two volumes of proceedings resulted: *New Challenges in the Modern Economic History of Indonesia*, and *Historical Foundations of a National Economy in Indonesia, 1890s-1990s* (Lindblad 1993a, 1996a). These volumes concentrate on a number of key themes, such as Geertz's concept of 'agricultural involution' in Java, and the notion of 'colonial state formation' (compare Lindblad 1995; Cribb 1994). Although the majority of the contributions deal exclusively with Java, the setting deliberately includes the surrounding archipelago, and the authors are aware of the increasing integration within the region. This applies in particular to the conference on 'Island Southeast Asia and the World Economy', held at Canberra in 1992. Proceedings of this conference appeared in part in a special issue of the *Review of Indonesian and Malaysian Affairs*.[22]

Other recent works deal with economic interaction in Southeast Asia. While several older studies analysed the common history of rubber in Sumatra and the Malay Peninsula (British Malaya), others have recently focused on other countries in the region, or even on the regional role of one city.[23]

[21] Thee Kian Wie 1989b; see also Thee Kian Wie 1977.

[22] *Review of Indonesian and Malaysian Affairs* 27 (1993) I-II.

[23] Allen and Donnithorne 1957; Barlow 1978, 1989; Brown 1994. In his book on Singapore, Huff (1994) also discusses rubber cultivation in the Outer Islands.

b. The Outer Islands as an entity

Recent research analyses the economic development of colonial Indonesia more systematically, paying specific attention to the Outer Islands.[24] J.Th. Lindblad has argued that the historiographer's light should be removed from under the bushel. Economic expansion in the Outer Islands has been recognized as a force which led to increasing integration within the colony. This integration sustained the rise of the 'late colonial state', which increasingly separated itself from the colonial mother country, by developing a political consciousness, opportunities for education, and an economy oriented towards other foreign countries. In his article 'Economic Growth in the Outer Islands 1910-1940', Lindblad argues that economic growth was principally a function of the integration of outer regions into world markets, rather than of the internal integration of the Indonesian archipelago under colonial rule. This process yielded a pattern of 'divergent regional fates' which continues to the present (Lindblad 1993b). A critical reader may want to take Lindblad's argument a step further, and argue that the Outer Islands should not be regarded as an isolated group, but ought to be studied in the wider context of Southeast Asia. In recent years Lindblad has in fact moved in this direction (Lindblad 1996c).

The advantages and shortcomings of various classifications of the Outer Provinces into clusters have been evaluated in articles by Clemens and Lindblad (Clemens 1992; Lindblad 1989c, 1990b, 1994a). In addition to the usual geographical division (Sumatra, Kalimantan, the eastern archipelago), the size and composition of the population of the individual provinces are taken into consideration. These exercises have inspired my elaborate treatment of the various attempts to cluster the provinces according to common features.

A stimulating introduction to economic expansion and colonial state formation in the Outer Islands is given in the collection *Het belang van de Buitengewesten* (Clemens and Lindblad 1989). Eight chapters, each by a different author, survey topics such as Western enterprise and indigenous rubber production in Jambi and Palembang. The book contains a useful and extensive bibliography of colonial literature on the Outer Islands.

c. Regional studies

A number of studies focus on one province. A book that places the study of one province in a broader theoretical context is the dissertation of Thee Kian

24 There is an ample range of pre-war studies on the Outer Islands. A provisional bibliography can be found in *Het belang van de Buitengewesten* (Clemens and Lindblad 1989). For further detailed references on the individual provinces the footnotes in Chapter II of the present study may be consulted.

Wie (1977), which analyses the economic development of East Sumatra using Baldwin's export technology hypothesis (see further below). A pattern of development for a plantation economy is described, in which an export industry is established by foreign firms with foreign capital. Although this leads to a large capacity for exports, the economic structure is one-sided and generates no balanced growth. As the first study of what can be regarded as the modern economic history of Indonesia, Thee Kian Wie's dissertation, defended in 1967 and published in 1977, is an important book.

Pelzer gives a well-written account of the estate agriculture of East Sumatra in his book *Planter and Peasant*, which also devotes ample attention to the indigenous smallholders in this province. More specifically, Stoler analyses labour relations in the estate area of East Sumatra. Building upon these studies, Breman launched a vigorous debate on the living conditions of estate coolies.[25]

In his dissertation *Patches of Padang*, Colombijn describes the history of Padang in West Sumatra. After enjoying several successful decades in the mid-nineteenth century, Padang increasingly lagged behind the trading centres on the eastern coast of Sumatra, Palembang and Medan (Colombijn 1991, 1994). Other analyses of individual regions in Sumatra can be found in a number of publications. Clemens gives a perceptive account of indigenous rubber in southern Sumatra. O'Malley looks at economic and political events in Indonesia during the Depression. Purwanto's dissertation deals with the wider region of southern Sumatra, focusing on indigenous rubber cultivation. I myself have stressed the centre/periphery features of two southern Sumatran provinces, Palembang and Jambi, during the late colonial era.[26]

Southeast Kalimantan, a vigorous residency on the large island of Borneo, is the subject of Lindblad's *Between Dayak and Dutch*. This economic history also deals with socio-political aspects of economic development, and describes how Western rule manifested itself in various fields, including the relationship with the sultans, the levying of taxes, and local infrastructural growth. The pillars of export growth are oil and rubber, the former produced by European and the latter by indigenous producers. The growth effects of export trade are analysed from the perspective of a dualist economy (Lindblad 1988a).

The smaller islands of the archipelago have also been subjected to scrutiny. Somers Heidhues has written a thorough study of Bangka, where tin exploitation led to a large influx of Chinese immigrants. Van der Kraan has written a monograph on Lombok. Heersink's dissertation on Selayar, a small island south of Sulawesi, incorporates much new material on the inter-

25 Pelzer 1978 (see also Pelzer 1982); Stoler 1985, 1988; Breman 1992b.

26 Clemens 1989; O'Malley 1977; Purwanto 1992 (see also Purwanto 1993); Touwen 1991.

regional copra trade in the eastern archipelago. Parimartha analyses trade and politics in the Lesser Sunda Islands.[27]

d. Specific aspects of the colonial economy

The colonial economy was predominantly an agricultural economy, but agriculture underwent changes over the years. Booth and Van der Eng have written studies on agriculture in Indonesia (Booth 1988; Van der Eng 1993a, 1996c). Although European agricultural entrepreneurs imported technology, changes in agrarian technology did not stimulate industry and only a few industries developed in the wake of trade. A well-documented industry in Java, which was significant to copra cultivation in the Outer Islands, is the N.V. Oliefabrieken 'Insulinde'. During the First World War, this copra factory developed into the largest single industrial firm in colonial Indonesia, only to go bankrupt shortly after 1920 (Kamerling 1982).

The best-studied European enterprise in the archipelago is no doubt the Koninklijke Paketvaart Maatschappij (KPM, Royal Packet Navigation Company). In his voluminous dissertation, A Campo has examined the role of the KPM in the Indonesian archipelago from three different perspectives: as an outgrowth of political imperialism, the fruit of economic expansion, and a burgeoning maritime network (A Campo 1992). His book analyses the increasing economic integration within the archipelago, and the imperialist role of the KPM. It elaborates systematically, but also rather long-windedly, on the maritime network as a system, and treats the extension of shipping routes, monopolization, government backing, and the relevant decision making. Post's dissertation also approaches one aspect of the colonial economy from a broad angle, analysing the increasing influence of Japanese enterprise in colonial Indonesia begun long before 1942, in particular outside Java (Post 1991, 1993).

A thorough study of the local expansion of railways in northern Sumatra, though perhaps rather narrow in focus, is Weisfelt's dissertation on the Deli Spoorweg Maatschappij (DSM, Deli Railway Company) (Weisfelt 1972). With other European companies as their theme, articles have been written by Gevers and Van Kommer (Deli Maatschappij), and Baks and Scholte (coal mining).[28] Lindblad has studied foreign investments and the petroleum industry in the archipelago (Lindblad 1988b, 1989a, 1991).

Potting has thoroughly studied the relation between the arrival of European banks and the monetary supply in Sumatra. Van Ark analyses the price fluctuations and the volume of aggregated exports from colonial Indonesia between 1823 and 1940, using an index figure to generate time series (see Ap-

27 Somers Heidhues 1992; Van der Kraan 1980a (see also Van der Kraan 1980b); Heersink 1999; Parimartha 1995.

28 Gevers 1991; Van Kommer 1989; Baks 1989; Scholte 1989.

pendix C). Korthals Altes's dissertation is on the balance of payments of colonial Indonesia between 1822 and 1932.[29]

There is an extensive literature on Dutch imperialism in the archipelago. In fact, this topic incorporates an important aspect of the economic history of the colony: the perception of economic profitability of colonized regions and the efforts made by the colonizers to exploit or develop the colony.[30] In the debate carried on in the literature about the nature of Dutch imperialism, some choose to stress the political factors behind expansion, while others emphasize economic factors alongside political factors.[31] More broadly speaking, imperialism can be said to have exerted a large influence on the economy. As a motivating concept it has an obvious connection with colonial state formation, and the latter is essential in the unfolding of a national economy. In the consolidation of Dutch rule in the archipelago, a distinction can be made between the periods 1808-1870 and 1870-1942. In the second period, after the abolition of the Cultivation System, interest revived in private enterprise, in exploring the Outer Islands, and in strengthening and modernizing government administration in the colony. The Pax Neerlandica allowed European firms to establish estates in the Outer Islands and promoted economic development by facilitating trade and commerce in the Outer Islands (Cribb 1994).[32]

Dualism revisited

A few additional remarks should be made on the historiography of 'dualism'. The observation that parallel production lines existed side by side in colonial Indonesia touches upon an old theme.[33] As argued above, Boeke's antithesis of a dynamic Western sector and a stagnant Eastern sector has been by and large invalidated. Ever since Boeke coined his concept of a dualist economy, dualist development has not lacked attention. Even dependency theories are built on a dualist point of view by assuming that traditional economies will not interact favourably with Western capitalism.

No matter how strong its *prima facie* appeal, dualism as an explanatory theory has been replaced. The contrast between the large, 'rational' estate enterprise and the small, subsistence-oriented indigenous smallholder has

[29] Potting 1987, 1989, 1997; Van Ark 1988; Korthals Altes 1986.

[30] For recent historiography on the imperialism debate, see Lindblad 1989b; Locher-Scholten 1994b; Kuitenbrouwer 1994.

[31] Kuitenbrouwer 1986; Lindblad 1986; Wesseling 1988b; A Campo 1992:21-30. Kuitenbrouwer's book focuses on political motives behind expansion. See also Kuitenbrouwer 1994. An interesting case-study on expansion in one outer province is: Locher-Scholten 1994.

[32] For a more detailed survey of colonial state formation, see Chapter VI.

[33] More recently, the negative perspectives on Asian societies by European observers have been studied by Edward Said in his influential book *Orientalism* (Said 1978).

been shown to disregard the importance of developing peasant cash-crop cultivation. Peasants did not belong to a stagnant, pre-capitalist subsistence sector. Smallholder rubber production in Sumatra and Kalimantan was incontrovertibly the main element in the expansion of indigenous export production. Even though the Depression 'nipped that development in the bud', Boeke's dichotomy in mentality and entrepreneurship quickly became obsolete (Mackie 1980:302-3, Elson 1997).

After exhaustive criticism by Higgins in 1955, the discussion on Boeke's dualism largely came to an end (Higgins 1955-56). Many later publications have examined important aspects of economic dualism, often referring to the segmented or two-tiered nature of the economy to avoid misunderstanding.[34] New contrasts have been added to the traditional dualism, for example, modern versus traditional modes of production; poor-quality versus high-quality production; high-technology enclaves versus labour-intensive, low-capital agriculture; indigenous entrepreneurship versus foreign (European or Chinese) entrepreneurship. The interaction between European trading houses and Chinese, Arab, Bugis, Minangkabau, and other traders can also be mentioned. Avoiding the term 'dualist economy', scholars have written about the 'plural', 'segmented', 'multi-layered', or 'fragmented' economy and the 'plantation-peasant dichotomy'. Some authors prefer Furnivall's concept of a 'plural society' (a concept originally based on different population groups, and not on economic characteristics). Although these concepts are useful in an attempt to avoid Boekean thinking, it is questionable whether these terms are helpful in the analysis of economic development. Fundamentally, as will be shown throughout this study, the economy indeed was split into two sectors. I use the term 'dualist economy' to describe, not to explain, the segmented economy.

The important question is: how wide was the gap between the two sectors? The regional economy of, for example, East Sumatra, Bangka and Belitung, Palembang, and Southeast Kalimantan was greatly changed by the arrival of large European companies. Did the European estates, mines, or trading firms have an impact on the development of indigenous export agriculture and trade, and can that influence be considered as 'bridging the gap' or 'reducing the enclave economy'?[35] It can be argued that, even if European export enterprise did have some linkages with the surrounding economy, the indigenous export economy developed independently from the estates. In-

[34] For example in Booth 1988; Garnaut and McCauley 1980; Lindblad 1988a; Somers Heidhues 1992.

[35] Dualism was incorrectly put forward by Boeke as the basic cause of the contrasts. In the words of Mackie: Boeke's 'Kiplingesque assumption that "East is East and West is West and never the twain shall meet" was a subordinate fallacy' (Mackie 1980:296).

digenous products only reached European wholesalers through intermediary traders. Smallholders generally gained little from the Western presence in the province. According to this view, a considerable contribution to economic development may have been made by the efforts of non-European entrepreneurs, who were running part of the economy independently, in fact fairly isolated from the European enterprises. These questions lie at the core of the definition of a dualist economy, and will be further explored in this book.

Theoretical background

In this theoretical review, I will discuss the essential literature on the theory of economic growth and development. The survey is not exhaustive, because the number of theories of, trends in, and approaches to economic development is very large.[36] As one author wrote, 'economic growth is about as little understood as the human mind' (Rohwer 1995:50). In the final subsections the concepts and analytical framework used in the present study will be introduced.

Theories of economic growth and development

The initial motivation behind theories on economic growth was the ambition to arrive at an explanation of the Industrial Revolution in Western Europe and the United States. After the Second World War, economists also started to direct their attention to economic growth in the Third World. A divergence ensued between those who described and analysed economies scientifically and those who worked on policy guidelines for future economic development.

Despite all these efforts, there is no comprehensive theoretical model that can explain the process or pattern of all economic development. Nevertheless, theoretical models have an important function in understanding economic development, and in identifying the determinants of that development. In historical analysis they should be used carefully. As Thee Kian Wie reminds us: 'Theoretical models are abstractions and distortions of reality, in which often the facts are squeezed and manipulated in order that they might fit into the theoretical construct of the model' (Thee Kian Wie 1980:56).

Three major approaches in the study of economic development can be discerned. In the 1950s and 1960s, the 'stages of growth' theories held sway. Next, in the 1960s and 1970s, theories emphasizing international interdependence gained ground. These 'dependency' theories strongly condemned the effects of capitalism on countries in the periphery. The 'free mar-

[36] For this survey I used Todaro 1989, 1992; Gillis et al. 1987; Muchie 1989; Brookfield 1975.

ket theories' which became all the rage in the 1980s and 1990s took the opposite point of view and stressed the favourable effects of the free market (Todaro 1992:98-9). It is tempting to relate these theories to the attitude of economists and politicians towards the Third World: in 1945-1955 the periphery barely impinged on their consciousness. The Bandung Conference in Indonesia in 1955 changed this, and inaugurated a period of optimism and high expectations. The end of optimism came with the UNCTAD Conference of 1965. The escalation of the Vietnam War may have been one of the reasons for growing scepticism in the late 1960s and early 1970s. The fourth period, which started with the Third World Forum in Karachi (Pakistan) in 1975, was one of increasing pessimism and a re-evaluation of goals (Reitsma and Kleinpenning 1985:4-22). From then on, ideals have been adjusted, although pessimism was not eliminated entirely. In the meantime, the economies of East Asian countries have continued to grow steadily. In 1989, the most recent turning point, the Soviet Union collapsed. Since then, the democratic-liberal system has been advocated by many with renewed enthusiasm as the definitive solution to world economic development (Fukuyama 1992:12). It must be acknowledged that fifty years of economic efforts have far from solved world poverty, and that a democratic-liberal world system also gives pessimists abundant reason to warn against corruption, misuse of power and natural resources, and economic imperialism as was also shown during the Asian Crisis in 1997.

Growth models in colonial history

'Much study of economic growth is statistical in character, the investigators seeking to measure inputs and outputs with great care and to range the resulting data against various theories of growth and development', Kindleberger (1990:20) writes. These words are essentially true of model-based growth theories and of descriptive growth theories. Since the 1980s, scholars have applied modern growth theory to colonial history. Colonial history presents a special combination of a pre-industrial society under the influence of an industrial mother country. As might be expected, the historiography of the colonial economy follows a path separate from the economic historiography of Western Europe. One of the reasons for this difference is that for the construction of almost any econometric growth model, a large quantity of statistical data is required. In the colonial archives, macroeconomic data are scarce.

An interesting example of the use of an econometric model in colonial history is Lindblad's application of Klein's 'Model I' to the economic development of Southeast Kalimantan in the late colonial period, in *Between Dayak and Dutch* (Lindblad 1988a). The author sets out to show that in the economy of Southeast Kalimantan, expansion was induced by trade. The fact that many assumptions and estimations are required shows that this is a hazardous venture, leading to cautious conclusions only.[37] Such an exercise is not feasible for an agglomeration of eighteen individual provinces and will not be attempted here.

But what is economic growth?

A recent textbook on economic theory proposes three objectives of 'development', which constitute a multi-dimensional process that ought, in theory, to be pursued by any country: (a) an increasing availability of basic life-sustaining goods, such as food, shelter, and health services; (b) an improving quality of life, as reflected in increasing incomes, a good educational system, and a wider acceptance of cultural and humanitarian values; and (c) an expanding range of economic and social choices for individuals and nations, freeing them from servitude or dependence.[38] It is generally acknowledged that healthy economic development increases the chance of attaining these objectives - although, of course, other factors such as the political system or environmental pollution may interfere with some of the benefits of growth.

With these objectives in mind, we return to the question how to define 'economic growth'. Economic growth is usually defined as an increase in real national income per capita.[39] Kuznets defines 'modern economic growth' as a sustained increase in per capita income, combined with rapid population growth and broad cultural changes. Growth is sustained when it is no longer interrupted by short-term cyclical fluctuations. This process is the result of an increase in productivity in all sectors of the economy, accompanied by an increase in the scale of production and consumption (due to specialization and concentration of output, and infrastructural improvements). Such growth can be observed in the economies of Europe and North America since about 1820 (Kuznets 1966).

This is a current but broad definition of economic growth. It is also used nowadays by economic historians (Van Zanden 1985). As a concept of eco-

37 Klein's 'Model I' is a relatively simple model, using six equations. Lindblad cautions: 'Operationalization of the variables bridges the gap between theory and reality, but may only be attained at the cost of some additional assumptions' and: 'Slightly more methodological acrobatics are needed [...]'; 'A certain boldness is indispensable [...]' (Lindblad 1988a:202-11).

38 These three objectives originate from Michael Todaro, and constitute a summary of ideas and opinions of such economists as D. Goulet, W.A. Lewis, and D. Seers. (Todaro 1989:14-9, 1992:102). The latter objective also includes being freed from 'the forces of ignorance and human misery'. One could remark that broad statements such as these are time-relative and culture-relative concepts; nevertheless, such objectives are superior to the mere pursuit of economic growth in the narrow sense, and express an ethic which is often lacking.

39 Originally, the United Nations used annual growth of GNP as a measure of economic growth. For example, the official development goal was 6% growth of GNP. Since populations were growing even faster, growth per capita was introduced (corrected for price inflation) (Todaro 1992:98-9).

nomic growth it is more encompassing than earlier definitions, which emphasized industrialization and urbanization. Still, it neglects important indicators, such as regional differences, income distribution, and changes in income distribution (for example, increasing inequality) (Reitsma and Kleinpenning 1985:37-9; Myint 1980:8, 14). In this study such a definition cannot be used because of insufficient macroeconomic data, particularly on a regional basis. But even without quantitative backing, the researcher may observe that the Outer Islands did not experience 'modern economic growth'. Short-term cyclical fluctuations interrupted economic growth, and development was mainly in the primary sector.

Indications of income are scarce in the late colonial era: tax registration was unreliable for a large part of the period, and even if we could deduce a certain approximation of income from imports (which, of course, only partially reflect levels of consumption), the population figures for the Outer Islands would be too incomplete.[40] Although I will relate the population counts of 1920 and 1927 to the census of 1930 and interpolate the figures into a time series, these exercises do not justify using an estimated per capita growth of Gross National Product (GNP) as a sign of economic development (see Appendix A).[41]

Nevertheless, several Outer Provinces experienced economic growth, albeit a 'pre-modern economic growth', which was not sustained over long periods of time, and not necessarily the result of productivity gains. In my assessment of colonial economic growth, I build on the classical economic assumption that economic growth is the result of an increase in production capacity (by expansion of factors of production, or by increase in labour productivity, or by changes in technology). As a consequence, incomes rise (money or goods), taxes are paid, and opportunities are created for further development (such as housing, education, health care). This pre-war economic growth may have been tempered by economic fluctuations, but it nevertheless continued for extended periods over large areas. The acceleration of trade, the effects of which are analysed using the concepts of Hirschman and Myint (linkages and surplus exports; see below), resulted in colonial economic growth in some regions, while in poorer regions such an impact was absent.

40 Unfortunately, it is not possible to trace the destination of imports: the European sector or the indigenous population. This also weakens import figures as a possible indicator of per capita consumption.

41 Maddison and Van der Eng have made GDP estimates for Indonesia for 1880-1989. These estimates include many 'constructed' figures, which makes their reliability difficult to assess (Van der Eng 1992; Maddison 1989a, 1989b; compare Creutzberg 1979).

Economic dynamism

There is a subtle difference in meaning between 'dynamics' and 'economic dynamism'. The word 'dynamics' refers to the mechanism or the structure which lies at the core of the economy. It indicates the configuration of the parts, which also embodies a certain amount of change, because an economy is not static. The 'dynamics of export production' therefore focuses on the mechanism of export trade: for example, which entrepreneurs produced what products and how were they traded and transported? 'Economic dynamism', by contrast, refers to the presence of dynamic behaviour within the economy. 'Economic dynamism' is used in this study when the process of internal transformation gains momentum in response to external impulses and is not stagnant. For example, changes took place in the economy of several provinces as a consequence of world market demand and the developing trading network. Entrepreneurs profited from opportunities for economic growth by engaging in export agriculture, transport, or trade. An important question which will be studied is how such incentives for change were transmitted. Generally, this 'economic dynamism' refers to a climate in which the actors in the economy adapted quickly and flexibly to the changing economic situation, pursued profit maximization, and responded to external impulses. Many regions adapted quickly to the growing demand in foreign markets for raw materials, and to changes in international price levels. By examining the dynamism of indigenous production, it is possible to emphasize developments that can be seen as forerunners of the later economic expansion of Indonesia under the New Order.

Classical economists

One of the oldest axioms of classical economic theory is that trade lies at the core of economic growth. According to Ricardo, trade is based on comparative advantages, and thus leads to economic growth. Say's law states that supply creates its own demand, since every producer in the market wants to trade or spend his revenue on someone else's products. Of course, this notion presupposes that no capital is hoarded: this would cause demand to decline. This criticism is expressed by, among other schools, the neo-marxists, who argued that capitalist trade makes the rich richer and the poor even poorer. This is in opposition to Ricardo's theory of comparative cost, and would turn the degree of international trade into an unreliable indicator of economic growth.[42]

[42] A classical economist would put forward the defence that accumulated money is invested, and as such will re-enter circulation, and create new demand through salaries and payments resulting from new productive capital (the income effect of investment).

In the colonial economy foreign remittances may constitute a 'drain of capital', analogous to the hoarding of capital, which reduces the local income effects of an export industry. This may be the case with European export industries in the colony, but also with Chinese or Javanese immigrant labourers in the Outer Provinces who sent their earnings home. Different views are expressed in the discussion on the negative effects of a 'drain'. Incomes, pensions, and dividend payments were not necessarily spent in the colony nor could they be reinvested anywhere else.

During the inter-war period, refinements were added to the classical theory by Heckscher and Ohlin. Later Samuelson also worked on this model, which was subsequently named the H.O.S. model, or the 'neo-classical model of relative factor endowments'. The key concept of this model is: 'Each country is inclined to export those goods which use relatively many of the abundantly available factors of production' (Bläsing 1978:240; Todaro 1992:330). The model does not include effects from diverging technology or productivity in different countries, and centres on the endowment of factor supplies. Influential critics of this model were W.A. Lewis and H. Myint. In the 1950s, Lewis enhanced the neo-classical view by pointing out that a flow of capital towards the poorer countries, where labour was abundant and cheap, could give rise to new production (this was, in fact, a dualistic view). Hla Myint proceeded with this notion and reformulated Adam Smith's 'vent-for-surplus theory of international trade', which states that unutilized factors can be used to generate export revenues.[43] I elaborate on Myint's theory below.

Stages in development

An important contribution to the study of economic growth and development after the Second World War was made by W.W. Rostow, who revitalized the idea of different phases in history, in his *Stages of Economic Growth* (Rostow 1956, 1960).[44] Rostow's model identifies five stages in the economic development of an industrializing country. According to the model, each country moves from a 1. traditional society, after the 2. development of preconditions, to the phase of 3. take-off into self-sustained growth, after which a 4. drive to maturity takes place, which eventually leads a country to a state of 5. high mass consumption. Rostow states that the take-off into self-sustained growth is only possible when 'leading sectors' propel the economy. The preconditions which should be met in stage 2 are the accumulation of capital, the presence of modern management in entrepreneurship, a good infrastructure, and a completed agricultural revolution.

43 Myint 1958; Todaro 1989:386-7; Gillis et al. 1987:415.

44 Rostow 'revived the notion of stages, as earlier studied by Ashley, Hildebrand, List, Bücher and Sombart' (Kindleberger 1990:15-6).

The idea that every country has to pass through these five stages, of which the boundaries and requirements (such as the rise of the investment level from less than 5 to more than 10 per cent of the national income during the third stage) can be described exactly, has been refuted. Historical research has shown that the exact phases are extremely difficult to distinguish. Despite such flaws, Rostow's model does offer insight into the general process of development, and its concepts have permeated a wide range of historical writing.

Rostow's work was received in the optimistic atmosphere of the early 1960s, a period in which politicians hoped that economic development in the Third World could be achieved quickly. Hopes were dashed, however, because the precondition of agricultural growth formed an obstacle for many poor countries.[45]

During the early decades of the twentieth century, the economy of colonial Indonesia can be said to have been in the second phase. Several preconditions were met during these years, such as improved physical infrastructure, accumulation of capital (although mostly in European hands), and gradual modernization of agriculture and entrepreneurship. There was little industrialization, mostly confined to Java, but certain sectors of the export economy can be considered as potentially leading sectors, such as the oil industry (in European hands) and the rubber industry (in which indigenous and Chinese producers and traders also participated). The terminology of Rostow's model serves in this study to make general appraisals of the relative stage of development of the economy of the Outer Provinces.

With his emphasis on the role of leading sectors, Rostow allows for the occurrence of unbalanced growth, in which key sectors pull the economy forward. In doing so, Rostow renounces classical theory because, according to Say's law, all sectors of the economy must grow equally fast to keep supply and demand in balance, if excess supply cannot be sold abroad (Kindleberger 1990:17). Defending the necessity of balanced growth, other theorists have stated that only simultaneous growth in many sectors of the economy enables the transformation to a modern industrial economy.[46]

A.O. Hirschman, who defined the concept of 'linkages' of industries, also supports the admissibility of unbalanced growth in poor countries. He argues that the government should make initial investments, which must function as investment incentives. I will return shortly to the various types of

[45] Reitsma and Kleinpenning are surprised that single-minded industrialization policies have ignored Rostow's requirement that agricultural output should increase substantially in order to sustain a long-term drive towards balanced economic development (Reitsma and Kleinpenning 1985:12-3).

[46] One may object that Rostow requires a balanced development of preconditions in the second stage.

linkages that a 'leading sector industry' may have in the surrounding economy (Hirschman 1977).

Widening the scope: the structuralist school

Rostow's stages may constitute a wider perspective on economic growth than that offered by classical economics, but in the late 1950s an even wider scope was introduced. The structuralist school of development argued that economic development is much more than the development of market and production, noting that in the Third World the economic situation had worsened in spite of all previous efforts. Several new and complex growth models for poor countries were developed.[47] As Myrdal put it, the whole North-South problem was a consequence of a 'cumulative causal process', in which single causes could not be isolated. This terminology emphasizes the complex character of development (Muchie 1989:24). W.A. Lewis concentrated on the prevention of harmful dualism in developing countries (Brookfield 1975:53-5).

One example of the attention paid to the complex character of the effects of world trade is the Singer-Prebisch thesis, which states that in the long run the terms of trade of raw materials and manufactured goods will turn against their producers.[48] This is a consequence of Engel's law: demand for bulk goods rises more slowly than incomes grow. The consequence is that incomes in the industrialized world grow faster than in areas where income depends on raw materials exports.[49] Singer and Prebisch state that the cause of these problems is found in the monopolistic tendencies of industrialized countries. Kindleberger summarizes: 'My contention is that few generalisations on the terms of trade between the world manufacturers and the world primary producers are valid, but that they tend to turn against underdeveloped and in favour of developed countries.' These observations seem to be confirmed by statistical research.[50]

47 For example by G. Myrdal, R. Prebisch, H. Singer, D. Seers and A. Lewis.

48 Todaro 1989:397; Gillis et al. 1987:420; Muchie 1989:25.

49 Primary exports face sluggish growth of demand' (Gillis et al. 1987:420). There are two types of 'terms of trade':

1. Net barter terms of trade: Tn = Px / Pm. Here Px = the average price of exports = index of export value / export volume. This is an index of export revenue. Accordingly, Pm = average price of imports. However, this figure says little about resulting income effect.

2. Income terms of trade (Ti) gives more information about purchasing power, by relating the index of export revenue (Px*Qx) to an index figure of import prices (Pm). This, by definition, leads to the multiplication of the above formula by Qx:

Ti = Px * Qx / Pm = Tn * Qx. In other words, income terms of trade = net barter terms of trade * volume of exports. This reveals the effects of exports on incomes in the producing country (Todaro 1992:375).

Income terms of trade have been applied to colonial Indonesia several times (Booth 1990b:287-9; Lindblad 1988a:195).

50 Kindleberger 1958:73, 84. G.M. Meier objects in a reaction in the same issue: 'Foreign trade

Essential in the development of a country exporting raw materials is the dependence on a single product, or on a small number of products. The 'carry-over problem' implies that, owing to a one-sided production structure, market price fluctuations may slow down economic development in the exporting country. Monoculture necessarily creates a vulnerability to price levels on the world market. The Hirschman index of export concentration is a suitable yardstick for this development. It calculates the percentage of total export earnings accounted for by the most important commodities. Booth has shown that Indonesia did not have a monocrop economy during the late colonial period and that the export package was relatively diversified, but this conclusion is not valid for each individual province (see also Figures 23a-23q).[51]

Baldwin's 'export technology hypothesis' is a model suitable for the analysis of large-scale export economies in previously isolated regions (Baldwin 1963, 1966). This theory states that the technological nature of the production function of the export commodity determines the extent of the stimulation of growth in other sectors of the region's economy. The characteristics of the export function, for example labour and capital input requirements, or economies of scale, provide a checklist for the various linkages emanating from the export sector.

The 'export technology hypothesis' describes a pattern of development based on export industry using foreign entrepreneurship and foreign capital, in a sparsely populated region with little domestic demand and with a population predominantly employed in the subsistence sector. Baldwin extends Myint's vent-for-surplus theory, by including the linkages of the export industry with the surrounding economy. This model can be applied to a plantation economy, where large-scale agriculture depends on technology (or imported labour) because of the scarcity of labour. The original vent-for-surplus theory assumes a surplus of factors of production. The linkage approach is suitable for an analysis of consequences of estate production using technology and imported labour, as will be shown in the present study.

Thee Kian Wie successfully applied this theory to the development of East

---

need not limit the development of primary product producing countries, but on the contrary may be a dynamic stimulant to their development'.

51 The Hirschman export concentration index is obtained as follows: the exports of the major commodities can be expressed as percentages of total exports. The index is calculated by forming the sum of the squares of these percentages and by extracting the square root of the sum. (Likewise, the concentration of the trade of one country with one or more other countries can be expressed in one index figure.) However, one may leave out the squares and square root exercise and calculate the plain percentage accounted for by the most important commodity and the five most important commodities (as Booth does). In this way the inequality in the contribution of each of the five major commodities is not expressed (Booth 1992a:104-5; Hirschman 1980:xviii-xix, 98-9).

Sumatra during the late colonial era, a sparsely populated region with large-scale European entrepreneurship concentrated in the Deli estate area. One of his conclusions is that as a result of income effects, the tobacco industry in East Sumatra was more beneficial to the surrounding region than was the petroleum industry. But the growth effects of the estate economy were small, mainly due to the large foreign remittances and its technological nature, which was difficult for the indigenous population to copy. Hence there was a weak development of regional demand and, as Thee Kian Wie puts it, the formation of a domestic market did not take place (Thee Kian Wie 1977:46-50, 72, 130-2).

In the Outer Islands, East Sumatra is an exceptional province because of hosting the Deli estate area. Other provinces may be less suitable for Baldwin's approach because they did not constitute a plantation economy to the same extent.

Even more critical than the structuralists: dependency theories

After the relatively optimistic theories of the 1950s, it was acknowledged by economists that forced industrialization in poor countries was no solution for poverty in the Third World. A number of critical and pessimistic theories emphasize these countries' economic and political dependence on industrialized parts of the world. These theories are called 'dependency theories'. A well-known example is A.G. Frank's 'development of *under*development'. Frank argues that the position of Third World export economies deteriorated since their economic development was obstructed by the imperialist motives of the capitalist states (Frank 1973; compare Seers 1981). Other examples are P. Baran and P. Sweezy, so-called neo-marxists (even though in other regards they were not marxist) because of their emphasis on drain of surplus and on exploitation and domination by imperialist states. The centre-periphery theory, advocated by Galtung and Wallerstein (who developed his 'theory of the modern world system'), should also be mentioned here.[52]

These theories concentrate on the negative effects of the development of export industries in traditionally more self-sufficient economies. The colonial era in Indonesia in many respects resembled the dependent situation of post-war Third World countries, and many conditions for development of Third World countries originate from the colonial period. The power relationship between rich and poor countries which is stressed in the dependency theories was a formal bond between mother country and colony – so that, in a sense, dependence was legalized. However, recent research has shown that in many colonies commerce and trading networks preceded the arrival of the colonial powers. Pre-modern economies were not isolated and self-sufficient, but car-

52 Muchie 1989:29; Reitsma and Kleinpenning 1985:200, 221, 263.

ried on considerable levels of trade (Reid 1988, 1993). Therefore the picture of traditional, self-sufficient economies which Western trading companies brought into confrontation with foreign markets and with capitalism, as can be found in pre-war literature, is not correct. Nevertheless, the primary aspect of the dependency theories remains valid: the fact that, in contrast to Rostow's model of linear development through several stages of growth, the countries in the periphery were influenced by the industrialized countries.

From a survey of the literature, we can distil six general characteristics of a country in the periphery:[53]

1. The periphery (or satellite) exports raw materials and agricultural produce to the centre (or core, or metropole) country. Usually, there is a concentration on a small number of crops.
2. There are few growth effects of export production on local infrastructure. There is little import substitution. Raw materials are not processed but exported immediately. This means that linkages with processing industries are absent, and export revenues remain relatively small.
3. The periphery has a high surplus on the balance of trade, but this surplus is drained off to the centre countries. Little capital remains in the region to stimulate new economic activity. (A part of the surplus may remain in the periphery, but is in the hands of local élites, which may constitute a local centre.)
4. Entrepreneurship is predominantly Western, and only incidentally indigenous. Local governments do little to stimulate small-scale indigenous entrepreneurship.
5. Centre-periphery distinctions can be made at the international, the national, or the provincial level, or in specific sectors of the economy. Consequently, the share of European and indigenous entrepreneurship in the periphery may differ by sector.
6. The periphery is forced to import relatively expensive capital goods, which becomes harmful to economic development as soon as export prices decrease. Capital revenues from investments in the periphery flow towards the regional or national centre.

These criteria are met by late colonial Indonesia, which exported mainly unprocessed primary materials. In the Outer Provinces many regions displayed a local specialization in one product, for example copra or rubber. Revenues from the European estates as well as capital revenues flowed out of the country, although a certain proportion of earnings was reinvested. In the mining sector almost all of the (capital-intensive) industries were owned by Euro-

53 Dependency theories show a number of common traits, emphasizing different aspects. I base this summary on Meier 1984:131-4; Reitsma and Kleinpenning 1985:201; Todaro 1989:74, 289.

peans or Americans. Within colonial Indonesia, Java was a regional centre, characterized by a concentration of power and a relative lead in industry.[54] One interesting aspect is that in the agricultural sector indigenous entrepreneurship was strong. This export industry had many linkages with the regional economy and was in fact atypical for a periphery, even though, corresponding to the above-mentioned criteria, little processing industry developed and local import substitution was rare. Regional differences within the Outer Provinces were large: for example, in Sumatra the economy of Jambi constituted an archetypal periphery, while Palembang showed a more diversified economy. In several respects Palembang formed a centre (for Jambi and Bengkulu) and had an economy which was less vulnerable to the world economic situation (Touwen 1991). In both regions indigenous entrepreneurship was heavily tilted towards Singapore, which could be viewed as another centre in the international chain of dependencies at the time.[55]

The dependency theories have been criticized for being too vague and all-encompassing, for claiming injustice without pinpointing a specific mechanism, diagnosing abuse without suggesting a remedy. Some critics have suggested that there is an element of circular reasoning involved: 'Dependent countries are those which lack the capacity for autonomous growth, and they lack this because their structures are dependent ones.'[56] However, this criticism does not explain why some countries or regions in the periphery have developed more successfully than others, notwithstanding the paralysing constraints. For others, the trap of dependence was real, whether circular or not.

In short, the dependency theories draw attention to the injustice of several elements of the economic 'rat race', an injustice which is ignored in many policy and development models.[57] They may also serve to increase our insight into the negative aspects of an economic development which in the short run may seem to be beneficial.

In this study no explicit use will be made of the dependency theories. The

54 Another aspect which conforms to this theory is that in the Netherlands Indies, local élites were allowed a great deal of leeway by the Dutch in exerting power and earning tax revenues.

55 A.G. Frank states that urbanization and large cities have a negative effect on the periphery. Others, such as Hirschman and Friedman, believe that the city has a positive, prosperity-generating role in the economy. In practice, cities often have negative and positive influences simultaneously. In this study, Batavia and Singapore play an important role as trading centres.

56 P. O'Brien, as quoted in Reitsma and Kleinpenning 1985:254. Compare Muchie 1989:38.

57 More recent criticism on the loans supplied by the World Bank and the International Monetary Fund can be mentioned here. These merely cause the foreign debt of Third World countries to increase, which may be harmful to their economic development and increase their international dependence. Alternative ways of supplying micro-credit to entrepreneurs is reminiscent of the small-scale credit supply advocated by the Agricultural Extension Service in colonial Indonesia in the 1930s.

analysis is directed towards differences in economic development between provinces, not towards unequal power relationships. Strict application of dependency theory could lead to a fairly negative evaluation of certain aspects of export-led growth. I choose not to overemphasize these aspects. Even so, several concepts from these theories, such as the centre-periphery contrasts and the drain of surplus, are used throughout this study. They can be viewed as the contribution of dependency theories to economic development theory.

The neo-classical reaction: positive effects of export-led growth

Since the 1980s new ideas about economic development have gained ground, and these concentrate on the favourable effects of free competition, which is claimed to guarantee an optimal allocation of economic resources. The classical dogma 'trade is the engine of growth' was again given priority and has caused observers to speak of a 'neo-classical reaction' or 'neo-classical counter-revolution' (Bläsing 1978:243; Todaro 1989:85). The neo-classical writers have argued that government intervention has become dogmatic, and that less government intervention in the economy will encourage competition and favour rapid economic growth.[58] According to neo-classical thinkers, development economics does not exist as a separate discipline.

Critics have argued that this reaction is only an illusory innovation in the debate, since the neo-classical economists have merely re-introduced the classical 'laissez-faire' concept. The 'factor endowment model', which was developed by neo-classical economists, states that differences in factor endowment will lead to trade (Heckscher, Ohlin) (see above). Ricardean economics focused exclusively on labour costs as the variable factor of production. It has been acknowledged by many writers that the static neo-classical theory of international trade (as based on the Hekscher-Ohlin model) is ill-suited to explain the dynamic relationship between trade and growth (Booth 1990b:267).

The neo-classical reaction, or the free market approach, can be seen as an extreme in a spectrum of opinions and trends – but it has gained respectable support, especially since 1989 when the Soviet Union collapsed. 'Free markets make free people', said Milton Friedman, who has been called the apostle of the free market economy.[59]

The opposite in the spectrum is formed by the orthodox marxists, who fall back on the doctrine of Karl Marx, seeing capitalism as the logical outcome of the bourgeois era (Emmanuel, Warren).[60] Taking a line similar to the neo-

58 Influential writers are: D. Lal, I. Little, P. Bauer, B. Balassa, H. Johnson, J. Simon, J. Bhagwati, and A. Krueger (Muchie 1989:37; Todaro 1989:85-6, 1992:99).

59 Often called 'supply-side economics' because of its emphasis on generating new production by removing government constraints (Starink and De Waard 1993:11-8).

60 One may also name as the opposite extreme the neo-Keynesians, who advocate *more* government spending and more government intervention.

classicists, they state that capitalism was beneficial to the colonies and poor countries, since, despite all evils, it at least fostered development.[61] As a school, orthodox marxism has not gained much ground since the 1980s.

The neo-classical approach has also had repercussions in the discipline of history. Neo-classical economic theory has been liberally applied in the 'New Economic History', which uses economic theory more explicitly than was customary before, and also implements quantitative econometric techniques in the study of history. Although it has rightly been argued that neo-classical economics provides only limited answers, and that it is not designed to analyse long-run economic change, it may provide 'theoretical building blocks' for the study of economic development (Thee Kian Wie 1980:57). An econometric model of colonial development has been designed by Birnberg and Resnick. This model specifies endogenous government expenditure to promote the growth of foreign exports as the key internal force for development. Export earnings generate imports, and both direct and indirect taxation of exports and subsequent imports finance additional government expenditure. In a nutshell, the model describes colonial development as a basically circular process (Birnberg and Resnick 1975:36-55).[62]

Institutions and economic development

During the 1990s, research on economic development has moved away from the rigid application of neo-classical theory and has attempted to include additional dimensions of the growth process. For example, *endogenous* economic growth focuses on technological development within the economy instead of taking technology as an exogenous factor. Within institutional economics, the whole complex of values and ideas that influence economic activities are studied. These institutional factors can be defined as the humanly defined constraints that shape human interaction. Institutions can be shaped by government bodies, but also by property rights and by administrative regulations, or by the whole complex set of locally defined norms and values in the society. Thus the colonial legacy, along with its impact on relationships between social groups, can be viewed as an institutional factor. It has been observed that such factors play an important role in economic development.

These paradigm changes show that economists these days have more appreciation for the relevance of path-dependent patterns, in other words historical development. Bringing institutions into economic history means including the restraints of the late colonial state and colonial government policy. It also means paying attention to regional differences, particularly in

61 Dudley Seers called this the 'neo-classical Marxist argument' (Muchie 1989:37).
62 See Chapter VI.

such a diverse and segmented economy as late colonial Indonesia was.

Many economists have studied detailed aspects of economic growth and the effects of foreign trade on economic development. This brief survey has reviewed only a number of major trends and well-known examples. Broadly speaking, many universally applicable theories have been formulated, criticized, and refuted. The final result is the notion that different countries and regions display different characteristics, so that their development cannot be explained by one comprehensive theory. The degree to which development in a country is influenced by internal (or endogenous) factors also varies.

Theoretical concepts used in this study

Let me recapitulate the theoretical concepts that I will use in the analysis of export trade in the Outer Islands of colonial Indonesia. Rather than venturing to apply one single growth model (which is a hazardous enterprise when adequate data are scarce), several theoretical tools may serve to increase our insight into the economy of the Outer Islands.

As we saw, Hla Myint further developed Adam Smith's 'vent-for-surplus theory of international trade' (Myint 1958). This traditional (classical) model of trade presumes that there is no unemployment. If there is unemployment, which means that the labour factor is not fully utilized, this creates an opportunity to expand production for export markets, and goods can be produced for which no local demand exists. This may increase GNP without extra cost. Myint has gained attention with his hypothesis that under-utilized natural resources in underdeveloped nations can be exploited when they first enter the world market. In recent economic thinking, free trade is deemed extremely important in facilitating economic growth, and it has been argued that Smith's vent-for-surplus notion also pertains to manufactured goods (Bleecker 1997:529-30). Viewed in terms of the vent-for-surplus theory, economic growth is not the result of reallocation of factors of production yielding comparative advantages (Ricardean growth), but uses previously unutilized resources instead, by exporting surplus products. As I see it, this is what happened in indigenous export agriculture in the Outer Provinces. The inhabitants of the rich primeval forest were able to generate a surplus production of cash crops and sell this surplus in overseas markets.

Since labour reserves form the major possibility for growth, Myint included the aspect of population density in his research (Myint 1958:325). This leads us to one important characteristic of the Outer Islands: they were sparsely populated. Accordingly, the European estates which began to be established in Sumatra and Kalimantan in the late nineteenth century found an ample supply of land, but were confronted with a chronic shortage of labour. They solved this problem by importing coolie labour from China and Java. The estate economy benefited from the surplus of labour in China and Java, from the surplus of natural resources (fertile soil) in Sumatra, as well as from surplus capital and entrepreneurship from Europe (European pioneers bringing foreign investments) (Thee Kian Wie 1977:47).

Myint points out that the growth effects of vent-for-surplus production may be weak. These weak linkages constitute the main shortcomings of vent-for-surplus production as a favourable development. In the first place, in the colonial situation, the revenues from vent-for-surplus production usually accrued to entrepreneurs from the mother country and so this production was only marginally beneficial to the colony itself. In the second place, a structural dependence of the economy on the export of primary goods may be dangerous; an 'enclave economy' can develop, which obstructs development towards a more diversified and self-sufficient economy.[63]

In studying vent-for-surplus production, an analytical distinction can be made between two phases in the expansion of the indigenous export sector of the economy (Myint 1980:38-9). In the first phase export production is taken up by the peasant as a part-time activity, in order to obtain some additional cash income. This income is essential if taxes are levied in cash, but it can also be spent on consumption, including imports. During the first phase, such activities are carried out on a spare-time basis without replacing the subsistence economy. During the second phase, however, a number of smallholders specialize in export production, neglecting their former subsistence activities, which means that they need cash revenues to purchase food.[64] A cash demand for locally produced foodstuffs and other locally produced goods and services is thus developed. In this phase, the money economy spreads from the export sector to the domestic sector. Other households in the region specialize in food-crop production (division of labour). However, the reduction in subsistence output may lead to vulnerability to crop failure or to fluctuations in an unstable export market. Smallholders may grow increasingly dependent on money lenders. Often, a dependence on rice imports is generated.

It should be emphasized that this model serves merely to study one aspect of the economy, namely the development of foreign export production and its effects. Recent researchers have pointed out that the indigenous economy was subject to change, and displayed different types of economic dynamism during earlier periods when export production had not yet risen to high levels. Therefore, the stereotype of a 'traditional, isolated subsistence economy' (versus a dynamic export economy) should be avoided. For example,

63 This criticism is, of course, mainly heard from the side of the dependency school (Todaro 1989:386-7; Brookfield 1975:65).

64 Myint emphasizes that such smallholders took full advantage of market opportunities, but not necessarily of technical opportunities (compare Booth 1990b:267).

recent research has shown the relatively dynamic character of the economy of the Lesser Sunda Islands in the nineteenth century – even though income levels and export production of these islands remained very low compared with other provinces (Parimartha 1995). Similarly, when I examine the development of indigenous export agriculture in Palembang in the twentieth century, the characteristics of the earlier economy (before the boom in exports took place) will be evaluated as well.

According to Myint, there are two preconditions for a rapid expansion of peasant exports. The first of these is an improvement in transport and communication (in certain regions, as in Sumatra, traditional transportation by river did not inhibit expansion of exports). Under such circumstances, more remote districts can be expected to become accessible and colonial law can be established, thereby fostering the advent of traders. The second condition is the presence of firms specializing in foreign trade, which may serve as mediators between the peasants and the world market. Such traders may form an inducement to increase export production, for example by selling imported goods to the indigenous population (Myint 1980:34-5). This is an important condition. Especially in the Outer Islands, export production expanded much faster in the regions where many European or Chinese trading houses operated than in the more secluded regions of the archipelago.

Generally speaking, exports may generate imports in a region. The export industry requires capital imports, and export revenues generate imports of consumer goods. When discussing the growth effects of foreign trade, Hirschman states that imports provide market information and thus prepare the way for local production (Hirschman 1977, 1980). However, an export industry may have additional effects on the surrounding economy, which Hirschman defines as linkages. The following linkages of an export industry can be specified:

1. When a leading-sector industry makes use of input from other local industries, it generates 'backward linkages'. For instance, when the oil industry needs steel pipelines, this will stimulate local production of steel pipes. In practice, however, the pipelines may be imported from abroad (thus obliterating local growth effects). Other backward linkages may be supplied locally, such as building materials, and food and housing for workers. The construction of private railways, necessary for the transportation of export produce, can also be viewed as a backward linkage.[65] When import substitu-

[65] Thee Kian Wie also mentions 'the export industry's requirements for intermediate goods' as a backward linkage. Backward linkages are particularly effective when the leading industry becomes so large that supplying industries can achieve economies of scale on their own, thereby lowering their production costs and becoming more competitive in domestic or even export markets' (Thee Kian Wie 1977:50; Gillis et al. 1987:16, 66-7; Kindleberger 1990:17).

tion takes place, the backward linkages of an industry in the region expand.
2. When the output of the leading industry is used by other industries, we speak of a 'forward linkage'. When, for example, the rubber industry requires further processing facilities and a remilling industry develops, which processes the rubber into a cleaner and better product, this is a forward linkage. In colonial Indonesia, raw oil was refined in the petroleum production centres before being exported as gasoline, kerosene, lamp oil, or a variety of other derivatives. The large refinery complexes in Palembang and Pangkalan Brandan (Sumatra), Balikpapan (Southeast Kalimantan), and Cepu (Java) formed forward linkages of the oil extraction. The oil refineries, in turn, generated some local demand for supplies such as rice and construction materials, which in turn were backward linkages.

In a highly dualist economy, the linkages of an industry may lead to an isolated area of industrial activity, an enclave. In that case the linkages have only a limited effect on the economy of the region. The concept of the enclave indicates a relative degree of isolation; there will always be an influence to some extent. Even though negative disturbances in the regional economy may occur, an industry will never exist in total isolation. Viewed in conjunction with Rostow's stages of growth, Hirschman's linkages imply that leading sectors will pull other sectors into modernization and so a country will experience balanced growth. A leading-sector development balances out.
3. Thee Kian Wie, following M. Watkins, also specifies 'final demand linkages'. When an export industry has input requirements of primary factors such as labour, these will be attracted and result in a better income distribution and increasing consumptive demand (Thee Kian Wie 1977:50). It is also possible to speak of 'consumption linkage effects'. These are in fact indirect backward linkages. The demand created by salary payments may also be limited to a small radius surrounding the industry in question.
4. Finally, 'fiscal linkages' indicate the effects of government expenditure, which was facilitated by taxes paid by the export industry.[66] For industries which tend to form enclaves, such as technology-intensive oil production centres, the fiscal linkages may be their most important effect. Since the petroleum industry in Indonesia in the late colonial period generated enormous exports, tax revenues were substantial. Fiscal linkages may result in a longer-term impact of trade on growth (Booth 1990b:269-72). However, it is essential to consider the composition of government expenditure, and its effect upon infras-

66 'Large government revenues derived from exports (taxes, dividends) can be used to finance other sectors. This depends critically on the kinds of programs and interventions that the government undertakes.' Effects can be observed in the construction of social capital: roads, railroads, power, water, telecommunications. These lower the costs for industries, and open opportunities for other industries (Gillis et al. 1987:417-8).

tructure and economic growth, to trace these linkages (see Chapter VI).

Since linkage theory is oriented mainly towards production, it can be viewed as an extension of classical economics, which is supply-oriented. It is a structural approach to development and facilitates a careful examination of the growth effects of an export industry (Thee Kian Wie 1977:49-50 including note 15).

In this study, the development and the growth effects of export expansion are analysed using the two theories mentioned above. The vent-for-surplus concept and the extent and nature of changes in subsistence agriculture will be used to analyse indigenous export agriculture. The analysis of the various linkages will examine the growth effects of both European and indigenous Indonesian export industry. Other factors, such as drain of surplus and the effect of government expenditure, will be included in the explanation when necessary.

Archival sources

Trade statistics

The Central Bureau of Statistics (Centraal Kantoor voor de Statistiek, CKS) in Batavia registered trade flows at the administrative level of the province, specifying volumes and values of traded goods for all commodities on an annual basis. These figures allow the analysis of the specific character or 'profile' of trade in each province, indicating how the export package was composed and how export production developed over the years. For the years 1917-1937, in addition to foreign trade, interregional trade flows were published in the trade statistics.[67]

The series on interregional trade consists of three flows: a. the imports of each province from Java; b. the exports of each province to Java; and c. the exports of each province to the other Outer Islands, the latter listed as aggregate exports per commodity originating from one province destined for all other Outer Islands. These interregional trade statistics were published twice a year beginning in 1920 and starting with one comprehensive issue for 1917-1919. From 1923 on, totals per province for all traded commodities were included.[68]

A selection from the trade statistics was entered into a computer database, partly by myself, partly by students at the Department of History at

67 *Statistiek handel,* scheepvaart 1877-1909; *Statistiek handel* 1909-23; *Jaaroverzicht* 1925-1942; *Statistiek intergewestelijke handel* 1922-40 (in further references, these are referred to as 'trade statistics').

68 A selection of less systematic figures on the interregional trade before 1917 can be found in Korthals Altes 1991.

Leiden University. This data set can be accessed through the Internet and allows analysis according to the type of product, place of origin, destination, and through time.[69] A systematic evaluation of the data sets is presented in Appendix B.

Well-known to all Indonesianists is the series of source publications *Changing Economy in Indonesia,* which was started by W.M.F. Mansvelt in 1939, and published by P. Creutzberg and P. Boomgaard since the 1970s.[70] This series has developed into an indispensable tool for the study of Indonesian economic history. Unfortunately, the amount of information on individual Outer Provinces in the series is scarce. The computer data set of foreign trade statistics described above was used to compile Volume 12B of *Changing Economy in Indonesia,* on the trade statistics of the Outer Islands.[71] This volume is the basis of the quantitative analysis of Outer Islands trade presented in this study.

Memories van Overgave

The trade statistics do not specify whether exported agricultural products originated from indigenous smallholders or from European estates (except for rubber, after 1927). This distinction can only be traced by using qualitative source material, such as the Memories van Overgave. These reports of succession (comparable to the British 'valedictory despatch') were composed by the Residents or Governors (the administrative heads of a province) for the enlightenment of their successors. The reports describe all aspects of the province, from politics, government, trade and industry, to education, local tradition, and religion. After 1905 a standard table of contents was included, which was later revised.[72]

The annual reports of the trading agencies of the Nederlandse Handel

69 The NHDA/NIWI web site is at: http://www.niwi.knaw.nl/.

70 P. Boomgaard, W. Mansvelt and P. Creutzberg (eds), *Changing economy in Indonesia; A selection of statistical source material from the early 19th century up to 1940.* Vol. 1-16. Amsterdam: Royal Tropical Institute, 1975-1996. See the bibliography for a complete list of titles (listed by author). In the bulletin of the Royal Tropical Institute, one of the editors describes the series (Boomgaard 1991).

71 This is the only volume in the series which explicitly concentrates on imports and exports of each individual province (1911-1940) (Clemens et al. 1992). *Changing Economy in Indonesia.* Vol. 16 on forestry also lists separate Outer Islands (Boomgaard and De Bakker 1996).

72 In 1940, the last model for the standard contents of a Memorie van Overgave was drawn up, but very few Memories were handed in after 1939. The Algemeen Rijksarchief (ARA) in The Hague and the Koninklijk Instituut voor de Tropen (Royal Tropical Institute, KIT) keep a complete set of the Memories van Overgave of the Residents, as well as a number of Memories by lower-ranking officials. In the Arsip Nasional in Jakarta several hundred more of the *Memories van Overgave* (including photocopies) can be found. Algemeen Rijksarchief (ARA), Ministerie van Koloniën 1901-1963 (Kol), Memories van Overgave (MvO); De Graaff and Tempelaars 1991; Meilink-Roelofsz 1968:17.

Maatschappij (NHM) form an additional source providing general information on the economic situation in individual provinces.[73] These reports contain the annual accounts of the trading agency. They also give a brief description of the hinterland regions of the major harbour towns. The NHM was established in 1824 by King Willem I of the Netherlands, in order to transport and market the produce of the Cultivation System in Java. It survived the nineteenth century and specialized in banking, supplying credit through a network of trading agencies in the Outer Islands and Java.[74]

These sources provide a view of the economy of colonial Indonesia through the eyes of the European civil servant or trader. It has often rightly been argued that a more Asia-centric perspective should be adopted in historiography, in order to avoid the stigmatization of the peripheral regions as 'passive' or 'stagnant'.[75] However, it is impossible to write an economic history of dynamic indigenous regions and to study the development of foreign trade using only sources which are not 'Euro-centric', since these simply do not exist or are at best scarce and unsystematic. The 'Euro-centric' sources must of course be used critically. Appropriate and objective use of archival sources remains at all times the responsibility of the historian.[76]

Composition of this study

It is not feasible to write a history of an area as large and as diverse as the Outer Islands without carefully defining the perspective, and clustering the eighteen provinces into intelligible groups. In Chapter II, a survey is given of the economic history of the Outer Islands. I define a thematic grid in which the eighteen individual provinces are accommodated. To facilitate further analysis, the individual Outer Provinces are grouped according to common features. As a main ordering principle, the presence of European enterprise as opposed to the extent of indigenous activity in export agriculture is used. The main criterion is export performance. This leads to the distinguishing of

73 Algemeen Rijksarchief (ARA): Archief van de Nederlandsche Handel-Maatschappij (NHM) 9086-9240, *Jaarverslagen van de vestigingen van de Nederlandsche Handel-Maatschappij in het Oosten, 1860-1940: Verslagen van de Subagenten* (VvS).

74 It is still a major Dutch bank right now, but under a different name (ABN AMRO Bank). The first century of the NHM has been described in Mansvelt 1924-26.

75 A recent appeal for a stronger Asia-centric perspective can be found in Sutherland 1994:788; Heersink 1999:6-8; Post 1993:159-60.

76 The rise of an Indo-centric historiography started with B.J.O. Schrieke and J.C. van Leur. In recent historiography, it is Smail who gave the first thorough argument for a non-Euro-centric approach, which he named 'autonomous history' (Van Niel 1990:112; Vogel 1992; Van Leur 1955; Smail 1961).

three paths of development or typologies of change: European dynamics, Asian dynamics, and a relative absence of change. These are further explored in Chapters III, IV, and V.

In Chapter III, I analyse the effects of the arrival of European estates and mining companies, starting on the basis of export figures. I focus on the coexistence of European and indigenous export production in East Sumatra and several other provinces. I compare the indigenous production lines in provinces where there were many estates, with indigenous production in provinces where European entrepreneurship was absent. In Chapter IV, the dynamics of indigenous export agriculture in the Outer Provinces are examined. In chronological order the cultivation of coffee, pepper, rubber, and copra are described. The mechanism of interregional trade is examined, and the effects and consequences of indigenous export agriculture are surveyed. Chapter V examines the provinces that produced only a limited amount for foreign export. These provinces appear at first sight to have had relatively stagnant economies, but in fact they too exhibit a wide range of development paths.

Even in a colony officially adhering to the credo of 'free trade', the government was an essential factor in economic development. The government not only influenced economic development by redistribution of funds, it also represented the legal claims of the mother country over its territories, and set the rules in the economy. Therefore, the colonial government, in close cooperation with the government in the mother country, had a profound influence on the emerging colonial state and the developing national economy. Nor was the colonial government static; it continuously redefined its goals in the changing economy. It is necessary, when analysing the effects of export growth, to consider the measures that the government took to improve the economic situation. The colonial government's economic policy and its consequences in the Outer Islands are analysed in Chapter VI.

CHAPTER II

The Outer Islands
More diversity than unity

'Unity in diversity' is a phrase that was adopted by the Indonesian government after independence to express the ambition that, despite the great diversity of Indonesia in ecological, economic, cultural, and religious terms, the Indonesian Republic would subsume all of these. It is also a suitable and widely used title for textbooks on Indonesia, since it signifies that both common and diverging features can and should be recognized within the rich and fascinating compass of the Indonesian archipelago.[1]

In this chapter I give a brief survey of the economic history of the Outer Islands during the late colonial period. I will examine both the traits shared by the Outer Islands and the differences between them. To begin with, the characteristics of the economic development of the Outer Islands will be identified by assessing the growth of foreign and interregional trade. The provinces will be grouped according to common economic features. I will evaluate several methods for classifying or clustering, and then group the Outer Islands into four clusters, after which each cluster is briefly introduced. Specific attention to the nature of entrepreneurship leads to a characterization of three types of Outer Islands economic development. In the second half of this chapter, I briefly sketch the economic history and main characteristics of each province.

Development of foreign trade in the Outer Islands, 1900-1940

Historically, the attention paid by the Dutch to the Netherlands Indies, in political, cultural, social, and economic terms, was heavily tilted towards Java, manifest in the very definition of the rest of the archipelago as lying

1 For example: *Unity and Diversity; Regional Economic Development in Indonesia since 1970* (Hill 1991); *Unity in Diversity; Indonesia as a Field of Anthropological Study* (De Josselin de Jong 1984); *Regional Dynamics of the Indonesian Revolution; Unity from Diversity* (Kahin 1985); *An Introduction to Indonesian law; Unity in Diversity* (Gautama and Hornick 1972). The policy slogan 'Bhinneka Tunggal Ika' derives from Sanskrit.

'outside' Java. These islands invariably received a label reflecting their relationship to Java: 'Outer Provinces', 'Outer Islands', or 'Outer Possessions'.[2] In the late nineteenth century, the numerous islands of the Outer Islands formed a vast and largely unknown area, in which small Western trading posts and a few estate areas were specks in the wilderness. The Outer Islands were sparsely populated, although inhabited by a wide range of indigenous groups. Much of the Outer Islands was covered with primeval, inhospitable forest. At the turn of the century, private enterprise, an adventure anywhere in the colony, was considered a downright gamble in many Outer Islands.[3] As to the administrative organization, the Outer Islands were divided into eighteen 'residencies' or 'provinces', each headed by a Resident or a Governor who reported to the Governor-General in Batavia, and who was supported by Assistant-Residents and additional personnel.[4]

The economic development of the Outer Islands gained momentum shortly after 1900 and was based on the export of primary goods. The trade statistics show the impressive expansion of export to foreign destinations of agricultural produce such as rubber, coffee, copra, and pepper, and of minerals such as tin and oil (Figure 1). During the inter-war period, the position of the Outer Islands in the Indonesian economy changed irreversibly. The Outer Islands accounted for an increasing proportion of export earnings: in 1911/15 Java's average share in foreign exports was 57 per cent. In 1936/40 its share had dropped to 35 per cent, whereas 65 per cent came from the Outer Islands (Table 1). In Indonesia today this shift from Java to the Outer Islands is even more pronounced (Clemens et al. 1992:21; Thee Kian Wie 1994:146).

The aggregate pattern shows rapid growth in foreign trade after 1910, originating from both indigenous and European producers, but not all provinces show the same mix of these two sectors of export production. In some provinces European estates dominated the cultivation of export crops, while elsewhere there was scarcely a European estate to be found. In the latter provinces, the indigenous population produced cash crops for foreign ex port on a small scale with the use of unsophisticated technology. In some

2 It is the same today, when the Indonesian administration distinguishes between 'Java' and 'Propinsi luar Java'.

3 On the introduction of private capital in the colony after 1870 and the process of establishing Dutch rule in the far corners of the archipelago, see Van Goor 1986 and Lindblad 1993c.

4 I disregard minor changes in administrative division. Tapanuli belonged to West Sumatra until 1908. Belitung was administered as an assistant residency of Bangka (its trade was listed separately in the trade statistics until 1935). New Guinea was recorded separately in the trade statistics during 1908-1924; afterwards it belonged in part to Ternate and in part to Ambon. After 1924 Ambon and Ternate together formed Maluku. In 1936 the Outer Provinces were divided into three 'governments': Sumatra, Borneo (Kalimantan), and the eastern archipelago (the 'Great East'). The latter consisted of South Sulawesi, Manado, Maluku, Timor and Dependencies, and Bali and Lombok.

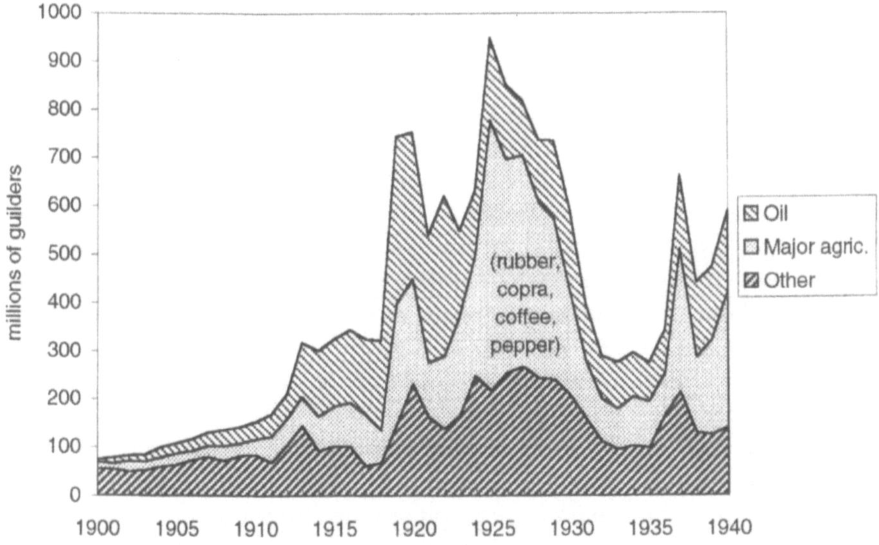

Figure 1. Foreign trade of the Outer Islands: Exports of oil and major agricultural products, 1900-1940 (Trade statistics).

provinces European companies were active in the production of oil, coal, or tin, while elsewhere such signs of industry were absent. In some provinces economic activity went forward by leaps and bounds, stimulated by large oil-production centres (Palembang, Southeast Kalimantan). Other provinces had oilfields that were merely exploited but did not lead to the establishment of production centres (Aceh, Jambi). Consequently they did not act as a large stimulus to the economy.

In aggregate exports of agricultural commodities, the share of indigenous production rose steadily. For colonial Indonesia as a whole, the share of indigenous production in total agricultural exports increased from 24 per cent

Table 1. Share of the Outer Islands in the total foreign trade of colonial Indonesia, 1911-1940 (average share in per cent)

	Exports	Imports
1911/15	43	30
1916/20	40	29
1921/25	47	29
1926/30	51	36
1931/35	55	33
1936/40	65	35

Sources: Trade statistics 1938(b); *Statistisch Jaaroverzicht* 1940, 1941.

in 1913 to 36 per cent in 1925. These percentages were much higher for the Outer Islands: Gonggrijp estimates that 44 per cent of agricultural exports from the Outer Islands in 1913 were indigenous, and that in 1925 smallholders supplied as much as 58.5 per cent! About 73 per cent of all coffee exports, 90 per cent of all copra exports, and 99 per cent of all pepper exports from the colony in 1929 were estimated to be cultivated by indigenous producers.[5]

In the first decade of the twentieth century, the market-oriented production of cash crops was poised on the eve of an unprecedented expansion. Even though many provinces had exported rice and forest products within the archipelago for centuries, the 'boom' in exports of raw materials such as rubber, copra, tin, and oil was still to come. It is instructive to examine the extent to which levels of exports and imports (as indicators of economic expansion) varied by province in the decades that followed. Did the differences between provinces increase, as some expanded more than others owing to the export trade?

In 1900/05 average exports per capita in the Outer Islands totalled about 9.4 guilders. The standard deviation, which measures the extent of variation among the export values in the provinces, was around 10.4 guilders. Therefore, the coefficient of variation (the standard deviation divided by the mean) measured 1.1 (Figure 2). In these years, agricultural production was spread relatively evenly throughout the provinces: West Kalimantan and East Sumatra, for example, had a very similar export production per capita. The major disturbance in this early picture was the small and thinly populated Belitung, which already had a very high export production per capita, mainly of tin (Table 26.1). A quarter of a century later, in 1926/30, average exports in the Outer Islands had risen to about 70 guilders per capita. At this time, the variation between the provinces had become much more strongly marked: the standard deviation had risen to 99.1, which results in a coefficient of variation of almost 1.5. Again Belitung heads the list, but we must keep in mind that the revenues from these exports were not distributed evenly among the population – and the economy of Belitung was very one-sided, being dominated by tin mines, characterized by a relatively high factor productivity. Falling prices during the Depression reduced export revenues, which caused the coefficient of variation between provinces to decrease slightly during the 1930s.

Surveying the export performance of the Outer Islands between 1900 and 1940, it is obvious that the gap between the provinces had widened. The larger variation, expressed by a larger coefficient of variation, meant a greater disparity between the provinces than before. The 'boom' of the 1910s and

5 Estimates are based on the value of exports (Gonggrijp 1938:209; Boeke 1946:23; Maas and Bokma 1950:259).

1920s had favoured the position of some provinces, and hardly affected the position of others.

Imports

As exports expanded, an increasing level of imports was generated, but imports lagged far behind exports in most provinces (Clemens et al. 1992:45, 53-9). The estate area in East Sumatra and the oil-drilling areas and tin mines imported large quantities of rice, construction materials, and additional capital goods such as iron and machines. But the surplus on the balance of trade remained large in East Sumatra, Palembang, Southeast Kalimantan, Bangka, and Belitung, because revenues from exports in the European sector of the economy remained much higher than imports.

The distribution of aggregate imports per capita over the individual provinces remained largely constant during the period studied (Figure 2). The coefficient of variation between provinces did not significantly increase over time, as it did for exports.

The indigenous population imported almost only foodstuffs and consumer goods, besides which the smallholders and Chinese traders introduced cars and trucks and small machines into the provinces. Unfortunately, domestic industry which could replace imports with locally produced goods failed to develop. Agriculture remained the most important indigenous sec-

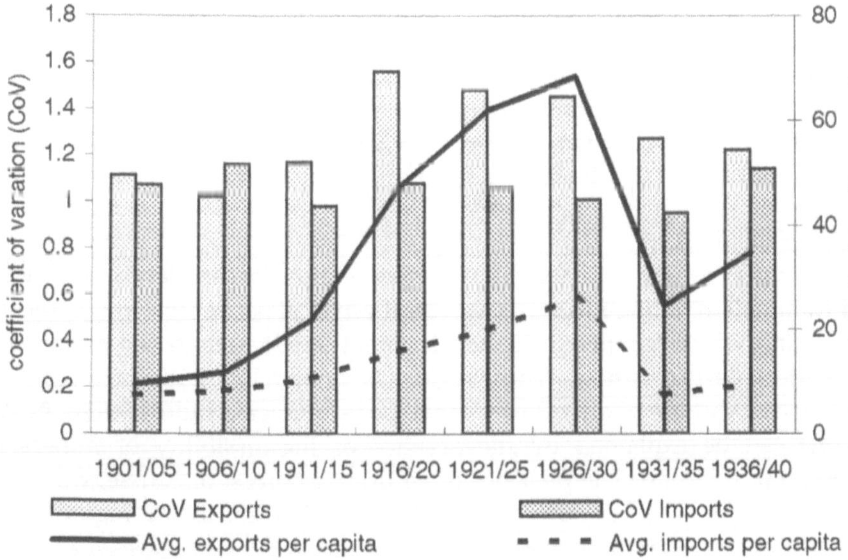

Figure 2. Coefficient of variation in foreign trade per capita by province, 1901-1940 (Trade statistics; reconstructed population figures (see Appendix A)).

tor of the late colonial economy, and export revenues were largely spent on foreign consumer imports.

In short, the late colonial economic development of the Outer Islands was characterized by:

- the presence of both European and indigenous entrepreneurship in market-oriented production;
- a sharp dividing line between agricultural exports and the non-agricultural sector (minerals);
- the revolutionary growth capacity of several 'new' export commodities (oil, tin, rubber, copra) which replaced traditional products, such as sugar and tobacco, in the export package of colonial Indonesia. These new products pushed the Outer Islands forward within the colonial economy.[6]

Conditions of growth

Examining the differences in export performance between the provinces, the contrasts in natural resource endowment and population density should not be overlooked. Many of the observed economic differences resulted from the ecological characteristics of the provinces. Naturally, soil fertility was a major factor in whether suitable cash-crop cultivation was feasible. With this in mind, it is possible to wonder why several other large provinces did not develop a level of export production comparable to the three 'giants', East Sumatra, Palembang, and Southeast Kalimantan. Was soil fertility the only reason why European estates preferred to settle in Palembang and not in Jambi? Was there no fertile stretch of land suitable for estate agriculture in Lampung, West Kalimantan, or even New Guinea? And was access so difficult for middlemen and traders in Tapanuli, or Timor and Dependencies, or Maluku, that they could not convince smallholders to produce more cash crops for the market?

Let us first review the natural environment of the larger islands, Sumatra and Kalimantan. In the former, the greatest physical barrier was the Barisan Mountains, which hampered the development of large plantation estates in the western part of Sumatra. These regions were literally on the 'wrong side' of Sumatra. Absence of other European export-producing industries in these regions can be explained by the absence or inaccessibility of minerals (petroleum, tin, coal). The presence of natural resources, of course, was the prime factor in whether successful and lasting interest in the region was

6 Sugar, for many decades one of the largest export commodities of the Netherlands Indies, originated almost entirely from Java and therefore will not be considered in this study. Clemens et al. 1992:60-1; Lindblad 1988b.

awakened among European industrial companies.

Rivers transected the rainforest and formed the primary means of transportation for many decades.[7] For the local economy, rivers carried the traditional trading routes: Chinese traders went up and down the river buying and reselling goods. Trading posts of the Chinese, Arabs, Indonesians, and Dutch were reached by prahu and steamer. Only in the 1920s did the use of cars and trucks for transport make any substantial progress; before that time, roads were limited or in bad condition. Railways and tramways were restricted mainly to the areas where European economic activity was well established. The 'growth provinces' therefore ranked first in the construction of roads, railways, and bridges. In East Sumatra and Palembang, large-scale rail transport became increasingly possible during the final decades of the colonial period.[8] Generally speaking, public expenditure in most Outer Provinces lagged far behind that in Java. Major rail and bridge construction, even in Sumatra, only gained momentum in the 1930s.[9]

Since rivers provided an important means of transportation, seaports and trading centres were often built near the coast on river deltas. The accessibility and navigability of its rivers increased the chance that a province would develop foreign exports. Traders sailed up the river and reached local inhabitants in the forest, and forest products and export crops were transported downriver to market towns and harbours.

This is well illustrated by southern Sumatra, where navigable rivers greatly enhanced smallholder economic activity. These long, deep rivers flowed through the eastern lowlands towards the east coast; by contrast, the rivers on the west side were mostly short and shallow. The rivers in Palembang, Jambi, and the northern part of Lampung were navigable far inland (the Batang Hari in Jambi has been called Jambi's 'lifeline'). The rivers in south and west Lampung and in Bengkulu were less accessible due to the steep mountain slopes.[10] In Lampung the rivers were full of meanders, and corvée labour was needed to clear them from obstruction by dead trees (Broersma

7 Van der Eng has stated that in Java, the importance of rivers for the purpose of transportation has been overrated, since road connections to the harbours were essential for economic integration (Van der Eng 1992:356-7). In the Outer Islands, shipping on rivers was dangerous during extended periods in the rainy season. Nevertheless, transport by river was essential for the expansion of the smallholder economy and trade within the archipelago.

8 Thee Kian Wie 1977:123; Weisfelt 1992; Wellan 1932.

9 For more detailed analysis of the navigability of rivers see the individual sections per residency. Government expenditure will be further explored in Chapter VI.

10 The Batang Hari was the most important river in Jambi, the Musi in Palembang. Many smaller rivers poured into these two large rivers. In Palembang and Jambi, *hulu* or *uluan* regions lay upstream, and *ilir* or *iliran* regions downstream, signifying the importance of the rivers (Purwanto 1992:41; Wellan 1932:28-31).

1916:7).[11] It is a safe generalization that in Sumatra, rivers that flowed into the ocean on the east coast were more easily navigable than the ones flowing west from the Barisan, where the terrain was more rugged and the coast was steeper.

In Kalimantan, the larger inland rivers could be accessed by prahus, although the rapids wrecked many of these craft during the rainy season. In West Kalimantan, rivers remained the principal means of transportation: even as late as 1938, Resident J. Oberman of West Kalimantan still emphasized the importance of rivers in this residency. The government-run Pontianak Rivier Vervoer (Pontianak River Transport) was one of the major improvements in transportation in West Kalimantan, in contrast to the relatively high number of roads that were constructed in the southern part of Southeast Kalimantan.[12] The rivers in South Sulawesi and Manado were only accessible a few kilometres upstream. This was not an economic disaster, as many locations in these provinces could be reached simply by navigating along the coast.

Although the importance of their ecological conditions cannot be underestimated, the fact that the Outer Islands were sparsely populated was also a major factor in their economic development. While labour was too scarce in many provinces to allow an increase in production, theoretically there was room for vent-for-surplus economic activity, since the natural resources were not fully exploited. Of all the Outer Provinces, only Bali was densely populated. Bali was the smallest province and had 148.4 inhabitants per km^2 in 1930, in an area smaller than 11,000 km^2. Southeast Kalimantan and New Guinea constituted the other extreme. These provinces stretched out over an area of 388,000 and 416,000 km^2 respectively, with 2.63 and 0.47 inhabitants per km^2. South Sulawesi and West Sumatra also had relatively large population densities. In 1930 South Sulawesi was the province with the highest population figure, more than 3 million inhabitants, but with only 31 inhabitants per km^2 it was not as densely populated as Bali or West Sumatra. Bangka, Riau, and Jambi were at the bottom of the list, being very sparsely populated (Table 14).

East Sumatra, West Kalimantan, and Bangka housed the largest numbers of Chinese. The largest concentration of Europeans was in East Sumatra (23 per cent of all Europeans in the Outer Islands in 1930). West Sumatra, Southeast Kalimantan, Maluku, and South Sulawesi each housed roughly 10 per cent of the Europeans who lived in the Outer Islands. The percentage of Europeans in the total population of the Outer Islands was everywhere less

11 In Lampung, the largest river was the Tulang Bawang. In Bengkulu, one could only sail inland on the Ketahun River.

12 ARA Kol, MvO 265, J. Oberman 1938:7, 88-9.

than 1 per cent. It was the highest in Amboina, East Sumatra, and Bangka. In the latter two areas, this was due to the European agricultural estates and the tin mines respectively (Tables 15 and 16).

There was little urbanization in the Outer Islands. In 1930, Palembang ranked first in population size of all Outer Islands cities (with some 108,000 inhabitants), surpassed in colonial Indonesia only by Batavia, Surabaya, and Semarang in Java (Table 17). Macassar, a trading town of importance in the eastern part of the archipelago, ranked second in 1930 with around 85,000 inhabitants. In 1890, Palembang had already been the largest city in the Outer Provinces, with 50,000 inhabitants, comparable in size to Semarang and Yogyakarta. In 1890 Padang had 20,000 inhabitants and Banjarmasin 36,000. Padang lost its historic importance within the constellation of towns. In 1930 the towns of Manado and Pontianak were roughly of the same size, but Manado was home to three times as many Europeans, while Pontianak, as could be expected in West Kalimantan, had three times as many Chinese. Medan was the fastest growing town in the Outer Provinces. In 1890 it was still very small, with some 1,200 indigenous inhabitants. Given an enormous boost by the arrival of the agricultural estates, it quickly outgrew the older cities of Padang and Palembang (Boomgaard and Gooszen 1990:43, 245).

Periodization of export trade

Total foreign exports from the Outer Islands rose impressively during the period 1900-1930. Three phases of expansion can be distinguished during this period (Lindblad 1989c:8). The initial expansion took place from 1909 to 1913, when exports rose from 142 to 320 million guilders (in current prices). This expansion can be ascribed mainly to the increase in oil exports from Southeast Kalimantan (Balikpapan), East Sumatra (Pangkalan Brandan, Pangkalan Susu), and Riau (oil depot on Pulu Sambu). The second stretch of growth followed upon the increase in demand resulting from the First World War: export levels rose from 300 to 750 million guilders at current prices in 1919-1921. Growth ended when these lagging demands were fulfilled, and world demand fell briefly during the recession of 1921-1922 (Figure 1 and Table 21).

After 1925, a new burst of expansion took place, this time climbing rapidly to unprecedented heights. Outer Islands exports reached an aggregate peak of more than 900 million guilders in 1927. These figures show that the first half of the inter-war period, 1922-1929, was a period of increasing prosperity and rising export volumes. Among planters and supervisors on the estates, this gave rise to feelings of euphoria, especially when bonuses were distributed on top of regular salaries. Repeating the history of the 1880s, ambitious planters and fortune-seekers from all over the world were attracted to Deli. 'The high prices had a bewitching effect', writes Gonggrijp.[13] In the meantime, rumours were rife about extravagant spending on clothes and houses by indigenous peasants, whose explosive participation in world trade did not go unnoticed by colonial officials and European entrepreneurs. The world economic depression following the Wall Street crash in October 1929 made short work of these unbridled trade revenues, and euphoria was replaced by shock. Bad as it may seem, it should be kept in mind that the price level had already decreased substantially after 1925. The Depression accelerated a process that was already underway: the world market was flooded by a continuously increasing supply of cheap raw materials (Aldcroft 1993).

Examining the exports of the different provinces, it is interesting to note that some provinces experienced a sharp peak in export revenues in 1925-1927, while others kept up a steady flow of income from exports for a longer period of time. When the Depression set in, the first group immediately felt the effects of the decreasing price levels (particularly in East Sumatra, Jambi, West Kalimantan, but also small producers in places like Indragiri and Bengkulu). The second group included West Sumatra, Palembang, South Sulawesi, and Aceh. These provinces expanded their exports faster than revenues could diminish, or exported products for which prices remained relatively stable. It is difficult to pinpoint one product or a combination of products that is responsible for these differences in market sensitivity – or, for that matter, that would make the 'ideal' export package. Generally speaking, revenues from petroleum exports suffered less from the Depression than other types of export revenue. Within agriculture, coffee did better than rubber and copra. I will come back to these differences in greater detail later (Figures 11 and 23a-23q).

In 1933 the government started intervening in foreign trade, initially only to counter the effects of the Depression, later as an integral part of economic policy. Imports were restricted and international cooperation resulted in export restrictions on rubber, tin, and tea. Meanwhile, realization of the indebtedness of indigenous smallholders prompted the colonial government to supply credit and to regulate sales. After 1936, world demand recovered and several provinces once again experienced expanding foreign export revenues. Palembang, Bangka, West Kalimantan, and Southeast Kalimantan were particularly favoured by a strong recovery in the late 1930s, owing to increased exports of rubber, oil, and tin. In 1940, six provinces were responsible for 78 per cent of total exports from the Outer Islands: the three highest-ranking (East Sumatra, Southeast Kalimantan, and Palembang) as well as three provinces with very active indigenous entrepreneurship (West Kali-

13 Gonggrijp 1938:197. Writings by planters offer fascinating accounts, for example Brandt 1948; Spaans-van der Bijl 1991; Van der Velde 1982.

mantan, South Sulawesi, and West Sumatra) (Clemens et al. 1992:11-2; Lindblad 1989c:10).

Interregional trade, 1917-1938

One limitation of the analysis of Indonesian trade by economic historians up to now has been the lack of insight into domestic trade. An analysis of domestic trade is essential for an understanding of the level of economic integration within the archipelago, but in most studies the analysis is restricted to direct foreign exports and imports, as recorded by province.[14] These shortcomings are often supplemented by additional (non-quantitative) information from the contemporary literature. For example, it is often stated in reports and articles that tin from Bangka was frequently first shipped to Tanjung Priok in Java, and then was re-exported, whereas tin from Belitung was shipped directly to Singapore or to foreign markets (Tables 37 and 41.1).[15]

Interregional trade flows can be added to the analysis, enabling more insight into the flows to and from Java, and supplementing quantitative data for regions with a fair amount of transit trade through Batavia. In many Outer Provinces, exports to Java supplemented foreign exports, and imports were also drawn from Java. Therefore, the impression of their economic functioning based on foreign trade statistics alone remains incomplete. Interregional trade with Java complements our picture of economic expansion based on foreign trade. The trade statistics registered three separate interregional trade flows: the imports of the Outer Islands from Java, the exports of the Outer Islands to Java, and the exports from the Outer Islands to other Outer Islands.

The part of domestic trade which took place in the inner regions of the islands, the internal trade, went unrecorded since it escaped official registration. Occasionally the Memories van Overgave did comment upon this trade. This unrecorded internal trade was mainly in food crops, other basic subsistence commodities, and handicraft products. It will not be given intensive consideration in this study.

Trade with Java

Exports from the Outer Islands to Java closely follow the pattern of foreign exports, corresponding to roughly 17 to 25 per cent of total foreign exports. From 1923 to 1930 these exports remained at a fairly constant level of 120 mil-

14 An exception is Dick 1990.

15 In 1924-1928, for example, 98.2% of Belitung's exports were foreign exports, while only 23.4% of Bangka's exports were foreign exports, with the rest of its exports going towards Java. See also Chapter III.

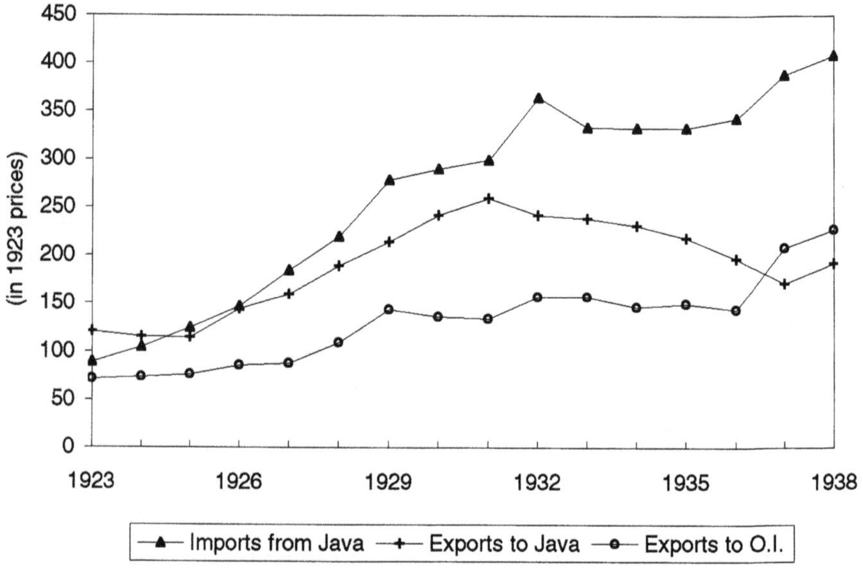

Figure 3. Aggregate interregional trade of the Outer Islands deflated with Van Ark price index, 1923-1938 (Tables 20, 22.1 and 22.2).

lion guilders. Interestingly enough, the peak in exports to Java was reached in 1929, a few years after the peak in foreign exports in 1925, at 135 million guilders. This can be explained by the different composition of the two export flows: the high rubber price in 1925 accounted for the peak in foreign exports in that year, but had no effect on exports to Java, as rubber was not traded interregionally.

Decline in aggregate exports to Java thus followed rather late. It was not as severe: after 1930 a steady decline reduced this value by about half, to a level of 60 million guilders. Foreign export earnings were reduced by the Depression to a mere 30 per cent of the top level, about 300 million guilders in current prices. The smaller decline in interregional exports can be explained by the fact that only a part of these exports was re-exported, while another part served domestic demand. During the period 1932-1936, exports to Java stabilized at around 60 million guilders. A strong recovery followed in the late 1930s (Figure 21).

Exports to the remaining Outer Islands were at a slightly lower level of 75-80 million guilders during 1923-1929. These exports fell to 20 million in 1930 and subsequently remained at about 35 million. After 1936, the recovery of exports to the Outer Islands was somewhat stronger than that of exports to Java (Figure 3).

Imports from Java show a pattern largely consistent with foreign imports.Their growth signifies an expanding market for consumer and capital

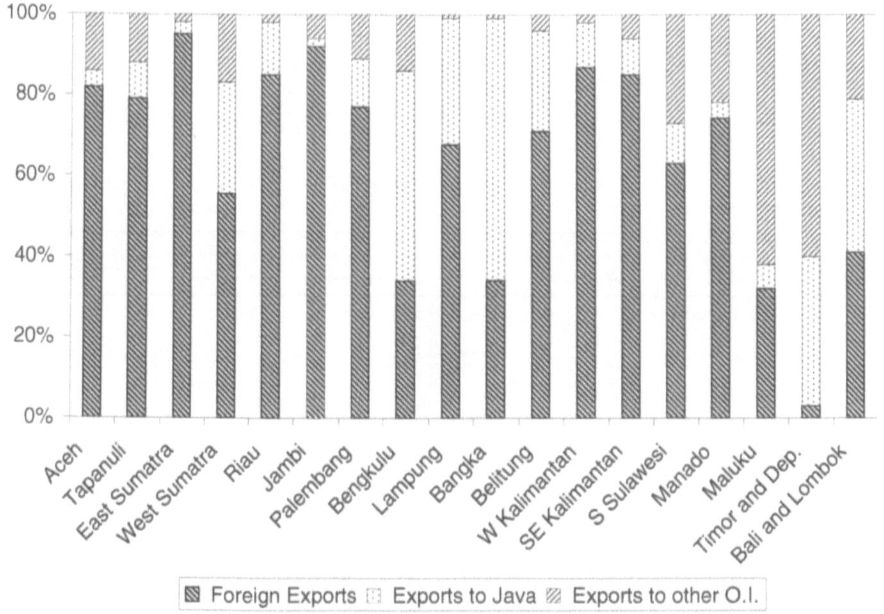

Figure 4. Types of exports by province, 1923-1938 (average percentage), 1924-1928 (Tables 25.1 and 25.2).

goods in the Outer Islands. Imports from Java grew steadily, rising from 90 million guilders in 1923 to 175 million guilders in 1929. In the latter year foreign imports added up to slightly less than 400 million. Then, a decline almost as dramatic as the decline in foreign import brought the level of imports from Java down to about 80 million in 1933, roughly half the level of 1928-1930. Concomitantly, foreign imports tumbled from about 300 million to a mere 100 million, which is an even more severe decline. Interregional imports from Java stayed at 80 million per annum for several years, but after 1935 these imports began to rise, reaching 150 million in 1937 (Table 22.2 and Figure 21).

We may conclude that both exports to and imports from Java had a mildly stabilizing effect on the fluctuations in foreign trade of the Outer Islands. This should be kept in mind when consulting earlier analyses that did not include trade to and from Java (Clemens 1992:33-6; Lindblad 1989c:8-10). In Java, the domestic consumption of raw materials such as rubber, oil, and tin was obviously not very high. These goods were mostly re-exported after a varying degree of processing. Crude oil was refined in the BPM refinery in Cepu at times when the capacity of the refineries in Balikpapan, Palembang, and Pangkalan Brandan proved insufficient. Batavia and Surabaya served as transit ports for other raw materials, where goods may have spent a certain

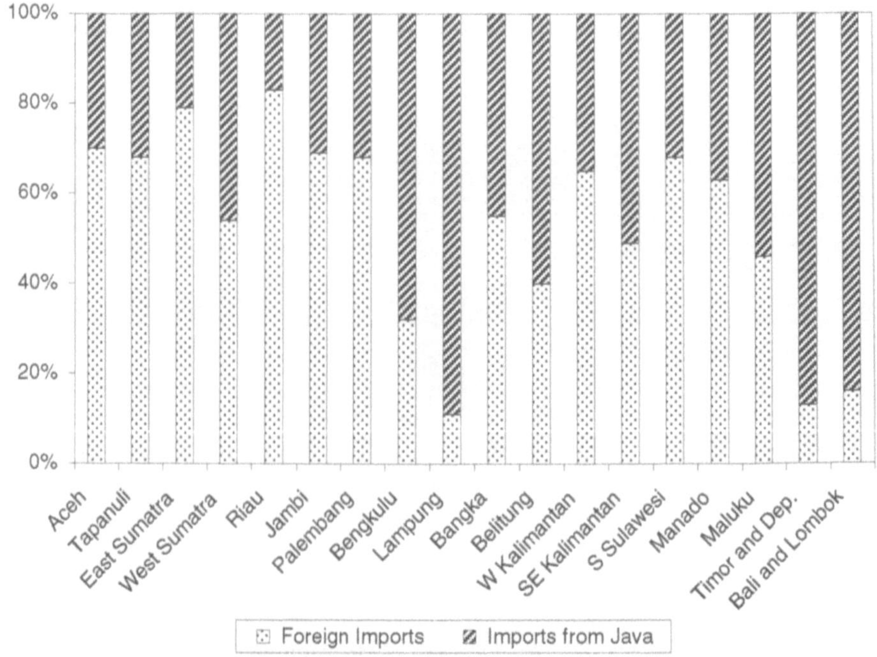

Figure 5. Types of imports by province, 1923-1938 (average percentage) (Tables 25.1 and 25.2).

amount of time in warehouses or may have undergone further processing before being exported elsewhere.

In terms of relative change from year to year, interregional exports to Java and to other Outer Islands displayed the same fluctuations as foreign exports. This is clearly illustrated in a graph using a semilogarithmic scale (Figure 22), expressing relative change on the vertical axis (using such a scale, constant growth is expressed as a straight, sloping line). At a level approximately one-fifth lower than foreign exports, interregional export values grew slightly faster than foreign exports and mirrored the post-1936 recovery.

The importance of Java as a trading partner

For each province individually, the importance of trade flows to and from Java varied widely – and not always, as one would expect, analogous to its distance from Java. Exports to Java were small in Aceh, East Sumatra, Riau, Jambi, Belitung, the two Kalimantans, and Manado. But from Bengkulu and Bangka, Lampung, Bali, and the Lesser Sunda Islands, a major part of the export trade went to Java. This implies that any analysis solely restricted to *foreign* trade severely underestimates export expansion in these provinces (Figures 4 and 5). Unfortunately, comprehensive aggregates on interregional trade flows are only given in the trade statistics from 1923 onwards (Tables 22.1 and 22.2).

The large trade flows between Java and the Outer Provinces also shed new light on the dominance of Java in the colonial economy, establishing the fact that Java had a role as a centre with respect to the peripheral provinces, supplying imports and processing raw materials. Nor should it be overlooked that a substantial part of Outer Islands foreign exports was shipped first to Surabaya or Tanjung Priok. When these exports were in transit trade destined for foreign ports, for example copra exports from Macassar, they were registered in the foreign trade statistics and not in the interregional trade statistics.[16]

In the import trade, the provinces of Lampung, Bengkulu, Bali, and Timor and Dependencies were again mainly oriented towards Java. More than half of their total imports were imported from Java, thus eluding the foreign trade statistics. It is striking that not only the residencies adjacent to Java, but also the provinces in eastern Indonesia (Manado, South Sulawesi, Maluku, Lesser Sunda Islands) relied heavily on trade flows via Java: roughly 30 per cent of the total imports of South Sulawesi, Manado, and Maluku originated from Java.[17] These provinces were situated further away from Java than were Sumatra and Kalimantan, but the lack of international harbours (such as Belawan in East Sumatra, and Palembang in southern Sumatra), compounded by the distance from Singapore (to which Sumatra and Kalimantan were orientated), explain this reliance on Java. Interestingly, Tapanuli and West Sumatra also showed a large inflow of goods from Java (while East Sumatra, Aceh, and Riau did not).

A distinction can be made between domestic trade within the archipelago serving local needs and interregional trade serving foreign trade. The latter accentuated the centre-periphery relationship between Java and the Outer Islands. It was caused by, amongst other factors, the presence of major Dutch trading firms and offices in Java and reveals Java's role as an intermediary in the foreign trade of the archipelago. In more general terms, the increasing trade within the archipelago can be viewed as a manifestation of the forma-

16 Transit trade was often billed at once, at a uniform charge, from the place of sale to its destination, disregarding transshipment or reloading. This was done with a 'delivery note', also called 'through-bill of lading' (*doorvoer-cognossement*). It was a form of cooperation between local freight transporters (often KPM) and international shipping companies, serving foreign purchasers. In the following I refer to this trade as 'transit trade' (Greene 1987:47, 261; Heersink 1999:165; A Campo 1992:249-51, 258-9).

17 As in export trade, the so-called 'through trade' in imports (on bills of lading) was registered in the foreign trade statistics: for example, when goods arrived in Tanjung Priok but had a through destination and were immediately re-exported, they were included in foreign trade statistics (De Graaff 1955:124).

tion of a colonial state. It was the outcome of growing economic coherence and improvement in the trading network within the archipelago (A Campo 1992:215-20, 526-7). Of course, many of the positive effects of trade in the region (such as regular shipping lines, communication, the spread of knowledge, the building of harbours) resulted from both trade flows. It is virtually impossible to untangle them and the distinction is largely theoretical. In the literature, a contrast has been made between foreign and domestic demand as incentives for growth and integration. It has been shown convincingly that domestic trade alone does not account for a major proportion of economic growth and income increase in the Outer Islands. But domestic trade constituted an essential corollary of foreign trade and should be included when analysing the individual regions. Lindblad emphasized the importance of foreign trade as an engine of growth (Lindblad 1993b:233). Domestic trade was enhanced by public expenditure on harbours, bridges, roads, and railways. One should not underestimate the growth capacity of the Indonesian population (43 million people in 1900, 70 million in 1940) as a market for trade (Van der Eng 1992:355-7).

In the following, when possible, I include exports to Java in the analysis of the export trade of the Outer Islands. Before I begin, a note about my methodology is in order. The interregional trade flows from the Outer Islands to Java are of course of a different order from the foreign exports of the Outer Islands, even if the goods traded were re-exported from Java. As is apparent from my previous observations, these trade flows are important for the study of the economies of the individual Outer Provinces.[18] By contrast, exports of crude oil to Java (as a consequence of temporary shortage of local refining facilities) should not be viewed as indirect foreign exports, since the value added by further processing in Java in fact turns this oil into a Javanese export product. However, by adding the value of pre-processed crude oil to the Outer Islands foreign exports, we gain a more complete picture of the local economy.

Incorporating Java among overseas destinations leads to an adjusted image of the export performance of the Outer Islands. This is best illustrated by the surplus on the balance of trade. For example, in 1924, the foreign exports of the Outer Islands amounted to 630 million guilders. Total imports in this year were 212 million guilders, so the overall trade surplus was 418 guilders (66 per cent of the export value!). Only a small part of export revenues was spent on imports. Typical import goods were rice, foodstuffs, and textiles, and in several provinces also included machinery and other capital

18 Again, tin exports serve as an example: tin from Bangka was exported via Batavia. To compare Bangka with Belitung, from which most of the tin was directly exported to Singapore and other foreign markets, it is important to include these interregional exports.

goods (Clemens et al. 1992:93-8). The interregional trade statistics show that the bulk of imports from Java also consisted of these commodities, amounting to 101 million guilders for all Outer Islands in 1924. Interregional exports to Java were mainly raw materials, similar to those exported in foreign trade, amounting to a total of 111 million guilders in 1924. Therefore, the total trade surplus, including Java, is 741 million minus 313 million, or 428 million guilders, which is 58 per cent of total exports. When trade with Java is included in the analysis, the export surplus is reduced from 66 per cent to 58 per cent of total exports. This significantly changes the balance of trade for individual provinces.

Colonial drain?

A persistent and substantial export surplus characterized the foreign trade of many colonial economies and has been described in the literature as a prominent feature of colonialism (Golay 1976:268). This aspect of nineteenth and twentieth century economic development has been labelled 'colonial drain'.

There has been a great deal of discussion in the literature on the question of whether revenue was 'drained' from the colony by Western and Chinese entrepreneurs and traders. The drain of capital reduced the favourable effects of the export industry and impeded the economic development of the colony. Much of the net gain from trade was not available for reinvestment in the colony. In his essay 'Een eereschuld' (1899), C.Th. van Deventer was the first influential advocate of repaying the colony for the profits extracted. He estimated the surplus to be 187 million guilders. Since then, others have tried their hand at calculating the net surplus. The best known is the estimate of Tinbergen and Derksen, who calculated that in 1938 the Netherlands had a profit of 700 million guilders from the Netherlands Indies (14 per cent of the national income) (Derksen and Tinbergen 1980; Baudet 1980).

Booth, and in her footsteps Maddison, speak of a double drain through both European and Chinese businessmen. The latter refers to the major role of the Chinese in the export of indigenous cash-crop production, resulting in substantial remittances made by Chinese immigrants to their families in China. Maddison estimates a 'drain' of 6 to 11 per cent of Indonesia's NDP during 1838-1938.[19]

Van der Eng has argued that it is premature to classify the trade surplus of the Netherlands Indies as a colonial drain, considering the fact that reinvestments by European enterprises in the colony were generally high in the

19 To make matters more confusing, the term 'double drain' has also been used for the drain of export earnings, to Java due to imports on the one hand, and to the rest of the world, due to remittances of profit, on the other (Booth 1990b:291-3).

1910s and 1920s, so that export earnings were not necessarily drained out of the colony. By estimating total net factor payments abroad, Van der Eng comes up with an annual average of 5.7 per cent of Indonesian GDP during 1914/29. He also notes that the opportunity cost of the services of foreign labour and capital employed in Indonesia should be deducted from overseas remittances when estimating the actual drain.[20] The problem is that this presupposes that the presence of European companies was beneficial or essential to the economy. To check this assumption, certain questions must be asked: For example, do Western oil companies drive the economy to higher levels, and does the economy benefit from the technologically advanced capital and the skilled labour employed in this industry? When European enterprises form enclaves, it is possible to postulate that the opportunity cost of their services is relatively small and that remittances are indeed drained from the economy (Thee Kian Wie 1977:71-2). The effects of the presence of European enterprise will be studied in more detail in Chapter III.

Generally speaking, foreign firms will always constitute a drain of profits. Some profits were reinvested or spent locally, for example for imports of services and goods such as insurance, construction goods and machines, or transport costs. However, net profits that were sent overseas in the form of dividends, salaries, and pensions were usually quite large and formed a drain by their very nature.[21]

This study does not provide detailed insight into the financial administration of foreign firms or balance of payments data. The annual trade surpluses of the individual Outer Provinces have been calculated at a macroeconomic level. These surplus figures become more meaningful when the statistics of interregional trade with Java are included, providing more insight into the expenditure on imports of each province. When studying the trade of the individual provinces, it is not surprising to find a large surplus on the balance of trade in those provinces in which many European enterprises were operating (Tables 32 and 33). The surplus was smaller in those provinces where the production of foreign trade goods was largely in the hands of indigenous producers (for example South Sulawesi, West Kalimantan, and West Sumatra). Indigenous products were largely traded through Chinese intermediaries; since there was a substantial flow of imports by the peasants, it can be concluded that these producers earned a substantial share and therefore that the intermediary traders did not reap the entire profit mar-

20 Van der Eng 1993b:21, 37-8; 1996b:94; Booth 1990c:291.

21 Lindblad has analysed dividend payments of the Java estates Michiels-Arnold and Wonolongan, as well as of Billiton Maatschappij and Deli Maatschappij, during the 1920s and 1930s. Of the latter two, dividend rates averaged 25% during the early 1920s; Billiton sometimes even paid out 70% or more (Lindblad 1996b).

gin. Under these circumstances, the 'double drain' was definitively biased towards European remittances. Colonial drain went much more in the direction of Europe than to China.

The dual character of agriculture

As in all pre-industrialized countries, small-scale indigenous agriculture was the most widespread economic activity in the Outer Islands – even more so than in Java, where Dutch involvement in agriculture and industry had exerted a stronger influence on peasant agriculture (Booth 1988; Van der Eng 1993a, 1996c). For centuries, agriculture in the Outer Islands had mainly served subsistence needs. Crops were only traded on local and interregional markets. There were a few notable exceptions in specific regions, such as pepper and nutmeg cultivation for foreign exports.

In the twentieth century, indigenous farmers turned on a massive scale to the cultivation of commercial crops such as rubber, copra, and coffee, which were traded on the foreign market. In indigenous export agriculture, the intermediary trader played an important role, bringing the smallholder producer in touch with foreign markets. Rubber and copra earned substantial profits in the inter-war years until 1929, when the effects of the Depression took a heavy toll and smallholders found that foreign markets were satiated. At this point indigenous production turned out to be very sensitive to price changes on the world market for raw materials. The rapid rise of smallholder rubber production during the preceding 'rubber boom' years (1923-1927) had been spectacular and brought substantial earnings to the population of several provinces (Lindblad 1989c:14).

In several provinces, indigenous smallholder agriculture coexisted with European estates. The estates often drew on the local area for their food supply and timber, and brought an influx of immigrant labourers, who often settled in the region as traders or peasants when their contract had expired. The extent to which the estates influenced local indigenous agriculture is difficult to determine, since Chinese trading networks and Indonesian and Arab traders were also of vital importance but went largely unregistered.

Relatively little is known about the production processes and productivity changes in the Asian sector of the archipelago. There are only estimates of productivity increases for aggregate agriculture. Van der Eng estimates that productivity growth in agriculture in colonial Indonesia was 1.8 per cent per year in 1880/1940 (it was 2.1 per cent in 1940/80). In the Outer Provinces alone, productivity growth in agriculture can be estimated to have been slightly larger: 2.5 per cent until the Second World War (Van der Eng 1990). While productivity growth in agriculture is a yardstick for growth in national income (agriculture had a share of more than 50 per cent in national income), it ignores all information on income distribution. The only detailed regional information on incomes is that which can be deduced from indigenous and European export production.

Estate agriculture is better documented. The abolition of the Cultivation System, which began with the passing of the Sugar Law and the Agrarian Law in 1870, can be viewed as the starting point for the establishment of large, privately owned agricultural estates. It was the result of the liberal economic atmosphere, the hegemony of laissez faire, which gained influence in the latter half of the nineteenth century. But despite such an encouraging economic atmosphere, European free enterprise in the Outer Islands depended on pioneers who ventured to start estate agriculture in the rainforest, far removed from Java. In 1863, J. Nienhuys selected Deli in East Sumatra as a site to explore the possibilities of planting tobacco. He turned out to be very successful. This formed an incentive for other European entrepreneurs to venture into the Outer Islands, but further export expansion was hindered by a shortage of labour. Planters started to recruit coolie labour. The passing of the Coolie Ordinance in 1880 allowed them to adopt measures to discipline the coolies and punish deserters (the poenale sanctie, a penal clause in labour contracts). Subsequently, the Outer Islands were opened up for private investment, resulting in large-scale estates that could compete with estates in Java in export earnings and profitability.

European estate crops were rubber, tobacco, and coffee, and to a lesser extent palm oil, tea, and fibres. Agricultural estates attained the highest levels of output in East Sumatra, but numerous European estates were also established in Palembang and Southeast Kalimantan. An important question is why European estate agriculture did not spread successfully to other provinces, such as West Sumatra and West Kalimantan, where indigenous producers were very active. Many European pioneers started planting rubber and coffee in Palembang. Why did they not choose Jambi? Why did they not settle in the vast stretches of rainforest in West Kalimantan? But one can also ask: What factors influenced the variation in degree of indigenous participation in export agriculture in provinces with plenty of arable land and fertile soil? These are the types of questions addressed in this study.

Mineral riches: Western hands

Oil was by far the most lucrative export commodity of the Outer Islands. In contrast to export agriculture, revenues from mineral riches accrued almost exclusively to European entrepreneurs and not to the indigenous population. The largest mineral products in terms of value earnings, oil and tin, expanded from a combined share in total exports of less than 1 per cent in 1900 to almost 40 per cent in 1940. Eventually, oil products alone accounted for an average of 29 per cent of all export revenues of the Outer Islands in 1935/40

(Table 37 and Figure 1).[22]

There are two main reasons why the exploitation of mineral riches remained largely in the hands of European companies: the capital-intensive technology involved, and the monopolistic policies of the large companies. Oil drilling and tin mining were large-scale industries requiring relatively advanced technology. The exploration, drilling, processing, and transport of oil was an especially capital-intensive industry and required a wealth of technological know-how. This put these industries financially and technically beyond the reach of the local indigenous population. After a series of fusions and takeovers, in 1907 the two leading producers in Indonesian oil, Royal Dutch and Shell, concluded an alliance. For several years, their joint subsidiary, the Bataafsche Petroleum Maatschappij (BPM), enjoyed a virtual monopoly on the production and marketing of oil from colonial Indonesia.[23]

Criteria for clustering

Heterogeneity

The economy of the Outer Islands was very heterogeneous, both in performance and in structure. Some provinces experienced an economic boom during the years up to 1930, while others were relatively stagnant. There were provinces where change had become a permanent phenomenon, and provinces where influences from the world economic situation permeated only very gradually into the regional economy. Some islands, such as Maluku, had known better times during the VOC era, stemming from the spice trade – and possessed at least the memory of a glorious past.

As we have seen, other contrasts in size and population figures can be noted. The Outer Islands differed not only in natural conditions and size, but also in production, involvement in trade, trade surplus, and economic and political stability. Contemporary residency governors were often promoted to larger or more affluent provinces after having served in 'backwater' provinces, which shows that some provinces were regarded as more rewarding than others – a larger province implied greater prestige.[24] To get a better

22 These figures refer only to foreign exports, excluding exports to Java. Clemens et al. 1992:68-9. See also Lindblad's article on the petroleum industry in Indonesia before the Second World War (Lindblad 1989a).

23 Lindblad 1990b:215. See also Lindblad 1989a:55; Gerretson 1971-3.

24 This was mainly a matter of prestige, since there were no separate salary scales for Residents of larger provinces (as there were for Governors). For example, Resident P.C. Arends moved from Tapanuli to West Sumatra in 1926, but kept the same salary of *f* 1,500 per month. When H.E.K. Ezerman moved as Resident from Jambi to Palembang in 1928, he also earned *f* 1,500 per month. When he was promoted to Governor of East Sumatra in 1930, his salary was

picture of the different economic features of the Outer Islands, I have divided the Outer Islands into four clusters.

Previous classifications

Several clusterings of the Outer Islands have been tried out before. My feeling is that they do not offer sufficient insight into the economic structure of the individual provinces to allow a systematic analysis of export trade and economic development. The main aim of my own classification is to group the provinces in such a way that provinces with corresponding features can be easily compared. For post-independence Indonesia, Hill and Weidemann used a clustering to analyse economic performance of individual provinces. 'For analytical purposes, simple geographic zones alone are inadequate', they state. They describe five groups: the 'resource-rich' provinces, the 'isolated' provinces, the 'densely populated' provinces, the 'settled' provinces, and the 'sparsely populated' provinces (Hill and Weidemann 1989:4). I have drawn up a different classification for colonial Indonesia, but before I present it, I will evaluate the classifications previously devised by Lindblad and Clemens. In his survey on the economic rise of the Outer Islands, Lindblad recognizes five clusters, which are grouped according to their geographic location in the archipelago (Table 2, column 1) (Lindblad 1989c).

Although this classification is imaginative, since it corresponds to the usual movement of the eye from West to East, it ignores important differences between provinces that fall within one cluster. In Sumatra, for example, the economic structure of Palembang differed greatly from that of the adjacent provinces of Jambi and Lampung, even though all are situated in the southeastern part of the island. The same can be said of West and Southeast Kalimantan: while in Southeast Kalimantan a number of European industries flourished, the economic development of West Kalimantan depended almost entirely on small-scale indigenous agriculture.

At a later stage Lindblad experimented with three other types of clustering, of which two are shown in Table 2 (Lindblad 1990b:218-25, Lindblad 1994a:108-10). He uses the following indicators to identify patterns of regional variation:

- absolute values of foreign exports and imports;

raised to *f* 1,800. Similarly, when Resident L.J.J. Caron left Bali to become Governor of South Sulawesi in 1929, he went from *f* 1,500 to *f* 1,800 per month. In 1930, all Residents earned *f* 1,500,whether they were stationed in Timor or Bali or in West Sumatra or Palembang. Other examples of Residents moving from one province to another were Resident W.J. Rahder, who moved from Riau to East Sumatra in 1910, and D.A.F. Brautigam, who earned *f* 900 as Assistant-Resident of Belitung in 1913-1914 and became Resident of Palembang in 1914 with a salary of *f* 1200. (ARA, Kol. 1901-1963, Stamboek Nederlandsch-Indische Ambtenaren, Z 539; E-1 591; I-1 823; M-1 177, 457, 769, 864; O-1 470, 727; De Graaff and Tempelaars 1991).

Table 2. Different clusterings of the Outer Islands

	1 Lindblad 1989c	2 Lindblad 1990b, 1994a	3 Lindblad 1990b, 1994a	4 Clemens 1992 (Lindblad 1990c, 1994a)	5 Touwen 2001
East Sumatra	I	I	IV	I	I
Palembang	III	II	IV	III	I
Southeast Kalimantan	IV	III	V	IV	I
Aceh	II	II	I	II	II
West Sumatra	II	II	I	II	II
Jambi	III	II	IV	III	II
Lampung	III	II	–	III	II
West Kalimantan	IV	III	III	IV	II
South Sulawesi	V	IV	II	V	II
Manado	V	IV	III	V	II
Bangka	I	II	–	I	III
Belitung	I	II	–	I	III
Riau	I	II	V	I	III
Tapanuli	II	II	I	II	IV
Bengkulu	II	II	I	II	IV
Bali	V	IV	IV	V	IV
Maluku	V	IV	II	V	IV
Timor and Dependencies	V	IV	IV	V	IV

– a combination of geographical proximity and economic structure (Table 2, column 2);
– the surplus on the balance of trade of each province calculated as a percentage of export revenues during the expansionary period 1905-1930 (Table 2, column 3).

The resulting classification is as follows: 1. Aceh, Tapanuli, West Sumatra, and Bengkulu showed a trade deficit instead of a trade surplus at certain times between 1900-1940; 2. South Sulawesi and Maluku displayed a surplus percentage significantly below average; 3. the surplus percentage of West Kalimantan and Manado tended to move towards the overall average; 4. East Sumatra, Palembang, Jambi, Bali, and Timor had a surplus percentage starting out at the level of the overall average and increasing from there; and 5. Southeast Kalimantan and Riau had a surplus percentage significantly above the overall level throughout the expansionary period (Table 2, column 3).[25]

The average surplus percentage, the third indicator in this classification, yields interesting results as it expresses the share of total export revenues that was not spent on imports. The unspent proportion of export earnings indicates the extent to which the rise of exports failed to generate regional demand or to stimulate consumption or investment at a local level. All well and good, but trade balances varied considerably even within these clusters and it is difficult to draw clear dividing lines between the clusters. One stumbling block is that the percentage surplus on the balance of trade does not tell us whether, for instance, a high surplus is due to a small surplus in combination with low exports, as in the Lesser Sunda Islands (Timor and Dependencies, Bali and Lombok), or a large surplus combined with high exports, as in East Sumatra. In the latter case, imports were at a substantial level while exports were even higher. In the former case the net weight of all trade was negligible in the total trade of the Outer Islands.

The fourth type of classification (Table 2, column 4) pays more attention to the relative size of export performance by considering economic structure, differentiating between European and indigenous production lines. The combination of geographical proximity and economic structure produces five clusters:

I. East Sumatra, Riau, Bangka, and Belitung: in these provinces along the eastern coast of Sumatra, economic expansion depended primarily on European enterprise;

II. Aceh, Tapanuli, West Sumatra, and Bengkulu: in these regions along the western coast of Sumatra, the pace of expansion was slower than in many other regions;

III. Jambi, Palembang, and Lampung: this southeastern part of Sumatra showed a characteristic combination of parallel European and indigenous production lines;

IV. West and Southeast Kalimantan: both regions had few inhabitants and considerable dynamism in both the European and the indigenous sectors;

V. South Sulawesi, Manado, Maluku, New Guinea, and Bali and the Lesser Sunda Islands (= Lombok, Timor and Dependencies): in these eastern regions, stagnation prevailed and expansion left few traces.

This classification gives clear insight into the economic structures of the Outer Islands. However, it can be argued that opposite pairs such as Palembang and Jambi, or West Kalimantan and Southeast Kalimantan, should not

25 Note that the boundaries are not very clear in all cases. Bangka, Belitung, and Lampung are excluded because of misleading figures: tin was not registered by customs officials as having been exported from Bangka and Belitung until after 1919; foreign imports often entered Lampung via nearby Batavia.

be grouped together in one cluster (the dynamism of the European sector was remarkably smaller in Jambi and West Kalimantan). Here the criterion of geographic proximity ignores differences in economic structure. Clemens, who uses the same classification, takes these contrasts within each cluster into account when analysing the foreign trade of each province (Clemens 1992:40-1). Gooszen has criticized the position of Riau in this clustering, arguing that mainland Riau (Indragiri) was an integral part of the central Sumatran economic region. In fact, she adds an economic region to the clustering of Sumatra: the central Sumatran mainland, Bengkalis-Riau-Jambi (Gooszen 1994:169). This appears to be a sensible correction with regard to Indragiri, although it abandons the use of colonial residencies as regional units. This region should preferably be named Bengkalis-Indragiri-Jambi, since the island part of the province of Riau was clearly different from these provinces. The latter had a relatively large presence of European activity (oil, tin, several agricultural estates) and exported different indigenous cash crops than Indragiri (such as copra).

Clusters based on dualist features

The twin basis of European and indigenous entrepreneurship constituted one of the most striking characteristics of late colonial economic development in the Outer Islands. I therefore chose to incorporate the dualist perception of economic development into my clustering of the Outer Islands. Before reaching conclusions on a. the degree of dualism, b. the differences in the effects of foreign trade on regional economies, as well as c. the possible gap between the two sectors, I grouped the provinces according to the extent to which each sector (the European sector and the Asian sector) dominated the economy. This 'dualist' approach does not proceed from any assumption about the interaction between the two sectors, and does not imply any judgement on the mentality or the social-economic behaviour within these sectors.

A second criterion of this clustering is economic performance. Economic development, increase in income and prosperity, construction of infrastructure, and the provision of other social overhead capital (like schools and hospitals), all differ strongly by province. This criterion also takes into account a degree of change: a province such as Palembang had a relatively good position in the ranking of the Outer Islands at the turn of the century, but income levels of all population groups (not only estate owners) increased substantially during the next three decades. Palembang thus maintained a relatively prosperous position even though other provinces also experienced economic expansion.

I prefer to form clusters of similar types of economies while disregarding geographic location. Using the comparative method reveals essential similarities and differences in economic structure. I distinguish four groups of

Outer Islands, each roughly characterized by type and level of export production (see Figure 6):[26]

I. Provinces where substantial European export production was located and also considerable indigenous export production took place: East Sumatra, Palembang, Southeast Kalimantan.
II. Provinces where exports almost entirely originated from the indigenous economy: Aceh, West Sumatra, Jambi, Lampung, West Kalimantan, South Sulawesi, Manado.
III. Provinces where European enterprise dominated export production: Bangka and Belitung, Riau.
IV. Provinces where there was hardly any foreign trade at all, stagnation prevailed, and little economic expansion took place: Tapanuli, Bengkulu, Bali, Timor and Dependencies, and Maluku.

		Export performance due to indigenous entrepreneurship	
		Low	*High*
Export performance due to European entrepreneurship	*High*	*III* Banka Belitung Riau	*I* East Sumatra Southeast Kalimantan Palembang
	Low	*IV* Tapanuli Bengkulu Maluku Bali, Timor	*II* West Sumatra Aceh, Jambi, Lampung West Kalimantan Manado, South Sulawesi

Figure 6. Clustering of the Outer Islands by export performance.

Export figures from the trade statistics show the composition, volume, and development of the foreign exports of each province. By combining quantitative data on export earnings with qualitative information on whether or not export commodities originated from indigenous smallholder agriculture, it was possible to assess the type of exports for each province. In the period 1900-1940, 63 per cent of all foreign export earnings in the foreign trade of the

26 I treat Belitung separately from Bangka (although it is placed in the same cluster). I include Indragiri in Riau (notwithstanding the Bengkalis-Indragiri-Jambi similarity), and combine Ternate, Amboina, and New Guinea (at times recorded separately in the colonial administration, each including some smaller islands) into Maluku. This results in eighteen Outer Provinces. These eighteen will be treated separately in the last section of this chapter.

Outer Islands was generated by Cluster I, whereas Cluster IV accounted for a mere 5 per cent of all export earnings in this period. On average, the annual share of Cluster I was 60 per cent of the exports and 50 per cent of the imports. Of the aggregate forty-year surplus on the balance of trade, Cluster I accounted for 70 per cent and Cluster IV for 5 per cent (Table 29).

Since the majority of the indigenous population was engaged in agriculture and hardly participated in industry, the evaluation of the agricultural and non-agricultural sectors in the economy also led to a distinction between indigenous and European producers (Table 59). Mineral exports (coal, tin, petroleum) were exploited almost exclusively by European companies. The regions that were almost solely dependent on the exports of tin (Bangka and Belitung) had only a small share of indigenous export production. Although both the Chinese and the indigenous population in Bangka grew pepper, these islands were mostly devoid of diversified peasant agriculture. On the other hand, regions that exported large quantities of oil products but also developed substantial indigenous export agriculture, such as Palembang and Southeast Kalimantan, belong to Cluster I. For an impression of the spatial distribution of the four clusters, see Map 2.

It should be noted that the clustering hinges predominantly on export production. Although it can be expected that income levels will coincide with the classification based on exports, regional incomes as such were not included as a criterion for clustering. There are two reasons for this. Regional income or income per capita (or, for that matter, regional imports or imports per capita) cannot be separated by population group: it would be difficult to calculate income per capita for Europeans, indigenous population, or foreign Asians. But even without this distinction, income levels per province are difficult to determine.[27] Per capita export and import figures, as presented in Appendix D, may serve as indicators of income (Tables 26.1 and 26.2). I have avoided complex calculations of a speculative character on macroeconomic variables such as aggregate regional production, income, and taxation. In the more detailed analysis of the economic situation of each province or group of provinces, several other aspects of standard of living will be evaluated. These features are mainly based on qualitative information from archival sources. In this manner, I will also attempt to determine the degree to which export earnings were distributed among the population.

Brief characterization of the clusters

Cluster I consists of provinces with both indigenous and substantial European export production: East Sumatra, Palembang, Southeast Kalimantan.

27 Rough estimates of the national income of the Outer Islands as a whole can be found in Creutzberg 1979; Maddison 1989a, 1989b; Polak 1943.

These provinces showed remarkable economic expansion during the period under study and can be characterized as 'growth provinces'. During the period of expansion, 1905-1930, the surplus on the balance of trade of these provinces was higher than the average trade surplus of the Outer Islands.[28]

Another resemblance within Cluster I is the physical environment. The area of all three provinces was large (East Sumatra 93,500 km^2, Palembang 85,918 km^2, and Southeast Kalimantan even 388,427 km^2) and for the most part the provinces consisted of swampy lowlands or fertile hills, both covered with rainforest. Despite such plenitude, the European sector tended to be concentrated in only a few areas. Indigenous export agriculture was more widely spread but also had stronger and weaker regions, for example Hulu Sungai in Southeast Kalimantan, which had a remarkable concentration of indigenous rubber cultivation. Physical size of the province should therefore not be regarded as an explanatory factor.

One province stands out in this cluster, East Sumatra, where the Deli estate area was situated. Here tobacco and rubber planters created a large cultivated area, which was populated by a peculiar society of roughnecks and forcibly subdued coolies. This was the only plantation economy in colonial Indonesia, that is, the only area in which the majority of the agricultural population (essentially Europeans, Chinese, and Javanese, outnumbering the indigenous Batak) worked on large estates. Part of the indigenous population took advantage of the expanded local market for foodstuffs; former estate workers also found employment in this sector (Thee Kian Wie 1977: 110, 119-21). Many smallholders outside the estate area participated in export production, exporting rubber, copra, and *pinang* (betel) nuts (from the areca palm). In Palembang, indigenous agriculture was better developed and produced a diversified package of coffee, rubber, pepper, rattan, and other products (Touwen 1991:140). In Southeast Kalimantan the major indigenous export crop was rubber. In these latter two provinces, agricultural estates were also established, but did not form such a large continuous area as they did in Deli.

In the second cluster of provinces, the bulk of the exports originated from the indigenous economy: Aceh, West Sumatra, Jambi, Lampung, West Kalimantan, South Sulawesi, Manado. In most cases these 'indigenous producers' concentrated on a narrow range of export crops, but this did not prevent them from displaying considerable economic dynamism. Within this cluster, surpluses on the balance of trade did vary, but this was mainly the upshot of

[28] The average trade surplus for the Outer Provinces during the expansionary period, 1905-1930, was 53%. Together with the far lower surplus percentage of Java (24%), this accounted for an average surplus percentage of 38% for all of the Netherlands Indies. Only Jambi, the Lesser Sunda Islands, and Riau had a surplus percentage starting out at or significantly above the overall level. These surpluses do not include trade with Java (Lindblad 1990b:219-20).

varying degrees of consumer demand. Indigenous exports destined for the foreign market were not consistently large, but in all of these provinces, exports had a large impact on economic life. In several of the provinces, particularly West Sumatra and South Sulawesi, exports were primarily destined for the domestic market. Lampung, in southern Sumatra, did not enjoy the reputation of being a dynamic province, but in fact had a fairly constant and relatively high level of exports per capita, especially when exports to Java are included (Table 26.1). Therefore it is also grouped with Cluster II.

These seven provinces exhibited an active indigenous economy that had passed the stage of subsistence agriculture. Smallholder agriculture produced large quantities of rubber, coffee, and copra, but also showed an interest in producing a variety of minor products for the export market. The production of handicraft goods such as *batik* or cane and reed items got off the ground only hesitantly, and played only a small role in the economy at large.

Apart from agriculture and handicrafts, forest products like rattan were collected and sold. These forest products signify the first stage of an export economy, drawing on a tradition from the nineteenth century. When the indigenous population started selling raw forest materials to visiting traders, these transactions increasingly introduced cash incomes. To obtain these export items, peasants did not have to invest in the construction of a *ladang* or rubber garden.[29] Exports of forest products occurred in almost all the Outer Islands, but were most characteristic of Clusters II and IV.[30]

Important factors in the development of indigenous trade were the presence of navigable rivers and fertile plains. But ecological characteristics varied within this second cluster: from wide, swampy plains and impenetrable rainforest to mountainous and hilly terrain. Although this did not form a major impediment to commercially oriented indigenous peasants, it did partly determine which cash crops could be cultivated. For instance, in West Sumatra, mountain-loving coffee flourished, whereas in West Kalimantan and Jambi indigenous rubber was omnipresent. Although mountainous South Sulawesi exported coffee as well, here copra developed into the major export commodity, especially in the 1920s and 1930s.

The third cluster of regions consists of Riau, Bangka, and Belitung. Here European enterprise dominated export production. In Bangka and Belitung, economic life was largely determined by European tin mines. Earlier studies postulate that European entrepreneurship was characterized by a drain of

29 *Ladang*: swidden agriculture, or slash-and-burn cultivation: primeval forest was first burned and cleared, the resulting fields were then cultivated for a few years (traditionally with rice, later also with cash crops), and then abandoned for several years before they were cultivated again.

30 Detailed figures on the trade in non-timber forest products (rattan, gutta, benzoin, damar, bird's nests, and wax) are given in Boomgaard and De Bakker 1996.

capital earnings, and that apart from infrastructure at industrial sites, few linkage effects resulted from these economic activities. It can be argued that East Sumatra, where estates dominated export earnings, should belong to this group. But this overlooks the fact that East Sumatra also had a separate sector of peasant agriculture cultivating export crops and therefore ought to be grouped with the 'dual growth provinces' of Cluster I (Table 59) (Thee Kian Wie 1977:110).

Riau's position was fairly extraordinary: the BPM oil depot on Pulu Sambu, close to Singapore, swelled foreign export figures, but only for a relatively brief period: 1911-1923. The Singkep tin mine is another reason why Riau is placed in the third group, and the relatively large presence of European estates cultivating rubber is another. The fly in the ointment is that in the mainland part of Riau, Indragiri, European economic activity was very limited. Here indigenous rubber agriculture was important. On average 56 per cent of the rubber exported by Riau was produced by indigenous smallholders in Indragiri.[31] As we have already seen, had it been a separate region, Indragiri would have been treated as belonging to Cluster II: it can be compared to Jambi. But the remaining 44 per cent of Riau's rubber was estate rubber. In combination with the tin and oil exports, this justifies Riau's classification in Cluster III.

The fourth cluster of provinces contains Tapanuli, Bengkulu, Bali, Timor and Dependencies, and Maluku. These were all provinces that produced little for export. Several of these provinces, Bali and Timor, as well as Bengkulu (and also Lampung), exported a large share of their export production to Java; when we consider the interregional trade with Java, their export production suddenly appears to have been much larger (Tables 25.1 and 25.2). If we rank the provinces of Cluster IV, Bali and Timor (the Lesser Sunda Islands) are always at the bottom of the list: they had little trade, little agriculture, and little prosperity, even during the 1920s, when revenues from indigenous exports were highest.

Bengkulu, by contrast, exported little before 1920 and did well in the period 1926-1935. Bengkulu belongs to Cluster IV, since its exports were small both as an aggregate and per capita, and because of its slow start. Nearby Lampung also had a late start, but performed much better in foreign exports in the 1920s. In Tapanuli, Maluku, Bali, and Timor and Dependencies, stagnation prevailed with few signs of economic expansion. Only on close scrutiny did these provinces show some modest local economic dynamism.

[31] Average percentage of exported rubber value in the foreign trade statistics of the years 1927, 1928, 1930, 1932, 1934, 1936, 1938.

Three paths of development

Since in this classification the 'dual growth provinces' (Cluster I) reflect the characteristics of both indigenous producers and provinces with European entrepreneurship, I have systematically compared European export industries in these provinces with European industries in Cluster III, and indigenous agricultural production in these provinces with indigenous smallholder agriculture in Cluster II. The extent to which these clusters corresponded I interpret as a degree of dualism: if local production and regional infrastructure were not affected by the large European companies elsewhere in the same province, the two sectors were clearly separate. This justifies the use of the term 'dualist economy'. For example, estates often used immigrant labour, imported rice, and other foodstuffs from foreign suppliers, and constructed infrastructure solely in the estate area, which meant it did not serve the rest of the regional economy. On the other hand, in several regions I found that smallholder agriculture was indeed affected by European export production. The influence was either positive (demand for food and construction materials, the spending of income) or negative (occupation of land, disturbing traditional subsistence agriculture). The contributions of European estates to the local and central government should not be ignored: in East Sumatra, the Malay sultans became very rich through the rents and concession payments of the estates. In these regions, the colonial government earned substantial revenues from export and import duties, and could thereby influence economic development more radically by expenditure on social infrastructure.

Following this line of thought, I discern three distinct paths of development, or scenarios, which describe economic change in the period observed. In the first scenario, a region possessed conditions suitable for attracting European entrepreneurs, either in mining or in agricultural estates. These European companies recruited workers, and constructed roads, railways, and buildings, which in turn may have spurred the arrival of competing firms. The arrival of European companies certainly raised the level of foreign exports and imports, since domestic consumption was too small in the Outer Islands to provide a market for the goods produced. Because this entrepreneurship was not confined to the local economy but dependent on world demand and the conditions and trading facilities of the wider region, I apply to this type of regional economic development the term 'European dynamics'.[32]

In the second scenario, the indigenous smallholder became involved in export agriculture. This usually meant a shift from food crops to export crops, and often also a change from barter trade (or trade using non-cash

[32] With regard to the use of European as signifying 'European and American' or 'Western', I refer to my explanations of terminology in Chapter I.

money) to cash income. Generally, peasants began by collecting and exporting forest products such as rattan and resins. Then, instead of cultivating rice and other food crops for subsistence needs, they planted Hevea rubber, coffee, or other crops to sell to the traders who ventured into the interior or were met in the towns. They expanded their original domestic consumption with purchased goods. In this development, Chinese trading networks played an essential role. In many Outer Islands, there was a sudden, sometimes even explosive, increase in export production. Just like European entrepreneurs, these indigenous producers made use of the opportunities offered by the expanding world market for raw materials, such as rubber and copra. They reacted to changes in world prices and adjusted their agricultural output to world demand. Although capital investments were small and production processes were low-capital and labour-intensive, indigenous entrepreneurship was also characterized by a dynamic character, which will be referred to in this study as 'indigenous dynamics' or 'Asian dynamics'.

In the third scenario, there was no arrival of European enterprises. Substantial indigenous export agriculture failed to develop and economic change did not filter into the subsistence economy. Although in theory, it is possible to 'defend' the provinces where little export production took place, by saying that indigenous peasants in a way reacted adequately to outside intrusion by preserving their traditional subsistence habits, I will concentrate on the lack of foreign trade and the poor level of integration into the surrounding economy. The term 'subsistence dynamics' will not suffice here. Since these provinces did participate in the domestic economy, and were exposed to the indirect effects of trade expansion such as the increasing opportunities for rice exports to other provinces, I have named this scenario 'development in the periphery of (economic) expansion'.

In this exercise, the four clusters of provinces have in a sense been reduced to three paths of development. We can observe the first type of development (European dynamics) in Clusters I and III, the second type (indigenous or Asian dynamics) in Clusters I and II, and the third type in Cluster IV.

Where it all happened

Before entering into a detailed analysis of Asian and European dynamics in the Indonesian archipelago, this section will briefly discuss the individual provinces. Short statements about indigenous agriculture and the presence of European estates will be supplemented by a summary of the most prominent ecological and cultural characteristics. The position of the province in domestic and international trading networks, including Chinese links with Singapore or the reliance on Java, will also be mentioned.

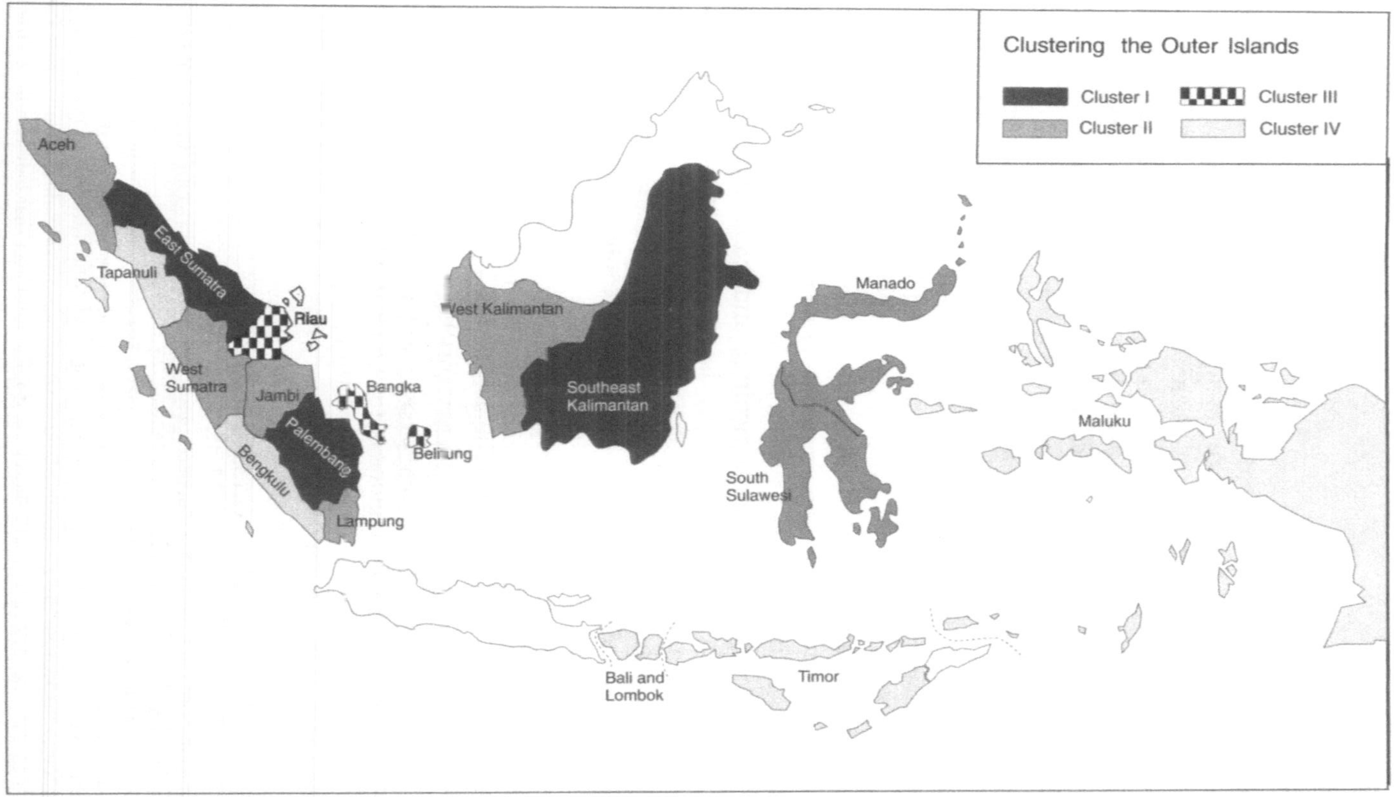

Map 2. Four clusters of residencies in the Outer Islands

Cluster I: The growth provinces

East Sumatra

'East Sumatra ['Oostkust van Sumatra'; today: Sumatera Utara] is a large and powerful province', was the appropriate description which B.C.C.M.M. van Suchtelen bestowed on it when he was inaugurated as governor of this province in 1933.[33] The estate area (Cultuurgebied), which had been consistently expanding since the 1860s, housed an influential group of European entrepreneurs in the export trade. In Western eyes, the estate area was the most striking characteristic of this large residency. It was located slightly north of the centre of the residency, near Deli and Serdang. Further north, in Langkat, oil was drilled and taken by pipeline to the BPM production centre in Pangkalan Brandan (Figure 23a).

Important though these were, especially in Dutch eyes, there was more to East Sumatra than just estates and oil production. Smallholders cultivated rubber, copra, and pinang nuts. On the Karo plains, vegetables were grown and sold by Karo Batak. In Asahan, peasants grew rubber. Javanese, Chinese, and other immigrant labourers settled in the region after having served their contracts, taking up smallholder agriculture and trade. Working together with indigenous population groups, they developed export agriculture, notably in rubber. South of Asahan, Bagan Siapiapi (district of Bengkalis), a small community that consisted almost entirely of Chinese, was one of the fishing centres of the Outer Islands. In 1905 5,000 Chinese lived here and exported fish and dried shrimp paste (trassi) to Java and elsewhere.[34]

In the nineteenth century, East Sumatran peasants had grown pepper and tobacco.[35] As elsewhere in Sumatra, rice was grown on ladang, or unirrigated fields, and in the south of the province fishing was an important source of income. The sparsely populated residency was originally inhabited by coastal Malays and inland Batak, and ruled over by Malay sultans and chiefs. As in most other thinly populated regions of the Outer Islands, the majority of the indigenous population were engaged in shifting cultivation. In the eighteenth and nineteenth centuries, the Malay sultans were already relatively wealthy

33 ARA Kol, MvO 190, B.C.C.M.M. van Suchtelen 1936:329.

34 ARA Kol, MvO 181, G. Schaap 1905:7; MvO 182, J. Ballot 1910:53; MvO 190, B.C.C.M.M. van Suchtelen 1936:263. Ballot called Bagan Siapiapi 'one of the world's most important fishing communities'. See also Vleming 1926:234; Boeijinga 1926.

35 Most of our knowledge of eighteenth-century East Sumatra is based on the reports of John Anderson, an Englishman who travelled extensively through East Sumatra in 1823 by order of the Penang government. As Pelzer put it, 'the observations made by Anderson in 1823 are of particular value to us because the European planters who entered East Sumatra forty years later were so busy carving their plantations out of the tropical rainforest that they had little time or interest in travelling about the country to make scientific observations, much less put such observations on paper' (Pelzer 1978:2-7).

– although under constant threat from Aceh and Siak (Bengkalis), the leading states in pre-colonial Sumatra. Around 1850, the region seemed destined to remain a forgotten and remote corner of the Indonesian archipelago (Thee Kian Wie 1977:4; De Waard 1934:215-7). When European planters came, things started to change rapidly. Estates were laid out, local chiefs received sums of money for land rent and concessions, and immigrant labour was imported into the estate area in large numbers. Entrepreneurs were attracted by the fertile soil and the favourable climate, which made it possible to cultivate tobacco and rubber – and in the 1930s tea, oil palm, and fibres. Cultivation took place on a large scale, and as a consequence, the largest concentration of Europeans in the Indonesian archipelago outside Java settled in the Deli and Serdang region. In 1930, 58 per cent of the population of East Sumatra was made up of Europeans and Chinese and non-local Indonesians, mainly from Java. Most of the last group were working or had worked as estate labourers.

In terms of estate agriculture, East Sumatra was the most important and most productive region of all the Outer Provinces. Even before 1900, East Sumatra had built up a reputation for providing good opportunities to make a profit. In 1925, East Sumatra supplied 32.8 per cent of the total export value of the Outer Islands (including smallholder exports and including non-agricultural exports such as oil) (Table 31). The concentration of European entrepreneurship made itself felt in the regional infrastructure: a network of roads and railways sprang from the economic activity, and Medan, originally a small provincial town, grew more quickly than any other town in colonial Indonesia during those fifty years (Boomgaard and Gooszen 1990:43, 245).

East Sumatra had a two-tiered or dual economy. The European presence was more pronounced here than in any other province, and was concentrated in the estate area of Deli and Serdang, and the oil production centre in Pangkalan Brandan. Smallholder export agriculture developed simultaneously. The Asian population (indigenous Batak and Malays, joined by Javanese and Chinese former estate labourers) developed their own independent production lines, which in the literature have unjustifiably remained in the shadow of European agriculture. The extent to which the presence of the estates infringed upon the expansion of indigenous producers, or stimulated them by increasing demand for food and construction materials, is an important question which is treated in Chapter III.

Palembang

A relatively affluent province, Palembang (today: Sumatera Selatan) had had a long history as a centre of local and domestic trade and handicrafts. During the famous Sriwijaya Empire in the seventh century, Palembang was an important region which dominated the southern part of Sumatra. When it was brought under the definitive control of the colonial government in the 1870s, it developed smoothly into one of the economically strongest provinces of the Outer Islands (Figure 23b). Inhabited by a population that took an active interest in agriculture and trade, Palembang had a relatively diversified economy. Smallholders produced coffee, pepper, and rubber, and exported a variety of other crops, such as pineapples.[36] As Resident J. Tideman wrote in 1928: 'For centuries Palembang has been known as a trading centre of great significance to South Sumatra. Important trade relations are maintained with Singapore and Batavia. In recent years, ocean steamers have managed to navigate the Musi River on a regular basis. In a sense, by their majestic appearance in the middle of the vast waterway right through the town, they accentuate the image of prosperity.'[37]

In the early twentieth century, the bustling economic activity of Palembang was attributed to the 'fine and energetic' character of the indigenous people of Palembang, who were 'reliable traders and orderly citizens'.[38] Although these impressions would seem to stand in contradiction to the earlier rebellious spirit shown by the people during the VOC era, they reflect the lack of political problems encountered in the province during the period under study – and the relatively strong economy (compare Wellan 1932:160-3). However, 'reliable' should not be taken too seriously: Palembang traders were notorious frauds with regard to the quality of their wares. Many Malay inhabitants of Palembang were active in intermediary trade. They were often peasants who produced cash crops themselves. The dependence of smallholders on Chinese middlemen for credit was lower in Palembang than in, for example, nearby Lampung or Jambi (Wellan 1932:399; Purwanto 1992:309).

As in East Sumatra, economic growth in Palembang had a dual basis. European entrepreneurship had gained a strong foothold in this residency – even though the humidity of the Palembang lowlands had the reputation of being more disagreeable than the climate of East Sumatra.[39] In Palembang there were coal mines (at Bukit Asem), several oil-drilling areas, and a number of European estates cultivating rubber, quinine, and tea, as well as some coffee.[40] In the 1930s BPM drilled oil at Muara Enim and Musi Ilir and a few other sites, and a subsidiary of Standard Oil drilled oil in Talang Akar. BPM constructed a large petroleum refinery in Plaju, near the town of Palembang.

The town of Palembang itself, which had been one of the first places in the

36 Other crops exported were resin (benzoin), pinang nuts, rattan, quinine, fibres (sisal), and gutta percha. ARA Kol, MvO 212, J. Tideman 1928:232; Atmodipoerwo 1934-35; Touwen 1991: 140, 171-73; Wellan 1932:168.

37 ARA Kol, MvO 212, J. Tideman 1928:232.

38 De Bruyn Kops 1919:42-3. See also Peeters 1994.

39 Interview Mrs T. Terpstra, Noordwijk aan Zee, 22 December 1994.

40 In 1932, there were 8 estates producing coffee in Palembang, compared with 21 in West Sumatra, 20 in Aceh, 14 in Lampung, and 5 in East Sumatra. Landbouwexportgewassen 1933:108.

archipelago to be frequented by the VOC in the seventeenth century (an honour shared with Jambi and Aceh), had been a trading centre for centuries. It was conveniently located on the Musi River, admirably accessible from the sea, which enhanced its trade relations with Singapore and Batavia. There were coffee-roasting factories and rice millers, as well as several rubber remillers. In 1928, when export revenues were at their highest, there were twelve coffee factories in the town of Palembang, two coffee-roasting facilities, and one factory processing both coffee and rubber (Creutzberg 1974:99; Wellan 1932:300). Most of the rubber and coffee from the interior were transported to the town of Palembang before being exported, including an unknown amount of Lampung rubber and Bengkulu coffee from the border regions of these provinces. This adds to our picture of a flourishing, relatively well-off economic centre.

Southeast Kalimantan

The island of Borneo was both larger and more unknown than Sumatra during the colonial period. About one-third of this island formed British Borneo, and the remainder was divided into two provinces: West Kalimantan and Southeast Kalimantan. At the turn of the century, Southeast Kalimantan ('Zuider- en Oosterafdeling van Borneo'; today: Kalimantan Selatan, Tengah, Timur) was almost the twin sister of West Kalimantan: an enormous area of largely primeval forest, speckled with a few coastal trading posts, usually on river inlets. Foreign trade consisted mostly of exports of forest products such as rattan and gutta percha (forest rubber). Trade was largely controlled by a handful of Chinese immigrants along the rivers. During the following decades, the economy of Southeast Kalimantan changed more rapidly under the forces of modernization than did that of West Kalimantan (Figure 23c) (Lindblad 1988a, Velsing 1925).

With the discovery of coal and oil, European industrial activity settled along the eastern coast of Southeast Kalimantan, in the sultanates of Kutai, Gunung Tabur, Sambaliung, and Bulungan. As in East Sumatra, European capital interests were quickly followed by the construction of infrastructural facilities. European entrepreneurs were engaged in oil, coal, and large-scale rubber and copra estates. Oil was produced in Kutai and on the island of Tarakan in the far north. In Balikpapan, BPM constructed and expanded a large production centre. Coal was produced on Pulu Laut, a small island located off the southeastern coast, by the East Borneo Company (OBM) in Kutai, and in Berau by the Parapattan company, a KPM subsidiary. In the 1930s, agricultural estates in the residency cultivated rubber, palm oil, gambir, and coffee.[41]

While European and American companies exploited oil, indigenous rub-

41 Lindblad 1988a:78-99; ARA Kol, MvO 277, B.C.C.M.M. van Suchtelen 1933:176.

ber cultivation reshaped Hulu Sungai. Almost all smallholder rubber cultivation was concentrated in this populous region in the south.[42] The rubber was transported to Banjarmasin and from there exported to Singapore, which served as the major transit destination for all smallholder rubber in the archipelago. By the 1920s many small-scale entrepreneurs were relatively prosperous. Other indigenous smallholders exported copra, ladang (swidden) rice, or forest products.[43] In regions where both copra and rubber were cultivated, coconut palms were neglected during the rubber boom, since wages for rubber tappers were too high to keep them employed in coconut groves. But after the rubber price fell in 1925, copra revived.[44] Prahus and steamboats navigated the Mahakam River to reach the interior (frustrated by numerous sandbanks in the rivers), while in the better-developed areas short canals were dug and maintained by corvée labour. Only in the districts of Hulu Sungai and Banjarmasin in the south, which were relatively densely populated, was there a network of roads.[45] In contrast to the Dayak and Malay population groups in the interior, many Banjarese inhabitants participated actively in trade and were known for their 'exceptional diligence' and their 'enterprising commercial spirit'.[46] Like the Bugis from South Sulawesi and the Minangkabau from West Sumatra, the Banjarese were known for their migratory habits and also showed their commercial spirit elsewhere in the archipelago (Potter 1993). Within Southeast Kalimantan, the main centres for both European and Asian trade were Samarinda and Banjarmasin.

Foreign trade was the motor of expansion in Southeast Kalimantan. The simultaneous success in two sectors (oil and rubber) was based on dualism, but increased the vulnerability of this twin-based economy to fluctuations in the world economy (Lindblad 1988a:172-88, 217-21).

Cluster II: Indigenous performers

Aceh

In the nineteenth century, pirates descending from their lairs in the independent sultanate of Aceh ('Atjeh') had often wrought havoc on Dutch trading routes. The Anglo-Dutch treaty of 1824 stipulated that Aceh should remain

[42] In contrast to for example Jambi and Palembang, indigenous rubber was concentrated in one region and did not spread over the entire residency. ARA Kol, MvO 225, Ph.J. van der Meulen 1936:74.

[43] Such as gutta percha, damar, rattan, and benzoin. ARA Kol, MvO 271, L.J.F. Rijckmans 1916:32-5; MvO KIT 1031, G.L. Tichelman (Controleur) 1929:82-3.

[44] ARA Kol, MvO KIT 1031, G.L. Tichelman (Controleur) 1929:89.

[45] ARA Kol, MvO 271, L.J.F. Rijckmans 1916:51-3; MvO 273, A.M. Hens 1921:98; MvO 277, B.C.C.M.M. van Suchtelen 1933:198; ARA, NHM 9088, VvS 33 (Banjarmasin 1927):15.

[46] ARA Kol, MvO 225, Ph.J. van der Meulen 1936:74.

independent and that the Dutch should not intervene in its internal affairs. In 1871 this agreement was revised and the Dutch took steps to contain the expansion of Aceh in 1873, one of the fuses which resulted in the Aceh War (1873-1903/1912). It was this initially low-pitched struggle to subjugate Aceh which brought the province to the attention of the Netherlands government and of the Dutch in Java. After intensified efforts by Van Heutsz, Dutch authority was gradually established between 1896 and 1904 (Furnivall 1944:178; Pelzer 1987:10-3; Reid 1979; Ricklefs 1993:146). Even after the pacification in 1913, a 'fanatical spirit of freedom was brewing in this province'.[47]

The Acehnese remained rebellious. They were passionately Muslim and frequently engaged in political meetings, willingly joining organizations, although the government did its best to discourage and prohibit both of these activities. Allegedly, no government official would walk on the street without a weapon in his pocket. Although represented as a keg of gunpowder, the Aceh peasants in the meantime put their efforts into developing a relatively stable and diversified agricultural sector (Figure 23d). Although some estates from the adjacent estate economy of East Sumatra did venture to cross the border into Aceh, European companies were loath to invest in this region. Indigenous peasants enhanced their traditional subsistence economy with exports of copra, *pinang* nuts, pepper, and also various food crops (maize, potatoes, cassava), kapok, and rubber. At times, rice was exported to the Deli estate area – although complaints from estate labourers about the quality of this brown rice caused foreign rice imports to be favoured over Acehnese.[48]

In the nineteenth century pepper had been a flourishing trade crop in much of eastern Aceh. The *uleëbalang* (district heads) became rich and powerful on the strength of pepper revenues. The *uleëbalang* competed with each other and repeatedly found themselves in conflict with the sultan of Aceh. In the twentieth century pepper exports started to decline, even though the indigenous population persevered in cultivating new pepper tendrils. The downfall was mainly due to plant disease and local food shortages.[49]

Aceh was one of the few provinces where imports often exceeded exports: a vigorous demand for foreign consumer goods led to a trade deficit in 10 out of 30 years during the period 1911-1940.[50] The local colonial government believed that attracting European agricultural estates was the best way to

47 ARA Kol, MvO 159, A.H. Philips (Aceh 1932) 26-7; MvO 160, A.Ph. van Aken 1936:1-2.

48 ARA, NHM 9128, VvS 522 (Olehleh (Aceh) 1903) 1-2; ARA Kol, MvO 159, Governor A.H. Philips 1932:46, 56; MvO 160, A.Ph. van Aken 1936:49-51.

49 ARA Kol, MvO 160, A.Ph. van Aken 1936:67; Gade Ismail 1994a:281-9; 1994b; Ricklefs 1993:143.

50 There is no reason to suspect an extraordinarily high purchasing power amongst the local population. Possibly certain imports were procured by European companies which exported via East Sumatra, thus not balancing these imports with export revenues (Clemens et al. 1992:53).

maintain law and order: by opening up remote regions, bringing money, employment opportunities, and prosperity. Wooed by this policy, a number of estates settled in Aceh in the 1930s, exporting rubber, coffee, and palm oil.[51] Some of the exports went through Kota Raja, a small trading town, whereas Sabang, on Pulau Weh, although a duty-free harbour, remained chiefly a coaling station for ocean steamers. Interestingly, much of the indigenous rubber from Aceh was exported not to Singapore, but to nearby Penang. The oil drilled by BPM in eastern Aceh flowed through pipelines to Pangkalan Brandan (East Sumatra) and is not included in the Aceh export statistics.[52]

In Aceh, European enterprise had little impact on the economy. In eastern Aceh, oil palm estates developed after 1920 and there was also some economic activity in the drilling of petroleum. While European enterprise slowly expanded, indigenous agriculture gradually declined (Gade Ismail 1994a: 289). Owing to this decline in eastern Aceh and to political unrest, indigenous agriculture in Aceh generated a relatively meagre value per capita (even though total exports were fairly impressive). In the late 1920s, Aceh did only slightly better in exports per capita than Bali, and lagged considerably behind Sumatran 'tigers' such as Palembang and Jambi (Tables 25.1 and 26.1, Figures 24a and 24d).

West Sumatra

Although West Sumatra ('Westkust van Sumatra'; today: Sumatera Barat) was situated out of the general run of things on the west side of Sumatra, this residency, including the port town of Padang, had a tradition of active participation in trade in the archipelago (Figure 23e). In this regard, West Sumatra resembled Palembang. In the nineteenth century it had been an important centre of coffee production under the Cultivation System. Government coffee plantations lasted from 1848 until 1916 (Young 1990:109; Dobbin 1983:225-47). There was also a tradition of *sawah* or wet-rice production, which was exceptional in Sumatra, where most rice cultivation was done on *ladang* fields. The twentieth century saw Padang struggling to retain its share in the expanding trade, which was shifting eastwards to the Java Sea to the benefit of Singapore, Medan, Palembang, and Batavia. Colombijn describes how in the course of the nineteenth and twentieth centuries Padang lost its role as a main trading centre (Colombijn 1991, 1994:89).

In West Sumatra there were not many traces of European enterprise, although some industrial activity was generated by the Portland cement fact-

51 Palm oil, for example, was cultivated in Aceh by the Franco-Belgian company Société Financière des Caoutchoucs after 1926. Most agricultural estates preferred the border region near East Sumatra or were extensions of estates in East Sumatra. In 1932, there were 20 coffee estates in Aceh (ARA Kol, MvO 160, A.Ph. van Aken 1936:72-5; Van Gelder 1950:429).

52 Thee Kian Wie 1977:34; ARA, NHM 9128, VvS 522 (Olehleh (Aceh) 1903):3.

ory in Padang, the nearby Ombilin coal mines, and the Salida silver mine. The harbour at Emmahaven in Padang owed its existence to coal exports, but also served as a local trading centre in indigenous produce (Gonggrijp 1938:166). Indigenous peasants produced coffee, which thrived in the highlands of the Barisan Mountains. Copra, along the coast, made a good income supplement and also gained a substantial share in West Sumatra's exports, but it did not replace the more traditional coffee. Other exports were rubber, cassia, tea, and rattan.

In West Sumatra, Minangkabau culture strongly influenced the position of the smallholder in the economy. Under the pressures of the matrilineal *adat* system, the men travelled extensively and carried on trade. In this province, Chinese middlemen played a smaller role than elsewhere because so much of the trade was in the hands of Minangkabau men.[53] West Sumatra was relatively densely populated, especially since most of the population lived in the coastal areas, which constituted some twenty per cent of the total area. Most of the trade went through Emmahaven, although some imports came through Pakanbaru in East Sumatra. Only an alleged 1.5 per cent of the rubber exports of this region went over inland routes to Jambi.[54]

Jambi

During the VOC era, exchanges between Dutch merchants and the indigenous population in Jambi ('Djambi') were few and far between, unlike in Palembang, where trade flourished and a successful Dutch trading post had been established. The VOC trading post in Jambi had been abandoned for extended periods of time since its establishment in 1615 (Wellan 1932:161). During the final decades of the nineteenth century Jambi was politically restless and mutinous. In the eyes of the colonizers, it formed, as did Aceh, a threat to the political stability in the archipelago. The attention of colonial officials in Batavia and the Dutch government in The Hague was drawn to Jambi by the discovery of oil.[55] Jambi was put under strong military authority. After

[53] This well-known Minangkabau cultural trait of voluntary migration is called *merantau*. The first type of *merantau* was the migration of whole villages and was encountered until the nineteenth century but not afterwards. The second type is characteristic of the period under study: the temporary migration of men, which started in the late nineteenth century. The third type of *merantau* consists of permanent migration of nuclear families and has only come up since the 1950s (Colombijn 1994:53, 79-81). *Merantau* can be seen in connection with the matrilineal tradition: men occupy a marginal position in the household, which gives them the opportunity to migrate and carry on trade.

[54] ARA Kol, MvO 170, A.I. Spits 1937:2, 75, 98; Colombijn 1994:78.

[55] Locher-Scholten writes that Jambi supplied between 2.7 and 4.5% of total Outer Provinces exports between 1880 and 1895. In fact, Jambi's exports constituted only 1.5% on average during the years 1883-1890. After 1900 they dwindled to 0.3% in 1903 (Locher-Scholten 1994a:208, 219-40, 255-62).

the rebellious Sultan Taha had been killed in an ambush, Jambi developed quietly for a number of years.[56]

In 1907 the first Hevea Brasiliensis plants were imported into Sumatra and it was Jambi above all other provinces that dedicated itself to the small-scale production of rubber (Figure 23f). In the years following, rubber cultivation spread rapidly. Chinese traders brought seeds and seedlings into the area, but in the beginning the government also distributed Hevea plants among the indigenous peasants to test the possibility of its indigenous cultivation (Touwen 1991).

The main reason behind the success of rubber cultivation in Jambi was the high market price for rubber on the world market in the years 1910-1925. Yet this does not explain why it was especially in Jambi that indigenous rubber cultivation became so important. In earlier days, farmers in Jambi had shown no signs of (economic) interest in the outside world, in cultivating trade crops, or in changing traditional sources of income. Suddenly, more quickly than in any other Indonesian province, Jambi smallholders reacted to the market mechanism, seeking maximum profits for cash crops. Even with an investment period of six years (since it takes six years for the rubber tree to become productive), Jambi farmers throughout the province started to plant rubber. Resident Th.A.L. Heyting recounts his surprise at the 'rubber fever' in his 1913 report: 'The indigenous population plants Para rubber with true fervour; every inhabitant is eager to seek his fortune.'[57] In the 1930s, Jambi was known everywhere in the archipelago for the explosive expansion of smallholder rubber production during the rubber boom. The income from this economic activity was seriously diminished during the Depression, but was well on its way to recovery when the Second World War broke out. Rubber was a low-capital industry, requiring little more than some land, cheap labour, and planting material. Neither the Jambi peasant nor his Chinese middleman made efforts to invest in processing techniques or local infrastructure. The wet rubber slabs were transported submerged under rafts in the river. Serious improvement of Jambi's infrastructure took place only when revenue derived from the surtax on indigenous rubber exports was allocated to specific projects.

It took until 1921 before oil exploitation in Jambi was organized (see Chapter III). Since the oil flowed by pipeline to Palembang, where it was processed, Jambi experienced few growth linkages from the oil industry. It remained a typical 'indigenous producer', where the economy was dominated by poor-quality rubber produced at low cost with little capital.

56 Sultan Taha Saifuddin was buried in Muaratebo (Tideman 1938:340).
57 ARA Kol, MvO 218, Th.A.L. Heyting 1913:28.

Lampung

Lampung ('Lampongse Districten') was situated close to Java, but was not drawn into the relative hustle and bustle of the Javanese economy. The southeastern part of Lampung consisted of swampy lowlands (*lebak*), but further west, close to the Barisan Mountains, the province was higher in elevation. At the turn of the century, the forest along the southern coast was not as unspoilt as in other parts of Sumatra, because Lampung had experienced the full destructive power of the eruption of Krakatau in 1883 (every cloud has a silver lining: this disaster also brought fertile volcanic ash to the coastal soil). Lampung betrayed no signs of rocketing indigenous rubber production such as took place in Jambi. After decades of growing pepper, Lampung peasants only gradually shifted to coffee and rubber, at the same time increasing their output of pepper, which became more important than Aceh pepper after 1922 (Figure 23g). 'The Lampung man, with his conservative *adat*, does not show as much inclination to adopt unfamiliar ideas and cultural enrichment', Wellan (1932:11) wrote. In this politically calm residency, the Malay population was known for its refined culture, exemplified by the famous *jujur* weddings.[58] The whole population participated in pepper cultivation. Exports made a slow start during the early decades of the 1900s, but then began to flourish after 1920.[59] A relatively large share of Lampung's exports was exported to Java. During the pepper harvest, a Javanese workforce invaded Lampung and returned home afterwards.[60] Lampung was well known as a major immigration destination in the 'colonization' projects of the colonial government, which aimed to lighten Java's population pressure. Lampung was an obvious choice for these projects, being sparsely populated and close to Java. However, neither the immigration projects nor the establishment of European industries managed to fulfil the expectations of government officials.

One Resident cherished the hope that one day Lampung would become like a 'second Deli' – a forlorn hope, as little European enterprise came to Lampung.[61] In the 1920s, in Cisaat, a small textile factory languished until it was saved by an energetic entrepreneur who started producing good-quality

58 The wedding was a very important event, in which *jujur* referred to the brideprice that was paid by the bridegroom to the family of the bride. (ARA Kol, MvO 231, J. Breukink 1922:35; Broersma 1916:64-90.)

59 Unfortunately, the totals per province of the interregional trade statistics were only published from 1923, obstructing a clear view of Lampung's trade with Java before 1920.

60 ARA Kol, MvO 231, J. Breukink 1922:21; MvO 233, L. Berkhout 1926:30; MvO 232, Th. Volmering 1933:12-5.

61 'Extremely large applications from financially sound bodies raise expectations that this region will become a second estate area like Deli' (ARA Kol, MvO 233, L. Berkhout 1926:49).

rope. A plywood factory also struggled for survival, a fate it shared with the factory of the Nederlands-Indische Hoogoven Maatschappij.[62]

Government officials, who believed that Lampung was a promising residency, turned out to be right about indigenous exports. Exports from Lampung increased from around 1923, and even during the 1930s, seemingly unhindered by the Depression. Per capita exports, including a large flow to Java, were higher in Lampung in the 1930s than in Jambi, Aceh, West Sumatra, Tapanuli, or Bengkulu. Intermediary trade in Lampung was mostly in the hands of Chinese and Palembangese, which resulted in many Lampung peasants being dependent on creditors from outside the residency (Wellan 1932:399).

In the 1920s, when the railways of the Zuid-Sumatra Spoorweg (South Sumatra Railway, ZSS) advanced into the interior regions and eventually reached the harbour of the town of Palembang, traders and peasants settled alongside the tracks. The trains carried pepper, coffee, and timber. This took the wind out of the sails of the flourishing inland trading town of Menggala – an example of how the development of infrastructure, initiated by the Dutch, influenced local trading patterns.[63] The ZSS had a favourable effect on the export economy. Truck services, both leased and owned, extended the railway connections into the smallholder gardens and the estates, thereby making it possible to avoid recourse to unprofitable transport by middlemen (Wellan 1932:399).

West Kalimantan

West Kalimantan ('Westerafdeling van Borneo'; today: Kalimantan Barat), the smaller western division of Borneo, long remained an enormous, rather inaccessible, and largely unknown stretch of primeval forest, crossed only by explorers and anthropologists.[64] Unique in the archipelago (except for perhaps Bengkalis in East Sumatra) were the old settlements of Chinese on the coast, inhabited by the descendants of mineworkers who were imported around 1750 by the then reigning Panembahan of Mampawah. The Chinese kongsi, above all in Sambas in the northwestern corner of the province, formed an economically strong and independent population group. They had close ties with the trading centre of Singapore. At times, the Chinese had even subjected the upland powers, but generally they tended to cooperate

62 The name of this entrepreneur was Mr Synja. ARA Kol, MvO 233, L. Berkhout 1926:10, 39-40; MvO 232, Th. Volmering 1933:27 (appendix).

63 ARA Kol, MvO 231, J. Breukink 1922:21; MvO 233, L. Berkhout 1926:5, 45-6; Purwanto 1993:121.

64 For example the well-known Dutch physician A.W. Nieuwenhuis, who travelled in 1896 and 1898 from Pontianak to Samarinda in about fifteen months (Nieuwenhuis 1904-07).

with the Dutch.[65] They not only engaged in fishing but also formed an important peasant community, concentrating on copra exports, and participated in the trade with the interior of Kalimantan, where Dayak and Malays lived along the riverbanks (Vleming 1926:256, 260-4).

Although the Malay population was Muslim, the province was too sparsely populated to develop any serious political organizations or political awareness as in Aceh. According to their governors, the Malays were not exceedingly industrious, but neither were they inclined to criminality. In exchange for certain favours from the Malays, the Dayak sometimes agreed to convert to Islam, although they generally held animist beliefs.[66] It seems the Dayak population cooperated more easily with the Chinese than with the Malays. The indigenous groups, spread throughout the inland forest, occasionally had traditional tribal feuds, but did not cause the colonial government any serious problems.[67]

The European presence was centred in Pontianak, where Chinese inhabitants were also numerous (Table 17). Pontianak was roughly the same size as Manado, but housed three times as many Chinese (however, in Manado there were three times as many Europeans). Slowly, Pontianak had developed into a trading harbour of some importance. Owing to its central location, it had regular shipping connections with Batavia, Belitung, and Singapore in the 1930s, even though the harbour remained small in size.[68]

As a large province in which the population of the unknown interior actively participated in foreign trade, West Kalimantan resembled Jambi. Although, unlike in Jambi, copra accompanied rubber as a major export product in West Kalimantan, export performance followed a similar path (Figure 23.h). This may be explained by the fact that copra was produced mainly along the coast, while rubber was the major export product in the interior. The rapid growth of rubber exports in the 1910s and 1920s, followed by a peak in 1925, a severe downfall in 1932-1936, and surprising recovery in 1938-1940, made these two provinces models of indigenous rubber production (Ozinga 1940.120, 289-300; Ranken 1989).

South Sulawesi

The strange shape of Sulawesi ('Celebes en onderhorigheden'; today: Sulawesi Selatan, Tengah, Tenggara) has been compared to a dishevelled orchid, a drunken spider, a scarecrow in a storm, or the letter K written by a

65 ARA Kol, MvO 265, J. Oberman 1938:26, 107; Ricklefs 1992:38.

66 ARA Kol, MvO 261, H. de Vogel 1918:15-9; MvO 265, J. Oberman 1938:26.

67 ARA Kol, MvO 265, J. Oberman 1938:107.

68 ARA Kol, MvO 265, J. Oberman 1938:55. In those days Pontianak was called at by KPM, Straits Steamship Company, and the trading company Thong Ek. Also, Madurese prahus provided transport to Java and Madura.

child.[69] Sulawesi consists of four peninsulas, giving it a very long coastline in proportion to its area. The maximum distance to the coast is 90 km, but most places lie less than 50 km from the seashore. Although the coastline favours shipping and easy access to all sides of Sulawesi, its geomorphology does not: most of inland Sulawesi consists of mountain peaks, one-fifth of which reach a height of more than 1,000 metres. Sulawesi was a jumble of inaccessible forests and mountain ridges, making inland transport by road or river hazardous, so that the best way of reaching the various coastal settlements was by circumnavigating the island by sea.

We can distinguish two dynamic centres on the island of Sulawesi. In the far northern part of Manado, Minahasa was an exceptional province where Dutch presence and influence were very strong (see below). Its opposite number in the south was Macassar (today: Ujung Pandang, Makassar), the traditional trading town on the west coast of South Sulawesi. This was the most important trading centre of colonial Indonesia east of Java and Kalimantan. Referring to Macassar, the Resident of Timor and later of South Sulawesi, A.J.L. Couvreur, remarked in a 1924 political report: 'Whoever has psychological domination over Macassar – and whoever, in the present context, says Celebes says Macassar, and will do so even more in the coming years – controls the eastern part of the archipelago.'[70] There was little that unified Sulawesi. Both the provinces South Sulawesi and Manado were home to numerous local peoples, local languages, and cultures, which were kept apart by the impassable physical infrastructure of the island.[71] In the nineteenth century, the princely statelets of South Sulawesi had bitterly resisted the intrusion of Dutch power. Only in 1904-1905 was the resistance of the Bugis and Macassarese states finally broken. The animist, head-hunting Toraja people of Central Sulawesi gradually came into touch with colonial power.

South Sulawesi was a net exporter of rice and maize, and exported small quantities of coffee, rattan, and resin (copal) as well, mostly through Macas-

69 Cubitt et al. 1993:150. 'Sulawesi barely seems to hold its sprawling limbs together even on the map' (Henley 1989:31).

70 'He dominates the whole Timor archipelago, from Sumbawa to Timor, directly and completely. In connection with Manado's southward push and endeavour to gain hegemony over Celebes, of which Macassar will nevertheless always remain the natural emporium, he can exercise a decisive influence upon Manado, and he will also influence Ambon, albeit more weakly than the above-mentioned areas, since Ambon is a natural commercial centre [emporium] itself – specifically of the Moluccas', as A.J.L. Couvreur wrote in his Communication to the Governor-General of the Netherlands Indies on 8 April 1924. Cited in Henley 1989:25.

71 Sulawesi 'failed its last test of unity' after independence, when events following the Pemesta uprising in 1957 split the region into north and south. The disparities between the north (Manado) and South Sulawesi continue to exist: 'Manado and Macassar seem today to be as dramatic a pair of counterpoles as Indonesia has to offer' (Henley 1989:31).

sar.[72] Although this province showed little economic expansion on the foreign market, it was a relatively large domestic trader (Figure 23i). Macassar exported copra not only from South Sulawesi but also from Maluku and surrounding local harbours.[73] Much of this trade was shipped on special delivery notes called 'bills of lading', a system of charging a uniform fee for transportation of local produce to Europe, disregarding the exact local origin (transit trade). In contrast to copal and rattan, which were often processed in Macassar before shipment to Europe, copra was exported as a raw bulk material. 'Since most export cargo is transit cargo, very little is stored locally, and therefore the rows of *gudang* [warehouses] often appear deserted.'[74] This transit trade augmented Macassar's role as a trading centre but was not represented in the trade statistics of South Sulawesi. Interregional exports of Sulawesi to Java were large, largest of all domestic traders as far as registered exports to Java and other Outer Islands are concerned. Imports consisted mainly of consumer goods, which means that few foodstuffs or capital goods were imported. In this regard South Sulawesi resembles West Sumatra (in contrast to Southeast Kalimantan and Palembang, where imports of capital goods were larger).[75] Typical of South Sulawesi was that it had continuously expanding exports, with relatively stable revenues during the Depression years, but still remained unattractive to European entrepreneurs. On the whole, it was less accessible and was cursed with worse natural conditions than Sumatra. Another objection was that Europeans thought that the inhabitants of South Sulawesi were not suitable for working on estates (although in Sumatra this same objection was overcome by using imported labour). According to commercial agents, it was this factor that delayed economic development in South Sulawesi. A rubber estate in southern South Sulawesi attracted skilled tappers from the interior, but these workers always returned to their villages to grow rice or corn, and did not provide a stable labour force.[76]

Manado

In Manado ('Menado'; today: Sulawesi Utara, Tengah), the most remarkable region in the eyes of the Dutch was Minahasa; the northern tip of the Manado residency was for centuries the favourite destination of missionaries and civil servants. As early as the seventeenth century, there were intensive trad-

72 Rice exports came mainly from the southern part of the residency. *Indisch Verslag* 1939:62; ARA, NHM 9122, VvS 447 (Macassar 1923):6; NHM 9123, VvS 456 (Macassar 1932):10.

73 For an analysis of the copra trade in the region, see Heersink 1999:159-86.

74 ARA, NHM 9122, VvS 448 (Macassar 1924):22. See also Heersink 1999:165; A Campo 1992:249-51, 258-9.

75 Largely due to European economic activity (Clemens et al. 1992:44, 97-8).

76 ARA, NHM 9122, VvS 448 (Macassar 1924):3; VvS 449 (Macassar 1925):4; VvS 452 (Macassar 1928):3.

ing contacts between the Dutch and the Minahasans.[77] In 1657 the VOC built a trading post on the site of the town of Manado, where armed protection was exchanged for local deliveries of rice and wood. Later, Minahasans supplied corvée labour and grew coffee and coconuts. In the wake of this trade, VOC preachers and the missionaries of the Nederlandsch Zendeling-Genootschap (NZG, Dutch Missionary Society) spread Christianity actively and established relatively well-developed educational opportunities. All this meant that the population of Minahasa received extraordinary attention from the Dutch, which is illustrated by its well-known epithet 'the Twelfth Province of the Netherlands'. Good schooling enabled Minahasans to work as civil servants or with the KPM. Many enlisted in the Netherlands Indies army (KNIL), earning, as did the Moluccans, a good reputation for military service.[78]

Minahasa was the only region in Manado where there was a good road system, on which private motor services provided regular transportation of goods and persons. The rest of Manado was less developed. Anyone travelling from Minahasa to the west, to Bolaäng-Mongondou, found that the roads gradually degenerated and were badly maintained, crossing many rivers without the benefit of bridges; the border river, the Poigar, even formed a serious hindrance. It was far more advisable to travel to Bolaäng by sea, which was a dangerous expedition during the West Monsoon because of the sudden 'Barat' storms. N.R. Pekelharing remarked after a trip to northern Sulawesi that, if large firms should gain interest in the region, the first condition would be improvement of its transport facilities.[79] In fact, European companies showed little interest in establishing agricultural estates in Manado. Its coast could be called capricious, the fertility of the land varied considerably, and, as a consequence of the mountainous terrain of the island, the climate was unpredictable and rainfall irregular.[80] None of the

77 For recent surveys of the history of Minahasa with more attention to cultural and social aspects, see Schefold 1995, Schouten 1998.

78 Minahasa soldiers were showcase pupils of their Dutch commanders, but the sympathy was reciprocal: during independence negotiations, several Minahasa groups aimed to achieve a special Minahasa status, with strong ties with the Netherlands. Of course, Minahasa ethnic and regional identity is of a more complex nature than can be outlined here. In his study on the internal unity and communal identity of Minahasa, Henley writes that the historical picture is complicated by 'a respectable crop of heroes of Indonesian nationalism, an integral contribution to the final independence struggle', complicated by 'an equally uncompromising myth of Dutchness - Minahassa as the "twelfth province" of the Greater Netherlands, a lonely outpost of Western culture and Christianity, a bastion of loyalty to the colonial power'. Although Dutch influence may not have been the singular or dominating characteristic of the indigenous identities of Minahasa, Minahasa received more social and cultural effects of Dutch presence than any other region among the Outer Provinces (Henley 1996:41-2).

79 ARA Kol, MvO KIT 1175, N.R. Pekelharing 1921:4-5 (*Report of an official tour through North Sulawesi*).

80 ARA Kol, MvO 304, F.H.W.J.R. Logeman 1922:11-3; MvO KIT 1175, N.R. Pekelharing 1921:4-9.

rivers was suitable for larger ships, and indigenous prahus sailed only a few kilometres upstream from the mouth of the river.[81] Except for a few estates growing copra, rubber, and coffee, there was no European estate agriculture in Manado.[82]

The indigenous population of Manado, like that of South Sulawesi, exported copra, rice, maize, coffee, and rattan (Figure 23j). Copra was the main product throughout the 1920s and 1930s, but food crops such as maize and rice made headway when copra prices were low.[83] Often smallholders signed the infamous 'copra contracts', in which they ceded the harvest or even the use of their coconut grove to their creditor if they could not pay back the loan in time. Falling into this trap, many Minahasan peasants found themselves indebted to their Chinese creditors. This prompted the government to make efforts in the 1930s to reorganize credit and sales. Apart from the Chinese, there were also many Arab traders in Manado, who had expanded their trade in the nineteenth century.[84]

Cluster III: European dominance in exports

Bangka

The shape of the island of Bangka ('Banka'), roughly equal in size to Bali, has been compared with a seahorse. The traditional links of Bangka to the Sumatran mainland are illustrated by the old geographical names: while in the past Bangka was called 'Chinapata', the southeastern part of Sumatra was named 'Bangka-Palembang' and the area towards the Barisan Mountains was called 'Bangka-Ulu', which explains the later name Bengkulu.[85]

Bangka was swampy with outcrops of granite hills, such as Menumbing, near Mentok, and the Maras Mountains. Its soil was mostly infertile. The typical stretches of *alang-alang* grass and young forest, which often formed the landscape in parts of Sumatra and Kalimantan where the forest had been cleared for *ladang* (swidden) agriculture, were rarely found on Bangka. Rice harvests were poor, and pepper grew only after intensive manuring of the stony soil.[86]

Bangka and Belitung were famous as the tin islands of colonial Indonesia

81 ARA Kol, MvO 304, F.H.W.J.R. Logeman 1922:15; MvO 305, J. Tideman 1926:8, 103, 128.
82 ARA Kol, MvO 305, J. Tideman 1926:115.
83 Trade statistics; ARA Kol, MvO 309, W.J.D. van Andel 1917:21; MvO 306, A.Ph. van Aken 1933:153.
84 ARA Kol, MvO 304, F.H.W.J.R. Logeman 1922:11-3; Clarence-Smith 1998:36.
85 ARA Kol, MvO 246, J.E. Edie 1928:1-3. Note that *(h)ulu* usually refers to (lands at) the upper course of a river, analogous to *ilir* for downstream.
86 ARA Kol, MvO 246, J.E. Edie 1928:51, 54.

(Figures 23k and 23l). In previous centuries the tin mines in Bangka had been exploited with the aid of Chinese organization and technology.[87] Chinese mining technology using water wheels and aqueducts struck the European foreigners as peculiar, but even more striking was the cooperative form of organizing labour and capital in the mines, the *kongsi*. As Somers Heidhues points out, *kongsi* can mean the territorial organization of labour, or the person in charge of the mine, or the cooperative organization which worked a single mine and within which earnings were evenly distributed (Somers Heidhues 1992:37-9). In the nineteenth century, Europeans adopted this labour system, making only slight adaptations. Around 1920, there were some 20,000 labourers, primarily Chinese coolies, supervised by only a small group of Europeans, some 200 persons in all. In 1928, the whole island housed 91,262 indigenous inhabitants, 77,242 Chinese (almost half of the total population!), and 893 Europeans.[88] In 1913 the Banka Tin Winning (BTW) was founded, a government undertaking, of which the Resident of Bangka was appointed head.

It is interesting that even at an early stage, tin processing took place on the island itself. Only a small part of the tin ore excavated was exported as such and smelted in Singapore (or elsewhere). The smelting, a forward linkage, provided additional industrial activity. In 1928 Bangka had five tin-smelting works.[89] This industry needed wood (charcoal) for fuel, which resulted in an active forest service that sometimes clashed with the indigenous population, who needed land for their traditional *ladang* cultivation. In Bangka, there was a dichotomy between the *peranakan* Chinese and the newly immigrant *singkeh* Chinese. After 1900, the former increasingly dedicated themselves to pepper cultivation, either as hired hands or as owners. The new Chinese immigrant labourers, attracted by the tin mines, formed a culturally separate population group from the *peranakan* Chinese (Somers Heidhues 1992:69). Many *peranakan* worked in pepper cultivation, alongside the indigenous population. The white Bangka pepper, often exported from the main town, Mentok, was sold by Chinese traders and earned a reputation for high quality.[90]

Belitung

Roughly one-third the size of Bangka, the island of Belitung ('Billiton') lies about 80 km to the east. Belitung was an assistant-residency to Bangka. In the

87 A recent study on the economic history of Bangka is Somers Heidhues 1992.

88 ARA Kol, MvO 246, J.E. Edie 1928:26.

89 ARA Kol, MvO 246, J.E. Edie 1928:67-9.

90 ARA Kol, MvO 246, J.E. Edie 1928:41-3, 53; MvO 247, D.G. Hooyer 1931. According to these officials, 80% of Netherlands Indies pepper exports originated from Bangka, and the quality was so good that on average it earned a 90% better price (compare Tables 34 and 35).

literature it has been described as the antipode of Java: though a tropical island, it had none of Java's natural richness. Even more than that of Bangka, the soil in Belitung was infertile: 'it bode a home mainly to snakes and crocodiles' (*Eiland Billiton* 1918:393). The indigenous inhabitants of Belitung, *orang darat*, were traditionally known for their manufacture and export of iron nails. They were not inclined to seek employment in the tin mines. Nor did this work appeal to the *orang sekah* (or *orang laut*), the indigenous inhabitants of the coast of Belitung. The Belitung nail was popular in many nearby regions, and besides the nail industry, there was some fish processing and preparation of dried shrimp paste (*trassi*) (Van der Ploeg 1945:91).

In previous centuries, when both Bangka and Belitung belonged to the sultanate of Palembang, Bangka supplied tin to the sultan and Belitung attracted little attention. It was known only as a pirate lair and a bolt-hole for villains.[91] When Prince Hendrik, the younger brother of King Willem III, applied for a tin concession in 1850, mineral experts had, notwithstanding the rumours, not yet found substantial amounts of tin ore on Belitung. This changed in 1852, when tin ore was found, and after a laborious start, complicated by the ambivalent attitude of the local heads, the Billiton Maatschappij (Billiton Company) was founded in 1860.

Tin mining in Belitung started out as a private undertaking. The Billiton Maatschappij initially produced about as much tin and tin ore as Bangka. After 1890, production stagnated at a level of 5,000 tons per year. In 1924, the government increased its influence in tin mining and the Gemeenschappelijke Mijnbouw Maatschappij Billiton (Joint Mining Company of Belitung) was founded (Somers Heidhues 1992:97-102). In contrast to Bangka, almost all Belitung tin was exported as ore to Singapore and smelted there, entering the market as 'Straits Tin'. From 1933, tin ore was also shipped to Arnhem in the Netherlands, where it was smelted and processed. The working conditions of coolies in Belitung were better than in Bangka, as the death rates and figures for desertion and sickness indicate (Somers Heidhues 1992:79-80, 125-6, 182; Allen and Donnithorne 1957:171).

91 After the British interregnum, when the Netherlands regained their colonies, Raffles hoped that Belitung would escape the attention of the Dutch, it being merely 'a dependency of Bangka', and remain in British hands. In 1822, after some discussion on this subject between the two colonizers, the government in Batavia sent two officers and 100 soldiers to occupy the island. Two years later England renounced its claims. The first Resident, J.W. Bierschel, immediately set out exploring the possibilities for tin mining. But in 1826 civil administration was withdrawn for financial reasons, to Bierschel's displeasure, and Belitung was placed under Bangka, where it remained largely unknown until 1851 (*Eiland Billiton* 1918:393-4).

Riau

The residency of Riau ('Riouw en onderhorigheden') consisted of the like-named archipelago off Sumatra's east coast and part of the mainland, Indragiri. In thinly populated Riau, both the local population and European estates produced copra and rubber. Total export values reached only a modest 28 million guilders during the affluent second half of the 1920s (Figure 23.m).[92] On the island of Singkep, the Sinkep Tin Maatschappij (Singkep Tin Company) produced modest quantities of tin. It was founded in 1890 and stayed in business until 1933, when it was bought up by the Billiton Company. In the late 1930s, the Nederlands-Indische Bauxiet Maatschappij (Netherlands Indies Bauxite Company) started exporting bauxite from its concession in Bintan.[93]

Inland Indragiri remained relatively backward, until in the 1930s the surtax on indigenous rubber exports had its effect on local infrastructure in Indragiri, facilitating the construction of roads and bridges.[94] In the 1920s, European estates showed surprising interest in Indragiri, which had relatively bad transportation connections with Palembang, Belawan, and Pakanbaru (Wynaendts van Resandt 1928:78). Due to these bad connections, the fertile lowlands of Indragiri remained beyond the reach of most European agricultural estates.

Export figures for Riau were heavily influenced by the fact that during the brief period from 1911 to 1923, shipments leaving the BPM depot at Pulu Sambu, near Singapore, were registered as foreign exports from Riau (while in fact this oil was produced elsewhere; compare Table 24). This practice means that before 1923 both export figures and the share of oil within these exports were considerably inflated: total exports amounted to 66 million guilders in 1916/22, but fell to a mere 8 million guilders in 1923/29 (Clemens et al. 1992:39). In order to take over some of the lively trade going on in Singapore, the Dutch government made the Riau Archipelago into a free trade area in 1928. Since these decisions were not accompanied by the construction of harbour works or other measures, though, they had little effect (De Graaff 1955:98).

Indragiri's average share in exports from Riau was 10 per cent of the foreign export value in 1911/20. The share changes if we ignore the Pulu Sambu oil exports and focus on the indigenous economy, for which Indragiri's average annual percentage was 38 per cent.[95] Between 1921 and 1930, the rubber

92 ARA Kol, MvO 240, L.R. Wentholt 1921:7-9; Clemens et al. 1992:39; Clemens and Lindblad 1989:17; Haga 1920 (on the Anambas and Natuna Islands).

93 ARA Kol, MvO 242, J.M. von Schmidt auf Altenstad 1936:22-5; Broek 1942:47.

94 ARA Kol, MvO 242, J.M. von Schmidt auf Altenstad 1936:8, 15.

95 Interregional exports were merely registered for Riau, including Indragiri. However, the

boom worked its magic: Indragiri's share increased to 53 per cent (without oil, 60 per cent). The Riau islands exported copra and various other crops, but rubber was a negligible quantity. Between 1927 and 1938, an average of 68 per cent of foreign rubber exports originated from Indragiri, which amounted to fully 73 per cent of exported volume. Of Riau's total rubber exports, 43 per cent was estate rubber, significantly more than estate rubber production in Jambi or Lampung.

Another consequence of Riau's proximity to Singapore was a high level of activity in the *panglong* enterprise: logging for the production of lumber and charcoal.[96] In the Riau-Lingga archipelago, as well as in Indragiri, Bangka, and Bengkalis (East Sumatra), Chinese businessmen (*tauke*) from Singapore exploited the forest, paying export duties on the wood and paying taxes on charcoal-burning facilities and labour (Erman 1994a, 1994b).

Tanjung Pinang (in Pulau Bintan) was a small city where little money was made available for public expenditure. For instance, the construction of waterworks between 1926 and 1932 created a great many problems.[97] Local government also tried to improve the quality of smallholder rubber by stimulating the construction of drying huts and mangles for dried rubber sheets. But the Chinese traders, who traded mainly with Singapore, impeded conversion to sheet production, offering only a slightly higher price than they did for wet slabs.[98] Riau was politically untroubled and life was uneventful but poor. We should consider the backward linkages of the oil depot, and the possibility that European activity was an incentive to local sea-fishers, tradesmen, and farmers in rubber and copra. Had BPM not selected Pulu Sambu as its major oil depot, Riau would have been classified – Indragiri's rubber production notwithstanding – with the poor provinces of Cluster IV.

Cluster IV: The small ones

Tapanuli

Tapanuli ('Tapanoeli'; today: part of Sumatera Utara) was a poor, little developed residency, populated mostly by Batak.[99] Although it was not as sparse-

---

interregional trade statistics include separate tables on oil imports and exports from the Pulu Sambu entrêpot.

96 In fact, *panglong* originated from Hakka Chinese and meant 'warehouse for storing planks'.

97 ARA Kol, MvO 242, J.M. von Schmidt auf Altenstad 1936:150-4.

98 ARA Kol, MvO 240, L.R. Wentholt 1921:1; MvO 242, J.M. von Schmidt auf Altenstad 1936:88.

99 The name 'Tapanuli' probably derived from 'Tapian na oeli' which means 'nice or beautiful bathing place'. ARA Kol, MvO 177, U. Fagginger Auer 1933:3.

ly populated as most of the other Outer Islands, there was little trade in Tapanuli, and exports per capita were small (Table 26.1, Figure 24e). In 1932, the Pak-pak road, which formed the north-south connection in this residency, was so badly maintained that government officials going north or south preferred to travel through adjacent East Sumatra. Not only roads, the other infrastructural provisions were also primitive: in 1933 there were waterworks to supply drinking water in only three towns, and there were no irrigated rice fields.[100] Sibolga was the only town of any importance, housing some 30,000 inhabitants in 1920 and having a small harbour that administratively fell under Emmahaven in Padang. From 1922 to 1926, when Resident W.K.H. Ypes allowed indigenous rubber to be exported duty-free, this port was attractive to indigenous rubber exports.[101]

During the 1920s there was indigenous coffee and rubber cultivation in Tapanuli (Figure 23n). The volume of rubber produced decreased quickly after the Depression set in: almost everywhere, smallholders stopped tapping latex. Coffee smallholders reacted much more slowly: part of the coffee grown in Tapanuli was Arabica coffee, for which the price remained relatively stable. This coffee was exported directly to foreign markets, while a large part of the Robusta coffee was sold to Aceh. Only in rice cultivation did Tapanuli enjoy some (local) renown: as a consequence of the equable rainfall, rice harvests rarely failed.[102] There were hardly any European estates in this residency, which was largely mountainous, except for the lowlands on the west coast, south of Sibolga. Tapanuli illustrates the vulnerability to world prices of relatively primitive and remote regions, where indigenous smallholders concentrated on cultivating only a small range of cash crops.

Bengkulu

Bengkulu ('Benkoelen') was a small, sparsely populated residency stretching along the southwest coast of Sumatra. It was roughly twice as large as Bali, but mostly mountainous and impassable for travellers. After establishing a trading post on the Bengkulu River in 1685, the British East India Company gradually gained control of this small province in the eighteenth century. Perhaps its location on the outermost edge of the archipelago explains why, in contrast to the eastern coast of Sumatra, the earliest Asian trade passed through Bengkulu. After having resided in Java during the British interregnum, Raffles did his best as lieutenant-governor of the region in the late 1810s to launch Bengkulu into a more awe-inspiring development. He soon gave up these efforts and directed his energies to Singapore. In 1824, after the

100 ARA Kol, MvO 177, U. Fagginger Auer 1933:19, 28.
101 ARA Kol, MvO 176, P.C. Arends 1926:15.
102 ARA Kol, MvO 177, U. Fagginger Auer 1933:58-62.

Treaty of London had been signed, local economic life in Bengkulu did not amount to much. Under the Cultivation System, compulsory cultivation of coffee was prescribed, but this did not persuade the indigenous population to participate actively in export agriculture. Politically, as well, Bengkulu was a peaceful residency.[103]

Little change could be observed in Bengkulu until after 1923, when large numbers of smallholders rather suddenly began to cultivate coffee. This led to a peak export value of almost 7 million guilders in 1928 (Figure 23o). One gets the impression that, quite independently of what happened elsewhere in the archipelago, Bengkulu gradually got involved in the international economy. Different types of vegetables were marketed (such as cabbage and beets) as well as coffee, cloves, pepper, and (on the coast) copra. These goods were brought to market and then transported to other destinations by truck and by the ZSS (South Sumatra Railway). Rubber was only cultivated in the border regions with Palembang; these smallholders probably marketed their produce in Palembang as well.[104] In those later years after 1923, Bengkulu's exports per capita became relatively high, even though they amounted to a mere 2 million guilders in 1928 (Bengkulu was sparsely populated). In fact, including the exports to Java, for several years in the 1920s, Bengkulu's per capita trade figures were better than those of some of the provinces of Cluster II (Tables 26.1 and 26.2).

There were some European estates near Rejang. In the early 1930s they tried to maintain their level of income by substituting tea and quinine for coffee, but several enterprises had to close down. Referring to this incident, Resident W.J.R. Zieck wrote that the smallholders probably did not even notice it, and only the toko keepers and taxi drivers did, since the departure of the contract coolies meant a reduction in the number of their customers.[105]

Bali

Bali ('Bali en Lombok'), even closer to Java than Lampung, was densely populated and small, and as such it was different from the other Outer Islands. There were no large agricultural estates in Bali, but the indigenous population had a reputation in the archipelago for breeding and exporting cattle, as well as supplying *sawah* rice to other provinces, and exporting some coffee and copra (Figure 23.p).[106] In previous centuries the aggression displayed by Balinese chiefs against Lombok had caused poverty and hardship, and the re-

103 In the 1930s, Sukarno was exiled to Bengkulu. He tried to stir up the local 'Mohammadijah' but after several warnings from the Resident, he held his peace. ARA Kol, MvO 204, P.M. Hooykaas 1939:111, 208.

104 ARA Kol, MvO 202, W.J.R. Zieck 1932:26-7; MvO 204, P.M. Hooykaas 1939:75-9, 113, 117;

105 ARA Kol, MvO 202, W.J.R. Zieck 1932:34.

106 ARA Kol, MvO 355, J. Eschbach 1905:31; MvO 362, H. Beeuwkes 1932:20.

lentless resistance to Dutch rule from the late nineteenth century until 1908 had resulted in two cruel *puputan* ('final battles'). The massacres in 1906 and the last uprising in Klungkung in 1908 were well remembered.[107] Also, in the nineteenth century the trade by *bandar* (harbourmasters; usually representatives of the king of Bali) had led to some wealth (in the years before 1850) (Van der Kraan 1993). Although per capita exports were not high, government officials report a relatively affluent indigenous society, where people wore colourful clothes and festive rituals were held for weddings and tooth-filings. Officials believed the people also held substantial savings in gold and silver, which helped them during the Depression.[108] This prosperity may have been the result of the export of slaves or of Balinese piracy and plundering of shipwrecks in the nineteenth century, which brought wealth to Balinese chiefs. Impressions of relative prosperity may also have been the consequence of the rich Hindu cultural heritage, and the additional fact that Bali, in contrast to many other Outer Islands, was so densely populated and relatively accessible. Whereas in several of the sparsely populated provinces of Sumatra and Kalimantan, the vast, impenetrable stretches of forest made it hard to imagine that substantial rubber and copra revenues flowed into those regions, Bali was relatively well opened up but remained economically passive.[109]

Timor

The Lesser Sunda Islands to the east of Bali ('Timor en onderhorigheden', today: Nusa Tenggara Barat, Timur) were poor. Here the traditional economy was not significantly supplemented by revenues from new exports or additional economic activities (Figure 23p).[110] The islands of Timor, Flores, Sumba, and Sumbawa were sparsely populated, dry, and not very fertile. In colonial times, Timor was known for the beautiful fossilized sea-creatures that could be found there. The limited participation in world trade was, according to the Resident in 1938, mainly owing to Timor's nonstrategic, remote location 'on the far eastern horizon'.[111] In the 1910s, the southernmost island, Sumba, was considered to be the most promising of the Timor De-

107 ARA Kol, MvO 355, J. Eschbach 1905:31; MvO 363, G.A.W.Ch. de Haze Winkelman 1937:92-4, 98; Ricklefs 1993:132-6; Van Goor 1986b:19-20.

108 ARA Kol, MvO 355, J. Eschbach 1905:21, 31; MvO 362, H. Beeuwkes 1932:25-7. See also Schulte Nordholt 1991, 1996; Wiener 1995.

109 ARA Kol, MvO 362, H. Beeuwkes 1932:183, 209-10.

110 Exports per capita, including those to Java, averaged a mere *f* 1.14 in 1924-1928 and *f* 0.45 in 1934-1938. Per capita exports of East Sumatra or Southeast Kalimantan were 100 times greater (Table 26.1). The 'Lesser Sunda Islands' in the archival sources or the literature sometimes include Lombok, even though I follow colonial convention and treat Bali and Lombok separately.

111 ARA Kol, MvO 345, J.J. Bosch 1938:2, 38. A certain degree of change could be observed in the nineteenth century when trade relationships with the outside world expanded, as Parimartha argues in his dissertation (1995).

pendencies, exporting rice supplemented by forest products such as sandalwood and beeswax. It was also known for its lively horse trade. However, on the eve of the Second World War it was Sumbawa that had developed the most voluminous and diversified export agriculture: rice, maize, onions, and *kacang hijau* (mung beans). Most of these products, as well as the horses, cows, and goats that were bred, were shipped to South Sulawesi and Java by Bugis prahus. In 1938, Bugis transported eight times the volume of the KPM. Bugis and Macassarese settlers could be found along the entire northern coast of Sumbawa and Flores. They carried on the trade in which the KPM showed no interest.[112] Flores exported some copra, but Timor itself exported hardly any goods. One Resident wrote: 'One is satisfied with the economic situation if the harvests succeed and the local population has enough food.' There was no incentive whatsoever, another Resident wrote, to produce more than what was strictly necessary.[113]

In the early twentieth century, the quality and education of government personnel in the poorer provinces gave rise to complaints. Resident J.F.A. de Rooy complained about his personnel, stating that the civil servants in Timor in 1906-1908 had received hardly any education, and possessed neither professional zeal nor any sense of duty. 'They are little more than flagkeepers', he wrote, and complained that they never surveyed or visited the vast areas they had been appointed to.[114] Poor and politically restless, Timor and Dependencies may not have been very attractive to civil servants, as illustrated by the fact that in 1908 some 6,000 illegal guns were seized by the government.[115]

Maluku

Maluku ('Molukken, Amboina, Ternate en onderhorigheden') was the best-known part of the Indonesian archipelago in the sixteenth century, but has gradually retreated to a status so peripheral that most modern historians have had no patience with its complexities' (Reid 1995:132). Thus Anthony Reid states the position of Maluku in a nutshell. The ten small islands around Banda, about 42 km^2 altogether, were already known for nutmeg cultivation when the Dutch first arrived in the archipelago. In 1621, J.P. Coen maltreated the population in order to obtain a VOC monopoly on nutmeg. In 1626 *perken* (gardens) were planted, run by a Dutch *perkenier* who cultivated the spices with slave labour and delivered the product to the VOC at a fixed low price

112 ARA Kol, MvO 339, J.F.A. de Rooy 1908:15; MvO 340, C. van Rietschoten 1913:90-3; MvO 345, J.J. Bosch 1938:38-40; MvO 344, E.H. de Nijs Bik 1934:7. Compare A Campo 1992:386; Post 1996:612.

113 ARA Kol, MvO 340, C. van Rietschoten 1913:87; MvO 345, J.J. Bosch 1938:40.

114 He was not the first Resident to complain. ARA Kol, MvO 339, J.F.A. de Rooy 1908:2, 13. Compare MvO 174, F.C. Vorstman 1921:8.

115 ARA Kol, MvO 339, J.F.A. de Rooy 1908:6, 13.

(G.J. Knaap 1987). In 1864, when free sale of nutmeg was permitted, planters enjoyed a few affluent decades, since spices still made good prices on the market. Around 1900, nutmeg prices dropped and economic decline set in. During the early decades of the twentieth century, the Banda Islands produced only some pepper, nutmeg, cloves, and honey. When nationalist leader Sutan Sjahrir was exiled to Banda in the 1930s, he wrote:

> All these fairy-tale islands seem to have only one aim, serving our country as a decoration. Their value is too insignificant for the production of prosperity. However, in the times of the East India Company, this was all quite different. [...] Now it looks peaceful and in harmony with its surroundings. (Sjahrir 1987:48.)

During his journey to Banda, Sjahrir saw hardly any economic life of importance. Only in Tual, he recounts, did several Chinese and Arab traders come aboard the ship and trade goods. Later he arrived in Dobo, the centre of pearl fishery. 'Some traffic and economic activity are present here, as is proved by the iron warehouses on the quay', he observed (Sjahrir 1987:49). But that was not much. Although some government officials continued to hope for favourable economic development in Maluku, especially in Ceram and Buru, by the 1930s this seemed definitely unrealistic (Figure 23q). The soil of the islands turned out to be less fertile than expected. Other causes contributed to Maluku's insignificance in the late colonial economy: its poor accessibility (made worse by the high freight prices charged by KPM steamers, which maintained the indispensable link with the outside world), the general shortage of investment capital, and the alleged incompetence of government officials who were posted to this remote corner of the archipelago.[116]

An important reason for the absence of European estates was the local labour shortage. Estates had difficulty attracting labour from outside the r-egion. In the years during which the penal clause in labour contracts was in the process of being abolished, the recruitment of workers from the Kei and Tanimbar Islands, the regular source of labour for the estates in Amboina, became increasingly troublesome. Contract coolies from Java were expensive, their wages compounded by the high cost of their transportation. Workers from Buton (South Sulawesi) were generally preferred; they came to the estates voluntarily to work for a few months a year and to earn some cash income. Buton seasonal labourers arrived in Banda packed into tiny boats.[117]

In the late colonial period, the major export commodities of Maluku,

116 ARA Kol, MvO 335, B.J. Haga 1937:70, 77; Habiboe 1989:267-70.

117 Their journey could last up to one month, during which they had to eat, drink, and sleep standing up. Earning 20 cents per day in the 1930s, they would work for three months, save *f* 10 to 25, and then head back to South Sulawesi, paying *f* 3 for the trip (Sjahrir 1987:119; Habiboe, 1989:268-71).

especially Ambon, were not cash crops but soldiers and clerks. Because of early Christianization, education was widely available and many Maluku inhabitants held government jobs. While in 1905, there were 5,000 Ambonese (21 per cent of almost 25,000 Indonesians) in the colonial army (KNIL), by 1916 this had risen to 39,000. This was a large proportion of the total population of Maluku of less than half a million (see Table 10). In 1936, total payments in government pensions to Ambon were more than 700,000 guilders.[118] Of course, the export of manpower did not generate much infrastructural spin-off, and although it generated income, it drained the islands of an important factor of production. There were some roads on Halmahera and Tidore, but only in 1921 was the first stretch of road paved in Ambon.[119]

New Guinea

The vast western part of the island of New Guinea ('Nieuw Guinea'; today: Irian Jaya, Papua) that belonged to colonial Indonesia came late into the orbit of the colonial state. With only 0.47 inhabitants per km^2, it was extremely sparsely populated. The Papuan population had lived in isolation for centuries and had only fleetingly participated in the regional trade of the Southeast Asian archipelago. In large parts of New Guinea the soil was infertile on the mountainous terrain, and the sparse population presented a labour shortage that was difficult to solve in this remote area. All this meant that estate agriculture held little appeal. After the abandonment of earlier settlements, the province was brought under permanent Dutch occupation in 1898. In 1919-1928, efforts were undertaken to increase control over the area. Only in the northern part was the land flat and relatively accessible, and in the 1930s rubber cultivation was introduced in these areas. By the time the government had made plans to encourage such cultivation, the rubber restriction scheme was in full progress and further expansion of rubber cultivation in colonial Indonesia was not permitted.[120] 'The major source of income in this province, unfortunately, is merely hunting for birds of paradise', wrote Resident C.C. Krom in 1924. Later, the government prohibited bird hunting, but to little avail.[121] There were some exports of copra and damar, which were mostly traded by barter. The people ate sago and cultivated little rice. Although the government continued efforts to develop West New Guinea, economically speaking this area was not of great interest during the period 1900-1940. According to Governor B.J. Haga: 'Despite long years of government endeavour,

118 ARA Kol, MvO 335, B.J. Haga 1937:70; Habiboe 1989:247; Ricklefs 1993:147.
119 ARA Kol, MvO 321, K.H.F. Roos 1909:24; MvO 322, E.J. Gerrits 1912:31; MvO 335, B.J. Haga 1937:70; Habiboe 1989:269.
120 ARA Kol, MvO 335, B.J. Haga 1937:99; Ricklefs 1993:137.
121 ARA Kol, MvO 327, W.A. Hovenkamp 1931:14, 28; MvO 371, C.C. Krom 1924:1.

the economic significance of this area is to say the least futile.'[122] The province was perhaps best known for its notorious prison camp in Boven Digul, which in 1927 was constructed specifically to house deported PNI nationalists.

122 ARA Kol, MvO 335, B.J. Haga 1937:111.

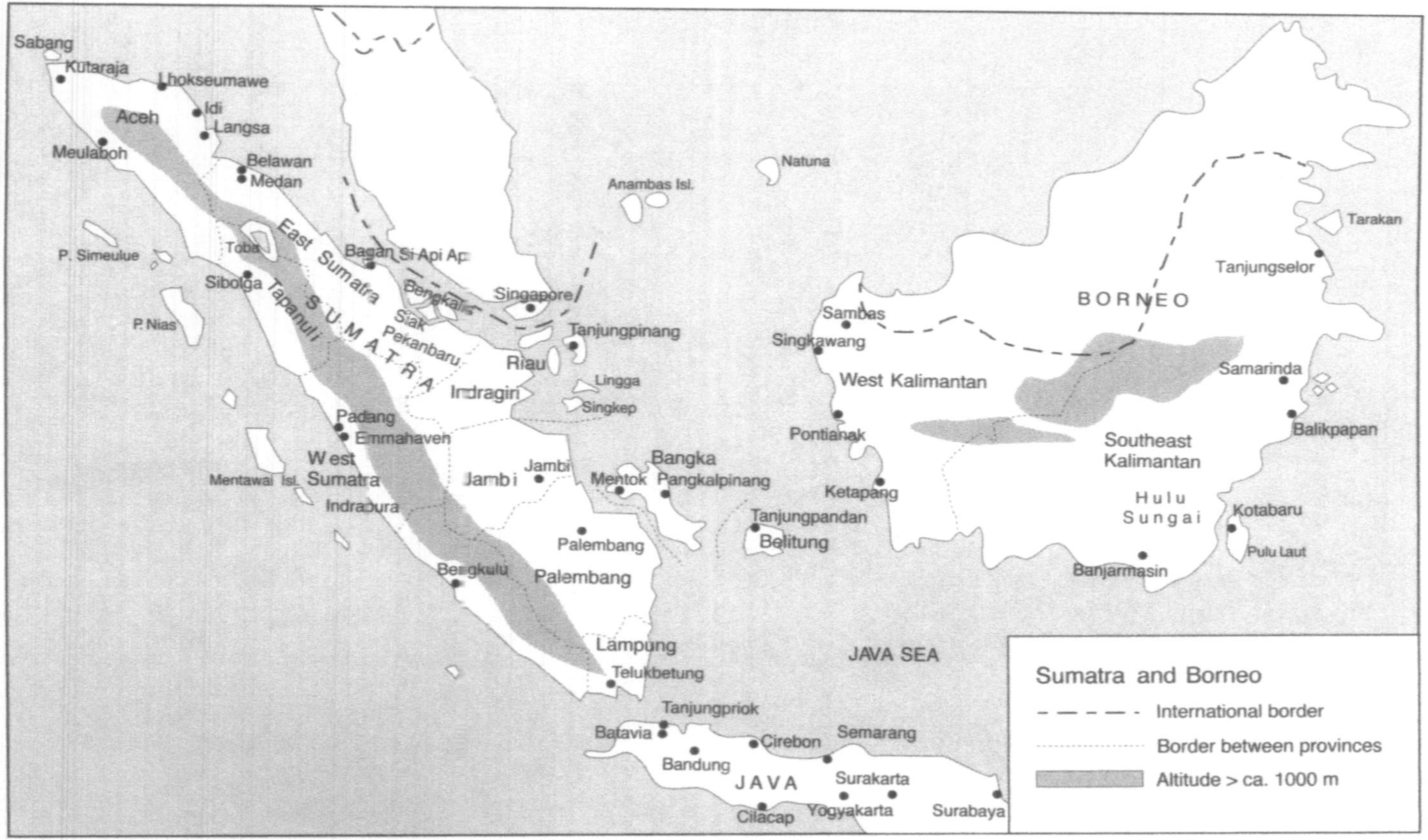

Map 3. Sumatra and Borneo

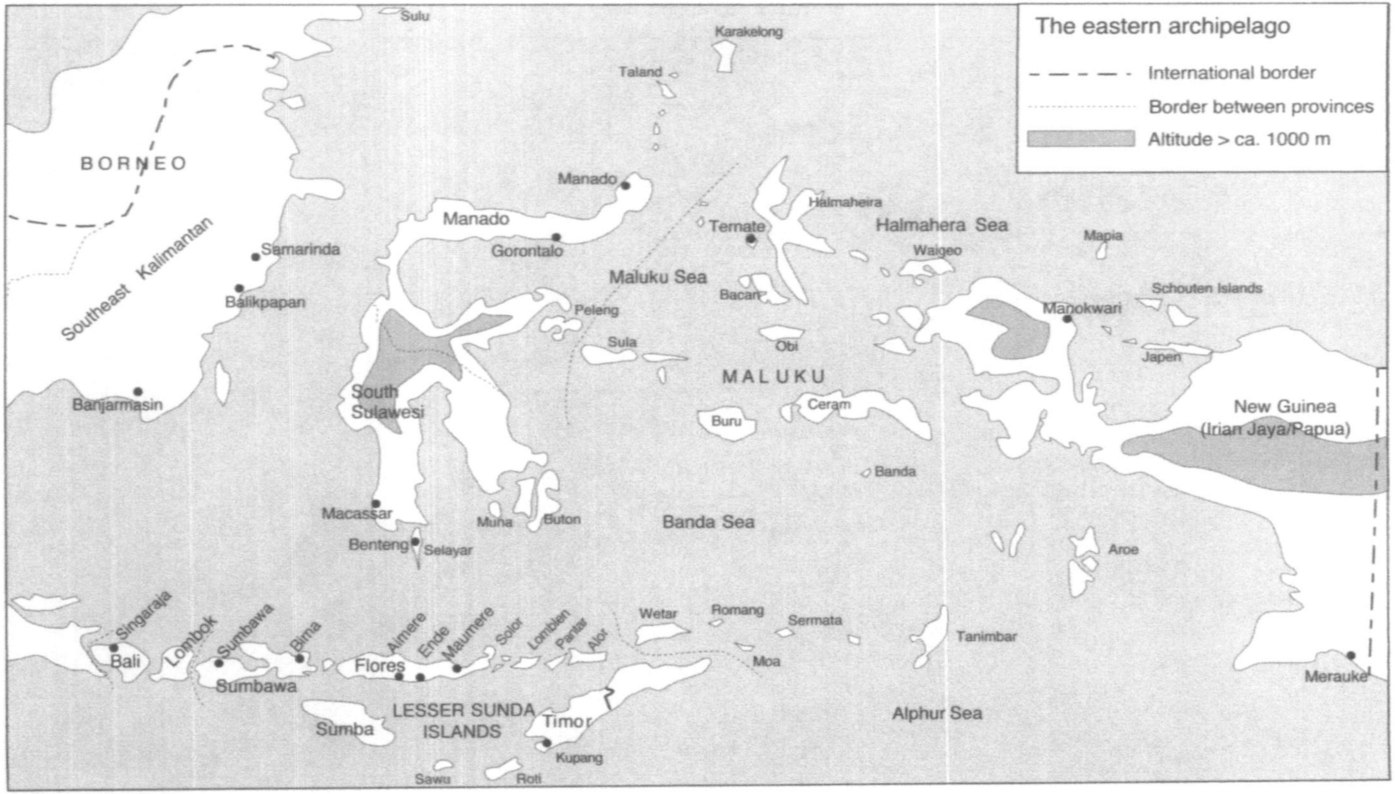

Map 4. The eastern archipelago

CHAPTER III

European dynamics

In 1926, a commercial agent attached to the NHM visited East Sumatra on a business trip. He described his impression of the estate area in the following words:

> [I saw] endless deserted roads, well maintained but bare and devoid of shade trees. Quiet and monotony enveloped the entire landscape. One meets no pedestrians, no livestock; but frequently cars and buses, and a single hand-cart. Only sporadically does a small settlement of traders come into view, in the proximity of which some activity may be perceived. On both sides of the road, interrupted every now and then by patches of uncleared forest, the rubber, tea, and oil palm gardens slip past the traveller. In the tobacco area, on the harvested lands, one sees nothing but fallow fields, partly covered with leaves for mulch, partly by encroaching jungle. The whole estate area forms a mosaic of plantations and forest, devoid of any significant villages, devoid of the vast paddy fields which occur everywhere in Java.[1]

According to this account, the landscape had been drastically transformed by the presence of European agricultural estates, and the original indigenous economy had been forced to retreat. Instead of inducing gradual change, European enterprise simply pushed the traditional economy aside. But to what extent is this true? Did the coexistence result in no incentives whatsoever to indigenous enterprise? This chapter analyses European export production in the Outer Islands in the agricultural and mining sectors. It will investigate where in the archipelago the European agricultural estates and mining companies were established. What products did they export? Which factors of production were amply available, and which were lacking? What effects did these enterprises have on the surrounding economy?

As I have argued in Chapter II, a clear distinction should be made between European and indigenous export production. The analysis of foreign exports, and the effects these had on economic development, shows that European export industries were engaged in (relatively) capital-intensive export production in both agriculture and mining. In addition to subsistence

1 ARA, NHM 9126, VvS 502 (Medan 1926):5.

agriculture or domestic trade, the indigenous sector was engaged in widespread small-scale export agriculture (Table 3). To establish the effects of export production on economic development, therefore, the linkages between these two sectors will have our specific attention. In other words, we will concentrate on the growth effects or spillover effects of the economic activity of European private enterprise on the surrounding economy. This will also lead to an analysis of the proportion of indigenous and European production in a single export crop, rubber. A more complete survey of the development of indigenous export production is given in Chapter IV.

When dealing with European enterprise in the Outer Islands, the estate area of East Sumatra is the first to spring to mind – as illustrated by the quotation cited above. The estate area was the largest concentration of European companies outside of Java, and provided the stage for the most hotly debated issues of the late colonial period – expectations of profit, the rise and fall of rubber prices, and the treatment of coolies and abolition of the penal clause.

Table 3. Major European and indigenous agricultural exports in the Outer Islands (p = peasant, e = estate)

	Rubber	*Copra*	*Coffee*	*Pepper*
Aceh	p			p
East Sumatra	p/e	e		
Tapanuli	p			
Riau	p			
West Sumatra		p	p/e	
Jambi	p	p		
Palembang	p/e		p/e	p
Bengkulu			p/e	
Lampung	p		e	p
Bangka				p
West Kalimantan	p	p		
Southeast Kalimantan	p		e	
South Sulawesi		p		
Manado		p		
Maluku		p		

Other European companies ventured into the Outer Islands with the aim of exploiting mineral resources. The petroleum industry generated an enormous output volume during the early decades of the twentieth century. Almost all petroleum drilling and refining, as well as the exploitation of tin, was in European hands. As a catalyst for economic change in the Outer Islands, and the most obvious sign of the invasion of Western capitalist entrepreneurship in remote regions, these industries were an essential component of European dynamics in the archipelago. In most instances, the indigenous population was involved in the industrial sector mainly as an occasional source of labour. I will briefly examine the growth effects of these industries on the regional economy.

I distinguish three separate aspects of European export production. The first two are based on the importance of European economic activity in two economic sectors, and the third is a general aspect of foreign economic activity in the colony:

1. Estate export agriculture, which dominated in East Sumatra, but could also be found in several other provinces.
2. Mining activities: the petroleum industry, which was concentrated at several locations in Sumatra and Kalimantan, and other important mining activities such as tin mining on Bangka and Belitung, and the coal mines in Sumatra and Kalimantan.
3. Growth effects on the indigenous economy: the effects of European export production on the economy, such as stimulating the flow of capital imports into the various regions where European export production expanded, and the influence of large-scale coolie migration.

In my survey of these three aspects, I will concentrate on the export commodities. I will examine the provinces where cultivation took place and the growth effects of estate agriculture on the surrounding economy. The European trading houses and banks formed a network for expanding trade, and they supplied imports. They consolidated their position alongside the efforts of small-scale Chinese, Arab, Bugis, and other traders. Part of a chain of continuous expansion from the time of the earliest ventures in the sixteenth century, the European trading firms developed into a tightly woven network of enterprising contacts with Chinese intermediaries, indigenous producers, and other traders, providing the link to large overseas buyers of raw materials.

A legacy of the Cultivation System, there were still some government enterprises cultivating cash crops, but their share in total exports gradually decreased to a negligible proportion. When the government participated in mining companies, this will be included in the analysis.[2] The economic policy of the Netherlands Indies government will be treated in Chapter VI. Government policy directly concerning European enterprise, such as the Coolie Ordinances and the mining concession policy, will be touched upon where relevant.

2 Another category of government companies remained active throughout the colonial period: post, telegraph, telephone; railways and air services; the salt and opium monopolies; electricity supply and so on.

From tobacco to palm oil in East Sumatra

By the late nineteenth century East Sumatra had already acquired a reputation for providing good opportunities for profit. Private enterprise in the Outer Islands raised high expectations, but was inseparable from the notion of high risk. This favoured the spearhead region where the first pioneers had proven their success. Legally speaking, the starting point for pioneers venturing into the unknown regions of the Outer Islands was the year 1870. In this year the Sugar Law marked the beginning of the end of the Cultivation System in Java, and the Agrarian Law enabled private entrepreneurs to obtain land for agriculture (Gonggrijp 1838:119; Allen and Donnithorne 1957:25). The way was open, but ineffectual control by the colonial government in many provinces meant that not everybody was tempted to head into the unknown (Lindblad 1989b). Only in Deli, in East Sumatra, did European entrepreneurs manage to establish successful estates cultivating tobacco. When the first tobacco estates sold their harvests, many planters began to believe in the myth of unequalled opportunity and easy fortune. European private estates also began to move into other provinces, but none of these ever surpassed East Sumatra's primacy in agricultural exports.

East Sumatra in the nineteenth century

Before the arrival of Dutch planters, East Sumatra had been populated by Malays and Batak. The Malays, who were descendants of Minangkabau migrants or had immigrated from Malacca, lived almost exclusively in the coastal regions. The Batak carried on trade with Malays at fixed exchange spots near the banks of rivers, mainly offering pepper, copra, gambir, coffee, or tobacco in exchange for textiles, ironware, salt, or weapons. In the early nineteenth century, Langkat, Deli, and Serdang experienced a boom in pepper production – which did not have as long a history in this region as it did in Aceh or Lampung. Some tobacco was grown by these peasants, but on a much smaller scale than pepper. Fishing was an important source of income. Rice was traditionally grown on *ladang* fields in the forest. The peasants in Deli had cultivated mainly tobacco and pepper, but had also tried their hand at copra and nutmeg, since around 1840.

Deli, Serdang, and Simalungun, in the middle of East Sumatra, was where the estate area would develop. Here the Batak population had to contend with the arrival of European planters. Land would be transformed into a valuable asset and the region would become densely populated with estate coolies. The settlement of Javanese ex-estate workers and Toba Batak, who cultivated wet rice instead of traditional Simalungun *ladang* rice, would be the catalyst which changed the traditional economy. The sultans quickly discovered that the European planters who came to the region were interested in leasing the land and buying locally cultivated food crops. Later on, when Chinese immigrants leased land that they legally could not own, there were coastal Malays who would live off the rent and concentrate on fishing (Stoler 1985:5; Pelzer 1978:2-7, 36-7).

Arrival of the first tobacco planters

In 1863 Jacobus Nienhuys headed the first generation of tobacco planters in East Sumatra when he started to cultivate tobacco in Deli. The first good tobacco harvests in 1868 came as a surprise, because the initial years had been scarred by struggle. Using capital supplied by Nienhuys's financiers and the NHM, the Deli Maatschappij (Deli Company) was founded in 1869. This became one of the largest and most influential tobacco estates (Gonggrijp 1938:123; De Waard 1934:218; Blink 1918:94).

Deli Maatschappij initially exploited only one estate, the Medan Estate, but expanded quickly until it controlled 21 estates in Deli and Langkat. Expansion and consolidation were the prime goals of Deli Maatschappij. It was successful right from the outset: as early as 1870 it paid out a dividend of 20 per cent. This inspired many other entrepreneurs to finance the establishment of tobacco estates in the fertile and climatically favourable regions of Deli and Serdang.[3] By the turn of the century, Deli Maatschappij had achieved a turnover of some 10 million guilders. Among the 25 largest Dutch limited liability companies in colonial Indonesia (*Indische NV's*) it occupied the eighth place (Bossenbroek 1996:88). In 1918 Deli Maatschappij cultivated 120,000 hectares in Deli and Langkat. After the recession following World War I, the following boom period benefited all estate cultivation. In 1923 Deli Maatschappij had a peak revenue of almost 36 million guilders, based on a production of 5,600 tons of tobacco (Blink 1918:95; Lindblad 1994b:64-6).

For reasons of accessibility, the first estates were situated along the rivers, as there were no roads yet. Since the government did little to improve this situation, the estates were compelled to finance a large part of road construction themselves. The estate area expanded more quickly than the government could keep pace with, but gradually the number of officials and police officers increased. As this happened, many aspects of economic life underwent changes. Trading agencies were established by the Chartered Bank (1888) and the NHM (1892). Monetary exchange took a firm hold, first in Spanish *mat*, then in Mexican dollars, and finally in Straits dollars, despite the fact that government taxes were levied in Dutch guilders. In 1906, the government of East Sumatra decided to carry out an extensive purge of the coinage with the assistance of the Java Bank (simultaneously with that conducted in West Kalimantan), in order to replace dollars with guilders. Even

3 For a more extensive history of the Deli Company, see Gevers 1991; Van Kommer 1989.

the Straits dollar, which was a stable currency, linked first to the silver standard and after 1903 to the gold standard, was banned from Sumatra. The first prohibition of the use of dollars was issued in Bengkalis in January 1907, followed in January 1908 by a ban on the use of dollars throughout the entire province. Dollars could be traded for Dutch coins at the agencies of the Java Bank: in two months, about 3.5 million guilders was dispensed in exchange for dollars. These stringent measures ensured that after 1908 the Dutch guilder made good headway in Sumatra.[4]

In 1871 J.T. Cremer, who would become the Dutch Minister of Colonial Affairs in 1897, was appointed chief administrator of Deli Maatschappij. In this capacity he made an important contribution to the development of Deli tobacco (Taselaar 1998:70-3). Referring to Cremer, Nienhuys said somewhat self-consciously: 'Even though I myself laid the basis for the establishment, I am very happy to grant him a major role in the unequalled way in which this cultivation has risen above all others.'[5] The society of the planters in Deli was rough, competitive, and smug. The approximate total revenue from tobacco exports from Deli was 11.3 million guilders in 1880, 27 million in 1885, and more than 40 million in 1889.

The late nineteenth century can be typified as the era of pioneers. Tobacco exports from Deli, Langkat, and Serdang grew rapidly throughout the 1880s, responding to favourable prices on the world market. As production expanded, the cigar wrapper from Deli achieved world-wide fame.

Problems loomed in 1891 when excess supply on the world market and import duties imposed by the United States forced the expansion to grind to a halt (Thee Kian Wie 1977:9). De Waard discerns two periods in early tobacco cultivation: from 1868 to 1890, the period of experimentation, and from 1890 to 1905, the period of stagnation, afflicted by declining tobacco prices (De Waard 1934). As De Jonge has observed, the tobacco trade is not only dependent on the world economic situation, it is also hit by fluctuations in the volume and quality of the harvests (more so than, for example, rubber and copra), aspects which are to some extent beyond the planter's control. Even when demand is strong, prices may follow their own course (De Jonge 1968:64-5).

Until 1916, tobacco remained the prime export commodity (in terms of value) of East Sumatra, a position it regained after 1931, when rubber and petroleum prices had dwindled in the wake of the Depression (Table 36.1). East Sumatra was essentially the only Outer Province from which tobacco was exported, but it did not surpass Java's older and larger estate production. What Deli did produce was a unique kind of tobacco, and it exported rough-

4 Potting 1987:129-33; Potting 1997:125-66; Breman 1992b:36-7.

5 In the memorial issue of the Sumatra Post to mark the occasion of the Golden Jubilee of Deli (1863-1913), as quoted in Blink (1918:94). For more about Cremer, see Lenstra 1986.

ly between 25 and 30 per cent of the total volume of tobacco exports from the Netherlands Indies between 1911 and 1940. The bulk still came from Java, where tobacco followed sugar and coffee as a major export commodity (Clemens et al. 1992:62-3).

The next estate products: coffee and rubber

At the turn of the century, when the heyday of tobacco was over, planters started to search for new crops to diversify their cultivation activities. Several companies started to experiment with coffee, but this failed to generate the desired expansion. Rescue came in 1907 with the advent of a rubber plant called Hevea Brasiliensis, which brought recovery to the estate area. In the late 1890s, Deli Maatschappij had already started growing the less suitable variety Ficus Elastica. A decade later, in 1918, Hevea Brasiliensis already covered some 50,000 hectares, mainly in Langkat (Blink 1918:95; Van Hall 1942:55).[6] Rubber brought recovery to the estate area when tobacco prices were low, and planters realized the vulnerability of dependence on one crop. Although coffee was planted as a so-called catch crop in the rubber gardens (to utilize the ground and provide shade during the years in which the new rubber plants were maturing), coffee exports from East Sumatra never reached great heights. After a promising start in 1900-1905, coffee exports stayed below two million kg. By contrast, after 1911 rubber exports quickly reached 13 million guilders, leading eventually to a peak in revenues of 184 million guilders in 1925 (Tables 36.1 and 36.2).

All over Sumatra and Kalimantan, the indigenous population also started to plant Hevea rubber soon after its introduction. Simultaneously with the beginning of Hevea cultivation on the estates, Chinese traders brought Hevea plants from Malaya to indigenous smallholders. Below, I will go into more detail about the 'dual' character of rubber exports. Since rubber was cultivated on a large scale both by the estates and by indigenous producers, this raises the question of whether there was any interaction between the two. How strong were possible linkage effects of estate cultivation? Was indigenous rubber in East Sumatra in a favourable position, which differed from that of other indigenous rubber producers, like those in Jambi and West Kalimantan?

Two reasons reveal why rubber estates were more profitable than tobacco estates. Rubber trees formed a stable investment, because once the gardens had been planted, a planter could collect latex for many years, providing he kept up basic maintenance like weeding and fertilizing. This is in contrast to tobacco, which is an annual crop, so that the area under cultivation could vary from year to year, and investments fluctuated each year bowing to mar-

6 In East Sumatra, 1916 was the first year with substantial rubber production, which was 6,432 tons (Thee Kian Wie 1977:11).

ket prices. Secondly, rubber tapping is not radically affected by bad weather – the product does not suffer bad harvests, even though growth and latex yields may vary a little from year to year (De Waard 1934:219). Rubber exports began in 1911 and had already reached more than 37,000 tons in 1919. The rubber industry also attracted many foreign investors, more so than tobacco (Lindblad 1989c:13; Burger 1975, II:87). It accounted for the steady growth of the estate area after 1910. Rubber estates were located mainly in Serdang and Simalungun, immediately south of Deli, and further south again, in Asahan (see Map 5).

Any survey of the regional distribution of estate rubber production shows that East Sumatra was by far the leader, followed at some distance by Southeast Kalimantan and Palembang. Index figures give further insight into the strategies of the rubber estates during the Depression. East Sumatra kept its output at almost the same level during the years 1927-1938. It concentrated on reducing costs more than on cutting output volume. Southeast Kalimantan estates, in contrast, increased their output in 1927-1934. In Palembang, there was also an increase in the production of rubber estates. During the Depression years, the growth rate of estate rubber in Palembang was smaller than in Southeast Kalimantan, but it quickly moved upwards after 1934, in the wake of the distribution of rubber quotas under the International Rubber Regulation Agreement (Figure 27, see also Figure 26).

New developments: tea, copra, fibres, and palm oil

Shortly after the cultivation of rubber had been established, tea was introduced. Initially, tea exports remained relatively low, but in 1929-1930 they formed 5 per cent of East Sumatra's export value. Gradually increasing from 1914, tea exports reached a value of 10 million per year in 1923 (Table 36.1). During the 1920s, European estates extended their range of crops and also started to produce tea, fibres (sisal), and palm oil. The estates expanded into Aceh and to the southern part of East Sumatra. The latter was still a relatively inaccessible region, but in the 1920s tax revenues from the estates had risen to such levels that the government actively assisted expansion by constructing roads and telephone and telegraph connections.[7]

Palm oil and fibres were new estate products that gained importance after 1920. The share of non-Dutch investments in these new crops was remarkably higher than in the older commodities, particularly tobacco (Burger 1975, II:87). Palm oil was clearly the most lucrative export commodity of the three, reaching values of up to 25 million guilders in 1937. This commodity was not produced by indigenous peasants, since it depended on elaborate techniques and required large-scale organization: the oil had to be extracted soon after

7 ARA, NHM 9126, VvS 5093 (Medan 1927):6, 16.

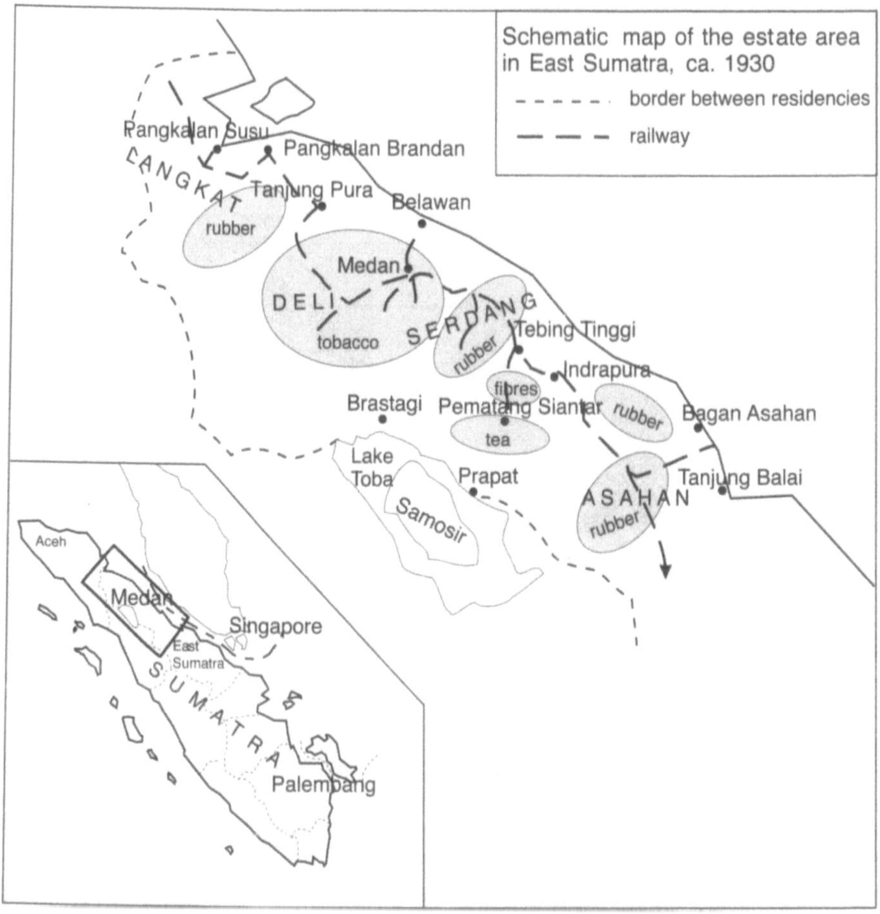

Map 5. Deli estate area (Atlas van Tropisch Nederland 12a)

the gathering of the fruit. This processing took place in highly mechanized plants, for which bulk storage and handling facilities were constructed. Smallholders with palm gardens preferred the production of copra, in which small-scale production could compete with estate production (Allen and Donnithorne 1957:145). Fibres such as sisal generated export earnings similar to the export value of tea, on average fluctuating between 5 and 15 million guilders per year (Table 36.1).

During the Depression, overproduction of tea put extra pressure on tea prices, which were already low. After an extended period of consultation between producers, the government and the other important tea-producing countries, India and Ceylon (Sri Lanka), an international restriction on tea

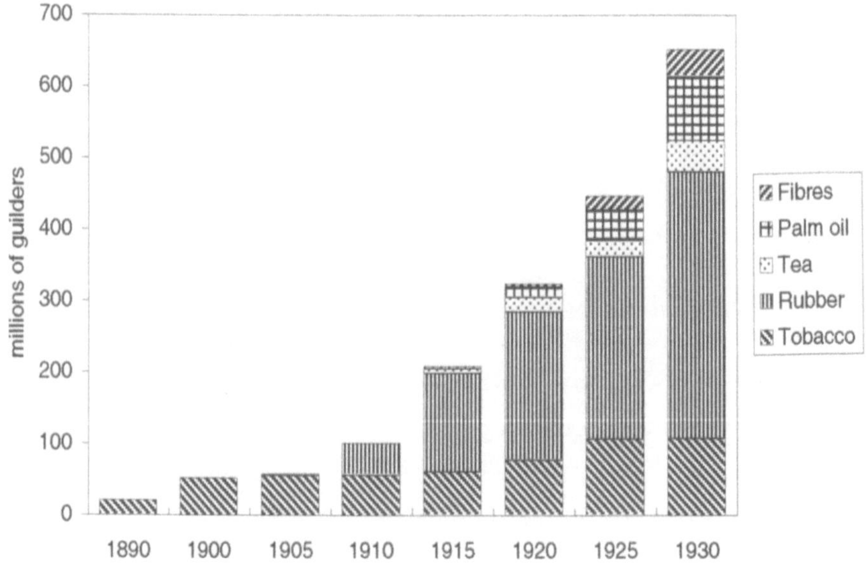

Figure 7. Capital investments in the East Sumatra estate economy, 1890-1930 (De Waard 1934:256).

took effect on 12 June 1933. During the first restriction year (April 1933-April 1934) export was initially restricted to 85 per cent of the Netherlands Indies tea exports of 1931, which eventually resulted in a restriction of the production to 50.8 per cent of total production capacity. Unfair to some tea producers was the measure exempting exports from April until 12 June, so that bona fide companies which had taken heed of the restriction as soon as the preliminary announcement had been made were harmed.[8]

Although the cultivation of the later export crops of tea, fibres, and oil palms resulted in substantial export volumes (Figure 23a), the amount of capital invested in these crops remained small compared to investments in rubber. Reviewing capital investments in tobacco, rubber, tea, palm oil, and fibres, rubber easily emerges as the export product with the highest investments. Investments in rubber amounted to more than 350 million guilders in 1930 (Figure 7) (De Waard 1934:256).

While the cultivation of tobacco was to a large extent a Dutch undertaking, rubber companies were often British or American. Of all the estates together, the most capital invested was Dutch: 48 per cent of all invested capital in East Sumatra in 1913 and 53.7 per cent in 1932 was Dutch capital. This

8 ARA, NHM 9127, VvS 509 (Medan 1933):12-3.

percentage was highest in tobacco (up to 96.4 per cent in 1932). In rubber, American and British companies challenged the Dutch: in 1913, 34.4 per cent of invested capital was British and 16.1 per cent American. In 1932, these percentages were 26.6 and 18.0, thus leaving the Dutch with a share of only 36.2 per cent of all invested capital.[9]

Since the late nineteenth century, a process of concentration and increase in scale had forced out most smaller companies. The bulk of the production of tobacco and rubber was in the hands of the so-called 'Great Four' and their subsidiaries: Deli Maatschappij, Deli-Batavia Maatschappij, Senembah, and Arendsburg Maatschappij. The process of concentration and monopolization was an ongoing process. It speeded up during the Depression, when many small companies could no longer compete.[10] This process of concentration shows a parallel with the oil industry, which had also been pioneered by many small companies in the late nineteenth century, only a few of which emerged as survivors in the early twentieth century. Among the trading houses the number of leading companies was restricted to five (Jacobson Van den Berg, Geo. Wehry, Lindeteves, Borsumij, and Internatio). However, in wholesale trade, a very large number of smaller traders also flourished (Allen and Donnithorne 1957:235-42).

Labour shortage in the estate economy

In contrast to Java, where land had become increasingly scarce at the end of the nineteenth century, colonial production in the Outer Islands was inhibited more by shortage of labour than of land. The early tobacco planters in East Sumatra tried in vain to recruit the labourers they needed amongst the local Batak and Malay population. Soon they started recruiting Chinese contract labourers. In 1875 the estates employed 4,500 Chinese and 1,000 Klingalese and Javanese workers. In 1900 this number had risen to roughly 100,000, and by 1919 there were about 250,000 coolies employed on the estates in East Sumatra (Langeveld 1978:296). At the outset, Chinese workers were contracted in Malaya (in Penang and Singapore), but after 1888 this changed to direct immigration from China (Phoa Liong Gie 1936:118). Coolies were also recruited from Java. In 1893, 19 per cent of the coolies were Javanese, 3 per cent were Indian, and 67 per cent were Chinese.[11] When World War I broke out, and cre-

9 There were also Belgian, French, Swiss, German, and a few Japanese companies in tobacco and rubber (De Waard 1934:257; Stoler 1985:20).

10 The total number of European companies settled in East Sumatra was 265 in 1933, 261 in 1934 and 256 in 1935. ARA Kol, MvO 190, B.C.C.M.M. van Suchtelen 1936:30; De Waard 1934:257.

11 In 1930 Chinese workers made up only 10 per cent of the labour force in East Sumatra, although their number still amounted to 26,000 (Thee Kian Wie 1977:39; Stoler 1985:30).

ated an impediment to international labour recruitment, this gave an impulse to large-scale immigration of coolies from Java. After the war, Java remained the most important source of labour (Rothe 1950:330; Scheltema 1929).

Hundreds of thousands of coolies were brought into the estate area during the ensuing decades (Houben and Lindblad 1999). The planters were not scrupulous about their methods for recruiting, disciplining, and punishing immigrant labourers. Often labourers were lured onto ships, enticed there under false pretexts, transported to Deli, and forced to sign a contract which left them entirely at the mercy of their employer. Recruitment could take place in three ways: through intermediary agencies, by so-called *laukeh* enlisting, and by the estate itself. Recruitment agencies resorted to deceit to trick workers into signing a contract. Their dubious activities were brought to an end in the late 1920s. According to some contemporary observers, *laukeh* recruitment was the fairest, since it employed veteran workers to recruit and break in new workers from their own hometowns. The snag was that it was an option open only to existing estates. The majority of *singkeh* coolies enrolled after recruitment by the estate itself. In this matter the Deli Planters Vereeniging (DPV, Deli Planters Association) cooperated with the organization of rubber planters, the Algemeene Vereeniging van Rubberplanters aan de Oostkust van Sumatra (AVROS, General Association of Rubber Planters in East Sumatra). They jointly established the Algemeen Delisch Emigratie Kantoor (ADEK, General Deli Emigration Office), which existed side by side with the recruitment organization of the Zuid-Sumatra Landbouw- en Nijverheidsvereeniging (ZUSUMA, South Sumatra Agriculture and Industry Association) (Langeveld 1978:305-13).

In 1900 there were more than 59,000 Chinese coolies and 30,000 Javanese coolies working on estates in Deli.[12] Most of the coolies were tied to their estate by three-year contracts which contained the infamous 'penal sanction' clause. Essential to these contracts was the regulation that enabled employers to apply disciplinary measures should the coolies abscond, refuse to work, or violate their contract in any other way. The Coolie Ordinance, which was first issued by the government in 1880, allowed such measures. The ordinance initially applied only to East Sumatra, but later it was extended to all provinces outside Java.[13] Corporal punishment was often employed to discipline coolies. Hamstrung by the penal clause, they had little opportunity and no legal backing to complain about unfair treatment.

[12] In 1900 also roughly 3,500 Indians (Klingalese), about 1,000 inhabitants of the island of Bawean, about 3,000 Banjarese from northern and western Sumatra, 1,500 Batak, and 400 Malays worked on the East Sumatra estates (Breman 1992b:84, 169-75).

[13] The penal clause was introduced in the Coolie Ordinance of 1880, and was elaborated in the Ordinance of 1889 (Langeveld 1978:297).

As the estate economy expanded, the numbers of coolies kept pace. In 1920 there were some 300,000 coolies working on the estates of East Sumatra, and in 1930 roughly 360,000, most of them originating from Java, but also including Chinese and Indians. Smaller numbers of coolies were employed in other provinces. In Palembang there were roughly 40,000 coolies in 1929, in Southeast Kalimantan about 36,000 (Tables 60.1 and 60.4).

The penal clause and the coolie debate

Around 1900, any public discussion about forced labour or indentured labour was rare in East Sumatra. But in the Netherlands, Van den Brand's brochure *De millioenen uit Deli* (The millions from Deli) caused shock waves in public opinion, reminiscent of the impact of Multatuli's *Max Havelaar* some fifty years earlier.[14] Voices raised in indignation and protest about the maltreatment of coolies on estates and in mines in the colony were increasingly heard, and in 1903 led to an investigation by J.L.T. Rhemrev, who described in full detail the systematic application of violence on Deli estates. This report was not made public at the time. Both reports were published in 1987 by Breman, who gives an extensive account of the shocking conditions and lack of justice under the coolie labour system around 1900.[15]

The labour problem was an important issue, affecting not only the economic organization of estate agriculture, but also the policy measures of the government and discussions between government and planters (Taselaar 1998:261-96). It has been in the limelight a great deal in recent years. In the following subsection, I will first make brief historiographical remarks on the coolie debate. These will be followed by a survey of the attitude adopted by the government towards coolie labour. With respect to the estate economy, the abolition of the penal clause was the main concern of government officials; in most other matters, the estates were largely left alone until 1930. This will be rounded off by an examination of the effects of the large inflow of estate workers on the surrounding economy.

14 Van den Brand wrote these reports in 1902 and 1904. See also Breman 1992b:25-7; Furnivall 1944:353.

15 Breman criticized the fact that the Rhemrev report was not made public. However, its existence and some reference to its contents can be found in earlier literature. For example, both Van den Brand's and Rhemrev's reports were referred to in Langeveld (1978:298). Also Pelzer (1978:138-9) extensively discusses the shocking contents of both reports, to which he had no access. This aside, Breman's thorough study is a valuable contribution to historiography, not in the least because it emphasized shocking injustice during 'a wave of nostalgic literature about *tempo doeloe*' in the 1980s (Breman 1992b:4-5). See also Kamphues (1988).

Scholarly discussion on the living conditions of coolies

The publication of Breman's book in 1987 aroused substantial debate amongst Indonesianists on the question of whether Rhemrev's report was unjustly hushed up by the government in 1903. Was this symptomatic of matters concerning the maltreatment of coolies and other injustices during the colonial period? The discussion centred on the question of whether the estates and the government were blinded by profit, and should be blamed for this attitude. Was the government too little concerned with living conditions on the estates and in the mines? Or did social malpractice diminish over time, after the government had put the estates under surveillance of the Labour Inspectorate (in 1908)?

Some scholars have criticized Breman's methodology. Houben, for example, argues that Breman did not underpin his conclusions with a systematic (and statistical) examination of the sources.[16] He proposes the use of a model to analyse the various aspects of the coolie labour system systematically (Houben 1995). A distinction should also be made between the goals of the planters and the policy of the government. The gradual improvement in labour conditions on the estates cannot be ignored, as attested by a drop in the number of attacks on supervisors. Improvement or not, the earlier bad living conditions on the agricultural estates cannot be excused.

The coolie debate has also led to more far-reaching standpoints on the European presence in the Indonesian archipelago. In this regard some speak of an Amsterdam school (centring on Breman's view of colonial abuse) and a Leiden school (consisting of the historians Wesseling, Fasseur, and others, and typified by Wesseling's remark that the civil servant thought of himself as a 'development worker *avant la lettre*'). The debate on the beneficial or detrimental effects of colonialism can probably never be resolved. It stresses two opposite but nevertheless ineradicable aspects of colonial presence in the archipelago: a certain amount of beneficial influence, and at the same time a certain degree of injustice.[17]

Discussion between government and planters: the three phases

Matters of injustice exercise many minds, even when the outcome of the discussion may be disappointing. During the first three decades of the 1900s, the

16 Houben 1988, 1993; Breman 1992a. In the introduction to the third edition of Breman's *Koelies, planters, koloniale politiek* the discussion is summarized (Breman 1992b).

17 Breman 1990, 1992b. Langeveld examines improving circumstances (Langeveld 1978). Wesseling's remark can be found in his 'classic' collection of essays (Wesseling 1988a:42). For a summary of the discussion see Van Doorn (1994:11-7). A discussion of the role of the colonial government in the economy will be given in Chapter VI. See also the section on historiography in Chapter I.

colonial government conducted a strenuous debate with planters. As a consequence, in the DPV and the AVROS, the issues of the abolition of contract labour and the potential colonization of labourers in the estate area were discussed extensively. In fact, the views on the abolition of the penal clause, free labour, and labour settlements (colonization) were closely related. Repeatedly, ideas were voiced from the side of the government or the planters advocating the development of rural settlements in East Sumatra, which could serve as a permanent labour pool and obviate the need to use contracts to compel coolies to work (Taselaar 1998:297-300).

Three phases can be distinguished in the views of planters on the penal clause and labour settlements:

a. 1880-1903, the pioneering phase,
b. 1903-1931, the phase of policy alternatives,
c. 1931-1942, the phase of priority of economic policy.

The pioneering phase

The first phase was in the nineteenth century, the pioneering era, roughly a quarter of a century from circa 1880 to 1903. The estates had started to recruit Chinese, Javanese, and Indian labourers to work on contract for three years. Wages were low, but included living in barracks on the estate as well as food and some medical care. After three years, in principle, the workers were sent back or given the opportunity to re-enlist. During this first phase, the poor living conditions of coolies were not widely criticized by the outside world and protests against the penal clause remained negligible. As Breman states, the end of the pioneering era was marked by the fact that the coolie scandals became more widely known.[18]

The phase of policy alternatives

The second phase was a phase of discussion and concern. It started in 1903, when Rhemrev wrote his report. Under the influence of the Ethical Policy, and impressed by the reports of Van den Brand, Van Kol, and Rhemrev, Dutch politicians acted to improve legislation. In 1907 a government Labour Inspectorate (Arbeidsinspectie) was established to investigate labour conditions and check for abuses of the penal clause. In the Coolie Ordinance of 1909 the penal clause was weakened and limited, and in 1911 a regulation for free wage labour was included.

Despite such amendments, the planters were in no hurry to abolish the

18 Breman analysed the pioneering period, studying labour conditions in Deli at the turn of the century. He does not survey the improvement of circumstances in the 1920s and 1930s achieved by the Labour Inspectorate and the increase of free wage labour (Breman 1992b:30, 33, 314.)

penal clause – and the government accepted this. For another twenty years, a large number of contract coolies and a small number of 'free' workers were employed simultaneously, usually for equal wages (Breman 1992b:301, 324; Stoler 1985:43). This phase lasted until 1931, when the penal clause was finally abolished.

Plans for abolition of the penal clause sparked off a rash of heated discussion amongst the planters, who kept arguing that the coolie system was an economic necessity without which the plantation economy would crumble. As early as 1928, Colijn remarked that the polemic discussions of planters for and against the penal clause already filled bookshelves (Langeveld 1978:294). In the meantime, the estates propagated the image of a 'model society' in the rainforest, where autonomous hospitals and laboratories were set up and different racial groups worked together harmoniously.

Several government plans were launched to deal with the labour shortage in the Outer Islands in another way: by establishing 'labour settlements'. This idea ran parallel to other plans to develop 'agricultural settlements', but constituted a different solution to a different problem. The first colonization plans were conceived in 1902 and their chief purpose was to relieve population pressure in Java. Under these plans Javanese peasants and their families were offered transportation costs and initial loans to move to Lampung, Palembang, or Manado. Labour colonization was specifically intended to create local labour pools for the estates.[19] The planters in East Sumatra agreed with the concept of labour colonization, but were opposed to agricultural colonization, because the latter implied that the settlers would be granted a larger area of land. They argued that there was no room for such settlements in the estate area, and effectively blocked the issue of agricultural colonization (Stoler 1985:38-41).[20]

The phase of priority of economic policy

The third phase began with the onset of the Depression in 1929. Suddenly, when the Depression necessitated cuts and lay-offs, there was an oversupply of labour. Like most other industries caught in the Depression, the estates fired large numbers of workers. The number of coolies laid off continued to increase until 1932 (Table 60.1). Free labour now presented a sound advantage to entrepreneurs on the estates. 'Free' workers could be laid off before the

19 There were agricultural settlements in Lampung, Palembang, and Manado, as well as smaller ones in Bengkulu, East Sumatra, Southeast Kalimantan, and South Sulawesi. Eventually, the numbers of settlers amounted to several tens of thousands, thus not reaching the large scale that the colonial government had envisaged. The largest were in Lampung (Furnivall 1944:252; Coolhaas 1943:59-61).

20 The results of government efforts to promote these types of colonization is treated in more detail in Chapter VI.

three-year period had elapsed, they would not have to be paid when there was no work to be done, and they did not have to be transported back to Java after the contract period had expired.[21]

International pressure speeded up the abolition of the penal clause, which eventually took place in 1931. A tariff agreement in the United States, contained in the Blaine Amendment (1929), threatened to prohibit imports of goods produced under indentured labour. The measure was to come into force in 1932.[22] In 1930 the International Labour Office in Geneva also pressed the Dutch government to abolish the penal clause entirely.[23]

In short, the influence of the Depression and (in the case of tobacco) the Blaine Amendment led to the final abolition of the penal clause. In 1931 tobacco planters issued a statement that they would no longer use contract labour under penal sanctions. The 1931 Coolie Ordinance contained a scheme for phasing out contract labour, stipulating the minimum percentage of non-contract workers for the coming years.[24] To expedite the process, a Registratiekamer (Registration Office) was set up in Medan. This office registered all labourers, to circumvent the possibility that workers from one estate could be tempted away by rival estates wanting to avoid expensive recruiting costs. The Registratiekamer restituted a sum of money to the estates for each immigrant worker recruited. In the course of the 1930s, when the number of coolies attracted to work increased again, this sum was decreased correspondingly (Table 60.2).[25] Production cuts, made unavoidable by the Depression, meant the labour shortage in East Sumatra was less acute. This fact played an important role in the abolition of the penal clause. It is possible to debate whether it was the Coolie Ordinance or the impending threat of the Blaine Amendment that speeded up the abolition of the penal clause; but the circumstances engendered by the Depression obviously helped. The fact is that in 1929 only 13.5 per cent of the coolies in the estate area were 'free' workers, but this percentage changed quickly to 96.3 per cent in 1934 (Table 60.3).[26]

21 ARA Kol, MvO 188, H.E.K. Ezerman 1933:48-50; Langeveld 1978:323.

22 Exceptions were made for goods that could *not* be produced in the United States. Only after a period of uncertainty did the American Congress decide that the costly Sumatran cigar wrapper leaf could not be grown in the United States and therefore was excluded from the tariff agreement. Thus, the American Congress in fact converted the amendment into a clever trade-protection device, which merely applied to certain competitive imports (Blaine amendment, section 307 of the Tariff Law of 1929). ARA Kol, MvO 188, H.E.K. Ezerman 1933:97; Homan 1987:145, 153; Rothe 1950:323; Thee Kian Wie 1977:40.

23 ARA, NHM 9127, VvS 506 (Medan 1930):2-5.

24 For estates established before 1923: 25% after 1 January 1932, 40% in 1934, 50% in 1936. ARA Kol, MvO 188, H.E.K. Ezerman 1933:96; Langeveld 1978:302.

25 ARA, NHM 9127, VvS 513 (Medan 1937):7; VvS 514 (1938):9; VvS 515 (1939):4; Langeveld 1978:304; Rothe 1950:322.

26 ARA Kol, MvO 190, B.C.C.M.M. van Suchtelen 1936:31; Rothe 1950:323.

The Depression implied one other major change in labour policy. Looking ahead to better times, planters decided to try to settle workers' families near the estate area, and to send back only the single workers. The agricultural family settlements should be self-sufficient, and were to provide labour for the future when times got better. For example, in 1933 Deli Maatschappij, Deli Batavia Maatschappij, and Cultuurmaatschappij 'De Oostkust' offered the following deal to their coolies after termination of their contracts: the use of 5,000 m^2 land on the estate, accommodation in their own huts on the estate, and a six-month allowance of 3.50 guilders per month, on condition that they would re-enter estate service after one and a half or two years. About 1,200 coolie families accepted this proposal.[27]

In general, government policy on coolie labour had only a limited effect. Planters were more sensitive to the economy than to government plans, and during the liberal period the colonial government was only moderately interested in delaying the expansion of private enterprise. In the meantime, the planters brought enormous numbers of immigrants into the region. It is interesting to examine the effects of these immigrant population groups on the local economy (see further below). But let us first examine estate agriculture in other Outer Provinces.

Estate agriculture outside East Sumatra

Many European and American companies obtained land concessions in provinces outside East Sumatra. Estates were established in Palembang and Southeast Kalimantan, as well as in Lampung and South Sulawesi, provinces with ample space and relatively little European economic activity. Outside Deli, tobacco estates were few and far between, but there was no shortage of companies cultivating rubber, coffee, copra, or other crops. In the early twentieth century, since the political unrest in Aceh made business there too precarious an undertaking, expansion to the north of the estate area of East Sumatra was not attractive, although a few estates were established in the southern part of Aceh. Only in the 1920s did estate agriculture in Aceh expand.[28] In West Sumatra and Lampung, as well as in Palembang, European estates successfully cultivated coffee. There were also several small coffee estates in South Sulawesi and Manado. Besides East Sumatra, rubber was grown by European estates in Palembang, Riau, and West and Southeast Kalimantan. Small copra estates could be found in South Sulawesi, Manado, and

27 ARA Kol, MvO 188, H.E.K. Ezerman 1933:65-7.

28 A number of rubber, coffee, and oil-palm estates in Aceh were owned by the Franco-Belgian Société Financière des Caoutchoucs. ARA Kol, MvO 160, A.Ph. van Aken 1936:75.

Maluku.[29] A small number of European estates cultivating coffee, copra, and rubber could also be found in Maluku, Bali, and the Lesser Sunda Islands. As a whole, compared to East Sumatra, estate agriculture in the other Outer Islands reached only modest levels. In the late 1920s, around 70 per cent of all coolies employed in agriculture could still be found in East Sumatra (Table 60.4, corrected for coolies in oil, tin, and coal). The conclusion is that most estate agriculture was located in Sumatra. At the end of the 1930s, European estates on islands other than Sumatra and Java still cultivated only 57,000 hectares – while in Sumatra it was estimated at more than 500,000 hectares.[30]

Versatility in Palembang

Probably the most active province with regard to indigenous dynamics, Palembang had an old tradition of trade and handicrafts. Roughly speaking, Palembang had four productive regions: Banjuasin, the Kubu districts (the lowlands), the Pasemah districts, and Musi Hulu (the uplands). Rubber was predominantly grown in Banjuasin and the Kubu districts, mostly the lowland areas, but there was some rubber in Musi-Hulu, along with fibres. Both indigenous and estate coffee was cultivated in the mountainous regions (Pasemah and Ranau). In the highlands, after 1925, tea and quinine were also grown (for example in Pasemah).[31] The largest share of agricultural exports was indigenous. Peasants produced pepper, *pinang* nuts, and rattan in the early decades of the 1900s, and after 1915 added coffee, rubber, rice, pineapples, and a wide range of smaller products.

The European estates produced mainly rubber and coffee. In 1928 one Resident estimated the area under cultivation by European estates to be roughly 6 or 7 per cent of the total area under cultivation by the indigenous population.[32] The estate sector in Palembang was much smaller than in East Sumatra, which is illustrated by the number of coolies. In 1922, there were about 9,000 coolies in Palembang and 189,000 coolies in East Sumatra. In 1929, 41,000 coolies were counted in Palembang, versus 303,000 in East Sumatra (this includes coolies working in mining) (Table 60.4).

It is interesting that indigenous agriculture in Palembang was diversified

29 In 1922 in Manado: the coffee estate Modajaq (in Mongondou). In 1926 several copra estates, one rubber and one coffee estate. (The trade statistics did not register the distinction between smallholder and estate products, except for rubber after 1927.) ARA Kol, MvO 304, F.H.W.J.R. Logeman 1922:93; MvO 305, J. Tideman 1926:116.

30 At the same time, European agriculture on Java covered 1 million hectares, of which about 600,000 hectares was planted (Van Hall 1942:53, 56).

31 Quinine, in colonial times also called *kina* (derived from the Spanish 'quina'), is extracted from the bark of the Chinchona tree, and used for medical (febrifugal) purposes. The Netherlands Indies was by far the largest quinine producer in the world during the pre-war years.

32 ARA Kol, MvO 212, J. Tideman 1928:278; MvO 214, J.L.M. Schwaab 1933:184.

and not dependent on one or two main cash crops, as it was in Jambi (rubber) and West Kalimantan (rubber and copra). In its crops, Palembang resembled West Sumatra, where the export package was varied and trade was also an important occupation, although the volume of exports from West Sumatra was smaller than from Palembang. Palembang coffee exports, almost completely of indigenous origin, made up 20 to 30 per cent of all Netherlands Indies coffee exports in the 1920s. Initially, most of Palembang's coffee was shipped to Batavia, where it was auctioned to European and American buyers. This had changed by 1923, when three-quarters of Palembang coffee was sold directly to overseas purchasers and merely transhipped at Tanjung Priok.[33]

As in Southeast Kalimantan, petroleum exports accounted for the highest volume of European export activity in Palembang, but European agriculture was dispersed throughout the whole region. Palembang's estate production of rubber moved along levels similar to West and Southeast Kalimantan: volumes of 500,000 to one million kg, leading up to 2.6 million kg in 1938. These figures were lower by roughly a factor of 100 than the estate rubber output of East Sumatra (Table 44.4 and Figure 26).

Referring to Palembang, it is possible to use the term multi-segmented economy. A strong indigenous agricultural sector produced coffee, rubber, and rattan, which was balanced by oil and coal mines, and European estates that produced rubber and coffee. The segments were also spatially integrated, more so than in Southeast Kalimantan (where the mining enclaves were situated along the east coast). The oil refinery at Plaju, the coal mines in Bukit Asem, and the agricultural estates provided local employment and economic stimuli (Touwen 1991).

Dualist Southeast Kalimantan

Southeast Kalimantan also ranked amongst the first three export producers in the Outer Islands in the late colonial period. This is slightly misleading, as the presence of European private enterprise in Southeast Kalimantan was restricted largely to the enclaves of oil production (Balikpapan and Tarakan) and the trading towns (Banjarmasin and Samarinda). The largest share of export agriculture was in the hands of indigenous peasants. There were only a few European estates and they produced mainly rubber. Generally speaking, there were more people and more commercial agriculture in the south of Southeast Kalimantan, but more capital and more mining centres in the east of the province.[34]

33 ARA Kol, MvO 212, J. Tideman 1928:257; MvO 215, W. Steinbuch 1936:204.

34 Resident Rijckmans wrote: 'For a large province such as Southeast Kalimantan, the num-

If we ignore petroleum exports, which raised total export revenues from Southeast Kalimantan to a peak value of some 220 million guilders in the years 1919-1920, we get a picture of a province that resembled West Kalimantan in product mix and export volume. Gutta percha, rubber, and other exports remained below 25 million guilders until 1923. Exports of agricultural and forest products reached peak values in 1926 at about 80 million guilders. These consisted mainly of rubber and rattan, and smaller products such as gutta, pepper, damar, copal, dried fish, wood, and copra.

In Southeast Kalimantan, planters tried to cultivate tobacco as an estate crop, but it turned out to be no match for Deli tobacco, because the soil in Kalimantan was not as good. Although Kalimantan planters assiduously tried to cultivate tobacco in the early 1900s, the poor tobacco prices in those years made it a hopeless struggle. The consequence was that indigenous tobacco (producing *kerftabak*) assumed a stable position in the economy of the region, while the few Western tobacco estates disappeared completely.[35]

Southeast Kalimantan lagged far behind East Sumatra in development of infrastructure. Although European traders had settled in Banjarmasin in the 1870s and succeeded to a modest degree in purchasing forest products and marketing these in Singapore, the inland areas remained vast and inaccessible for many years. Trading was mostly done on the coast. The NHM agency in Banjarmasin fell under Singapore as a sub-agency until 1907. It had been opened in 1877, but closed again in 1885, only to be reopened in 1903.[36] In 1903, when Deli tobacco exports already exceeded 14 million guilders, Southeast Kalimantan was still largely unknown territory which exported little more than forest products. As the NHM sub-agent put it, 'because of the scarcity of the industrial enterprises and the insignificance of agriculture in Banjarmasin and its hinterland, this part of Kalimantan produces almost nothing except forest products'.[37] The NHM purchased forest products: rattan, various sorts of gum and resin, wax, gutta, as well as some dried fish. No one yet produced copra. Only a little export revenue outside oil was earned in Southeast Kalimantan at that time.

Dismal as the picture may seem, export production gradually and steadily increased. In 1907 three trading firms exported copra to the European market. All exports of copra to Singapore in those years were in the hands of Chinese

---

ber of European estates can be called disappointingly small [...]' ARA Kol, MvO 271, L.J.F. Rijckmans 1916:47. See also Lindblad 1985a, 1988a:177-88.

35 ARA, NHM 9086, VvS 9 (Banjarmasin 1903):2; NHM 9087, VvS 10 (Banjarmasin 1904):12; NHM 9088, VvS 11 (Banjarmasin 1905):13; ARA Kol, MvO 270, H.N.A. Swart 1906:16. Compare Lindblad 1988a:29.

36 ARA, NHM 9086, VvS 3 (Banjarmasin 1877/78); VvS 7 (1885); VvS 9 (1903).

37 ARA, NHM 9086, VvS 9 (Banjarmasin 1903):1.

traders. Ficus Elastica, the forerunner of commercial rubber, was not only tapped from wild trees in the forest, but was increasingly being planted in gardens by both Europeans and Dayak.[38] When Hevea rubber came, as almost everywhere else in the western part of the archipelago, both indigenous peasants (first in Banjarmasin) and European firms started planting seeds and seedlings. The densely populated region in the south, where indigenous rubber was concentrated in Hulu Sungai, was more accessible than the northern part of Southeast Kalimantan. Here, in 1920, the indigenous population amounted to around 430,000, almost half of Southeast Kalimantan's total indigenous population, which was about one million at that time.[39] Transport in Hulu Sungai was facilitated by a relatively well-developed network of roads. In comparison, indigenous rubber peasants in Jambi and southern East Sumatra, in Asahan, and in West Kalimantan were scattered over relatively large, inaccessible areas from where the rubber had to be transported by rafts along rivers. This situation lasted longer in Jambi and West Kalimantan, where infrastructural provisions came later and more hesitantly than in the more affluent provinces of East Sumatra, Palembang, and Southeast Kalimantan. In the course of the twentieth century, the European presence exerted itself favourably at least in the construction of better roads.

It is interesting that in both Southeast Kalimantan and Palembang, the share of the European estates in rubber exports averaged only 13 per cent over the years 1927/38. In East Sumatra, 88 per cent originated from the estates and in Jambi and West Kalimantan, 0.4 and 7 per cent respectively (Table 44.7).[40]

As in all other rubber provinces, the rubber smallholders in Southeast Kalimantan earned more money during the rubber boom than they had ever done before. After 1926 rubber prices started to decrease, and the indigenous demand for luxury goods such as motor cars and clothing immediately dropped, causing problems for Chinese import traders. A good indicator of indigenous welfare is the annual number of *haji*, those making the pilgrimage to Mecca; this number decreased immediately. But the imports of luxury foodstuffs continued, and the standard of living remained high, according to the NHM sub-agent.[41] When the economic situation worsened, 'a large number of people from Hulu Sungai, the rubber region par excellence, left for other places, heading especially for the eastern coast, to look for a better

38 ARA, NHM 9086, VvS 10 (Banjarmasin 1904):4; VvS 14 (1907):4-5; ARA Kol, MvO 271, L.J.F. Rijckmans 1916:31.

39 In 1920, only 104 of the 2,690 Europeans lived in Ulu Sungai. The main concentration of Europeans lived in Banjarmasin (841) and Samarinda (1,478). Foreign Orientals (or foreign Asians) were also concentrated in these towns (5,737 and 10,525 out of a total 19,550, only 549 in Ulu Sungai) (see Table 17 for 1930).

40 Calculated over the years 1927, 1928, 1930, 1932, 1934, 1936, and 1938. See Tables 44.1-44.8.

41 ARA, NHM 9088, VvS 32 (Banjarmasin 1926):1; VvS 33 (1927):2.

means of making a living'.[42]

Indigenous agriculture in Southeast Kalimantan was not severely hit by the Depression, and prosperity seems to have returned quickly. The range of possible occupations was relatively large in this province, where employment in trade or at the coal mines or the oil production centres formed an alternative to cash-crop cultivation. In 1937 the NHM sub-agent summed up the range of choice as follows: 'Southeast Kalimantan is a prosperous province. There are many means of subsistence for the population: rubber cultivation, food crops, pepper, and copra, the gathering of forest products (such as wood, rattan, damar, gutta jelutung, katiauw, hangkang) supplemented by fishing, kacang and purun weaving, duck breeding, gold and diamond mining, and diamond cutting. Over and above this, the department for the maintenance of roads and waterways, several oil companies, and the forestry all provided employment for many. There was no reason why anybody should suffer from poverty.'[43]

Roughly speaking, the Europeans in Southeast Kalimantan produced oil or carried on trade, while the indigenous population cultivated agricultural products, alongside only a small number of estates. Western influence in the economic sphere also stemmed from European banks and trading firms. The main providers of credit to Europeans were the NHM and the Javasche Bank (Java Bank), whereas the Borsumij lent funds to the Chinese merchants and retailers. An increasing number of European trading firms took the plunge in Southeast Kalimantan, occupying a disproportionately large share in officially registered trade: of the 44 formal trading firms in operation prior to 1940, many were unmistakably European, among which were the well-known names Hagemeijer, Lindeteves, Wehry, Jacobson van den Berg, and Handelsvereeniging Bandjermasin (Lindblad 1988a:183-5).

Lindblad speaks of a 'twin basis of expansion in Southeast Kalimantan', which increased the potential of the region but also exposed its vulnerability to adverse developments abroad. This implied a lopsided distribution of returns for the factors of production and a drainage of profits away from the region.

> Preciously little was achieved in terms of infrastructural provisions. Ironically, such accomplishments began to materialize somewhat only after the mid-1930s, when expansion had long since passed its zenith and tighter budgetary constraints compelled the government to appropriate more of the gains from indigenous rubber (Lindblad 1988a:219).

42 ARA, NHM 9088, VvS 35 (Banjarmasin 1929):2.
43 ARA, NHM 9088, VvS 43 (Banjarmasin 1937):6-7.

Southeast Kalimantan resembled East Sumatra with regard to its dual economy, but the European sector was less emphatically present in the interior regions and occupied less space. The active indigenous population created its own export production, without the benefits of European presence leading the way, and without utilizing Western-made infrastructure to increase export trade.

Adventures in estate agriculture: Aceh, West Sumatra, or Lampung

Although Deli in East Sumatra was undoubtedly the favourite region for European companies wanting to venture outside Java, agricultural estates were established in several other provinces in Sumatra and Kalimantan. In Aceh, the government favoured the coming of European estates because they were seen as a means to keep the peace in this rebellious province: isolated areas were opened up, employment opportunities improved, and the amount of cash in the hands of the indigenous population increased. The government hoped that entrepreneurs from neighbouring East Sumatra would apply for concessions in Aceh. Hopes were dashed because Aceh's unfavourable political reputation deterred entrepreneurs. A small number of estates on the western coast of Aceh grew rubber, coffee, and oil palms. In eastern Aceh, rubber cultivation began in 1907, and oil palm plantations spread quickly during the inter-war period.[44]

Further south along the western coast, in West Sumatra, the establishment of Western enterprise was most apparent in Emmahaven, the harbour of Padang: here, in addition to European wholesale trading houses, oil and copra factories could be found. There were only a few estates in West Sumatra, growing tea, quinine, coffee, and (a little) rubber, for example in the departments of Lubuk Sikaping and Solok. Another symbol of Western presence was the Portland cement factory, owned by the Nederlandsch-Indische Portland Cement Maatschappij (Netherlands Indies Portland Cement Company).[45] Rubber was relatively unimportant and many coffee gardens were closed after 1929, when the Depression set in. Tea and quinine developed strongly in West Sumatra in the 1930s.[46]

Lampung, being the nearest to Java, was the most obvious target of the government's policies of agricultural colonization. In Java, government offi-

44 ARA Kol, MvO 160, Van Aken 1936:72-5; Gade Ismail 1994:288-90.

45 ARA Kol, MvO 165, J.D.L. le Fèbvre 1919:56, 57; MvO 166, W.A.C. Whitlau 1926:83, 123, 131; MvO 170, A.I. Spits 1937:12-9. See also Colombijn 1994:89-91.

46 In 1937, tea plantations employed about 5,000 workers, whereas coffee employed about 2,600, quinine 1,000, and rubber only 100. Estates with mixed crops employed another 1,400 workers. ARA Kol, MvO 170, A.I. Spits 1937:12-5.

cials promoted Lampung as 'the land of the future', and the government spent several hundred thousand guilders on the settlement of several thousand Javanese immigrants in Gedung Tanaan and Kota Agung. During the early decades of the 1900s, Lampung remained a somewhat rural province, although its road system was relatively well developed. Substantial estate agriculture did not get off the ground. Several Western entrepreneurs experimented with growing tobacco and rubber in the early 1920s, but without success.[47] A few years later, during the rubber boom, more land was given in concession to estates: Resident L. Berkhout estimated the total area given in concession to estates to be 264,000 hectares, which was about 11 per cent of the province. But land in concession was not always cultivated, as the applicants often overestimated their ability to obtain capital.[48] Lampung remained a land of high hopes.

Estates and the surrounding indigenous economy

The economic effects of European estates are a topic emphasized in this chapter, in particular the effects of the large-scale immigration of coolies to the estate area. Four major consequences of large-scale estate agriculture can be noted. These linkages constitute the major effects of the presence of the estates on the surrounding economy:

a. demand effects created by the estates,
b. infrastructural development in the region,
c. the economic role of ex-coolies who did not return to their home country,
d. scarcity of land for indigenous smallholders.

Undeniably, the estates created a new demand in the surrounding region for construction materials and foodstuffs. The large-scale immigration of workers created a new population group, which created a demand for a variety of goods, ranging from foodstuffs to clothing. While the estates supplied some of these goods, other were bought by the workers themselves.

East Sumatra's export economy may also have had favourable demand effects on the domestic economy of the Netherlands Indies at large. Compared with other provinces, East Sumatra had a substantial flow of imports, a portion of which originated from Java and other islands. East Sumatra's export economy thus had favourable economic repercussions for the country as a whole. These effects could be observed in particular in Java, where East Sumatra's rapid growth stimulated the growth of 'final demand linkage' industries,

47 ARA Kol, MvO 231, J. Breukink 1922:1-3, 7-8, 12, 13, 23; MvO 233, L. Berkhout 1926:1-4, 10.
48 ARA Kol, MvO 233, L. Berkhout 1926:36.

such as the textile industry, the cigarette industry, and rice mills.[49] Nonetheless, caution is advised; it has been argued by Thee Kian Wie that these effects should not be overrated. A large proportion of the factor inputs involved in European estate production in East Sumatra were 'foreign' and remitted a goodly proportion of their earnings abroad. The trade balance showed a large export surplus for all years between 1900 and 1940. The development of a domestic market, vital to integration within the archipelago and an important factor in stimulating growth in the region's economy outside the export sector, failed to evolve in East Sumatra, at least to the extent that might have been expected with such an export performance (Thee Kian Wie 1977:132-4).

Income effects in the region followed directly from local demand linkages. Peasants sold agricultural goods, and retail traders in the region supplied the estates with such goods as wood and construction materials. This small trade earned them a money income, which they could spend on imports. Sultans earned money by leasing land to the estates. Usually, a number of Chinese shops sprang up near the estates, supplying goods to the estate area and the coolie population. Such opportunities to earn money had previously been unknown in the region.

The wages of estate workers were a catalyst through which substantial flows of income were distributed in the region. These backward linkages reached substantial heights, due to the fact that there were hundreds of thousands of Javanese coolies in the region, who, although concentrated in small estate areas, outnumbered the original Batak and Malay people (Tables 18 and 58). This can be illustrated by examining the expenses generated by the tobacco industry. In 1926, the tobacco estates alone paid more than 24 million guilders in wages to Indonesians – and their overall expenditure on salaries (including European salaries, the largest part of which was also spent locally; they do not include bonuses). Medical care and other social costs, taxes, supplies, and immigration costs added up to almost 49 million guilders. In the face of cost reductions and lay-offs, this amount was reduced to an average of 18 million guilders over 1932/38, which is still a substantial sum, since the price level had also declined during these years (Table 58).

Taxes paid by tobacco estates, particularly those paid to the local authorities, were also indirectly beneficial to the indigenous population. The percentage of these taxes in total tax revenues averaged 7.3 per cent (De Ridder 1935:81). The resulting social benefit per planted hectare (the sum of all expenditure on wages, transportation costs, community services such as forest clearing, and taxes), as given by Pelzer, was as high as 2,500 guilders in

49 Final demand linkage: effects in income distribution and consumer demand, due to input by an industry of primary production factors (consumption linkage) (Thee Kian Wie 1997:133).

1926. It decreased steadily in the 1930s, to about 1,400 guilders in 1938.[50] The percentage paid as wages to indigenous and Chinese workers amounted to roughly 60 per cent of this amount. Even though wages per worker were low, aggregate payments in the labour-intensive tobacco industry amounted to a considerable sum. In the same way, the other agricultural estates also had an economically beneficial effect on the region.

Infrastructural development in the region

The most important backward linkage of the European estates in East Sumatra was in infrastructure. Roads, railways, and ports were built to serve the needs of the estates. The whole economy around the estates served the needs of the estate economy. For example, the Deli Maatschappij initiated the establishment of the Deli Spoorweg Maatschappij (Deli Railway Company) in 1883 for the transport of harvested and dried bales of tobacco to the coast (Thee Kian Wie 1977:44; Weisfelt 1972:41-61). This is a clear example of infrastructural development as a backward linkage of the estate economy.

When roads were constructed, a new opportunity was created for the transport of indigenous products, alongside the traditional use of the river. Interior traders quickly adapted to the use of trucks and buses. Foreign imports of motor cars into East Sumatra amounted to around 2.2 million guilders annually in 1925/27. In Palembang, this average was almost 0.6 million guilders and in Southeast Kalimantan 0.26 million guilders, in Jambi 0.12 and in Aceh 0.16 million guilders (these figures refer only to foreign imports).

Another linkage effect is the so-called 'fiscal linkage'. The duties that were paid by the estates on their imports and exports as well as company taxes and income taxes generated a substantial flow of income into the treasury of the colonial government. This facilitated government expenditure on infrastructural development. The degree to which these revenues favoured the economically strong provinces or were redistributed to provinces with a weaker economy is addressed in Chapter VI.

Settle, re-enlist or return?

The third effect of European estates was that a number of immigrant workers did not return to their home country but settled in East Sumatra. Some of these workers became peasants or traders. Labour colonization (or border colonization) of estate workers who became part-time peasants also belongs to this category of linkages: it created a new group of agricultural producers – in addition to the indigenous peasants and the estates.

50 Pelzer's data originate from a report by Van Beukering in 1939, based on annual reports of DPV and AVROS. Similar figures are given by De Waard. Pelzer 1978:107, 110; De Waard 1934:282. See also Table 58.

The original contracts stipulated that after the contract period ended, workers would be shipped back to their native place. But often workers wanted to stay in the area, having little hope of making a good living in the impoverished areas from which they came. Javanese former contract workers settled in kampongs on the estate area (intermingled with the indigenous population), but also in clandestine, exclusively Javanese kampongs, on the borders of the estate area, or in agricultural settlements established by the estate (De Ridder 1935:51). From the point of view of the planters and the government, labour settlements created a possible solution to the labour problem by providing a more or less stable labour reserve. In discussions about the living conditions of coolies, defenders of the estate labour policy argued that coolies who had earned a small sum of money could start a business as a local trader. It seems unlikely that this took place on a large scale, since coolies often ran up debts by gambling or spending advances on their pay, which forced them to extend their contracts.

The immigration of Javanese to East Sumatra was by far the largest migration flow that took place in the Netherlands Indies during the late colonial period. In 1930, about 432,000 Javanese were living in East Sumatra (of whom 182,000 were coolies). There were some 335,000 Malays and 381,000 Batak (Table 18).[51] It is difficult to assess the number of ex-estate coolies who found a place to live in East Sumatra each year, or to specify whether they found a living as peasants or as part-time coolies, or in some other occupation. Often, coolies living in kampongs were still hired to work on the estates, for example during the tobacco harvesting season.[52]

According to the census of 1930, the total number of Javanese living in East Sumatra was 590,000. There were 357,000 coolies registered on the estates, many of whom had brought their families with them (Table 60.1). Taking account of this, Pelzer estimates that close to half a million inhabitants depended on estate agriculture for a living.

In the census of 1930, almost 30,000 of the remaining roughly 90,000 Javanese living in East Sumatra stated their occupation to be 'peasant'.[53] This may not seem a large number, but it constitutes 45 per cent of all Javanese peasants in the Outer Islands. In Lampung, only 13,000 Javanese stated that

51 Javanese immigrants made up 40.1% of the indigenous population of East Sumatra. In Deli and Serdang, it was 54%, and in Langkat and Asahan it was also higher, 49 and 42% respectively. By comparison, the number of Chinese in East Sumatra in 1930 was much smaller: 12% in East Sumatra, 17% in Deli and Serdang (see also Langeveld 1978:165).

52 Unlike rubber, tobacco was harvested only a few months a year. Interestingly, after World War II, Javanese squatter settlements on estate lands developed into permanent Javanese villages. Fewer estate workers lived in *pondok* (simple housing on estates) and many lived in Javanese villages clearly separate from Malay and Batak settlements (Stoler 1985:4).

53 Of these, 25,716 were male and 3,671 were female. *Volkstelling* 1933, IV:94.

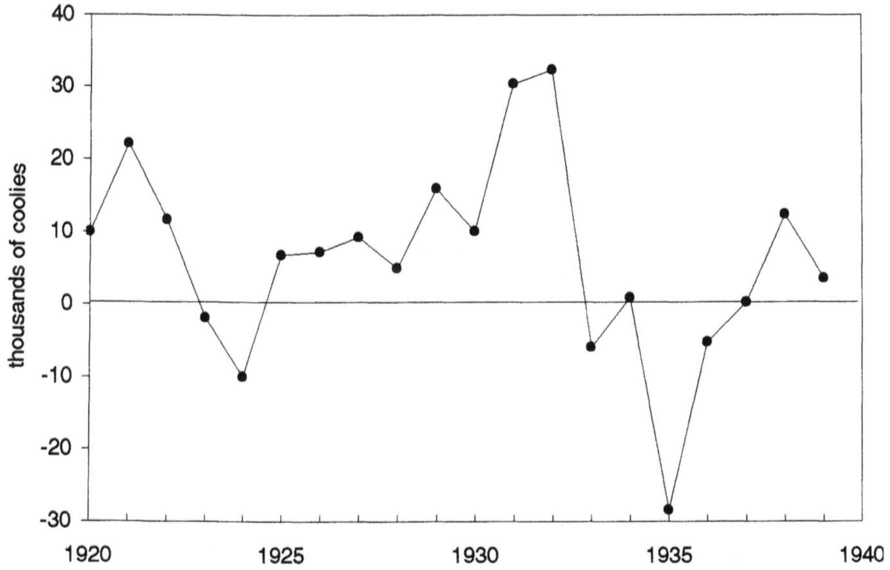

Figure 8. Reconstructed numbers of coolie settlers, 1920-1940 (Table 60.5).

they were peasants (19.8 per cent), in Jambi 4,000, and in Aceh only 2,000. Half of all (registered) Javanese peasants in the Outer Islands in 1930, then, lived in East Sumatra, which also constituted 12.5 per cent of the total indigenous population who stated 'peasant' as their only occupation. Including the number of inhabitants with multiple occupations would raise the actual number of Javanese peasants. Since almost all Javanese in East Sumatra had originally immigrated as coolies, it is indisputable that substantial numbers of ex-coolies became peasants in Sumatra.

We can go one step further in estimating the number of coolie settlers. Labour Inspectorate reports state the number of coolies who returned each year to their home country, as well as the number of new coolies recruited in Java. Langeveld gives approximate death rates among coolies (on average 9.57 per 1000 per year during 1917/32; the death rate was lower in the 1930s, due to improved living conditions).[54]

The newly recruited coolies served a. to replace those coolies who had passed away, b. to replace coolies who did not extend their contract, and c. to

[54] These figures taken from Langeveld 1978:308, 310, 312, 340, 363 (tables I, II, III and X and appendix III). The figures are represented in Table 60.5. No Chinese coolies are included, only Javanese (after 1910 the largest number were Javanese). No distinction is made between contract coolies and free coolies. Cf. Boomgaard and Gooszen 1990:54.

expand the workforce (during the years 1917-1929). Using the total numbers of Javanese estate coolies, it is possible to calculate the annual change in respect to the previous year. Subtracting from this number the net result of recruitment, deaths, and returning to Java yields an annual figure of ex-coolies that settled in East Sumatra (Table 60.5). In some years, as in 1924 and 1935, the estates recruited from this local labour pool. The average of this figure (Column 8 in Table 60.5) is 6,300 workers. This means that each year, 6,300 coolies left the estates without returning to Java. This amounted to 126,700 coolies over the period 1919-1939. In the years preceding the Depression, 1920-1930, the average was 7,800 coolies per year, amounting to 86,300 settlers in the 1920s (Figure 8).

After 1929, large numbers of coolies were laid off, only a small part of whom went back to Java (Tables 60.1 and 60.5). During these years, 1929-1933, tens of thousands of ex-estate coolies dispersed over Sumatra, in search of a means to make a living.

Many settlers colonized as peasants, shopkeepers, or small traders. They joined Batak kampongs or migrated to other places in Sumatra, for example to offer themselves as rubber tappers to indigenous smallholders. Some of these immigrants also had families. We may conclude from these figures that substantial numbers did not renew their contract, but remained in Sumatra. Langeveld has argued that the coolie had little reason to leave the estates, because indigenous agriculture was a poor alternative. This may explain why 'free' coolies, who were not contracted under the penal clause, did not run away. Whatever the case, to many Javanese, becoming a peasant in East Sumatra must have been more attractive than going back to Java, where living conditions were worse (Langeveld 1978:327).

Indigenous agriculture: cornered by sultan and estates

The local rulers, the sultan of Langkat and the Malay princes, granted concessions in return for land rent or other profits. As a consequence, the indigenous population near the estate area, who had a tradition of swidden agriculture on *ladang* in the forest, found the amount of land at its disposal shrinking. Ultimately, by 1940, the concessioned estate area in East Sumatra had expanded to 10,000 km^2. But as early as 1930 it had a population density of 107 inhabitants per km^2.[55] While the estate area expanded, traditional subsistence agriculture had to seek new tracts of land in remote uplands or in coastal areas. As De Ridder writes, 'the formerly thinly populated parts of the country became relatively densely populated in the course of the years, since the area of free settlement had shrunk considerably through the practice of concessions' (De Ridder 1935:43). Concessions were valid for wastelands and

55 De Ridder 1935:37; *Volkstelling* 1933, IV. East Sumatra's total area was 93,500 km^2.

could not be issued on kampongs or indigenously cultivated fields. However, concessions could cross *marga* fields, areas traditionally available to municipalities, without regard to their status.

The model contract of 1878 stipulated that residents living within the estate borders at the time of the initial agreement were allowed to cultivate plots of 4 *bouw* (2.8 hectares), which was grossly inadequate for subsistence needs under the swidden system.[56] Their alternative was to choose the use of a slightly larger area of *jaluran*, harvested tobacco fields. *Jaluran*, literally meaning 'strip of land', was the land from which the tobacco had been harvested, after which it had to lie fallow for several years; indigenous peasants who already lived on the concessions or returned from elsewhere were given the right to cultivate rice or maize on these fields. This possibility was first included in the 1884 model contract. Problems still abounded, as the area available was limited, there were many claimants, and estate policy was to give *jaluran* rights to as many as possible, since this was seen as a way to tie indigenous workers to the estate. The upshot was that *jaluran* fields were small, and the system was not a resounding success (De Ridder 1935:43, 47; Stoler 1985:23). While the model contracts were refined, reducing the rights of the peasant, the estate area expanded and left less land for indigenous agriculture.

Although the peasants had only small patches of land to cultivate, they did not switch to irrigated agriculture. The government did little to stimulate, let alone finance, irrigation projects and *sawah* construction. The office of the Landbouwvoorlichtingsdienst (LVD, Agricultural Extension Office) was even temporarily liquidated between 1933 and 1935. A second, and probably more serious, drawback was that permanent field cultivation required the daily attention of the peasant – and since planters offered only upland or coastal areas to inhabitants of large kampongs in the estate area, these plots were too remote for intensive cultivation. It was impossible to practice swidden agriculture on two or four *bouw*, or even on four hectares.[57]

Besides occupying land, the presence of European estates in East Sumatra did have another direct effect on the indigenous agriculture of Malay and Batak peasants in Deli, Serdang, and Simalungun. The traditional cultivation of tobacco had been forbidden by planters' regulations in the late nineteenth century, out of fear of theft of estate tobacco by coolies. This prohibition prevented peasants from expanding their traditional tobacco cultivation. Had tobacco planters in Deli not prevented peasants from growing tobacco, an economic activity that was widely practised in East Sumatra in the early nineteenth century might perhaps have expanded. This prohibition was imposed by the estates to avoid soil exhaustion on *jaluran* fields. The Deli

56 One *bouw* is 0.7 hectare. See also Stoler 1985:23.
57 ARA Kol, MvO 181, G. Schaap 1905:73-5; Pelzer 1978:102.

cigar wrapper, which made Deli so famous, was the result of careful cultivation and drying methods. Indigenous tobacco growers elsewhere in the archipelago had no share in this market, but supplied tobacco to the indigenous cigarette industry. In Southeast Kalimantan, the opposite happened: when tobacco planters arrived in Hulu Sungai and Samarinda in the 1890s, they found little indigenous cultivation. To monopolize supply, European producers began to purchase the tobacco which was cultivated by their workers, thereby sustaining indigenous cultivation. Various Residents complained that European tobacco cultivation could not survive because of the 'zealous and unfair' competition of the Deli estate area. This was not the whole story. The soil in Southeast Kalimantan was not as fertile as in Deli, and this was the main reason why all European tobacco estates eventually disappeared there. The indigenous population continued small-scale tobacco production. Malay smallholders near Tanjung and Barabai in Hulu Sungai stayed in business for years, aiming mainly at the domestic market.[58]

Attracting labour and occupying space

The establishment of agricultural estates in the Outer Islands did not necessarily disturb indigenous agriculture. The two most important effects of European estates in East Sumatra were the large influx of coolies immigrating to the region and the increasing land area reclaimed from primary forest.

The large immigration flows of coolie labourers had a profound influence on the indigenous economy of East Sumatra. The net inflow of ex-estate coolies who found a permanent home in the region induced higher population growth in East Sumatra than in most other provinces, and the settlers spread out over various occupations. In thinly populated Sumatra, the inflow of coolie-settlers was not a negative backward linkage. Outside the estates, land was abundant and on the whole coolie settlers contributed favourably to the local economy. We may call this effect the 'migration linkage'.

The expenditure of the estates on labour, as reviewed above, can be viewed as a special backward linkage. Nevertheless, on the whole, the backward linkages of the estate economy were limited. More particularly, the impact of estate agriculture on the local indigenous economy was not always positive. The occupation of land, often leased from local sultans, may have hindered the expansion of smallholder export agriculture, but this was only the case in East Sumatra.

One potential effect of the estates has not been listed in this section. In the literature the role of the estates as 'agents of change' is sometimes mentioned. This effect may also be termed the 'information linkage'. However, as I will

58 ARA Kol, MvO 270, H.N.A. Swart 1906:16; MvO 277, B.C.C.M.M. van Suchtelen 1933:166. See also Lindblad 1988a:29.

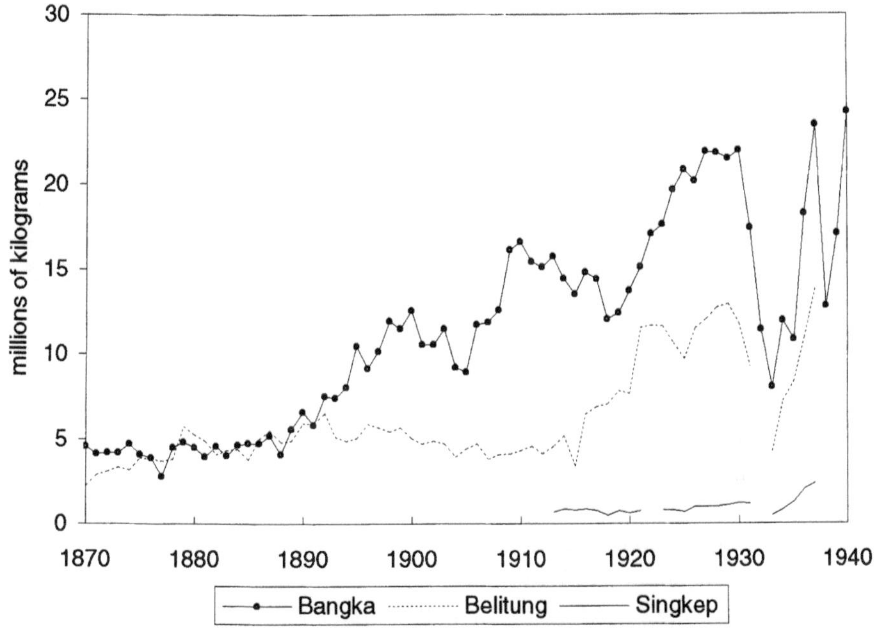

Figure 9. Tin production of Bangka and Belitung, 1870-1940
(*Jaarboek Mijnwezen* 1900-1939; Somers Heidhues 1992:80, 129)

argue in Chapter IV, in the Outer Islands this effect was practically negligible. Chapter IV will discuss the reasons smallholder export agriculture expanded as it did.

Mining: capital, coolies, and strange locations

Strongholds of tin

Tin was one of the oldest mineral exports from colonial Indonesia. Tin mining was already under way during the VOC era, but increased considerably during the nineteenth century, when tin became the major mineral exported from the archipelago (Boeke 1946:81; Gonggrijp 1938:185). The tin mines were concentrated in even fewer locations than the fairly exclusive petroleum industry: tin was produced under supervision of Europeans from the middle of the nineteenth century on Bangka and from 1860 on Belitung and the even smaller island of Singkep in the Riau Archipelago. Indigenous and Chinese tin exploitation was older, but is beyond the scope of this research. At first, tin was found only on Bangka. For many years rumours were rife that tin could be mined in Flores, and almost everywhere else in the archipelago tin was feverishly prospected (for example in the Siak sultanate in East Sumatra), but to no avail. In the late colonial period, the only other substantial producers of tin were Belitung and Singkep.

Bangka: state mines, peasant pepper

In the second half of the nineteenth century, the annual production of the government tin mines on Bangka increased almost imperceptibly. It averaged 5,000 tons per year. After 1860, Belitung's production fluctuated at much the same level. At the turn of the century, when Belitung was subject to concessionary hassles, production in Bangka increased to an average of around 11,000 tons per year in 1900/10 (Figure 9).

Tin mining on Bangka had been under government supervision since 1816. The administration of the tin mines resulted in a steady production of tin, but suffered from difficulties in coolie recruitment, epidemics, and the slow improvement of primitive tools such as drills and pumps. In 1913 tin mining was brought under the Banka Tin Winning (BTW). The Resident of Bangka was appointed head of this government undertaking, but a separate director was installed at Mentok. Bangka tin had a good name and earned good prices. Prices were highest just after the First World War, in 1918-1920. In 1928 the BTW supplied 14 per cent of the world's tin.[59] Stimulated by mechanization and the opening of new mines, annual production increased to about 22,000 tons in 1928-1930 (Figure 9). This was beneficial to the state treasury: for example, in 1926 earnings from Bangka tin amounted to roughly 56.4 million guilders.[60]

At an early stage, tin processing took place on the island itself. Only a small part of the tin ore excavated was exported as ore and smelted in Singapore. The smelting, a forward linkage, provided additional industrial activity in Bangka. There had been over a hundred small smelting locations at the turn of the century, but a conscious process of concentration and centralization resulted in five large tin-smelting works in 1928, of which only three were left by the 1930s.[61]

The tin industry radically transformed the relatively poor, infertile island. The influx of large numbers of Chinese, who formed the labour force of the mines, increased when tin production expanded. In 1920, around 20,000 labourers worked in the tin mines on Bangka. This labour force consisted primarily of Chinese coolies, organized in the *kongsi* system. They were supervised by a small group of Europeans consisting of about 200 persons.

59 ARA Kol, MvO 246, J.E. Edie 1928:65; Somers Heidhues 1992:110-5.

60 Gonggrijp 1938:185. For a more detailed review of government profits, see Houben 1994. See also Chapter VI.

61 ARA Kol, MvO 246, J.E. Edie 1928:67-9; Somers Heidhues 1992:128.

The tin coolies settled on the islands, in many cases integrating into local economic life, carrying on trade, and, on Bangka, cultivating pepper and rubber. As examined in more detail in Chapter IV, exports of Bangka pepper reached a considerable volume. For example, in the peak year 1934, Bangka exported more than 16,000 tons of pepper (black and white), almost as much as Lampung exported in that same year.[62]

Belitung and Singkep: private exploitation

On Belitung, tin exploitation started out as a private undertaking. Billiton Maatschappij (Billiton Company), which was founded in 1860, endured the slow decision-making process and bureaucratic delay to which a company that was partly state-owned was heir (broadly similar to the NIAM in Jambi much later) – but the problems were largely of its own making. Billiton Maatschappij caused a scandal in 1882 when it secretly tried to extend its concessions, which were due to expire in 1892. The Dutch Parliament did not appreciate the company's efforts to arrange this matter with Governor-General F. s'Jacob. Tedious discussions in Parliament led to the dismissal of the latter and when the concession was extended, the company had to pay a much higher dividend rate to the Dutch state: 62.5 per cent instead of the earlier 3 to 4 per cent of gross profits.

With tin prices continuing to fall, the prospects were bad, but the sky cleared when prices rose in the early 1900s and mechanization increased productivity. The need to extend the concession caused trouble again in 1915-1917, when Dutch politicians preferred full state exploitation. The ensuing negotiations resulted in the decision to set up a mixed company, jointly owned by private investors and the government. The Gemeenschappelijke Mijnbouw Maatschappij Billiton (Joint Mining Company Belitung) was founded in 1924 (Allen and Donnithorne 1957:169-71; Van der Ploog 1945:97-102).

This history in a nutshell shows that Belitung's development was more independent of the government than was Bangka's. Initially, the exploitation of Belitung was a matter for private capital. Labour was organized differently and working conditions on Belitung were better, as indicated by rates of death, desertion, and sickness. A substantial part of the tin was not smelted locally but exported as tin ore to Singapore, which meant that much of Belitung's tin was eventually brought onto the market as 'Straits tin'.[63]

Singkep, in the Riau Archipelago, was the third tin island. In 1890 Singkep Tin Maatschappij (Singkep Tin Company) was founded. It had moderate suc-

62 ARA Kol, MvO 249, J.C. Mann 1938:2; Clemens et al. 1992:72. See also Somers Heidhues 1992:103.

63 Somers Heidhues 1992:79-80, 125-6. The title of Somers Heidhues's book, *Bangka Tin and Mentok Pepper*, refers to the 'two-track economy' that developed in Bangka (217)

cess, producing between 300 and 1,000 ton per year (Van der Ploeg 1945:111; Somers Heidhues 1992:80). The Depression weakened the company, and in 1934 it was bought up by Billiton Maatschappij, which set up the Singkep Tin Exploitation Company 'Sitem'. Production remained small: between 1932 and 1935 an annual average of 650 tons of tin was exported from Singkep.[64]

Constancy of tin production

The world's tin producers managed to cooperate more harmoniously than did rubber producers. During the recession of the early 1920s, the 'Bandung Pool' was formed, in which the Netherlands Indies participated along with British Malaya. During this tin restriction, the production of tin did not decrease, but the supply was withheld from the market in order to induce a rise in price. When prices recovered in the mid-1920s, the stock of tin was gradually sold. In 1931 a tin-restriction agreement was again signed, between the Netherlands Indies, Malaya, Bolivia, and Nigeria, later joined by Thailand. The International Tin Pool stockpiled tin, and liquidated the stocks after 1933, when prices had recovered slightly (Figure 28).[65] Production and exports decreased during the Depression, to a mere 8,000 tons in 1933. After 1935 a quick recovery took place, although prices remained low (Table 41.1 and Figure 9).

Tin production showed steady but modest growth during the first three decades of the 1900s, in sharp contrast to the vast expansion of petroleum. Tin exports occupied a substantial share of total exports from the Outer Islands, at times reaching more than 7 per cent (Table 37). Most of Bangka's tin was shipped to Java, from where it was exported. Tin from Belitung was exported directly to foreign markets (Table 41.1).[66] Before 1925, Bangka tin earned better prices than Belitung tin: from 1910 to 1915, Bangka tin sold for about 2,000 guilders per ton, while tin from Belitung fluctuated at around 600 guilders per ton.[67] From 1916 to 1920 Bangka prices rose to more than 3,000 guilders per ton. After 1927 a decline followed, in spite of the Tin Pool of 1931-1933. In the 1930s the average price of all Netherlands Indies tin was about 1,000 guilders per ton (Figure 28).

64 ARA Kol, MvO 240, L.R. Wentholt 1921:21 appendix 2; MvO 241, L.M.F. Plate 1924:6; MvO 242, J.M. von Schmidt auf Altenstad 1936:21-2; Allen and Donnithorne 1957:170.

65 ARA Kol, MvO 249, J.C. Mann 1938 chapter III. See also Boeke 1946:80-1; De Graaff 1997: 524-49.

66 The interregional trade statistics do not specify separate tin flows from both islands, stating one entry for exports from both Bangka and Belitung. Most of this flow obviously consisted of tin from Bangka. Thus Tables 41.1 and 41.2 in Appendix D are slightly misleading in regard to Bangka's share in tin production, because Bangka's tin was exported to Java and was therefore not included in the foreign trade statistics, on which this table is based. See also Clemens et al. 1992:74.

67 Gross weight, including ore; prices calculated from the foreign trade statistics.

Tin production provided more backward than forward linkages, since there was hardly any existing infrastructure on the bare and desolate tin islands. As was the case for the oil industry, every road or railway had to be constructed. Beginning in the 1860s, when tin mining became a serious proposition, a network of roads and tramways was constructed in close co-operation with colonial authorities. Unfortunately, on Belitung these investments were of little use to indigenous export agriculture, since the island was unsuitable for agrarian activities (Figure 23.1).

Very little smelting was done on the island of Belitung itself. This forward linkage therefore remained much smaller than on Bangka. Some tin was initially smelted at Tanjung Pandan and Manggar (1910-1921), but afterwards this was increasingly taken over by the Straits Trading Company in Singapore. Some of the tin ore was also smelted in the United States. Plans for a central tin smelter in Java, which was to serve both Belitung and Bangka, failed to materialize. Had it been constructed, it might have become an important forward linkage in the colony. Eventually, after 1933, tin smelting also took place in the Netherlands, at Arnhem.[68]

Billiton Maatschappij had a high profit-to-equity ratio: it pursued a conservative policy with respect to equity. Equity was kept artificially low, despite high profitability levels. The company paid out high dividends.[69] However, the cost price of Belitung tin was slightly higher than Bangka tin: in 1930/35 the average cost price of 100 kg tin from the government-owned BTW was 101 guilders, considerably less than the average cost price of tin from Belitung, which was 129 guilders.[70]

Labour in tin mining

The most important effect on the regional economy of the tin islands was not the construction of infrastructure, but the immigration of Chinese workers. From 1911 to 1930 a fairly constant number of around 20,000 coolies were employed in the Bangka tin mines and a similar number in Belitung (Houben and Lindblad 1999:209-30). The majority of these mineworkers were Chinese, since Chinese workers were preferred to Javanese or Malays. Chinese were cheaper, more productive, and more often without family. Attempts were made to employ more indigenous labourers, but these failed. In contrast to the estates in East Sumatra, where Javanese were already being hired in the nine-

68 This tin smelter was exploited by NV Hollandsche Metallurgische Bedrijven, which was founded in 1928. Allen and Donnithorne 1957:171; Somers Heidhues 1992:182.

69 See case study of Billiton Company in Lindblad 1996b:219-20.

70 This difference played an important role in the discussions in the late 1930s about a possible merging of the tin enterprises in the Netherlands Indies (Hövig 1937:503; Gerritsen 1935: 141; 1938:420).

teenth century and after 1910 increasingly replaced Chinese coolies, in 1938 98 per cent of Bangka's mineworkers were Chinese and 76 per cent of these were immigrants (Somers Heidhues 1992:130, 178-9). As a result, 47 per cent of the population of Bangka and 39 per cent of Belitung were Chinese (Table 16).

Under circumstances resembling those of estate coolies, tin coolies often had no choice but to re-enlist when their contract ended, because of debts or because they had sent their earnings overseas. Even if a coolie incurred no debts, he could only leave the mines at the earliest after two years. If he had saved enough, he could return to China, but he could not yet settle on the island. He did have the chance of moving to another mine, but if he signed another contract in order to receive a new advance on his pay, this would deprive him of his freedom for a further three years. Only if a coolie had worked in the mines for five years did his release allow him to settle and work elsewhere in the Indies.[71] During the Depression years many coolies were laid off, and the labour force decreased from 20,000 to a mere 4,000 workers in 1933. Recovery did not bring back demand for pre-crisis numbers of Chinese, as mine managers turned increasingly to mechanization. The number of workers employed in 1937/40 averaged roughly 9,000 (see also Table 40). In Bangka, the penal clause was slowly phased out during the 1930s, when recruitment declined. Although the abolition of the penal clause was stipulated in the Bangka Chinese Labourers Ordinance of 1932, there were still new Chinese recruits whose contract contained the penal clause as late as 1940.[72]

The labour system was different from that used on the agricultural estates. The BTW had made the shrewd decision to maintain the traditional supervision of Chinese coolies exercised through the *kongsi* system. On the estates, Chinese and Javanese coolies were supervised by European assistants. Work in the Bangka mines was contracted to management committees (*mijnbesturen*), which were led by Chinese managers or overseers. Mine workers were supervised exclusively by fellow countrymen (although many overseers were *peranakan* Chinese, born on Bangka). The *kongsi* grew its own vegetables, adjacent to the mines, and in the late 1920s, the Labour Inspectorate reported nutritional and accommodation conditions at the mines to be relatively good. The labour system gained a good reputation amongst gov-

71 It took three years' of work and the payment of a small fee to be allowed to settle on Bangka and work outside the mines. Somers Heidhues 1992:115.

72 For example in 1937, 72% of the workforce of 12,000 in the tin mines of Bangka were Chinese under contract with the penal clause, only 28% without the penal clause, and a mere 1% Javanese on contract without the penal clause. In 1938 59% of the 8,100 workers were still under the penal clause. ARA Kol, MvO 249, J.C. Mann 1938 chapter V sub 4 p. 1; Somers Heidhues 1992:115-9.

ernment officials; one administrator used a putatively Arab saying – 'Kind over kind, *that* is mercy!' – to show his approval.[73]

When tin exploitation started on Belitung, the *kongsi* system was imported from Bangka, but the system changed quickly because these workers were strangers to each other and, besides, there were outside shareholders. Under the Belitung system which replaced it, coolies could change their place of work freely after the expiration of their first year's contract. The work team was called a *numpang* and shared the profits of tin production, gradually eliminating outside shareholders. As a consequence, there was little direct contact between the European personnel and the mineworkers. More importantly, as a result of this system the working conditions for coolies on Belitung were much better than those on Bangka (Doorman 1910:916; Somers Heidhues 1992:79).

Tin mines and the indigenous economy

Apart from the tin mines, Bangka and Belitung were small, rather poor provinces. The local government could spend only a little on infrastructural projects or other social expenditure. Looking back on the good earnings from tin in the 1920s (the year 1926 had yielded net profits of 0.56 million guilders), Resident J.C. Mann complained about the paucity of public expenditure that this money had brought to Bangka. Referring to Van den Brand's brochure about Deli, he wrote the spiteful words: 'One might as well talk about the Millions of Bangka'.[74] In 1928, there was a 1,021 km network of roads on Bangka, displaying various degrees of maintenance and quality. Most of these roads led to mines, and were used and maintained by the tin company. The pepper and rubber regions were considerably less accessible by road. There were no major railways or tramways outside the mines, but the lower courses of the rivers were navigable by prahus for long distances.[75]

As a result of immigration labour at the tin mines, large numbers of Chinese coolies settled on the island, gradually integrating into local economic life. They carried on trade, became household servants, or were engaged in the cultivation of pepper and rubber. 'Trade rests almost solely in Chinese hands, only a single indigenous retail trader can be found,' wrote Resident J.E. Edie in 1928.[76] Chinese on the coast earned a living from fishing. While the traditional *ladang* cultivation was practised mainly in the south, pepper and rubber gardens were situated everywhere throughout the whole island,

73 ARA Kol, MvO 246, J.E. Edie 1928:66. The saying had gained currency due to C. Snouck Hurgronje.

74 ARA Kol, MvO 249, J.C. Mann 1938 chapter II p. 11.

75 ARA Kol, MvO 246, J.E. Edie 1928:15-6, 18.

76 ARA Kol, MvO 246, J.E. Edie 1928:41, 43.

set up by both indigenous and Chinese peasants. Besides their ventures into pepper and rubber, many Malay inhabitants of Bangka earned a living from the tin industry: cutting and sawing trees and supplying timber, transporting firewood for the smelting works, or burning charcoal. Others were employed at the drills, or worked as contractors for construction of buildings around the mines or in administrative functions at the mines.[77]

Repeating the pattern in the estate area in East Sumatra, indigenous slash-and-burn agriculture on Bangka was challenged by the non-indigenous export sector. On Bangka this was the consequence of logging, which provided the fuel for tin-smelting. The tin mines needed charcoal to smelt the tin ore. Since most of the ore in Bangka was smelted on the island itself, a sizeable forest reserve was needed to provide this indispensable charcoal. Hemmed in, traditional indigenous agriculture had less area at its disposal. It was for this reason that pepper was introduced from Riau in 1869 by a Chinese entrepreneur, who saw it as an additional means to earn a livelihood. Pepper cultivation spread rapidly just after the turn of the century. Many *peranakan* Chinese left work in the mines to the *singkeh* and started their own pepper gardens, or worked as hired hands in other pepper gardens (Somers Heidhues 1992:69).

In the twentieth century, the *kongsi* lost its original social and distributive significance and developed into a means to bring the greatest possible profits to the mine owners and the tin company. The *numpang* system on Belitung succeeded better in guarding the interest of the coolies, but did not prevent company interests from dominating and seizing the majority of profits (Somers Heidhues 1992:79).

A major similarity between Bangka and East Sumatra is that *ladang* peasants were evicted from their traditional forest agriculture, pushed aside by the mining company and the government forestry reserve. In both provinces, European entrepreneurship resulted in the influx of new population groups, land scarcity, and an inflow of ex-coolies. The government had to mediate to arrange plots of land for the Chinese (who were not allowed to own land), and to stay alert to make sure that the forest reserves that were vital for tin exploitation were not reduced. Clandestine occupation of land was a recurring problem. On several occasions, indigenous groups turned nasty and unruly when areas of traditional forest were suddenly designated as forest reserve and declared closed to swidden agriculture.[78]

On Belitung, smallholder agriculture failed to develop as it did on Bangka. The indigenous population neither produced cash crops nor enlisted at

77 ARA Kol, MvO 246, J.E. Edie 1928:41, 45; MvO 247, D.G. Hooyer 1931.

78 ARA Kol, MvO 247, D.G. Hooyer 1931 appendix A.A., appendix 'Bosreservering op Banka'; MvO 249, J.C. Mann 1938 chapter IV pp. 1-2, appendix III p. 3.

the mines. However, many *Sekah* men, who lived on the shore, were reportedly engaged as porters and dock-hands, and transported goods for the mines by prahu (Doorman 1910:916).

Bangka pepper exports constituted an important segment of the Bangka economy and Chinese inhabitants contributed significantly to the development of these exports. The fact that large groups of Chinese settled permanently, in contrast to the situation in the estate area of East Sumatra, is a major difference between the tin mines and the agricultural estates. The *peranakan* Chinese who became peasants and traders played an important role in the development of pepper cultivation on Bangka.

Coal: fuelling domestic transport

Coal production was regarded as vital to the economy, because the fuel was essential to the whole network of steamships and railway transport. Coal was not primarily an export product. The reverse was the case: the coal mines had to face competition from coal imports. Since many cargo ships used coal as a ballast freight in order not to steam eastwards from Europe with empty holds, supply was relatively cheap. It was precisely to avoid one-sided dependence on these imports that the government judged domestic coal production to be important. In plans for development of a coal industry, the discussion of cheap imports versus domestic production was as much an issue as the choice between state exploitation versus private exploitation. In 1913, almost as much coal was imported (487,000 tons) as produced (568,000 tons), but by 1922 domestic production had risen to 75 per cent of total consumption (1,032,000 tons produced and 327,000 tons imported). In 1922 770,000 tons was produced in state mines.[79] It is therefore not surprising that coal 'dominated inter-island trade' (Dick 1990:306-7).

Coal mines were located in provinces where indigenous economic activities in other sectors were relatively dynamic. The most profitable coal mines were state-owned: Ombilin Mines in West Sumatra (1891), Bukit Asem in Palembang (1919), and, from 1913 till 1931, Pulu Laut on the island Pulu Laut in Southeast Kalimantan.[80] The oldest profitable, privately owned coal mine was that of the Oost-Borneo Maatschappij (East Borneo Company, OBM) dating from 1888. It was located near Samarinda in Southeast Kalimantan. Also situated in Southeast Kalimantan, but in the remote northeastern sultanate of Sambaliung, was Parapattan mine (1914), which was a subsidiary of the KPM (Lindblad 1988a:89-95, 231-2; Van der Ploeg 1945:123-42).

79 Allen and Donnithorne 1957:172; Gonggrijp 1938:186; Lindblad 1989c:12.

80 The coal mine in Pulu Laut was established in 1903 by A. Janssen, but after a period of continuing losses was sold to the colonial government in 1913 (Baks 1989).

A link in the chain

Because of their supplying fuel for the domestic infrastructure, coal mines can be regarded as a valuable link in the chain of an expanding economy. The coal itself was important, but quite apart from this, the economic activity of the mines helped to encourage the local economy. For example, in 1892 Ombilin Mines near Sawah Lunto in West Sumatra formed a major incentive to construct port facilities at Emmahaven near Padang. A narrow-gauge railway was constructed from the mine to the coast over a distance of more than 150 km. Government mines produced satisfying results, but only with government backing. Private mines show a more troubled picture, averaging only a few thousand tons annually, although Parapattan increased its output to about 300,000 tons a year in the 1930s.[81] In 1931 Ombilin Mines produced 507,545 tons, followed by Bukit Asem with 303,246 tons. Parapattan produced almost as much, 229,752 tons in that year, while the OBM produced 146,420 tons at Batu Panggal. There were several smaller mines in Southeast Kalimantan: Pulu Laut produced 96,298 tons, Gunung Batu Besar 50,560 tons, and Erven Pangeran Mangku Negoro (near Samarinda, in Loa Bukit) 37,454 tons (*Indisch Verslag* 1933:128; Van der Ploeg 1945:142). It is interesting to note that coal was the only mineral that was also produced by the indigenous population in considerable quantities. For example, in Kutai (Southeast Kalimantan) in 1931 33,033 tons of coal were sold to local traders. In West Kapuas (West Kalimantan) coal was dug by the indigenous population.[82]

More than 50 per cent of coal produced in Palembang (Bukit Asem), West Sumatra (Ombilin), and Southeast Kalimantan was consumed in the colony itself. The trade statistics show that a large proportion of coal exported from these provinces went to Java (Tables 42.1 and 42.2).

Ombilin Mines employed not only contract coolies but also convicts. Taking the year 1924 as an example, 3,269 convicts were employed, alongside 5,163 contract coolies and 1,602 'free' labourers (Houben 1994:200-1). Supervision in the mines was in European hands. Work underground was not much to the taste of Javanese coolies, which led to recurring problems with labour supply. During the 1920s in the Bukit Asem mines in Palembang,

81 Allen and Donnithorne 1957:173; Furnivall 1944:327; Gonggrijp 1938:185-6.

82 These figures may give an impression (coal production in tons):

	Kapuas-Barito	Samarinda
1933	9,091	25,441
1934	18,871	29,216
1935	19,638	31,846
1936	26,133	52,019

(Source: ARA Kol, MvO 271, L.J.F. Rijckmans 1916:42; MvO 278, W.G. Moggenstorm 1937:336; Van der Ploeg 1945:142.)

coolies often ran away to earn a better living in smallholder rubber production. The mines employed both contract coolies and free workers, and tried to retain the latter by building small houses in the kampong where workers could live with their families.[83]

Drilling for black gold

The boom in oil exports came several decades after the upsurge in agricultural exports. When tobacco was experiencing its initial years of growth, A.J. Zijlker (a manager of a tobacco firm) applied for an oil concession near Telaga Said, a site along the Lepan River in Langkat, East Sumatra – not far from the estates. In 1883, this first concession for drilling petroleum was granted.[84] Zijlker managed to attract financiers, but without the help of the government it was impossible to launch exploitation. In 1890, the 'Koninklijke' (Royal Dutch) was established. The company was located at Pangkalan Brandan, on the Balbalan River, where provisions were constructed for processing, storage, and shipment. It was destined to become one of the major players in the game of oil exploitation. Its full name was Koninklijke Nederlandsche Maatschappij tot Exploitatie van Petroleumbronnen in Nederlandsch-Indië (Royal Dutch Company for the Exploitation of Petroleum Resources in the Netherlands Indies). Founding capital amounted to a mere 1.3 million guilders, of which Zijlker himself brought in 371,000 guilders.

Crude oil drilled at Telaga Said was collected in tanks and carried to the refinery in Pangkalan Brandan by pipeline. Because the Balbalan River was not navigable for large vessels, kerosene was taken by prahu to Sembilan Island, which lay close to the coast in Aroë Bay, north of Pangkalan Brandan. The kerosene was sealed in tins and put in wooden packing cases; later, it was shipped in barrels. Bulk oil was transported by pipeline to Pangkalan Susu also in Langkat, north of Pangkalan Brandan. The initial years were plagued by infrastructural problems arising from production and transportation in these then undeveloped areas. Success did not come easily, but, even though production was laborious and capital-intensive, oil turned out to be an attractive asset. Many small entrepreneurs applied for oilfields in the 1880s and 1890s, justly anticipating a large growth in the oil market. The government issued large numbers of oil exploration concessions in Java, Sumatra, and Kalimantan.[85]

83 ARA Kol, MvO 212, J. Tideman 1928:304-10.

84 *Telaga* means 'source'. Allen and Donnithorne 1957:175; *Mijnbouw* 1917:839; Van der Ploeg 1945:144-6.

85 Oil was also found in Java. This had happened at Cirebon, as early as 1871. An important

In Southeast Kalimantan, the earliest oil reserves were found near Kutai in 1897 by J.H. Menten. These fields were exploited by the Shell Transport and Trading Company. Shell operated under the name Nederlands-Indische Industrie en Handelsmaatschappij (Netherlands Indies Industry and Trade Company) to meet the requirement that firms in the colony have a 'Dutch' nationality. In 1898, this company built a large modern refinery at Balikpapan, in Kutai. Southeast Kalimantan developed into the largest petroleum-exporting province of the late colonial Netherlands Indies; oil constituted the largest proportion of its total export value (Figure 23c).

It had been surmised for years that oilfields also existed in Palembang. In this province, indigenous traders knew of natural sources of petroleum near Muara Enim. Many entrepreneurs applied for concessions to explore for oil in Palembang, and in 1899 the first concession at Muara Enim was granted. Of all the concessions in Palembang, this turned out to be the most successful, more so than later concessions in Iliran, Banjuasin, or Babat.

At the turn of century, Royal Dutch had not yet secured its future position. In 1898, the survival of Royal Dutch was threatened when the sites in Telaga Said (East Sumatra) appeared to be drying up. New oil reserves were found in Aceh, but this province was not very suitable for industrial expansion as the Aceh War was still raging there. Later, after war efforts were intensified, Aceh was brought within the compass of European enterprise. In 1901 the rich concession in Perlak (in East Aceh) began to be exploited, ensuring the survival of Royal Dutch. Pangkalan Brandan remained the site of its refinery (*Mijnbouw* 1917:839-41; Lindblad 1989a:58).

In terms of output volume, oil really started booming after 1914. The petroleum industry in northern Sumatra quickly developed an enormous production of both crude oil and oil derivatives (Tables 36.2 and 38). The share of petroleum products in aggregate export revenue rose to more than 40 per cent of the grand total in the years 1914-1922 (Table 37). Volume kept increasing, even though the share of oil revenues decreased in relation to other commodities in the 1920s.

In 1917, 19.5 per cent of all Netherlands Indies oil exports came from East Sumatra, but by 1929, its share had declined to 9.4 per cent. In this year, around 4,200 million litres of petroleum distillates were exported from the Outer Islands, of which only 416 million litres came from East Sumatra (Clemens et al. 1992:68). In value, petroleum exports in 1929 amounted to 160

Java-based oil company was Dordtse Petroleum Maatschappij (Dordrecht Petroleum Company), with its refineries in Surabaya and Cepu, near Rembang, established by A. Stoop. This company profited from the local market for lamp oil and petrol in Java but remained relatively small. In 1911 it was taken over by Royal Dutch.

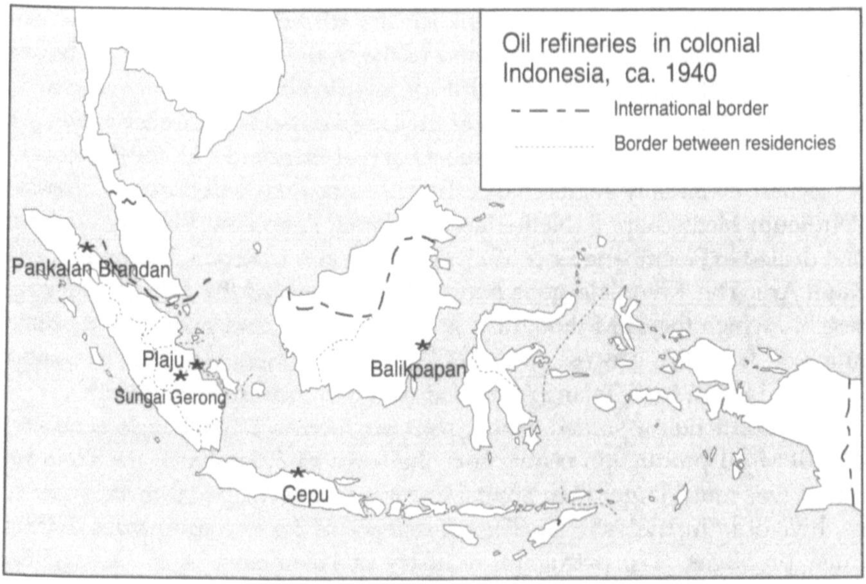

Map 6. Oil refineries in colonial Indonesia

million guilders, of which 26 million guilders were earned by exports from East Sumatra (Table 38).

In Southeast Kalimantan the two large production centres were at Balikpapan and on the small island of Tarakan, some 500 km north of Balikpapan. The latter oilfield contained crude oil which became known as Tarakan crude, suitable for use as liquid fuel without any further processing. The exploitation of Tarakan by the BPM began in 1908. In the period 1912-1933, Southeast Kalimantan was the largest oil exporter of the Outer Provinces (Table 38).

Since 1902 Royal Dutch had been drilling in Southeast Kalimantan where it had joined Shell, and geographical proximity led the two giants to cooperate. (In fact, Royal Dutch was attracted by the modern Shell refinery at Balikpapan, and Shell fancied cooperation with a Dutch company.) This was effectuated in their alliance in 1907, when the joint production company BPM was established. The BPM was 60 per cent Dutch and 40 per cent English. The BPM soon dominated and virtually controlled all production and exports of oil from the Netherlands Indies. With its labour force of several tens of thousands, it became the largest single company in colonial Indonesia (Gerretson 1971:91-106, 1973:140-62; Lindblad 1989a:55).

Major competition to the BPM was offered only by the American company Standard Oil (Esso), which tried to gain a foothold in the Indonesian archipelago. The door was anxiously kept shut on the Americans. In 1898 Standard Oil tried to take over Muara Enim in Palembang, but was prevented from doing so by the government. Rivalry stirred again when oil was discovered in Jambi in 1904, but because of the shaky position of Dutch power in Jambi and the initial irresolute attitude adopted by the Dutch government, it was 1921 before the exploitation of the Jambi oilfields got under way.[86]

It was in Palembang that the subsidiary of Standard Oil, the 'Koloniale' (Colonial), eventually got its chance. Its full name was Nederlandse Koloniale Petroleum Maatschappij (Netherlands Colonial Petroleum Company) and it had drilled in Palembang since 1913, at concessions in Redan, Klumpang, and Kayu Aru. The 'Koloniale' got a boost when it acquired the Talang Akar concession, which the BPM thought was unproductive, and managed to obtain much oil from this concession in 1915. A small refinery was built in Sungai Gerong, 140 km from Talang Akar near the coast, not far from Plaju.[87]

Oil production assumed a dominant position in Palembang's economy. The BPM oil production centre near the town of Palembang, the Plaju refinery, was much larger than Sungai Gerong and developed into an impressive hive of industrial activity. The coexistence of the two companies did not cause problems. 'The petroleum industry in Palembang is, in view of the value of the product which sees the light of day, undoubtedly the most important branch of industry in this province', said Resident J. Tideman in 1928. 'The world's two largest petroleum concerns, which often treat each other less benevolently in other countries, cooperate very harmoniously in a relatively small area.'[88] For many years the BPM remained the largest company, producing about 364,000 tons of oil in 1923, up to 996,000 tons in 1939. The 'Koloniale' increased its production from a mere 531 tons in 1917 to 152,000 tons in 1924, rising to 2.1 million tons in 1939. In 1939, The NIAM in Jambi produced about 1.2 million tons of oil.[89]

The oil sector showed an unequivocal tendency towards monopolization. Before 1900, many small companies had explored oil concessions. After 1900, this fierce competition and segmentation gradually evaporated, resulting in two major actors, Royal Dutch and Shell, which established a strong position in their joint BPM. The only other company was Standard Oil, but it did not increase its output substantially until the 1930s.

By that time, the scene became even more complex. In 1910, Standard Oil had been split into several smaller companies. The NKPM was a subsidiary of American Petroleum Company (APC), which belonged to Standard Oil of

[86] Recently two extensive accounts have been written of the (political) backgrounds of the NIAM concessions and oil exploitation in Jambi: De Graaff 1997:453-93; Locher-Scholten 1994:225-39. See also Lindblad 1989a:54; Touwen 1991:146, 154.

[87] ARA Kol, MvO 212, J. Tideman 1928:298.

[88] ARA Kol, MvO 212, J. Tideman 1928:292.

[89] ARA Kol, MvO 212, J. Tideman 1928:301; Lindblad 1989a:77; Touwen 1991:177.

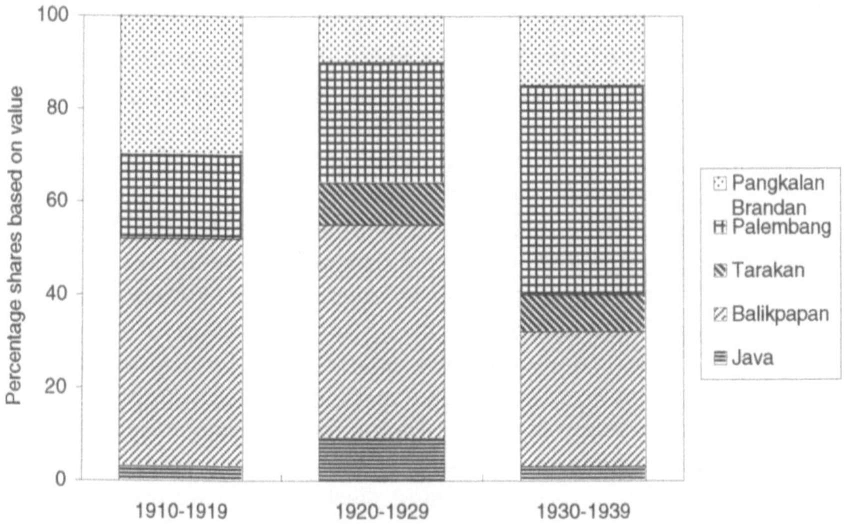

Figure 10. Regional composition of foreign oil exports, 1910-1939 (Trade statistics).

New Jersey. Nederlandse Pacific Petroleum Maatschappij (NPPM), which became an important oil producer in the 1930s and exploited petroleum in Southeast Kalimantan, was a subsidiary of Standard Oil of California (1934). In New Guinea, NPPM, NKPM, and BPM jointly established the Nederlandse Nieuw-Guinea Petroleum Maatschappij (NNGPM) (1934). In the 1930s, Gulf also applied to enter the Indonesian oil market, hoping to become the fourth major player, but it was denied access (De Graaff 1997:454-91).

Importance of the oil industry

These Western activities did not pass unnoticed in the indigenous economy. Although the oil industry employed relatively many Europeans, it gave work to large numbers of Asian workers as well. In 1928 the BPM in Palembang employed 512 Europeans and 13,954 Asians.[90] In 1929, the total payroll for Asian workers in the Palembang oil industry amounted to an estimated 8.8 million guilders, providing work for about 23,000 labourers.[91] In this same year, in Pangkalan Brandan, the refinery employed 8,200 immigrant workers and 350 European supervisors. The oilfields in northern Sumatra gave work to an additional 1,500 men, mostly of local origin. In Balikpapan, 9,300 men

90 This includes the NIAM, operating in Jambi. ARA Kol, MvO 212, J. Tideman 1928:297.

91 These figures exclude NIAM in Jambi (additional 4,000 labourers) but they include Colonial Petroleum. Wellan 1932:347; Touwen 1991:147. See also Lindblad 1989a:58.

worked in the oil refinery and around 8,400 in the oilfields. In 1921 12,000 workers lived in the extreme isolation of the island-enclave on Tarakan.[92]

Refinery centres continuously expanded their capacity to process crude oil. Gradually, exports of crude oil almost totally disappeared. The main refinery complexes were constructed in Pangkalan Brandan (East Sumatra), Plaju (Palembang), and Balikpapan (Southeast Kalimantan), and produced kerosene, petrol (benzine), lamp oil, motor oil, lubricating oils, paraffin, and candles (see Map 6). The share of Java, with its major refinery at Cepu, near Rembang, remained below 10 per cent of total volume for almost all years between 1911 and 1940 (Figure 10) (Clemens et al. 1992:69). The capital-intensive refinery centres formed a major forward linkage of the oil-extraction industry. Unfortunately, the favourable effects of these forward linkages on the local economy were small, since there was no local supply of machinery and steel construction materials. Their most important effect was the upswing of secondary backward linkages, such as the construction of local infrastructure (roads, airports), housing, electricity and waterworks, and an enlarged demand for foodstuffs. These growth effects were the most important linkages of the oil industry. At one remove, the fiscal linkage of considerable tax payments should not be disregarded.

Unquestionably, the discovery of oil and the construction of oil production centres influenced government policy. For example, the discovery of oil increased pressure on the government to intensify campaigns to 'pacify' those regions, as in Aceh (the Aceh War escalated in 1898) and Jambi (1901). In Jambi the ambitious Sultan Taha was deposed in 1858 but did not relinquish his control over the indigenous population, effectively limiting Dutch rule to the town of Jambi and impeding the entrance of private entrepreneurs into the region. Authorities held back until oil was discovered in Jambi in 1900. In 1903, with applications for concessions piling up, a military expedition penetrated the interior and in 1904 the aged Sultan Taha was killed in his retreat.[93]

Economic expansion was not the principal motive behind the extension or consolidation of Dutch rule, but it certainly did play a role. The fact is that the oil from Jambi was pumped to Palembang and exported from Plaju. Much more important to Jambi than its oil was its vast indigenous rubber production during the late colonial era. Similarly, Aceh missed out on becoming an oil-refining centre several decades earlier, when Royal Dutch decided to process Perlak crude oil not in Aceh but in East Sumatra (Touwen 1991:155).

The geographical position of the major oil production centres is also relevant. In Balikpapan and Tarakan (Southeast Kalimantan) the oil industry had transformed isolated specks on the map into boom towns dominated by the

92 ARA Kol, MvO 273, A.M. Hens 1921:13; Lindblad 1989a:58-9.

93 Lindblad 1989b:11-2, 23-4; Locher-Scholten 1994a:208-12, 284.

oil companies. In contrast, the principal indigenous rubber regions in Southeast Kalimantan were situated in the south, in Hulu Sungai. The oil industry in Pangkalan Brandan (East Sumatra) was situated further inland, but also remote from the indigenous production regions. Similarly, petroleum drilling near the Aroë Bay in East Aceh resulted in little direct contact with the local population and did not directly influence that region's economy (De Ridder 1935:38). Only in Palembang were the oil companies situated more centrally in the province, close to areas of smallholder export agriculture. Many peasant households that produced rubber or coffee may have had family members working in the oil industry (or, near Bukit Asem, in the coal mines). The roads constructed by the BPM in Palembang were used by the indigenous population to bring goods to the market, more so than the roads in Pangkalan Susu or near Tarakan.

The conclusion is that the influence of the oil industry on the local economy was largest in Palembang, where the dual powers BPM and Standard Oil were in competition with each other. Nevertheless, one Resident reported that the petroleum industry (comparable to the coal mines) 'formed so much a world of its own that its success or failure had only a limited effect on business life in Palembang'. Be that as it may, the same report emphasizes that the BPM set up a network for local sales of petrol for trucks (by supplying petrol pumps) and steamships, and that the company offered employment to a large number of European and Asian workers.[94]

As with agricultural estates, we can evaluate the effects of the oil industry in terms of demand effects (through wages and the need for construction materials), development of infrastructure, and tax payments. We have seen that demand for technological capital imports, typical of an economic enclave, meant that there were fewer backward linkages than in the estate areas. During the years 1924-1938, foreign imports of typical capital goods such as machines, iron, cement, and freight trucks were significantly higher in the three oil-producing provinces than elsewhere, except for the tin provinces (Table 54.2).

Location in remote areas clearly decreased growth effects on the smallholder economy. Tributary payments for concessions were made to local sultans, but this income was rarely used for purposes of public policy.[95] Little is known about the response of the indigenous population to the establishment of European oil industry. There is documentary evidence that in Palembang the indigenous population preferred to burn new *ladang* near oil-drilling

94 ARA Kol, MvO 212, J. Tideman 1928:233-4.

95 These payments were fixed for long periods and were relatively small compared to total profits in the oil industry. For example, in Southeast Kalimantan, the sultan of Kutai required 50 cents per ton crude oil from concessions granted by him. Other concessionary charges were paid to the Dutch state and the Oost-Borneo Maatschappij (OBM) (Lindblad 1988a:140-1).

areas, even when there was enough suitable land elsewhere. This move was prompted by the hope that the mining companies would enlarge their concessions and pay generous compensation to the local peasants. The remedy against such speculative land use by calculating peasants was to introduce a prohibited zone of 200 metres around test-drilling areas, allegedly to prevent oil drills accidentally catching fire.[96]

The fact that the companies were European-owned meant that net foreign remittances (capital drain) were high. Some of the profit were reinvested or spent locally, but most of it never re-entered the original supply regions. Infrastructure was built mainly to serve the specific needs of the industry. Unfortunately, in contrast to estate agriculture, the mining industry was barely challenged by indigenous entrepreneurship. Because there were no indigenous oil-producing companies, transfer of technology from colonizers to the indigenous economy was rare. The oil industry employed large numbers of indigenous workers, but these skilled workers were not able to transfer their skills to enterprises of their own, because the capital needed was beyond their reach.

The oil industry had a relatively high 'enclave' character. Although it had a powerful impact on the national export economy as a whole, it did little to stimulate the indigenous side of the economy.[97]

Growth effects of European export production

Exports expanded and pushed the economy in new directions. European entrepreneurs generated a massive output of raw materials, yielding lavish profits even at times when the economic situation was unstable. The government received its share in taxes. Did the indigenous economy gain anything from these developments? In the previous section several effects of European export expansion on the local economy have been commented upon. The establishment of European export companies, both in agriculture and in mining, did not go unnoticed by the local population. More roads and bridges were constructed in these four decades than during the previous two centuries, motorized traffic increased, and in several parts of Sumatra railways provided additional local transport. Another effect was the substantial migration flows, brought about by the system of coolie labour. The number of imported coolies was so large that, even though most of them lived on the

[96] These restrictions were based on Article 514 of the Mine Ordinance, as interpreted in a memorandum of the 'Dienst der Mijnverordeningen', 21/3/1929 no 2301. ARA Kol, MvO 214, J.L.M. Schwaab 1933:193.

[97] Lindblad 1988a:213, 219; 1989a:71; Touwen 1991:147.

estates or near the mines, their presence was felt in the indigenous economy; many immigrants became rubber tappers or traders and a few settled as peasants. In this section I will give a brief review of these and other growth effects of the export trade.

Spending export revenues

As we have seen, foreign imports to the Outer Islands were generated largely by foreign exports. This is illustrated in Figure 20: fluctuations in foreign imports reflect fluctuations in foreign exports. To some extent this is due to price levels on foreign markets, which affected the value of both exported and imported goods. But there is also a structural coherence between the two trade flows. The export industry needed capital goods, and foodstuffs (rice) for its work force. Imports tend to follow exports with a lag of two to four years. Consequently, the rise in aggregate exports after World War I led to an increase in imports only after 1920. The situation in the world economy is apparent in the trade figures for the 1920s: while prices of raw materials were already declining after 1925 (four years before the 1929 stock market crash), imports continued to rise for another few years. This growth came to an end in 1929, when the World Depression set in (Figure 20).

This lag in aggregate imports is illustrated by the Pearson correlation coefficients of the values of aggregate foreign imports and exports of the Outer Islands. The correlation coefficient is high (R = 0.89 for 1904-1940, N = 37), indicating a strong systematic relationship between imports and exports, but even higher if we calculate the relationship between imports and exports of the previous year (R = 0.91 for 1904-1940, N = 37). However, for many individual provinces the correlation coefficient is stronger between imports and exports of the same year. In most instances, this correlation is very strong. Only for Tapanuli, Bangka, Bali, Manado, Aceh, and Timor and Dependencies is the value of R not significant (Table 57).[98]

Because most European companies relied on rice imports to feed their workers, rice was one of the most important import commodities in provinces with European export production. In the estate area of East Sumatra, in the oil production centres in Sumatra and Kalimantan, and in the Bangka and Belitung tin mines, large quantities of this staple were needed. This is reflected in the fact that in 1924/28, rice imports constituted almost 24 per cent of the value of average annual imports in East Sumatra (Table 54.1). In volume, East Sumatra took by far the largest share of rice imports entering the Outer Islands. Of course, there was additional demand from the local population, particularly where there was indigenous export production. In

98 If R > 0.7, more than 50% of the variation in the dependent variable is explained by the variance in the independent variable.

Table 4. Estimated rice consumption and rice imports in Cluster I in the 1920s (in thousands of kg)

	East Sumatra	Palembang	Southeast Kalimantan
1922:			
Number of coolies	189,321	8,900	21,000
Estimated coolie rice consumption	43,500	2,000	4,800
Estimated indigenous rice consumption	240,700	171,400	207,000
European rice consumption	n.a.	n.a.	n.a.
Total estimated rice consumption	284,200	173,400	211,800
Foreign rice imports	134,700	8,500	40,500
1929:			
Number of coolies	320,700	40,800	36,300
Rice needed for coolies	73,800	9,400	8,300
Estimated indigenous rice consumption	248,800	179,700	223,200
European rice consumption	n.a.	n.a.	n.a.
Total estimated rice consumption	322,600	189,100	232,500
Foreign rice imports	362,700	36,600	32,700
European population in 1930	10,000	4,000	5,000

Notes: Annual rice consumption per coolie is estimated to have been 230 kg. Annual rice consumption per Indonesian is estimated to have been 170 kg. Reconstructed population figures have been used for indigenous consumption (Appendix A). n.a. = not available.
Source: Tergast 1931-32:232; Table 60.4; Trade statistics; *Volkstelling* 1933, VIII.

East Sumatra, Chinese and Javanese ex-coolies who worked in trade, fishing, and forestry were also dependent on rice imports.[99]

Turning to Palembang and Southeast Kalimantan, where export production was very high due to a twin-based economy, the huge need for foreign rice imports in both provinces is remarkable. In 1917/26, Southeast Kalimantan on average had net annual rice imports of roughly 36,000 tons. Palembang imported 26,000 tons. The lower number of contract coolies in

99 In the southern part of East Sumatra, in Bengkalis, forestry (or *panglong*) was important. *Panglong* literally means 'storage for timber or planks'. Van de Koppel 1946:375; Vleming 1926:11-3, 227-39.

Palembang in the early 1920s may account for smaller rice imports in Palembang, but it is remarkable that rice imports exceeded the average volume needed for coolies, which indicates a large regional demand for imported rice (see Tables 4, 56.1 and 60.4).

How can we explain this foreign supply of rice? In Southeast Kalimantan, domestic food production often failed to meet local needs. Large quantities had to be imported to supplement domestic production (Lindblad 1988a:23, 26). It is plausible that the widespread use of *ladang* for rice cultivation in the Outer Islands prevented the development of large surplus production. Rice production on irrigated fields or near rivers had a higher yield than on upland *ladang*, sometimes twice as high. In Palembang, *renah* and *lebak* areas usually produced ample rice harvests, and *lebak* rice was of good quality.[100] Traditionally there had been enough rice to feed the indigenous population, and the local rice surplus was sold to the estates and industry (oil, coal). This generated extra cash income in the lowland regions and can be regarded as a backward linkage of European industry in Palembang. In the 1920s the rice *ladang* were increasingly being planted with cash crops, mostly rubber and coffee, but also fruits such as durian and pineapple, as well as rattan, for which local demand increased owing to a higher standard of living. As a consequence, surplus rice production declined, and rice imports in Palembang increased (Table 4). The net volume of rice imports in Palembang over the years 1924/38 was smaller than in Southeast Kalimantan, but the share of rice in total imports was comparable (Tables 54.1 and 56.1).

Rice imports in Southeast Kalimantan in 1922 were relatively high, as seen in Table 4. Rice imports were considerably higher than the volume of rice theoretically needed for coolies. Apparently, a substantial volume of rice was consumed outside the estates. Table 4 also shows that in these benchmark years, European enterprise (as measured by number of Europeans and number of coolies) was of similar proportions in Palembang and Southeast Kalimantan. In these two provinces foreign rice imports constituted a smaller proportion of total rice consumption than in East Sumatra, which indicates that indigenous smallholders produced enough rice for local consumption (alongside rubber and other cash crops).

While the share in total imports of consumer goods was not significantly higher in the three largest export producers, the proportion of capital goods was larger than in the provinces of Cluster II (Table 54.2).

100 *Renah* is land alongside the river, naturally irrigated. *Lebak* is land in river bends that was inundated during the rainy season and that was used for traditional *sawah* rice cultivation. *Talang* is higher ground that was less fertile and yielded only moderate rice harvests. ARA Kol, MvO 214, J.L.M. Schwaab 1933:174; MvO 215, W. Steinbuch 1936:194-5.

Infrastructure: of more than local use?

Oil, tin, and coal mining required large capital investments and generated extensive infrastructure only in the immediate vicinity of the mines and refineries – except for pipelines to the oilfields. In contrast, construction on the estates concentrated mainly on buildings (sheds, and *pondok* as living quarters), and a wider area of forest was cultivated. One major repercussion of the estate area in East Sumatra was the network of roads and railways which was constructed. The Deli Spoorweg Maatschappij (Deli Railway Company, DSM) is a good example of this backward linkage, as although it was originally established to transport tobacco it quickly earned half of its revenues by transporting passengers. Outside Java, Sumatra was the only island where a railway system was constructed; it is instructive to briefly survey the expansion of railways in East Sumatra.[101]

Deli Spoorweg Maatschappij

The DSM, established in 1883, owed its origins to the need to transport tobacco to the coast. Its early development was dependent on the ups and downs of the tobacco industry. The first railway lines ran from Medan to Belawan, Deli Tua, and Timbang Langkat. Before these lines could be constructed, many problems had to be tackled, not only related to the technical building of the railway through the uncleared region, but also providing the labour supply needed, negotiating with the government, and dealing with trenchant opposition from the inhabitants of Aceh. Most railway labourers were Chinese, but Javanese and Malays were also recruited.

The next expansion of the railway network was to the south, from the Deli region to Serdang and Selesai. By 1890 there was a total of 103 km of railroad track. In the meantime, the estates constructed their own 'feeder lines' to connect the plantations to the DSM railroad. The most practical way of achieving this was to build narrow-gauge railways for which no concession was needed, using a gauge of 0.70 metres. Sometimes the DSM granted subsidies for the construction of these lines, since they were beneficial to the exploitation of its own railway. During this period DSM already enjoyed a high return on both freight and passenger transport. After 1890, profits deteriorated in the wake of the tobacco crisis. No new tracks were constructed until 1902. Before 1900, passenger transport accounted for almost half of all returns, but in the twentieth century the share of freight transport gradually increased, until it constituted more than 80 per cent in the 1930s. One of the causes of this development was the increasing competition in passenger transportation offered

[101] This paragraph is based largely on Weisfelt 1972:41-61, 170-4, 215.

by motorbus companies and shipping companies engaged in coastal trade, which really stepped up in the 1920s. In 1930 DSM operated about 500 km of railroad, and had another 44 km under construction. In that year, revenues for passenger transport amounted to 1.7 million guilders (6 million passengers) and freight transportation to 6.9 million guilders (925 million kg). In 1930 the company employed 3,834 workers, but in 1932 only 2,904 workers.[102]

A backbone of railways

As early as 1897 plans were made for a backbone of railways through Sumatra, beginning from Pangkalan Brandan in the north, and all the way across the island to Padang in West Sumatra. Much discussion was needed to decide whether this should be a cheap narrow-gauge tramway or a normal broad-gauge railway (1.097 metres wide). Ultimately, with a future line to Lampung in mind, it was decided to construct normal broad tracks. The gauge had been decided, but Padang was not yet within reach. Priority was given to opening up the Deli region and the petroleum fields in the north, which meant that after the construction of the Deli lines (Serdang, Selasai, Deli) the Bedagai and Langkat lines were given priority.

From 1907 to 1915 DSM railway construction experienced another period of stagnation. Only when the cultivation of new crops – rubber and tea – in the south had proven to be rewarding were lines constructed to transport these products. During these years, the difficult decision about whether to choose Belawan, hampered by natural shortcomings, as a main harbour also influenced the slow expansion of railways. After 1915 the first lines to the new rubber areas south of the Asahan River (the Asahan line) were constructed, and these were extended in the 1930s. When the South Asahan line was finished in 1937, it turned out to be the last railway built by DSM. At that moment the total length of its tracks added up to 553 km. Reaching Lampung, through the relatively desolate mid-Sumatran regions, was not a feasible goal.[103]

The facts indicate that tobacco cultivation stimulated railway construction from 1883 until 1914, whereas after 1915 it was other crops that provided the main stimulus to extend lines in a southerly direction. Weisfelt, who analysed DSM as a factor in the economic development of East Sumatra, observes that although the petroleum industry was of great economic import-

102 The DSM also constructed several telephone lines, which were connected to the government telephone system. ARA Kol, MvO 188, H.E.K. Ezerman 1933:337-9.

103 During the Japanese occupation, in 1944-1945, the construction of the 220-km long Pakanbaru railway, from Pakanbaru in East Sumatra to Muara in West Sumatra, took place under atrocious conditions. This railway, for which plans had existed since 1870, would allow the transport of coal from the Ombilin Mines to East Sumatra, by rail and via the Siak River, from where it could be shipped to Singapore. Hovinga 1996:56-9; Wijnands van Resandt 1928:78.

ance in East Sumatra, because of its out-of-the-way location it was not as influential as the agricultural estates. The transportation of oil by DSM was of much smaller significance to the railway company than the transport of agricultural products (Weisfelt 1972:69).

In the meantime, East Sumatra's road network had also expanded more than that in other provinces, stimulated by the estates. In 1933, there was a total of 930 km of roads in the estate area, of which 260 km was paved. An annual budget of roughly 500,000 guilders in 1931-1933 was spent on maintenance, major repairs, and the construction of new bridges. 'The majority of the smaller roads are not paved, but many of these are so insignificant that asphalting them is out of the question,' wrote Resident H.E.K. Ezerman.[104]

The cost of transport over land invariably dropped in regions where a road or railway network had been constructed in the wake of European export industry. Yet it should not be overlooked that for many interior regions, transport overland merely offered an alternative to well-established river transport. Rivers had been the major means of reaching distant markets for centuries, and this should be kept in mind when evaluating the infrastructural growth effects of the agricultural estates. Similarly, it has been observed in the literature that an island economy has natural advantages over a land economy in developing international commerce, stressing the importance of navigation.[105]

Technological dualism

Dualist characteristics can be shown for each factor of production in the export industry. Of all factor inputs in the estate export industry (land, labour, capital, and entrepreneurship), land was the most essential. Fertile land in the right climatic zone turned out to be a valuable asset to tobacco planters. It was for lack of suitable land that initiatives to establish tobacco estates elsewhere in the Outer Islands, outside Deli, failed. Owing to the abundance of land in the Outer Islands, indigenous and European export production could usually coexist (only in East Sumatra did land become scarce). The indigenous population had traditional land rights and practised non-intensive *ladang* cultivation (slash and burn) in primary or secondary forest. Cash-crop cultivation changed this, and led to a more permanent use of *ladang* fields. The estates acquired their land on long-term lease and introduced labour-intensive agriculture, entirely clearing the primary forest and profoundly changing the ecology.

It was the labour factor that received the most attention from entrepren-

104 These 930 km roads in the estate area were distributed as follows: Langkat 161 km; Deli 232 km; Serdang and Simalungun 221 km; Batu Bara, Asahan, and Labuan Batu 316 km. ARA Kol, MvO 188, H.E.K. Ezerman 1933:1901.

105 Dick 1996:31. See also Baudet and Fennema 1983:49; Van der Eng 1992:355-7.

eurs. Capital was imported when necessary, but formed no impediment. The immigration of Chinese coolies (and later Javanese coolies) and the means to retain them after the expiration of their contracts caused the planters major concern, especially when public opinion was putting pressure on them to abolish the penal clause.

European export industry used considerable amounts of invested capital. The technology was European and therefore the value added was earned by companies that were owned by Europeans or Americans. Oil refineries, tin mines, and palm oil processing factories were beyond the reach of indigenous entrepreneurs. Estate products were sold on overseas markets as primary goods, although a certain amount of local processing was necessary.

Entrepreneurship was closely linked to capital. The higher levels of technology involved in European export agriculture and mining created a major technological gap between the European sector and the indigenous sector. There was hardly any transfer of technology. Unfamiliar with the product, the indigenous population lacked the knowledge and the organizational skills to cultivate, dry, select, and package tobacco, to grow high-quality tea, or to export palm oil. Such ignorance meant that in these agricultural products and in oil and tin, indigenous entrepreneurship did not have the wherewithal to develop. After the establishment of large tobacco estates in East Sumatra, high-quality export tobacco was monopolized by Western producers. When they became involved in rubber, European companies produced a product radically different from the contaminated, poor-quality indigenous rubber. Various rubber-processing techniques introduced different sorts of machinery (mangles, latex tanks, spray rubber installations). Indigenous rubber producers sold their products largely unprocessed, at best converted to dried sheets (Higgins 1955-56).

Estate agriculture was labour-intensive rather than capital-intensive. In the petroleum industry, production was highly capital-intensive, so that large companies with a lot of capital had a comparative advantage. This is the main reason indigenous and Chinese enterprises could easily be bought up by large European companies. The scope for new jobs was restricted, but considerable investment was required. As Lindblad says, 'the growth in oil production probably stimulated demand for capital goods more than that for consumer goods, but this is difficult to ascertain for individual supply regions, as the evidence of incoming and outgoing trade flows is blurred by a fair amount of intra-insular trade. Machinery for the oil industry often entered north and south Sumatra or East Kalimantan via Batavia or Surabaya.' (Lindblad 1989a:70.)

The large refineries and production centres of petroleum in the Netherlands Indies were concentrated in roughly five locations: Pangkalan Brandan in East Sumatra, Plaju in Palembang, Tarakan and Balikpapan in Southeast

Kalimantan, and Cepu in Central Java, not counting the smaller refineries and oilfields such as Sungai Gerong in Palembang and Kapuan in Java (see Map 6). The refineries were located near oilfields, and formed enclaves of modern industry.

In the Outer Islands, oil derivatives were the largest export commodity, but their impact on the indigenous economy was small. Like oil, tin and coal mining formed European enclaves, but their effects on the local economy were greater. Due to their central location, the coal mines contributed most to local infrastructure. Their demand for unskilled labour created employment for indigenous workers. The tin mines on Bangka and Belitung attracted an influx of Chinese labourers, of whom many, like the Javanese ex-coolies in Deli and Serdang, settled in the local economy as peasants, traders, or fishermen.

Linkages

We have distinguished between two types of growth effects of European export industry: backward linkages and forward linkages. As we have seen, the export of raw materials generates few forward linkages. The main forward linkages of the export industry were the oil refineries. In their impact on the indigenous economy, backward linkages were more important than forward linkages.

Normally, the essential investments in infrastructure (usually financed out of export earnings) can be seen as backward linkages. European estates invested in roads and railways, which were an added stimulus to the indigenous economy. The DSM railway lines are a good example of a railway system constructed by European planters that served the wider rural area of northern Sumatra. The availability of new means of transportation improved market access for indigenous producers. Elsewhere in Sumatra, the railway network took longer to develop, but better roads enabled Chinese and indigenous traders to travel by car or bus. Infrastructure built by the mining industry was less useful to the indigenous economy. Not only was the locations of mines often out-of-the-way, but many infrastructural improvements such as waterworks and harbours served only the production centre itself.

A different backward linkage, which was most apparent in the estate area but also played a role on the tin islands, was the immigration of Chinese coolies to supply the export industry with labour. In addition to the economic role of ex-estate coolies, the European export industry exerted a demand for food and construction materials, which formed an important backward linkage in the direct surroundings. Local consumption increased owing to the distribution of wages in the local economy (this is called a 'final demand linkage') and the import of luxury and consumer goods by European estates and mines. These effects were much greater in the estate area and near the coal mines, due to the more labour-intensive character of the agricultural estates and the coal mines, compared to oil and tin mining.

One backward linkage which could theoretically constitute a positive growth effect of an export industry is the development of local industries to achieve import substitution. This failed to emerge in the Outer Islands. The foreign character of the companies and the free trade regime effectively prevented import substitution from developing. It would have been far too costly to produce locally the technology that could be imported cheaply from elsewhere. Outside East Sumatra, demand for such goods was also fragmented over a very large area. The government did not pursue any protective policies to stimulate the emergence of import-substituting industries. Government protection of new industries might have had a positive effect on import substitution; for capital goods, however, such as the highly technical refinery installations, it would have been difficult to find the expertise or sufficient demand to establish import-substituting industries, either in Java or in the Outer Islands.

Peasant versus estate

The smallholder learnt little from the estates directly, in terms of agricultural technology or large-scale production, but what was the contribution of the ex-estate workers who settled in the province? As noted earlier, it is difficult to determine the exact number of ex-coolies who integrated into the local economy. Certainly only a small proportion of the total number of coolies became traders or (more likely) peasants. Considering the large number of coolies involved, my conclusion is that the several thousands of ex-coolies who settled in the region must have had a significant influence on the thinly populated local economy, for example by providing skilled labour in rubber tapping. In addition, the estates attracted newly immigrant *singkeh* traders from China. Coolies and ex-coolies created extra demand for local products, particularly during the 1920s, when there was a large inflow of immigrant labour. During the 1930s, many coolies were laid off and had to look for a livelihood elsewhere, and the low market prices for export crops reduced earnings and subsequent expenditure.

Such demand effects were a backward linkage of the estates. We have seen that the arrival of European companies brought wealth to specific indigenous groups: sultans profited from long-term leases of land, some Batak peasants sold locally grown food crops, coastal Malays rented land to Javanese and Chinese immigrants. Estate workers' wages also ensured that flows of income were distributed in the province. The local indigenous economy sold foodstuffs and timber to the estates and developed an indigenous export production, mostly parallel to the estate export production.

Government attempts to solve the labour shortage on the estates by stimulating labour colonization, border colonization, or agricultural colonization did not amount to much, except during the Depression, when the estates offered married Javanese coolies small allotments of land with the two-edged purpose of diminishing the costs of wages and creating a labour reservoir for better times.

In the estate area, near Deli, Serdang, and Simalungun, and to the south in Asahan, traditional indigenous *ladang* agriculture was pushed aside by estate concessions. Despite such intrusions, indigenous rubber production generated substantial volumes, comparable to indigenous rubber production in Palembang and Jambi. Indigenous agriculture developed independently of the large estates in all of the Outer Islands except in East Sumatra, where indigenous export agriculture was thwarted by the large area already occupied by Western concessions. This reduced the possibilities for Batak, Malay, and Javanese peasants to expand their rice or rubber cultivation. In most other provinces, land was abundant.

Conclusion

This chapter has surveyed the advent of European enterprise to the Outer Islands, examining estate agriculture and mining industries and their effects on the local economy.

In East Sumatra, estate agriculture dominated economic development, at some places infringing on indigenous agriculture, but also facilitating economic growth by stimulating the ongoing expansion of infrastructure. On the horns of a dilemma, the indigenous economy simultaneously benefited from the estates and was hindered by them. The entrepreneurial behaviour of the smallholder did not alter significantly owing to the nearby presence of European estates, an issue which will be further explored in the next chapter.

Elsewhere in the Outer Islands, estate agriculture was practised on a much smaller scale and thus played a more limited role in the indigenous economy. The mining industry in many respects led a life of its own. Although a great deal of infrastructure and technology was involved, economic activity was confined largely to the mining enclaves. Interaction with the indigenous economy was very limited.

The provinces of Cluster I (East Sumatra, Palembang, and Southeast Kalimantan) were the most affluent of all Outer Islands – in terms of export revenue and per capita exports, but also with regard to the prosperity of the indigenous economy as described by colonial administrators. The largest share of export revenues was earned by European companies; therefore, export figures alone do not reveal much about the standard of living of the indigenous population. But the relative wealth of indigenous peasants in these provinces can be inferred from various sources.

These provinces left the others behind in economic expansion and trade: trading towns and ports expanded and developed into crowded centres of economic activity, where large warehouses were built near concrete quays at which large ocean-going steamers were moored. Railways, telephone systems, and waterworks were initially built in these centres, and later expanded to the nearby periphery. In this way Palembang, Medan, and Banjarmasin developed into the most sizeable urban centres of the Outer Islands.

Especially in and around cities and industrial centres, infrastructure was relatively well developed. European industries and estates in East Sumatra formed enclaves, which had only weak linkages with the local economy and which were clearly separate from peasant smallholder agriculture (Thee Kian Wie 1977:109). Likewise, the economy in Southeast Kalimantan has also been characterized as 'dualist' – since the twin foundations of its economic expansion, European oil and indigenous rubber, tended to diverge rather than assimilate (Lindblad 1988a:215, 219).

There were few direct linkages between indigenous agriculture and the estates, although traders and middlemen did benefit from infrastructural improvements. In several provinces, such as Bangka and East Sumatra, agriculture was practised by a new population group of ex-coolies, of Chinese origin in Bangka and of Javanese origin in East Sumatra. On Bangka and Belitung coolies who were laid off in the tin mines often tried to earn a living by cultivating pepper or rubber, thereby participating in the local economy.[106] The proximity of European estates does not appear to have stimulated the production of indigenous rubber or other cash crops. The indigenous population followed its own path of development into export production, running largely parallel to European activity in the estate area. Demand on the world market was transmitted through intermediary traders, and as such formed the main economic incentive for these peasants to produce. This theme is the subject of the next chapter.

106 ARA Kol, MvO 249, J.C. Mann 1938 chapter V sub 4 p. 2; MvO 259, J.H.M.L. de Wilde de Ligny 1931:2.

CHAPTER IV

Asian dynamics

After his visit to Palembang in 1919, R. Broersma wrote an account of his travels in *De Locomotief* under the title 'Palembang explorations'. 'However successful the indigenous entrepreneur may be in his industry', he wrote, 'it will never have a solid foundation. It will always be like a booth at a fair, it can be taken down in one night' (Broersma 1920:58). In this manner, Broersma describes the low-capital nature of indigenous enterprise in a rather negative tone. However, it could be argued that it was precisely this low-investment character that enabled the development of a small-scale Asian export sector, and allowed this sector to compete with European companies. Or perhaps it is better not to say 'compete with', but 'produce parallel to': due to differences in quality, the products of the two kinds of suppliers differed substantially, making them suitable for different markets and allowing for differences in productivity.

Indigenous producers adapted quickly and flexibly to the changing economic situation. They pursued profit maximization and were capable of accommodating external impulses, such as the growing demand for raw materials on the world market. A network developed consisting of indigenous producers, intermediary traders and middlemen (often Chinese but also Indonesian), and trading agents of large trading houses, who all interacted in their effort to produce and sell as much raw materials as possible. In its own way, the indigenous sector of the economy rivalled European export production: in flexibility of cash-crop cultivation and in dynamic interaction with overseas markets. This is why I speak of Asian dynamics.

In this chapter I analyse those provinces in late colonial Indonesia which had a dynamic indigenous economy. Several provinces in Sumatra, Kalimantan, and Sulawesi contributed substantially to Netherlands Indies foreign exports. Important indigenous export production sometimes arose under its own steam, sometimes parallel to European estate agriculture. The latter situation occurred in Palembang, East Sumatra, and Southeast Kalimantan. In Aceh, Jambi, West Sumatra, West Kalimantan, South Sulawesi, and Manado indigenous export production developed of its own accord with hardly any European counterpart.

A brief survey of the trade statistics reveals the impressive, sometimes even sensational character of the export performance of these provinces. In Jambi, export revenues escalated from less than 3 million guilders in 1915 to a peak of 46 million guilders in 1925, mainly due to rubber exports. West Kalimantan made a similar jump to more than 70 million guilders in 1925, exporting rubber and copra. In West Sumatra, export revenues grew from an average of below 7 million guilders in the 1910s to almost 30 million guilders each year in 1925/30 – here coffee, not rubber, was the major export product. In South Sulawesi, copra exports raised export revenues to more than 40 million guilders for several years in the decade between 1919 and 1930 (Figures 23a–23q).

This chapter studies the composition, the origin, and the development of these remarkable foreign exports. Which export crops did each province produce? Did they specialize in one commodity or was the export package diversified? To whom did smallholders sell their cash crops, and how important was the role of the intermediary traders, the suppliers of credit? I will examine the role of the different ports in the archipelago and the degree of processing of the export products. In the major ports, after selling the export commodity, the Indonesian or Chinese intermediate traders paid back their loans or obtained import goods from European trading houses, which were taken to local producers in inland areas. A separate section will be devoted to the intermediary trade, which was largely in Chinese hands. This was an essential element of the indigenous economy that has received scant attention in recent literature.[1]

My aim is to obtain a picture of regional differences in export production. Therefore, I will examine the different strategies which were applied in the 1930s when prices on the world market dropped and revenues were much smaller than in the 1920s. Regional variation in local processing, quality control, and credit supply will also be discussed.

Besides this, I will study the growth effects of export production by analysing imports, innovation and expansion of production, labour supply, and infrastructural developments. I will examine whether there were regional differences between the six provinces with predominantly indigenous export production in terms of imports and export surplus.

All this will lay the foundation for an evaluation of the provinces in terms of economic development: were these provinces the true winners in the process of economic integration, adapting dynamically to new markets, reaping the benefits of shrewd trading networks? Or did they only experience the short-term blessings of world market demand?

1 The recent translation of a useful book on Chinese business by Vleming (1926) into English testifies to the growing interest in this theme. It is included in Fernando and Bulbeck 1992. For other literature on intermediary trade see notes below.

Indigenous cultivation of export crops

The main indigenous export crops during the period under study were rubber, coffee, copra, and pepper (Table 5). These were supplemented by smaller quantities of tea, fibres, *pinang* nuts, tobacco, and various other products which were sold by smallholders. Quantities of forest products such as rattan and gutta percha were also included. In order to study regional patterns of indigenous export agriculture we have to analyse the export figures, since no record was kept of the production figures of smallholders. Some methodological reflection is required at this point.

Table 5. Major European and indigenous export crops in the Outer Islands

	Indigenous producers	European estates
Coffee	West Sumatra, Palembang, Bengkulu	Palembang, Lampung (West Sumatra, Bengkulu)
Pepper	Aceh, Palembang, Bangka, Lampung	
Rubber	Jambi, Palembang, West Kalimantan, Southeast Kalimantan	East Sumatra, Palembang (Southeast Kalimantan)
Copra	West Sumatra, West Kalimantan, Manado, South Sulawesi	East Sumatra
Tobacco	(Southeast Kalimantan)	East Sumatra

Note: Provinces with small shares are given in brackets.

There was no registration of production in indigenous agriculture. In contrast, the production of European agricultural estates was well documented. The registration of European production was in most cases carefully conducted by company officials and reported to the administrators of the CKS (Centraal Kantoor voor de Statistiek, Central Bureau of Statistics). Exceptional cases required inspection by government officials to estimate production and revenues – not least to make sure the correct amount of taxes was paid (*Landbouwexportgewassen* 1933:2-3, 906). Statistics on indigenous agriculture are scarce. The sources mainly offer qualitative information about the indigenous sector of the economy. It was difficult for government officials to assess the area of land planted in rubber, coffee, or coconut. The number of trees per hectare, the frequency of harvesting, and the yield per tree all varied. Consequently, in the rubber provinces there were only rough estimates of the number of households that tended rubber gardens, the size of these gardens, how many rubber trees were planted, and how often they were tapped, and, finally, whether the rubber trees were interspersed with other crops or cultivated as a single crop (Broersma 1926:157; Luytjes 1925b). Only in 1937 was a serious effort made to count rubber trees in sample areas in each province and to compare these figures systematically with earlier estimates.[2] Only foreign and interregional exports were registered on a regular basis. Internal trade flows and deliveries from stock were not observed by customs officials, so they could not establish exact figures for production and stocks based on export figures. In order to assess the production of export crops, government officials deduced production estimates from export figures.[3] There is no indication of how much was held in stock awaiting a more favourable price level during periods when prices were low, or how much was sold from stock when prices were better.[4] As a rule, low prices often formed an incentive for the peasant to sell the product before prices could decline even further. Admittedly, the trader often had paid an advance for the deliveries and therefore the producer had another reason not to stockpile.[5]

When dealing with products that were also consumed domestically, such as coffee, reconstruction of indigenous production figures becomes even trickier, since there was no record of local consumption within the region and only a limited record of interregional trade. In 1928 the Arabica coffee harvest reached top levels, but only when prices were relatively strong in 1932 did exports show a sharp increase.[6] This shows that indigenous peasants and Chinese traders were price-conscious and kept a calculating eye on the world market, analogous to the careful scrutiny of European planters.

Another complicating factor is the degree of processing. The amounts of rubber and copra that were dried and cleaned locally varied, as well as the degree to which this was done. Rubber export statistics, for instance, were fairly precise in stating whether export figures referred to wet rubber slabs or dried rubber sheets, but the quality of both wet and dry rubber varied widely, as did the percentage of water in slabs and sheets, which makes the precise production figures hard to determine. The percentage of water contained in wet rubber slabs varied by region. The statistics list these percentages, and give only dry equivalents for rubber produced (Table 46). The production

2 This was done in order to establish individual export quotas for the international rubber restriction. *Landbouwexportgewassen* 1933:2-3. See also Maas and Bokma 1950:416-7; Van Gelder 1950:464-7. On the counting of rubber trees, see Tergast 1932.

3 In principle, exports to Java were included in these estimates, which were published by the CKS in Batavia. See *Landbouwexportgewassen* 1931, 1933.

4 Although output could be easily reduced by tapping the trees less frequently, in some provinces peasants kept rubber in stock, speculating on a rise in prices. Luytjes reports that in Palembang in 1925, an estimated 600,000 kg was stored in sheds. Luytjes 1925b:6.

5 For rubber traders in Southeast Kalimantan, this is described in Broersma 1927:215.

6 *Landbouwexportgewassen* 1933:113. See also Figure 30.

figures based on export figures were particularly rough estimates in the case of the toll-free trading area in Riau, which is noted in the statistics.

My quantitative analysis of the Outer Islands economy is based on foreign and interregional exports. Production figures of indigenous cash crops will only occasionally be examined. When regional differences in production are studied from export statistics, we must be conscious of the fact that we are looking at the outward and visible signs of what was happening in the interior regions. That we know anything at all is due to the surviving qualitative evidence recorded by colonial government officials.

Which provinces grew what

In order to study the mechanisms of smallholder export agriculture and the effects of this activity on the local economy, I concentrate on four major indigenous export crops: rubber, copra, coffee, and pepper. The export of these products substantially increased overall export revenues. There were more - economic activities than export agriculture alone. For example, several kinds of food crops were cultivated and were sold mainly on the regional market. Quite apart from agriculture, forest products such as rattan and gutta percha were collected, and timber was sold. Fishing also provided a means of livelihood for many. However, these types of trade are outside our major interest. Collecting forest products required less commitment from the smallholder and offered fewer possibilities for expanding output or increasing revenues. More specific attention to the export of forest products is given in Chapter V, which studies the provinces in which this type of trade predominated.

Rubber, copra, coffee, and pepper were the cash crops which permitted the expansion of the provinces with strong indigenous exports in Cluster II (Aceh, West Sumatra, Jambi, Lampung, West Kalimantan, Manado, and South Sulawesi). Jambi specialized in rubber and achieved the status of - single most important indigenous rubber producer during the 1920s. Manado and South Sulawesi produced mainly copra, although some rattan, coffee, and several other crops were grown there as well. In the other provinces, peasants divided their attention between various crops, cultivating either mixed crops or different crops in adjacent gardens: in Aceh pepper, rubber, *pinang* nuts, and copra; in West Kalimantan rubber and copra. West Sumatra excelled in the cultivation of Robusta coffee, but also produced rubber and copra (Clemens et al. 1992:40-4).

How does this compare to the provinces of Cluster I? In Palembang, we also find a mixed range of export crops: mainly coffee and rubber, with a sprinkling of various other crops. Parts of Southeast Kalimantan produced little else but rubber, while elsewhere a more diversified combination of crops was grown. In East Sumatra peasants also exported various agricultural and forest products.

In some provinces, the cultivation of export crops yielded relatively small quantities compared to other provinces, but nevertheless formed a significant part of the regional economy. For example, Lampung and Bangka were important producers of pepper. Bengkulu had substantial coffee exports in the years 1925-1932.

I shall begin by treating the two more traditional crops, coffee and pepper. These will be followed by an analysis of the two tree crops whose importance for exports was relatively new: copra and rubber. Exports of copra will be discussed briefly, while rubber will be subjected to a more elaborate analysis.

Major traditional export crops: coffee and pepper

Coffee: relatively robust

Coffee had a long tradition in Indonesia. When the VOC brought the first coffee plants from India to Java, in the late 1690s, no one suspected that a hundred years later, at the time of the liquidation of the Company, coffee would be its major export product (Bulbeck et al. 1998:142-78). Alongside sugar, coffee became one of the pillars of the Cultivation System - earning excellent prices on the European market and contributing considerably to the finances of the Netherlands government.

State coffee cultivation was found mainly in Java, where 'Coffea Arabica' came to be called Java coffee, but had also been established in several regions in the Outer Islands. During the nineteenth century, Arabica coffee was planted in the Padangse Bovenlanden in West Sumatra and in Tapanuli. Although Sumatran peasants allegedly treated the sensitive plants with relative nonchalance, coffee gardens in West Sumatra produced about 9,000 tons of Arabica annually in 1860-1864. Forced cultivation in Sumatra had a less compulsory character than that in Java, which may have encouraged local producers to carry on with the cultivation (Dobbin 1983:225-47; Van Hall 1943:94-103; Young 1990).

Disaster struck in 1878 when the notorious coffee leaf-blight (*bladziekte*), which originated in Africa, was brought to the colony. Both in Java and in West Sumatra, coffee suffered severely. The damage caused by this plague is one of the reasons government coffee cultivation in Java disappeared.[7] Even though coffee plants in mountainous regions had been less affected, indigenous coffee production in Java had also vanished almost completely by the

7 The last government coffee estates were eventually closed in 1916. Van Hall 1943:100.

turn of the century.[8] Measures taken to combat the leaf-blight included the introduction of new types of coffee. The first step was taken in 1876 when the Dutch consul in Greenville, Liberia, sent seeds of a new species of coffee to 's Lands Plantentuin in Buitenzorg (Bogor). Although sturdier, Liberia coffee also turned out to be highly susceptible to plant disease. Then, in 1900, several estates started experimenting with *Robusta*, a species of coffee originating from the Belgian Congo. Robusta coffee was less prone to epidemic diseases and was less demanding of soil fertility. After successful testing in Java, the first Robusta in the Outer Islands was planted in 1910 at Pagar Alam (Palembang) (Van Hall 1943:104-5). Smallholders in Ranau and Pasemah (southern Palembang), and on the other side of the Barisan Mountains in Bengkulu quickly changed to cultivating Robusta.[9] After 1915, Arabica ('Java coffee') held only a small share of Indonesian coffee exports. For example, in 1932, the Outer Islands exported approximately 70 million kg of coffee, of which 65 million kg was Robusta, 4.9 million kg Arabica, and a mere 5,000 kg Liberia. Arabica was grown in small quantities in Bali, Tapanuli, South Sulawesi, and West Sumatra.[10]

The cultivation of coffee was stimulated by the government, especially through the availability of credit for planters. Agricultural credit was paid back in instalments, in contrast to trade credit, which usually had to be paid back in full after one year. The Palembangsche Volksbank (Palembang Credit Union) was founded in 1925 and played an important role in supplying these loans.[11] The fall in incomes and prices in the 1930s led the government in the Netherlands to levy a tax on all coffee imports entering the mother country. The revenue accruing from this tax (the Coffee Fund) was spent on improving indigenous coffee cultivation and doing research on coffee cultivation techniques. This fund was later converted into a central purchasing and sales agency with monopolistic powers (similar to the Producten Verkoop Centrale in Minahasa) (Allen and Donnithorne 1957:89-91). The contribution of government policy to the rise of indigenous export agriculture will be addressed in Chapter VI.

8 Estate coffee in Java constituted on average 50% of the coffee exported from the Netherlands Indies in 1900-1940.Traditionally coffee had been grown in the hilly countryside of East Java. But even though coffee did not suffer as much as sugar from the Depression, the emphasis in Java in the inter-war period shifted towards other types of exports. Clemens et al. 1992:30, 64-5.

9 This change was made remarkably quickly, which shows that the peasants knew what they were doing. Touwen 1991:142, 177 (Table V).

10 Not surprisingly, most Java coffee came from Java. Between 1911 and 1924, total coffee exports from Java (including both Arabica and Robusta, mostly estate coffee) amounted to 60 to 90% of total coffee exports. In later years, Java's share decreased and settled at an average of roughly 35% until 1940. Clemens et al. 1992:65; *Landbouwexportgewassen* 1933:103, 111.

11 ARA Kol, MvO 212, J. Tideman 1928:160.

Adulterated Robusta production

In 1900-1942 indigenous coffee was grown mainly in Palembang and West Sumatra, but was also found in Bengkulu and to a lesser extent in Tapanuli and Lampung. In Bengkulu, it was the main export commodity (Figure 23o). Palembang's coffee exports gained momentum after 1920. In the preceding decade, annual exports ranged from a mere 100,000 to 600,000 guilders, but in the 1920s coffee export revenues reached peak levels of about 14 million guilders in 1924 and 1927 (Figure 23b). In the total coffee exports of colonial Indonesia, Palembang coffee occupied an increasingly important place: in 1916/20 it exported an average of 6 per cent of total export volume, in 1921/25 19 per cent, and in 1926/30 21 per cent. During the 1930s the figure hovered at slightly above 20 per cent. Most of it was smallholder coffee. West Sumatra closely followed Palembang, being second in Outer Islands coffee exports. Also in West Sumatra, the largest part of the coffee production was cultivated by peasants and not by estates (Tables 48, 49, and 50).[12] Before 1920, West Sumatra, South Sulawesi, and East Sumatra had been the main coffee exporters in the Outer Islands, each exporting between 0.8 and 2 million guilders.

A large proportion of indigenous coffee production, particularly from Bengkulu and Palembang, was sent to Batavia where it was put up for auction (Table 53.1). Because of its variable quality, Palembang Robusta quickly earned a dubious reputation in Batavia. This was partly due to careless treatment by smallholders, who often allowed the accumulation of moisture and mildew in the coffee beans, but can also be blamed on manipulation by traders, who sometimes added sand and grit to increase the weight. Another factor contributing to the poor quality of this type of coffee beans was the dry preparation method used, which is less suitable for Robusta.[13]

The producers of Palembang Robusta were repeatedly accused of exporting an inferior quality of coffee. In 1928, the French even threatened to ban further imports of Palembang Robusta. A French wholesaler wrote angrily: 'On estime que la Hollande est sur la route de tuer sa poule aux oeufs d'or!' (one would think that Holland is on its way to kill the goose that lays the golden eggs).[14] In 1928-1934, auction prices for Palembang Robusta were on average 29 per cent less than those for Robusta from other areas (Rudin 1935-36:258).

12 ARA Kol, MvO 212, J. Tideman 1928:257; Clemens et al. 1992:64-5.

13 Smallholder Robusta coffee was usually processed according to the 'dry preparation' method, in contrast to the West Indian method (W.I.B.), which washes the pulp away with water instead of merely drying the beans and pounding the dried pulp. Applied to Robusta, the dry method often fails to eliminate the hulls. Van Hall 1943:101, 107.

14 As quoted in ARA Kol, MvO 212, J. Tideman 1928:261. By 'la Hollande' the author means the coffee peasants in Palembang. See also Van Hall 1943:108.

Not all coffee was auctioned: large shipments of (mainly plantation) coffee were sent straight to foreign buyers, after transshipment in Tanjung Priok.[15] In 1925 prices were so high that – echoing what happened in rubber regions – peasants abandoned rice production. Rice was imported along with other food crops, and paid for with the revenues from coffee exports (Rudin 1935-36:283). The years 1928 and 1929 were peak years, with more than 16 million guilders' worth of coffee exports from West Sumatra. From the Outer Islands, more than 45 million guilders' worth of coffee was exported overseas in 1928, to which can be added interregional exports of about 8 million guilders from the Outer Islands to Java.

After 1925 Lampung produced an increasing volume of coffee, at times challenging Bengkulu in terms of volume.[16] Lampung exported on average 5,700 tons of coffee per year in 1927/40, compared to a meagre 150 tons in 1900/26, earning an annual 1.5 million guilders in 1927/40, compared to 92,000 guilders in 1900/26. Bengkulu started exporting substantial amounts of coffee after 1923, reaching a peak output in 1928 of more than 10,000 tons, earning 6.6 million guilders. Finally, Bali exported a constant, relatively small amount of coffee, with a value between 0.5 and 1.5 million guilders per year between 1900 and 1940. By including exports to Java, coffee exports from Bali are roughly doubled.

One harmful consequence of low coffee prices during the Depression was the tendency of peasants to neglect the maintenance of their coffee gardens – which resulted in decline in quality, and the spread of diseases. Coffee cultivation in Tapanuli almost vanished when it was struck by the 'bessenbubuk' disease. Another effect was that traders in Palembang started to stockpile coffee, waiting for better prices (*Landbouwexportgewassen* 1931:121).

Despite such hiccups, compared to other primary export goods, the price of coffee remained relatively strong. It dropped neither as quickly nor as deeply as rubber and copra prices. For example, in 1933, when the rubber price had fallen dramatically to 8 per cent of its price in 1927, the coffee price was still 40 per cent of the price in 1927 (Figures 11 and 30). When all is said and done, during the Depression, coffee turned out to be a relatively strong commodity. In those regions where coffee was cultivated alongside rubber or copra (in certain regions of Palembang and West Sumatra), peasants could reduce their loss of income in rubber by cultivating the relatively robust coffee.

15 ARA Kol, MvO 212, J. Tideman 1928:257.

16 Although some rubber estates in Lampung planted coffee while waiting for young rubber seedlings to grow, almost 75% of Lampung's coffee exports originated from coffee smallholders. However, pepper (not coffee) was the most important indigenous crop in Lampung. ARA Kol, MvO 232, Th. Volmering 1930:13. See also Figure 23g.

Pepper: still going strong

As a commodity with a long tradition, pepper was of great influence in colonial trade. Pepper was not only used for consumption, but also for the preparation of leather and the fabrication of perfume.[17]

In VOC times, Bantam (Java) was the centre of the pepper trade, and Lampung and Aceh were the most important supply regions. Pepper was traded in almost every trading post in Sumatra and Kalimantan. In the late colonial period, its significance did not abate, even though new commodities were added to the export package. Lampung and Aceh remained important pepper regions. At the turn of the century, other provinces where pepper was a substantial indigenous export product were Palembang (the Komering region), Bengkulu, and West and Southeast Kalimantan. A conspicuous newcomer was Bangka, where pepper cultivation was introduced by Chinese.

The total volume of foreign pepper exports from the Outer Islands remained at a markedly constant level from 1900 to 1920: roughly between 6 million kg and 10 million kg were exported annually, averaging 10 million kg in 1901/10 and 13 million kg in 1911/20. In the following decades, pepper production increased: in 1931/40, an average of 44.6 million kg of pepper was exported from the Outer Islands each year (Table 52). Java's share in total pepper exports declined: in 1916/20 an average of 47 per cent of total exported volumes, in 1936/40 an average of 10 per cent (Clemens et al. 1992:72-3).

Major changes occurred in the regional composition of Outer Islands pepper exports. Aceh gradually lost out in importance in the pepper trade, its share dropping from more than 36 per cent in 1901/10 to less than 3 per cent of average annual foreign exports in 1931/40.[18] Lampung, by contrast, kept augmenting its pepper output until it had reached top levels in 1936 and 1939 of more than 60 million kg per year. On average Lampung pepper constituted 63 per cent of total pepper exports from the Outer Islands in 1931/40. Bangka built up an increasing share in pepper exports after 1913, and expanded its pepper production significantly after 1930 (Table 52).

Pepper from Aceh was grown mainly in pepper gardens in East Aceh, which dated from the nineteenth century. Here the rich and powerful *uleëbalang* (district heads) competed for the revenues from the pepper export trade. Indigenous pepper cultivation in East Aceh went into a steady decline, reaching its lowest point in 1920, the year in which this area almost completely stopped exporting pepper. The origins of this decline were chronic diseases of pepper plants, poor living conditions in the region (leading to

17 ARA Kol, MvO 232, Th. Volmering 1932:16; Bulbeck et al. 1998:142-78; Van Hall 1943:131-2.

18 Aceh had been dominant in Indonesian pepper exports in the nineteenth century. Bulbeck et al. 1998:92-6.

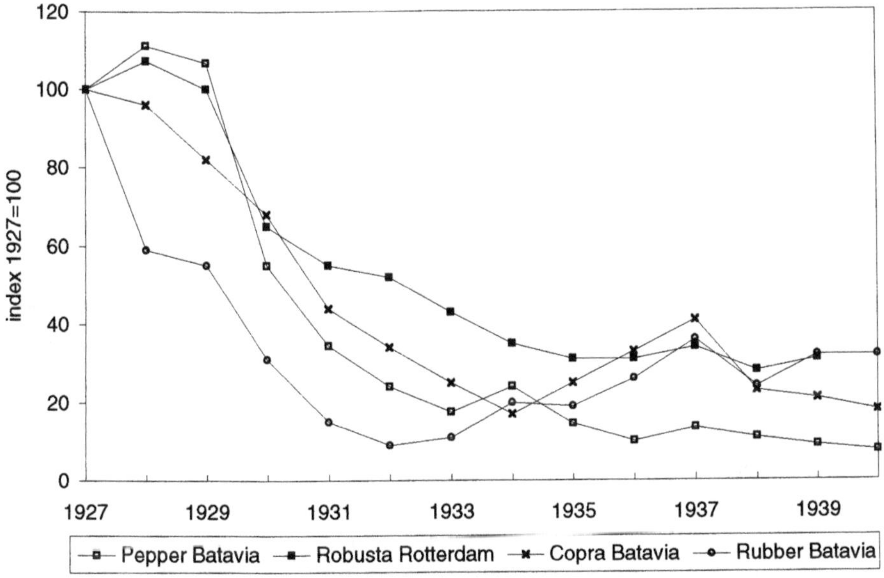

Figure 11. Index of market price (1927 = 100): rubber, copra, coffee, and pepper, 1927-1940 (Table 35).

recurring famines), and the poor credit facilities offered by the Credit Union in times of food shortage (Gade Ismail 1994:281-300). Undeterred, elsewhere in Aceh, the indigenous population continued cultivating pepper.[19]

In Lampung, as early as 1914 pepper was reported to be a product that contributed 'to the wealth of the population'.[20] Pepper was traded by indigenous traders in Menggala, a booming indigenous trading town, and by more powerful Chinese traders and European trading houses in Telukbetung. The construction of a railway around 1920, which made pepper transport by train possible, turned Menggala into a ghost town, robbing it of its pepper trade.[21] Afterwards, Kotabumi became the centre of the indigenous pepper trade.

Lampung produced roughly 14 million kg of pepper in 1928. About 3.4 million kg was exported directly to Singapore (of which 1 million kg passed through Palembang). Roughly 6.8 million kg was shipped to Europe and the United States and 3.7 million was sent to Java.[22] This indicates that even a province like Lampung, which was relatively close to Java, had strong ties with Singapore through Chinese intermediary traders.

19 ARA Kol, MvO 160, A.Ph. van Aken 1936:67.
20 ARA, NHM 9193, VvS 1257 (Telukbetung 1912):4-5.
21 ARA Kol, MvO 233, L. Berkhout 1926:5; Purwanto 1993:**121-2.?**
22 ARA Kol, MvO 232, Th. Volmering 1930:17.

On Bangka, Chinese and Indonesian peasants grew pepper supplemented by some rubber. Poor soil generally made agriculture an uphill battle, but pepper did well in this province. A *ladang* field produced only one rice harvest per year, which supplied only enough rice for five or six months. In such a situation not only the labour force in the tin mines but also the smallholder population was dependent on rice imports. Pepper cultivation was a resourceful way of supplementing income in an otherwise poor region.[23]

Mirroring the price of coffee, the price of pepper was relatively stable during the first years of the Depression, particularly in comparison with the price of rubber. In 1927-1929, the price of pepper maintained an even better level than rubber, copra, and even coffee (Figure 11). Later, after 1929, export revenues from pepper also fell quickly (Figures 23g and 23k). Nevertheless, smallholders in Bangka and Lampung continue their export trade during the Depression years (Table 52).[24]

Just like indigenous coffee and rubber, pepper harvests reached the auctions badly adulterated. One Resident in Lampung discovered that the peasants did in fact bring a relatively clean product to the market, where all loads were inspected thoroughly by intermediate traders. When the cargo was brought to the wholesaler in Telukbetung, however, the administrator found that the middleman had added kapok, stones, or small clay pellets especially made for the purpose. These impurities at times constituted up to 30 per cent of the traded product![25]

Pepper gardens required fertile soil and considerable attention. Indigenous pepper growers knew that it made no sense to plant pepper on unsuitable land, for example on heavy clay or very wet swamps (Van Hall 1943: 132). With reference to this, Ozinga added an interesting proposition to his dissertation of 1940: 'Because pepper gardens soon perish when neglected, pepper cultivation lacks the element that has contributed most to the establishment of a restriction in rubber cultivation' (Ozinga 1940). Unbridled expansion of pepper gardens was not feasible as long as labour was scarce.

New export crops: copra and rubber

Copra: speciality of the East

Copra was a relatively 'new' product in colonial Indonesia. Beginning its rise in the late nineteenth century, it became an important indigenous export commodity. Most of this copra was produced in South Sulawesi and Mana-

23 ARA Kol, MvO 249, J.C. Mann 1938 chapter V pp. 1-3, chapter VI pp. 1-2.

24 ARA Kol, MvO 159, A.H. Philips 1932:65; MvO 160, A.Ph. van Aken 1936:47.

25 ARA Kol, MvO 233, L. Berkhout 1926:32.

do, West Kalimantan and West Sumatra (Clemens et al. 1992:70-1). Coconuts were husked and the dried copra served as a raw material for margarine and vegetable oil.[26] Of course, the use of the coconut palm was not new in Indonesia: in the literature, it has even been compared to the role of the cow in Western Europe: the cow is important in European consumption by providing milk, meat, fat, butter, and even leather. Similarly, coconut palms in Indonesia were found everywhere and were used for many purposes: the coconut water (or *albumen*, from the *kelapa muda*), the pulp, and the coconut oil (*kelapa sawit*) served as foodstuffs, whereas the fronds, bark, fibres, and tree trunks were used for various purposes. The value of the coconut palm for the indigenous economy has even been expressed in the nickname 'green gold' (Heersink 1999:14). The coastlines of Kalimantan, Sulawesi, and Maluku were seamed by irregular rows of these indispensable trees.

The use of copra as a raw material for industrial processing started in the late nineteenth century. Most of the copra came from South Sulawesi, Manado, and West Kalimantan (the European estates in East Sumatra produced a relatively small share). In these provinces indigenous and Chinese copra production generated considerable demand effects – causing a relatively high level of imports, which were more strongly linked to exports than in more diversified provinces.[27] West Sumatra and Riau also contributed substantially to the copra trade. These five provinces accounted for more than 80 per cent of all Outer Islands copra exports between 1900 and 1938. Java's share in copra decreased steadily from about 35 per cent in 1911 to an average 0.7 per cent of the annual copra export volume in 1936/40. Total Indonesian copra exports did not increase as dramatically as rubber but nevertheless grew impressively throughout 1911-1940, from 200,000 to 500,000 kg per year (Table 51) (Clemens et al. 1992:70-1).

Domestic consumption of copra in colonial Indonesia is estimated to have been about 9 kg per capita, which amounted to 540 million kg in 1930. This means that in 1930 about 42 per cent (395 million kg) of the 935 million kg of copra cultivated in the colony was exported (Tammes 1947:9-12).

In West Kalimantan, the Chinese were skilful in implementing draining and irrigation techniques, preparing the land for the growing of coconut palms. Malay inhabitants of West Kalimantan quickly imitated these methods and started producing copra as well. West Kalimantan copra came almost entirely from the coastal regions and was exported to Java, Singapore, and after 1920 increasingly to Europe and Japan (Ranken 1989:199). Ozinga highlights the fact that because copra was produced mainly along the coast,

26 Lindblad 1989c:11; Ranken 1989:199; Tammes 1947:7-10.

27 See also the statistical correlation between imports and exports, as in Table 57.

it did not affect the level of income in the interior, where rubber was the major export product (Ozinga 1940:120).

In Manado and South Sulawesi, copra was the single most important indigenous export product (Figures 23i and 23j). In the 1850s, the forerunner in the cultivation of coconut palms had been the small island of Selayar, south of South Sulawesi. For this island, copra was the principal economic asset during much of the late colonial period. Coconuts could be easily and flexibly cultivated alongside *ladang* rice fields, the palms needing little fertilization or maintenance (Heersink 1999:69-84, 159-93). Manado's copra was produced mainly in the Minahasa region. Copra cultivation also expanded in Lampung in the 1920s when people realized that there was a good market for this product (within the region as well as outside). Copra palms were planted on strips along the coast and on the islands, such as Sebuku and Sebesi. A well-known *haji*, Jamaludin, was the owner of many trees. But, according to Resident L. Berkhout in 1926, he spent regrettably little time on the maintenance of his gardens and planted his trees too close together. Often the coconuts were not processed but just sent to Java, after merely peeling off the outer husk.[28]

The major copra-producing provinces did not ship their exports to Java. In 1918/22 the proportion sent to Java from South Sulawesi and Manado averaged 12 to 14 per cent, but after the 'Insulinde' (De N.V. Oliefabrieken Insulinde) went bankrupt in 1922, interregional trade in copra dwindled to less than 5 per cent (Table 53.4).[29]

During the Depression, the price of copra fell considerably. The decline may not have been as serious as that in rubber, but nevertheless in 1934 the copra price was only 17 per cent of what it had been in 1927 (Tables 34 and 35). After 1934, the copra price started recovering significantly. All was not yet rosy in the garden as the copra price remained subject to great instability.[30] This prompted government intervention in the late 1930s (see Chapter VI).

Rubber: the power of change

Rubber was a product that changed the lives of many smallholders in Sumatra and Kalimantan. In Chapter III, rubber was discussed in connection with its production by agricultural estates. In this section I will review the history of this tree crop, which turned out to be so important for the indigenous smallholder.

28 ARA Kol, MvO 233, L. Berkhout 1926:32-3; ARA, NHM 9193, VvS 1261 (Telukbetung 1916):9; VvS 1262 (1917):10; VvS 1264 (1919):14.

29 Dick 1990:306; Kamerling 1979, 1982.

30 ARA Kol, MvO 285, L.J.J. Caron 1933:154; MvO 306, A.Ph. van Aken 1933:153, 157; MvO 308, M. van Rhijn 1941:40.

Hevea rubber has a relatively young history. Previously, rubber from the indigenous gutta percha plant was collected in the forest. In 1876 an Englishman called H.A. Wickham brought 70,000 new seeds of Hevea Brasiliensis, also called Para Rubber, from Brazil to England. In the same year 2,000 small seedlings of this crop were carefully shipped to Ceylon and Buitenzorg.[31] The new rubber species had many advantages: it grew quickly, even on relatively poor soil, and frequent tapping stimulated latex production instead of wounding the trees. After several years of testing and improvement, large quantities of seeds and seedlings were shipped to colonial Indonesia and distributed. The first smallholder plantings were reported in West Kalimantan in 1903, in Jambi in 1904, and in Southeast Kalimantan in 1905.[32] In Palembang, the first rubber plants were imported in 1907, culminating in Hevea production six years later in 1913.[33] In Southeast Kalimantan, E.A. Hilckes imported Hevea seeds from the Straits Settlements and established two plantations in Martapura, which together had more than 100,000 young trees in 1907 (Lindblad 1988a:58).

The cultivation of rubber started with local heads and spread to the peasants. When Malay chiefs and wealthier inhabitants started the cultivation of rubber in the 1910s, selling the product to Chinese traders, peasants saw that this was a lucrative trade, and started to plant rubber on their fallow *ladang* rice fields.[34]

On the world market, demand for rubber grew consistently during the early 1900s. Rubber was used in all kinds of new industries and for a variety of consumer products: for insulating wires and cables, for the tyres of carriages, bicycles, and motor cars, for conduit pipes for gas and water, for fan belts, buffers and bumpers, draught-protectors, rubber mats, billiard tables, and boots and shoes (*Caoutchouc* 1917:437-8; McFadyean 1944:17). Demand was rising and prices were high, until 1920. In that year, prices started falling for the first time. But they recovered again in 1923, and years of further expansion of the rubber trade followed, until in 1926 a decline in rubber prices, which eventually turned out to be dramatic, set in (Table 35).

Cheap capital, poor quality

The indigenous cultivation of rubber was characterized by its low-capital (and, compared with other crops, relatively labour-intensive) production techniques. Farm households required few capital goods, mainly seeds or

[31] Contrary to popular belief the seeds were not secretly smuggled out of Brazil, but shipped strictly legally. *Caoutchouc* 1917:437; McFadyean 1944:7-8.

[32] Clemens 1989:214-5; Van der Eng 1996c:233; Van Gogh 1983:127.

[33] ARA Kol, MvO 212, J. Tideman 1928:55-7; Clemens 1989:215; Touwen 1991:144.

[34] ARA Kol, MvO 215, W. Steinbuch 1936:194, 207. See also Thee Kian Wie 1977:18.

seedlings, knives and cups, and an occasional oil drum for collecting and coagulating the latex. The main expenditure for producing rubber from an existing garden was the coagulation material (acid, alum).[35]

Rubber production required a small initial investment and a lot of patience. The rubber tree took five to six years to mature and an even longer period before it was yielding its best (McFadyean 1944:x). When the tree was tapped, the white, moist latex (lump-rubber) was carried to a collecting point, where it was treated with acids or alum to make it coagulate. Rubber sap that had thickened on the trunk of the tree was collected as 'scraps', sap that was spilt as 'earth rubber', and even the thin strips of bark, which were cut away to allow the latex to flow out, were collected. From the latter two kinds, 'crêpe rubber' was made. Coagulated clean rubber could be traded as wet 'slabs', containing a lot of water, or be milled into 'sheets', which were dried in drying huts or in smoking huts, or by mangling them.[36] These different sorts of unprocessed and half-processed rubber show that because of the high demand for the product (and, initially, the high prices) as much latex as possible was sold regardless of its condition (Table 46).[37] It will come as no surprise that indigenous crêpe rubber was of poor quality. The same could be said of the wet rubber sold as slabs: it was coagulated 'in any shape or form' and into it 'everything was mixed, even old boots'. Several additions, such as stones and iron sand, posed a danger to machines in rubber-milling factories. A sensational list of other illegal ingredients sometimes found in wet rubber included: clay, flour, sago, bark, Ficus Elastica, newspapers, cigarettes, soles of old shoes, glass, and even dead monkeys.[38]

Indigenous rubber from the eastern provinces of Sumatra was usually transported by river on rafts. Many traders kept the wet rubber slabs under the raft, submerged in the water, so that they would remain wet instead of losing weight by drying (*rakit* trade).[39] Indigenous rubber from Tapanuli and

35 ARA Kol, MvO 223, J.R.F. Verschoor van Nisse 1931:131; Van der Eng 1996c:234.

36 ARA Kol, MvO 212, J. Tideman 1928:256; *Caoutchouc* 1917:437-8; Ozinga 1940:297-8.

37 Before 1925, this distinction was not included in the trade statistics: all rubber was included under one item: 'Caoutchouc, raw or processed'. Huff argues that all rubber exports from the Netherlands Indies during 1906-1932 should be reduced by 20-30% because the export statistics do not differentiate between wet and dry rubber. I do not agree, since it is repeatedly reported that rubber statistics were underrecorded in the early 1920s, which may compensate for the loss. Important conclusions in this study are all drawn from the data after 1927, which were expressed in the trade statistics in dry equivalents. W.G. Huff 1994:196, 204; Luytjes 1925b:15; Ozinga 1940:293-4.

38 The governmental 'rubberkeur' did little to prevent this practice. ARA Kol, MvO 212, J. Tideman 1928:253; MvO 225, Ph.J. van der Meulen 1936:70; Tideman 1938:192; W.G. Huff 1993:298.

39 This happened mainly in Jambi and in Palembang (Rawas region, and along the Barumun) and resulted in slabs containing 50% water. ARA Kol, MvO 223, J.R.F. Verschoor van Nisse 1931:122-5; Luytjes 1925b:11.

West Sumatra had to be carried over long distances by land, which made it more profitable to process the rubber into dried sheets. Tapanuli indigenous rubber was considered to be so good that it approached estate rubber in quality.[40] However, neither Tapanuli nor West Sumatra were large producers of indigenous rubber (Table 44.1).

In Palembang, the bulk of the rubber was shipped into the city of Palembang along the Musi River. Other rubber came by rail or by road, in small trucks, coaches, or personal cars. Rubber traders from the city of Palembang frequently travelled to the interior, usually on market days, to purchase rubber. Palembang was an important centre of indigenous business. In the rubber gardens, tappers collected the latex and brought it to the home of the garden owner. At times, traders also bought rubber from *toko* owners in villages, a *cintu* (cargo clerk) on a paddle boat, a truck owner, or a village head. They often received credit from the Palembangsche Volksbank (Palembang Credit Union). BPM agents or agents of firms importing textiles or foodstuffs sometimes acted as intermediary traders in the interior, buying rubber from producers and selling it to traders in the city. Allegedly, during the mid-1920s, import traders were so anxious to buy rubber that they sometimes accepted a loss on the sale of their import goods to obtain ready cash for new rubber transactions. In the city of Palembang, rubber was stored in the large *gudang* (warehouses) of wholesale traders, or in a shed on a large raft, called *rumah tumpak* or *tumpakan*. The *tumpakan* functioned as a rubber exchange. Often the owner acted as a broker and was paid a commission of about 1 guilder per picul sold. He offered the producer or supplier of the rubber free board and lodging. Sometimes the owner of the *tumpakan* acted as a trader himself and bought up the rubber supply, particularly when it was a small quantity. One *tumpakan* could store roughly 125 picul (7,712 kg). When trade was lively, the owner could earn as much as 100 to 125 guilders per day. Buyers from wholesale trading companies visited the *tumpakan* every morning. The market price of rubber was telegraphed from Singapore to these agents, but their offer was only made after carefully recalculating the price, taking due note of the water content and the degree of adulteration of the rubber in question. Then most of the rubber was shipped to Singapore. In the mid-1920s about 12 per cent was processed in Palembang.[41]

Most of the rubber from rubber-producing provinces was shipped to Singapore. Very little rubber was transported to Batavia. This was in contrast to copra and coffee exports, of which a large percentage was exported to Java. Only during and shortly after the First World War were rubber exports to Java a little higher. In 1923-1937, of all Outer Islands rubber exports, less than

40 Brook, Doffegnies and Slotemaker 1926:43; Van der Kolff 1929:121; Luytjes 1925b:10.
41 ARA Kol, MvO 212, J. Tideman 1928:254-6.

1 per cent went to Java. This confirms the impression that Batavia played a very marginal role as a rubber entrepôt trading centre (Table 53.3).

In Singapore the rubber was remilled, cleaned, and processed into sheets. It was then sold to local rubber factories for more sophisticated manufacturing, or exported. Since the remillers were highly competitive and their profitability depended on a large turnover of rubber, good prices were offered the smallholder for his unprocessed rubber (Van der Eng 1996c:234). This gave rubber growers little incentive to process their own rubber.

Only after 1930 were Palembang and Jambi able to increase their percentage of processed rubber exports, thanks to the rubber factories of Internatio and the Nederlandse Rubber Unie (Netherlands Rubber Union) in Palembang. Overall this constituted only a small improvement, from about 10 per cent to 20 per cent of all rubber.[42] Also in Southeast Kalimantan, where the rubber areas were concentrated in Hulu Sungai, there was virtually no processing of indigenous rubber in the 1920s and early 1930s. In 1926, an NHM sub-agent wrote that all indigenous rubber from Southeast Kalimantan was exported to Singapore as a raw, insufficiently dried product (scraps, lumps, wet slabs of variable water content). It was hoped, he remarked, that the government would intervene, because all the profits of 'remilling' were now being earned in Singapore, instead of by local rubber factories (of which there were several in Banjarmasin).[43] (This issue will be explored further in Chapter VI.) In Jambi and West Kalimantan, smallholder rubber producers were scattered throughout the interior. The Chinese settlements in West Kalimantan played a role in the dissemination of rubber cultivation. Their rubber was mostly of better quality than the rubber produced by the Dayak and Malays.[44] It is clear that the widespread cultivation of Hevea by indigenous smallholders resulted in a type of rubber very different from European estate rubber. It was rubber of poor quality, but it was cheap; and simply by virtue of the huge quantities, it generated enormous revenues for the rubber regions.

Export revenues: rise and decline

Indigenous rubber exports made up an impressive proportion of total Outer Islands exports in the 1920s. After a steady increase, rubber exports in 1927 amounted to 304 million guilders, which was 37 per cent of total foreign

[42] Resident Schwaab estimated the rubber exports from Palembang as follows. In 1927 1,500 tons dry and 20,500 tons wet rubber; in 1929 2,500 tons dry and 19,500 tons wet rubber, in 1930 tons 3,000 dry and 11,000 tons wet rubber, in 1931 2,600 tons dry and 10,400 tons wet rubber. ARA Kol, MvO 214, J.L.M. Schwaab 1933:107, 201; *Landbouwexportgewassen* 1931:79.

[43] ARA, NHM 9088, VvS 32 (Banjarmasin 1926):4; VvS 33 (1927):3-5.

[44] ARA Kol, MvO 225, Ph.J. van der Meulen 1936:74; Loos and Van Beusechem 1925:45; Johan 1934-35:189-204.

exports (818 million guilders). Of these rubber exports, 49 per cent originated from indigenous smallholders. In dry equivalents, total rubber exports in 1927 were 228 million kg. Because indigenous rubber was sold at a lower price than estate rubber, in 1927 the former constituted 65 per cent in terms of volume (Table 43).

The dual character of rubber led the colonial government to levy a separate tax on the export of indigenous rubber, starting 1 June 1925.[45] Estate rubber was exempted from taxation. This injustice may have something to do with the fact that European companies paid company tax and income tax, while indigenous peasants often evaded income tax. But the saturation of the rubber market and subsequent decline in price may also have influenced the decision-making process. An export excise would perhaps lower indigenous production and encourage smallholders to limit their activities to food production.[46]

As a consequence of the decision to impose a tax on indigenous rubber exports, the trade statistics kept a separate record of estate rubber and indigenous rubber from 1927. Therefore rubber is the only product for which the exact proportion of indigenous and European exports was recorded (Table 43).[47] (These export values also suggest the income effect of indigenous rubber exports, provided we can determine how much of the revenue ended up with the producer.)

As long as world demand for rubber was rising more quickly than supply, prices were high and producers flourished. Indonesian rubber production rose rapidly between 1911 and 1919, reaching a post-war height of 54 thousand tons with a value of almost 130 million guilders in 1919. Jambi won the race to reach impressive indigenous production levels, but Palembang, Southeast Kalimantan, and West Kalimantan caught up and also developed

45 *Indisch Staatsblad* No. 218 (13 May 1925). *Koloniaal Verslag* 1925:144. Fiscal and statistical definitions were not entirely compatible. When a peasant cultivated rubber on his own land, this was indigenous rubber. When a peasant rented or leased land from someone else, his rubber would, fiscally speaking, be registered as estate rubber. The latter situation only happened on a very small scale and in practice would often be registered as indigenous rubber when exported (which in fact it was). The result of the tax was an increase in rubber excise revenue from a mere 14,103 guilders in 1924 to 6,233,714 in 1925. *Koloniaal Verslag* 1926, Bijlage S:3.

46 Barlow and Drabble incorrectly state that there was no export duty on smallholder rubber until the mid-1930s. Barlow and Drabble 1990:205.

47 Since the rubber was exported in various qualities ranging from wet to dry, the statistics calculated dry-equivalent volumes. Three categories were registered: dry rubber; wet rubber; and raw, unprocessed or unpurified scraps and earth-rubber (the lowest grade). For each of these categories a percentage of water was determined for each province in order to calculate the *dry equivalent*. This meant estimated export volumes were constructed. Although different percentages were used for each province, based on samples, these approximations were not exact (see Table 46). Usually, the amount of rubber of each of the three different categories was stated in the trade statistics. ARA Kol, MvO 212, J. Tideman 1928:256; *Landbouwexportgewassen* 1933:90, 95.

substantial levels of smallholder rubber exports (Figures 23b, 23c, 23f, 23h). Heavy world demand during these years is one of the reasons. Indigenous producers could afford to pay scant attention to the quality of their product, choosing to concentrate simply on quantity.

The crest of the wave was short-lived. World demand was soon matched by supply: in 1920-1921 rubber prices began to fall, setting off a tendency to sell increasing quantities against lower prices.[48] In the period 1914/20, the average rubber price in the Outer Islands had fluctuated between 2.00 and 3.00 guilders per kg. It sank to 0.85 guilders in 1922, but showed some hesitant recovery, mainly due to the Stevenson Restriction Scheme (1922-1928). The Netherlands Indies declined to participate in this restriction plan, and profited from reduced competition from producers in the British empire. Dutch refusal led to a permanently larger share for colonial Indonesia in world rubber supply.[49] Rubber prices remained high until 1925, when they started to fall again. After 1929 the World Depression sent rubber prices into a steep decline. This marked the end of the rubber boom years. In 1932 the average rubber price was somewhere in the region of 0.10 guilders per kg (Tables 34, 35, and 44.5). When international rubber-producing countries decided to limit world supply and signed the International Rubber Regulation Agreement (IRRA) in 1934, rubber prices gradually recovered, but they never again reached the level of the mid-1920s.

Labour in indigenous rubber

Peasants who cultivated rubber often planted more trees than one household could manage, and relied on hired workers for the tapping. Yet regional differences influenced the demand for labour in rubber areas. The smallholder in Jambi usually owned more trees than the smallholder in Palembang and was therefore more dependent on hired labour. The population of sparsely populated Jambi was also unevenly spread. Tappers could be recruited in the town of Jambi, but in the interior, hired labour was scarce. Sometimes tappable trees were left untapped for lack of labour. Leaving the tapping to hired labourers sometimes led to rough treatment of the trees, resulting in loss of latex.

In Palembang, rubber smallholders had to compete with indigenous coffee cultivation for hired labourers: tappers would hire themselves to whichever crop offered the best wages. Apart from local tappers, many Javanese were employed as tappers by indigenous rubber producers. Some of them came directly from Java in search of work. Others were colonists, or former estate or mine coolies who had finished their contracts, or labourers who had run away from their employers because indigenous rubber gardens offered

48 For example in Hulu Sungai. Lindblad 1988a:63.

49 Lindblad 1988a:63, 68; Touwen 1991:145; Thee Kian Wie 1977:22-4; W.G. Huff 1993:297.

better pay (Pekelharing 1925:28; Purwanto 1992:261). Recruitment of workers from China or Java was beyond the financial capacity of smallholders, which made them dependent on the supply of free labourers offering themselves for work in the province. East Sumatra and Palembang profited from the fact that there were many ex-coolies from the estates, who would offer to work for smallholders. This made labour in these residencies generally cheaper than it was in Jambi or West Kalimantan.

When rubber prices were high, the *bagi dua* system was used, under which hired tappers were paid half of the amount of latex they brought in. The owners and the workers negotiated about who would provide the tapping equipment, buy the acid, and prepare the latex. Usually, these expenses were shouldered by the owner, who also provided lodging for the tapper. Circumstances which could influence the deal ranged from the rubber price and the productivity of the gardens, the supply of labour in the region, the remoteness of the rubber holding, and the presence of wild animals, particularly tigers (Pekelharing 1925:12-4). Sometimes the owner would supply additional perks, such as free meals or consumer goods (rice, salted fish, lamp oil, or salt). As an added gesture, the tappers would sometimes be allowed to pick up the scraps, the earth-rubber (*bekuan*).[50]

The *bagi dua* system was not without its shortcomings. It was in essence an effective system of sliding scales, adapting the salary of the worker to the revenue, so that the tapper shared the market risk. The system became precarious in times of high prices, when the owner was dependent on help from tappers who were very much in demand. They might mistreat the trees by tapping too intensively: they cared for the revenue, not for the trees. When prices were low, there was no gain to be earned for tappers, unless they received a higher share. The whole system can be seen as a consequence of labour shortage. The strategy of the smallholders when trees were damaged by tapping too roughly (which decreased the latex production of the tree) was simply to plant more trees.[51] Not all observers were equally convinced that rough tapping was so bad. While some fumed that the trees were being tapped to death ('an alarming destruction of capital'), others observed that the trees could stand a remarkable amount of maltreatment (Ozinga 1940:253-4; Rutgers 1925:10).

In the 1920s, managers of estates frequently complained that coolies ran away before their contract had expired: the wages that could be earned in the smallholder rubber gardens were often higher, for example ranging from 1

50 ARA Kol, MvO 223, J.R.F. Verschoor van Nisse 1931:130.

51 ARA Kol, MvO 212, J. Tideman 1928:9; Boeke 1955:139; *Landbouwexportgewassen* 1931:97; Velsing 1925:210.

to 3 guilders a day in the early 1920s, compared to less than 0.5 guilders at rubber estates.[52]

Different types of indigenous cultivation also competed for labour. For example, in the early 1920s, when the price of coffee in Palembang was higher than that of rubber, tappers were inclined to move to the coffee gardens. When rubber prices were low, owners would tap the rubber themselves or with their families, since they could not find tappers who would work for 50 per cent of a product that was so hard to sell. Often they had too many trees and were forced to hire tappers, to whom a larger share of the product was paid to compensate for low prices. Thus, tappers could negotiate a larger share: *bagi tiga* (2/3) and even *bagi empat* (3/4) or *bagi lima* (4/5). If the worst came to the worst, owners pawned their rubber gardens to tappers.[53]

One consequence of this system was that supply was relatively inelastic in response to price changes in regions where there was sufficient labour supply. Even with a very low profit margin, rubber would still be offered on the market: the rubber garden was there without any extra cost (the peasant had waited for five to six years before the trees could be tapped), so he would settle with a tapper for a very small profit margin. Indeed, he was often forced to do so because of outstanding debts. This is important, and means that the output volume of indigenous rubber was not much influenced by the price level on the world market. As we will see, the surtax on indigenous rubber in force in 1934-1937, which in fact only lowered the profit margin though prices had recovered, failed to reduce the indigenous rubber output to the quota set in order to comply with the IRRA.

Smallholder reaction to the Depression

Cease or increase?

After 1927 the prices of raw materials dropped. In 1927-1932 the rubber price plummeted to its lowest level: to a mere 7 per cent (Figure 11). This makes it worthwhile to take a more detailed look at the individual rubber provinces during the Depression.

As the rubber boom in the 1920s had brought affluence, the Depression profoundly shocked the indigenous rubber economy. Prices kept on falling

52 ARA Kol, MvO 211, O.M. Goedhart 1926:11-3; Polak 1979:20, appendix 24.

53 According to Resident Verschoor van Nisse, the rubber price had to be 0.06-0.08 guilder per kg in order to allow a *bagi lima* deal. *Bagi dua* would require a rubber price of more than 0.2 guilder. He also estimated that wages had to be at least 1 guilder per day for Javanese tappers to offer their services; he suggests that this would imply a rubber price of around 1.3 guilders per kg in New York. ARA Kol, MvO 223, J.R.F. Verschoor van Nisse 1931:131-2; MvO 214, J.L.M. Schwaab 1933:184; MvO 224, W. Steinbuch 1933:183.

until the flow of easy rubber guilders, or *hujan mas* (gold rain) as the Malays called it, nearly dried up. Although import goods and foodstuffs had also fallen in price, many smallholders could not repay their debts and were severely hit.

We can observe two different reactions to the decreased revenue brought by low prices: cost reduction, and diversification to other food crops. Of course, imports of all kinds of luxury goods and textiles quickly came to a full stop. Cost reduction was achieved mainly by laying off hired tappers and using family labour for the tapping of the trees. Consequently, after 1930 the *bagi dua* system of equally sharing the produce between owner and hired hand was used less frequently. Also, as we have seen above, the share of the produce ceded to the hired hand increased when prices were low. This is one of the reasons that, in some regions, export volumes of products with declining prices still increased.[54]

Many smallholder producers switched back at least partially to the cultivation of food crops and other products, their sights set on self-sufficiency in rice or, if they cultivated other cash crops, choosing the crops that made the best prices. Even when self-sufficiency in food was feasible, selling export crops had become vital to earn cash needed to pay taxes and repay loans (*Markt* 1932:91-2). For example, in 1928 peasants in Palembang reduced rubber tapping, abandoning their rubber gardens, but continued to cultivate coffee, which retained a slightly higher price level.[55] Therefore, coffee export volumes from Palembang have a more constant character and show a peak quantity of 27 million kg in 1932, the year in which rubber reached a ten-year low in export volume (Table 44.3) (Clemens et al. 1992:64). Other Palembang peasants concentrated on crops that had already been planted as 'catch crops' between maturing new rubber trees. For example, pineapples, which had once been cultivated as a catch crop, achieved the status of a major export crop after 1927, leading to about 500 tons of exports in 1934 (of which 300 tons went to Batavia) (Atmodipoerwo 1934-35:468-9, 483).

In 1933 Resident J.L.M. Schwaab stated that, as a consequence of the decline in prices on the world market, rubber cultivation in Palembang had ceased to make sense to the indigenous population, whereas indigenous coffee cultivation (in the upland regions) was, at a lower level, still an important source of income. This quick response to world market prices was typical of Palembang. The volume of rubber exports declined steadily in 1927-1932 (Figure 12). Hounded by low prices, by 1933 many Javanese tap-

54 ARA Kol, MvO 265, J. Oberman 1938:39-40. *Bagi dua* becomes *bagi tiga* when the owner collects only one-third of the produce. Thus production could continue at no extra cost to the owner (only a smaller profit margin), at times of low prices.

55 ARA Kol, MvO 214, J.L.M. Schwaab 1933:172.

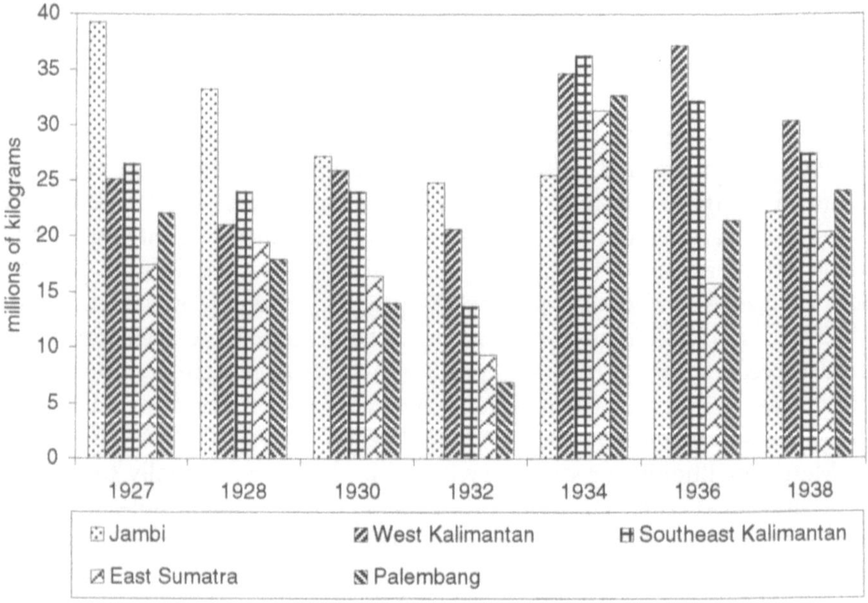

Figure 12. Indigenous rubber exports from major provinces, 1927-1938 (Table 44.3).

pers had returned to Java and many trees were left untapped. In Palembang, rubber was tapped only in areas where it was the only source of income, and peasants used family labour rather than hired workers (in Rawas, Musi Hulu, and Musi Ilir). The local government tried to entice Javanese tappers not to return to Java by exempting them from corvée labour or income tax and offering them pieces of land – to little avail, mainly because the best land was already occupied.[56]

In a situation similar to that in Palembang, indigenous rubber exports from East Sumatra also decreased quickly in 1928-1932 (Figure 12). It has been argued in the literature (Van der Eng 1996c:236) that coolie settlers from Java, who had formerly been employed on the rubber estates, maintained and increased their production of rubber because they lacked experience with other products. The output volumes in Figure 12 show no evidence for this.

Rubber exports from Jambi in those years declined as well, similar to those in Palembang and East Sumatra. Smallholders decreased their output of rubber in 1927-1932 from almost 40 million to less than 25 million kg (Figure 12). Smallholders in Jambi did not switch to other export crops, but turned their attention to the cultivation of food crops and the collection of

56 ARA Kol, MvO 214, J.L.M. Schwaab 1933:3-4, 173.

forest products, particularly rattan.[57] In response to lower incomes, imports quickly decreased in Jambi, from 11.5 million guilders on average in 1924/28 to 5.5 million guilders in 1929/33 (Table 25.2). The quick changeover in Jambi to self-sufficiency in rice is shown by the fact that rice imports decreased from 4.18 to 2.23 million guilders in these two five-year periods.

Jambi was a province where household labour quickly replaced hired workers. To reduce costs, the entire household was engaged in tapping, including the wife and children. The rubber gardens were still tapped, because the owner often had no other cash income (which he needed to pay taxes or to buy off corvée labour duty) or because he had debts to a Chinese middleman (Tideman 1938:195). These circumstances meant that Jambi rubber could be produced very cheaply with household labour, but production could not expand to compensate for the low market price. In 1923-1924, there had already been more rubber trees in Jambi than the population could possibly manage to tap (Pekelharing 1925:13-4; Rutgers 1925:16-7). Paradoxically, the scarcity of labour in this province and the absence of the *bagi dua* system with hired tappers conspired to produce a relatively sluggish, unresponsive supply of rubber in Jambi after 1927.

West Kalimantan maintained the most constant output volume of rubber during the years 1927-1932 (Figure 13). Of course, export revenues seriously decreased, but quantities were relatively stable. While Jambi had been the province with the largest indigenous rubber exports in 1927-1932, after 1934 West Kalimantan and Southeast Kalimantan stole a march on it (see also Figure 12). One of the explanations for this expansion is that the rubber trees planted during the previous rubber boom had now reached maturity and could be tapped. In Southeast Kalimantan, as in Jambi, household tapping replaced tapping by hired labour. Out of work, a large number of rubber tappers from Hulu Sungai (the main indigenous rubber region) left to try their luck in other places, especially on the eastern coast, hoping to find a better means of making a living.[58] The fact that the rubber output of West Kalimantan barely decreased during the Depression is also explained by the fact that rubber was cultivated in the interior, where – as in Jambi – smallholders did not switch to other export items. Copra exports from West Kalimantan originated from the coastal regions.

Copra was a different story: West Kalimantan copra had a high percentage of vegetable oil and fetched a relatively good price. Copra, like rubber, was produced using the *bagi dua* (*bagi tiga, bagi empat*) system.[59] Copra

57 ARA Kol, MvO 223, J.R.F. Verschoor van Nisse 1931:129; Pekelharing 1925:10; Rutgers 1925:21.

58 ARA, NHM 9088, VvS 35 (Banjarmasin 1929):2-4.

59 ARA Kol, MvO 265, J. Oberman 1938:40. See also Ozinga 1940:118-9.

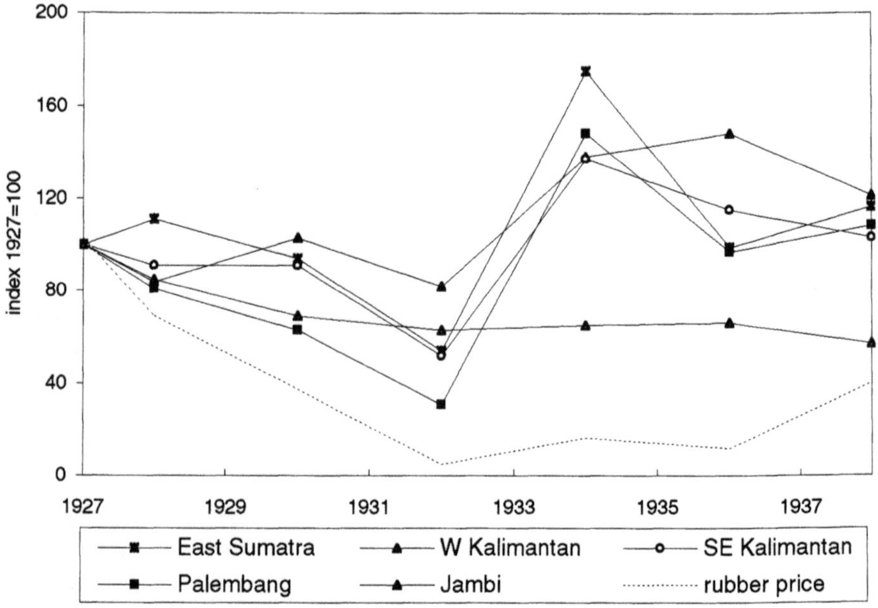

Figure 13. Volume index of indigenous rubber exports, 1927-1938 (1927 = 100) (Table 44.3).

exports increased from about 70,000 tons per year in 1929/31 to almost 77,000 tons per year in 1932/33. After 1934 this high level of copra exports was not reached again. Roughly speaking, the export volume of copra did not decrease in the 1930s (Table 51).[60]

The inevitable conclusion seems to be that the regions which had been highly dependent on rubber during the rubber boom years (and imported foodstuffs at that time) started growing food crops in a search for self-sufficiency (Jambi, West Kalimantan). In the meantime, by reducing costs, they kept up high levels of production. Regions that had alternative cash crops tended to oscillate between the various crops, choosing to harvest and market whichever product fetched the best price (particularly in Palembang). Interestingly, in Sumatra, rubber output decreased during the Depression, while in Kalimantan it did not.

It has been suggested in the literature that the peasant tended to increase his supply every time the price he received per unit dropped (because he depended on the sale of rubber for his living).[61] This does not hold true for

60 For figures including Java see Clemens et al. 1992:70-1.

61 Compare Oberman's remark: 'One had to increase production in order to maintain income.' ARA Kol, MvO 265, J. Oberman 1938:75.

the Depression years. In Palembang and Jambi particularly, smallholders gradually decreased their output of rubber between 1927 and 1932. Even in Jambi, often called a typical rubber province, output decreased (Figure 13). This underscores the importance of doing an analysis by province. Several years later, during the IRRA period, other rubber-producing provinces *did* increase their production, as we will see below.[62]

What happened after 1934: the rubber restriction

After 1934 the prices of rubber and copra slowly began to recover (Tables 34 and 35). But indigenous rubber producers immediately faced another hurdle which depressed their profits: the government's surtax on indigenous rubber. In 1934 international negotiations to restrict rubber supply resulted in the International Rubber Regulation Agreement, an agreement between Britain, France, India, Thailand, and the Netherlands Indies (McFadyean 1944).

The Netherlands Indies government had to restrict the rubber output of the colony to meet the agreed quota. A quota was set for each rubber estate based on its production in previous years.[63] But restriction of indigenous output was difficult to achieve, since there was no exact registration of rubber holdings (number of trees, productivity per garden). An individual quota for each smallholder was therefore not feasible. After lengthy discussions, the colonial government tried to reduce exports by levying a temporary surtax on indigenous rubber (*bijzonder uitvoerrecht op bevolkingsrubber*), in 1934-1937. The initially imposed export surtax was 10 guilders per 100 kg for dried sheets, 5 guilders for uncleaned scraps, and 7 guilders for all other types of rubber. Later, the rate was changed several times; in December 1936 it was 57 guilders for all types (Tideman 1938:198). Gonggrijp, in his well-known textbook on the economic history of colonial Indonesia, voices his criticism of the surtax as follows: 'This rubber restriction [...] constitutes a protection of European industry against the small indigenous enterprise, which generally holds a stronger position' (Gonggrijp 1938:230).

In spite of this, the taxation did not reach its goal. Smallholder production increased considerably, even after the tax rate had been raised repeatedly.

62 Thus, higher prices lead to larger supply and lower prices lead to smaller supply in the market. In the past, the 'backward-sloping supply curve of effort and risk taking' was often quoted as a sign of irrational market behaviour ('limited wants in Eastern society'). For example, if prices went up, quantities produced did not increase. When this occurred, however, it was not due to irrational behaviour but the result of a lack of social mobility, which reduced the incentive to increase earnings. This obviously was not the case in the rubber provinces. Boeke 1946:49; Higgins 1955:63, 72.

63 De Graaff gives an excellent account of the political background of the rubber restriction in Indonesia. De Graaff 1997:494-549. See also Van Vuuren 1941:12-7.

Rubber prices rose, and many smallholders wanted to use this opportunity to compensate for their smaller profit margin by producing more. They could do so because they produced with very flexible cost factors (Bauer 1948:56-73).

As the rate of the surtax was regularly adjusted by the government, it tended to rise month by month. This was an extra incentive for the peasant to hold no rubber in stock. The final levels of the surtax were quite dramatic: in December 1936 the surtax was 57 cents per kg at a time when the market price was 73 cents per kg, leaving the producer a meagre 16 cents for each kg sold (De Graaff 1997:512; Lindblad 1988a:74). The surtax yielded roughly 14 million guilders in Palembang and 10 million guilders in Jambi during 1934-1937. In Southeast Kalimantan, the revenue was 2.4 million guilders in 1934, 5.5 million guilders in 1935, and 11.5 million guilders in 1936. Eventually, total revenue from the surtax on indigenous rubber amounted to 83,146,624 guilders.[64] The top year of rubber output in the 1930s was 1934. One of the reasons was that in anticipation of the surtax (which became effective on 1 July 1934), many smallholders quickly raised their output, a move which can be observed in all major rubber-exporting provinces. Only in Jambi did the volume of indigenous rubber exports remain at a remarkably constant level, probably hamstrung by shortage of labour (Tables 43 and 44.3; Figures 12 and 13).[65] The planting of extra rubber trees must be ruled out as a reason for this suddenly expanding output volume, because a rubber tree takes five to six years before it begins to bear. There were many old rubber gardens which had been tapped irregularly during the Depression and were now put into full production. Furthermore, trees that had been planted during the rubber boom now came into production. Peasants who had other sources of income may also have hoarded rubber, which could now be sold.[66]

One of the outcomes of the discussion about the 'unfair' taxation of indigenous producers was the Rubber Fund. The revenue from the surtax on indigenous rubber was poured into this fund, which provided for all kinds of social overhead capital (roads, schools, hospitals) and agricultural extension projects, such as quality improvement techniques for indigenous producers. In Palembang, Jambi, West Kalimantan, and Southeast Kalimantan a great many roads, bridges, and irrigation works were constructed from this revenue (see also Chapter VI).

Another indirect effect of the surtax on indigenous rubber was that it served as an incentive for smallholders to start processing their own rubber. Initially the export duty was levied as a fixed sum per kg (adjusted upwards later on), whereas the dry rubber equivalents of slabs were fixed at a rate of

64 ARA Kol, MvO 278, W.G. Moggenstorm 1937:192; Van Suchtelen 1939:140.
65 East Sumatra estate rubber production also reached a peak in 1934 (Tables 36.2 and 44.2).
66 See for example Lindblad 1988a:68, 71-2.

70 per cent. Therefore, in practice, if a load of rubber slabs contained 80 per cent rubber, the additional 10 per cent could be sold untaxed. Not unnaturally, peasants started to dry their rubber to evade the rubber tax.[67] The percentage was raised several times by the government and when the norm was raised until it neared 100 per cent in 1937, it made no sense to export anything but dry rubber.[68]

With the surtax faltering, in 1937 another method was instituted to reduce rubber output: a system of individual quotas for each producer.[69] The registration of indigenous smallholdings during 1935 and 1936, which was essential for setting the quotas, was also financed from proceeds from the export duty (the Rubber Fund). This can be viewed as a violation of the government's pledge to spend this revenue on welfare projects benefiting the peasants (Thee Kian Wie 1977:28). A system using harvest licences ('coupons') was introduced, which quickly gave rise to a lively new type of trade: large numbers of smallholders chose not to harvest their rubber but to sell their coupons to others. Prices ran as high as 45-50 guilders for a coupon for 100 kg rubber, causing a large inflow of cash into Southeast Kalimantan in 1937, where the output quota was relatively high.[70] This is reflected in a slowly decreasing output of rubber in Southeast Kalimantan (Table 44.3).

When rubber smallholders started to dry rubber on a large scale, they were suddenly committing themselves to processing the raw material to a degree which had been inconceivable in the 1920s. They compressed the slabs using mangles, and dried the rubber sheets in smoking huts. This was an important step towards the development of a processing industry. Indonesian smallholders bought their rubber mangles mainly in Singapore, where a substantial Chinese industry of rubber mangles had emerged (W.G. Huff 1993:292, 298-300). The peasants could apply for rent-free loans for the purchase of mangles from the Rubber Fund. In Jambi, smallholders had bought 596 ribbed and 660 unribbed mangles by 1936. In Southeast Kalimantan, at the end of 1936 there were 380 smoking huts, and as 1937 drew to a close this number had risen to 734. Mangles aside, the Rubber Fund was also used to propagate the preparation of *smoked sheets* in smoking huts and to discourage the use of alum (which yielded rubber of poor quality). In every *marga* (municipality), a demonstration smoking hut was built.[71]

67 Clemens 1989:230-4; Lindblad 1988a:74-5, 1994b:74; Ozinga 1940:297.

68 ARA Kol, MvO 225, Ph.J. van der Meulen 1936:80; Lindblad 1988a:75.

69 ARA Kol, MvO 278, W.G. Moggenstorm 1937:192; Van der Eng 1996c:238; Thee Kian Wie 1977:26-9; Touwen 1991:145.

70 ARA, NHM 9088, VvS 43 (Banjarmasin 1937):1-6; Lindblad 1988a:75.

71 Many mangles were bought from Lindeteves and from the Industriële Maatschappij Palembang (Industrial Company of Palembang). Aside from discouraging the use of alum and stimulating the drying of 'smoked sheets' in demonstration huts, instruction was given on the

These were the ways the rubber restriction provided funds for social overhead expenditure and improved the quality of indigenous rubber. The surtax of 1934-1937 did not decrease output volume, while during the Depression output volume decreased drastically. Supply was a good deal more inelastic than demand. But on closer scrutiny, a small recovery in price could raise output even while profit margins were squeezed by export duties.[72]

Origins of smallholder export growth

Mentality of the rubber smallholder

Smallholder export agriculture expanded quickly and followed its own course in price, quality, and elasticity of supply. But why did it develop as it did, hardly influenced by European estates and generally finding its own path, thereby consolidating the dual basis of economic growth?

On occasion the rise of smallholder rubber in Sumatra and Kalimantan has been viewed in the literature as a reaction to the arrival of Western enterprise. Indonesian peasants, in this view, 'reacted to the challenge of the West'.[73] There are legitimate grounds for wondering whether the indigenous population in East Sumatra, more than in Jambi or West Kalimantan, was aware of any 'challenge of the West'. Few Batak people came across any Europeans. Indigenous peasants in East Sumatra probably encountered more (ex)coolies than Europeans, but it would be rather extreme to assume that such encounters constituted a major transfer of Western know-how, as the coolies by and large did unskilled labour. Moreover, the peasants may not have been well disposed to Western ideas, as they had to deal with bottlenecks created by the estates (such as shortage of land). This was compounded as government agricultural extension schemes were relatively rare in this province, most public expenditure being directed towards the estates.

Only in the techniques of rubber tapping did indigenous peasants benefit from the presence of the estates, taking advantage of the skills of ex-estate coolies. These were hired by indigenous smallholders to tap their rubber gardens. At the Hayup Estate in Southeast Kalimantan, it was possible to learn to

---

use of mangles, coagulation tanks, and acetic acid. ARA Kol, MvO 225, Ph.J. van der Meulen 1936:72; ARA, NHM 9088, VvS 43 (Banjarmasin 1937):3-4.

72 Contra: 'The supply by these producers, therefore, was *inversely* proportional to the price of rubber minus export duties.' Boeke 1946:49. Compare McFadyean 1944:x. That Boeke did not analyse the general problem of price elasticity of supply has been previously noted. Mackie 1980:300.

73 Booth 1988:17, 221; Thee Kian Wie 1977:17-8, 48; Wertheim 1956:96. (Booth mentions that the 'demonstration effect of the large European estates' has been widely accepted as one of the causes of the rapid growth of smallholder production.)

tap for the sum of 2.50 guilders. This is a concrete example of a demonstration effect, which of course only occurred during the initial rubber years. It should not be overrated as an example of technology transfer, because it stands to reason that ex-coolies were all too willing to spread the techniques themselves. And had there been no ex-estate coolies, rubber tappers from Malaya would have spread the technique, which was not very difficult anyway.[74]
East Sumatra Batak started cultivating and exporting rubber not in imitation of large estates, but because intermediary traders persuaded them to do so. The process was similar to smallholders in Jambi, Palembang, West Kalimantan, and Southeast Kalimantan. They were stimulated to plant rubber gardens by Singaporean intermediary traders, whose intention was to copy the success of rubber in the Malay Peninsula. There were historical ties, both cultural and commercial, between the Sumatran and Malayan Malays. *Haji* returning from Mecca, some of whom had worked in Malaya to earn money for their journey, spread the news about rubber. Also, Chinese traders in East Sumatra had close relations with the Chinese trading community in Singapore.

In this sense, smallholder export agriculture can be viewed as a continuation of Asian commerce as it had been functioning for centuries. Indigenous trade gained from continuing influence from Asian traders; although it may have been modified by the presence of European enterprise, it certainly was not swept away by it in the wake of colonialism.

Indigenous industry was less efficient. Careless tapping reduced the rubber output of indigenous trees considerably. Ex-estate coolies probably tapped a little more carefully than other tappers. Resident J. Oberman reported in 1938 that indigenous rubber production in West Kalimantan showed marked influence of European-learned skills, because former estate coolies were more practised, and tapped without inflicting wounds in the bark of the trees.[75] If this was the sole significance of the estates for local entrepreneurship, it was not much.

As Myint explains, the production of export crops is often stimulated by imports of consumer goods, which create new wants (Myint 1980:38). An example of this in the Outer Islands was Chinese and Arab traders offering rubber seeds and seedlings. These middlemen supplied credit, and placed orders for forest or agricultural products. They imported consumer goods to remote areas which they dispensed as advance payment for export crops. Also, peasants cultivated rubber as a cash crop, which provided money income that could be used for purchasing consumer goods. In this light, rubber cultivation was not inspired by the estates, but should be attributed to the close proximity of Singapore, the emerging rubber cultivation in

74 Lindblad 1988a:61; Velsing 1925:26. Compare Luytjes 1925a:27, 40.
75 ARA Kol, MvO 265, J. Oberman 1938 appendix 3 p. 2. Compare Luytjes 1925a:27.

Malaya, and the availability of consumer imports.[76]

In East Sumatra, the manifest presence of European enterprise must not distract our attention from the dynamic entrepreneurship of East Sumatran smallholders themselves. The latter were open to new crops, such as rubber, but had a tradition of a diversified package of agricultural exports. De Waard stresses the importance of smallholder copra production in North Asahan, of which almost 50 per cent was exported to the Netherlands, Germany, and Scandinavia – instead of, like rubber, being mainly directed towards Singapore. The indigenous population in East Sumatra also produced *pinang* nuts (De Waard 1934:285). Another crop produced was sago, mainly in Bengkalis, where Chinese owned the sago washeries and exported the produce to Singapore. Pepper, which had been an indigenous export product in the early nineteenth century, had almost completely vanished from East Sumatra in the 1930s.[77]

Copra, *pinang* nuts, and the various vegetables and potatoes cultivated on the Karo plateau were important to the indigenous economy since they remained relatively stable during the Depression. After 1930, smallholder rubber suffered badly, here as everywhere else in the Outer Islands. 'Many gardens were abandoned or only tapped sporadically. People awaited better times', writes Resident H.E.K. Ezerman describing these years. Although copra prices were bad as well, peasants kept on planting new trees, even against the express wishes of the Zelfbestuur (indigenous government) and the European government, who tried to promote the cultivation of food crops. On the Karo plateau, there was a relatively high number of Chinese peasants.[78]

Of course, these export figures do not give us any information about whether the revenues from trade were earned by peasants or by intermediary traders. But it is safe to conclude that East Sumatra smallholders did *not* produce significantly less for the export market than did smallholders in Palembang or Southeast Kalimantan. They showed a similar economic dynamism.

Who were the agents of change?

Chapter III surveyed the development of estate agriculture in East Sumatra and several other Outer Provinces. Let us briefly summarize the effects of estate agriculture on the indigenous economy in East Sumatra. Three conclusions stand out. First, infrastructural developments (the construction of

76 Van Gelder 1950:428; Thee Kian Wie 1977:18, 1989b:142.

77 Anderson reported that in 1822, 3.5 million kg of pepper was exported from Deli, Bulu Cina, and Langkat! De Waard 1934:286. See also Pelzer 1978:2-5.

78 ARA Kol, MvO 188, H.E.K. Ezerman 1933:260-1.

roads, railways, ports, and telephone and telegraph lines) were the most important structural growth effect of the estates. These provisions were constructed either as backward linkages by estates to facilitate transport, or funded by the government to attract new estate agriculture to economically backward regions.

Second, the influx of the enormous coolie population to East Sumatra had a large impact on the region itself ('migration linkage'), but the impact was smaller outside the estate area. It is difficult to determine how many ex-estate workers swarmed out into the wider region, offering labour to smallholders or engaging in small-scale trade. This group on its own was not very large, but was supplemented by traders and seasonal labourers coming directly from overseas destinations.

Third, the major *negative* effect of the estates on the indigenous economy was the shortage of land. In the estate area, around Deli, Langkat, and Simalungun, indigenous rubber cultivation could not expand because most of the arable land was occupied by the estates (and tobacco cultivation was prohibited). This was a problem only in the relatively small estate area in East Sumatra, however. In the south of this province, in Labuan Batu and in Asahan, indigenous agriculture expanded as it did in other provinces, producing large volumes of rubber and copra. Most of the rubber was exported from Siak, Bengkalis, or Pakanbaru and destined for Singapore (De Waard 1934:285).

The estates did not figure as 'agents of change'. There are few signs that the smallholder population imitated technology or production methods. The European estates did not encourage peasants to set up export production of their own. Smallholder export production developed along a path *parallel* to estate agriculture. Even though smallholders indubitably benefited from roads and bridges, or from increased government spending, they did not follow examples that were too complex and too alien to them to imitate. Only occasionally is it possible to speak of an 'information linkage'.

If it was not because of the estates, why did smallholders develop exports of rubber, coffee, or copra, and how did they come into contact with overseas buyers? The answer to these questions must be sought in the functioning of the network of intermediary trade. The intermediary trade in cash crops was both an essential precondition and a strong incentive for the growth of indigenous export production. The middlemen conveyed market demand, offered advance payments to smallholders, and stimulated the cultivation of export crops by the indigenous population. The middleman himself sold the goods to trading houses, trading agents, or other traders. For example, almost all indigenous rubber was sold by Chinese intermediary traders in Singapore. Before reaching Singapore, the product had often already passed through the hands of three or four traders, some of them Chinese, some of them Arab or Malay (Clarence-Smith 1998:32; Post 1996:612-3; W.G. Huff 1993:299). Everywhere in the archipelago, Chinese intermediary traders were part of the scene, but there were regional differences in the level of hegemony (which occasionally even resulted in a monopoly) of Chinese traders. Other population groups, such as the Malays, the Minangkabau, and the Bugis, also participated in small-scale intermediary trade, as did other foreign groups such as Arabs and Indians.

A slipshod style but a shrewd sense of profit

Intermediary traders must be viewed as the agents of change in the Outer Islands, much more so than European estates or colonial civil servants. Below, I will describe the credit and debt mechanisms functioning in intermediary trade, paying ample attention to Chinese middlemen. There was a lack of any alternative low-interest credit facilities in the Outer Provinces. The custom of exchanging future harvests for import goods or money sometimes led to permanent indebtedness during the Depression. Were the indigenous smallholders innocent and gullible producers who put themselves submissively into the hands of middlemen? The existence of a class of indigenous traders already contradicts such an assumption (Post 1996:612-3). Let us consider five examples of statements that can be made about indigenous entrepreneurship:

1. There was a very rapid expansion into new crops in many regions. This can be observed in rubber cultivation, which in the years 1912-1917 spread quickly, even though it takes 5 to 6 years before the trees start bearing. There was also a very quick change from Arabica to Robusta coffee in 1914-1915, when the latter, improved variety of coffee was introduced into the colony (Touwen 1991:142-3, 177).
2. There was widespread use of false scales (*dacin*): but the producer who sold, often negotiated an extra margin of profit, taking the deceit into account.[79] This prompted Luytjes to observe: 'The real weight of the picul often increases when one goes further into the interior' (Luytjes 1925b:11).
3. Initially, when prices were very high, both producer and intermediary trader tended to deliberately add impurities (stones, rubbish, old shoe soles) to the rubber, the coffee, or the pepper in order to increase its weight. This may not have been a very prudent move towards their purchasers in the long run, but it displays a certain shrewdness induced by high demand.
4. The surtax on indigenous rubber levied in 1934-1937 taxed wet rubber 'slabs' as containing a fixed percentage (initially 60 per cent) of dry rubber. Stung into action, producers started to dry their rubber, because if slabs contained a larger percentage of rubber, the additional percentage would be sold

[79] In rubber, the middleman could cheat the producer by 20 to 30%, according to Pekelharing. Pekelharing 1925:20-1; Rutgers 1925:13.

without being subject to taxation (and the customs official would not notice). Dry rubber exports developed as soon as it was profitable to the producer to do so.

5. After 1937, when the individual restriction was introduced and every peasant had an individual export quota imposed, a lively trade in coupons developed. The quota for rubber exports was based on the size of the rubber gardens, and many smallholders saw more profit in trading their export rights than in producing. In Southeast Kalimantan, where the rubber quota had been overestimated due to a miscalculation (this was later adjusted), an enormous trade in coupons arose in next to no time.

All this happened between 1910 and 1940, a relatively brief period. Before 1930 there was an open trade policy which allowed cheap imports and did not stimulate processed exports. This explains why there was little incentive for smallholders to invest in processing activities, and why import substitution did not get off the ground. These items are often used as indicators of incipient industrialization, of which there was little evidence in the Outer Islands. Also, smallholder production was admittedly primitive, adulterated, rather chaotic, and small-scale. Given the circumstances, there was little reason for smallholders to raise production to Western standards. Be that as it may, the above observations show that market incentives quickly led to revised strategies.

Naturally there were many regional differences in the Outer Islands in the commercial behaviour and business acumen displayed by smallholders. Reviewing the cluster of provinces which displayed successful indigenous entrepreneurship, it is no exaggeration to conclude that the entrepreneurial attitude of smallholders was intelligent and flexible. The indigenous entrepreneur was not irrational or passive, but had a highly dynamic and adaptable attitude towards the changing conditions of the smallholder economy. In order to get a better view of the situation in which smallholder exports developed, the next section analyses the network of intermediary trade.

The network of trade

The Chinese in the Outer Islands

Since the Chinese were so important in the intermediary trade, it is instructive to survey the distribution of the Chinese population in the Outer Islands and their history in the colony. Most (63 per cent) of the Outer Islands Chinese lived in East Sumatra, Bangka, and West Kalimantan: 29 per cent, 18 per cent, and 16 per cent, respectively, of all Chinese in the Outer Islands. In Riau, Palembang, and Aceh, close to Singapore, and Southeast Kalimantan and Manado, a smaller share of Chinese had settled (between 3 and 6 per cent).

Two factors may account for the distribution: distance from Singapore (Maluku and Timor and Dependencies) and the active trading acumen of the indigenous population (in West Sumatra and Tapanuli) (Table 16).

Among the Chinese who lived in the Outer Islands, four groups of occupations stand out. During the census of 1930, the largest group stated their profession as 'trader' (32 per cent of all Chinese in the Outer Islands). Among the other frequently mentioned occupations were 'peasant' and various activities in small industry and handicrafts (shopkeepers, artisans, craftsmen, mainly in the towns). It must be kept in mind that a census constitutes merely a static record. More importantly, a person could have various occupations at the same time. For example, a shopkeeper could call himself a trader; a trader could also be a peasant. Another large group of Chinese were employed in estate agriculture or tin mines (as coolies). Finally, in certain regions Chinese earned a living by fishing (*Volkstelling* 1933, VII:130). In contrast, the only major occupation of other foreign Asians (residents of Arab or Indian descent) was trading.[80] In Java, the Chinese also earned considerable sums in revenue farming, obtaining contracts from the government for a fee which was significantly lower than the incomes proceeding from them. Pawnshops, opium and salt distribution, and gambling houses were examples of revenue farming (*pacht*) (Brown 1994:143). Revenue farmers became rich entrepreneurs, envied especially by the poorer indigenous population. In the more sparsely populated Outer Islands, their position was less conspicuous (Vleming 1926:13).

The first large group of Chinese to arrive in the Outer Islands after 1850 were the coolies. They were mainly recruited between 1860 and 1914, and were concentrated in the estate area in East Sumatra. Large numbers of Chinese coolies were also employed in the tin mines of Bangka and Belitung. These immigrant Chinese (*singkeh*) were signed up to work for European companies on a three-year contract. Since only some of the coolies renewed their contract, while estate production expanded, a continuous inflow of more coolies was necessary.

Many Chinese traders were new immigrants from China and only a few had worked as coolies before they became traders.[81] In 1930, of all recent Chinese immigrants the number of *singkeh* Chinese (mostly traders or coolies,

80 Of all 36,153 other foreign Asians that lived in the Netherlands Indies in 1930 (mainly Arabs and Indians), 19,054 (52%) stated 'trade' as their profession during the census. *Volkstelling 1933*, VIII:33.

81 Some estate coolies got involved in trading after their contract had expired. It is difficult to determine the exact number of coolies who settled in the area. In Chapter III it was estimated that in 1919-1939 an aggregate of 127,000 coolies (Javanese, Chinese, and others) settled in East Sumatra and surrounding regions. Very few of these were Chinese. After 1900, the number of Chinese coolies decreased in comparison to Javanese coolies. In 1919, of the 250,000 coolies, only

some in other occupations) was the largest in Sumatra. Of all *singkeh* Chinese in Sumatra, 35 per cent worked on estates or in the mines.[82]

Of the Chinese who earned a living in smallholder agriculture and fishing, the largest number lived in settlements in Riau and West Kalimantan. Bagan Siapiapi, a flourishing fishing community in East Sumatra, should be mentioned here as well. In Riau, only a stone's throw away from Singapore, many Chinese, in addition to their trading activities, were active in cultivating rubber, gambir, and copra. They also earned money in the timber industry (*panglong*) (Vleming 1926:11-3, 227-39). On Bangka and Belitung, Chinese families that had lived in colonial Indonesia for several generations (*peranakan*) were engaged in pepper cultivation. Of the 11 *peranakan* and 7 *singkeh* smallholders per 1,000 in Sumatra, most of them lived on Bangka and Belitung, but a number of *singkeh* Chinese peasants were also counted in Riau (across the sea from Singapore). Most of the smallholders in Kalimantan lived on the west coast of West Kalimantan, either cultivating cash crops for export or vegetables in the vicinity of towns.[83]

While coolies and peasants were to be found in a few dominant areas, Chinese who were traders could be found virtually everywhere in the archipelago. The Chinese in trade were often Hokkien Chinese (from Amoy and surrounding areas), whereas in business and small industry, Hakka and Cantonese tended to predominate (*Chineezen* 1917:480-6; Vleming 1926:14). The indigenous population regarded them as 'aliens' in the sense that they were immigrants who seemed to belong to a different racial group, embraced a different religion, and spoke a different language. This perception is illustrated by the situation in Java. Although *peranakan* Chinese often spoke Malay and were closer to the Javanese than the *singkeh*, the Javanese considered them much more foreign than for example Batak, Minangkabau, or Ambonese. The Chinese belonged to what was considered to be a different ethnic group. They did not live in a specific region but were widely spread throughout urban areas, were usually excluded from Indonesian nationalist organizations, and were seen as having a homeland across the ocean (Suryadinata 1993:78-80). The Agrarian Law of 1870 ruled that Chinese were barred from owning land outside towns, which effectively prevented their integration with the peasant population. In a few areas outside Java, such as Padang and parts of eastern Indonesia, Chinese communities spoke Indonesian (or a regional Indonesian language) as well, but these

10% were Chinese and in the subsequent decades, this number decreased further. This results in approximately only 650 (or 5% of 127,000) Chinese ex-coolies in 1919-1939.

82 In Sumatra in 1930, there were 197,000 *singkeh* Chinese (in the other Outer Islands 37,000) and 29,000 *peranakan* Chinese (in the other Outer Islands 27,000). *Volkstelling 1933*, VII:130.

83 The Siauw Gap 1989:178; *Volkstelling 1933*, VII:130-1, 348.

communities were usually smaller and more isolated than those in Java. In Bangka and in West Kalimantan, however, *peranakan* Chinese communities spoke predominantly Chinese dialects, even if they had been in Indonesia for centuries. The *singkeh* Chinese in Belitung, Riau, and East Sumatra also spoke Chinese (Mackie 1976:7).

Present in the archipelago for many centuries

Chinese traders and seafarers had been visiting the Indonesian archipelago for many centuries. Although overseas trade and settlement were effectively forbidden by the Ch'ing dynasty between 1644 and 1894, several concentrations of Chinese immigrants developed, notably in West Kalimantan and on Bangka. Two surges of immigration increased the number of Chinese in colonial Indonesia: one between 1860 and 1890 with the inflow of Chinese labourers into the estate area in East Sumatra and into the tin islands, and the other after 1900 when the colonial government abolished restrictions on Chinese entry and settlement (Mackie 1976:4).

When Chinese merchants appeared, in the second half of the nineteenth century, it was not long before they took over the traditional export trade from other trading groups, such as the Bugis from South Sulawesi. Internal cohesion and mutual loyalty have been named as characteristics that facilitated their quick penetration of trading. They were helped by their willingness to adopt improvements in sailing techniques, such as European-style square-rigged vessels. The Bugis stuck to their traditional prahus and rapidly lost business to the Chinese. As the Chinese did not contribute to any Muslim revivalism, they enjoyed the favour of the colonial authorities (Lindblad 1988a:11).

Another important aspect of Chinese entrepreneurship is the Chinese tendency to form cooperative communities of common interest, or *kongsi*. Although Chinese culture is characterized by a large degree of individual independence and self-interest is never sacrificed, the Chinese had the reputation of organizing themselves into *kongsi* which could serve both family and commercial interests. On Bangka and Belitung, this cooperative tendency was recognized by the Europeans as a good way to organize the labour force for mining.[84] Profitable though it was, the *kongsi* should not be regarded as a reliable, well-organized business association – it was too loosely organized to develop a major role in capital investment or large-scale enterprises. Brown describes the attitude towards finance in these 'tight, family-controlled networks' as follows: 'Capital was a tool of *circulation* rather than for accumulation' (Brown 1994:255-6; Cator 1936:59-61). It has been generally acknowledged that the networks of family businesses in Southeast Asia did (and still

84 ARA Kol, MvO 246, J.E. Edie 1928:66; Somers Heidhues 1992:79.

do) exert a large influence; these firms had difficulty in making the transition from family to professional management. Chinese organizations, to the present day, are not group-oriented but family-oriented (Fukuyama 1995:74-95).

Credit and delivery

It was a sign of the importance of Chinese middlemen that indigenous rubber production in Jambi, Palembang, Riau, East Sumatra, and West and Southeast Kalimantan was almost completely directed towards Singapore. Chinese traders in East Sumatra and Kalimantan had close commercial relations with the Chinese trading community in Singapore. The Singapore connection supplied credit and eventually received the product (Thee Kian Wie 1977:18). How did this trade function in practice? Generally speaking, it is possible to differentiate between wholesale trade, intermediary trade, and retail trade. The retail trader bought export products from the smallholder and sold import goods in the interior regions. Wholesale traders, often members of European trading houses, shipped the export product to foreign markets and supplied the intermediary trader with credit or import goods for the domestic market. The function of the intermediary traders (or middlemen) was to serve as the link between wholesale trade and retail trade, or between trading houses and smallholder producers (Cator 1936:68, 175, 244).

Huff has described the trading system as 'the interlinked deal' or 'bookkeeping barter'. This arrangement emphasized the relationship between the Chinese middleman in colonial Indonesia and the Chinese buyer in Singapore. An interlinked deal implied that credit was supplied in the form of goods, mainly simple textiles and rice, which were advanced to finance the purchase of rubber output. The Chinese middleman who went into the provinces (also called an 'outport dealer') liquidated his debt in Singapore by delivering rubber, but usually incurred a new debt before the existing debt had been cleared away. The debt owed to the Singapore Chinese agent or trading house was never completely repaid and the credit relationship was usually perpetuated. This semi-barter relationship meant that high transaction costs were avoided; it was based on close personal ties (often family ties) between the trader and the agent, which involved a high degree of trust (W.G. Huff 1993:297-8, 1994:92-3, 96-7, 280).

Turning to the peasant, in addition to this semi-barter trade, the middleman also supplied advance payments (in goods and in cash). In this way, through a small chain of intermediary Chinese and indigenous traders, the smallholder rubber producers received payment for their deliveries. The middleman handed over goods up to a certain value, which the peasant could reimburse later. This was common practice in southern Sumatra, particularly among coffee and pepper growers and collectors of forest products. In the rubber regions of Sumatra, there were essentially three ways indigenous producers sold their product: to middlemen who penetrated the interior, or to local traders, such as *toko* holders and local sultans, some of whom were rubber cultivators themselves (or agents of other traders, or remillers); or they brought their rubber to a nearby market (or to an exporter or remiller in a town) themselves. Middlemen who bought rubber were often boat-owners, suppliers of goods to oil companies, agents for imported textiles, beverages, and foodstuffs, or car drivers.[85] This again shows that in Sumatra, many Malay traders were involved in trade in the interior. 'In most rubber provinces, a powerful indigenous class of traders develops, which is able to cope with the Chinese influence' (Luytjes 1925b:2, 10).

At a later stage, when the use of money had spread in the Outer Islands, peasants desired a money income to spend on luxury goods or house improvements. Advance payments in cash were given to smallholder producers as a loan, with the entire future harvest or even the peasant's land holdings as collateral. Through this mechanism, when harvests failed, the Chinese middleman could claim the gardens as his property, and the peasants were placed in a position of ever-increasing dependence.

Import trade

The discussion above shows how import goods served as credit goods in the semi-barter trade, or were traded by import traders who depended on loans from import firms and banks. In other words, the import trade was based mainly on credit. Import firms supplied wholesalers with goods on credit, trying to assess their creditworthiness beforehand. Wholesalers supplied retail traders, and these small traders, after having sold their goods, repaid the credit to their suppliers, either in money, or by supplying raw materials or forest products.

NHM agents often did business with Chinese retail traders. They repeatedly mentioned Chinese small traders in their annual reports, especially when times were rough. These Chinese traders, who sold European import goods to indigenous consumers, often received loans from the NHM. The information on the Chinese import trade in East Sumatra reflects the economic situation: the margins of import traders were so narrow that when prices fell, they could not sell without loss. The *singkeh* traders in particular often went bankrupt (Figure 14). The recession of 1921-1922 and the Depression of 1929-1934 resulted in two peaks of bankruptcies – amongst which almost 70 per cent were Chinese. Dramatic though this may seem, many of these bankrupt one-man trading companies probably bounced back after a while. As Brown writes:

85 Purwanto 1992:304, 1993:120; Thomas and Panglaykim 1976:143-7.

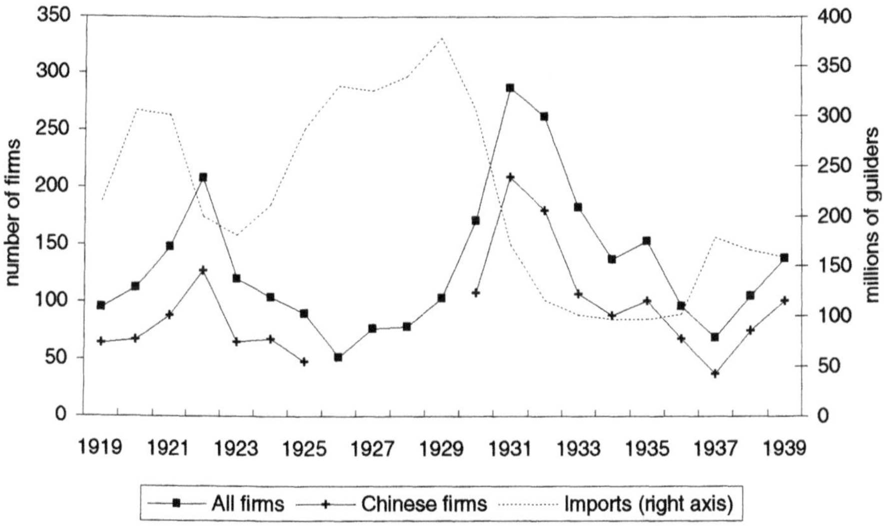

Figure 14. Bankrupt import traders in East Sumatra (NHM clients) as compared to total foreign imports, 1919-1939 (Table 61).

> Bankruptcy had only a vague meaning. Chinese social and business relations were so closely intertwined that bankruptcy did not necessarily mean the cessation of trading. But bankruptcy in one enterprise might mean the sudden collapse of numerous others, both large and small. (Brown 1994:256.)

East Sumatra was a slightly exceptional case in intermediary trade. In this province, Chinese middlemen also supplied rice and other import goods to the labour force on the estates. Amongst these traders there was cut-throat competition: there was no sudden burst of affluence in the 1920s when harvests were good or prices were high, as in the indigenous rubber regions, since the coolies earned a fixed income. The class of Chinese traders in Medan was not wealthy and powerful as some of the successful Chinese traders in Palembang, Banjarmasin, or Macassar, but consisted of a large army of small traders who secured only small margins of profit.[86] The high number of bankruptcies in East Sumatra also reflects the small-scale character of import trade. Those going bankrupt were middlemen who served small consumers. The large import firms, which supplied agricultural machinery, were less vulnerable (Figure 14).[87]

86 ARA, NHM 9126, VvS 502 (Medan 1926):88.

87 ARA, NHM 9122, VvS 448 (Macassar 1924):21; NHM 9124, VvS 484 (Medan 1908):1-2.

Weak position of foreign firms

How was the situation in a province where not estates but indigenous producers supplied the bulk of the trade? In many provinces, branches of European firms were set up to collect indigenous export products. For example, in Halmahera (Maluku), the Moluksche Handelsvereeniging traded with indigenous producers. Indigenous coffee producers in West Sumatra traded with both local and foreign trading firms in Padang. Local firms bought up coffee and other products, such as copra, directly from the growers. They were on close, personal terms with the indigenous peasants. Often cash advances were made, enabling the producer to plant seeds and cultivate a garden, thereby securing the trader's future supply. Foreign or 'outsider' firms could not do without intermediaries, since they were ignorant of the customs and trading techniques of the indigenous population. These firms therefore used Chinese or Minangkabau intermediaries, paying them in advance. They often had to pay a higher price for the export commodity, since intermediary traders kept their own profit-margin. Sometimes intermediary traders even sold their load for a higher price to another European export firm, claiming that this rubber belonged to a family member, and keeping the first foreign firm waiting for another few weeks. On the other hand, the big foreign firms had an advantage on the international market, being able to deliver directly to foreign buyers, which was out of the question for smaller local firms (Colombijn 1991:165-8, 1994:79-84).

The NHM and other Dutch trading companies often bought goods from Chinese and Malay intermediary traders in consignation and sold them in Europe. Thus, European wholesale firms transported from the major ports of the Netherlands Indies to Europe, and Chinese firms with agents in Singapore sold to Singapore. The coexistence of these two trading networks gave rise to increasing competition in the export trade.[88] The intermediary trader could choose whoever offered the best price, This competitiveness is illustrated by attempts to gain an edge, such as the establishment of the Rubber Union in 1926. The Rubber Union was an initiative of KPM and was intended as a way to bypass Chinese middlemen in the rubber trade and seize a share in the remilling industry. It had a starting capital of seven million guilders and established four rubber factories in Sumatra and Kalimantan. However, rather exceptionally in the history of KPM, the colonial government did not support the initiative: by issuing the Rubber Ordinance the government set standards for the quality of rubber and prohibited submerged transport

88 ARA, NHM 9086, VvS 14 (Banjarmasin 1907):4; NHM 9128, VvS 516 (Manado 1898):4.

under rafts in rivers (the *rakit* trade was the method used by the Malays).[89] This government intervention worked in favour of Chinese traders. The last remilling factory run by the Rubber Union was closed down in 1931.[90]

In Sumatra, Chinese traders had relatively easy access to peasants. Traditionally, Chinese peddlars (*klontong*) travelled to the remotest villages, selling all kinds of small goods. Later many Chinese opened small retail shops (*warung*) in villages, from which they also bought rubber from indigenous producers. They did not have a free hand in this, as many Malays were active in internal trade, preventing the Chinese from monopolizing it. In the late 1920s, rubber *pasar* were established – mainly for Chinese rubber traders, since Malay middlemen bought rubber directly from the individual producer (Thomas and Panglaykim 1976:142).

In Kalimantan, Chinese as well as Bugis and European traders concentrated on commerce with the outside world. They did not make easy contact with the Dayak of the interior. This trading arena was initially reserved for Malay merchants, who sailed up the rivers and employed business procedures that were in accordance with local custom and preference. In both West Kalimantan and Southeast Kalimantan, Chinese trading gradually moved further into the interior, sometimes outflanking the Malay intermediaries.[91]

Trade along rivers

A central role in internal trade on rivers was played by the *cintu* (*tjintoe* or *chinchew*), the cargo clerk who had an office on a paddle boat, often seated on the roof of the cabin. This clerk was employed by a trading house or by the company that owned the ship, and supplied credit to traders who travelled to the inner regions of the province. In the late 1920s in Southeast Kalimantan, he would carry as much as 6,000 to 10,000 guilders with him for this purpose. No interest was expected on the loans, but of course shipment costs had to be paid for cargo transported (Broersma 1927:206).

One example of how the river trade worked is given by Broersma (1927), who describes a trip on a small KPM steamer. He sailed inland on the Mahakam River in the Kutai area in eastern Kalimantan. During this trip he met a trader, Jinal. It is not clear whether Jinal was a Malay or a Banjarese, but he bought his cargo from a Chinese trader and sold it, in Samarinda, to another

89 In the expansion of its network of shipping lines in the archipelago, KPM was effectively-supported by the government, as is shown in A Campo 1992:364-5.

90 ARA Kol, MvO 212, J. Tideman 1928:257; MvO 223, J.R.F. Verschoor van Nisse 1931:122-5, 168; W.G. Huff 1994:204.

91 The fact that Chinese traders were often Buddhist, and as such more easily made contact with the animist Dayak than did the Malay traders who were Muslim, may have been one cause of the increasing penetration of Chinese traders into the interior. See also Lindblad 1988b:13, 185; Ranken 1989:189.

Chinese trader. Jinal aimed to buy rattan somewhere upstream and to sell this rattan in Samarinda. He borrowed 1,000 guilders from the *cintu*, to which he added 400 guilders of his own money. After some bargaining he bought 100 piculs of rattan for 13 guilders per picul (21 cents per kilogram) from a Chinese shopkeeper in Muara Muntai. The *cintu* gave Jinal a fair deal on the shipping fee, 100 guilders instead of the usual 1.20 per picul (which would have amounted to 120 guilders). Back in Samarinda, a few days later, the trader collected several bids on his load of rattan (but he kept them all secret). He eventually sold the rattan for 15 guilders per picul. However, his profit was not, as we would expect, a hundred guilders: the scales used by his client short-weighted his 100 picul load to 95 picul – resulting in a loss of 75 guilders for Jinal! This surprised Broersma (as it may surprise us), but Jinal himself was used to the differences in scales. He was content with his 25 guilder profit. Added to profit from his other deals, it made his trip worthwhile.[92]

This anecdote illustrates that, since the traders made their deals with borrowed money, they were more concerned with a quick turnover than with large profits. Taking advantage of the keen competition between European importers, intermediary traders could borrow large sums of money. In Java, cases were known of traders with private capital of less than 5,000 guilders who enjoyed credit with various wholesale dealers amounting to 100,000 guilders (Cator 1936:70).

The *cintu* had been typical for river trade during the latter part of the nineteenth century, and endured in Kalimantan. In Sumatra, the *cintu* disappeared gradually during the twentieth century, because Chinese intermediary traders, who had adequate financial resources, started to visit peasant producers frequently (Allen and Donnithorne 1957:243).

The trading system, based on a chain of credit and delivery obligations, was safe and simple, as long as prices were good. But it was not foolproof, and problems could arise at any link in the chain. Usually, the Dayak in interior Southeast Kalimantan did not have their supply of forest products or cash crops in stock, and had to be prompted by an advance payment from the Malay trader before they would start collecting or harvesting. Advances were supplied to them in tobacco, rice, or other foodstuffs like dried fish, or other exchange goods. If by some unforeseen circumstance the delivery was not ready in time, the trader ran the risk of not being able to collect the goods

92 1 picul = 61.76 kg. Broersma 1927:214-5. False scales in the hands of Chinese traders have been common practice for 2,500 years. Only recently, on 1 December 1995, the Chinese government stipulated that, at least in Beijing, verified scales have to be used. *NRC Handelsblad* 30 November 1995. Other mentions of false scales in rubber regions: Pekelharing 1925:20-1; Rutgers 1925:13.

and, in turn, pay back his own loans (Broersma 1972:217-8). Later, during the 1930s, cooperatives were organized to make the supply chain more efficient and less dependent on middlemen (for example in Minahasa, in Manado).

Competition in trade

European import firms counted on the Chinese trading network for the distribution of their goods. Before 1925 almost all imported products, such as rice and other foodstuffs, yarn and silk, and other consumer goods, as well as machines, were bought from the European import firms by Chinese traders. These traders then turned their attention to the inland peasants. After 1925, several European trading houses took the plunge and started delivering directly to indigenous buyers (Vleming 1926:241). The intermediary trade in peasant cash crops was handled by Chinese everywhere in the Outer Islands, but their role was not equally large in every region.

Cator wrote in 1936 that 'it may be said that every variety of trade and commerce of Riau, Indragiri, Lower Jambi, and East Sumatra, is almost exclusively in the hands of the Chinese' (Cator 1936:245). But elsewhere in Sumatra, the Chinese were challenged by other population groups which were experienced in trade (Post 1996:612-3). In West Sumatra, many indigenous Minangkabau were traders. Through their matrilineal tradition the women managed the family possessions and the men could roam the country and carry on trade.[93] They brought coffee, copra, and rubber to coastal trading centres, most often to Padang, but sometimes also to Palembang and even to Singapore. The number of Chinese inhabitants in Padang was therefore smaller than average in the Outer Islands: in 1930 the Chinese population in West Sumatra formed 0.9 per cent of the total population of the province, whereas the average in the Outer Islands was 3.7 per cent.[94]

In Palembang and Jambi, a large proportion of Malays were active in trade. The flourishing trade in Palembang offered a good occupation for all and sundry and there were many Arabs and Indians involved in intermediary trade. In the north of Sumatra Batak and Gajo were involved as well.[95] Nevertheless, while inland trading in Sumatra was carried on by Arabs or Minangkabau or Malays in Palembang, transport to Singapore was almost

93 ARA Kol, MvO 166, W.A.C. Whitlau 1926:132; MvO 170, A.I. Spits 1937:98; Colombijn 1991:167, 1994:53-4.

94 Other provinces in which the Chinese made up only a small part of the population were South Sulawesi (0.8%), Tapanuli (0.5%), Bali (0.6%), and Timor (0.4%). See Table 16.

95 Arabs had been coming to the Netherlands Indies since the introduction of Islam, for purposes of trade, or in connection with a pilgrimage to Mecca, or for other reasons. Most of these Arabs came from the South Arabian region of Hadhramaut. They originally settled in Palembang or on the north coast of Java. Eventually the largest concentrations of Arabs were on Sumatra and Kalimantan. *Arabieren* 1917:55-6; Fernando and Bulbeck 1992:216; Post 1996:617.

totally handled by Chinese. Interestingly, the rich trade from Palembang was divided into Chinese trade destined for Singapore and Batavia on the one hand, and trade directed towards the Javanese harbours of Semarang and Cirebon on the other, the latter mainly carried out by Malay traders.[96] Jambi was one area where the number of Chinese fluctuated strongly: in 1920, 2,780 Chinese were counted in Jambi; by 1930 this figure had risen to 8,830, but in 1933 it had dropped again to 5,200 (Cator 1936:245). The indigenous population in this province in the 1920s went from strength to strength in the rubber trade. Indigenous traders purchased the product as wet slabs in the interior, transported it using river rafts to the town of Jambi, and sold it to Chinese or other agents. By the late 1920s, the Chinese had regained most of the interior river transport.[97]

On Bangka and Belitung, where Chinese formed the largest ethnic category in the regional population in the Outer Islands, the Chinese ran practically all intermediary trade.[98] In West Kalimantan, likewise, the relatively high percentage of Chinese played an essential role in the economy. Almost all rice imports entered the province through the intervention of Chinese traders. These Chinese had originally been attracted to the gold found in West Kalimantan, or had been recruited by the sultans, but like the Chinese in the old settlements on Bangka, who had come for the tin but had got involved in pepper trade in the nineteenth century, the Chinese in West Kalimantan had taken up trade and agriculture.

West Kalimantan depended heavily on rice imports. During the years 1926-1937, West Kalimantan imported almost as much rice as Bangka, even though on Bangka, most of the tin mining coolies were dependent on rice imports and in West Kalimantan there was very little European enterprise.[99] Many Chinese trading houses in Pontianak concentrated almost solely on the import of rice. The local alluvial gold (washed from the river) was also bought by Chinese merchants, even though their prices were often reported to be lower than those of the Java Bank. Despite their entrenchment, while Chinese traders expanded their contacts in the interior, many of the traders who went up the rivers to trade with the Dayak were Malay. These Malays were long settled in West Kalimantan and during earlier times had ruled the Dayak.[100]

In Southeast Kalimantan, as in Palembang, trade was a field open to a large number of foreigners: Banjarmasin was home to Malays, Javanese,

96 ARA Kol, MvO 223, J.R.F. Verschoor van Nisse 1931:125; Vleming 1926:241.

97 ARA Kol, MvO 223, J.R.F. Verschoor van Nisse 1931:125; Cumming 1924:2; Pekelharing 1925:20-3.

98 ARA Kol, MvO 246, J.E. Edie 1928:43; MvO 249, J.C. Mann 1938 chapter I p. 2, chapter IV sub 4; MvO 259, J.C.M.L. de Wilde de Ligny 1932:5.

99 *Landbouwexportgewassen* 1931:247. Table 56.2.

100 ARA Kol, MvO 261, H. de Vogel 1918:25-6; MvO 264, K.H. van Prehn 1933:14.

Madurese, and Arab traders. These groups had already been trading in the archipelago in the many centuries before the Europeans arrived. As in West Kalimantan, the Chinese dominated the coastal trade (Broersma 1927:17; Reid 1988, 1993).

The further east we go, the farther removed we are from the dominance of Singapore. Analysis of interregional trade shows that South Sulawesi, Maluku, and the Lesser Sunda Islands sent much of their foreign trade to Java first (either directly or via Macassar), and also received most of their imports from Java. This is reflected in the ethnic groups involved in trade. In South Sulawesi, besides Chinese, many indigenous Bugis and Macassarese were very much involved in internal and interregional trade (Post 1996:612). Admittedly the well-known prahu traders could not reach all inland peasants, since the rivers in South Sulawesi and Manado were only navigable a few miles upstream from the sea, but all along the extensive coastlines of Sulawesi, Bugis prahus were a familiar sight.[101]

The Bugis, known from the nineteenth century for their inveterate trading tradition, sailed to every outport of the archipelago, occasionally even as far as Padang on the western coast of Sumatra. But their special domain was the eastern archipelago. In the voyage to and from Java, Bugis traders were important, providing a small-scale trading network. Bugis prahu captains generally undertook only a few trips per year (they were mostly peasants) (Pelras 1996:3, 254-68, 311-4). By contrast, Chinese traders were full-time transporters. They also travelled through the interior, opened up shops or started small industries or handicraft businesses. Nevertheless, the Bugis were a force to deal with in shipping. The KPM even had special, cheaper, freight rates during the east monsoon because this was the season that Bugis prahus competed with them. Chinese trading firms dealing with Bugis had a special contact-man, *papalele*, who took care that the prahu captain did not sell his load to someone else upon entering a port (Turpijn 1933:118). Thus, by dealing with small traders, several large Chinese trading firms flourished in Macassar, the trading centre of eastern Indonesia.[102]

Madurese and Bugis sailing vessels concentrated on domestic trade, including Java, but their role in transport to Singapore was much smaller. This is explained by the fact that Chinese money-lenders in Singapore preferred to do business with Chinese intermediary traders. While at some point Malay rubber traders did manage to find access to agents in Singapore, the Bugis did not (Cator 1936:176).

101 Around Macassar, some 80% of the prahus were Bugis, and 20% Macassarese. In 1934, 13,804 prahus were counted in Macassar. Turpijn 1933:118-20.

102 ARA, NHM 9122, VvS 448 (Macassar 1924):17; VvS 450 (1926):18; NHM 9123, VvS 456 (1932):12.

The power of the middleman

It often happened that the smaller entities in this chain of credit and purchase, the smaller traders or the peasants, could not repay their debts. Either by receiving advance payments for export production or by accepting too many import goods, they had become financially indebted to the middleman or trader. In several regions a dependency on Chinese middlemen developed, since more and more Chinese could claim to own part of a rubber or copra garden when loans were not repaid. When prices fell during the Depression, many businesses collapsed.

The 'copra contracts' in Minahasa (Manado) are an exceptional example of how Chinese middlemen fortified their position during the 1920s and increasingly gained power in the prevailing commercial situation. In this region, at times when copra prices were high, smallholders bound themselves to Chinese middlemen by written contracts. They promised future deliveries in return for a large sum of money. This form of credit was formalized in 'copra contracts'. The middlemen had the financial backing of European and Chinese trading houses, which supplied the credit and took the raw copra.[103] The smallholders received a loan amounting to 2,000 guilders or more. In return, they had to repay their creditor in quarterly instalments of copra up to a certain value (plus 6 per cent interest), either for the duration of the contract or until the loan was repaid. This long-term agreement, which could cover a period of up to 15 years, was usually made in writing, often by a notary public. Sometimes the creditor was given the right to set his own hired workers to work in the garden during the period of the contract. These contracts were called the *sewa kebun* (rented garden contracts). In other contracts, no period was specified and the smallholder had to make deliveries after every harvest, until the borrowed money was returned, tied to the local market price of copra. The upshot was that copra smallholders had committed themselves to deliver to middlemen for a long period, which made them vulnerable to changing circumstances (Van Hall 1943:124-5; Leirissa 1996: 269-72).

As long as the copra price was high, until 1929, the system benefited all parties. The contracts made copra cheaper for middlemen than at the *pasar*, and smallholders earned increasing amounts of money. The trouble set in after 1930, when Minahasa smallholders earned very little from deliveries at the local market price. They lost their income and struggled to pay the interest, let alone pay the quarterly instalments, which had to be made in copra to a certain value (Leirissa 1996:271-2). The middlemen could claim the harvest of the coconut groves for prolonged periods, up to many years. In consequence, Chinese traders practically owned the coconut groves (even though

[103] ARA Kol, MvO 304, F.H.W.J.R. Logeman 1922:66, 70; Van Hall 1943:124.

Chinese could not own land according to the Agrarian Law of 1870). Only after 1936, when the colonial government gave financial backing to the copra sales cooperative, the Producten Verkoop Centrale (PVC, Product Sales Organization), and improved the legal basis for the contracts in the Copracontracten Ordonnantie (Copra Contracts Ordinance) of 1939, was the financial situation of the Minahasa peasants ameliorated. Under such circumstances the Chinese middlemen dug themselves into a strong position, owning stores and storage houses in many villages.[104]

It should be remembered that Minahasa was a relatively well-developed region, where many missionaries were active and where education was widespread. Many Minahasa smallholders spent the money earned from copra contracts on education or housing. They often chose to work together in *mapalus*, cooperatives for agriculture or construction.[105] It does not seem justified to blame the situation on the mentality of the indigenous population.

As Resident M. van Rhijn wrote in 1941, cooperative banks rescued the region: there were many villages where a cooperative bank would 'forestall a peasant from borrowing at a warung, which would lay the foundation for a mountain of debts for many years'. But in 1941 there were only 35 of these banks. 'Far too few', judged Resident Van Rhijn. 'There should have been 20 times as many!'[106] Perhaps the government could have taken steps at an earlier stage to prevent the negative repercussions of copra contracts, but the government intervened only when indebtedness had occurred on a very large scale. Apart from issuing the Agricultural Ordinance in 1918 to regulate landownership, the government did little to prevent the Chinese hegemony in trade, or to protect indigenous producers.

Casting a cursory eye over the Minahasa situation may create the impression that indigenous peasants were led astray by sharp Chinese entrepreneurs, and that they were eventually saved by the various measures taken by cooperatives and by the government. Leirissa, who uses copra contracts to study the interaction between the traditional and modern sectors of the economy, argues that it was state intervention that 'prevented copra production from collapsing after the Depression years' (Leirissa 1996:276).

In my opinion, this picture paints the intervention of the colonial government in too positive a light. Undoubtedly the economic situation in Manado did deteriorate seriously during the Depression, yet it was only in 1936 that firm measures were taken. In the meantime, Minahasa smallholders had to lay off contract workers and cut down on all luxury expenses. They travelled

104 ARA Kol, MvO 308, M. van Rhijn 1941:104.
105 ARA Kol, MvO 306, A.Ph. van Aken 1933:94; Leirissa 1996:271.
106 ARA Kol, MvO 308, M. van Rhijn 1941:96.

so little that more than half of the public bus lines had to be discontinued.[107] Government officials had the authority to loosen credit relationships by supplying loans. Copra contracts were clearly identifiable IOUs in a region where Dutch influence was exceptionally high.

Chains of credit

In many other provinces, debt relationships might have been just as serious, and the government did little to intervene in the powerful networks operating in internal trade. For example, the Dayak in inland West Kalimantan were often in debt to the credit-supplying Chinese middleman, 'as if linked to him with a silver cord'.[108]

The dependency on Chinese middlemen was not so evident in other regions in the archipelago. In his recent study on Selayar, an island south of Sulawesi, Heersink concludes that in the emergent copra trade during the late colonial period, the Chinese did turn out to be a dominant economic group, linking Selayar with large European export firms – but on the island itself, they did not become real powerholders (Heersink 1999:10-1, 147-51, 166-71, 325-6). Similarly, in the Sumatran rubber provinces, rubber smallholders often depended on Chinese creditors, but had not bound themselves so completely and irreversibly to traders as Minahasa smallholders had done. Moreover, Chinese middlemen who imported goods were very vulnerable themselves, particularly when the Depression set in, as they had their own creditors to repay.

The rubber trade

In the rubber trade, the role of Chinese intermediary traders in providing market access may have been even more important than in the copra trade. To test this it is necessary to make a brief survey of the rubber trade. Middlemen provided market access. Through the credit system, they encouraged peasants to plant rubber trees. There were many indigenous traders in the internal rubber trade, which reduced the Chinese hegemony and its negative effects on indigenous peasants: the peasants were protected by the many links in the chain.

Rubber traders were very important in the introduction of smallholder rubber production in Sumatra. Since the rubber trade was concentrated in Singapore, traders stimulated the development of rubber gardens first in areas that were accessible by river from the sea south of Singapore, such as Riau, Jambi, East Sumatra, as well as West and Southeast Kalimantan. Although initial information on rubber cultivation in the 1910s was also spread by way of

107 ARA Kol, MvO 306, A.Ph. van Aken 1933:22-g, 72.
108 ARA Kol, MvO 265, J. Oberman 1938:75-6.

haji, Malay traders, and European estates, middlemen financed the further expansion of the rubber trade by supplying credit (Touwen 1991:144-6).

During the rubber boom years, in the 1920s, a growing number of indigenous (mostly Malay) traders brought rubber down from the interior to harbour towns. Transport of rubber by road was rare at that time. Rubber was mostly shipped by prahu or raft along the rivers. This method had the advantage that no loss of weight occurred, since the wet slabs were kept in the water. These traders sold the rubber in harbour towns, such as Palembang and Jambi, either through an agent or directly to an export trader.[109] In Palembang, the main export traders in 1925 were Firestone and three Chinese firms: Chie Sing Chan, Tan Kah Kee, and Chin Seng Chan. The latter two purchased rubber for their own remilling factory in Singapore.[110]

KPM took steps to block the development of a Chinese monopoly in the archipelago rubber trade. As noted above, it participated in the Rubber Union. Lining up for battle, KPM at first lowered freight prices to attract rubber exports by Malay traders to Singapore. When this did not produce the desired effect, it made efforts to mediate between Malay traders and the purchasers in Singapore, so that these two parties came into contact without the intervention of Chinese middlemen. Advances of up to 70 per cent of the freight value were given to traders, and Singapore agents were offered a free return journey to Singapore. Eventually, in 1926, KPM transported 40 per cent of all rubber exported from Jambi to Singapore.[111] This victory was short-lived, because in the late 1920s when the transportation of rubber under river rafts was prohibited and prices fell, the Chinese regained their position and KPM's share decreased. Increasingly, a division along ethnic lines developed: the Malay population produced the rubber, the Chinese traded it.[112]

Incomes of Chinese traders

It is difficult to estimate the income level of the Chinese traders. The aggregate data on incomes in colonial Indonesia include a number of other occupations in which Chinese were found. Also, there were many poor traders and relatively few wealthy traders. Most Chinese traders were not very powerful at the outset.[113] It has already been established that the small trader himself

109 A detailed scheme was drawn up by Thomas and Panglaykim, distinguishing tappers, collectors at the retail level, collectors at the wholesale level, and remillers. Thomas and Panglaykim 1976:144. See also Purwanto 1992:308-11.

110 ARA Kol, MvO 225, Ph.J. van der Meulen 1936; ARA Openbaar Verbaal 2868 (27 August 1926), Report A. Luytjes:4-5. An extensive case study on the enterprise of Tan Kah Kee can be found in Brown 1994:105-15.

111 ARA Kol, Openbaar Verbaal 2868 (27 August 1926), Report A. Luytjes:15-6. See also A Campo 1992:364-5.

112 ARA Kol, MvO 223, J.R.F. Verschoor van Nisse 1931:125; Clemens 1989:219.

113 The wealthy *comprador* (Portuguese: intermediary) were few and far between in the Outer

was often in debt to his supplier or creditor. Many of the small Chinese traders were *singkeh*, newcomers to Indonesia. They started their enterprise with little capital, mostly using money borrowed from relatives at high interest rates (Vleming 1924:139).[114] With the increased inflow of poor *singkeh* Chinese, the gulf between *singkeh* and *peranakan* Chinese widened. The immigration of new Chinese produced a flow of labourers, who were seldom skilled or trained in specific professions, and who definitely did not bring with them an influx of capital. This is in sharp contrast to European colonization, which was accompanied by capital and intellectually and technically highly trained personnel.[115]

Despite such drawbacks, the opportunities available to *singkeh* to acquire an influential position in the indigenous economy were numerous, even though they were vulnerable to price changes and associated developments. Since intermediary trade formed an indispensable link between wholesale trading houses (for both imports and exports) and the indigenous population, the position of Chinese traders was very important. They knew the needs and interests of the peasants, and developed a trading network that reached to the remotest corners of the Outer Islands (Vleming 1926:12, 140-1).

The income of Chinese and other foreign Asians in the Outer Islands in 1930 has been estimated by Polak at 320 guilders per capita, compared to 66 guilders per capita for the indigenous population. In Java, these figures were 310 and 55 guilders per capita. These are simply averages and the income distribution may have been very unequal: many *singkeh* Chinese were indisputably poor. Maddison estimates income per capita in 1929 in Indonesia as 301 guilders for Chinese and other foreign Asians, and 61 guilders for Indonesians.[116] According to Remer's (1933) estimates of inter-war Chinese transactions, remittances to China were running at 25 million guilders in 1930 (Maddison 1989b:24; Booth 1989:80). Polak estimates aggregate income of all 717,000 foreign Asians (including other Asians) in the Outer Islands in 1930 to be 229 million guilders (about 310 guilders per capita).[117]

Islands. These influential Chinese mediated between European banks and traders, and the Chinese trade. They looked after the Chinese personnel of European firms and were confidential agents for both parties. They played a more important role in China and Singapore and elsewhere in the Netherlands Indies. The comprador were usually of influential and wealthy descent. Vleming 1926:151-2.

114 At the beginning of the twentieth century, many Chinese left their home country tired of the poor living conditions, the risk of owning capital in China, and high unemployment. Many came from Fukien (Fujian) and Canton (Kwantung), provinces where agriculture was hampered by poor soil. *Chineezen* 1917:480-1.

115 Cator 1936:252. See also Van Doorn 1985:148, 1994.

116 Creutzberg 1979:77; *Volkstelling* 1933, VII; Van Ours 1995; Maddison 1989a, 1989b:24, 35.

117 Polak 1945:62, 70-1; Creutzberg 1979. All foreign Asians in Java in 1930: 196 million guilders. Total: 425 million guilders.

Chinese hegemony in intermediary trade

In 1933, Resident W. Steinbuch of Jambi wrote: 'The intermediary trade, which is exclusively in the hands of Chinese, is a very speculative and risky business. When prices are low, the profits are, in part owing to the relatively high transportation costs from the place of purchase to Singapore, extremely small.'[118] This quotation succinctly characterizes intermediary trade in the archipelago. Chinese traders were present everywhere but they did not make an easy living.

This section reviews the economic function of the Chinese in Outer Islands trade during the late colonial period. It looks at the role of Chinese traders in provinces that produced raw materials for the foreign market. The Chinese trading network and sales organization, which developed and extended into the most remote corners of the interior during these years, was of vital importance to the development of indigenous foreign exports. In many regions, Chinese traders had a hegemony in intermediary trade. Many of the traders were *singkeh* Chinese who were obliged to start small. Increasing affluence could be discerned among some traders, but there was great risk involved in trading.

The Chinese were often identified as a class of intermediary traders. But, contrary to Steinbuch's remark about Jambi, they were not the only intermediary traders. In Sumatra, besides Chinese middlemen there were also Minangkabau and a number of Arabs involved in small-scale trading. The Minangkabau, for instance, did not give an inch to Chinese competition. During the recession of 1920-1922 many Malay intermediary traders in West Sumatra went bankrupt, which allowed Chinese the opportunity to expand their business in this province. Although European traders expected that Minangkabau traders would also be replaced by Chinese, this did not happen. It was 'unthinkable' that Chinese could drive out the Minangkabau from small-scale intermediary trade.[119] In Kalimantan there were also Arab, Bugis, and Malay traders, both in the interior and along the coast. In Sulawesi, besides Chinese and Arabs, there were many Bugis, Banjarese, and Madurese active in internal and interregional trade.

In the literature, the strong position of the Chinese in colonial Indonesia has been attributed to their higher level of literacy and their large numbers in the nineteenth century, which gave them an advantage in the 'bazaar economy', where, unlike in the fragmented small-scale indigenous market, paper credit financed long-distance trade in an effective manner. This 'bazaar economy' developed in the nineteenth century throughout the Indian Ocean

118 ARA Kol, MvO 224, W. Steinbuch 1933:186-7.
119 ARA Kol, MvO 166, W.A.C. Whitlau 1926:20-1.

and East and Southeast Asia (Booth 1998:311; Ray 1995:552). In Sumatra and Southeast Kalimantan, it is clear that indigenous traders had a good position in interior trade, but could not expand in the interregional and overseas trade to Singapore, in which the Chinese dominated.

Not all the competition came from these indigenous trading groups. Chinese activities in retailing and imports during the inter-war period were also increasingly challenged by the Japanese (Furnivall 1944:430). Dick calls the Japanese economic penetration of colonial Indonesia after the outbreak of the First World War a dramatic shift in the balance of economic power (Dick 1989). Initially, instead of threatening it, Japanese trade complemented Chinese trade since the Japanese needed the Chinese distribution network. Japanese businessmen, often connected to large business conglomerates (*zaibatsu*), cultivated good contacts with Chinese traders, often offering them cheap freight rates on their shipping lines. The Japanese were much more involved in European industrial and financial centres than were the Chinese, but in order to reach the indigenous market, they were dependent on Chinese middlemen. To achieve this, many Japanese manufactured goods were imported via Singapore. Only in the 1930s did Japanese increasingly begin to deal with indigenous and Arab traders – soon to be hindered, as were the Chinese, by the Crisis Import Ordinance of 1933 (Post 1991:62, 71, 308, 1993: 149-53).

Chinese credit was more an incentive than an impediment to indigenous entrepreneurship. It enabled peasants to plant and harvest new crops, even though it tied them to their credit supplier. The absence of other forms of credit meant that they could not easily switch to other activities once a debt had been incurred – but as long as prices were not too low, they had no need to. The middleman earned a large slice of the total profits, but also opened up the regions and stimulated foreign exports. As discussed earlier, indigenous producers were in many regards shrewd entrepreneurs, particularly in Sumatra. A one-sided emphasis on the usurious character of intermediary trade underestimates the entrepreneurial capacity of the smallholders.

Growth effects of indigenous export production

So far this chapter has concentrated on the supply side of indigenous exports, reviewing the products, the provinces, and the complex pattern of intermediary trade. We have obtained a picture of rapid change in provinces with indigenous export production. In the initial stages, these provinces experienced increasing export revenues. Then they were confronted by the drop in prices during the Depression. In this section I survey consumer behaviour, levels of income, and the development of imports during the Depression.

Whether the steady growth of tax revenues from these regions also led to government expenditure to improve infrastructure, education, health care, and hygiene will be explored in Chapter VI.

Resident W.A.C. Whitlau of West Sumatra wrote in 1926:

> 'Whoever makes a journey through this province, and crosses the centre – going through Padang, Agan, Pajakumbuh, and Solok – seeing the solid houses, decorated with wood carvings, the cultivated lands, and – if he comes during the *sawah* season – the well-bedded paddy, with stalks bending under the weight of the ears, the well-dressed and usually well-fed and healthy looking Minangkabau people – who visits the pasar humming with lively trade [...] does not need any statistical information to be convinced that the country he is visiting is a country where the people live in prosperity.'[120]

In the 1920s, indigenous exports generated large revenues, which indubitably raised the standard of living, as illustrated by this quotation. Various types of expenditure by indigenous peasants were observed. As in Minahasa, much income was spent on better constructed, more solid houses (often with brick walls and corrugated iron roofs), and on cars, small trucks, and bicycles. There were also considerable imports of clothes and textiles (from Java and increasingly from Japan), and of small items of machinery such as sewing machines. Additional money was spent on food, sweets, high-quality tea, coffee, and sugar, and on tinned food and meat. During the heyday of export revenues in the 1920s, many houses in Lampung were reportedly furnished with mirror-fronted wardrobes, clocks, lamps, and carpeting, all of which had to be imported.[121] In Hulu Sungai (Southeast Kalimantan) the cinemas were crowded, wedding ceremonies were luxurious, and the number of *haji* visiting Mecca grew as prosperity spread.[122] A contemporary observer was convinced that these imports were largely a matter of unnecessary luxury: 'A calamity in rubber will hit only the luxury items. No one will mourn for it very long.' (Velsing 1925:227.) We may doubt the truth of this, because a substantial part of the above-mentioned expenditure was not on superfluous luxury, but served the local economy or provided basic subsistence needs. Nor should it be forgotten that imports of foodstuffs were often necessary because the cultivation of cash crops reduced self-sufficiency in food production. Many smallholders had specialized in export production and were consequently dependent on the purchase of rice.

Even though these smallholders often relied on internal rice trade (espe-

120 ARA Kol, MvO 166, W.A.C. Whitlau 1926:131-2.

121 ARA Kol, MvO 232, Th. Volmering 1930:20; MvO 165, J.D.L. le Fèbvre 1919:55.

122 Cramer 1934; Post 1996; Velsing 1925:226-7.

cially in Sumatra), their demand also stimulated additional foreign rice imports. In the import statistics, Jambi, West Kalimantan, and Manado stand out as provinces where a large share of imports consisted of rice (Table 54.1). Foodstuffs also formed a large share in Jambi and Aceh. West Sumatra and South Sulawesi spent a larger share on selected consumer goods such as textiles. As may be expected, expenditure on capital goods such as steel and machines was not as large in these provinces as in the provinces of Clusters I and III, where more European companies were established. Absence of capital investments in Aceh, Jambi, and West Kalimantan is obvious from the import statistics (Table 54.2).

Generally speaking, in provinces with large indigenous exports there was little drainage of profits earned by European companies; rather, a substantial share of the total profit ended up with intermediary traders, who were often Chinese. Imports followed exports more closely than in regions with heavy estate agriculture, since smallholder export earnings generated smallholder import expenditure on approximately the same level. In Lampung, Jambi, West Kalimantan, and West Sumatra, the statistical correlation between imports and exports in 1900-1940 was the highest of all Outer Islands. Only in Manado and Aceh was there no significant correlation between imports and exports (Table 57).

Another item of expenditure favoured by smallholders was buying themselves out of their obligation to do corvée labour ('Herendiensten'), a kind of work which was often seen as degrading (Tideman 1938:169). In most provinces (in the directly governed territories), indigenous residents were obliged to spend a fixed number of days per year working for the government, maintaining public works such as roads and bridges.[123] As soon as smallholders had earned enough money, they would pay a fee to the authorities to be released from this obligation. For example, in 1938 a total of 1.4 million people were liable for corvée labour. Of this total, 267,000 people bought themselves out of the obligation, which resulted in total payments of 1.5 million guilders. The largest sums were collected in Palembang (396,000 guilders in 1938), Jambi (237,000 guilders), and Tapanuli (209,000 guilders). Sometimes money from the Rubber Fund, which was financed by revenues from the export surtax on smallholder rubber, was used to release smallholders from their corvée labour obligation.[124]

Because of the large number of people buying out their obligation, there was little labour left for actual road maintenance. In Palembang in 1936, 85 per cent of the work was done by Javanese coolies, who earned 0.40 guilders

[123] The number of days varied per province, but was usually around 20 days per year. In Aceh and Timor it was only 15 days. In Bengkulu and Manado 26 days. *Indisch Verslag* 1939:468.

[124] ARA Kol, MvO 265, J. Oberman 1938 appendix 3 p. 14.

a day. (This cost the government a little more money per worker, since a Palembang peasant could pay off his 24-day obligation in 1936 by paying 6 guilders, or 0.25 guilders per day.)[125]

Nine years earlier, in 1930, a considerable pay-off sum for corvée labour amounting to 6.5 million guilders was collected in the Outer Islands. In 1931 this had dropped to 4.9 million and in 1933 to 1.4 million. This rapid drop shows that the effects of the Depression were quickly felt. One Resident remarked that, considering the aversion of Jambi smallholders to corvée labour, the declining percentage of people buying themselves out of corvée labour showed how sadly meagre the money income of the indigenous population in this province had become. Pay-offs had decreased from 26 per cent in 1931 to 6 per cent in 1932.[126]

The effects of the Depression

The Depression disrupted economic development in the Outer Islands and reduced all export revenues. The export economy was inevitably vulnerable to the overseas economic situation. Indigenous producers suddenly could not afford their luxury imports, since their cash income flow stopped almost completely when prices of raw materials slumped. Fortunately, many could switch back to subsistence agriculture and supply their own basic needs. Barter trade made a partial comeback and the use of money tended to recede. Prices of imports had dropped as well, so that expenditure on textiles and rice continued at a smaller level (although, under government restrictions, rice had to be imported from Java or Sulawesi). There are repeated remarks to the effect that exports continued because cash was needed to pay taxes.[127]

In 1932, Governor A.H. Philips of Aceh reported that there was hardly any money left among the indigenous population. There was very little purchasing power and (semi-)barter trade was increasingly replacing the use of money.[128] Aggregate imports in Aceh fell from over 10 million guilders in 1930, to 7 million in 1931, under 5 million in 1932, and slightly over 3 million in 1933. Still, these four years are characterized by a trade deficit, because output of cash crops declined even more. In 1924/28 a large share of Aceh imports had been consumer goods (such as textiles and clothing). In 1929/33, imports of consumer goods and rice still amounted to 27.7 per cent of its imports (Tables 32, 54.1 and 54.2).[129]

125 ARA Kol, MvO 212, J. Tideman 1928:158-9; MvO 215, W. Steinbuch 1936:390; MvO 223, J.R.F. Verschoor van Nisse 1931:161-8.

126 ARA Kol, MvO 224, W. Steinbuch 1933:188-90.

127 ARA Kol, MvO 223, J.R.F. Verschoor van Nisse 1931:128; MvO 264, K.H. van Prehn 1933: 13-5.

128 ARA Kol, MvO 159, A.H. Philips 1932:44-5; Clemens et al. 1992:53.

129 There are solid grounds for suspecting that BPM imported construction materials (steel,

Loss of income in export revenues was most prominent in the rubber and copra provinces of Jambi and West Kalimantan and Manado. Among smallholder export crops, coffee and pepper were relatively strong products. Many middlemen and import traders also suffered heavily from the sudden fall in prices. Import traders suddenly found that their stock had become worthless because clients did not have the means to buy any goods. The middleman who had supplied advance payments for deliveries of rubber or copra found that he owned a stack of raw materials of which the value had seriously depreciated. Matters could be even worse, as we have already seen in Minahasa (Manado), where the middlemen who supplied credit could claim ownership rights because their debtors were not able to pay back their debts. Such ownership claims, which included claiming the entire harvest, could be profitable for the middleman even at low prices.

Index figures on the value of foreign and interregional imports display the fall in import value during the Depression years. For many provinces, 1933-1934 was the low record of imports, represented as a percentage of imports in 1923. In Maluku, imports in 1934 were only 19 per cent of imports in 1923, in Manado 25 per cent. In Jambi this was 42 per cent. Of all provinces in Cluster II, Lampung and South Sulawesi were the provinces with the most stable imports compared to the 1923 value. In terms of current value imports in Aceh reached their deepest point in 1936, when in most other provinces a recovery could already be observed (Table 55).

Long-term effects of the Depression are more difficult to assess. Government cuts caused a major discontinuity in infrastructural development, but a permanent change in the government's attitude in the 1930s created a more beneficial climate for the development of indigenous processing industry and export agriculture. For example, after 1934 the revenue from the rubber surtax was largely spent on social overhead capital. Therefore, the rubber provinces were not as badly off as suggested by the severe decrease in prices. Various other government measures such as credit regulations and the backing of sales cooperatives were favourable to the indigenous economy. Unfortunately, the major disruptions of the Pacific War brought recovery to a halt and made the outcome of these measures impossible to observe.

Conclusion

Indigenous Indonesian agriculture reached impressive results during the 1920s in rubber, coffee, copra, and pepper in particular. In the mountainous

---

machines) for the Aceh oilfields. But the share in Aceh imports of iron and machines was relatively small (Table 54.2). These imports probably entered the province through East Sumatra.

areas of Palembang and West Sumatra, coffee was the most important indigenous cash crop. Pepper was cultivated in Aceh, Lampung, and Bangka. In Jambi, Palembang, West Kalimantan, and Southeast Kalimantan smallholder rubber production became the most profitable sector of the indigenous economy. South Sulawesi and Manado exported large volumes of copra, as did West Kalimantan and West Sumatra.

This chapter has analysed foreign and interregional exports from the provinces where indigenous entrepreneurship generated widespread export agriculture. The chapter concentrated on the production of rubber, because it was the most important export product for which indigenous exports and estate exports can be analysed separately. Rubber exports generated high incomes in the 1920s. I have examined dualist policies of the government, and different strategies used by entrepreneurs in various provinces. Over and above this, rubber was a product that was not consumed domestically, and therefore gives the most clear-cut example of the development of foreign export production.

Although Broersma observes that indigenous enterprise had no solid foundation, export agriculture was successful – in spite of being low-capital. Indonesian peasants had hardly any capital to invest, but were quick to adapt to the small-scale cultivation of rubber, new types of coffee (Robusta), or copra, when the market for these products expanded. Using labour-intensive production techniques, they often relied on hired labour, although in many regions family labour would be substituted for migrant workers when the profit margin shrank. In the 1920s many peasants hired coolies to tap rubber or harvest coffee. In the 1930s these labourers were either laid off, or given a larger share of the product, leading to a supply with a high price inelasticity.

A versatile process of change

Flexibility enabled indigenous producers to live through periods of depression and low prices. Provinces that cultivated a diversified package of export goods changed to those crops which had a stable price, thereby securing for themselves more consistent earnings. Provinces that specialized in one crop (such as Jambi in rubber or Manado in copra) switched, as needed, to the cultivation of food crops or the collection of forest products. Because food prices fell as well, and peasants were often self-sufficient in food crops, subsistence was not immediately endangered by fluctuations in world prices. But when prices were low, foreign trade earnings almost vanished. By increasing their output, some smallholders could still generate some money income at a minimal level. There is no doubt that the Depression limited further economic expansion and made peasants increasingly dependent on their credit suppliers.

Indigenous dynamics were only feasible in interaction with Chinese and (later) Japanese trade. The intermediary trader supplied credit to the peasant in the form of money, import goods, or seeds and seedlings. He conveyed information on prices and products. In many regions, a chain was formed from the producer to the internal trader to the middleman in the harbour, who in turn sold to an agent who would deliver the goods to a wholesale company. Although the Chinese had no monopoly in intermediary trade, they were dominant in many regions. During the Depression many smallholders found themselves in a debt trap to these creditors. But the middlemen themselves also suffered from the low prices, since their stock of import and export goods lost its value before it could be sold.

Little was invested by smallholders in crop variation, production techniques, or processing. The credit system, under which money was often immediately spent on consumer goods even before delivery of export products to the creditor, may have impeded investments in increased productivity, although this may also have been a question of mentality.

Although it was firmly rooted in the regional economy, indigenous export agriculture did not develop as many linkages in the macroeconomic sense as would have been needed for an economic takeoff:

a. *Forward linkages* such as the rubber remilling industry only developed on the eve of the Second World War.

b. Crop improvement laboratories and agricultural education, which can be interpreted as *backward linkages*, were only established by the government or the European agricultural estates. Only the Chinese businesses made substantial investments in schools (Vleming 1926:8-9).

c. In many remote areas, major effects of export production, apart from rising incomes, were *fiscal linkages*: revenues from export duty and income tax, augmented by the surtax on indigenous rubber. These revenues contributed to gradual improvements in the social infrastructure of the Outer Islands.

Although in many provinces the local government made efforts to spread new agricultural techniques, promoting cooperative marketing boards and the People's Credit Bank system, these efforts were too weak to prevent the expanding power of the Chinese middlemen. The economic policies of the government will be explored in depth in Chapter VI.

During the Depression years, a difference can be observed in strategy between provinces that produced only rubber or copra and provinces with a more diversified economic structure. The latter provinces, particularly Palembang and Southeast Kalimantan, tended to reduce their production of rubber radically in 1930-1932, when the average rubber price was at its lowest. In 1934, when rubber prices had risen and news spread about the introduction of a surtax on indigenous rubber, producers in these provinces quickly expanded their production, up to five times the output volume of 1932. In West Kalimantan, where only rubber and copra were produced, smallholders maintained a more constant output of rubber. In Jambi, where rubber was the only export crop, export volume remained at a surprisingly constant level in 1932-1938. Peasants in Jambi did not increase production to maintain their income. They continued tapping the rubber trees they had and went back to growing rice and local foodstuffs.

Indigenous export agriculture was neither primitive, vulnerable, nor essentially traditional. It can be more appropriately characterized as flexible, profit-oriented, and adaptable. In the regions of Clusters I and II, studied in this chapter, export agriculture reached very large volumes. The next chapter examines the provinces of Cluster IV, where foreign exports were much smaller. Did these provinces lag behind, as a vulnerable periphery in an archipelago full of dynamic producers?

CHAPTER V

In the periphery of economic expansion

Sweet repose in calm regions

On 27 July 1912, the NHM opened a branch office in Telukbetung, which at that time was the main town of Lampung. In his first annual report, the agent wrote that this residency was suspended in a state of 'sweet repose, which was never disturbed by any important event'. He recalled that an acquaintance, visiting him after forty years of absence, had remarked that neither change nor progress were to be traced in Lampung after all those years. Such tranquillity was not to the liking of the NHM agent, who hoped that things would change once the plans to found the South Sumatra Railways (Zuid-Sumatra Spoorwegen, ZSS) had been realized.[1]

Before 1920 Lampung and Bengkulu exported very little to foreign markets directly. While the peasants in Jambi feverishly planted Hevea gardens and Palembang smallholders diligently produced goods for export and Western oil companies busily hummed away, the southernmost regions of Sumatra appeared to be sunk in a deep inertia. But were they really?

The NHM did not even bother to open an agency in the province called Timor and Dependencies, situated virtually at the other end of Java. In 1908, the Resident of Timor decided that it was premature to levy taxes on indigenous peasants 'because of the impoverished situation in which they live'.[2] Five years later, his successor was more optimistic and did introduce an income tax. 'Without reservation I can proclaim hopeful expectations for the future', he wrote in 1913, boasting that the best horses of the archipelago were bred on Sumba.[3] This seems to have been a flash in the pan, because in the following decades economic life in Timor and Dependencies remained substandard, and cattle breeding was only a minor source of income in Timor's economy. Foreign exports remained under 300,000 guilders per year for practically all years between 1911 and 1940 (Clemens et al. 1992:58). Further east, in Ambon,

1 ARA, NHM 9193, VvS 1257 (Telukbetung 1912):1-2.
2 ARA Kol, MvO 339, J.F.A. de Rooy 1908:24.
3 ARA Kol, MvO 340, C. van Rietschoten 1913:55, 59.

one Resident suggested that the government officials of the BB (Binnenlands Bestuur) there could just as well be appointed park-keepers or foresters, since the residency reminded him of a national park. 'It seems as if all plans for the future have to be discarded here', C.C. Ouwerling wrote in 1930.[4]

A third path of development

In Chapter II, three scenarios for economic development were outlined, corresponding to the dominant type of export production in the various Outer Provinces. The third path of economic development is characterized by little economic development in infrastructural innovation, little government expenditure, low tax revenues, and a low standard of living as these were perceived by government officials. Foreign and interregional exports – either from European estates or from indigenous producers – were lower than in other provinces, both in absolute value and per capita. Tapanuli, Bengkulu, Maluku, and Timor and Dependencies were small residencies with small populations. They formed a periphery to the ongoing expansion in nearby provinces. Bali was a different case. Although Bali was an easily accessible, small, but densely populated island, it should still be classified among the smallest economies of the Outer Islands. In this chapter, the time has come to examine the economic development of provinces which had no more than a small involvement in world trade.

A separate section in this chapter is devoted to the rice trade and rice production in the Outer Islands. The importance of rice, as the main food crop of the archipelago, is of course not restricted to the smaller provinces, but rice is a major factor in the subsistence economy. In an economy where the production of food crops (as opposed to commercial crops) was the central agricultural activity, self-sufficiency in rice (or, in Maluku, sago) was vitally important since there was little money income to supplement the home-grown diet.

The provinces that shifted to export agriculture often partially abandoned their traditional cultivation of food crops. Exports to the world market often started with a surplus production of agricultural products, but many smallholder provinces shifted to export specialization and stopped cultivating rice, especially during the heyday of export production in the 1920s. This left them needing to import rice. From this need emerged a market that boosted the rice trade within the archipelago.[5] Did the small provinces profit from this process and develop a role as suppliers of rice?

It is essential to deal with the position of Java within the trading network,

4 ARA Kol, MvO 315, C.C. Ouwerling 1930:1-2.

5 In fact, surplus export production often developed under the influence of the demand exerted by middlemen who wanted to purchase from smallholders. Vink 1946:277.

since several small provinces traded intensively with this island. Over and above this, Java held an important position in the rice trade in the archipelago. Bali and Lampung, close to Java, had little foreign trade, but had a substantial trade volume with Java. Per capita exports including interregional trade indicate whether or not these exports were in fact of the same magnitude as in the more successful provinces.

Around 1900, except for the estate area of East Sumatra, the cultivation of cash crops in most Outer Islands had hardly begun to develop. Disregarding a few small areas with an older tradition of export cultivation, such as West Sumatra (coffee) or Aceh (pepper), the main exports from many Outer Islands consisted of forest products. These included rattan, resins (damar and copal), and gutta percha. Did the small provinces, which did not participate in the subsequent explosive export agriculture of the 1910s and 1920s, have a substantial share in these early exports? Did this initial share turn out to be an advantage or a drawback in the development of foreign exports? I will explore whether the presence of forest rubber (gutta percha) paved the way for the later cultivation of Hevea, and to what extent the small provinces, while not making the transition to perennial tree-crop cultivation, continued collecting forest products.

Natural endowment

A glance at the map reveals the economic disadvantages of the location and topographic features of most of the small provinces. The coastal plains west of the Barisan Mountains in the mountainous province of Bengkulu, in southwest Sumatra, were even narrower than those in Tapanuli. This land was relatively infertile and unsuitable for irrigated rice cultivation (Benkoelen 1917:269). One contemporary observer mentions that Bengkulu's coastal areas were even poorer than the highlands.[6] Both Tapanuli and Bengkulu lagged behind in export expansion in comparison to adjacent provinces, and can be viewed as peripheries which were drawn into the orbit of trade by the centres (East Sumatra and Palembang).

The Barisan Mountains formed an impediment to economic life from north to south, favouring the provinces on Sumatra's eastern side. Trade flows from the mountain regions were directed towards adjacent provinces, crossing the residency border by mountain trail and footpath, conveniently escaping the attention of government officials. For example, coffee and benzoin[7] from northern Tapanuli were often exported via Lake Toba to East

6 ARA Kol, MvO 202, W.J.R. Zieck 1932:19.

7 Benzoin was used as medicine and as perfume. Benzoin is a resin obtained from certain trees, and is sometimes erroneously referred to as a gum, as in the British name 'gum Benjamin'. *Benzoë* 1917:274.

Sumatra or to Aceh, since the Tapanuli coast was on the other side of the mountains.[8] Smallholder rubber in Bengkulu, which was cultivated on the east side of the Barisan Mountains (the Palembang side), was taken to Palembang. Even when there were no mountains in the way, accessing the nearest harbour was preferable to prolonged transport overland, with the result that exports escaped provincial registration. A good example of this was the pepper and rubber from northern Lampung, which were brought to the Palembang harbour by *haji* or by Chinese traders.[9]

Similarly, Maluku and the Lesser Sunda Islands were small and located far from the busy trading areas around Singapore and Batavia. In the eastern archipelago, the major export crop was copra. In addition, Ambon and Ternate had some coffee and rattan for export. Macassar was the centre of economic activity for these provinces, and there was substantial trade in rice and other commodities between these eastern islands. Timor and Dependencies, for example, exported some timber as well as copra and various other commodities, such as rice, forest products, and cattle in smaller quantities; there was an especially lively trade in horses from Sumbawa (and, to a lesser extent, from Sumba).

It would be easy to be misled if one looked no further than foreign trade statistics, since regional and internal trade may have been substantially higher than was recorded. Exports of rice and cash crops supplemented local income. The level of consumer imports may give an indication of whether this 'hidden prosperity' was spent, but only in so far as the imports came through provincial harbours. Since many Chinese traders supplied import goods as well as purchasing forest products or rubber, the chances are that such imports may also have gone largely unnoticed.

When regarded as a group, the Outer Islands have often been typified as a vast area which was sparsely populated. The most remarkable exception to this picture is of course Bali, which had 175 inhabitants per km^2 as early as 1930.

The fact that indigenous export cultivation did not develop in certain provinces was not due to their low population density, however. While successful indigenous export provinces of the Outer Islands such as Palembang, East Sumatra, Lampung, and Manado had a population density of only 13 to 17 inhabitants per km^2, Tapanuli and Timor – provinces with less trade – were more densely populated, with around 26 inhabitants per km^2. Sparsely populated provinces such as Jambi and West Kalimantan exceeded Cluster IV provinces both in per capita and in aggregate exports (except New

8 ARA, NHM 9165, VvS 940 (Sibolga 1930), 941 (1931):4-5.

9 ARA, NHM 9193, VvS 1264 (Telukbetung 1919):13; ARA Kol, MvO 204, P.M. Hooykaas 1939:78, 117.

Guinea, which had neither many inhabitants nor many exports). In Jambi (5 inhabitants per km^2 in 1930), average per capita export revenue in 1926/30 was 90 guilders; in West Kalimantan it was about 60 guilders.

Lampung showed a remarkable orientation towards Java. In this province (12 inhabitants per km^2), per capita foreign exports were about 50 guilders, but exports to Java earned an additional 30 guilders per capita. In comparison, Bali and Timor lagged far behind, with 12 and 3 guilders per capita foreign exports, including trade to Java. In 1931/35, the ranking of the provinces by per capita export revenue had hardly changed in relation to the preceding 1926/30 period (although revenues in contemporary currency were lower). Tapanuli, Bali, and Timor and Dependencies were among the provinces with the smallest per capita exports in 1926-1935 (Table 26.1 and Figures 24d and 24.e). It should be noted that Aceh also displayed low per capita exports. On account of other criteria, such as a versatile export package and relatively large exports in the 1920s, Aceh was included in Cluster II.

Successful subsistence or misery?

Economic life in the Outer Islands amounted to more than export production alone. In order to distinguish the local economy (production of food and basic living commodities) from commercial agriculture, I use the term 'subsistence economy'. Provinces where no significant export production took place often had a relatively well-functioning subsistence economy providing for basic living needs such as food and housing. Even though modernization in some cases disturbed traditional cultures and values (and has been criticized for this), foreign trade brought economic development in the form of roads, bridges, railways, schools, and hospitals in Sumatra, Kalimantan, and Sulawesi, which improved the quality of life (see Chapter I).

In studying the small provinces with little export agriculture, it is therefore necessary to determine whether the subsistence economy in these provinces provided sufficient income for a basic standard of living. Besides this, I will explore whether surplus production was feasible, allowing vent-for-surplus and enabling the provinces to increase exports.

The definition of subsistence economy

In theory, 'subsistence economy' can be defined as an economy in which (a) all production, usually agricultural, is consumed locally, and (b) the standard of living provides no more than the basic necessities of life (food, shelter, and clothing) (Todaro 1992:254, 506). Depending on the rigidity with which the second part of this definition is applied, two different types of subsistence economy can be discerned: in the first type, people live at a minimum subsistence level, having only the bare minimum to consume.[10] The second type emphasizes the self-sufficient character of the local economy and is not necessarily restricted to bare minimum consumption (Myint 1980:36).

In the first type of subsistence economy, resources and technology are only just sufficient to keep the inhabitants alive. This situation was rarely encountered in colonial Indonesia: the rich natural resources in most Outer Islands normally offered enough to enable the indigenous inhabitants to grow, gather, or hunt food.[11] Subsistence economy in this study refers to the second type, which emphasizes the self-sufficient character of the economy. Although there were no regular shortages of food and only infrequent famines, money played a secondary role and there was relatively little exchange with other villages or overseas regions.[12] While around 1900 in West Kalimantan and Sumatra all kinds of foreign dollars (Mexican dollar, British-trade dollar) were used as a means of payment, in the interior of Kalimantan, Sulawesi, and New Guinea there was another currency system in which rather sophisticated objects of exchange such as feathers, stones, and shells were used (Potting 1987:119, 1997:7, 60-9). This corresponds with the more self-sufficient (though there still was trade!), non-monetary type of subsistence economy as described by Myint (Myint 1980:36-7).

Recent studies have argued that within the pre-colonial Southeast Asian region, overseas (and inter-island) trade had long been important (Reid 1988, 1993). Whatever the truth of the matter, in the colonial period this pre-colonial trade receded and instead the colonizers increasingly dominated foreign trade, which consequently was redirected towards the Western world. After 1900, while exports of European enterprises in the Outer Islands reached unprecedented heights, a new development can be observed in indigenous trade: the contrast in volume between export-oriented regions

10 Scott discusses the ethics and social and moral arrangements of peasants living close to the subsistence margin ('standing up to their neck in water'). Scott 1976:1-90.

11 In textbooks Asian subsistence agriculture is often typified as suffering from overpopulation and scarcity of land (India, Java, Japan), whereas Latin American agriculture was subject to less harsh conditions but suffered from an inefficient landownership system (misuse of fertile land in 'latifundias'). In broad terms, this implies that the poor subsistence economy is situated in Asia, whereas the 'vent-for-surplus' type of subsistence economy occurred more frequently in Latin America (and parts of Africa). In Java, Taiwan, and Japan, for example, the cultivated area of land per agricultural worker was small, less than 1 hectare (Booth 1988:5). In the richly endowed, thinly populated Outer Islands, the latter, 'un-Asian' type of subsistence economy predominated. Colonial rule, in changing property rights and monetizing the indigenous economy, is said to have worsened conditions in rural areas, but whether this is generally and irreversibly true has been disputed. Myrdal 1968:1033-52; Todaro 1992:258-62.

12 In the extreme form, there was not even a market, although there may have been a margin of surplus productive capacity (mainly the occasional export of surplus rice or some handicrafts). This type of economy existed in several regions in the pre-colonial economy. From the mid-nineteenth century, such a degree of isolation became increasingly rare. Myint 1980:36-7.

and subsistence-oriented regions in the Outer Islands grew much larger.

The islands were a heterogeneous set of economies, some more integrated within the archipelago, others relatively backward and isolated. The use of the term 'subsistence economy' in contrast to 'export economy' incorrectly suggests a homogeneous indigenous economy. In fact, local differences abounded in the Outer Islands. Particular features of *adat*, heritage, cultural traits, and also tribe, village, or family organization within each province greatly influenced the economic behaviour of the indigenous population. Nevertheless, it is useful to distinguish between the commercial export economy and the more traditional economy that principally served subsistence needs.

Myint has argued that rapid expansion of the peasant export sector was an extension of the traditional economic organization and technology of the subsistence economy. It owed little to outside economic resources, required very little durable capital equipment (apart from land), and the necessary labour was supplied from the family and relatives of the peasant producers. He stresses that this economy was non-monetary, even though there was a market, where a margin of surplus production (occasional exports of extra rice) was traded (Myint 1980:34-6).

This picture applies very aptly to the situation in the Outer Islands in the late colonial era. In many provinces, the more traditional type of trade did not amount to a large share of total income, most efforts being directed towards cultivation of food crops. The *pasar* formed an 'essential lubricant' in the traditional exchange economy, and export production arose as an extension of traditional agriculture (Myint 1980:36-7). Leaving aside Western estate agriculture, the commercial farming activities of smallholders in the Outer Islands were not incompatible with the traditional pattern of production. Some scholars, such as Purwanto in his dissertation on southern Sumatra, have extended this argument and stated that the provinces with large indigenous exports in fact remained rural and primitive (Purwanto 1992:360-3). In this view, exports only supplemented subsistence, whereas subsistence remained the basis of the economy.

Production methods remained primitive, quality was poor, and peasants knew little about technology, credit, or investment strategies. Despite such handicaps, structural changes took place. Even during the Depression, peasants did not return completely to subsistence agriculture. In some provinces, smallholders kept on producing ever larger quantities of rubber and coffee to maintain their income levels (for example in Jambi). In other provinces, in addition to returning to food-crop cultivation, they shifted to other commercial crops (for example in Palembang). In these provinces, subsistence agriculture supplemented exports rather than the other way around, and agriculture shifted irreversibly to export production. This is also illustrated by the need for rice imports in Jambi in the 1930s (see the section below on the rice trade). The (partial) shift to commercial agriculture changed the traditional economy structurally and constituted the first step towards modernization of the economy.

The irreversible changes had their roots in an uncomplicated but nevertheless relatively powerful subsistence economy. Although foreign exports increased in this period on an unprecedented scale, there had been a longstanding participation in world trade. The regional and interregional trade that had been carried on within the archipelago for centuries provided a network of traditional links that could be expanded for a new, more intensive use. It is important to bear in mind that the traditional subsistence economy was not necessarily stagnant. In accordance with Myint's vent-for-surplus theory, there was room for expansion, since not all production factors were fully employed. The subsistence economy allowed indigenous export agriculture to develop, but the extent to which the local economy specialized in foreign trade was different in each province.

In the following discussion, I examine the characteristics of the subsistence economy in northern Sumatra, in southern Sumatra, and in the 'Great East' (eastern Indonesia). Within these regions, the continuation of the subsistence economy in some residencies can be compared with a more substantial shift to indigenous exports in adjacent residencies.

Regional variation in northern Sumatra

Tapanuli was hemmed in between Aceh, East Sumatra, and West Sumatra. Its foreign exports remained at a much lower level than those of the surrounding provinces: its share amounted to a mere 1 per cent of total exports for all Outer Islands in 1900-1940 (Table 27). In this section, I will give reasons to explain why this was so. Tapanuli's exports consisted mainly of rubber, supplemented by coffee and some copra and benzoin. The northern part of Tapanuli belonged to the Batak lands (Toba, Dairi region) and was relatively fertile. It produced Arabica coffee, benzoin, and rice. The southern part, in which a mixed population of Batak, Malays, and Minangkabau resided, was less fertile but produced rubber and Robusta coffee.[13]

By far the largest part of Tapanuli was mountainous and the coast was less accessible than on the eastern side of Sumatra. Sumatra's mountain range, the Barisan Mountains, hindered access and cash-crop cultivation, but natural resources alone do not account for the differences in export production. For instance, West Sumatra, which was also relatively poorly endowed with natural resources, did have a vigorous indigenous economy. This suc-

13 ARA Kol, MvO 176, P.C. Arends 1926:6; Hagreis and Vonk 1927-28:681-4.

cess may be explained to a certain extent as an exception based on two factors: the historically strategic function of Padang, and Minangkabau entrepreneurship in trade. But per capita figures show that, although Tapanuli's total exports were small, its sparsely scattered inhabitants were about as economically active as in West Sumatra and Aceh. Per capita exports in West Sumatra amounted to around 23 guilders in 1926/30; in Tapanuli this was 18 guilders (Table 26.1).

Aceh, to the north of Tapanuli, was better equipped for the challenges of the international market for cash crops. It was an area of wide stretches of fertile flatlands, covering the whole northern tip of Sumatra. It was more easily accessible for trade. In spite of all this (perhaps due to unremitting political restlessness), per capita exports in Aceh in 1926/30 averaged only 17 guilders, slightly less than in Tapanuli (Table 26.1).

Did Tapanuli show a hidden export expansion that is revealed by including the interregional trade statistics? Not all features of its economy were equally encouraging. Per capita imports in Aceh (and West Sumatra) were significantly higher than in Tapanuli (Table 26.2). Moreover, Aceh produced a consistently higher volume of exports during the earlier decades, 1900-1920, and also had a more varied export package, consisting of copra, pepper, *pinang* nuts, and rubber. In contrast, Tapanuli's major export crops were confined to rubber and coffee (Clemens et al. 1992:36, 53; Gade Ismail 1996: 245-6). The majority of the Tapanuli population consisted of politically tranquil Batak and Malays. Only in one respect did these two provinces have corresponding economic characteristics: both had little Western enterprise before 1920, one due to its mountains, the other due to political unrest.

Aceh's imports were more diversified than Tapanuli's and included more luxury consumer goods and textiles than did those of Tapanuli. This can perhaps be ascribed to the higher number of Europeans who lived in Aceh on agricultural estates and in the garrisons of the Dutch colonial army (in 1930 3,000 against 900 in Tapanuli). These imports at times exceeded exports, but the indigenous inhabitants of Aceh did not want to have anything to do with European economic activity. Local people were not willing to work for Western firms. The indigenous population of Aceh displayed an independent dynamic behaviour.

The Depression shows that export production in Tapanuli was vulnerable and that revenues evaporated as soon as prices dropped (Figure 23n). Tapanuli exported less than 5 million guilders per year until 1924, after which rubber income raised export revenues to a peak of 18 million guilders in 1925. After 1930, Tapanuli's export revenues quickly fell back to the pre-1924 level. Roughly half of the rubber exports were produced by European estates, slightly more in the 1920s, slightly less in the 1930s, when thousands of coolies were laid off and production capacity contracted substantially.

Because indigenous rubber was exported overland to East Sumatra instead of to Tapanuli's port town, Sibolga, it is difficult to estimate the production in inland Tapanuli.[14]

The sudden fall in prices of Robusta and Hevea after 1929 reduced the income of peasants in the south of Tapanuli as it did in other places where these items were the main export products. The only reason Robusta coffee was harvested was because the price of rubber was even worse, as an NHM agent remarked. When the rubber price 'neared point zero', almost all peasants stopped tapping rubber. Even if they had wanted to continue, it was impossible to find labourers willing to tap rubber, since their share of the product would have been virtually worthless. Where coffee planters cultivated the higher quality Arabica, the initial years of the crisis were not as severe, since Arabica maintained its price level much longer (Figure 30).[15]

The benzoin produced in northern Tapanuli was purchased mostly by Chinese traders, who transported it to Sibolga, where it was processed and packed. The Chinese traders worked in *kongsi,* which resembled trading partnerships. There were also several European firms that traded in benzoin, the bulk of it from Sibolga.[16] Most of the benzoin was exported to Batavia, and a smaller part (from Barus) to Singapore. When Chinese traders could not sell the product at a reasonable profit, they became more careful in supplying credit to smallholders and stopped buying benzoin, which caused peasants in the interior to stockpile large reserves.[17] At times, import traders had difficulty collecting older debts. In Tapanuli, according to *adat* law the Batak could not go bankrupt, so the government had to intervene by closing down shops and seizing goods.[18] In Natal, where copra was produced, Chinese traders were few. It was Malay traders who bought the copra and shipped it to Padang by prahu, where they sold it to Dutch firms.

In this way export revenues entered the interior and supplemented the subsistence economy. The rise in trade brought the need for money. Besides the Spanish dollar, which was so popular among the Batak that it was called *ringit Batak,* there was a plethora of small copper change in circulation. There was a repeated shortage of small coins and five- and ten-guilder notes in regions where indigenous trade had expanded.[19] In earlier times, the stand-

14 ARA, NHM 9165, VvS 940 (Sibolga 1930):2-6; VvS 941 (1931):1-4.

15 ARA Kol, MvO 177, U. Fagginger Auer 1933:30, 58; ARA, NHM 9165, VvS 940 (Sibolga 1930):2-6; ARA, VvS 941 (1931):2.

16 In 1916 there were four European firms trading in benzoin and coffee; in 1920 there were seven. ARA Kol, MvO 732, E.E.W.C. Schröder 1920:516, 574.

17 ARA, NHM 9165, VvS 940 (Sibolga 1930):3-4; VvS 941 (1931):3-4; ARA Kol, MvO 732, E.E.W.C. Schröder 1920:516, 575.

18 ARA, NHM 9165, VvS 940 (Sibolga 1930):11.

19 ARA, NHM 9125, VvS 485 (Medan 1909):12; VvS 486 (1910):15.

ard means of exchange in Tapanuli had been the 'rice measure', called *tumba* or *tuba*, containing some 2 litres and specified at each transaction. Dollars quickly spread, which prompted the government to prohibit the use of the dollar in 1908. In the interior, forest products were still traded for cotton fabrics, and these in turn could be traded for cows and water buffalo. Cattle, rice, and tobacco had long been traditionally accepted means of exchange.[20]

Various degrees of modernization coexisted in trade. Money largely replaced barter trade, but at times money disappeared and barter trade returned. Different types of intermediary trade were also prevalent. Coffee, which was exported by European trading houses in Sibolga, was bought at inland *pasar* by Malay and Arab middlemen. In contrast, in the Dairi lands there were no *pasar*: here all trade was controlled by the Chinese, who usually owned a small shop but concentrated on purchasing coffee, benzoin, or rattan from local peasants. In Mandailing, the indigenous trading class had connections with Padang and took charge of the distribution of coffee and rice, often using matches and cotton fabrics as means of exchange. They travelled from *pasar* to *pasar* and used money only to supplement barter trade, effectively preventing Chinese intermediary traders from stepping in.[21]

Undiscovered economic potential

Although the mountains were subject to regular rainfall, which made rice cultivation reliable and bad harvests uncommon, after 1926 the local government tried to stimulate irrigation and the construction of *sawah* fields. However, such attempts were short-lived, because when budgets were cut in the early 1930s most of the plans had scarcely got underway.[22] The same happened in road construction. In 1932 a road inventory was compiled and a road construction plan was designed. This was fine on paper, but afterwards the development of roads advanced only slowly. Most traffic had to take a long way round through East Sumatra to travel from north to south or vice versa.[23]

During the 1910s and 1920s road construction had been a recurrent theme in government reports. Resident F.C. Vorstman saw Tapanuli as a backward region with undiscovered economic potential, and complained: 'The Dairi lands still need a proper arterial road to East Sumatra that could open up this region, which is so very suitable to the cultivation of tea.' He went on, complaining that Padang Lawas was isolated; the road between Natal and

20 *Indisch Staatsblad* 1908, no. 404-6, 1919 no. 511; ARA Kol, MvO 732, E.E.W.C. Schröder 1920:532-5.

21 ARA Kol, MvO 732, E.E.W.C. Schröder 1920:519.

22 ARA Kol, MvO 175, W.K.H. Ypes 1926:27; MvO 176, P.C. Arends 1926:16; MvO 177, U. Fagginger Auer 1933:60.

23 ARA Kol, MvO 177, U. Fagginger Auer 1933:19.

Mandailing was not ready yet. Even though the Residents of all provinces at times complain in their reports about the scarcity of funds to invest in infrastructure, Tapanuli was especially unlucky and was full of undisclosed potential.[24] Thanks to the efforts of this Resident, freight trucks, motor cars, and motorcycles were imported. Their number grew from a mere 11 in 1915 to 238 in 1921, expanding the possibility for the Batak to transport their products.[25]

The economic potential of Tapanuli did not pass entirely unnoticed. As early as the 1910s entrepreneurs sought to expand the success of the estate area of East Sumatra. Resident W.K.H. Ypes wrote in 1926 that he had 'learned from a reliable source that the interest of big capital and high finance in the Dairi lands was still unflagging'.[26] Assistant-Resident E.E.W.C. Schröder, who wrote an almost 900-page-long document on the residency, counted 21 companies and entrepreneurs which had concessions of around 28,700 hectares in Tapanuli, although he was unsure how much was actually under cultivation. He concluded: 'Nevertheless, it is the indigenous population that dominates the trade in this residency, and it is thanks to them that business in Sibolga is still gaining ground.'[27]

Small but not stagnant

All this goes to show that Tapanuli was a small export producer, but not stagnant and not especially poor. While regional differences were undeniable both in the volume of export production and the ways trade was carried on within the residency, Tapanuli's indigenous economy was not so very much smaller than those of several Cluster II provinces in the 1920s and 1930s. Tapanuli is a good example of the misleading impression obtained by analysing only aggregate export figures. Per capita export trade (including interregional exports to the other Outer Islands and Java) in Tapanuli rehabilitates this province with regard to export performance, especially in the 1920s. Quite apart from this, there was a hidden export trade to adjacent provinces. The impression of a stagnant province is too negative and should be refuted. Careful analysis of trade statistics and sources reveals that all over Sumatra smallholders displayed dynamic behaviour in export production. Even Tapanuli peasants contributed substantially to Sumatran smallholder exports.

24 ARA Kol, MvO 174, F.C. Vorstman 1921:8-9. Compare MvO 175, W.K.H. Ypes 1926:1-2.
25 ARA Kol, MvO 174, F.C. Vorstman 1921:9.
26 ARA Kol, MvO 175, W.K.H. Ypes 1926:2.
27 ARA Kol, MvO 732, E.E.W.C. Schröder 1920:239, 576.

Hidden trade in southern Sumatra

Indigenous smallholders in Jambi and Palembang were large exporters of rubber, as were smallholders in Indragiri, West Kalimantan, and Southeast Kalimantan (Chapter IV; see also Tables 44.1 and 44.3). Here, I will review the smallholder rubber production of the other residencies of southern Sumatra: Lampung and Bengkulu.

In Lampung and Bengkulu, peasants grew pepper and coffee, respectively, on the abandoned *ladang* fields that had once been used for rice. Besides these crops they marketed a number of smaller commodities such as tobacco, vegetables, cloves, cotton, copra, and forest products like benzoin, gambir, and rattan. Smallholders in Palembang, and particularly Jambi, owed their success in export production largely to the widespread cultivation of rubber. Why did the cultivation of rubber not spread to Bengkulu and Lampung as well? Since rubber was the motor behind the expansion of indigenous exports, the absence of rubber may help answer the question why Lampung and Bengkulu lagged behind in the fast growth of export cultivation in the 1920s.

Bengkulu

In general terms, Bengkulu was too mountainous to be very suitable for Hevea Brasiliensis. In spite of poor accessibility by river, Bengkulu peasants managed to cultivate and export coffee, which grows well on higher ground. More coffee than rubber was grown in the highland regions in Palembang, too (rubber reigned in the lowlands). These circumstances explain why Hevea was not an obvious cash crop for Bengkulu peasants.

In aggregate exports, Bengkulu played a modest role. In the older literature, this is explained by the fact that Bengkulu was a British territory up till 1825, isolated from the Dutch trading posts in other provinces (see, for example, Wellan 1932:170). This superficial argument does not hold water in the face of a century of hesitant development afterwards. More importantly, its remote location on the outer rim of the archipelago may have stood in the way of its economic development. Trade settlements on the coast, which formed the link to overseas markets in other sparsely populated provinces, were largely absent. (These arguments are also valid for Tapanuli.)

It was in the 1920s that Bengkulu developed a substantial production of smallholder Robusta coffee. The province was sparsely populated (about 12 persons per km^2, which is about the same as in Lampung and Palembang, but more than twice as many as in Jambi) (Table 14). It should be noted that, although Bengkulu was situated on the west side of Sumatra, it depended heavily on Java: the interregional trade figures show that a considerable part of Bengkulu's exports went through Java, either for consumption (coffee) or for re-export (the same holds for imports from Java) (Tables 25.1 and 25.2). Although the Resident promoted the cultivation of high-quality Arabica, the peasants stuck to Robusta. Several Bengkulu districts developed their own export cultivation: cloves in Seluma, pepper in Kroë, cloves and pepper in Manna and Kaur. Along the coast small quantities of copra were produced and often locally processed, mainly in Kroë, Pulau Pisang, and Enggano.[28]

Two factors explain why Bengkulu had a relatively high value of exports per capita in the period 1923-1938: its low population density and the relatively strong market position of coffee. Until 1930 per capita exports of Bengkulu were considerably less than those of Jambi and West Kalimantan, but nevertheless exceeded those of Manado, South Sulawesi, Aceh, and West Sumatra. Owing to the good market position of coffee in comparison to rubber and copra, Bengkulu displayed a stronger per capita export performance in the 1930s. In 1930-1934, Bengkulu smallholders were exporting even more than smallholders in other provinces of Cluster II (West Kalimantan, Jambi, Lampung, South Sulawesi, Manado, Aceh, and West Sumatra) (Figures 24c–24e).

Lampung

In the mountainous areas of Lampung, it follows that Hevea was not a widespread crop. But Lampung's wide stretches of swampy lowlands were comparable to those of Palembang and Jambi. Four reasons have been suggested in the sources and the literature to explain why Hevea did not develop much in Lampung.[29] These four reasons are:

1. There was little inclination among the peasants to replace traditional pepper cultivation with Hevea.
2. There was some rubber cultivation in the border regions but it was marketed in Palembang and went largely unnoticed by European observers.
3. Government policy discouraged Javanese settlers in Lampung from cultivating rubber since it wanted to steer them towards the production of rice.
4. Lampung was sparsely populated and there were very few Chinese traders.

Of these four points, only the first two stand up to close scrutiny. The first factor might be largely a matter of attitude. Since, historically, Lampung peasants had cultivated pepper on their abandoned rice *ladang*, they did not seem to be willing to replace pepper with Hevea.[30] The whole population participated in pepper cultivation, which flourished in the second half of the

28 ARA Kol, MvO 202, W.J.R. Zieck 1932:27.

29 ARA Kol, MvO 234, F.J. Junius 1933:56; MvO 199, L.C. Westenk 1920:125-32; Broersma 1916:139; Van Gelder 1950:429. Several of these arguments are also given in Purwanto 1992:161-5; see also Purwanto 1993, 1996.

30 Economists would call this 'path-dependency': specific developments dictated by history rather than by laws of economic profit.

1920s. Although pepper fields were to be found everywhere, the main centres of production were the Way Lima region, along rivers (Kota Bumi and Menggala, later abandoned), and on the coast (Kota Agung, Kalianda, and Labuan Meringgi).[31]

Rumours of high revenues from rubber, which circulated in Jambi in the early 1910s and prompted many peasants to plant rubber seedlings, did not convince Lampung peasants to do the same, since they already had a good alternative. While there were hardly any European estates in the province, many Lampung peasants already cultivated pepper fields.[32] In Jambi and Palembang, smallholders bought seedlings from Singapore traders, thereby making investments (often on credit) in the full conviction that this would be profitable. In Lampung, peasants were not tempted to invest in rubber plants to the same extent. Although the post-war recession of 1920-1922 hit pepper cultivation fairly seriously, the trade revived soon afterwards. In 1923-1925 the Resident reported that Lampung was a 'prosperous province', and was 'economically strong'. Each year, a large group of workers from Bantam came from Java to earn money harvesting pepper, and returned home afterwards.[33]

Turning to the second factor, rubber cultivation in both Lampung and Bengkulu did take place in the border regions near Palembang. These areas were accessible by the rivers, some of which flowed to Palembang (Wellan 1932:15-44). It follows that this indigenous rubber was marketed in Palembang, in trading centres such as Muara Dua, Lubuk Linggau, Tebing Tinggi, and Lahat. It is impossible to estimate the amount of indigenous rubber production that escaped the attention of the colonial administration through internal trade. Nevertheless, the existence of this unrecorded trade flow means that we would be wrong to assume that rubber was not grown in the Lampung lowlands.

Although it was the policy of the Dutch government to stimulate immigrants from Java, who were part of the government colonization programme, to start cultivating rice, their numbers were small and cannot have been very influential.[34]

The government also granted land concessions to European companies. Despite such official largesse, there were not many foreign estates in Lampung in comparison with Palembang. Estates as such would not have prevented Lampung peasants from cultivating rubber. Nor does the absence of

31 ARA, NHM 9193, VvS 1257 (Telukbetung 1912):4-5; VvS 1263 (1918):10.

32 ARA Kol, MvO 231, J. Breukink 1922:9-10, 21; ARA, NHM 9193, VvS 1257 (Telukbetung 1912):3.

33 ARA Kol, MvO 233, L. Berkhout 1926:21, 30, 48-9.

34 Booth estimates that the area of land opened up through the establishment of these *sawah*-based settlements amounted to only 40,000 hectares in Lampung, with an additional 10,000 hectares elsewhere in Sumatra and Sulawesi. Booth 1988:93.

estates explain the failure of commercial agriculture to develop. As I have argued in Chapter III, the incentive which peasants may have derived from the proximity of European estates should not be overrated: estate production differed in quality, in scale, in the amount of investment, and in labour organization. The incentive to grow rubber came from middlemen, not from European examples. As the peasants in Jambi and Palembang showed, the absence or presence of agricultural estates did not really make a difference in the indigenous propensity to develop export agriculture.

Finally, previous explanations for Lampung's slow involvement in export cultivation have focused on its low population density. Again, a glance at sparsely populated Jambi shows the weakness of this argument. Broersma states that the absence of Chinese middlemen was the major cause for the absence of Hevea production in Lampung (Broersma 1926:149). The absence of traders meant that the incentive for indigenous peasants to start growing Hevea was missing. This should be seen in conjunction with the difficulty of access that traders had to inland Lampung, from where they were unable to ship the rubber out to the main trading centres. As Purwanto has argued, this explanation does not hold water (Purwanto 1992:161-5). Indeed, according to the 1930 census, the Chinese population in Bengkulu and Lampung was relatively small, but the number of Chinese in Palembang and Jambi was smaller still (Table 16). Moreover, in southern Sumatra the participation of indigenous middlemen (Malays and Minangkabau, often *haji*) in trade was proportionally high and trade did not depend solely on the presence of Chinese.[35] In past centuries, the traders from outside Lampung who had purchased pepper had been from Bantam or from Palembang, or from further afield, Madurese or Bugis traders. Chinese traders came only after 1856, when conditions were safe (Broersma 1916:177). These Chinese were mainly retailers and supplied imported consumer goods.[36] The cultivation of pepper shows that export production was indeed feasible in Lampung.

'Amply self-sufficient'

In spite of its slow start during the 1910s and 1920s, and in spite of the absence of widespread rubber cultivation, the economic performance of Lampung was not stagnant. The traditionally minded Lampung peasant preferred pepper cultivation to rubber, not least because pepper continued to fetch a good price. Part of Lampung's export activity, including rubber, has escaped our attention since it left the residency on overland trade routes through the rainforest. In this overland trade, Lampung, as a periphery, depended on the trading centre of Palembang. Another portion of Lam-

35 ARA, NHM 9193, VvS 1257 (Telukbetung 1912):4-5; VvS 1263 (1918):11.

36 ARA, NHM 9193, VvS 1259 (Telukbetung 1914):6; VvS 1264 (1919):2; Vleming 1926:244-8.

pung's export production was exported to Java. When these latter export flows are included in the analysis, per capita export figures (including both foreign trade and trade with Java) indicate that the Lampung peasant did quite well.[37] Average per capita exports in 1926/30 were 80 guilders, which is almost as much as the 91 guilders in Jambi. This was considerably more than per capita exports in Manado, South Sulawesi, West Sumatra, and Aceh. Even during the Depression years 1930-1934, Lampung did relatively well in the cluster of indigenous producers (Table 26.1).

Although there was no explosive participation in exports as in Jambi, there are no grounds for claiming that peasants in Lampung and Bengkulu lived in hardship. In the 1930s, when several of the rare European estates in Bengkulu were threatened with closure, Resident W.J.R. Zieck remarked: 'One cannot say that the indigenous peasant will suffer from the closing of the estates. Only toko owners and taxi drivers will notice that the number of contract coolies among their customers has been reduced.' In the inaccessible and mountainous province of Bengkulu, the indigenous population was 'amply self-sufficient', according to this Resident.[38] Lampung, which benefited from roads and railways constructed by the colonial government, had a consistent though not excessive income from indigenous pepper. Even though some rubber was planted, pepper remained the 'basis on which the whole economy of Lampung rested', as the NHM agent in Telukbetung put it in 1939. In the late 1930s, the coupons that allowed individual rubber quotas to be exported were often sold to Palembang and rubber gardens remained untapped.[39]

Rubber occupied only a small share in these economies, and consequently export production during the 1920s and 1930s was less sensational than in Jambi or Palembang. But, largely unnoticed by the outside world, hidden trade generated steady flows of export revenues in these regions, enriching the traditional subsistence economy.

Western versus eastern Sumatra

With minor exceptions, the provinces of eastern Sumatra occupied a more favourable position than those on the west side. Viewed from East Sumatra, Tapanuli was a periphery. Similarly, from the point of view of Palembang, Bengkulu (and initially Lampung as well) was a peripheral province. On the relatively accessible east side of Sumatra, several provinces developed an impressive indigenous export production. The most successful provinces

37 Contemporary chroniclers based much of their judgement of economic behaviour exclusively on production for foreign export. An exception is Wellan, who includes interregional trade statistics in his study on Lampung, Palembang, Bengkulu, and Jambi. Wellan 1932:169, 391.

38 ARA Kol, MvO 202, W.J.R. Zieck 1932:27, 34.

39 ARA, NHM 9193, VvS 1268 (Telukbetung 1939):10, 18.

were Palembang, East Sumatra, and Jambi – the latter being an exceptional case since all rubber production originated from indigenous smallholders. Indragiri was the only eastern province that seemed to lag behind. Its lameness is explained by its situation as a no-man's-land between East Sumatra and the Jambi/Palembang area: since infrastructural developments (roads, railways, harbours) grew from the trading centres in north and south, the middle area was neglected. Initially Indragiri produced relatively little for foreign or domestic markets, but eventually developed into an important indigenous rubber producer in the late 1920s. Whereas the Riau Archipelago attracted European capital, in Indragiri (mainland Riau) there were only indigenous rubber smallholders.

For all its mountains, the population on the western side of Sumatra was economically very active. The Sumatran peasant, whether Malay, Batak, Minangkabau, or from Lampung, participated almost everywhere in commercial export agriculture. Although exports ranged from pepper to coffee to rubber, or a combination of these, there were no regions devoid of export agriculture. This even distribution stands in sharp contrast to Western estate agriculture, which was concentrated in a few locations and favoured a few provinces by generating an accelerated development of roads, railways, and harbours. Smallholders in provinces that lacked such benefits managed to reach foreign markets either through their own indigenous or Chinese trading networks.

While all Sumatran smallholders seem to have keenly focused on expanding trade, there was a much larger discrepancy between them and the smallholders in the 'Great East'. In the eastern archipelago, conditions were quite different. Here copra was the main indigenous product. Export revenues were small and the distances to be covered to reach buyers were large. As we will see in the following section, indigenous export participation in the eastern archipelago displayed less dynamism.

Isolation in the eastern archipelago

The third group of small economies was situated in the east: Bali and Lombok, the Lesser Sunda Islands, Maluku, and New Guinea. In contrast to Bengkulu, Lampung, and Tapanuli these economies were not only small, they were also hampered by the fact that there were no active centres nearby from whose development they could profit. As Broek wrote:

> The eastern islands of the archipelago have not shared to any great extent in the recent commercial development. Plantation agriculture is almost nonexistent [...]. This may be in some measure a consequence of the tumultuous past, with its suppression, mismanagement, and constant wars over the spice

> monopoly. But the natural environment is largely responsible for much of the present-day backwardness. The islands are mountainous and, apart from New Guinea, small so that there is little arable land. The pronounced dry season limits the number of crops that can be grown. Moreover, these islands are greatly handicapped by their unfavourable location away from the major shipping lanes. (Broek 1942:50.)

These were the harsh features of the provinces in the periphery, as sketched by J.O.M. Broek in 1942. The out-of-the-way location of eastern Indonesia provides an obvious clue towards understanding the slow development of foreign exports. Whereas Tapanuli profited from East Sumatra's roads or from Minangkabau traders from Padang, and Bengkulu peasants could find a ready market for rubber in Palembang, the isolated islands in the eastern archipelago had no such advantages.

The Lesser Sunda Islands formed the bottom row in all trade statistics. Close scrutiny of these statistics reveals hardly any change over the period 1900-1940. More than 90 per cent of Timor's trade was directed to Java, substantially improving the picture that would be obtained by examining the foreign trade statistics alone. The latter show no overall surplus on the balance of trade for the period 1900-1940, in contrast to all other provinces, where foreign exports exceeded imports (Tables 28 and 32) (Clemens et al. 1992:58). Including interregional trade, Timor and Dependencies had an average positive surplus on its balance of trade of almost 3 million guilders in 1924/28, 1.6 million in 1929/33, and 1.4 million in 1934/38. As a percentage of export value, the surplus was between 50 and 60 per cent.[40]

The low volume of exports failed to generate imports among the indigenous population. Much of the revenue ended up in the pockets of traders, who took advantage of the fairly inexperienced trading skills of smallholders in these islands. In Sumatra and Kalimantan, Chinese traders put British-trade dollars and Mexican dollars into circulation, but in the small-scale economy of Timor there was hardly any money. 'Upon my appointment to the residency, barter trade prevailed almost everywhere', Resident J.F.A. de Rooy wrote in 1908.[41] De Rooy banned the trade monopolies of foreign traders, and

40 Average surplus on the balance of trade in Timor and Dependencies in five-year periods, including exports to Java and exports to other Outer Islands (in millions of guilders):

	Exports	(Foreign exports)	Imports	Surplus	Surplus as % of exports
1924-1928	4.9	(0.08)	1.9	3.0	59
1929-1933	3.1	(0.25)	1.4	1.7	51
1934-1938	2.3	(0.08)	0.9	1.4	60

(Source: Tables 25.1 and 25.2)

41 ARA Kol, MvO 339, J.F.A. de Rooy 1908:21.

introduced small copper coins in Maumere (Flores), Alor, and central Timor, where money was either hardly known or entirely absent. A recurring problem was usury and the corrupt trade practices of foreign traders and Dutch merchants and missionaries, who reportedly took advantage of innocent inhabitants by lending money at very high interest or by selling gunpowder and arak in exchange for large quantities of local products.[42]

Where no expansion took place, vulnerability to the world economic situation remained small, but only in a relative sense. Timor's average per capita export revenue in 1931/35 fell to a level of 35 per cent of its average exports in 1926/30. As a comparison, in Jambi per capita export revenue had-dwindled to a mere 20 per cent. Despite such a fall, even during the Depression years per capita export revenue in Jambi was much higher than in Timor and Dependencies (Table 26.1). Only an assessment of subsistence income, which is difficult to attain, would reveal the true economic situation.[43]

In Maluku, some government officials attributed the low production of cash crops to the abundant cultivation of sago, which dominated smallholder agriculture and provided a relatively effortless supply of food. Agricultural consultant E.P. Wellenstein advised attempting to change the mentality of the population towards agriculture. But he conceded that high KPM freight costs impeded all export agriculture in this province.[44]

As in South Sulawesi and Manado, coconut groves formed the major source of export products on several of the islands of Maluku. Chinese traders purchased the copra from smallholders. When advances turned into unpaid debts, the owner had to rent his coconut groves to the Chinese trader. In Buru (today an island of dubious reputation) in some villages 90 per cent of the coconut groves were reported to be run by Chinese traders.[45]

The soil in Ternate was relatively fertile. The forest supplied ironwood, resins (copal, damar), and rattan. In 1900-1920, roughly 20 to 30 per cent of Maluku's exports consisted of forest products. Ternate provided a fluctuating share of these, varying from 70 per cent in 1906 to 20 per cent in 1922.[46] In Halmahera, the indigenous population collected large quantities of damar,

42 ARA Kol, MvO 339, J.F.A. de Rooy 1908:22; MvO 340, C. van Rietschoten 1913:113. Rietschoten mentions the better educated Rotinese and Sawunese (from the southernmost islands of Roti and Sawu) who competed with Chinese and Endehnese traders in 'usury and unfair credit'.

43 For the Outer Islands as a whole, per capita exports declined to 40 per cent in 1931-1935, compared to 1926-1930. This reduction is not as dramatic as that in Jambi or Timor, largely due to the relatively constant character of oil and tin revenues (which were not earned by the indigenous population).

44 ARA Kol, MvO 335, B.J. Haga 1937:69-70. In 1933 Wellenstein became director of the Department of Economic Affairs.

45 ARA Kol, MvO 335, B.J. Haga 1937:75-7; Habiboe 1989:253.

46 Habiboe 1989:252. For additional trade figures on forest products, see Boomgaard and De Bakker 1996.

which was sold to European and Chinese traders.[47] Sago cultivation provided an easy supply of food, but it was reported that every peasant owned his own plot for cultivating tobacco, sugar cane, and other crops in addition to sago. Tidore provided an even slightly higher export production. Resident K.H.F. Roos stated in 1909 that the Maluku population managed to earn considerable sums of money – often silver dollars – which were saved and hidden in the ground, to be dug up for marriage festivities or other rituals.[48] Currency thus remained out of circulation for prolonged periods. At this time, non-barter trade was conducted at an unhurried pace, as these 'considerable sums' were not needed for imported goods or taxes. The little trading that was done went via three trading centres: Ternate, Pulau Bacan, and Fakfak (western New Guinea). A small number of concessions were issued on Halmahera, Obi (to the Obi Gom Maatschappij (Obi Gum Company)), and New Guinea, for timber cutting, damar collection, and pearl fishing. Damar collection in Halmahera, Morotai, and Bacan provided a constant source of supplementary income, which meant the effects of the Depression were felt in these islands when the damar price fell in 1930.[49]

Dutch administrators judged the subsistence economy they observed to be fairly primitive. 'Looking at Ambon and Saparua, one is often at a loss to know how the local population make a living', wrote Governor B.J. Haga in 1937. Fishing was another important subsistence activity in this area. It sounded promising but, according to Haga, people were handicapped by primitive methods and lack of technological progress, and therefore fished mainly for their own consumption. Any exports of fish to Java were few and far between, and Japanese fishers using motorized vessels easily earned high revenues.[50] The sea formed a natural resource almost comparable to the Sumatran rainforest. While 'many islands are not fertile and lack the resources to encourage modernization', the land and the sea 'offer everything that is needed for subsistence, circumstances which have made the population very easygoing', according to Resident G. Sieburg. A corresponding statement was made by Resident C.C. Ouwerling, who quoted an Ambonese proverb: 'Whoever has once sated his appetite with fresh fish will not climb the mountain to eat *dengdeng*.'[51]

47 *Damar* is the Malay word for resins. Copal is a cheaper type of damar. Both were used to prepare varnish, shellac, synthetic leathers, and linoleum. Indigenous uses of damar were to make torches and caulk the keels of prahus.

48 ARA Kol, MvO 321, K.H.F. Roos 1909:20-1.

49 ARA Kol, MvO 321, K.H.F. Roos 1909:23-4; MvO 322, E.J. Gerrits 1912:34, 36; MvO 327, W.A. Hovenkamp 1931:27.

50 ARA Kol, MvO 335, B.J. Haga 1937:70, 72.

51 ARA Kol, MvO 312, G. Sieburg 1910:25; MvO 315, C.C. Ouwerling 1930:2, 25. *Dengdeng* or *dendeng* is dried, spiced meat, often venison (deer).

In his book on Lombok Van der Kraan emphasizes that the consequences of Dutch rule in this island were predominantly negative. He describes the impoverishment of the peasants, the increasing concentration of landownership in the hands of Balinese and Sasak landlords, and the worsening of the food situation for Lombok inhabitants. Resident J. Eschbach was not concerned about such underdevelopment: he remarked that the poverty which could be blamed on the Balinese rulers had been alleviated. One of his successors, H. Beeuwkes, also stressed that subsistence food production was adequate in Lombok. Whatever their opinions, it is obvious that improved prosperity due to export production, as observed in such provinces as Jambi or West Kalimantan, was scarcely visible in Lombok. Van der Kraan shows that the burden of the land tax in Lombok grew. Already heavily burdened, peasants had to surrender large parts of their harvests to their landlords. Resident Beeuwkes stated that the land tax remained more important than income tax in Lombok. This is interesting, since after 1900 in colonial Indonesia as a whole, income tax and excises assumed greater significance as a source of government revenue than land tax.[52]

In a nutshell, in Maluku and Timor indigenous inhabitants were less engaged in commercial activity than in Sumatra. The small provinces of Sumatra were assiduously engaged in various trading activities. The eastern periphery, on the whole, lacked the production factors that might generate vent-for-surplus production. There was little European activity.

No exports without rice

Both in Java and in the Outer Islands, rice has been the most important single food crop since time immemorial. Rice was the main staple crop in most of the archipelago, except Maluku, New Guinea, and Madura, where sago was the main crop, and Sulawesi and Timor, where in addition to rice other food crops such as maize were important (Van der Eng 1993a:27, 152; 1996c:18, 165; Tergast 1931-32:195; Booth 1988). It is difficult to estimate the total production of rice in colonial Indonesia. In the Outer Islands, production was not recorded systematically, as it was in Java during this period.[53] The only indication of the degree of self-sufficiency in food production in the Outer Islands is that obtained from the trade statistics.

In Java, in addition to local rice cultivation, substantial imports were necessary until the 1930s. The agricultural statistics estimate an annual rice har-

52 ARA Kol, MvO 355, J. Eschbach 1905:21; MvO 362, H. Beeuwkes 1932:28, 44-5; Van der Kraan 1980b:166-74. See also Booth 1990a:220.

53 Van de Koppel 1946:373; *Landbouwexportgewassen* 1931:245, 1933:204.

vest of about 3.4 million hectares in Java in 1926/30. Booth estimates the annual rice availability in Java as 89 kg per capita in 1921/30, and slightly less in subsequent years.[54] Van der Eng, who concentrates on production, estimates a total production of paddy rice in Java of between 5.4 and 7.3 million tons per year during 1921/30, which amounts to roughly 2.7 to 3.6 million tons of clean rice. This leads to production estimates of about 85-90 kg per capita in the 1920s and 1930s (Van der Eng 1996c:169, 295).

In the Outer Islands, dependent on *ladang* cultivation with its lower yields, rice cultivation per capita was not as high as in Java and rice imports were concomitantly higher. But food was in ample supply; rice available per capita in the Outer Islands is estimated by Van der Eng to have been 27 per cent higher than in Java (using a post-war proportion between 10 of the Outer Provinces and Java in 1954-1957). He calculates a total production of 4,574 million kg of paddy rice in the Outer Islands in 1930 (Van der Eng 1996c:295). This would mean that per capita clean rice production may have been as high as 120 kg – but again, this production was supplemented by substantial imports.[55]

The share of imported rice in total domestic consumption in colonial Indonesia increased from approximately 6 per cent on average in 1900/09, to 9 per cent in 1920/29, according to Van der Eng. It declined to 5 per cent in 1930/39 in the wake of government restrictions on rice imports.[56] The proportion of imported rice to total consumption was higher in the Outer Islands than in Java. In 1920/29, the Outer Islands imported on average 11 per cent of their total rice consumption. In 1929, a peak year of foreign rice imports, imports into the Outer Islands were about 765,000 tons (Figure 15). Total production of rice is estimated to have been around 2,200,000 tons in that year. In Java, imports amounted to 346,000 tons in 1929, while approximately 3,400,000 tons of rice were produced. Thus, in 1929 the Outer Islands import-

54 Harvested area in husked rice equivalents; 87 per cent of harvested area was *sawah* and 13 per cent dry land; 93 per cent of the production was from *sawah*. Booth 1988:123; *Landbouwexportgewassen* 1931:245.

55 Van der Eng estimated Outer Islands rice production by using per capita food supply approximations, multiplied by reconstructed population figures, to which exports were added and from which imports were deducted. This reconstruction hinges on the annual per capita food supply, which is difficult to determine. Van der Eng concedes that 'the whole procedure used for the Outer Islands is undoubtedly rough'. Nevertheless, he argues convincingly that production was slightly lower than suggested by earlier estimates from the 1930s and 1950. Van der Eng estimates that in 1910-1940 total paddy rice production in Java slowly increased from circa 6 million tons per year to 9 million tons per year. Likewise, he estimates that aggregate paddy rice production in the Outer Islands increased from circa 3 million to circa 5 million tons per year in 1910-1940. Van der Eng 1993a:282-4, 1996c:293-7.

56 Clemens et al. 1992:79-80; Van der Eng 1996c:182-4. See also Creutzberg 1972-75:119-20, 203-5.

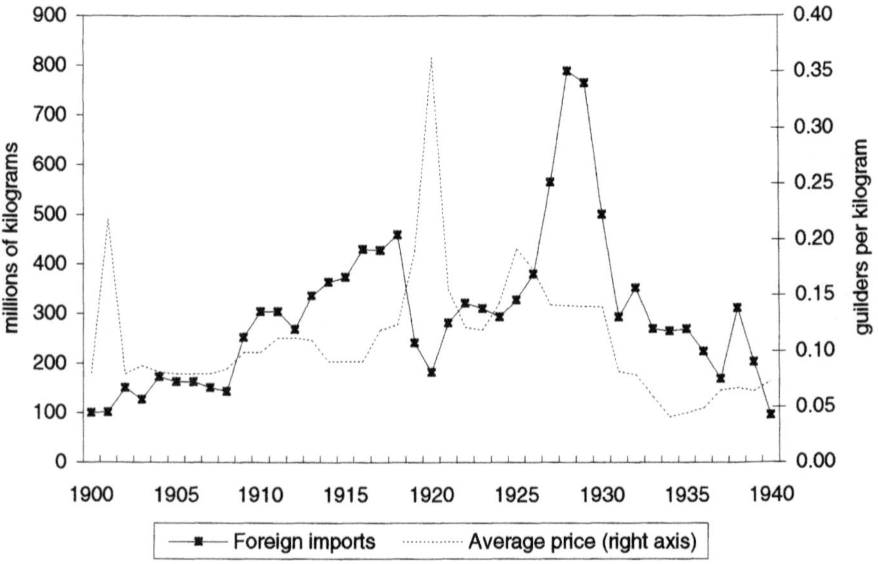

Figure 15. Foreign rice imports and average rice prices, 1900-1940 (Trade statistics).

ed approximately 15 per cent and Java 9 per cent of its rice consumption (not taking into account interregional rice trade between Java and the Outer Islands (Clemens et al. 1992:75; Van der Eng 1996c:297). This larger proportion of rice imports in the Outer Islands can be explained by a concentration on cash crops, much infertile land, and the employment of coolie labour by European enterprises. Imports varied considerably per province, but on average imports account for only about 0.3 kg per capita per year.

In Chapter III, I reviewed the imports of rice that were generated by European enterprise in East Sumatra, Palembang, and Southeast Kalimantan. In this section I will concentrate on the rice trade in the archipelago in general, and indigenous rice production in the Outer Islands. In many Outer Islands, rice was cultivated on *ladang*, but in West Sumatra, Tapanuli, Aceh, South Sulawesi, and Bali a lot of rice was produced on *sawah*. *Sawah* were also cultivated in Minahasa (Manado), as well as in Hulu Sungai (Southeast Kalimantan), and in Sumbawa (Lesser Sunda Islands) (Tergast 1931-32:196).

Under the free market conditions, colonial Indonesia depended increasingly on imported rice until the 1930s. Per capita rice imports in the Outer Islands increased from 13 kg in 1900/09 to 17 kg in 1910/19. (For Java the figures were 4 kg and 8 kg.) Foreign imports increased steadily, mainly because in the 1910s the cultivation of export crops by the indigenous population necessitated imports of rice previously grown locally. Another factor affecting imports was the steady increase of coolie labour in the Outer Provinces, reaching an initial peak in 1919 of 300,000 workers (of whom roughly 250,000 were employed in East Sumatra) and a higher peak in 1929 of about 540,000 (about 300,000 of them in East Sumatra). Incontrovertibly, increasing urbanization and the growth of production centres of the petroleum industry also raised the demand for imported rice.

It was not always convenient to rely on imports. In 1919, after a period of continuously mounting rice imports, a rice shortage on the world market caused the price to soar. The colonial government reacted by promoting self-sufficiency in rice and encouraging rice cultivation, with the result that until 1925 imports were lower than in 1918 (Figure 15; Prince 1989:213-4). During the years 1925-1929 a rapid expansion in rice imports reflected the explosion in indigenous exports and the simultaneous boom in estate agriculture, which automatically triggered a rise in the number of coolies. The number of Javanese coolies hired for public construction works also increased when rubber smallholders paid off their obligation to do corvée labour.[57] Indigenous export agriculture not only pushed rice cultivation into the background, in the 1920s it also brought Javanese tapping coolies to the Outer Islands.

After 1929 demand for rice fell. The rubber-tapping coolies were forced to return home as soon as the Depression robbed smallholder exports of their profit margin. Large numbers of estate coolies were laid off and many indigenous peasants returned to the cultivation of food crops. Imports did not fall immediately, as harvest failures in Bali, South Sulawesi, and Aceh in 1929-1930 delayed the reduction of foreign imports.[58] Since under the influence of the crisis the price of rice in mainland Asia fell faster than the price of indigenous export commodities, smallholders continued to import foreign rice. The government introduced licences and taxes designed to restrict rice imports and stabilize the domestic rice price, in order to protect domestic rice-producing households, especially those in Java. By 1931 the rice price had fallen to a record low. In Palembang the ban on foreign rice imports drove up the price of rice from 4 cents to 6.5 cents per kg in 1933.

During the whole period, at times when there were international rice shortages, the government banned rice exports to avoid the depletion of rice stocks within the colony. This happened for instance in 1911, 1912, 1914, and between 1917 and 1920, when three calamities coincided: harvest failures, an influenza epidemic, and a blockade of sea transport. In 1921 this export ban was lifted.[59]

57 ARA Kol, MvO 212, J. Tideman 1928:156-7; MvO 215, W. Steinbuch 1936:390; MvO 223, J.R.F. Verschoor van Nisse 1931:126.

58 Coolie labourers were estimated by Tergast to consume about 230 to 240 kg of rice per year. Others arrive at similar estimates. Tergast 1931-32:199, 201; Potting 1997:91; Thee Kian Wie 1977:116.

59 ARA Kol, MvO 215, W. Steinbuch 1936:198-9; Boomgaard 1986:68-9; Van der Eng 1996c:184. See also Chapter VI.

Rice trade in the archipelago

Within the domestic economy of colonial Indonesia, the rice trade assumed an important place. Almost all provinces imported rice occasionally, but several also exported rice – to Java or to other Outer Islands.[60] The major rice exporters within the archipelago were Java, Bali, and South Sulawesi (Tables 56.1–56.4). Several ports in Java imported and exported rice simultaneously. The major importers of domestic as well as foreign rice were the European estates in East Sumatra and the tin mines on Bangka and Belitung. Only a little rice was cultivated locally on the tin islands.

Two ten-year periods were studied, 1917-1926 and 1929-1938, to find out whether the interregional rice trade changed when the 'boom years' before the Depression turned into a decade of economic malaise compounded by government intervention. Although rice flows varied in volume and direction from year to year, averages were calculated to reveal structural differences (Tables 56.1 and 56.2).

Provinces where smallholders concentrated on the cultivation of export crops in the 1920s and 1930s, such as Jambi and West Kalimantan, depended heavily on rice imports from other parts of the archipelago. The fact that in both provinces the average imported volume of rice increased after 1929 (from 15 million kg and 35 million kg in 1917/26 to 19 million kg and 45 million kg in 1929/37) indicates that the employment of family labour instead of hired labour when rubber prices were low left little room for raising food crops (Tables 56.1 and 56.2). Commercial agriculture thus appears to have changed the economy irreversibly, because even with small profit margins, exports continued and rice imports remained high. In Palembang, smallholders were more flexible in cultivating their own food crops. Here surplus rice imports diminished from 26 million kg in 1917/26 to 15 million kg in 1929/38, owing partly to reductions in coolie labour in estate agriculture and mining.[61] The same happened in Southeast Kalimantan, where rice imports declined from 36 million kg to 17 million kg.

In West Sumatra rice cultivation had once been an important activity. Until the 1920s, West Sumatra was a net exporter of rice, but in the 1930s, the cultivation of copra, coffee, and rubber replaced cultivation of rice, and concomitantly the expansion of the estate area enlarged the number of labourers

[60] During most of the period 1900-1940, a relatively small proportion of domestically grown rice in Java was exported to the Outer Islands. In 1929-1938, for example, circa 22,000 tons of rice was exported to the Outer Islands. In the Outer Islands, these rice imports from Java were supplemented by a much larger volume from abroad (in 1929-1938: 425,000 tons per year on average) (Table 56.3).

[61] 'Since the fall in the prices of agricultural products, the indigenous population has devoted itself to the cultivation of rice.' ARA Kol, MvO 214, J.L.M. Schwaab 1933:183.

dependent on imported rice (Van de Koppel 1946:375).

Several provinces in Sumatra supplied rice to the agricultural estates in adjacent regions. From Aceh, rice was exported to East Sumatra and West Sumatra, from Tapanuli to Aceh and West Sumatra. Likewise, interregional exports from Palembang went to Jambi and Lampung, and from Bangka to Palembang.[62] This illustrates the division of Sumatra into a northern and a southern market. In the north, East Sumatra functioned as a centre which drew on Aceh and Tapanuli for supplies. In southern Sumatra, Palembang was the centre, trading with Jambi, Lampung, and Bangka. Since overland transportation in mid-Sumatra was difficult (roads were bad and railways absent), these two areas can be viewed as two separate trading zones (Wijnaends van Resandt 1928). Southeast Kalimantan's exports to the other Outer Islands went to South Sulawesi and Manado; from South Sulawesi, exports were directed towards Maluku and the Lesser Sunda Islands; and from Bali, to South Sulawesi and Manado.

The small provinces of Cluster IV (outside Sumatra) imported little rice, less than 4 per cent of total rice imports in 1911-1940 (Clemens et al. 1992:80). Statistics on the interregional rice trade clearly show that Lampung, Bengkulu, Maluku, and Timor were oriented towards Java for their rice imports. Rice imports from Java were higher than foreign rice imports in 1917/38 for Lampung, Bengkulu, and Timor. Remarkably, before 1929 this was also true of West Sumatra. Bali and South Sulawesi had a consistent flow of rice exports to other Outer Islands in 1917/38. Bali not only supplied rice to other Outer Islands, but also exported it to Java (Table 56.4).

The heart of domestic rice trade

Of the other provinces, South Sulawesi held an interesting position as far as the rice trade is concerned. Here rice was a transit commodity. South Sulawesi did not require large rice imports for the food supply of European enterprises. Nevertheless, it imported rice from abroad (from Saigon and Thailand (Siam)), and imported more rice from Java than it exported to Java. Sulawesi also exported rice to other Outer Islands (mainly to Manado, Maluku, and the Lesser Sunda Islands) – on the whole, in the period 1918-1937, South Sulawesi imported slightly more than it exported. This confirms the important function of Macassar as a transit port for the 'Great East'.[63] Although it was important as an entrepôt port, it also exported rice grown in inland

62 In a note with each table, the early interregional trade statistics state major destinations. See for example *Statistiek intergewestelijke handel* 1921:180-9 [Mededeelingen van het Centraal Kantoor voor de Statistiek 3].

63 In terms of value exported, Macassar was the fourth largest port in the Outer Islands in 1938, after Palembang and Belawan in Sumatra and Balikpapan in Southeast Kalimantan (Table 23).

South Sulawesi. At times, so much rice was harvested in South Sulawesi (there were 227,000 hectares of *sawah* in 1936) that it piled up and new markets had to be found.[64] Sulawesi formed the heart of the rice trade in the eastern archipelago.

Dick remarks that 'in terms of both value and tonnage, the most spectacular growth in inter-island trade during the 1930s was in the rice trade from Java to the Outer Islands' (Dick 1990:310, 1996:43). Indeed, interregional exports from Java increased substantially towards the end of the 1930s. In contrast, Java's net interregional exports decreased from an annual average of 20 million kg in 1917/26 to 14 million kg in 1929/38 (Tables 56.3 and 56.4).

Rice supply from the periphery?

The small provinces of Cluster IV played a minor role as rice suppliers to the provinces that concentrated on the cultivation of cash crops. Of Cluster IV provinces, only Bali enjoyed the remarkable position of having a well-developed (*sawah*) rice production. Its exports were directed to both Java and other Outer Islands. *Sawah* rice in Bali was characterized by a high productivity, which was facilitated by its high population density. Its function as a rice supplier was relatively recent: although in the 1910s Lombok exported some rice, until 1923 Bali and Lombok needed extra rice imports: their net annual imports of rice amounted to 5,000 tons. Their increasing output of rice was due largely to government stimulation of irrigated rice cultivation.[65]

Tapanuli, Bengkulu, and Lampung did not produce much surplus rice, although they occasionally exported to adjacent provinces. Maluku frequently depended on foreign imports – but here rice was only a supplementary food and not a staple. The Lesser Sunda Islands were self-sufficient in rice in the 1930s – which was a major accomplishment considering the climatic and soil conditions on some of these islands (Table 56.2).

Collectors of forest products

Forest products such as rattan, forest rubber (gutta percha), damar, and copal were simply collected in the forest and sold to traders. Although the share of these products decreased when tree-crop cultivation was introduced, they maintained a fairly constant volume within total exports. Collection of forest products was a common secondary activity for the local population in the interior, whose main occupation was cultivating subsist-

64 ARA Kol, MvO 286, L.J.J. Caron 1933:99, 259, 262-4; MvO 287, J.L.M. Swaab 1936:187-9.

65 ARA Kol, MvO 355, J. Eschbach 1905:31; MvO 362, H. Beeuwkes 1932:25; Van de Koppel 1946:376. See also Booth 1988:30, 119-21; Van der Eng 1996c:168-82.

ence crops (Cohen 1939).

The share of rattan in total foreign exports of the Outer Islands was not very large, and it decreased steadily: on average, about 5 per cent of the export value in 1900/10, 2 per cent during 1910/20, and 1 per cent in 1920/40.[66] It is worth taking a closer look at who supplied rattan within the archipelago. Large rattan exporters were South Sulawesi, Southeast Kalimantan, and Palembang – provinces where the indigenous inhabitants were heavily engaged in the cultivation of cash crops. In 1921/30 South Sulawesi had an average annual export of almost 12 million kg of rattan, and in 1921/30 this swelled to 16 million kg. In the latter decade, Southeast Kalimantan exported 11 million kg and Palembang about 5 million kg. In Southeast Kalimantan, gutta percha and rattan constituted roughly 70 per cent of foreign exports in the 1880s and 1890s, but the revenue seldom exceeded 1 million guilders.[67]

While West Sumatra exported relatively large quantities of rattan, Bengkulu and Tapanuli did not. But the importance of this forest product in the smaller provinces is revealed when we consider per capita foreign exports of rattan by the indigenous population. Now Manado and Jambi appear at the top of the list, exporting roughly 10 kg of rattan per capita per year in the first decade of the 1900s. Even though producers in Jambi started to develop rubber cultivation during the 1910s, average per capita rattan exports increased to 20 kg and remained at 12 kg in the 1920s. In Manado, in 1911/20, rattan exports decreased to about 5 kg per capita. This level of rattan production was also found in Palembang, Riau, West Kalimantan, Southeast Kalimantan, and South Sulawesi. In three provinces the per capita volume of rattan exports increased during 1900-1930: Riau, Palembang, and South Sulawesi. Jambi was the only province in which rattan occupied a substantial share in the export package: 30 per cent in 1900/10, 20 per cent in 1911/20.

Since the nineteenth century there had been a strong tradition in colonial Indonesia of exporting gutta percha. Gutta percha was used mainly for the insulation of electrical and telegraph wires, as well as for shellac. The Goodyear company also produced funnels, flasks, fan belts, and shoe soles from gutta percha. In the nineteenth century the latex was acquired by cutting down the trees, but at the instigation of M. Treub in 1883, the colonial government stimulated its preparation from the leaves (*Getah pertja* 1917:784).

Gutta percha was exported mainly from Palembang, West Kalimantan, and Southeast Kalimantan, although most other provinces also exported some gutta percha. From Palembang and West Kalimantan, average exports

66 Trade statistics. Additional figures on interregional and foreign trade in forest products are presented in Boomgaard and De Bakker 1996.

67 ARA Kol, MvO 277, B.C.C.M.M. van Suchtelen 1933:178; Lindblad 1988a:14, 1001.

of gutta in 1900/20 were about 3 million kg. From Southeast Kalimantan the average exports in 1900/20 amounted to more than 5 million kg. After 1920, gutta percha exports decreased, as it was increasingly replaced by Hevea or synthetic products. Jambi also exported gutta percha, albeit at a much lower level than rattan. Most of this gutta was collected by Kubus, who made a living from this economic activity (Tideman 1938:217).

The export of resins such as damar, copal, and benzoin was more widespread throughout the archipelago. For many centuries, the indigenous population of Palembang and Southeast Kalimantan had sold damar and benzoin alongside rattan and timber. After the First World War, the coastal regions embarked on new kinds of trade, but the interior remained focused on the collection of forest products.[68] Benzoin from the interior of Palembang was processed in small Chinese-owned factories in the town of Palembang. During the Depression, exports of damar, benzoin, *pinang* nuts, and rattan were reportedly marketed by smallholders to supplement their dwindling rubber revenues.[69] Benzoin was also an important export commodity in northern Tapanuli, a trade, as in Palembang, mostly pursued by Chinese entrepreneurs.[70]

Forerunner of success or consolation in poverty?

Almost all provinces participated in the sale of forest products. Damar and gambir supplemented rattan and gutta in West Kalimantan. In South Sulawesi, gum copal and agar-agar (dried seaweed) were being collected in addition to rattan even before World War I. Collection of damar, ebony, and rattan in conjunction with copra and food-crop cultivation formed the basic economic characteristics of Manado, according to Resident A.Ph. van Aken.[71]

Maluku and Timor produced small quantities of resins, which formed a limited but essential supplement to the cultivation of food crops. Again, much of this trade was in the hands of Arab and Chinese intermediary traders. Resident G. Sieburg complained that this was the consequence of careless chiefs, who signed 'foolish' concession contracts in order to pocket large advance payments.[72] Damar and copal were produced in Halmahera, Morotai, and Bacan. Of the Lesser Sunda Islands, it was Sumba, the most promising island

68 ARA Kol, MvO 215, W. Steinbuch 1936:194, 278; MvO 271, L.J.F. Rijckmans 1916:31, 35; Lindblad 1988a:14, 101.

69 ARA Kol, MvO 215, W. Steinbuch 1936:276-8. In Sumatra and Kalimantan, the traditional collection of gutta and rattan gave way to modern logging – a more permanently damaging form of collection of wood products.

70 ARA Kol, MvO 732, E.E.W.C. Schröder 1920:516, 575.

71 ARA Kol, MvO 265, J. Oberman 1938:42-4; MvO 261, H. de Vogel 1918:26; MvO 264, K.H. van Prehn 1933:6; MvO 284, Th.A.L. Heyting 1916:75, 98; MvO 306, A.Ph. van Aken 1933:22a.

72 ARA Kol, MvO 312, G. Sieburg 1910:35.

of the Timor Archipelago, which exported the most forest products.[73]

One essential question remains. Did the collection of forest products function as a forerunner of cash-crop cultivation? By 1900, several provinces had developed considerable connections with outside markets and exported large quantities of rattan and gutta percha, which were collected in the forest. In Southeast Kalimantan and Palembang, these exports persisted in the interior, whereas more accessible regions converted to cash-crop cultivation. In Jambi rattan was the next favourite export product of rubber growers. In this province the collection of rattan alternated with export agriculture. But except for rattan, the collection of forest products as a commercial activity did evolve into the cultivation of export crops. Several provinces, such as Aceh, Bengkulu, and Lampung, barely participated in this type of trade. In other provinces in the periphery, resins were collected and sold to supplement subsistence agriculture. Maluku exported damar and a little rattan. Tapanuli exported benzoin. In these provinces, the collection of forest products did not develop into commercial export agriculture. It was instead a way to supplement subsistence agriculture with money income.

Tempted by traders?

Development of export production may arise as the consequence of consumer demand and the wish to expand money income. In the Outer Islands, export revenues generated imports of consumer goods and necessitated imports of rice. Consumer demand for most foreign goods in most provinces was very low before export agriculture and intermediary trade gained momentum. Besides this, there was an autonomous demand for import goods such as rice. Reviewing the case of the provinces with low exports, it can be surmised that expanding horizons, personified by KPM and small Bugis and other traders, and the subsequent acquaintance with a variety of potential imports, generated an appetite for consumer goods before export revenues were earned. In this section I examine imports and the trade surplus in these provinces to identify patterns of import and export trade development.

In the small provinces, imports did not follow exports the way they did in provinces with large export production. The statistical correlation between imports and exports in these provinces is generally low: the value of the Pearson correlation coefficient is not significant for Timor (and Dependencies), Aceh, Bali, Manado, Bangka, or Tapanuli. In Timor there was no systematic statistical correlation between imports and exports at all ($R = 0.03$) (Table 57).

Not surprisingly, provinces near Java drew their imports from Java. Lam-

[73] ARA Kol, MvO 335, B.J. Haga 1937:252; MvO 339, J.F.A. de Rooy 1908:90-2.

pung, Timor, and Bali imported the largest share of their imports from Java: more than 75 per cent in 1924/38 (Table 25.2). In 1934/38, Maluku also imported 71 per cent of its imports from Java.

Average annual imports in Timor were very low: less than 2,000 guilders per year in 1924/28, less than 1,400 guilders and 1,000 guilders in 1929/33 and 1934/38. Demand in Timor was undeniably small. Per capita imports were absolutely the lowest of all Outer Islands (Table 25.2). Maluku, Tapanuli, and Bali precede Timor on the list of average annual per capita imports.

Most provinces had a surplus on the total balance of trade exceeding the average of 47 per cent for all Outer Islands in the period 1923/38 (Table 33). It is remarkable that the provinces with very low foreign exports display a positive surplus on the balance of trade even when interregional trade is included.

In his analysis of foreign trade, Lindblad (1990) calculates these surplus percentages on the basis of foreign trade statistics alone. He classifies Tapanuli and Bengkulu as displaying at one time or another a deficit rather than a surplus. My figures including trade with Java result in a rehabilitation for these provinces, which at that time, instead of a deficit, showed a relatively large surplus. These are minor adjustments, but they are essential for the provinces with small volumes of foreign exports: they reveal more export trade in Tapanuli and Bengkulu than has previously been surmised (Clemens et al. 1992:43-4; Lindblad 1990b:220-1).

With regard to the distribution of imports in different categories, rice and textiles formed the main expenditures. In Maluku the percentage of additional foodstuffs in imports was remarkably small, which confirms the impression that these islands were largely self-sufficient in foodstuffs other than rice (for example fish and sago) and there was little extra money to spend after rice had been bought. In most small provinces, the share in imports of consumer goods such as textiles and clothing decreased quickly when the Depression set in (Tables 54.1 and 54.2).

Bali, Timor and Dependencies, and Maluku taken together accounted for a very small percentage of total Outer Islands imports, within which the share of capital goods was tiny. The average annual percentage of foreign textile imports into these provinces was 0.83 per cent of Outer Islands textile imports in 1911/30. Their foreign imports of iron and steel were very small: these constituted only 0.4 per cent of total Outer Islands iron and steel imports. Likewise, their imports of machines were a mere 0.3 per cent (Clemens et al. 1992:82-6). This observation confirms the impression that in these provinces the economy changed only very slowly.

Conclusion

In a classification based on the criterion of European or indigenous export growth, there is a temptation to underestimate the performance of the economy in provinces with very little export production (the provinces of Cluster IV). Increasing levels of foreign and interregional imports, as well as the collection of forest products indicate that at a lower level the economy of these regions was affected by many changes.

The absence of fiscal or backward linkages from an export industry, either European or Asian, meant relatively little investment in infrastructure and social overhead capital in these provinces. Provincial tax revenues were small; the Residents often complained about the difficulty of committing funds to the construction of roads. Some of these regions were far away from the active trading centres of the late colonial era. But how bleak was the economic situation here?

In this chapter I have evaluated three subgroups of provinces with little export production: those in northern Sumatra, those in southern Sumatra, and those in eastern Indonesia. East and west form a contrast in this regard, revealing essential differences in character and development.

The Sumatran provinces profited from the proximity of centres such as East Sumatra and Palembang, which furnished infrastructural improvements and drew them into their orbit of trade. The economies of the mountainous regions of small export producers in Sumatra were relatively promising and dynamic. Tapanuli and Bengkulu had a late start (as did Lampung and Indragiri (mainland Riau), which were grouped in Clusters II and III) but showed much more economic change than Bali, Timor, and Maluku, especially when per capita exports are calculated. Some exports of rubber and coffee from these provinces went by overland trade, unnoticed by government registration. The collection of rattan and gutta percha and resins such as damar, copal, and benzoin formed a supplementary commercial activity in the subsistence economy of these small provinces. Bengkulu and Lampung had the good fortune to benefit from the relatively stable character of pepper and coffee prices during the Depression.

Examination of interregional trade statistics reveals that Bali, Timor, Bengkulu, and Lampung exported a large share of their export production to Java. After including the interregional trade with Java, they did a lot better (Table 25.1), but the Lesser Sunda Islands (Bali and Timor and Dependencies) were always at the bottom of the list: they produced few exports and enjoyed little prosperity expressed in consumer demand, not even during the 1920s, when the revenues from indigenous exports in most provinces were highest. Only in the rice trade, after the First World War, did Bali win a central position between Java and the Outer Islands, being densely populated and having a high yield per acre.

When compared to provinces with large indigenous exports, such as Jambi, West Sumatra, West Kalimantan, and Southeast Kalimantan, Cluster IV provinces were hindered by unfavourable natural resources and their remote location. In the provinces of Cluster II, subsistence economy was partly replaced by export economy, a commercial mentality, and a widening market for imports. Changes in Cluster IV appeared on a much lower level.

In those Cluster IV provinces that were situated in the eastern archipelago, there was little vent-for-surplus trade. Indigenous agriculture in Maluku was hindered by its out-of-the-way position in the east, at a time when the comparative advantage of having low transport costs to Singapore was as important as being located within the sphere of influence of Singapore's Chinese trading community. These islands were also small and less fertile; there was no abundant rainforest to supply products attractive to local trade. They carried on trade on a much smaller scale, less oriented towards the international market.

What changes in the traditional situation were brought by foreign trade and modernization?[74] When foreign traders entered the economy of the Lesser Sunda Islands, they sometimes swindled the indigenous population, taking unfair advantage of the latter's lack of trading experience. The government, on the other hand, tried to protect trade and to stimulate irrigated rice cultivation, as well as the planting of suitable cash crops, such as *kacang*, coffee, and cotton on Amboina, or coffee and kapok in New Guinea. But all these efforts could do little to change an economy which seemed to stick to its own pace of change. In Timor and Dependencies, promotion of cattle breeding was successful, partly because low KPM tariffs encouraged exports to Sulawesi and Singapore.[75] Even though within the archipelago as a whole, the trade of Bali, Timor and Dependencies, and Maluku was very small, the trade in rice, forest products, and cattle showed a certain dynamism in these regions. Remoteness and lack of natural resources lay at the core of a slower pace of change.

74 From a neo-marxist point of view, the economic situation could have worsened under influence of the changing situation in the surrounding economy – if the provinces in the periphery of expansion found themselves in a position of subservience to and dependency on the core (or metropole). But the weakness of the small producers lay mainly in their autonomous character – either inaccessible because of the Barisan Mountains, or isolated by long distance. Isolation was not favourable, even when subsistence provided enough to allow a small margin of trade in supplementary products such as rattan, damar, or fish. Analysis of the Memories van Overgave and NHM reports shows that positive aspects of relative isolation were scarce. Touwen 1991:136-7 (on dependency theories see also Chapter I).

75 ARA Kol, MvO 312, G. Sieburg, 1910:27; MvO 327, W.A. Hovenkamp 1930:28; MvO 362, H. Beeuwkes 1932:22; MvO 340, C. van Rietschoten 1913:4-6.

CHAPTER VI

Economic policy
Beyond the reach of ethical intent

In 1938, Resident J. Oberman of West Kalimantan, in his final report for his successor, dedicated a few words to the challenge of achieving a successful economic policy in his residency. 'The economic structure of West Kalimantan,' Oberman wrote,

> is very simple. The course of events is easy to keep an eye on and uncomplicated. But the task of the government, as regards promoting the planting of food crops, is extremely difficult. And it is particularly hard to accomplish when rubber and copra prices are relatively high.[1]

This remark reveals that the Resident underestimated the complexity of the economic dynamics of West Kalimantan. As an administrator, he considered the main goal of government intervention, stimulating production of food crops, hard to achieve. He believed that stubborn peasants who grew export crops should plant food crops to increase the food supply, and he found it difficult to convince them to do so. Even though Oberman held office in the late 1930s, his view echoes the thrust of the Ethical Policy: to stimulate cultivation of food crops as the most direct means of raising the indigenous standard of living. Were there no other objectives that the government could have pursued to improve the economy in West Kalimantan?

Until 1930, free trade prevailed and measures to protect local industries were out of the question. Despite this, the economic potential of the Malay and Dayak population, who marketed large quantities of rubber and copra, should not be underestimated. There was no shortage of food, at least not in most of the region.[2] The flourishing indigenous export agriculture competed with the rubber exports of European estates, leading government officials to

1 ARA Kol, MvO 265, J. Oberman 1938:77.

2 Oberman remarks that in a few Dayak areas (North Landak and parts of Semitau), famines and harvest failures occurred frequently. In other Dayak areas (such as Melawi, Sanggau, Sekadau, and Sintang) and among the Chinese and Malay population, the food situation was stable. It has been observed that the subsistence economy of West Kalimantan was poor com-

refrain from any encouragement of indigenous cash-crop cultivation. Resident Oberman was aware of the vulnerability of an economy that depended on two export products only, while having a relatively weak subsistence economy. He acknowledged the fact that there had not yet been any systematic agricultural extension work for rubber cultivation, and stressed that in spite of this, rubber had developed 'on its own'. This was his way of justifying not taking any concrete measures to improve indigenous methods of tapping and processing.[3]

This example demonstrates how interesting it is to study the role of government in a colonial economy that was changing so quickly.[4] As Trebilcock says of pre-industrial Europe, 'all the actions of government, however humdrum, have an economic outcome, however minor' (Trebilcock 1981:18). In a large colony where a colonial state and a national economy were gradually taking shape, this is even more true. Putting the Cultivation System behind it, the government's aim in 1870 switched to the creation of a modern, nationally integrated economy in the Netherlands Indies, with an eye to optimizing the colony's economic profitability. The economic policy of the colonial government was liberal for most of the period under study, but in 1930 the World Depression triggered off major changes in government policy: the ensuing export duties and import restrictions signalled the end of the liberal era.

A colonial government had to juggle the interests of several groups. European companies formed a strong lobby trying to influence government policy. This was counterbalanced by a growing awareness of government responsibility towards the indigenous population, especially in Java, where the Ethical Policy was implemented at the beginning of the century. The idea was that the government should stimulate economic expansion not only to serve the interests of the mother country, but also for the sake of the colony itself. The question now confronting us is: what was the consequence of this attitude for the Outer Islands economy? Undoubtedly, estates and small-scale indigenous producers both benefited from investments in economic infrastructure, such as roads and bridges, but these investments were often concentrated in the vicinity of ports and European production areas. Likewise, large European export companies, such as BPM, installed electric lines and piped water in their employees' living areas, but such measures had only

---

pared to other regions in the Outer Provinces. ARA Kol, MvO 265, J. Oberman 1938:38-9; Ozinga 1940:102.

3 ARA Kol, MvO 265, J. Oberman 1938 p. 75, appendix 'Rubbernota' p. 6.

4 According to Van Doorn, a colony is essentially a project which stems from a colonizing national government. Therefore, colonial policy is the essence of the presence of the colonizer in the colony (or, one might say, colonial policy stands for the influence the colonizer exerts on the country being colonized). The colonizing national government, in close cooperation with the government of the mother country, in a sense 'defines' the colony. Van Doorn 1994:83-104.

a limited effect on the economy as a whole and mainly served the economic enclaves. Did the government spread out infrastructural investments so that remote areas of the interior also became accessible by road? And did it conscientiously set itself the goal of 'developing' backward regions?

Tackling these problems requires a careful approach. Critics of the colonial regime charge that every newly constructed road served the colonial military in patrolling the area, or enabled new agricultural estates to occupy more land. Others argue that the indigenous economy was able to expand because the economic infrastructure improved.

As the situation in West Kalimantan shows, the government's attitude towards 'autonomous' indigenous trade and economic change is important. Therefore I will evaluate the government's role in the indigenous sector. It is difficult to assess to what extent economic policies of the colonial government contributed to sound economic development in provinces with high levels of indigenous exports. However, it is useful to analyse the government's attitude towards economic development, especially in provinces where government intervention had traditionally been rare.

The first point to be made is that government measures were of different types. Quite clearly a distinction can be made between (subsistence) food production and export cultivation as areas of economic policy. In this regard agricultural extension work was very important. Other areas of government intervention were credit supply and the protection of domestic trade.

Secondly, did the government intentionally and effectively stimulate economic activity or agricultural development in those remote regions where European enterprise was absent and indigenous export agriculture occurred only on a small scale? Did, for example, the demonstrations given by the Landbouwvoorlichtingsdienst (LVD, Agricultural Extension Service) favour the development of economically 'backward' regions, to allow them to catch up with economically more advanced provinces? Evidence of this would be that the local government in the Outer Islands managed to attract funds (usually from Batavia) to spend on roads and bridges in regions that were inaccessible, remote, and relatively backward. Another way to phrase the question is: did the central government consciously aim at balanced growth within the colonial economy (even though it may be anachronistic to presuppose an economic growth policy in the modern sense) (Prince 1993:177)? Related to these questions is the issue of whether economic policy was guided by European economic activity, the major source of tax revenues. Did the government favour provinces where European export production took place?

In theory, when development policy succeeds, the result is that (technical) knowledge is spread, income inequality within the country decreases, and balanced, self-sustaining economic development is facilitated. A region can benefit from its (domestic) comparative advantage only when a more or less uniform domestic market exists. A healthy economic policy should have a unifying effect on a fragmented economy. My intention is to examine whether unifying effects of this kind can be observed in the Outer Islands.

In this chapter I will investigate how and to what extent colonial economic policy influenced the economic development of the Outer Islands. After a brief section on the historiography of economic policy, I will turn to the government budget, its capacity to influence or improve the economic situation, and the effects of export trade on government expenditure per province. Next, I will outline the major economic concerns of the colonial government after roughly 1870, addressing the impact of the Ethical Policy and the types of intervention most relevant for the Outer Islands.

Recent historiography on economic policy

Recent historiography has not produced a systematic study of the political economy of colonial Indonesia. Burger, in his textbook on the social and economic history of Indonesia, describes the changes in government policy implemented after 1929 as the outcome of a process of increasing institutionalization in the economy. He notes that both government intervention and private entrepreneurship increasingly committed themselves to observing regulations and agreements in individual branches of industry, even though in the developing economy there was barely a beginning of organized labour and only a few cooperatives of indigenous producers.[5] Booth has proposed an approach for analysing fiscal policy, but as yet no one has followed up on it (Booth 1990a). Prince has characterized the activities of the government in colonial Indonesia, repeatedly focusing on economic policy and political goals (Prince 1989, 1993, 1995, 1996).

Boomgaard has published an article on welfare services in colonial Indonesia, describing the organization of agricultural extension work, education, and health services. He deals mainly with Java, where the most significant efforts in these fields took place (Boomgaard 1986). Government intervention during the recession of 1921-1923 has been examined in detail by Van Anrooij (1979).

A more elaborate analysis of government measures to improve agriculture can be found in Van der Eng's dissertation, *Agricultural Growth in Indonesia since 1800* (1993a, 1996c). Van der Eng notes that such topics as agri-

5 Although published in 1975, Burger's book was actually written in the early 1950s. Burger mentions the various production restrictions, but largely ignores the rubber restriction policy (the most influential measure related to indigenous export production), which he describes only briefly in another section. Burger 1975:32 (rubber), 126-36 (government policy).

cultural research and agricultural extension work are often difficult to disentangle, for example when both deal with the development and extension of seed improvement in rice cultivation. Until 1910, the colonial administration gave little thought to irrigation in the Outer Islands.[6] Java remained the major area of activity. Until 1938, only 7 per cent of the irrigation budget was spent in the Outer Islands. Often irrigation was part of transmigration projects, which involved a relatively small number of peasants. On the whole, the amount of land under irrigation in the Outer Islands did not expand significantly during the colonial period.[7] Van der Eng also analyses the results of the LVD and private research stations in colonial Indonesia. The LVD studied indigenous agriculture, collecting a wealth of fundamental knowledge, and at the same time instructed smallholders in the use of better farming methods.[8]

The response of European companies to government policies, and their efforts to influence matters by setting up their own associations, are treated in Taselaar's dissertation (1998). Finally, both the Ministry of Colonial Affairs in the Netherlands and the civil service (Binnenlands Bestuur) in Java have each been the subject of an extensive study. Of these two books, the first contains a thorough analysis of the political and institutional background of issues such as government exploitation of oil and tin, and the rubber restriction policy of the 1930s (De Graaff 1997). In the second book, only scant attention is paid to economic policy other than the Ethical Policy, and the focus is almost entirely on Java (Van den Doel 1994).

The birth of a colonial state

After 1870, the Netherlands Indies can be viewed as a large, fragmented colony in the process of unification. The government played an increasingly important role in the economy. Cribb gives a recent view on the development of the late colonial state.[9] He defines the late colonial state as an important stage in the Indonesian polity, an interim stage between earlier colonial rule (under the Cultivation System) and eventual independence in the 1940s. His assumption is that late colonial state formation took place roughly between

[6] The Department of Agriculture, established in 1905 by M. Treub, was located in the botanical gardens of Bogor until 1910. Van der Eng 1996c:41, 57, 71. In the *Memories van Overgave*, I only found frequent mention of irrigation plans after about 1920.

[7] ARA Kol, MvO 233, L. Berkhout 1926:57-8; Van der Eng 1996c:57, 68.

[8] Van der Eng 1996c:72-91. Van Hall and Van de Koppel 1946-50 takes stock of agricultural knowledge at the end of the colonial era.

[9] In Chapter I, the historiographical connection between colonial state formation and the debate on Dutch colonial expansion is explained. In this section, I do not refer to Dutch expansionist policies since I am less concerned here with the motives of expansion than with the (narrower) goals of economic policy in the colony. It should be borne in mind, however, that when colonial expansion occurs for economic reasons these goals may overlap.

1880 and 1942 (Cribb 1994b).[10] The colony became more independent of the mother country, and offered growing opportunities for education, intellectual development, and the use of technology – from which the indigenous populace was not entirely excluded. This gradual process represents an interesting paradox. The late colonial state grew stronger, both economically and politically, but in doing so it generated forces that threatened its very existence. Decolonization gradually became inevitable, because the desire of the Indonesian populace to become self-governing was bolstered by the late colonial state itself. The process was a slow one, and many contemporary observers either failed to notice it or refused to acknowledge it.

Two developments were basic to the formation of the late colonial state. The Netherlands Indies began to disengage itself from the Netherlands. Simultaneously, the Outer Islands began to integrate economically into the well-established Java-based Dutch colonial economy. During the late nineteenth and early twentieth centuries, both the economy and the colonial administration became more complex and more highly organized.

From the turn of the century, the colonial government was alert in guarding the 'Pax Neerlandica' and intensified its efforts to introduce a new system of justice and administration in the archipelago. Government officials computed statistics, collected taxes, and supervised the expenditure of an increasing number of social programmes, such as education, the health service, and the construction of economic infrastructure. While government administration in the colony expanded, the political-administrative system branched out; one example is the introduction of the system of *landschapskassen* (indigenous state treasuries).

Genuine efforts were made, but many differences remained in the extent and pace of development in the various provinces. It was difficult for the central government to draft laws and regulations that were equally suitable for all areas. As Cribb says,

> 'to produce regulations and administrative structures which were appropriate at the same time for the regimented plantation regions of East Sumatra, the uncoordinated smallholder plantation regions of Maluku and Sulawesi, and the barely developed islands of Nusa Tenggara, as well as for the rice basket and basket case of the archipelago Java itself, was difficult and demanding' (Cribb 1994b:7).

In fact, this process of government modernization had already got underway in the nineteenth century. Between 1860 and 1870, several highly placed administrators, such as two ministers of colonial affairs, I.D. Fransen van de

10 It can be argued that the concept of a 'colonial state' places too much emphasis on national borders, while economic development was much more dependent on regional political or institutional initiatives in which 'national' borders were not relevant.

Putte and E. de Waal, and the governor-general, L.A.J.W. Sloet van Beele, recognized that colonial policy had to be turned in new directions. Government, infrastructure, and economy were reorganized and acquired a more modern character. An important concrete expression of this change is, of course, the Agrarian Law of 1870, which signalled the end of the Cultivation System and marked the beginning of an increasing flow of private capital and entrepreneurship into the Outer Islands. It formed the key to the opening up of and increasing intervention in several regions of the archipelago which had previously received scant attention.

The subsequent decades have been characterized as the 'liberal period'. The major issue in government regulation of European entrepreneurship was taxation – a matter that led to heated discussions and repeated adjustments of taxes. Another source of contention was the Labour Inspectorate, which was set up in 1908 as a separate branch of the Department of Justice. Its task was to inspect labour conditions on European estates, mediate in labour disputes, and generally supervise the implementation of the various Coolie Ordinances, which regulated relations between European employers and coolie labourers after 1880.[11] Even after 1900, when the Ethical Policy was implemented, interference with European private enterprise was limited. It was only after the 1929 Depression that the government assumed a greater role, having reached the conclusion that its grip on the economy should be extended. Consequently, in the 1930s European enterprise in the archipelago faced more regulations and restrictions than ever before.

Many government officials also became increasingly aware of the intricacies of the indigenous economy. The network of indigenous producers and Chinese traders, the various debt relationships, the rapidly increasing degree of monetization in the interior, and the expanding demand for consumer goods raised issues that could not be ignored.[12] The colonial administration faced a complex, quickly changing indigenous economy.

The upshot was that new and more complex tasks were required of the government of the late colonial state – both in regulating and in guiding the economy. Economic considerations aside, a new attitude developed towards the indigenous populace. Resident Oberman of West Kalimantan, quoted at

11 The Labour Inspectorate is described in Chapter III. The development of regular tax legislation (as opposed to the surtax on indigenous rubber, for example) will not be treated here. Houben 1995, 1996; Taselaar 1998:219-60.

12 For example, in West Kalimantan, Resident De Vogel describes the credit system used by Chinese intermediary traders who traded with Singapore. In 1933, Van Prehn recounts the lack of legal tender and difficulties of collecting taxes; he emphasizes the need to accept Straits dollars. Oberman describes the 'silver thread' which links the Dayak and Malay petty trader to the Chinese creditor. ARA Kol, MvO 264, K.H. van Prehn 1933:13-5; MvO 261, H. de Vogel 1918:28; MvO 265, J. Oberman 1938:75.

the beginning of this chapter, hoped the government could lead the peasant to a better life by teaching him to cultivate food crops and increase productivity. Oberman thus shared the desire of many civil servants to 'elevate' or 'raise' the indigenous peasant. This is reminiscent of the paternalistic attitude of the colonizers during the nineteenth century, which also influenced much of colonial thinking during the twentieth century. It is succinctly expressed in Bousquet's remark: 'The Dutch administration considers the native to be a child and meddles with the pettiest trifles in native life.'[13] Even when the results were not impressive, this frame of mind was important, as it represented a sense of colonial responsibility for economic and social development.

More interesting than the discussion of whether or not Dutch presence was beneficial is Legge's remark that 'the nationalist movement was the product of the virtues rather than the vices of Dutch rule'. He argues that the colonial state, by offering the Indonesians education and various kinds of technology, worked towards its own termination. This accords with Cribb's view on the formation of a late colonial state. The good intentions of the civil servant may have nurtured the seeds of independence - an ironical side-effect of which not all officials were conscious (Legge 1964:114; Wesseling 1988:41-5).

The government budget

Composition of revenues and expenditure

Before examining the projects and priorities of the political economy of colonial Indonesia, I will first review the organization of finances and the levels of government expenditure. How much was spent by the government and on what was it spent? Before 1930 there was a laissez-faire policy. In the 1930s production restrictions, import protection, and rice policy emerged as significant components of government intervention. Nevertheless, the colonial government had substantially increased its expenditure long before 1930.

This section looks at the composition of government revenues and expenditure. After this, I examine the regular expenditure of the government, and analyse how government subsidies were distributed among the individual Outer Provinces.

13 The author continues: 'Sur ce point, les auteurs sont d'accord. Chailley parle avec courtoisie du "personnel instruit, devoué, nombreux, mais faisant de la philantropie, au lieu de faire l' administration [...]"'. Bousquet 1939:90; see also Booth 1991:49.

Revenues

What were the main sources of revenue for the colonial government? The bulk of the receipts in the twentieth century were taxes. For example, in 1924/29 combined taxes constituted on average 65.2 per cent of total receipts (in these years of expansion, tax revenues averaged 520 million guilders annually) (Table 62). Other sources of revenue were the government monopolies and the government estates and industries (electricity and railway companies, harbour works, post and telegraph, the Banka Tin Winning) (Houben 1994). Of the various taxes, import duties formed the largest share in the 1920s. In 1924/29, receipts from import duties averaged 79 million guilders. In the same period export duties averaged only 13 million guilders and the various excise taxes (on petroleum, matches, tobacco) averaged 33 million guilders per year. After the passing of the 1925 tax legislation, income tax and company taxes (*vennootschapsbelasting*) increased rapidly. These two items rose from 30 million guilders each in 1924 to 54 million each in 1929.[14]

Revenues came to be dominated by tax receipts, especially foreign trade duties, replacing revenues previously obtained from government monopolies and sales of products on government account, which had been substantial in the nineteenth century. The share contributed by excise taxes and income tax rose quickly, whereas the share contributed by *landrente* (tax on agricultural land owned by indigenous inhabitants) fell. The principle of land taxation stemmed from the Raffles administration, and the land tax in the nineteenth century had been the most important single tax (the revenue from which, however, was always small compared to the revenue from the sale of products).[15] In the twentieth century income tax and excise taxes consistently formed a larger share of tax revenues. These taxes, by their very nature, constituted a more equitable tax burden than the land tax. This situation prevailed until the Depression years, when indigenous money income fell faster than land tax revenues, and the burden of taxes on the indigenous populace increased (Booth 1990a:225).

Expenditure

As the years from 1905 to 1930 were a period of substantial real growth in the economy, it is not surprising that government expenditure in colonial Indonesia also increased. Expenditure rose even faster than revenues. The composition of expenditure shifted in favour of public works – including buildings, roads, bridges, irrigation works, port facilities – and government

[14] Creutzberg 1976:86-8; Statistisch Jaaroverzicht 1929:441-2.

[15] Land tax never amounted to more than 12 per cent of total revenues between 1846 and 1875. Booth 1990a:214. See also *Overzicht der geldmiddelen* 1916:16-21.

enterprises, of which railways and post and telegraph facilities were the most important (Booth 1990a:219-25, 239).

Beginning in 1907, a distinction was made in government expenditure between regular and extraordinary expenses. Recurring annual expenses essential to the carrying out of routine government responsibilities were called the 'ordinary service' (*gewone dienst*) in the public accounts. The 'extraordinary service' (*buitengewone dienst*) included expenditure on long-term productive activities and on durable assets. This includes the fixed assets of the Staatsspoorwegen (State Railways), the PTT (Post, Telegraph, Telephone), and also the repurchasing of previously sold private domains, large-scale irrigation projects and civil works, and other expensive projects (Creutzberg 1976:10). To finance this last category, the government could borrow funds.[16]

During the slight recession of 1921, government expenditure declined moderately, but they increased again after 1925. Expenditure fell again in the early 1930s, both in absolute and in real terms. Compared with total expenditure, the share of expenditure for social overhead capital decreased even more substantially in the period 1921-1939 (Booth 1990a:239).

Decentralization

Because of several changes in bookkeeping it is difficult to compare public accounts over longer periods of time. The 1903 Act separated the Netherlands from the Netherlands Indies financially. The distinction between regular and extraordinary government expenditure adds to the problems of comparing time series. The Indische Bedrijvenwet of 1927, a set of accounting rules for public services and government enterprises, reduced the information given in central government reports. For example, instead of recording both revenues and expenditure, the new rules specified for many items that only the balance of the two be listed. A further problem in the analysis of public accounts is that the distinction between directly governed and indirectly governed territories does not correspond to the administrative division of the Outer Islands into provinces.[17]

In colonial Indonesia, revenues and expenditure of directly governed territories were accounted for by the central government in a system of public accounts. In the twentieth century, there was a growing tendency to institute indirectly governed districts (such as sultanates, principalities, and urban regions). The central government handed over tasks and responsibilities to these 'autonomous, self-governing' districts under the *ontvoogdingspolitiek*

[16] After the change in the Indische Comptabiliteitswet in 1912, the Netherlands Indies government could do so independently of the mother country. Van Anrooij 1979:119.

[17] The indirectly governed territories were often called 'native states', or areas under 'zelfbestuur', which can be translated as 'self-governing states' (a somewhat misleading term). See also Houben 1987.

(detutelization policy). They were financed partly by their own revenues, partly by the central government. In 1905, financial control of them was transferred to district treasuries (*landschapskassen*). From 1903, in the directly governed territories, government responsibilities were transferred to local autonomous bodies (*locale ressorten*). City councils were set up in urban areas to broaden the scope of local governance. After 1925, the Netherlands Indies was gradually divided up into larger provinces. In a steady stream after 1935, a large number of government tasks in agriculture, public works, health, and education were delegated to the individual provinces.[18]

In addition to taking over existing taxes and levies, these local and regional bodies were allocated new ones. Expenditure was accounted for separately in each decentralized district, and did not appear in the national budget. However, public expenditure in these areas was included in the central government accounts in the years 1903-1930, 1938, and 1940.[19] Consequently, public expenditure in the national budget was increasingly understated. Mansvelt estimates the amount of understatement at around 2 per cent in 1910, 8.5 per cent in 1930, and 16 per cent in 1938. Of course, this figure is different for each residency, making it difficult to determine government expenses in each province. National finances became 'less and less representative of government in general' (Creutzberg 1976:60). This means that the analysis of government expenditure in the Outer Islands is hampered by the changes in administration and accounting. In the next section, I will examine several aspects of the government budget, but a detailed macroeconomic analysis per province is not feasible. Using benchmark years, I will compare the regional budgets, after having simply added the figures for the indirectly governed territories to each province's budget (Tables 63.1 and 63.2).

For protracted periods, the expenses of the Netherlands Indies government were not covered by its receipts – as was the case in 1901-1906, 1913-1924, and 1929-1939.[20] As Keynesian 'deficit spending' was not yet common policy, it was not a deliberate decision for the colonial government to spend more than was received. In 1923, when severe budgets cuts were deemed necessary, the director of government enterprises, P.A. Roelofsen, wrote a fierce protest against budget cuts during a recession period. Subsequent debate in the Dutch parliament, however, did not persuade Minister of Colonies S. de Graaff to change his policy of balanced budgets (Van Anrooij 1979:126-8). Between 1924 and 1929, the years of major export expansion, there was an

18 Creutzberg 1976:11; Cribb 1993:227; Van den Doel 1994:238-66.

19 For the years 1931-1937 and 1939 there are no financial data for the indirectly governed areas. Creutzberg 1976:12.

20 Creutzberg 1976:221 (Graph 10.4). For a graph of long-term revenues and expenditure, see Creutzberg 1976:89.

average surplus of 67 million guilders per annum on the budget of colonial Indonesia, which was almost 13 per cent of the average annual government income of 520 million guilders (Table 62) (*Statistisch Jaaroverzicht* 1929:441). On the whole, the costs of the growing body of government officials had picked up a momentum that could not easily be stopped. During the recession of the early 1920s and the Depression of the 1930s, the government made substantial use of overseas loans to maintain real levels of expenditure while revenues were declining. In these two periods the composition of expenses shifted away from economic infrastructure and towards general administration (salaries) and defence (Booth 1990a:240).

Regional inequalities in expenditure and export trade

Since the Outer Islands formed an enormous area with a much smaller population than Java, the task of creating an infrastructure, of agricultural extension work, or of maintaining a corps of civil servants there was a great deal more demanding. Differences in the degree of government influence on the economy depended on several factors, including the number of European inhabitants and presence of European companies (as in East Sumatra), the military presence (as in Aceh), proximity to Java (as in Lampung and Bali), and cultural or historical factors such as the activities of Christian missionaries (as in Maluku and Minahasa).

Government policy as a function of export trade

An influential argument in the literature on colonial economic development is that government expenditure was largely dependent on revenues, and that revenues, in turn, were a function of export earnings in an undeveloped, open economy. According to this view, provision of infrastructure was almost entirely directed towards the export sector, with government expenditure leading to new export earnings. Exports generated new revenues, mainly accrued through export taxes, which led to further government expenditure. Turning to the geographical distribution of government expenditure, this argument suggests that the government did not set itself the task of redistributing income.[21]

In nineteenth-century colonial Indonesia, the government-run Cultivation System in fact determined the level of exports. Then, after 1870, when

[21] Booth 1990a:240. This model is used in Birnberg and Resnick 1975:36, 52-4, 240. Applied to the provincial level, one can argue that it does not result in a fair distribution within one country. Provincial budgets in post-colonial Indonesia were distributed according to provincial contribution to national export revenues during Repelita I (1969/70-1973/74). This system was called the SPP-ADO (Sumbangan Pemerintah Pengganti Alokasi Devisa Otomatis) (Azis 1991).

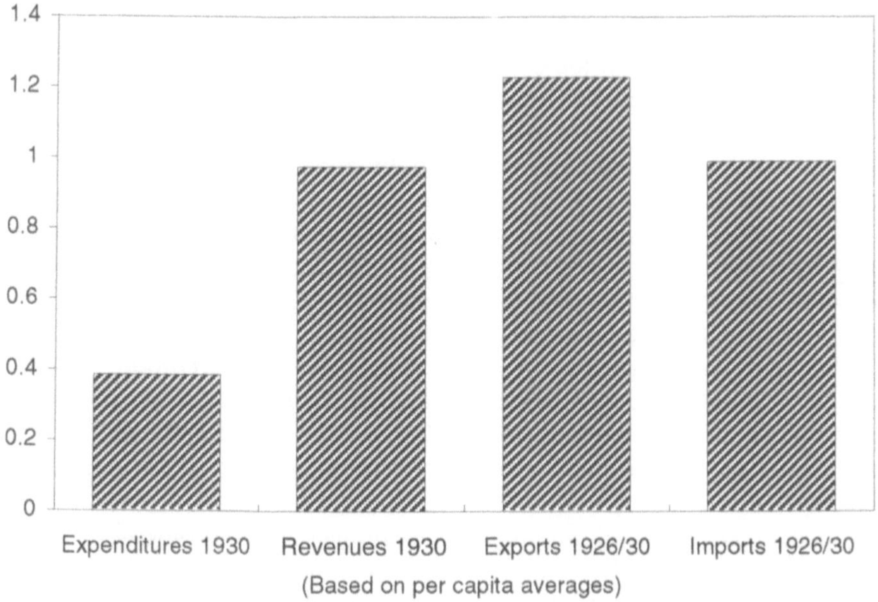

Figure 16. Coefficient of variation by province, for per capita government revenues and expenditure in 1930 and average per capita import and export value in 1926/30 (N = 18) (Table 65).

the period of liberalization commenced, the government gradually stopped spending money on organizing the cultivation and sale of cash crops. Government revenues became dependent on tax revenues, which in turn depended on the commercial success of free enterprise. The Aceh War and subsequent expansion of colonial control prompted higher military expenses and, after 1900, the introduction of the Ethical Policy led to higher public expenditure. Nevertheless, there is a strong statistical correlation between total exports and total government expenditure over the period 1874-1939.[22] I use this correlation as a starting point for an examination of government expenditure in the Outer Islands.[23]

22 The Pearson correlation coefficient between total exports and total government expenditure for this period is R = 0.89 (N = 66). Also during the shorter period 1900-1939, the correlation is high: R = 0.83 (N = 40). Likewise, the statistical correlation can be calculated for total government *revenues* as a dependent variable depending on total exports. As may be expected, this correlation is slightly higher: for 1874-1939 R = 0.92 (N = 66) and for 1900-1939 R = 0.87 (N = 40). Government revenues and expenditure are aggregate totals, including extraordinary expenditure. Creutzberg 1976:56-9, 64-7; Korthals Altes 1991:69-75.

23 It has been pointed out in the literature that government expenditure and revenues in nineteenth-century Indonesia did not correlate very strongly with export revenues and were probably influenced by deliberate government actions, such as military expeditions. Booth 1990a:240.

Comparison of provincial budgets

A preliminary glance at the coefficient of variation in government budgets and exports in 1929 and 1930 suggests that provincial budgets showed much less variation among provinces than exports did.[24] For example, the coefficient of variation (the standard deviation divided by the mean) of export revenues in the Outer Islands in 1930 was 1.3 (and 1.2 for per capita exports 1926/30). For per capita government expenditure it was only 0.4. This means that there was less variation among the eighteen provinces in per capita expenditure, and that government expenditure was more evenly spread over the provinces than export revenue (Figure 16).

Regional inequalities in provincial budgets in 1930, as reproduced in the statistical reports, did not reflect the regional distribution of provincial export values for the preceding years 1926/30. Statistical correlation between per capita expenditure and average per capita exports is not significant (Table 65).[25]

Closer analysis of the 1929 and 1930 accounts reveals considerable variety in government expenditure and revenues among the individual provinces. Using 1930 as a benchmark year, I calculated total revenues and expenditure per km^2, per capita, and as a percentage of average annual exports (Table 64). Total government expenses and receipts were aggregated from both the *landskassen* (state treasuries) and the *landschapskassen* (regional treasuries), in order to compensate somewhat for incompleteness owing to decentralization. However, these figures cannot be accepted as anything more than an estimate: the Annual Statistical Reports emphasize that the annual accounts per province do not exactly mirror the provinces to which these expenses and receipts relate. 'They therefore do not yield a straightforward, mutually comparable picture of the economic life or the statistical position of the provinces themselves' (*Statistisch Jaaroverzicht* 1930:460). The figures in Table 64 should be read with this reservation in mind.

24 Regional specification of the total government budget is rare in the Statistical Reports (*Statistisch Jaaroverzicht*) in the *Koloniale Verslag* and *Indische Verslag*. The years 1929-1930 were chosen because in these years, the government budget had gradually been adjusted to the large revenues earned during the boom years 1925-1928, so that the possible effects of export growth in the individual provinces would have been most evident. The severe budgets cuts due to the Depression had not yet been enforced, as is obvious from Tables 63.1 and 63.2. Also, since the first reliable census was held in 1930, budget figures per capita can also be calculated (Table 64, columns F and G).

25 The correlation between per capita expenditure and average per capita exports is very weak (R = 0.44, N = 18). Average exports per capita in 1926-1930 was chosen because exports tend to fluctuate over the years. Government expenses, by contrast, tend to be more stable because of a fair amount of fixed expenditure, such as salaries.

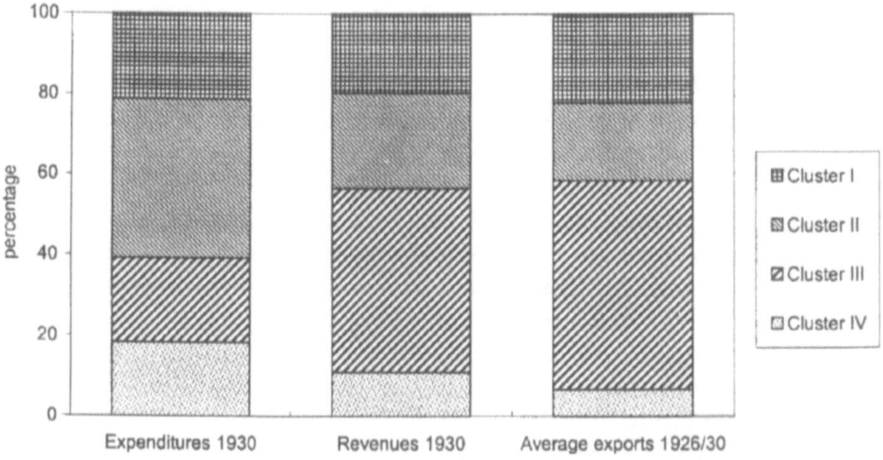

Cluster I: East Sumatra, Palembang, Southeast Kalimantan; Cluster II: Aceh, West Sumatra, Jambi, Lampung, West Kalimantan, South Sulawesi, Manado; Cluster III: Bangka, Belitung, Riau; Cluster IV: Tapanuli, Bengkulu, Maluku, Bali, Timor.

Figure 17. Per capita government expenditure and revenues in 1930 compared to per capita exports 1926/30, by cluster (Table 65).

The *landskassen* and *landschapskassen* show a relatively even balance among provinces of expenses and receipts per capita, particularly as more public expenditure might have been expected in provinces with a large export production. Per 1,000 inhabitants, expenditure varied between 10 and 16 guilders for nine of the eighteen provinces. The extremes were Bali and Timor and Dependencies, with only 3 guilders per 1,000 inhabitants spent by the government in 1930 (in the case of Bali this is related to high population density). Expenditure was highest in Aceh, with 16 guilders per 1,000 inhabitants. On the whole, residencies in Sumatra had significantly higher government expenses per capita than those in the eastern archipelago (Table 64, column F).

Expenditure seems to have been triggered by receipts, but not entirely so. The large per capita revenues in East Sumatra, Bangka, and Belitung were not matched by proportionately higher government expenditure in these provinces, although these provinces contributed a large surplus to the treasury. Likewise, in provinces where exports were low, the government nonetheless spent considerable amounts of money, for example on the salaries of government officials. Therefore, the ratio of government expenses to exports was disproportionately high in Timor. As may be expected, the ratio was smallest in the provinces with more exports: in Bangka, Belitung, East Sumatra, and Southeast Kalimantan. Export tax revenues were obviously not all spent in the province of origin (Table 64, columns F and H; see also Figures 16 and 17).[26]

The reason the ratio between government receipts and exports was not automatically constant (or receipts equivalent to exports) was because the central government reallocated funds to the different provinces. Let us review the distribution of government expenditure and export performance by province. In a sparsely populated province such as Jambi, government expenses per km^2 were low. Government expenses were also low in proportion to export value, but government expenses per capita were relatively high. This indicates that export taxes did lead to increased government expenditure on health, education, and infrastructure – even before the surtax on indigenous rubber in 1934 led to a more direct linkage between exports and social expenditure.

Generally speaking, the infrastructure in large provinces remained more primitive than in smaller provinces, because expenditure on infrastructure was not made a major priority. Subsidies per km^2 were small in Kalimantan and New Guinea (included in the table under Maluku). Per capita expenditure was the highest in Aceh, where the military presence added to costs (Table 64, column F). This again illustrates that export revenues were not the primary reason for expenditure: the proportion of government expenditure in Aceh was high compared to export revenues (Table 64, column H, and Table 65), and even higher in Timor and Dependencies. Conversely, in provinces where per capita export revenues were very high, such as Bangka and Belitung, the government did not increase its spending. In this regard, the provinces with substantial indigenous exports (Cluster II) were actually favoured by per capita government expenditure (such as Jambi, West Sumatra). Per capita government expenditure was higher in Cluster II than per capita export revenues (or per capita government revenues) would account for (Table 64 and Figures 16 and 17).

We may conclude that, with regard to provincial treasury budgets, export revenues were not the primary factor determining government expenditure, even though at a macro level a strong statistical association is observed. Government attention was not disproportionately oriented towards European enterprise in estate agriculture and mining, or to provinces where indigenous exports were large. But per capita expenditure in provinces with indigenous exports was generally higher than export tax revenues would account for.

26 For exports I have used average annual aggregated exports (including trade with Java) over 1924-1928. It is reasonable to conclude that, if it was the case that government budgets were led by revenues from export surtaxes, government budgets needed some time to adjust to a sudden growth in exports. Since the aim is to compare provinces with each other, the use of exports over a range of years to establish their relative position is justified.

Ethical Policy: effective or rhetorical?

From the turn of the century, the colonial government faced an important new task: the responsibility for indigenous welfare. The Ethical Policy was an unprecedented phenomenon in the annals of the colonial administration. It was largely aimed towards Java, as the situation in Java was what had given rise to 'ethical' concerns. Despite its focus on Java, I will treat the Ethical Policy fairly extensively, because it affected the official attitude of the colonial government towards the indigenous sector of the economy, not only in Java but also in the Outer Islands.

The Ethical Policy was announced in Queen Wilhelmina's speech to the States General in the Netherlands in 1901. Technically, the policy was in force until the late 1930s, but after 1920 it had lost most of its original momentum. It is therefore more useful to say that it lasted until the early 1920s, when conservative political criticism of this enlightened policy (which was thought to be too supportive of the nationalist movement) made the term unpopular.[27]

Various meanings have been attached to the term Ethical Policy, depending on the time or the person using it. In its narrower sense it stands for a 'welfare policy', which aimed at raising the standard of living of the indigenous population.[28] But in fact the Ethical Policy embraced a more complex set of ideas and goals, which arose from a sense of 'ethical', or moral, responsibility towards the colony:

1. limited participation in government for indigenous population groups and a certain degree of tolerance of the nationalist movement;
2. expansion of educational opportunities for Indonesians;
3. welfare policy for the indigenous population, to raise the standard of living.[29]

These three aspects all involved further government intervention. More intervention meant more staff, so the Ethical Policy led to a growing number of offices and functionaries in the civil government, both Dutch and indigen-

27 Locher-Scholten takes a wide view of the Ethical Policy and dates it from 1894 (the Lombok expedition) to 1942. Locher-Scholten 1981:176-208; Cribb 1993:225.

28 The publication of the essay 'Een eereschuld' (A debt of honour) by the well-known ethical publicist and ex-Semarang lawyer, C.Th. van Deventer, in *De Gids* in 1899, is usually viewed as the starting point of the public debate that something should be offered to the Indies, in return for the large surplus that had flowed into the Dutch treasury between 1830 and 1878. Van Deventer estimated this surplus at 187 million guilders. His 'eereschuld' arose mainly in Java, where, during the latter half of the nineteenth century, these revenues were earned. Van Deventer 1899.

29 Cribb 1993:227-9; Locher-Scholten 1981:176-9. Van Doorn notes that there were very few engineers among the proponents of government's moral responsibility, which strengthens the impression that the Ethical Policy consisted more of ideals than of pragmatic decisions. Van Doorn 1994:149-51.

ous, the former often technically trained. Besides a department of agriculture established in 1905, the departments of education, public works, and public health were also expanded.

In Locher-Scholten's view, the Ethical Policy aimed at not only the development of the country and its people under Dutch guidance, but also the expansion of Dutch control in the archipelago. This is a rather broad definition. It does not leave much room for other reasons for expansion, such as political and economic motives not associated with the moral obligation felt by original proponents of the Ethical Policy. On the other hand, it may be argued that the Ethical Policy found fertile soil in the complex structure of colonial concerns precisely because it was not merely a government matter. For instance, Dutch business interests were served by improvement in the health of their Indonesian labourers and a higher disposable income for them, thus ensuring an expanding market for Dutch products.[30]

Dutch colonial policy, in the approach adopted for the duration of the Ethical Policy, has been called 'scientific', or even 'scholarly'. Most Dutch civil servants had the benefit of a full university education in Indonesian Studies (known during the colonial era as 'Indology') (Fasseur 1993). They spoke Indonesian (Malay) and many of them were devoted to the cause of raising the living standard of the Indonesian people (Thee Kian Wie 1994:155). The best example of the scientific approach taken by government officials was the enquiry into the causes of the 'mindere welvaart' (declining living standard) in Java.[31] A very extensive field survey was conducted in Java between 1902 and 1914, which eventually produced a 33-volume report.[32] This report was widely quoted, but led to few concrete measures to improve the indigenous economy. This may also be due to the fact that living conditions improved in the years between the alarming first survey and the final observations ten years later.

Three major themes of welfare policy evolved under the Ethical Policy: migration, irrigation, and education. Migration programmes to alleviate population pressure and irrigation plans to increase agricultural productivity were both intended to raise the standard of living in overpopulated Java,

30 Cribb 1993:226; Van Goor 1994:269-70; Hüsken 1994:217; Locher-Scholten 1981:176-9.

31 In Dutch, 'mindere welvaart' has a double connotation, meaning either (a) a lower standard of living compared to elsewhere, or (b) a standard of living which is declining. Sometimes it is translated as 'declining welfare' or 'diminishing welfare'. The Dutch word *welvaart* has also acquired the meaning of 'prosperity', whereas the English word *welfare* nowadays often denotes 'assistance to the disadvantaged'. See also Cribb 1993:230-1.

32 *Onderzoek mindere welvaart* 1905-14. Since much had changed after World War I, a new enquiry into the standard of living was ordered in 1924. The newly established Centraal Kantoor voor de Statistiek in Batavia (1916) published a useful report called *Verslag over de Economische Toestand der Inlandse Bevolking 1924* (in two volumes). Boomgaard 1986:59; Coolhaas 1943:23; Hüsken 1994:215-6.

but in the end they did not amount to much. Education involved not only the establishment of village schools in 1906, but also the dissemination of new farming methods, and the propagation of knowledge of hygiene. The activities of the LVD vied in importance with the establishment of schools.[33] Other aspects of welfare policy designed to assist the indigenous population were the setting up of credit facilities and agricultural cooperatives, both in Java and in the Outer Islands. Several other government activities, such as road construction and some slight encouragement of local industry, can be mentioned as undertakings which also benefited economic development, but these were not explicit goals of the Ethical Policy.

In several ways, the Ethical Policy came at the right time. In the emerging colonial state, it allowed for a loosening of ties between the mother country and the colony, since the colony was allowed to 'mature'. Imperialist expansion and subsequent enlargement of government influence in the colony had fostered ideas of a greater government responsibility for the economy. And, finally, the sincere efforts made by civil servants trying to educate and 'elevate' the indigenous population could now find an outlet.

Superficially everything was fine, but according to Higgins and others, the welfare policy was half-hearted in its efforts to gear up the indigenous economy. This was in line with the cultural aspect of Boeke's view of Indonesia as being incapable of development along Western lines. Many Dutch officials may have agreed. Boeke himself felt that efforts to promote such development would serve only to hasten the disintegration of traditional society, without replacing it with any other unified social system. Higgins stresses that Boeke should not be considered an old-fashioned colonialist, intent on keeping the indigenous population subjugated. 'Within the limits of his own analytical framework', Boeke can be regarded as a progressive thinker (Higgins 1894:56-8).

Boeke's sociological concept of the irrational indigenous peasant was not accepted by all of his contemporaries. Several scholars in the 1930s observed that smallholders displayed rational market behaviour. Increasing production at lower prices for example, typical of 'Boekean behaviour', could be explained by reasonable causes, such as the peasants' debt relationship to traders, and the low variable cost of production. Before the war, such a critical attitude led to vigorous attacks on Boeke's ideas by G. Gonggrijp, R. Kool, R. Slot, E. de Vries, and E.P. Wellenstein (Van der Eng 1991).

33 Boomgaard 1986:59-67; Van den Doel 1994:163-76, 227-30; Van der Eng 1996c:94-100, 113-8.

Raising welfare through food production

The measures enshrined in the Ethical Policy were directed towards raising the standard of living among the indigenous population – without inconveniencing Western enterprise. The political influence exerted by organized Dutch business interests in the Netherlands was strong. To a critical observer, Van Deventer's respectable ideas and the subsequent political propagation of the Ethical Policy would have earned more credibility had they not been advocated simultaneously with a 'hurrah for private enterprise' (as Multatuli called it) (Alberts 1992:30). As it stood, such a welfare policy was a dualist policy, improving conditions for the indigenous sector of the economy while not wanting to upset the applecart in the European sector. Pragmatically, indigenous food production became the major goal. European entrepreneurs did not oppose welfare policy measures as long as free enterprise in the Western sector was left alone. In fact, they were in favour of welfare policy because it would boost the purchasing power of the indigenous population. From a practical point of view, education was welcomed by European companies because it created cheap personnel for the lower ranks (Poeze 1982:xi-xvii; Prince 1989:210).

Rather confusingly, the government's policy was characterized by paradoxical objectives. Incontrovertibly, the main stated goal of the Ethical Policy was to raise the indigenous standard of living, but the government intended to keep a low profile. Since 1870, the beginning of the 'liberal period', there was an unwritten rule that free enterprise should not be obstructed in developing export trade. An 'open door' policy was pursued, giving trade free play and – at least until the early 1930s – viewing government intervention as undesirable. It might be argued that other measures, for example protecting the domestic market or stimulating import substitution, might have been more beneficial to indigenous prosperity. But such measures were not politically interesting to the colonial government, because it was in the contradictory position of having to function as an intermediary between European enterprise in Java and the population that needed to be protected. The fact that the Ethical Policy focused on indigenous food production, and not on stimulating export production, can be viewed as a compromise between these contradictory government objectives.[34]

[34] In Java, matters were more complicated. The cultivation of sugar cane competed with subsistence agriculture and was therefore more sensitive to government actions to promote indigenous well-being. For example, the sugar industry feared that the government would decide to limit the area planted with sugar cane or to force sugar mills to pay higher lease prices. Hüsken 1994:217-8.

Impact of the Ethical Policy in the Outer Islands

The Ethical Policy was a major factor in the views of civil servants in the Outer Islands on the government's role in the indigenous economy. Resident Oberman's remark in 1938, quoted at the beginning of this chapter, is typical of government views in the decades preceding 1930. Fighting famine and stimulating self-sufficiency in food production was the main task Oberman set himself. The export of commercial crops, which could also be viewed as a sign of modernization, was seen as a hindrance, because it drew resources away from food production. New planting methods, supply of fertilizer, and work of the Agricultural Extension Service, as well as (minor) improvements in credit facilities for peasants, were all directed towards raising food production. In 1937, an LVD official in Jambi argued that intensification of food production was not even feasible as long as rubber prices were good. He asserted that, although it had been set as a major aim, intensification should be replaced with diversification of agriculture and improvement of rubber seedlings.[35]

The emphasis on food production in indigenous areas may also have been characteristic of the way the centre viewed the periphery. Be that as it may, there were also government officials in the Outer Islands who had more promising ideas about how to bring their regions into the orbit of modern economic life. For example, Resident F.C. Vorstman of Tapanuli, a residency whose economic potential was frustrated by difficult transport in its mountainous terrain, stated succinctly: 'The construction of main roads is one of the most powerful means to improve economically backward regions.'[36]

In many Memories van Overgave, agricultural extension work and road construction are mentioned as the most important means for improving the local economy. Most Residents gave agricultural extension high priority as a government task. Other policy objectives, such as maintaining political stability or alleviating food shortages, were often not meant to improve the economy but merely to sustain law and order.[37]

Was a perceived economic dynamism of the Outer Islands, which must have seemed to contrast sharply with economically troublesome, overpopulated Java, another reason for lack of government intervention in the Outer Islands? In many Memories van Overgave, indigenous adaptability in trade was praised and the need for improved rural credit supply or agricultural

35 Nota F. van Gogh, as quoted in Tideman 1938:261-3.

36 ARA Kol, MvO 174, F.C. Vorstman 1921:8-9.

37 For example, in Aceh, superficial calm would vanish as soon as even part of the 4,000 military troops left the residency, according to Resident Van Aken. Expenditure on health services in Aceh was seen as 'one of the most effective means of pacification', and agricultural estates also functioned as a means to avoid political unrest, by bringing in money and employment opportunities. ARA Kol, MvO 160, A.Ph. van Aken, 1936:1, 72-5; MvO 159, A.H. Philips 1932:17.

extension was observed without displaying a condescending or overtly patronizing attitude. The fly in the ointment was that in the vast area of the Outer Islands, funds and civil servants were much scarcer than in Java, at any rate too small to promote economic development significantly. Many government officials in the provinces observed that there were important responsibilities awaiting the government, but they did not often receive the funding for initiating large projects.

Incomes in the Outer Islands did rise, but this was primarily due to the economic dynamism of the indigenous population – entrepreneurship in export agriculture and trade, and flexibility in adopting new economic activities. Measures taken by the colonial government did little to trigger new economic activity when development was slow or international contacts were poor. This can be illustrated by the relatively backward regions in the Outer Islands, where indigenous incomes were below average, and where there was only limited (local) trade. In those provinces of this cluster which were situated in Sumatra, indigenous production rose because of other incentives – influence from neighbouring provinces, contacts with middlemen. Resident F.C. Vorstman of Tapanuli confirmed this by saying: 'Because of a shortage of staff in almost all branches of the service, not only is a powerful stimulation of economic progress hindered, but at times it is even impossible to keep our own business going.'[38]

In provinces of the 'Great East' where local stimuli from trade in adjacent provinces were absent, the government could do little to strengthen the economic situation (see Chapter V). Resident J.F.A. de Rooy in Timor complained about having too few officials to carry out effective policy. In New Guinea, Resident K.H.F. Roos lamented in 1909: 'No shred of progress can be traced anywhere in any way whatsoever'. Even as late as 1930, Resident C.C. Ouwerling of Ambon noted that all plans for large projects had to be discarded in the quiet southern Maluku islands.[39]

Short-term effects of the three major goals of the Ethical Policy (migration, irrigation, and education) on the Outer Islands were limited. These goals had been conceived with Java in mind and, moreover, budgets were too restricted to carry out major plans effectively outside Java. This was a consequence of the origins of the Ethical Policy, for which the immediate cause had been the 'lesser welfare' in Java between 1890 and 1910. The shift of economic activity to the Outer Islands, as described in Chapter II, introduced a complication into government policy. The cinderella Outer Islands emerged as the major field of investment and the major earners of export revenues, while

38 ARA Kol, MvO 174, F.C. Vorstman 1921:8.

39 ARA Kol, MvO 339, J.F.A. de Rooy 1908:2; MvO 321, K.H.F. Roos 1909:26; MvO 315, C.C. Ouwerling 1930:1.

the main welfare problems (poverty) as well as the alleged 'debt of honour' (the Cultivation System) were located in Java.

Efforts by government officials in the Outer Islands to create favourable conditions for economic development were hampered by lack of funds rather than by a lack of good intentions. For the colonial government in Batavia, the continuation of a profitable exploitation of the colony diluted the sense of urgency to 'develop' the indigenous population. Creating favourable economic conditions in the Outer Islands was not an urgent goal. The sheer magnitude of the archipelago, only recently having come entirely under colonial rule, was decisive in limiting the efficacy of the available budget.

Major aspects of economic policy

This is an appropriate moment to outline the major aspects of economic policy in the Outer Islands. Before the onset of the Depression, the main issues in government were agricultural extension, cooperatives, credit supply, colonization plans, and of course the construction of infrastructure. Several of these items were vital for creating favourable conditions for export growth. After 1931, production restrictions and import limitations brought government intervention into new areas of the economy. These subjects will be discussed briefly in this section. I will treat neither government policy concerning forestry nor the complicated matter of taxes (except for the surtax on smallholder rubber). I will not deal with the concessionary laws on exploitation of natural resources (farming land, oil, tin) by foreign companies (this subject is addressed in Chapter III), nor will issues such as the circulation of money (commissioned by the government to the Java Bank) and revenue farming of monopolies (opium, salt) be treated here. The attitude of the government towards indigenous export trade will be discussed later in this chapter.

Agricultural extension

The Landbouwvoorlichtingsdienst (LVD), established in 1910 as a special section in charge of demonstration fields, carried out research on smallholder crops (kapok, sisal, copra).[40] Associations of European estates gradually established their own research institutes for coffee, tea, and tobacco, either in Java or in East Sumatra. Research carried out by the LVD led to substantial growth in basic knowledge of peasant agriculture. Agricultural consultants (*landbouwconsulenten*) were appointed to each province to study indigenous agriculture, advise local civil administrators, and instruct peasants on the use

40 The establishment of the LVD is recounted in Van den Doel 1994:163-76, 227-30.

of new methods. Van der Eng states that, especially during the Depression, considerable government involvement in the Indonesian economy yielded tangible results (smallholders becoming increasingly interested in improved seed varieties, fertilizers, improved cultivation techniques, and ways of combating pests and diseases) (Van der Eng 1996c:72-4,77-91,94-100). As a consequence of enforced cutbacks in the civil service, the LVD was less active in the Outer Islands than in Java.

In many regions, government efforts to increase food production centred on irrigation techniques and stimulating *sawah* cultivation through both large-scale and small-scale projects (Boomgaard 1986:70-2). For example, the provincial government in Southeast Kalimantan encouraged the construction of *sawah* by organizing contests among the peasants in Kandangan-Rantau and Barabai as well as in Kutai. The stated aim was to diversify cultivation of food crops and cash crops.[41] In West Kalimantan, Resident H. de Vogel reported in 1918 that the construction of *sawah* was encouraged with a view to promoting the cultivation of secondary crops, but to little avail. Resident Oberman confirmed that only Chinese peasants bothered with rice *sawah*.[42] Resident L. Berkhout in Lampung remarked sadly that government subsidies spent on *sawah* construction often led owners to arrange for their *sawah* to be farmed by Javanese sharecroppers, while 'the [Lampung] owners are content with one-third of the harvest'.[43] In Bangka, results were very disappointing; the soil was too dry and infertile. All experiments with *sawah* construction failed, notwithstanding the diligence of Chinese peasants.[44]

Although the estates in East Sumatra had their own research stations, the estate area also drew more than its fair share of the attention of government officials and policy makers, overshadowing indigenous agriculture. One of the signs that indigenous agriculture received little attention in this province is that the government abolished the East Sumatran branch of the LVD in 1933 in a round of budget cuts.[45] Although the agricultural extension service in East Sumatra was reestablished in 1935, the new consultant, P. Mansvelt Beck, was only allowed two assistants.[46] This was quite different from some other provinces, where LVD personnel kept expanding, even during and shortly after the Depression. The total number of LVD field workers and surveyors in Java increased from 68 in 1930 to about 150 in 1936.[47] Since the

41 ARA Kol, MvO 278, W.G. Moggenstorm 1937:191.

42 ARA Kol, MvO 261, H. de Vogel 1918:20-4; MvO 265, J. Oberman 1938:38.

43 ARA Kol, MvO 233, L. Berkhout 1926:27.

44 ARA Kol, MvO 246, J.E. Edie 1928:3, 44.

45 ARA Kol, MvO 188, H.E.K. Ezerman 1933:263.

46 ARA Kol, MvO 190, B.C.C.M.M. van Suchtelen 1936:208.

47 Van der Eng 1993a:94. In the rubber provinces, the Rubber Fund allowed for extra LVD officials.

planters' associations had their own experimental stations, the government gave less priority to agricultural extension for the local population.

In provinces with high levels of indigenous exports, such as Palembang and West Kalimantan, the LVD played an important role in preventing the deliberate adulteration of exported coffee and rubber by peasants. The regional government considered this issue important, since foreign purchasers accused the trading firms of cheating, and threatened to go elsewhere. It stands to reason that in a province where indigenous export production was the dominant economic activity, the government had an interest in protecting and securing these exports. This may explain the relatively high government expenditure per capita in the provinces of Cluster II, observed in the late 1920s. In these provinces the LVD also contributed to fighting plant disease. In Southeast Kalimantan, in 1937, 14 employees were working at the LVD, which is considerably more than Mansvelt Beck's two assistants in 1935.[48]

Cooperatives and credit: the constraints of colonial finance

As we have seen in Chapter IV, the cultivation of coffee in Palembang was stimulated by the government, especially through a system of planters' credit. The loans supplied had to be paid back in annual instalments, in contrast to credit to traders, which usually had to be paid back in full within one year. The Palembangsche Volksbank (Palembang Credit Union) was founded in 1925 and played an important role in supplying these loans. In 1928, it had 21 offices in Palembang and charged a low rate of interest, only 12 per cent. The Resident of Palembang remarked that it was very difficult to find personnel for these small offices. Much depended on the motivation and commitment of the indigenous *marga* heads (heads of municipalities).[49]

How were formal credit facilities for the indigenous population in colonial Indonesia arranged? In theory, indigenous peasants could obtain credit from the large commercial European banks, such as the Java Bank and the NHM, but in fact the commercial banks were not geared towards providing adequate credit for smallholders. They were out of touch with village communities, and potential indigenous clients had to overcome a psychological barrier before approaching them. With the gradual upsurge of monetization, the need for money expanded. Apart from earning cash (for example in export agriculture or in government jobs such as road construction), there were several other ways to obtain money: borrowing from relatives, obtaining loans from moneylenders or intermediary traders, or using the credit facilities created by the government (Van Laanen 1990:257).

48 ARA Kol, MvO 212, J. Tideman 1928:261; MvO 265, J. Oberman 1938:40; MvO 278, W.G. Moggenstorm 1937:136; MvO 277, B.C.C.M.M. van Suchtelen 1933:163.

49 ARA Kol, MvO 212, J. Tideman 1928:160-3.

In 1904 the Volkscredietwezen (People's Credit System) was established to supervise the founding and running of private district banks in Java; such banks would be accorded tax relief if they accepted supervision by this service. The Volkscredietwezen established village banks as well as larger district banks, the so-called *volksbanken* (credit unions).[50] In 1924 the credit service was privatized and renamed the People's Credit Service, in which the only government involvement was a government-appointed advisor. In 1934 this service changed its name again, to the Algemeene Volkscredietbank (General People's Credit Bank). This new private bank was an officially recognized institution and acted without government interference. One of its tasks was to supervise the village banks. It also supplied credit to these smaller banks.[51]

Village banks (in contrast to district banks) were accessible to individual smallholders. They were usually run under the supervision of local civil administrators. These banks granted small loans at lower interest rates than those charged by moneylenders, often for a matter of only a few weeks and without collateral. Such banks were scarce in the Outer Islands; more than 90 per cent of the village banks were in Java. In 1930 there were almost 6,000 village banks in Java and only 624 village banks in the Outer Islands (of which 537 were in Sumatra). In the same year there were 71 district banks in Java and only 18 in the Outer Islands (11 in Sumatra, 2 in Kalimantan, and 4 in Sulawesi).[52]

The People's Credit Unions (or district banks) had total assets of about 90 million guilders, of which 19 million formed the assets of district banks in the Outer Provinces. More importantly for peasants, in 1929 the village banks in the Outer Provinces had a capital of 1.4 million guilders. In this year these village banks had 429,000 guilders on loan from district banks, and 86,000 guilders on deposit by indigenous inhabitants. Considering that the total indigenous population in the Outer Islands was more than 18 million in 1930, it is obvious that formal credit supply was still very much in its infancy.[53]

In the Outer Islands, even more than in Java, many smallholders depended on intermediary traders or moneylenders for credit. The high interest rates paid on these loans, both in Java and in the Outer Islands, were notorious. As we have seen in Chapter IV, smallholder products were often sold to the

50 In Java, there were also village rice banks (or paddy banks, *lumbung desa*), run by village officials, where rice was stored and could be borrowed as seed paddy.

51 It is the forerunner of the present Bank Rakyat. Cribb 1993:236; Van der Eng 1996c:128-30; Van Laanen 1990:259.

52 In 1940 there were some 5,600 village banks, only 500 of which were in the Outer Islands. Boomgaard 1986:76; Van der Eng 1996c:130-3; *Statistisch Jaaroverzicht* 1929:199-209; *Statistisch Jaaroverzicht* 1930:203-6.

53 Boomgaard 1986:76; Coolhaas 1943:128; Ranken 1989:189; *Statistisch Jaaroverzicht* 1929:199-209.

trader even before they were harvested, resulting in dependence of the peasant on his creditor when the harvest did not meet expectations. Such a situation is hard to reverse. Often, the credit banks were hamstrung because most of their funds were tied up in outstanding loans, paralysing them in any attempt to service more clients. This made Resident A.Ph. van Aken of West Sumatra wonder whether putting pressure on clients to meet their overdue loan repayments might not result in the opposite to what the bank intended to do; the main objective of the banks, after all, was to supply credit, not to be obsessed with demanding it back. 'The People's Credit Unions could work beautifully, provided that every case is thoroughly researched.'[54] Looking at the situation from the smallholders' point of view, there was a discrepancy between the informal ways by which the old-style moneylenders supplied loans, and the more bureaucratic procedures of the Volkscredietwezen, which may have alienated peasants. The success or failure of formal credit facilities depended to a large extent on the ardour of local government officials.

The colonial government not only supported the People's Credit Union system, in the 1930s it also turned its attention to stimulating cooperative marketing boards. Such an intervention was much better attuned to local production methods, and cooperatives were more readily accepted by peasants.

In themselves, these measures were appropriate and useful, but they were too weak to push the indigenous economy to expand (Potting 1997:269-70). They could not fulfil the growing demand for credit, which explains the expanding role of intermediary traders and unauthorized moneylenders. It can be argued that a larger and more accessible system of People's Credit Unions, and the introduction and support of smallholder cooperatives at an earlier date, would have given peasants more opportunities to obtain sound financial backing.

Colonization programme

Immigration projects had been a favourite theme of policy makers since the launching of the Ethical Policy. Resettlement of Javanese peasants to the sparsely populated Outer Islands should alleviate the population pressure in Java. Colonists were given a bonus, their passage, and a loan in order to start farming on a new piece of land in the colonization area, where they were expected to cultivate rice in the same manner as they had done in Java. The construction of irrigation facilities was an integral part of the projects. The oldest colonies were near Kota Agoong and Gedung Tataan in Lampung, established in 1905. Although these settlements grew from a thousand families to roughly 24,000 settlers in 1927, this was only a drop in the bucket towards relieving population pressure in Java. To have achieved this, migration flows

54 ARA Kol, MvO 306, A.Ph. van Aken 1933:22-j.

of more than half a million people would have been necessary. The new settlers cultivated rice and copra, and mingled little with the indigenous inhabitants of Lampung. By 1941, Javanese settlements in Lampung had roughly 175,000 inhabitants. Other settlement projects in Sumatra, Southeast Kalimantan, and South Sulawesi provided new homes for around 80,000 Javanese.[55]

In the 1930s there were several small Javanese colonization areas in Bengkulu, each amounting to less than 1,000 Javanese immigrants. These very small settlements were expected to become self-sufficient in food production very rapidly and to cost the government little in advances.[56] Resident P.M. Hooykaas aired his scepticism when he reported that the colonization projects in Wonosobo (Lampung), which provided the example for the small experiments in Bengkulu, were characterized by maladministration, mismanagement, abnormally high loans to immigrants, and therefore high costs to the government. The government had to offer employment in the form of expensive irrigation projects. Loans to settlers were not paid back on time. The only positive effect, according to Hooykaas, was that indigenous farmers were exposed to new farming methods.[57]

In Palembang, the government had a slightly different reason for promoting Javanese settlements. Javanese immigrant labourers, who had come to the province during the rubber boom, tended to move back to Java during the Depression. Government efforts to keep these migrants in the province, in order to have a supply of labour for better times to come, were not successful. Even exemptions from the twin burdens of income tax and corvée labour could not entice Javanese tappers to settle in Palembang as peasants. Exempting them from corvée labour was rather ironic, since another reason for attracting colonists to Palembang and Jambi was the need for a labour force to work on road maintenance. Many local peasants bought off their corvée obligations, and with these revenues the government hired Javanese coolies.[58]

Plans for labour settlements near the estates

During the entire period of this study, there were protracted discussions between the government and the estates about the working conditions of contract coolies, the necessity for a 'penal clause', and the possibilities of cre-

[55] ARA Kol, MvO 231, J. Breukink 1923:23-5; MvO 233, L. Berkhout 1926:50-64; Broek 1942:22; Cribb 1993:237; Van der Eng 1996c:57.

[56] In Perbo (Lais, Bengkulu), established in 1933-1934, 429 people. In Kamumu (Lais), established in 1935, 410 families. And in Lubuk Mumpo (Dorian Mas, Rejang), established in 1935-1936, 370 families. ARA Kol, MvO 205, P.M. Hooykaas 1939:35.

[57] ARA Kol, MvO 205, P.M. Hooykaas 1939:10-2.

[58] The major cause of the failure of colonization in Palembang, according to Resident Swaab, was the fact that *marga* offered only less-fertile plots to the immigrants. ARA Kol, MvO 214, J.L.M. Swaab 1933:4; MvO 223, J.R.F. Verschoor van Nisse 1931:141, 161-8.

ating labour settlements near the estates (see also Chapter III). Labour colonization was intended to create labour pools around the estates. This would eliminate the need for contract coolies and make the penal clause redundant, since coolies who had settled with their families would not run away or show other forms of misconduct. In principle the planters in East Sumatra accepted government proposals to stimulate labour colonization, but they were fervently opposed to another type of settlement called agricultural colonization, which assigned larger plots of land to settlers. The planters argued that there was no room for such settlements in the estate area, and effectively blocked the issue of agricultural colonization in their own backyard (Stoler 1985:38-41). To help persuade the government, they wrote a report which concluded that 'agricultural colonization could not contribute to the solution of the labour problem on the estates'.[59] The alternative solution, establishing labour settlements with considerably smaller plots of land, was put forward with much more vigour. A reservoir of estate workers would live near the estates, working partly on the estate and partly on their own allotments. A much discussed topic was the absolute minimum size of a plot of land from which a Javanese settler could live. In almost all plans, the proposed allotments were too small for subsistence agriculture, so that settlers would remain economically dependent on the estates, needing to supplement their income by working as hired labourers. Proposed plot sizes ranged from a mere 100 m^2 to 700 m^2 per household (Stoler 1985:39-40).

The labour settlements remained small in comparison to the number of coolies employed on the estates. Nevertheless, many firmly believed that this would solve the labour shortage, as illustrated in a 1922 report by the NHM agent in Medan: 'The coolie contracts with the penal clause will be abolished in 1926. It is expected that by that time colonization will have advanced to the extent that a sufficient number of free coolies will apply for work on the estates'.[60] This sounds a little naive, considering the failure of earlier labour settlements.

Another short-lived initiative in labour relations was put forward by the Cultuurraad (Cultivation Council). It suggested appointing confidential agents among the workers who could mediate between coolies and managers. Referring to this idea, the NHM agent quoted above could barely contain his scepticism: he doubted whether 'this well-meant plan would achieve a shadow of success in practice'.[61] Not to be swayed, officials continued to

59 ARA Kol, MvO 187, L.H.W. van Sandick 1930:65 and appendices following page 65 (report by J.J. Priebee and J.F.A.M. Buffart). Priebee was head administrator at the Deli Maatschappij, Buffart was chair of the AVROS.

60 ARA, NHM 9126, VvS 497 (Medan 1921):19.

61 Two years later, in 1924, the same agent states that the reports of the Labour Inspectorate

believe firmly in colonization plans.

The Depression in the 1930s speeded up the abolition of the penal clause. Inevitable lay-offs suddenly led to an oversupply of labour. After the abolition of the penal clause in 1932, many estates in East Sumatra started providing workers with plots of land, so that they could become self-sufficient peasants and form a labour supply when times got better.

Simultaneously, the Kantoor van Arbeid (Labour Office) distributed pamphlets among estate coolies, warning those who planned to return to their hometowns about the sorry state of living conditions in Java. In November 1932, 2,670 copies of a booklet called *Rungokno ceritaneh tanah wutah getihmu* ('Listen to the story of your native land', obviously meant to be read aloud) were distributed, recounting the poverty and unemployment in Java.[62]

The discussion between planters and the government now focused on the question of whether these new settlements, the so-called *randkolonisaties* (border colonies), should be located on or off the estates. Located on the borders of an estate, families could grow their own food when they were not employed, but they were not meant to become independent peasants. The major drawback to this plan was that planters feared they would be an obstacle for future expansion of the estate area.

In June 1933, just after the government had declared itself in favour of border colonies, Dr W. Brokx, the Assistant-Resident, who was charged with implementing the colonization policy, published a report stating his rejection of border colonization as an official policy. Apparently unconvinced, after lengthy discussions the Volksraad declared its support of border colonization.[63] All the while, the government promoted colonization in order to accomplish the provision of a free labour market and to reduce the 'one-sided structure' of the province with regard to supply and demand of labour. Even voluntary settlement by Javanese families was encouraged, for example in Sisir Gunting, a flourishing settlement of ex-coolies from neighbouring tobacco estates; in adjacent Pulu Gurau, Banjarese from Southeast Kalimantan grew rice and kept goats and poultry.[64]

After 1934 world demand started to regain its strength. As production picked up, so too did the demand for labour. Various methods were now used to prevent a renewed labour shortage: priority was given to the recruitment of married couples, who would settle permanently in Deli, and to improving living conditions on the estates. All workers were officially 'free'

---

show that he was right about 'those silly mediator plans'. ARA, NHM 9126, VvS 497 (Medan 1921):19; VvS 499 (1923):14.[62] ARA Kol, MvO 188, H.E.K. Ezerman 1933:62-3, 656.

63 ARA, NHM 9127, VvS 509 (Medan 1933):9-10; ARA Kol, MvO 190, B.C.C.M.M. van Suchtelen 1936:22. See also Tideman 1918:63-6.

64 ARA Kol, MvO 190, B.C.C.M.M. van Suchtelen 1936:22-3, 57.

workers by now. As Langeveld has shown, the position of coolies on estates in East Sumatra improved between 1930 and 1940, which may have been a spin-off of the transition to free labour. The main improvement was in the treatment of workers: less imprisonment and better recruiting methods. Salaries, medical care, and accommodation improved only marginally (Langeveld 1978:346-62).

What can be learnt from all these proposals and the protracted discussions between planters and government officials? It is clear that, officially, the colonial government shared the ardent concern of those in the mother country about the maltreatment of coolies. As to taking action, a critical observer may reproach the government for a lack of efficacy. Stoler says about the colonization plans:

> The reams of paper generated over these proposals belie the fact that most of these schemes never got beyond the experimental stage and were certainly never implemented on a region-wide basis. The largest concentrations of such efforts came at critical economic junctures – during World War I, the economic malaise of 1921-1923, and the Depression of the 1930s: that is, when it became mandatory to reduce labour costs, in part through massive dismissals of managerial and coolie personnel, in part by allocating more of the maintenance costs of labour power to the workers themselves. (Stoler 1985:41.)[65]

In its efforts to improve the lot of coolie labourers, the government's main leverage was through the Labour Inspectorate, which contributed to improving the living conditions of coolies. The Depression (and, in tobacco, the Blaine Amendment) was needed to achieve the final abolition of the penal clause. It is difficult to escape the impression that government plans for colonization were well meant but not entirely realistic, particularly in the 1920s when the estates attracted hundreds of thousands of contract labourers, while colonization programmes only involved a few tens of thousands.

Roads

The construction of roads served a political as well as an economic goal. Good connections were essential to a properly functioning government. Agricultural estates and mining companies also built roads and bridges, of course primarily only for their own use, but inevitably to the benefit of the region. Roads and railways did not merely serve the colonial power, whether they were constructed by large capitalist estates or by the expanding government. Roads facilitated the transport of indigenous cash crops on carts and

[65] In her book Stoler focuses on the communities of Javanese immigrant workers in the plantation periphery, in a conscientious analysis of labour relations among the different generations of plantation workers in East Sumatra in the twentieth century.

trucks, even though regulations sometimes prevented peasants from using certain traditional cart designs or prescribed certain ratios between wheelbase and tonnage, in order to prolong the life of the roads (Cribb 1993:239).

Road construction also contributed to the monetization of the economy, since unskilled labourers on road construction work were often paid in cash. Road maintenance, by contrast, was carried out by corvée labourers. In certain regions, when this formed an incentive for peasants to earn cash to pay off their corvée duties, it stimulated monetization in a slightly different manner.

Though not all regions profited from such developments to an equal degree, infrastructural development was beneficial to the economy of the region. Unpaid corvée labour, used in the construction and maintenance of roads and bridges, represented a significant savings to the Netherlands Indies government (Van der Kraan 1980a:6). In the late 1930s, the Rubber Fund was also used to cover additional expenses for roads and bridges.

Roads and bridges were not the only form of social overhead capital investments by the government. In all residencies, efforts were poured into the construction of harbours, airports, and telephone, telegraph, and postal services, as well as waterworks and electrification schemes, the latter two mainly in the larger towns.

More weight on economic matters during the Depression

The Depression called for a change in attitude towards the economy at large. In the 1930s, the government suddenly felt compelled to intervene in trade and industry. This is illustrated by the fact that many older textbooks only start treating economic policy seriously after 1930, largely ignoring welfare policy in the early twentieth century.[66] In a sense, this is legitimate, because the European sector felt the effects of government intervention only after 1930.

As stated at the beginning of this chapter, the Depression of the 1930s was the first occasion on which it is possible to speak of any far-reaching government intervention. 'This was wholly contrary to the traditions of the Dutch since 1870', Furnivall writes. He continues: 'They were firm believers in individual enterprise and in free competition and free trade and they were encouraged in these views when the rubber interests [...] made huge profits by standing out of the Stevenson Restriction Scheme' (Furnivall 1944:435). But after 1930, production restrictions, import limitations, and the rice policy were used to regulate the free trade which had been so important to the expansion of the economy of the Outer Islands. There were three reasons for the government to intervene more strongly in the economy after 1930 than before: the low prices for raw materials on the world market in the wake of

66 Boeke 1953:216-8; Broek 1942:52-75; Furnivall 1944:435; Gonggrijp 1938. This point is also made by Prince (1993, 1995:26).

the Depression; the mounting debts weighing upon the shoulders of producers; and, finally, the expansion of Japanese economic influence in the archipelago (Burger 1975:126-8).

The first of the industries brought under government control was the sugar industry in Java. Regulations were formulated in the Chadbourne Plan (1931). Shortly thereafter, the International Tin Pool (1931), the International Tea Committee (1933), and the IRRA rubber restriction (1934) were established, with profound repercussions for both indigenous and European production in the Outer Islands.[67]

The production restrictions were based on international agreement, as the international community realized that systematic overproduction and subsequent oversupply of the various export goods on the world market were the prime causes of slumping prices. However well intentioned, such restriction agreements were not always effective. The expensive, overvalued Dutch guilder, which was linked to the gold standard until 1936, weakened the position of Netherlands Indies export goods on the international market (Baudet and Fennema 1983:38-40; Ricklefs 1993:187).

The government tried to stimulate trade by establishing export cooperatives and central organizations for buying up smallholder crops and products such as copra, kapok, tobacco, cassava, and resins. In some cases these were effective (for example in Minahasa, as discussed below) and at least showed some concern for the indigenous economy. But cooperatives can only have had a marginal impact on the economy. Krafft lists 56 indigenous credit and production cooperatives in the Outer Islands in the 1920s (most of them in West Sumatra). In 1939 there were 574 cooperatives, with a total membership of a mere 52,555 peasants. Some 75 per cent of these cooperatives were credit cooperatives, to assist heavily indebted smallholders (Van der Eng 1996c:137-8; Krafft 1929:305-9).

Indigenous production, linked to the market through a network of Chinese traders, was largely beyond the reach of local and central governments. Registration of production or land use were inadequate and primitive, so that imposing quota restrictions based on production figures was impossible. Unfamiliarity meant government insight into the mechanisms of production was poor. For example, the *bagi dua* system discussed in Chapter IV, which gave tappers an equal share of the harvest, caused supply to be very price inelastic. *Bagi dua* could switch to *bagi tiga, bagi empat,* or *bagi lima,* offering tappers a larger share when prices were low, thus maintaining an ample supply. Supply could also be inelastic because indebted producers were forced to keep selling in order to pay back their debts. These factors explain why the

67 Broek 1942:62. On government decision-making regarding the tin and rubber restrictions, see De Graaff 1997:494-549.

rubber restriction initially caused the output of indigenous rubber to expand rather than contract.

Imports, too, were subjected to regulation during the Depression. During the preceding few decades, Japan had been aggressively entering the import trade in the archipelago. By supplying cheap consumer goods (textiles) and cooperating with the Chinese distribution network, Japanese import traders penetrated the indigenous market and began competing with Dutch import trade. This especially threatened Dutch textile exports to the Indies. In 1933 the Crisis Invoer-Ordonnantie (Crisis Import Ordinance) restricted foreign imports and established a quota system (Prince 1989:217, 1993:171). This enabled the government to put a temporary embargo on the import of specific goods and served to enlarge the Dutch share of Netherlands Indies imports, which was suffering from the high gold-standard exchange rates (Van Hall 1943:161; Post 1991:112, 307-9). It was an important measure, because it constituted the first profound break with the free-trade policy which had been pursued since 1870. Admittedly, the intention of this measure was to restrict Japanese imports (and protect Dutch imports) rather than to protect the developing domestic industry. Imports from Java during these years did however increase. Interregional trade statistics show that the percentage of aggregate imports originating from Java increased from 42.6 per cent in 1933 to 47.4 per cent in 1936 (Table 22.2 and Figure 21). In 1924/28, the share of imports from Java had averaged 31 per cent for all Outer Islands; in 1929/33 this was 62 per cent and in 1934/38 it was 45 per cent (Table 25.2).

Rice policy in the 1930s

Of the imports from Java, rice was particularly important. Rice imports from Java to the Outer Islands averaged roughly 30 million kg per year in 1917/26 and 167 million kg per year in 1929/37 (Tables 56.1 and 56.2) (Dick 1996:43).

In the early 1930s, rice prices had been low, to the benefit of the estates, which had an interest in keeping food costs for their workers low. In 1933, when a large quantity of Japanese rice was dumped on the market in Macassar, the government was forced to intervene to stabilize the domestic price level of rice and to encourage surplus production by peasants. The intention was to replace foreign rice imports as much as possible by domestic rice production. In contrast to the 1910s, when a shortage of rice led to high rice prices and a government ban on rice exports in 1911-1919, there was now an ample supply of rice on the international market at a very low price. The government introduced a ban on rice imports in 1933 (Prince 1989:213, 1993:168).

Rice imports were restricted through a system of licences and taxes, in order to stabilize the rice price at an economically viable level. Revenues from the rice import tax were used for various purposes, such as purchasing rice in surplus areas (to be sold in deficit areas) and subsidizing KPM and

State Railways freight rates for food crops (Van der Eng 1996c:185; Prince 1989:213-4). After 1939 the rice policy was explicitly aimed at attaining self-sufficiency. Generally speaking, international restrictions greatly stimulated inter-island trade between Java and the Outer Provinces, especially in rice (Dick 1990:320-1).

Evaluation of priorities

In the preceding sections on the Ethical Policy I have analysed the policy measures affecting the Outer Islands: agricultural extension, credit unions, colonization programmes, and rice policy. In this section I will reflect on the government's attitude towards the development of indigenous export production in the Outer Islands. Finally, I will briefly evaluate the role of the colonial government in the colonial economy in more general terms.

Java-based policy

The most general but nevertheless valid observation is that a large part of economic policy was developed in Java and with Java in mind. Much of the information on which economic policy was based was collected in Java. Inescapably, the trio of themes 'migration, education, and irrigation' was inspired by the Javanese situation, and the welfare policy was largely directed towards the Javanese peasant, who had suffered under the Cultivation System and the repercussions of the sugar industry.

Undeniable though this Java-centrism was, the expanding body of government officials in the Outer Islands slowly but steadily increased its influence. Regions with a large European presence gained the attention of civil servants. Here government officials had to keep European entrepreneurs happy. When smallholder export agriculture expanded in other provinces, such as Jambi, West Kalimantan, or South Sulawesi, administrators and agricultural engineers wrote reports on these economic developments. Knowledge of the economy of these previously not-very-well-studied regions grew.[68] Although the government budget in these regions was not insignificant, there were restrictions on what the civil service could do.

Government measures to increase agricultural production had the favourable side-effect of raising revenues from land and income taxes (Van der Kraan 1980a:2). But on the whole, the effects of policy measures in the large Outer Provinces were unpredictable. My impression is that many local

68 For example the series on smallholder rubber (*De bevolkingsrubbercultuur in Nederlands-Indië*) summarized in Luytjes 1925b (Cumming 1924; Luytjes 1925a; Bailie 1925; Loos and Van Beusechem 1925; Slotemaker 1926; Brook et al. 1926; Warren and Van Staalduinen 1925).

government officials and field workers sincerely intended to improve food production and to raise the standard of living of smallholders, but on the whole, the civil service in the Outer Islands was restrained by small budgets. There was a great deal that escaped the notice of civil servants. In a note from the Ministry of Colonial Affairs in December 1925 A.A.L. Rutgers wrote: 'Rubber cultivation has been entirely withdrawn from government control, facts are unregistered, and the government misses the points of reference to influence it'.[69]

Civil service versus European enterprise

It is by now well established that the colonial government rarely intervened in European industrial life in the Outer Islands before 1930, adhering to a strict laissez-faire policy. The worlds of the civil servant and the Western entrepreneur have been characterized as worlds apart: European export companies almost by definition disliked the civil service, and regarded it as an institution which was out to put a spoke in the wheel of economic progress, as a former government official put it.[70]

Before 1930, the issue of the treatment of coolies was the most striking example of government intervention in European enterprise (see Chapter III). Labour legislation on coolie contracts and the establishment of the Labour Inspectorate in 1908 were the outcome of the political indignation about the living conditions of coolies which flared up around 1900. As early as the 1910s the colonial government began talking about abolishing the penal clause in coolie contracts, but it was 1931 before this actually happened. A series of revisions of the Coolie Ordinance between 1923 and 1931 faithfully mirrored a continuous struggle between government officials and employers' organizations, a struggle focused mainly on the amount of coolie wages. The slowness of this decision-making process can be seen partly as the consequence of a lack of efficacy, or perhaps even a government bias towards European enterprise.

Ambivalence towards smallholder rubber production

The government's attitude towards indigenous rubber cultivation, the most dynamic phenomenon in the indigenous economy of the Outer Islands, can be typified at best as ambivalent. Unquestionably, export duties and tax rev-

[69] He advocated that the government should become more involved. See also the section below on government indifference. Creutzberg 1972:595-605, in particular 600; Rutgers 1925.

[70] In Leiden University's long-standing training programme for government officials, when Snouck Hurgronje added the ethical element of propagating European civilization, dissenting views on what constituted proper training for colonial officials led to the establishment of a Utrecht faculty for colonial administration, sponsored by private capital in 1925. Alberts 1989:30; Fasseur 1993.

enues in the rubber provinces soared, allowing government officials to embark on all kinds of projects. The downside was that the government had no grip on the booming production, while being under considerable pressure from European estates to limit it. Commencing in 1927, the government began to favour European companies by levying an export duty on indigenous rubber, from which agricultural estates were exempted. This move was defended by emphasizing the difficulties of collecting income or company taxes in the indigenous sector, whose rubber exports generated large revenues in the 1920s, while European companies were taxed more systematically.[71]

In 1934 the IRRA required limiting the volume of total rubber exports. Therefore, a surtax on indigenous rubber was introduced, in order to reduce the volume of indigenous rubber exports.[72] This surtax was justified by the government on the grounds that the lack of production data made a quota system, such as was used for estate rubber, impossible. But critics have pointed out that while the rubber surtax was in effect, from 1934 to 1937, government efforts to register rubber gardens for setting up an individual restriction system were less than vigorous. In the meantime, the estates enjoyed a favoured position, being allowed to sell their rubber quota at the full market price.

The surtax taxed wet rubber slabs disproportionately, and while it did not succeed in cutting back rubber production, it did, as an unintended side-effect, increase the proportion of dried rubber exports (Lindblad 1988a:75). After 1937, under the individual restriction scheme, almost all rubber was dried in smoking huts and mangled into sheets. Only then, on the eve of the Second World War, did smallholder producers take the first steps towards a processing industry. However, this should not be viewed as a deliberate government policy to encourage an indigenous processing industry. In fact, in the 1930s observers were already criticizing the unfair treatment of indigenous rubber producers under the restriction scheme. Governor B.C.C.M.M. van Suchtelen of East Sumatra even lost his position when he expressed fierce indignation about the rubber surtax, stressing how unfair it was to spare the rubber estates and burden rubber smallholders (Van Suchtelen 1939). Many reports were written on indigenous rubber production, commissioned by the government, but little actual policy was developed and pursued to guide the growth of indigenous export production. Even during the rubber boom years, the government showed little interest in promoting a

71 In June 1925, a 5% export duty on smallholder rubber was introduced. This duty led to considerable revenues for the Dutch government from 1927 on.

72 The rate of the surtax was regularly adjusted by the government and it tended to rise month by month. The surtax yielded about 19.4 million guilders in Southeast Kalimantan, 14 million guilders in Palembang, and 10 million guilders in Jambi during 1934-1937. Total revenues from the surtax amounted to more than 83 million guilders (see Chapter IV).

local processing industry or manufacturing industries in the Outer Islands (see also De Graaff 1997:521-2).

To meet the demands of opponents of the surtax on indigenous rubber, revenues from the surtax were poured into the Rubber Fund, and spent on infrastructural projects in the rubber provinces. In his survey of provincial expenditure on roads, bridges, irrigation works, and telephone lines, Resident Oberman wrote: 'It goes without saying that during the years 1931, 1932, and 1933 the budget in this region had to be cut drastically. All leeway could be made up, however, and a great number of new public works could be executed besides, by using the funds from the surtax on indigenous rubber'.[73]

With the benefit of hindsight, it is tempting to say that the surtax on indigenous rubber resulted in almost Keynesian, and previously unimaginable, expenditure on infrastructure in the rubber provinces. But this does not take into account the inequitable burden of the tax on rubber smallholders. Besides, other activities, such as the cost of introducing an individual registration system, were also financed by the surtax revenues (Thee Kian Wie 1977:27-9). It would have done credit to the government in Batavia had it forced the rubber estates to pay at least their share of regular export duties.

Government indifference towards indigenous trade

In the 1910s and 1920s, smallholder export agriculture in the Outer Islands grew rapidly with hardly any assistance from the government or the estate sector.[74] Although the basic colonial objective was to create favourable economic opportunities for the colony at large, the colonial government was primarily concerned with the exploitation of natural resources by large-scale European enterprises.

Smallholder agriculture was facilitated and stimulated not by the government but by the Chinese trading network. Chinese traders acted as the indispensable link between indigenous producers and the destination of their products. During the 1910s and 1920s the Chinese trading network and sales organization extended to the most remote parts of the interior. As a result of their efforts, Chinese traders formed a considerable economic power, possessing a hegemony in access to the indigenous population and market networks. The middlemen manipulated their suppliers through a system of advances and loans. Increasing affluence amongst traders did not make this population group well-liked, a situation which continues even today. As seen in Chapter IV, many of the traders in the Outer Islands started out in a small way as *singkeh*, newly arrived from China. The risk of the trade meant many

73 ARA Kol, MvO 265, J. Oberman 1938: 'Overzicht gewestelijke uitgaven en inkomsten 1913-1937. Dienst van wegen, bruggen, waterwerken en telefoonlijnen'.

74 Booth 1990b:290. See also Chapter IV.

made an uncertain living, but those who were successful built up sound financial positions.

It should be emphasized that the Chinese trading network supplied credit, functioned as an incentive to indigenous entrepreneurship, and enabled peasants to plant and harvest new crops. The opportunities arising from this trading network were of great significance to the development of the indigenous export sector, as argued in Chapter IV. The fact that smallholders were often tied to their credit supplier, and had committed themselves to high interest rates, was the price that smallholders had to pay.

During the 1920s there were also indigenous traders who participated in the intermediary trade, especially in interior regions, for example in the Sumatran rubber trade. Chinese traders remained a powerful force, however, because they had strong links with the Singapore market and with trading agencies owned by overseas Chinese. This raises the question of whether the government felt any obligation to protect smallholders against foreign traders or moneylenders. The short answer is: it took no concrete measures to restrict the powerful position of the Chinese in intermediary trade. With the importance of the Chinese trading network in mind, it may reasonably be argued that this was largely advantageous to the smallholder economy, or at least that the negative aspects of the Chinese intermediary trade were counterbalanced by the positive ones. However, if the government had supplied alternative, legitimate ways of obtaining credit, it would have played a more helpful role for smallholders.

In early 1925, the forester A. Luytjes was commissioned to travel to Palembang, Jambi, and Singapore to study the rubber trade, and to formulate a proposal for introducing a new excise tax on rubber, based on an improved estimate of the Singapore market price. In his extensive study of the situation in the rubber provinces, Luytjes also recommended that the government should establish rubber-processing (remilling) factories in the Outer Islands.[75] This would reduce the Chinese dominance in the rubber trade, or at least build up the rubber revenues of peasants by improving the quality of their exports. He hoped that in this way a growing share of the profits would end up with indigenous traders. Luytjes reported that both indigenous and Chinese traders transported rubber slabs from the interior to the harbour, where the rubber was sold by agents to export traders, all of whom were Chinese. He also reported that the Residents of Jambi and Palembang were in favour of local rubber processing, although it would be difficult to establish the necessary fixed *pasar* for rubber. In Palembang, for example, there were no rubber *pasar* except in the harbours. Luytjes also formulated several pro-

[75] ARA: Kol. 1901-1963, Openbaar Verbaal 2868 (27 augustus 1926): Report A. Luytjes. Luytjes published more on indigenous rubber cultivation, for example Luytjes 1925a, 1925b.

posals for stimulating local rubber processing and reducing the power of the Chinese. For example, he suggested that the increase allowed in rubber production over the next few years could be assigned to local processors in order to increase their share.

Despite the cogency of his arguments, the government rejected all plans to promote local rubber remilling. In fact, the ordinance that was issued in 1927 set a standard for quality control and prohibited the transportation of rubber in water (*rakit* trade). This measure was detrimental to indigenous traders, who normally used this type of transportation, and thereby effectively favoured Chinese traders, who used boats. In subsequent years, Jambi rubber traders disappeared from the rivers. 'Poor, very poor, are those who by plying that trade had thousands in their hands for a brief time', the Resident of Jambi wrote, referring to the wealth that internal trade had brought to Jambi traders. This government measure also cut KPM's participation in the rubber trade, painfully achieved through a company called the Rubber Union.[76]

Several arguments were put forward for the rejection of Luytjes' proposals. The government feared that assigning the increase in rubber production to local processors would give Chinese traders the chance to raise the price of the remaining quota artificially. It would also mean a violation of the 'open door' policy promulgated by the government, damaging international prestige. And, finally, how would it be possible to exclude powerful Chinese firms in Palembang and Jambi from participating in local remilling?

In a letter to the governor-general, the director of the Binnenlands Bestuur wrote: 'There is no reason to protect rubber planters against the Chinese. On the contrary, the indigenous population owes a lot to the Chinese trader and to the Singapore remilling industries. The Residents say, there are no serious cases of abuse when the products are purchased. The indigenous peasant is well able to look after his own interests'. We know that this was not exactly true: as we saw in Chapter IV, in the section that analysed the powerful position of the traders/moneylenders, indigenous peasants were often dependent on Chinese intermediary traders (even Sumatran smallholders, who were more commercially shrewd than other population groups in the Outer Islands).[77]

The governor-general's decree of 14 May 1926 merely stipulated that

[76] See Chapter IV. These measures were taken because of complaints from Singapore remillers about the poor quality of the rubber. Not surprisingly, the Rubber Union tended to ignore the rubber ordinance and continued buying adulterated indigenous rubber. The Rubber Union was established by the KPM in order to trade directly with indigenous producers and to take some of the intermediary trade out of the hands of Chinese traders. ARA Kol, MvO 212, J. Tideman 1928:257; MvO 223, J.R.F. Verschoor van Nisse 1931:119-25, 168.

[77] ARA, Mailrapport 1150/26, Letter from the director 'Binnenlands Bestuur' to the Governor General, 3 april 1926; Creutzberg 1972:606-7.

measures should be taken to prevent adverse effects of the unconditional admission of any new rubber industry. The Rubberbereidingsordonnantie (Rubber Processing Ordinance) of 1926 merely provided for the issuing of licences for remilling factories, in fact opening up the region to Chinese remillers, whose participation in this type of activity had been restricted by resolutions dating from the nineteenth century.[78] This example shows that the government had little desire to intervene in the situation, preferring to continue its laissez-faire policy.

In this context the rubber restriction measures of the 1930s can be mentioned again. The proceeds from the surtax on indigenous rubber, which was levied in 1934-1937, were put into the Rubber Fund, and covered many government expenses in the rubber regions. Fortunately, this burden on smallholder producers resulted in more expenditure on social overhead capital, from which they would ultimately benefit. (The Rubber Fund financed irrigation projects, bridges, roads, and other infrastructure.) Another interesting observation is that after 1937, when wet rubber slabs began to be taxed more heavily, it stimulated rubber smallholders to process the rubber and export dried rubber 'sheets', thus boosting the domestic processing industry. These developments contributed to the economic recovery in the late 1930s.

In spite of this bright side, it could be argued that the rubber provinces would have had better prospects had they not been unfairly muzzled by the rubber restriction measures. They could produce more cheaply than the estates and, in theory, might have been able to beat the latter in the international competition in rubber supply in the 1930s, even though their rubber was poorer in quality. The positive effects of the rubber restriction (the Rubber Fund and incentives for local processing) do not make up for the loss of income in rubber regions.

The inescapable conclusion is that the colonial government was indifferent to indigenous export agriculture and valued it less highly than estate agriculture. Until the 1930s, indigenous trade had a low priority on the government agenda. This is illustrated by Hevea cultivation. The government did not actively support or protect smallholder rubber production, in spite of its important role in the growth of the domestic economy. The low priority of the development of smallholder rubber may have been a result of the threat it constituted to the European sector, or of historical indifference to the indigenous economy. Although in the mid-1920s various government officials were given the task of documenting the smallholder rubber industry, the principal active government intervention was the smallholder rubber

[78] 'Rubberbereidingsordonnantie' of 1926: *Indisch Staatsblad* 1926 no. 211. Older regulations: *Indisch Staatsblad* 10, 3 februari 1836.

restriction, which for smallholders was a blessing in disguise.

Copra contracts in Minahasa

A second example of government indifference to indigenous trade is the case of copra production in Minahasa (Manado). As shown in Chapter IV, 'copra contracts' virtually transferred ownership of coconut groves in Minahasa to Chinese traders (even though the Agrarian Law of 1870 prohibited Chinese landownership) (Leirissa 1996:265-77). The negative effect of long-term copra contracts emerged during the Depression, when, with their hands effectively tied by the low market price, smallholders could not make their monthly debt repayments. Because of their control over so many coconut groves, Chinese middlemen were very powerful in this region. What was the role of the government in this matter?

In 1918 the Agrarisch Reglement (Agricultural Ordinance) came into effect, regulating landownership and settling the dispute between pioneers in the region and the indigenous inhabitants, who adhered to the local *adat* stipulating that land was family-owned. The new rules set the duration of copra contracts at five or ten years.[79] In the booming mid-1920s, the government made token efforts to prevent some Chinese middlemen who had drawn up misleading contracts from acquiring ownership rights to indigenous groves.[80]

The presence of the colonial government was hardly felt until 1936, when local efforts were made to assist smallholders. A locally established credit bank, Volksbank Tonsea (1914), assisted people in paying off their debts to middlemen. Also, the People's Credit Unions made efforts to assist peasants. But both institutions had to be careful not to endanger their own financial situation, which was not very strong. In 1930, the Minahassaraad (Minahasa Council, the local governing body founded in 1919) took the initiative of establishing a sales cooperative, the Copra Verkoop Centrale. This initiative led to the establishment of the much larger Producten Verkoop Centrale (PVC, Product Sales Council).[81] The PVC bought copra from smallholders, guaranteed a minimum price, and held the copra in stock when prices were low. 'By ruling out the intermediary trade, a larger part of the low price is left for the producer', wrote Resident A.Ph. van Aken in 1933. But the PVC was not a strong enough body to solve the problems, even with some assistance from the residency treasury.[82]

79 ARA Kol, MvO 304, F.H.W.J.R. Logeman 1922:66; Leirissa 1996:270.

80 ARA Kol, MvO 305, J. Tideman 1926:29.

81 Officially called the Inlandse Coöperatieve Producten Verkoop Centrale 'Minahassa'. ARA Kol, MvO 1176 (1934): Statuten van de Inlandse Coöperatieve Producten Verkoop Centrale 'Minahassa'.

82 ARA Kol, MvO 306, A.Ph. van Aken 1933:22-j, 95-6.

It was 1936 before the PVC was given the aid of the Algemeene Volkskredietbank (General People's Credit Union), which allowed it to expand and become the main copra trader. At this time, steps were taken to regulate the legal basis of copra contracts. This resulted in the Copracontracten Ordonnantie (Copra Contracts Ordinance) of 1939. After 1940, when copra exports could not reach purchasers in Denmark and the Netherlands in war-torn Europe, the Copra Fund bought the surplus copra in the Outer Islands and stored it in warehouses. This policy helped smallholders, and operated until the Pacific War broke out in 1942 (Burger 1975:133; Tammes 1947:9, 51-3).

We may conclude that the colonial government reacted rather tardily to the debt situation in Minahasa, which had been very imbalanced because of the large debts incurred by smallholders to Chinese middlemen. The use of contracts in indigenous copra cultivation seemed harmless in the 1920s, but its pernicious financial consequences came to light in the changed economic climate of the Depression. Looking back on government intervention in the late 1930s, Egbert de Vries said in 1988: 'The cooperative settled a price with copra exporters and within a year the money we had furnished was paid back, and the seemingly permanent debt had vanished just like that' (Van der Eng 1991:49). Earlier, some officials had doubted the benefit of such intervention. For example, when B.J. Haga studied copra cultivation in Riau in 1920, he found that 'the majority of the copra producers are not eligible for membership of a new cooperative, because they have tied themselves to the Chinese middleman by written contract, while it is out of the question that their debts can be paid off by the cooperative or the Credit Union' (Haga 1920:318). Haga obviously was somewhat pessimistic on this point. If sound credit facilities had been available at an early stage, smallholders would have had an alternative way of obtaining cash, and the government could have played an important role in providing this credit. But again, it should be realized that the scale of indigenous copra production in the archipelago was so large that providing sound credit facilities would have required really large assets. Like its rubber counterpart, smallholder copra did not have such a high priority on the government agenda.

More than a 'nightwatchman'?

All in all, the government's influence on economic change in the archipelago was small, despite all the efforts of individual civil servants. I have argued that government efforts to stimulate the economy of the Outer Islands were limited, and protection of smallholders was almost totally nonexistent. In most matters regarding the economy, the government kept a low profile. All this is in spite of the fact that the Netherlands Indies government spent quite large amounts of money compared to other colonial powers. Booth formulates this paradox as follows:

> Almost certainly the government was a much more important economic actor in late colonial Indonesia than it was in British India, or indeed in many other colonial territories. Furthermore it is at least arguable that the aim of fiscal policy in Indonesia in the late nineteenth and twentieth centuries was more consciously 'developmental' than in many other parts of the colonial world. But in spite of both rhetoric and the accomplishments of the half century up to 1930, the total achievement was disappointing, as influential scholars and colonial administrators were forced to acknowledge even before the onset of the Depression of the 1930s. (Booth 1990a:241.)

In other colonies, the government assumed the role of 'nightwatchman', turning its hand to little else than maintaining law and order and levying taxes. Indonesia, in the last four decades of Dutch colonial rule, was the main exception to this. The Dutch colonial government did make an effort to do more. Government expenditure during this period even reached 25 per cent of GNP (Booth 1991:33, 49; De Graaff 1997:613-8).

A large share of this was spent in Java, where about 70 per cent of the total budget was spent in 1930, compared with 30 per cent in the (much larger) Outer Islands (Table 63.1). To what extent was the role of the colonial government in the Outer Islands economy more than that of a nightwatchman?

Any doubts that government intervention in the economy during the liberal era was small must by now have been put to rest. Until 1920 the Ethical Policy gave rise to intervention, but the Ethical Policy was directed mainly towards Java; for the Outer Islands it amounted to little more than the stimulation of food-crop cultivation (apart from a few small colonization projects). During and after the brief recession of 1921, indigenous export agriculture continued to expand, but the government's attitude can be characterized as one of indifference to this development. The 'open door' policy, in effect until 1930, allowed for the unbridled expansion of indigenous export agriculture, but without any support from economic policy.

The 'open door' policy may also have frustrated the development of local import-substitution industries and slowed down the development of a domestic market. Local industries probably would not have developed very rapidly, however, even if the government had actively protected them with import restrictions, as shown by the failure of the 1930s import restrictions to generate large-scale industrialization later in that decade. Import protection made textiles and consumer goods more expensive. Although theoretically this can stimulate domestic industry, the Javanese textile industry was by no means yet strong enough to meet the demand for cheap textiles in the Outer Islands. Although the indigenous inhabitants had gone back to self-sufficiency in food production during the Depression, they suffered from the import restriction measures when it came to buying clothing, textiles, and building materials. Finally, the interregional trade statistics show that the domestic market expanded even during the preceding laissez-faire period.

I have evaluated the various government measures concerning the economy of the Outer Islands. Initially, infrastructural provisions in the Outer Islands had a low priority in the colonial budget. Often the construction of roads, railways, and harbours was initiated by European enterprise for their own benefit. Later, maintenance of roads and bridges, and the construction of airports, waterworks, and irrigated fields was accorded a small but permanent place in the national budget. In the early 1930s this funding was severely cut. Many regions were so large and impenetrable that constructing infrastructure was very expensive, and this at a time when the government was spending relatively large amounts on salaries for civil servants, which may indeed have served the development of the colonial state but only indirectly benefited the economy. In relation to other provinces, smallholder rubber provinces had a slight advantage because the outlays from the Rubber Fund in the mid-1930s expanded public expenditure in rubber regions.

The indigenous economy in the Outer Islands of course made grateful use of new infrastructure such as roads and railways. Although much of the export trade took place by river and as such was not dependent on overland transport facilities, intermediary trade made increasing use of buses, trucks, and cars.

Initiatives such as the agricultural transmigration programmes (colonization), as put forward by the government, had no major influence on the economy of the Outer Islands. Sound credit facilities (Credit Unions) in the Outer Islands were scarce and their scope of action remained limited. The LVD probably constituted one of the best efforts to increase agricultural productivity and boost food production.

In a nutshell, Outer Islands economic development followed its own course, largely uninfluenced by the colonial government. The European sector was not disturbed and the Asian sector was mostly left alone. Asian trading networks in the Outer Islands operated largely beyond the scope of the civil service. Special issues such as the abolition of the penal clause and the rubber restriction scheme were isolated incidents in an overall policy of abstinence. Under the influence of foreign demand, Asian export agriculture opened up new economic perspectives. Weaknesses in this development were not actively combated. For example, some provinces became largely dependent on a single export crop. Formal credit facilities were scarce and not widely used. There was little incentive for smallholders to invest in processing techniques, because poor-quality products still fetched a fairly good price. Besides, output was often sold before the harvest was in, in which case the price received served mainly to pay off an existing debt. Smallholders had a low propensity to save, and did not accumulate sufficient capital to move into other sectors.

The Outer Islands economy did not gain much from paternalistic intentions to 'elevate' or 'raise' the Indonesian (read Javanese) peasant. Government officials reported on many disadvantageous developments but could exert only limited influence on economic growth. In the Outer Islands, like a nightwatchman, the government levied taxes and maintained law and order. In some respects the late colonial state still appeared to be in its infancy.

Conclusion

In the nineteenth-century world economy, economic liberalism reigned supreme. In colonial Indonesia free enterprise ruled from about 1870 until 1930, and was subjected to government regulation only in the matter of concessions and taxes. This situation was the result of a process of state formation, during which government power was consolidated and extended into previously uncontrolled areas. At the turn of the century, the Ethical Policy focused increasing attention on the government's role in dealing with indigenous poverty in Java. The Ethical Policy assigned more tasks to the allegedly one-sided, profit-oriented approach to government. These tasks were predominantly aimed at Java: it was Java's 'lesser welfare' (poverty) between 1890 and 1910 that had been the impetus for the Ethical Policy, and it was in Java that the Netherlands incurred its alleged 'debt of honour' (by reaping profits from the Cultivation System). In the meantime, the Outer Islands emerged as the major earners of export revenues and a major field of investment. Efforts of the colonial government to 'elevate' the peasant constituted the sum total of government intervention in the economy until the 1930s, and these efforts were directed almost exclusively towards Java.

On two levels, the colonial government's economic policy displayed a certain bias. First, with respect to economic development in general, the government's aim of encouraging profitable exploitation of the colony reduced the urgency to 'develop' the indigenous economy. Secondly, with respect to ethical intentions, the focus was on Java and not on the Outer Islands. Creating favourable economic conditions for the indigenous economy in the Outer Islands was viewed by the colonial government as a subordinate task. In spite of good intentions, efforts made by government officials in the Outer Islands to create favourable conditions for economic development came to nothing because of lack of funds. Looking at the budget available, the sheer magnitude of the archipelago was decisive.

In the 1930s the alleged need for protectionist measures in the wake of the Depression changed views on the desirability of government intervention. The most profound change in government regulation was the Crisis Invoer-Ordonnantie of 1933, which restricted foreign imports. During this decade sugar, tea, rubber, and tin were subject to export restrictions. The European export sector, after having dealt with the Depression, was not severely hindered by these measures, especially when production restrictions led to price recovery.

In the indigenous sector, rubber smallholders had to deal with the surtax on indigenous rubber (1934-1937), which was meant to decrease indigenous market supply. This proved to be a blessing in disguise for smallholders. Even though the surtax took away much of smallholders' profits, the revenues from this tax were poured into the Rubber Fund, which made possible additional regional expenditure. The government did not actively support or protect smallholder rubber production, although this was one of the dynamic developments that played an important role in the growth of the domestic economy. The low priority assigned to the development of smallholder rubber may have been a result of the threat it posed to the European sector, or of deep-seated indifference towards the indigenous economy.

Apart from coping with the rubber restriction problem, the colonial government paid little attention to the indigenous economy in the Outer Islands. Particularly during the Depression, budget cuts prevented extended government assistance to the struggling smallholder economy. Except for typical 'nightwatchman' activities such as levying taxes and maintaining law and order, the government did little that could be interpreted as 'economic policy'. Major government activities in the Outer Islands were the construction of infrastructure, providing agricultural extension services, and arranging for formal credit supply. Agricultural extension supported the development of indigenous agriculture, but the number of LVD officials posted to the Outer Islands was small. The colonial government failed to offer the indigenous economy sound credit facilities on a sufficient scale. Supporting cooperatives, which had hesitantly started in the 1930s, proved to be a more effective way to promote indigenous agriculture.

A pre-war colonial government should not be judged by the standards of a post-war government pursuing industrial development policy, even though certain parallels can be drawn between the colonial government and the post-war New Order regime.[83] Especially in the Outer Islands economic development was not an explicit aim. Moreover, the integration of the Indonesian economy was the result of participation in foreign trade, which

83 An interesting comparison between the Ethical Policy and the New Order eras has been made by Booth. She points to the similarity in objectives and argues that the New Order has been successful in certain areas of development policy where the Dutch government failed (particularly in food-crop production and in education). Conditions from the late 1960s through the early 1980s were more favourable due to rapid and sustained improvement in the commodity terms of trade. Through the 'oil company tax', much of the growth in oil revenues accrued directly to the government, facilitating an increase in development expenditure. Booth 1989.

was stimulated by the liberal economic policy of the Netherlands Indies during most of the late colonial period. As shown in Chapter IV, export growth had a large impact on the indigenous economy. In short, colonial economic policy was neither a primary stimulus of indigenous economic expansion in the Outer Islands, nor a powerful force in protecting the peasants.

The Outer Islands economy can be characterized by enclaves of European export industry and widespread Asian trade. This large area was largely beyond the reach of ethical intentions. Low priority was given to government intervention in the economy. This stemmed either from a firm belief in a laisez-faire approach, or from a conviction that there was no need to intervene, or just from sheer indifference.

CHAPTER VII

The integration of economic extremes

Java challenged by Outer Islands export growth

'The term "Outer Provinces" may persist, but these islands are no longer merely an insignificant periphery of the Indies', J.O.M. Broek wrote in 1942 (Broek 1942:13). Broek was right. Even though politically speaking the centre of gravity remained in Java, the economic role of the Outer Islands in the colony increased enormously during the last four decades of Dutch colonial rule. Foreign trade was the catalyst that triggered off this process of rapid economic expansion.

This chapter will briefly summarize the conclusions of the foregoing chapters and put them in a larger perspective. In the previous chapters, different types of economic development in the individual Outer Islands were analysed. The development of an export industry formed the essence of economic change in this period, followed by a flow of imports and increasing domestic integration generated by specialization and rising demand. European companies mined minerals and produced agricultural commodities; a dynamic and flexible indigenous export agriculture formed their Asian counterpart in trade.

In terms of total export revenues, by 1925 foreign exports from Java had fallen to 47 per cent of total exports from colonial Indonesia. Beginning in the 1920s and continuing thereafter, more than half of total export earnings were generated in the Outer Islands. Oil and rubber exports were the main components of the export package which swung the advantage to this area.

Since the end of the Cultivation System in 1870 European companies had been established in several Outer Provinces, producing large volumes of tobacco, rubber, petroleum, and tin. The first pioneering initiatives opened up previously unknown regions to European entrepreneurs, but European enterprise never expanded beyond a small number of regions. While the growth effects of these European estates on the immediate surroundings should not be overestimated and linkage effects with the regional economy turned out to be limited, the establishment of European estates was of the utmost importance in the economic development of the Outer Islands.

Cultivation of cash crops occupied an increasingly important place in indigenous smallholder agriculture. Foreign trade in commercial crops such as rubber (Hevea Brasiliensis), coffee (particularly Robusta), and copra (dried coconut kernel used in the manufacture of vegetable oils) led to profound changes in the indigenous economy. In many provinces, a strong indigenous export agriculture developed at a remarkably fast pace. Indigenous smallholders planted cash crops in large quantities, and earned substantial incomes by exporting these crops, especially during the 1910s and 1920s. They employed resilient and adaptive entrepreneurial strategies. Modern export production in these smallholder provinces led to a much larger flow of cash income than in those regions where trade was small and subsistence-based.

The indigenous economy was far more dynamic than was appreciated in the older literature. For colonial Indonesia as a whole, this conclusion has been reached by several recent writers, although mainly based on the situation in Java (for example Booth 1988:28-60; Van der Eng 1996c:10-29; Lindblad 1995:6). Little specific attention has been given in recent historiography to the Outer Islands or to regional variation within the Outer Islands. Also, a thorough analysis of the parallel existence of European and Asian entrepreneurship in this area and the ways in which the former may have influenced the latter has been lacking. My study has focused on the dualist aspects of the Outer Islands economy, and I have found that European entrepreneurship was not a precondition for the expansion of Asian export production. The two types of economic activities, European and Asian, coexisted with relatively little mutual interference. While certainly the Asian trading network was linked up to the European trading network in all major harbours, Asian trade nevertheless developed independently and had its roots in disparate origins. It utilized indigenous resources and traditional trading links, but this did not prevent it quickly exploring the new opportunities of world trade.

While many islands in the archipelago were drawn into the orbit of the world market, displaying an impressive performance in export production, a few provinces lagged behind and profited only to a limited extent from the demand for raw materials in overseas markets. The differences between the various regions have lain at the core of this study. I set out with the aim of identifying and explaining differences in the economic development of the individual Outer Provinces in the late colonial period. One of the core questions was: how did differences in development relate to the accelerating process of integration into the world market? Additional research questions were designed to elucidate the research goal and provide insight into the economy of colonial Indonesia. This made it possible to examine the ways in which both European and indigenous entrepreneurship in the Outer Islands developed. Hirschman's linkage theory was brought to bear on the growth effects of export production, and proved useful in identifying different types of growth effects. The price movement of the major export commodities, the important role of Chinese intermediary trade, and the contribution of the maritime trading network in the archipelago were included in the analysis, and the priorities in the economic policy of the colonial government were also examined.

The importance of foreign and interregional trade in the archipelago

As the only reliable quantitative source in this period, the trade statistics offer insight into the regional diversity and the flexible adjustment to world demand in a number of provinces. After the end of the nineteenth century, customs officials meticulously recorded foreign and interregional trade flows. In this study interregional trade flows between the Outer Islands and Java have been subjected to quantitative analysis for the first time, in addition to extending the analysis of foreign trade statistics.[1]

Interregional trade in colonial Indonesia was very important in the economies of provinces in which direct foreign exports were small. Whether or not they reached foreign markets, a variety of their products were traded within the archipelago. Interregional trade was recorded as the trade of each province in the Outer Islands with Java. The bulk of the export trade from Bengkulu, Bangka, Lampung, Bali, and Timor and Dependencies went to Java. Exports to Java were relatively small in East Sumatra, where estate products were shipped directly to foreign destinations, nor did exports ever reach great heights in Aceh, Riau, Jambi, or Belitung, as well as in West Kalimantan, Southeast Kalimantan, or Manado. Conversely, in imports, the smaller provinces were also more strongly dependent on interregional trade from Java. The analysis of interregional trade sheds new light on the economic development of the provinces in the periphery.

It is generally acknowledged that trade was of immense significance to the colonial economy. While I endorse this, trade as an indicator for economic development in a colony should be used with care. Not all effects were beneficial. For example, the European estate area in East Sumatra incontrovertibly interfered with local indigenous agriculture. Furthermore, much of the indigenous export in raw materials remained unprocessed. In several provinces, such as Jambi and Manado, a one-sided dependency on the exports of one crop (rubber and copra respectively) created a relatively unbalanced and vulnerable economy. Dire problems were usually averted because the export of cash crops could be supplemented by the cultivation of food crops, thereby reducing the dependence on the world economic situation.

1 Clemens et al. 1992; Lindblad 1993b, 1994a.

The growth effects of export trade and the changes in the regional economy were traced using government reports and economic reports of NHM agents stationed at trading posts throughout the archipelago. The effects of trade on economic development were studied using the vent-for-surplus theory of Adam Smith as reformulated by Myint, in addition to Hirschman's concept of linkage.

Quite apart from foreign and interregional trade, the interior of the islands was the scene of internal trade, which has escaped registration. This indigenous trade, often carried out on a small-scale basis in areas which could be reached only by river, was likely to be overlooked or underestimated by Western observers, even though government officials periodically mentioned which goods were traded in which direction. Internally traded export goods eventually ended up in nearby harbours. Nevertheless few data are available on this trade. Likewise, local consumption and products held in storage were not recorded. Bearing this in mind, it would be invalid to assume that exports were equal to production, particularly when goods were also consumed locally. This also explains why regional estimates of income (or GDP) cannot be constructed.

An estimation of exports and imports per capita was made with the use of reconstructed population figures. Exports per capita offer a valuable indication of indigenous incomes, provided there was little European entrepreneurship in a province (since this intrusion caused a large inequality in income distribution). For example, several provinces, such as West Kalimantan, Jambi, and Bengkulu, displayed relatively high per capita export revenues during the Depression years in the early 1930s (Table 26.1). In these provinces trade derived from indigenous smallholder agriculture. In general, exports per capita were largest in the tin provinces (Bangka and Belitung) and in those provinces where European exports were dominant but where indigenous participation in export trade also played a role (East Sumatra, Southeast Kalimantan, Palembang). In the ranking order of per capita trade performance, these provinces were followed by a large group of successful indigenous export producers. In these provinces export earnings changed local income levels significantly and caused the indigenous economy to transform rapidly.

Clustering the Outer Islands

A clustering of the individual Outer Provinces according to two criteria (export performance and origin of exports) was functional in the analytical approach to the eighteen individual provinces. A thematic grid was defined in which the eighteen provinces were placed to facilitate the appraisal of

export performance. Four clusters of provinces were formed:
1. Provinces where European enterprise was established alongside indigenous activity in export production;
2. Provinces where indigenous export production was large, but hardly any European companies were present;
3. Provinces where European export production dominated the economy with relatively little indigenous export production; and
4. Provinces in the periphery of expansion where foreign trade played only a minor role.

The two different types of export production, European and Asian, provided a criterion for the analysis of the great variety in economic features displayed in the individual Outer Provinces. For example, regions where economic change due to foreign exports was predominantly the consequence of economic activities in the Asian sector could be compared with each other (Cluster II). The clustering does not claim to be the ultimate grouping of the Outer Islands (for example, it does not explicitly refer to size and geographic location, which also influenced economic development) but it serves the analysis of the effects of different types of export trade. The success of any clustering depends on the degree to which individual observations match typologies. (Some provinces, such as Riau, Bangka, and Lampung, did not fit entirely or should have been moved to another cluster in the course of time.) On balance, the clustering has provided insight into the different types of economic development in the archipelago, and served as a useful tool to distinguish common aspects of the development in the European sector of the economy on the one hand, and the Asian sector on the other.

Cluster I consists of the provinces in which many European companies were active and indigenous export agriculture prospered alongside them. Of these provinces, Palembang (with its relatively affluent past) had the most balanced, diversified, and multi-faceted economy. East Sumatra was dominated by the Deli estate area, and its export revenues were raised even higher by large exports of oil. Despite this seeming European domination, smallholder export agriculture was also dynamic in this province, particularly in the south, where rubber was cultivated. In Southeast Kalimantan the oil production centres were located along the eastern coast, at Tarakan and Balikpapan. The indigenous economy in the interior was not as diversified as that in Palembang. Hulu Sungai was an exceptionally busy region in this province, producing mainly rubber.

The provinces of Cluster II (West Sumatra, Jambi, Aceh, Lampung, West Kalimantan, South Sulawesi, and Manado) displayed the characteristic features of indigenous dynamics: rapidly developing, flexible smallholder export agriculture in one or more products. These regions boomed in the 1920s, as long as export prices remained high, but were severely hit by the

Depression. In consequence, food-crop cultivation partly replaced cash-crop cultivation and money incomes dwindled. The economically diversified provinces fared better than those provinces where large areas were entirely dependent on a single crop (such as Jambi and West Kalimantan). Export revenues per capita including interregional exports are the main indicators of the large incomes earned by the indigenous population during the heyday of export revenues in the 1920s. Archival sources supply additional information on indigenous prosperity. Dependence on rice imports varied strongly within this cluster, depending on the level of specialization in export crops (creating a dependence on food imports) and the traditional priority given to the cultivation of rice and other food crops.

In Cluster III, Belitung was the only province where almost all export production, and therefore most economic activity, was derived from European export industry (the tin mines). On Bangka, a successful and productive indigenous cultivation of pepper emerged, but both in revenues and in the development of regional infrastructure, the tin mines put their indelible stamp on the economy of Bangka. When all was said and done, pepper cultivation on Bangka was an indirect consequence of the tin mines, because it was Chinese former mineworkers who had taken the initiative and had begun to cultivate this successful export crop in the nineteenth century. Indragiri (mainland Riau) resembled Jambi and southern East Sumatra with its indigenous rubber production, although its output was smaller. The BPM oil depot at Pulu Sambu, the mining of tin and bauxite, supplemented by several European agricultural estates in island Riau explain its place in Cluster III.

The main characteristic of the provinces of Cluster IV is that they were located in the periphery of economic expansion. The provinces in Sumatra with little export trade (Tapanuli, Bengkulu) were still much more dynamic than Maluku, Bali, or Timor and Dependencies. To a certain extent, natural resources explain the regional variation in export production in these so-called 'backwater provinces'. In the Sumatran provinces a 'hidden' potential was discovered. Export products grown near the borders of Tapanuli, Bengkulu, and Lampung was often exported to the adjacent provinces on the eastern side of Sumatra. Per capita export values in 1923/38, including exports to Java, display a better export performance for these provinces than that achieved by analysing foreign exports alone (Figures 24a-e). Unquestionably, a convergence of economic features can be observed in the Sumatran provinces with indigenous export production. In the 1930s, when the economic advantage of cash-crop cultivation began to fall in the wake of low prices, the boundary between Cluster II and Cluster IV seems to have become blurred. Maluku and the Lesser Sunda Islands suffered from their geographic position remote from the centre of economic activity, and from scarcity of natural resources. These factors go a long way towards explaining the small per capita exports in these eastern provinces. Bali deserves specific mention for its high population density and large production of rice. In 1917-1937, Bali's surplus production of rice was exported in equal proportions to Java and to other Outer Islands. In general, trade in the provinces of Cluster IV formed only a small segment of economic life. Most economic activities in these provinces were directed towards subsistence. Exports of forest products and cash crops from Cluster IV provinces took place on a smaller scale than elsewhere, but nevertheless showed a minor dynamism which should not be ignored.

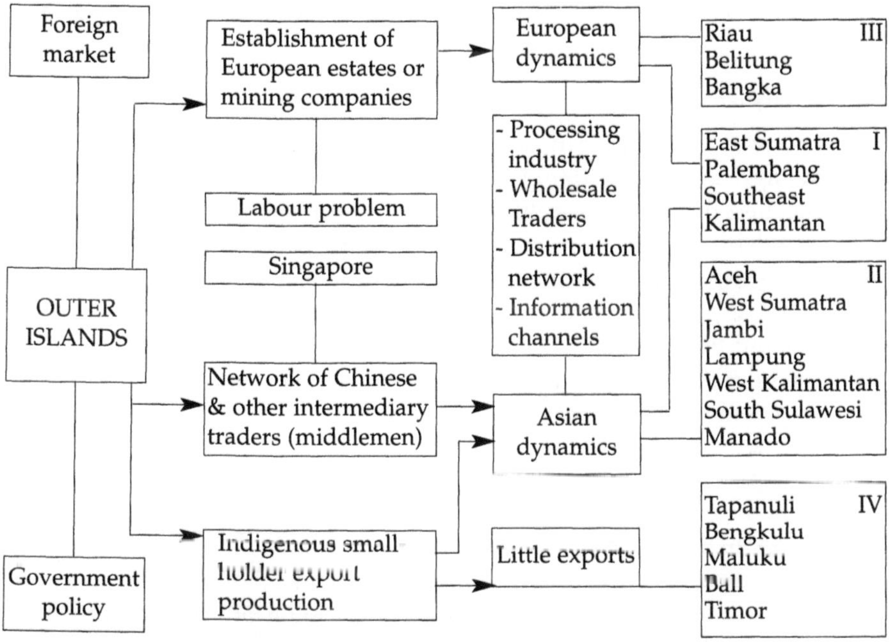

Figure 18. Paths of development in the economy of the Outer Islands.

Three paths of development

The presence of a European export industry, the scope of indigenous export production, or the absence of spectacular export growth lead to the distinguishing of three paths of development, depicted in Figure 18. A situation with relatively little foreign trade (with the exception of Deli in East Sumatra) represents the Outer Islands at the turn of the century. Change took place along three paths. Government policy and the foreign market are represented as exogenous factors in this diagram. The establishment of either European agricultural estates or mining companies was the most important manifestation of European dynamics. Intermediary trade was an essential precondition for the development of indigenous economic dynamism. Because of this importance of middlemen, who were often Chinese (and sometimes Arab, or Malay, Minangkabau, Macassarese, Banjarese, or Bugis), we speak of Asian dynamics.

Many intermediary traders were backed up by trading houses, for example rubber factories in Singapore or European trading houses in the larger ports in the archipelago. The large trading houses bought export products from the middlemen and provided credit. They also supplied import goods. The middlemen were vital in setting up distribution networks, as well as forming a link between European enterprise and indigenous producers and consumers.

European dynamics

The European and American export industry led to substantial investments in estate agriculture and mining technology. Expansion and diversification were dictated by the market: like the tobacco estates, European estates developed where rubber, palm oil, or other products could be cultivated. Oil production expanded and offered an increasing range of refined products, constituting a growing share of total export revenues. The oil industry was characterized by a tendency towards monopolization and increase in scale. Since the oil industry had a high tendency to be an enclave, it had a powerful effect on the national export economy at large, but only a limited ability to stimulate the indigenous sector of the economy.

Export production prompted by European enterprise formed a special segment in the economy, which exerted various growth effects on the regional (meso) and national (macro) levels. Regional growth effects of European estate agriculture included a rise in local demand for foodstuffs and construction materials, a contribution to the construction of infrastructure, and also (particularly in East Sumatra and the tin islands) the introduction of a new population group (a large number of immigrant coolies and ex-coolie settlers). A negative effect was the encroachment on indigenous land, but in the Outer Islands this was a problem only in East Sumatra. A branch of industry dominated by Europeans, the oil industry was concentrated in relatively few, isolated locations. It was highly capital-intensive. Although it generated large export revenues and as such was of considerable importance to the colonial economy (and to the colonial treasury), its regional linkages were largely limited to infrastructural provisions and wage payments to workers. The transfer of technical knowledge ('information linkage') from the European sector to the indigenous sector was small.

Asian dynamics

Demand on the world market and good prices for raw materials nurtured the unbridled expansion of cash-crop cultivation during the 1910s and 1920s (Table 6). The subsistence economy was pushed into the background and products were sold to intermediary traders either for money or in exchange for import goods.

The major stimulus to indigenous production was the intermediary trading system. Intermediary trade conveyed incentives, supplied credit, and generated a demand for import goods with money earned by export production. In this regard, Myint's mechanism of vent-for-surplus (of previously unused production factors), which leads to import demand, can be observed. The trade and transportation network, the Pax Neerlandica, and uniform government measures were all conditions which enhanced economic development, but were not the principal cause of it, as is illustrated by the provinces in the periphery of expansion. Nor were the 'challenge of the West', as the presence of European enterprise has been called, or 'estates acting as agents of change' of large influence on indigenous dynamics. Instead, indigenous export agriculture was receptive to stimuli of Asian origin. Nor should the presence of a tradition in entrepreneurship be overlooked as an important factor (see Table 6).

Table 6. Main factors determining export dynamics in the Outer Islands

	Demand factors	Supply factors	Market factors
European dynamics	Price levels World demand	European capital & technology Coolie labour Natural resources	Maritime network Government policy Expanding infrastructure
Indigenous dynamics	Price levels World demand	Middleman credit & information Local tradition in entrepreneurship Natural resources	Intermediary trading network European wholesale traders Government policy Expanding infrastructure

The most important group in intermediary trade was the Chinese traders. Although they had no complete trading monopoly since there were many groups who challenged the Chinese middlemen, there was a hegemony of the Chinese in certain types of trade. Because planter's credit was often provided by the trader, in many cases a dependent relationship developed, which forced the smallholder to pay high interest rates, and hindered investments, savings, or switching to other crops, especially when future harvests had already been promised in return for large loans or imported consumer goods. During the Depression, in many regions the use of money largely vanished and people reverted to an exchange economy. The remaining money income was spent mainly on tax payments or repaying outstanding debts to creditors. In short, the credit system necessitated continuing foreign exports at lower prices. The large debts incurred by producers postponed recovery of incomes in the mid-1930s.

Dependence on middlemen was larger in those provinces where the indigenous smallholder traded directly with a Chinese intermediary trader who was connected to a wholesale trading company. Where there were more links in the chain and other small traders brought the products from the interior to the harbours, as in the Sumatran rubber trade, the smallholder was more self-reliant.

In the periphery of expansion

Close examination shows that subsistence agriculture in the Outer Islands was for the most part neither primitive nor inadequate for local food production. At this time, the remote regions where export agriculture remained insignificant were also being opened up to outside influence. Better infrastructural facilities were constructed funded by the government and more frequent transportation service (such as the KPM lines) were provided. This improved trading conditions and allowed isolated areas to be more fully integrated in the Netherlands Indies economy – a process which boosted the formation of a colonial state.

The export of forest products often supplemented subsistence agriculture with some money income in these provinces. Even though export expansion was not as remarkable as in the other Outer Islands, the periphery of expansion had its own dynamism.

Dualist features of the Outer Islands economy

Reviewing export production and economic development, a large number of dualist features show up clearly. Although the European export industry did have linkages with the regional economy, it was not embedded in local society with regard to ownership, share-holding, capital investments, and division of profits. Quite apart from the limited linkages, the concentration of European enterprise in relatively few locations also widened the gap between the European and the indigenous sectors.

In this regard the segmented character of the colonial economy was an impediment to economic development in the archipelago. A survey of dualist features in the Outer Islands economy is given in Table 7. This survey

Table 7. Dualist features of the Outer Islands economy

	Asian dynamics (smallholders)	European dynamics (estates, mines)
Mode of production	low-capital little division of labour relatively low-labour (ladang)	capital-intensive much division of labour labour-intensive
Technology	simple	more advanced
Investment	expansion on credit no future investment	foreign investment
Output increase	planting more trees	increasing productivity (improving seeds and seedlings, mechanization)
Quality	low quality (many impurities)	high quality
Internal trade	small-scale, intermediary trade (indigenous/Chinese) often along rivers	directly to ocean harbours by railways / pipelines European trading houses
Interregional trade	prahus / small steamships	steamships
Landownership	traditional rights	long-term lease
Linkages	well-rooted in the region fiscal linkages	some backward linkages few forward linkages fiscal linkages
Remittances	China / Java (rubber tappers, middlemen)	profits/dividends/salaries: overseas (Europe/America) salaries: China / Java (coolies)

illustrates that the parallel lines of production each had a viability of its own. The dualist economy was far more complex and well-balanced than was proclaimed in the pre-war literature. Dualist features permeated the economy but did not inhibit modernization.

Economic policy for the Outer Islands

The predominantly liberal economic policy pursued by the government until 1931 displayed little concern for emerging indigenous export production, and favoured European export industries. Throughout these years, the Ethical Policy (1901-1920s) was aimed mainly towards raising food production. It was both triggered by and oriented towards the situation in Java.

In addition to general expenditure on education, health services, and the construction of infrastructure, the most important contribution made by colonial economic policy to the indigenous economy in the Outer Islands was in terms of agricultural extension and the improvement of credit supply (even though in the latter, as well as in the stimulation of cooperatives, the scale of intervention was small). Regarding such measures, and those taken in education and infrastructure, the intentions of regional government officials were good, but budgets were limited. In the vast area of the archipelago, government efforts in agricultural extension and the stimulation of formal credit supply had only a limited effect.

Economic policy had a low priority. The government was primarily concerned with the profitability of the colony. On another level, when ethical concerns resulted in policy measures aimed at raising indigenous welfare, these were implemented predominantly in Java (where Van Deventer's 'eereschuld', or debt of honour, was generated). In the Outer Islands, government economic policy was an important force neither for indigenous economic expansion nor for the protection of the indigenous peasant. The liberal policy of refraining from intervention was the government's main contribution to the development of trade.

Reflections on the dynamic indigenous economy

Export performance implied a dynamic attitude towards trade, which is characterized by orientation to world demand, determination to profit from opportunities for growth, flexibility in accommodating setbacks, and quick adjustment to changing external factors. There was a remarkable economic dynamism in provinces with high levels of indigenous export agriculture.

Inhabitants of the Outer Islands had been active in subsistence and commercial agriculture for centuries. Tobacco and foodstuffs were cultivated, there was a trade in buffaloes, cattle, and horses, and there were exports of pepper, salt, and salted fish. Textiles, ornaments, tools, and a range of other essentials were sold at the market. These subsistence economies were not economically self-contained, but participated in domestic and inter-island trade. Even when no typical export cash crops (such as rubber, coffee, or copra) were cultivated, there was still a substantial trade in locally consumed goods. In this study, the term 'subsistence economy' includes cultivation of food crops as well as various other types of economic activity, such as fishing, forestry, and small domestic trade. Some economic activities, such as the collection of rattan and resins (benzoin, damar, copal), also generated foreign exports. The earnings gained from these exports were of a much smaller scale than the export agriculture of cash crops. Small economies also had an inherent continuous vulnerability to harvest failures and epidemics, and hardly profited from the opportunities for economic expansion.

Export revenues brought prosperity during the 1910s and 1920s. The Outer Islands were sparsely populated, and the population pressure and land shortage which plagued Java were unknown. Paradoxically, in several cases labour shortage inhibited the exploitation of rich natural resources. Surplus of land created a vent-for-surplus capacity for growth in abundant fertile areas. In provinces where export revenues allowed the indigenous population to generate an increasing flow of imports, the standard of living rose during these decades, even though the credit system often forced people to spend before they had actually earned. Apart from luxury items, many of the imported items were sensible purchases. People bought bicycles, sewing machines, and small trucks. They invested in building better houses. This sort of expenditure certainly occurred in the rubber regions, but was by no means absent in provinces from which coffee, pepper, or copra were exported. Rice and food imports often became necessary because the peasants had stopped growing these crops themselves, in order to generate a higher output of export crops.

Entrepreneurial strategies

During the 1910s and 1920s, smallholder producers did not bother to invest much in ways to increase productivity. Nor did much import substitution develop in the Outer Islands. Smallholders were happy to spend their income on import goods – both consumer goods and construction materials for houses. To a certain extent, the open trade policy may be blamed for the relative absence of economic growth effects such as import substitution and investment in production methods. The open trade policy did not stimulate the processing of exports or prevent cheap textile imports. But much more important as a cause of consumer spending was the credit relationship with traders: it facilitated easy spending, which led to indebtedness that inhibited more structural expenditure.

World market demand for products of poor quality persisted, partially as a consequence of Asian trading links. For example, reprocessing ('remilling') of poor-quality rubber was a separate industry in Singapore. This encouraged the export of adulterated indigenous rubber, which Western overseas industries would not accept as such. Entrepreneurial strategies were different from those employed by the European export industry: low-investment, low-capital production dominated (Table 7). This type of production could survive on a very small profit margin and could be combined with food production or cultivation of other crops. The latter was an important characteristic of indigenous export agriculture, because it created a flexibility which reduced the harmful effects of low prices during the Depression.

Other indicators typify the entrepreneurial attitude of the smallholder in the period 1910-1940. This entrepreneurial attitude can be characterized as sloppy, but nevertheless shrewd and adaptable. Examples include the deliberate adding of impurities, weighing with false scales (a disadvantageous feature of dealing with middlemen, which forced producers to negotiate an extra profit margin in compensation), and making smart deals with hired labourers in the *bagi dua* system. Other examples reveal smallholders' rationality and adaptability: the very swift change from cultivating Arabica to cultivating Robusta coffee in 1914-1915, and the rapid spread of rubber cultivation in 1912-1917, even though it took five to six years before the trees came into bearing. The behaviour of rubber producers during the international rubber restriction (IRRA) after 1934 can also be seen as displaying a flexible and shrewd mercantile instinct on the part of producers and traders alike: smallholders sold stock just before the surtax was instituted, changed to a higher percentage of dry rubber, and after 1937 generated an extra trade in coupons. As a side-effect of the 1934 regulations, peasants shifted from the export of wet slabs to that of dried sheets, which contained a smaller percentage of water. Initially this was done in order to export an additional percentage of untaxed rubber (wet slabs were taxed as containing a fixed percentage of rubber), later to increase the amount of rubber exported under the required certificate. In 1937, when individual rubber quotas were introduced, indigenous rubber production could finally be controlled in order to meet international agreements on export volumes. In these years, not only was the rubber itself traded but there was also a brisk market in the certificates ('coupons') that were required to export rubber, a relatively 'modern' type of trade, which supports the view that Asian traders were keen on exploiting any avenue of profit. Particularly in Southeast Kalimantan, where due to miscalculation of the size of the rubber gardens the rubber quota had been overestimated, traded export rights caused a large inflow of cash (Lindblad 1988:75).

Indigenous rubber cultivation serves as a good example of indigenous entrepreneurship developing parallel to European exports. Separate taxation of indigenous rubber exports led to accurate registration of indigenous and European export flows after 1927. In indigenous rubber production, we can discern two major strategies during the Depression (1930-1936): a. a substantial reduction of output volume (Palembang, Southeast Kalimantan, West Sumatra) and b. a relatively constant output (or only slightly decreasing) in provinces where production costs could be lowered and a very small profit margin was acceptable, which made supply relatively inelastic (Jambi, West Kalimantan). Later, during the initial years of the international rubber restriction (1934-1937), strategies also diverged: in Palembang, West Kalimantan, and Southeast Kalimantan peasants quickly expanded their rubber exports, first in anticipation of the surtax on indigenous rubber (which was instituted in mid 1934), later because the price recovery influenced their productive behaviour more than the low profit margin due to the surtax. By contrast, in Jambi smallholders did not expand their output but kept their rubber production at a relatively constant level during 1930-1938. The major cause for this deviant production strategy must have been shortage of labour (the maximum output by household tapping had been reached).

Indigenous entrepreneurship in post-war Indonesia

Indigenous entrepreneurship was an issue of great importance during the early decades of Indonesia's independence. The new Indonesian government in 1949 faced the challenge of reducing entrenched Dutch economic interests in Indonesia, and dealing with the heavy inherited debts that burdened the state (Booth 1998:63; Mackie 1971:482). Various policy measures were initiated to stimulate indigenous entrepreneurship. The well-known Benteng Plan (*benteng*, 'fortress') of 1950, which was designed by the Natsir Cabinet (1950-1951), aimed to promote indigenous participation in the non-agricultural sector of the economy by restricting imports (particularly the import of textiles) exclusively to Indonesian entrepreneurs. This plan was not very successful, because it attracted many bogus importers who sold their import licenses to Chinese or other traders (they were sometimes called *importir aktentas* because they posed as importers by carrying briefcases) (Thee Kian Wie 1996:317). This kind of entrepreneurship is reminiscent of the trade in rubber coupons after 1937. In the context of the Benteng Plan, the (illegal) trade in import licenses shows a similar type of entrepreneurial shrewdness. But it did not particularly advance the rise of an indigenous class of traders.

There were various other policy measures in post-war Indonesia which aimed at strengthening the indigenous economy. For example, new credit institutions were established, such as the Bank Industri Negara (State Industrial Bank), Bank Negara Indonesia 1946 (State Bank of 1946), and the Yayasan Kredit (Credit Foundation). An ambitious state-directed industrialization plan was devised, the Economic Urgency Plan (1950). Also, small-scale cooperatives were stimulated. A useful initiative (although prone to corruption), it followed in the footsteps of the pre-war introduction of agricultural cooperatives, and was strongly favoured by Mohammad Hatta (Thee 1996:317-8; Booth 1998:168-8).

Such special measures to encourage indigenous entrepreneurship were only partially successful. Why did the shrewd and adaptable indigenous entrepreneurship as encountered in the pre-war Outer Islands not lead to an influential class of farmers and traders in post-war decades? The answer may be found in the political turmoil, the strong position of European trading houses, the patrimonial distribution networks, and the persisting Chinese interests in the archipelago which hindered further 'Indonesianization' of trade. In further research on this subject, more emphasis could be placed on individual indigenous entrepreneurial groups in the Outer Islands before and after the war. For example, it has been stated in the literature that Sumatran traders expanded their business and flourished during the Japanese occupation and the early period of independence (Post 1996:615-8). The problem of indigenous entrepreneurship is still present in contemporary Indonesia. It is connected with the problem of the Chinese population group owning a disproportionate share of economic power, an aspect of Indonesian economic development which constitutes a continuity in its economic history.

Contributing to an emerging national economy

In retrospect, several aspects of this economic dynamism in indigenous export agriculture warrant consideration. What were the beneficial effects of these exports on Indonesian economic development? To what extent did indigenous export agriculture profit from external influences?

Dick has argued that the fact that industrialization failed to materialize in Java towards the end of the nineteenth century, despite increasing export diversification, was due to the small and fragmented domestic market and the open trade policy. The latter was beneficial to the export-import economy but did not protect new domestic industry (Dick 1993b). On the eve of the Pacific War, the economy of colonial Indonesia had left this stage behind. In the late 1930s, hesitant steps towards more systematic support for industrialization were made by the government and by European companies, which were not always in favour of changing the role of the colony from that of provider of raw materials to that of a competitor in international trade. Only in the decades after independence did further industrialization take shape. A relevant question in this context is: to what extent did economic development in the Outer Islands contribute to economic growth in colonial Indonesia?

The economy of the Outer Islands became integrated with foreign markets in three ways: directly, through Asian trading links, and as a consequence of the domestic integration of the colonial economy. The result of export growth was a rise in domestic trade, as was shown among other evidence by the interregional trade statistics. The domestic market within the regional economy gained from the improved physical infrastructure (transportation facilities), from the influx of Chinese traders, and from increasing foreign export revenues creating consumer (import) demand. Intermediary Chinese trading networks, oriented towards Singapore, expanded the volume of domestic trade on the Java Sea. For example, rubber was exported mainly to Singapore, but other export products such as copra and coffee were also shipped to Batavia. In the eastern part of the archipelago, Macassar formed a trading centre where overseas trade and trade with Java (Surabaya) were linked to the smaller islands in the 'Great East'.

In East Sumatra, European estate agriculture generated relatively little domestic demand. European estates and oil companies were orientated towards overseas purchasers and import suppliers, although they also imported via Java. Until 1934, East Sumatra's imports from Java averaged less than 20 per cent (Table 25.2). Only after 1934 did average imports from Java increase to about 30 per cent. Thus domestic demand effects, which might have induced investment in new economic activities in Indonesia, thereby stimulating growth in the economy of the region outside the export sector, remained limited.[2]

The development of a domestic market, vital to integration within the archipelago, was largely the consequence of indigenous export production. Smallholders who became active in export agriculture interacted with the wider economy of the archipelago. The domestic market remained relatively small and fragmented, partly because of the drain of revenues to overseas Chinese destinations, but the integration of the colonial economy was also enhanced by the Asian trading network. Dualist features may have restricted the effects of export growth because the economy was so segmented. It is fair to say that, outside Java, the formation of a 'colonial state' lagged behind. Still, boosted by the expansion of foreign exports, a more coherent 'national economy' was emerging.

Authenticity of the smallholder economy

An essential feature was the authenticity of indigenous export agriculture. The strength of the smallholders, let me stress, was their ability to combine more 'traditional' forms of agriculture with 'modern' types: the difference between subsistence agriculture and export agriculture was not a clear-cut line but a gradual one without distinct borders. Myint distinguishes two consecutive phases in peasant export production: part-time export production and full-time specialization in market-oriented cash-crop cultivation (the second phase includes a larger dependence on money income). These two phases of export production were not irreversible stages in a linear process, but closely intertwined and coexisting forms of economic activity. Increasing market demand created more opportunities to earn money (effectively conveyed by the intermediary trader). This generated more supply to export abroad. Rubber and copra replaced rattan, copal, or gambir, but the mechanism of selling export commodities to local traders remained the old and familiar one. The scale expanded, new cash crops and new traders arrived, but combining export trade and food-crop cultivation was not essentially new. These trade dynamics were authentic to and institutionally embedded

2 See also Thee Kian Wie 1977:130-2.

in the Southeast Asian region, where trade had been going on for centuries.[3]

When the prices of raw materials declined after 1927, export agriculture was often kept up only as a part-time occupation – to harvest trees already planted, or to pay off outstanding loans. The way back to food cultivation, collection of forest products, or cultivation of crops for the local market was not cut off because of one major condition: an ample supply of land. Here an important difference can be observed between the Outer Islands and Java. In Java, smallholders had more difficulty adapting to a situation of low prices for raw materials, and did not have the rich resources of the Sumatran or Kalimantan forests to rely upon. Many landless peasants in Java lived close to the poverty line, with little defence against disaster. Smallholders in Java who owned some land survived the Depression more easily, due to the same flexibility for reducing costs as that of smallholders in the Outer Islands (Elson 1984:239-47).

During the Depression, government officials in the Outer Islands did not always notice this resilience of the smallholder economy. While some contemporary observers thoughtfully wondered whether it was unexpected savings that were being used to carry households apparently effortlessly through these hard times, others lamented that trade had come to a standstill and harbours and market places were poverty-stricken. Indeed, when barter trade partly replaces cash, it cannot be taken as a sign of balanced modern economic growth. But exports quickly recovered and, even with their small profit margins, smallholders again generated considerable earnings during the second half of the 1930s. This may indicate that in the smallholder economy, adaptability was an important prerequisite of growth and that the authenticity of indigenous supply, well-rooted in the local economy, improved its chances for recovery more than any forced export agriculture would have.

What would have happened had there been no European enterprise in colonial Indonesia? This question is related to the presence of the colonial power. The standard answer is, economic development in colonial Indonesia would probably have been much slower and would have lacked many of the impulses generated by European enterprise and colonial government. Nevertheless, except for a few linkages in their immediate environment, the agricultural estates did not exert much direct influence on the indigenous economy. The main benefits of the colonial presence to the Indonesian economy were often in interaction with the government: investments in social overhead capital as well as fiscal linkages. Indigenous export agriculture, although infrastructure was not a prerequisite for it, did profit from the in-

3 Elson puts forward the hypothesis that intensive commercialization of peasant agriculture in Southeast Asia during the nineteenth and twentieth centuries changed peasants into farmers, workers, and citizens, thus undermining traditional peasant society (Elson 1997).

creased possibilities to reach overseas markets at less cost. Estates and mining companies constructed roads and railways, and, profiting from their tax payments, the government had increasing funds to do the same. Even taking all these benefits into account, the indigenous economy had the potential to expand on its own under the influence of world demand for export products. The European presence may have helped, but was not a prerequisite.

The literature on the premodern era has emphasized the substantial internal dynamism of non-Western actors in the Asian economy (Klein 1989; Reid 1993). In the long-term perspective of Asian trade, the fruitful interaction of Chinese, Japanese, and Indonesian traders belonged to an old tradition.

Asian entrepreneurship has also been of great importance in the worldwide expansion of Asian economies in the period 1965-1997. Since Indonesia became an independent state, and especially since 1957, the role of European entrepreneurship in the economy has been more restricted. The striking economic performance of East and Southeast Asia after the 1960s was rooted in Asian entrepreneurship; and in Indonesia, the interaction of Indonesian and Chinese entrepreneurs became very important for the economy. In the post-war economy of export-led growth and consciously pursued industrialization, Asian trade mechanisms thus played an essential role.

Through its stimulation of local entrepreneurship, distribution of imports, and its role as a banker for credit, the intermediary trading network was important in increasing the cohesion of the pre-war Indonesian economy. The strong development of the Asian trade sector in colonial Indonesia formed the foundation for post-war economic development. Several specific aspects of this Asian entrepreneurship have recently received attention, for instance the importance of informal overseas networks of emigrant Chinese.[4] Many questions are left unanswered about Chinese and indigenous traders in the Indonesian archipelago in the late colonial period. How large were their credit facilities? What was their standard of living, particularly compared with indigenous smallholders? What differences can be observed in freight charges, credit provided, volumes traded, and specific crops, when compared for instance with the NHM? More research will be necessary to study these matters. In addition, other important trading groups, such as the Arabs, should be studied as well.

The Pacific War and the subsequent struggle for independence disturbed the development of indigenous export agriculture and delayed the expansion of Asian entrepreneurship. It would be incorrect to assume that, had the world economy regained full strength after the Depression in 1930-1936, Asian trade would automatically have followed a path to modern economic growth and industrialization, resembling the 'economic tigers' in contemporary Asia dur-

4 For example Seagrave 1995; Weidenbaum and Hughes 1996.

ing recent decades. Several other conditions are essential for such development: for example foreign investment, effective government industrialization policy, booming world trade, and advantageous terms of trade. Had decolonization taken longer, it might not have been in the direct interest of the colonial government to take the relevant measures. It might have aimed to prevent Indonesia's industrialization and preserve its role as a market for Dutch goods. Such speculations aside, the late 1930s saw a favourable turning-point in colonial policy. The measures taken in the late 1930s, such as the industrialization policy, import protection, increasing promotion of sales and credit cooperatives, as well as ongoing agricultural extension, would have had an effect. The Outer Islands stood a good chance of becoming an even more successful growth region than they had been in the 1920s, had the economy not been disrupted so dramatically by political events.

Extremes in the Outer Islands

In the Outer Islands, contrasts abounded and there was more diversity than unity. Different types of extremes could be observed. There was the contrast between high technology and low technology, for example between the ultramodern latex-spray installations used by rubber estates to process and transport liquid latex, and the simple smokehuts used by smallholders. There was also the spatial contrast between for instance the estate area in East Sumatra, where the forest was cut down and cars and trucks travelled on roads, and the inaccessible interior of Kalimantan, where indigenous Dayak grew Hevea Brasiliensis on small plots in the rainforest. There were extremes in living conditions: next door to the modern BPM refinery complexes, compounds for European employees were fitted with electric lighting and running water, providing a luxury unknown to the coolie huts (*pondok*). During the 1920s, pepper and rubber cultivators in southern Sumatra frequented cinemas and lived in brick houses financed by the sales of their profitable product. During the Depression, in many places this money economy gave way to subsistence agriculture and barter trade. There was also the contrast between extreme luxury in the indigenous export regions in the 1920s, and the poor islands in the periphery, where life did not change at such a high speed and the economy developed at a much slower pace.

Many Outer Islands had a dynamic, industrious indigenous sector which interacted successfully with other Asian traders. These provinces quickly developed a very effective cash-crop production, discovering the possibilities offered by the world market. The Asian sector was dynamic and adapted quickly to changing circumstances. Production of cash crops was labour-intensive in the laying out of fields, but required relatively little labour for upkeep. It was its low-capital character that facilitated exploitation at very low cost. Smallholders in the Outer Islands were dedicated and adaptable entrepreneurs, even though to European observers their rubber and coffee plots may have looked chaotic and badly kept. These provinces needed no European incentives. Their exceptional growth in export production demonstrated their 'indigenous dynamism'.

APPENDIX A

Extrapolation of population figures

The diversity of the Outer Islands is proverbial not only in terms of ecology, trade, and culture, but also in population density. In general, the Outer Islands were sparsely populated, especially in comparison with Java. But population density varied widely. It is necessary to have annual population figures for calculating per capita trade, in order to make comparisons between provinces and over time. This appendix discusses methods for obtaining reasonable estimates of population figures per province.

The population figures for the Outer Islands before 1900 are largely unreliable. So-called 'population recording' by civil servants started in 1879, but outside Java this was only done in Minahasa and around Padang, and later in the directly governed territories.[1] After 1905 the government decided to shift from these primitive attempts to real censuses. Because of the high costs of a census, the first census was delayed until 1920 (Gooszen 1994:41). The data before 1920 are complicated by the fact that the directly governed area was extended significantly between 1905 and 1917. Boundary changes were rarely well enough documented to allow an estimate of their effect on the size of the population figures (Boomgaard and Gooszen 1990:43). The upshot was that in 1917 an administrative enumeration was drawn up in the Colonial Reports (*Koloniale Verslagen*) of which the figures were neither complete nor very reliable. The 1920 census was the first complete census, but it was not entirely reliable due to misreporting and misregistration (Gooszen 1994: 51). In 1927, another enumeration of figures drawn from the civil administration was compiled, but as in 1917, it was not complete. The census of 1930 is the first census that can be considered both complete and reliable.[2]

In my attempt to reconstruct population figures per province, I use a method suggested by Boomgaard and Gooszen in *Changing Economy in Indonesia*, volume 11. This method was also used and refined by Lindblad. I

1 Boomgaard and Gooszen 1990:42; Gooszen 1994:37-8; Van de Graaff 1955:142; Nitisastro 1970. See also Gooszen 1999:9-16.

2 Van der Eng expands the 1930 census results by 3% to correct for nonreporting in the 10-14 age group. I decided not to do this. Van der Eng 1993a:267-8; *Volkstelling 1933*).

reconsider several choices, and expand the reconstruction to earlier years and all population groups.[3]

Indigenous population

Although the counts of European and Chinese population in 1905, 1917, 1920, and 1930 were reliable, the recording of the indigenous population before 1930 was not. In 1927, there was an administrative enumeration preceding the 1930 census. Crucial to my reconstruction is the assumption that the methods used for the 1920 and 1927 counts were of equal inaccuracy and incompleteness. These figures provide a growth rate that can be applied to the reliable 1930 figures, in order to extrapolate backwards and forwards from 1930.[4]

Table 8. The population of the Outer Islands in 1930

	Indigenous	European	Chinese	Other Asian	Total
Aceh	975,945	3,067	21,795	2,255	1,003,062
Tapanuli	1,035,382	809	5,704	688	1,042,583
East Sumatra	1,470,395	10,207	192,822	19,776	1,693,200
West Sumatra	1,887,866	4,969	14,962	2,501	1,910,298
Riau	257,439	516	39,084	1,186	298,225
Palembang	1,064,117	3,653	26,076	4,879	1,098,725
Jambi	234,533	427	8,843	1,469	245,272
Bengkulu	316,312	704	5,716	391	323,123
Lampung	351,378	865	8,838	482	361,563
Bangka	107,764	952	96,098	549	205,363
Belitung	44,096	653	28,614	66	73,429
West Kalimantan	689,585	922	107,998	3,942	802,447
Southeast Kalimantan	1,327,487	4,084	26,289	8,354	1,366,214
South Sulawesi	3,063,217	4,305	21,380	4,349	3,093,251
Manado	1,110,386	2,772	20,022	5,475	1,138,655
Bali and Lombok	1,788,843	518	10,949	2,373	1,802,683
Timor and Dep.	1,646,101	965	6,867	3,443	1,657,376
Maluku	876,128	4,247	8,726	4,299	893,400
Total Outer Islands	18,246,974	44,635	650,783	66,477	19,008,869
(Java	40,891,093	188,590	582,431	56,250	41,718,364)

Source: Boomgaard and Gooszen 1990:224-330.

[3] Lindblad concentrates on the reconstruction of indigenous population figures, whereas I calculate figures for all population groups, in order to arrive at per capita data for the whole population. Even though non-indigenous figures are small, it would not be sensible to calculate total exports per person for the indigenous population in East Sumatra, since a large share of those exports were in fact produced by the European and Chinese population in the estate area. Lindblad 1993b; Boomgaard and Gooszen 1990:45.

[4] Boomgaard and Gooszen 1990:44-5. The census of 1930 was so much more exhaustive that it would yield improbably high growth rates when compared with 1920 figures.

In order to assume stable and continuous population growth, four necessary conditions must be met by the indigenous population of the Outer Islands (Lindblad 1993b:245):

- fairly large size;
- normal sex distribution;
- normal age distribution; and
- negligible migration movements.

That migration flows in the late colonial period were small compared to the total population (except for coolie migration) is obvious from the scarce data on migration included in the colonial administration (Boomgaard and Gooszen 1990:42-7, 233-5).

It is unfortunate that the census planned for 1940 did not take place (Gooszen 1994:50). Since the economic situation changed dramatically during the crisis, it would have been valuable to have a more precise impression of population development during the 1930s. For example, the numbers of Europeans in the archipelago show a steep increase between 1905 and 1920; it is not likely that this growth continued in the 1930s.

For the indigenous population, I reconstructed figures in the following manner. When the population shows *continuous* growth with a growth rate of '*a*' (expressed as a fraction of 1), the population in year 1930+n can be calculated with the formula:

$$Pop_{(1930+n)} = Pop_{(1930)} * e^{a*n}$$

Taking into consideration the (artificial) situation that a population grows by a fixed annual percentage (instead of displaying continuous growth), the formula for annual growth becomes:

$$Pop_{(1930+n)} = Pop_{(1930)} * (1 + a)^n$$

In my reconstruction, differences between continuous and annual growth are marginal. Theoretically, a population experiences continuous growth (Ohler 1980:162-9).

Table 9. Reconstruction of the indigenous population by province, using constant growth rates

	1920 census	1927 census	Growth rate (1)	1930 census (2)
Aceh	718,444	783,629	1.24	975,945
Tapanuli	839,515	899,264	0.98	1,035,382
East Sumatra (6)	1,042,930	1,077,830	0.47	1,470,395
West Sumatra	1,505,209	1,594,320	0.82	1,887,866
Riau	199,615	204,704	0.36	257,439
Palembang	810,353	849,450	0.67	1,064,117
Jambi (3)	203,116	234,533	1.11	234,533
Bengkulu	253,639	276,740	1.25	316,312
Lampung	229,608	252,763	1.37	351,378
Bangka	85,774	91,646	0.95	107,764
Belitung	39,188	43,607	1.53	44,096
West Kalimantan (4)	535,516	620,300	2.10	689,585
Southeast Kalimantan	998,282	1,076,924	1.08	1,327,487
South Sulawesi (6)	2,329,123	2,517,646	1.11	3,063,217
Manado	745,985	967,715	3.72	1,110,386
Bali and Lombok	1,556,154	1,576,168	0.18	1,788,843
Timor and Dep.	1,140,708	1,160,872	0.25	1,646,101
Maluku (5)	418,270	544,980	2.65	544,980
New Guinea	193,856	331,148		
Outer Islands (7)	13,871,144	14,818,137	0.94	18,246,974

Source: Boomgaard and Gooszen 1990:224. Compare Lindblad 1993b:246, 252.

Comments on Table 9:

1. Growth rate a = 1/7 * ln(Pop1927 / Pop1920).
2. Figures were reconstructed using: $Pop_{(1930+n)} = Pop_{(1930)} * e^{a*n}$
3. For Jambi, the growth rate is based on the years 1917-1930, since it is unlikely that in this booming rubber province the population actually decreased in the 1920s.
4. West Kalimantan figures are regarded as being inaccurate, but since the less reliable figures originate from the interior, which was very sparsely populated, we can still accept them as estimates.
5. Maluku: Ambon and Ternate are taken together, and New Guinea is left out. Stated figures refer to 1920 and 1930. Since the explored area of New Guinea increased and recordings were very superficial, we have stated these estimates separately (Boomgaard and Gooszen 1990:223).
6. Lindblad correctly calculated growth percentages 1920-1927 for East Sumatra and South Sulawesi, which differ from those used by Boomgaard and Gooszen (Lindblad 1993b:247; Boomgaard and Gooszen 1990:45).

7. Total Outer Islands: census totals taken from Boomgaard and Gooszen (1990:224) (not recalculated). The population growth for all Outer Islands, as calculated from the aggregates, is 0.94 per cent, which corresponds to the percentage arrived at by Boomgaard and Gooszen (0.95), who exclude West Kalimantan with its allegedly rapid growth but include a higher percentage for Ternate.

Table 10. Reconstruction figures on the indigenous population of the Outer Islands in 1900, 1905, 1920, 1930 (in thousands)

	1900	1910	1920	1930	1940
Aceh	672	761	862	975	1,104
Tapanuli	771	850	938	1,035	1,142
East Sumatra	1,276	1,338	1,402	1,470	1,541
West Sumatra	1,475	1,601	1,738	1,887	2,049
Riau (including Indragiri)	231	239	248	257	266
Palembang	869	930	994	1,064	1,138
Jambi	168	187	209	234	261
Bengkulu	217	246	279	316	358
Lampung	232	267	306	351	403
Bangka	81	89	98	107	118
Belitung	27	32	37	44	51
West Kalimantan	367	453	558	689	850
Southeast Kalimantan	959	1,068	1,191	1,327	1,479
South Sulawesi	2,194	2,452	2,740	3,063	3,423
Manado	364	527	765	1,110	1,610
Bali and Lombok	1,693	1,724	1,756	1,788	1,821
Timor and Dep.	1,527	1,565	1,605	1,646	1,687
Maluku	246	321	418	544	710

Note: The figures for the early years 1900-1910 are estimates of increasingly dubious nature. I use them with care, for lack of better estimates.
Source :Based on Table 9.

Non-indigenous population

We can safely assume that, contrary to the indigenous population, the European and Chinese population groups were accurately reported in the period 1900-1930. Both were recorded by the colonial registration service (Gooszen 1994:55). The figures for 1900, 1905, 1920, and 1930 are given in Tables 11 and 12.

There are several methods for attaining an annual reconstruction of these non-indigenous population groups. We must bear in mind that they were immigrant minority groups, and therefore of a less stable nature. However, since they formed only a small portion of the total population, I used a slightly more crude reconstruction. Since there is no reason to presuppose a continuous growth rate, I applied linear interpolations between the four points of measurement (Table 11). Another method would be to take the percentage of the non-indigenous population in relation to the total population, as Lindblad suggests. However, it is not at all self-evident that the European and Chinese populations increased at the same rate as the indigenous population. The arrival of European or Chinese settlers in the Outer Islands was not related to the indigenous population density (compare Lindblad 1993b:246).

Table 11. Non-indigenous population of the Outer Islands in 1900, 1905, 1920, 1930: Europeans

	1900	1905	1920	1930
Aceh	701	684	2,370	3,067
Tapanuli	369	431	704	809
East Sumatra	2,079	2,264	7,093	10,207
West Sumatra	2,298	2,858	4,077	4,969
Riau (including Indragiri)	238	201	409	516
Palembang	618	638	1,621	3,653
Jambi			221	427
Bengkulu	214	351	557	704
Lampung	121	146	575	865
Bangka	269	309	605	952
Belitung	84	136	399	653
West Kalimantan	314	330	633	922
Southeast Kalimantan	696	974	2,375	4,084
South Sulawesi	1,525	1,549	3,497	4,305
Manado	1,125	1,255	2,066	2,772
Bali and Lombok	114	116	322	518
Timor and Dep.	225	248	740	965
Maluku	2,366	2,626	3,449	4,247
Outer Islands	13,356	15,116	31,713	44,635

Source: Boomgaard and Gooszen 1990:226.

Table 12. Non-indigenous population of the Outer Islands in 1900, 1905, 1920, 1930: Chinese

	1900	1905	1920	1930
Aceh	5,139	8,575	13,919	21,795
Tapanuli	1,695	1,607	2,904	5,704
East Sumatra	103,768	99,236	134,750	192,822
West Sumatra	11,261	8,267	11,094	14,962
Riau (including Indragiri)	13,737	18,491	22,542	39,084
Palembang	8,958	9,248	12,793	26,076
Jambi			3,531	8,843
Bengkulu	804	2,336	2,756	5,716
Lampung	879	1,186	3,510	8,838
Bangka	39,849	43,723	67,398	96,098
Belitung	11,577	2,522	28,968	28,614
West Kalimantan	41,440	48,348	67,787	107,998
Southeast Kalimantan	6,426	7,174	15,231	26,289
South Sulawesi	5,309	5,656	12,708	21,380
Manado	4,489	6,206	10,723	20,022
Bali and Lombok	1,576	1,807	7,215	10,949
Timor and Dep.	1,547	1,560	3,755	6,867
Maluku	1,597	2,314	4,138	8,726
Outer Islands	260,051	268,256	425,722	650,783

Source: Boomgaard and Gooszen 1990:228.

Table 13. Non-indigenous population of the Outer Islands in 1900, 1905, 1920, 1930: Other Asians (Foreign Orientals)

	1900	1905	1920	1930
Aceh	513	1,439	1,632	2,255
Tapanuli	615	324	462	688
East Sumatra	9,208	15,976	12,781	19,776
West Sumatra	2,129	1,765	1,860	2,501
Riau (including Indragiri)	247	209	556	1,186
Palembang	2,383	3,209	3,237	4,879
Jambi			617	1,469
Bengkulu	193	67	188	391
Lampung	62	106	210	482
Bangka	287	304	364	549
Belitung	11	19	27	66
West Kalimantan	1,814	1,919	1,466	3,942
Southeast Kalimantan	2,289	2,064	4,711	8,354
South Sulawesi	589	532	2,317	4,349
Manado	549	882	1,918	5,475
Bali and Lombok	697	850	1,323	2,373
Timor and Dep.	325	323	1,457	3,443
Maluku	973	1,375	2,349	4,299
Outer Islands	22,884	31,345	37,475	66,477

Source: Boomgaard and Gooszen 1990:230.

Notes onTables 11-13:

1. Jambi is included in Palembang in 1900 and 1905. I have taken the ratio Palembang/Jambi of 1920 in order to split up the Palembang figures for 1900 and 1905.
2. In my reconstruction, intermediate years were calculated as linear growth between these four anchor years. It is not realistic to expect that these figures for the non-indigenous population are accurate, but since they are small, they may serve as reasonable estimates.
3. Other Asians were mostly Arabs and Indians. The Japanese were grouped under 'Other Asians' during the period 1905-1930. In earlier years they were presumably included under Europeans. In 1920, the majority of Japanese in the Outer Islands lived in East Sumatra (789) and Southeast Kalimantan (325) (Boomgaard and Gooszen 1990:229).

Table 14. Area and population density in 1930

		Population per km²:				
	Area (km²)	Europeans	Chinese	Other Asians	Indigenous	Total
Bali and Lombok	10,290	0.05	1.06	0.23	173.8	175.2
West Sumatra	49,778	0.10	0.30	0.05	37.9	38.4
South Sulawesi	100,457	0.04	0.21	0.04	30.5	30.8
Tapanuli	39,077	0.02	0.15	0.02	26.5	26.7
Timor and Dep.	63,338	0.02	0.11	0.05	26.0	26.2
Aceh	55,392	0.06	0.39	0.04	17.6	18.1
East Sumatra	94,583	0.11	2.04	0.21	15.6	17.9
Bangka	11,942	0.08	8.05	0.04	9.0	17.2
Manado	88,578	0.03	0.23	0.06	12.5	12.9
Palembang	86,356	0.04	0.30	0.06	12.3	12.7
Lampung	28,784	0.03	0.31	0.02	12.2	12.6
Bengkulu	26,249	0.03	0.22	0.02	12.1	12.3
Belitung	4,833	0.14	5.92	0.01	9.1	15.2
Riau (incl. Indragiri)	31,688	0.02	1.23	0.04	8.1	9.4
West Kalimantan	146,760	0.01	0.74	0.03	4.7	5.5
Jambi	44,924	0.01	0.20	0.03	5.2	5.5
Southeast Kalimantan	392,700	0.01	0.07	0.02	3.4	3.5
Maluku	496,456	0.01	0.02	0.01	1.1	1.1
Outer Islands	1,772,186	0.03	0.37	0.04	10.3	10.7

Source: Boomgaard and Gooszen 1990:243.

Note: The area changed over time as the result of redrawing boundaries and improved measurement. Maluku here includes New Guinea (Irian Jaya). This table states area and population figures in 1930. The total area of the Netherlands Indies in 1920 was 1,900,142 km² and in 1930 1,904,159 km².

Table 15. Distribution and composition of the population of the Outer Islands in 1930: Europeans (as a percentage)

	Share of Europeans in total European population of Outer Islands	Share of Europeans in total population of each province	Share of total provincial population in total Outer Islands population
East Sumatra	22.9	0.60	8.9
West Sumatra	11.1	0.26	10.0
South Sulawesi	9.6	0.14	16.2
Maluku	9.5	0.49	4.7
Southeast Kalimantan	9.1	0.30	7.2
Palembang	8.2	0.33	5.8
Amboina	7.3	0.89	2.1
Aceh	6.9	0.31	5.3
Manado	6.2	0.24	6.0
West Kalimantan	2.1	0.11	4.4
Timor and Dep.	2.1	0.06	8.7
Bangka	2.1	0.46	1.1
Lampung	1.9	0.24	1.9
Ternate (+New Guinea)	1.8	0.17	2.6
Tapanuli	1.8	0.08	5.5
Bengkulu	1.6	0.22	1.7
Belitung	1.5	0.89	0.4
Riau (incl. Indragiri)	1.2	0.17	1.6
Bali and Lombok	1.2	0.03	9.5
Jambi	1.0	0.17	1.3

Table 16. Composition of the population of the Outer Islands in 1930: Chinese (as a percentage)

	Share of Chinese in total Chinese population of Outer Islands	Share of Chinese in total population of each province
East Sumatra	29.6	11.4
West Kalimantan	16.6	13.5
Bangka	14.8	46.8
Riau (including Indragiri)	6.0	13.1
Belitung	4.4	39.0
Palembang	4.0	2.4
Southeast Kalimantan	4.0	1.9
Aceh	3.3	2.2
South Sulawesi	3.3	0.7
Manado	3.1	1.8
West Sumatra	2.3	0.8
Bali and Lombok	1.7	0.6
Jambi	1.4	3.6
Lampung	1.4	2.4
Maluku	1.3	2.1
Timor and Dep.	1.1	0.4
Bengkulu	0.9	1.8
Tapanuli	0.9	0.5

Table 17. Population figures of the twelve largest cities in colonial Indonesia in 1930

		Indigenous	European	Chinese	Other Asian	Total
Java	Batavia	325,978	31,130	71,688	6,388	435,184
	Surabaya	271,275	25,900	38,871	5,629	341,675
	Semarang	175,457	12,587	27,423	2,329	217,796
Outer Islands	Palembang	86,882	1,895	15,492	3,876	108,145
	Macassar	65,445	3,447	15,363	600	84,855
	Medan	41,270	4,293	27,287	3,734	76,584
	Banjarmasin	57,822	947	5,014	1,915	65,698
	Padang	40,744	2,592	7,263	1,455	52,054
	Pontianak	27,160	541	15,275	2,220	45,196
	Balikpapan	23,411	988	4,327	1,117	29,843
	Manado	20,047	1,392	5,519	586	27,544
	Teluk Betung	20,518	421	3,921	310	25,170

Source: Boomgaard and Gooszen 1990:245.

Table 18. Population groups in East Sumatra in 1930

	Malay	Batak	Javanese	Other	Total indigenous	Chinese
Langkat	40,451	37,595	107,220	32,591	217,857	30,292
Deli Serdang	61,953	81,012	231,044	57,590	431,599	88,740
Asahan	120,596	37,679	129,246	21,391	308,912	23,975
Simalungun/Karo	2,157	219,378	114,364	16,842	352,741	15,632
Bengkalis	109,707	5,685	8,062	35,832	159,286	34,192
East Sumatra	334,864	381,349	589,836	164,346	1,470,395	192,822
Percentage of the total indigenous population per area						
Langkat	18.6	17.3	49.2	15.0	100	
Deli Serdang	14.4	18.8	53.5	13.3	100	
Asahan	39.0	12.2	41.8	6.9	100	
Simalungun/Karo	0.6	62.2	32.4	4.8	100	
Bengkalis	68.9	3.6	5.1	22.5	100	
East Sumatra	22.8	25.9	40.1	11.2	100	

Source: *Volkstelling 1933*, IV:165; VII:12.

APPENDIX B

Computerizing trade statistics

The foreign trade statistics, as compiled by the Central Bureau of Statistics at Batavia, specify imports and exports for Java (and Madura) and for the Outer Islands, as well as differentiating by region for areas outside Java. In 1926-1928 the statistics were reorganized, first for Java and subsequently for the Outer Islands as well. Commodities were to be stated with origin and destination if their value exceeded 1,000 guilders. In the years 1930-1934, the listing of exports and imports in the Outer Islands by residency was suppressed, as costs had to be cut. For these years the trade of each individual residency can be calculated by adding up the exports and imports of the individual harbours of origin and destination, which are stated next to the commodity totals of the Outer Islands (Touwen 1992).

During most of the period covered by this study, from 1914, the trade flows were registered in accordance with the 'continental system', which registers foreign trade at customs points as opposed to national borders, as is the case under the preceding 'Anglo-Saxon system'. The main difference between these two methods is the treatment of goods in entrepôt. The Anglo-Saxon system counts these goods as imports upon entering a freeport and again as exports when leaving. The continental system includes such goods only when destined for distribution in the country in question. It has been demonstrated that the difference was of marginal importance in the registration of the foreign trade of colonial Indonesia (Korthals Altes 1986:21 2).

Yet, even if the continental system did prevail in the colony from 1914, the freeports in the archipelago were treated like any other ports. As a consequence, foreign trade entering or leaving freeports was normally included in the official statistics. This was the case, for instance, for Sabang and the islands of Riau prior to 1923 (Korthals Altes 1987:25-7, 30-3). A different procedure was followed only in certain special cases, such as the oil shipments to and from the Royal Dutch/Shell reservoirs on Pulu Sambu near Singapore. These exports and imports were added to the trade statistics as if Pulu Sambu had been a foreign country.

As a remnant from the time of the Cultivation System in Java, when the colonial government monopolized exports, a differentiation was made between private trade and government trade. This distinction gradually disappeared from the foreign trade statistics, as government trade constituted an increasingly unimportant proportion of the total. In the analysis, it may be safely left out.

After 1917 additional statistics were published by the Central Bureau of Statistics on interregional trade between Java and the Outer Islands. These data appeared in three sections, each broken down by residency: the imports of the Outer Islands from Java, the exports of the Outer Islands to Java, and the exports from each residency of the Outer Islands to other Outer Islands. From 1923 on, aggregates of these trade flows were included. When studying the Outer Islands, the interregional trade with Java supplements our picture of economic expansion based on foreign trade.

The computer database

The analysis of trade statistics in this study makes use of a computer database in which selected foreign trade statistics were entered by students at the Department of History of Leiden University under supervision of Thomas Lindblad. Interregional trade flows were entered into the computer by myself, with the assistance of several trainees of the Transnational Postgraduate Training Programme in Historical Information Processing 'Data Bank for Urban and Regional History (DABURH)' in Leiden.[1] I constructed a separate data file containing export figures of indigenous rubber and smallholder rubber for the years 1927, 1928, 1930, 1932, 1934, 1936, and 1938. This data set contains the values and volumes of rubber, as listed by harbour, aggregated by residency. The trade statistics list dry-equivalent volumes of indigenous rubber, which were calculated on the basis of its moisture percentage. A standard percentage was assigned to each category of rubber, and this varied by province, taking into account local production methods.

The data set of foreign trade statistics was used earlier to compile a volume on the trade statistics of colonial Indonesia in *Changing Economy in Indonesia* (Clemens et al. 1992). I subsequently made several minor corrections and improvements in the data set. An updated version is available on the Internet and can be obtained at the web site of the Netherlands Historical Data Archive.[2] The additional data sets on interregional trade and indigenous and estate rubber are also available, as well as extensive documentation on the data sets.

1 I express gratitude for the efforts put into this data entry and conversion process to T. Dijksterhuis, J. van Droffelaar, M. Gosselink, L.W. Nolten, and H.M. van Wuijkhuijse.

2 The address of the NHDA/NIWI web site is: http://www.niwi.knaw.nl/

Selection of commodities

For the data set on foreign trade, an initial selection was made of 40 key commodities, for which values and quantities were entered by region. This selection of import and export products was carefully chosen to contain the major import and export products, but of course it covers less than 100 per cent of total trade. From the interregional trade statistics, a slightly different selection was entered into the computer, in which some typical indigenous products were added (for example gambir) and others appeared in a different category (for instance rice, separately listed as Saigon rice, Indian rice, Siam rice, and unhulled rice). The data set includes the following products:

Foreign exports: Copra, *pinang* nuts, pepper (black and white), rubber (dry equivalents), coffee (Arabica, Liberia, Robusta), tea, tobacco, palm oil, timber, rattan, gutta percha, fibres (including sisal and hemp fibres, jute, fibres of kapok and cotton), oil (crude oil, kerosene, petrol, liquid fuel, bunker oil, other fuel oil, batching and solar oil, turpentine, lubricating oils, paraffin, candles, and other refined oils), coal, and tin.

Foreign imports: Rice, coconut oil, imported oils, flour, fish, cigars, cars, textiles (including unbleached, bleached, undyed, and dyed textiles, and clothing), machines, metal products, iron (including bars, roof material, pipes, nails, rivets), fertilizer, tinned iron, and cement.

Interregional trade: Copra, rubber, coffee (Arabica, Liberia, Robusta), gambir, coal, tin, rice (including Saigon rice, Indian rice, Siam rice), textiles (including dyed and woven cottons, sarongs, kain, slendang, and shawls), machines and tools, cars, trucks, cement, iron and steel (including bars, rods, plates, roof iron, wires, cables, pipes, nails, rivets).

Totals: For each year, total foreign exports and total foreign imports by region (1900-1940), as well as total interregional imports and exports by region (1923-1938), were entered into the data base, to facilitate analysis of aggregate trade flows.

The average coverage for the period 1900-1940 was 85 per cent for foreign exports leaving the Outer Islands, and 62 per cent for foreign imports entering the Outer Islands. For several individual provinces, the selection turned out to cover only a small proportion of the trade. However, the selection did not aim to cover total trade, but to identify to what extent the important trading commodities were traded by the various provinces. Foreign exports were well represented in the selection, but the product selection of imports from Java did not nearly cover the total trade flow, mainly because this trade was highly diversified (which would require a very large data input). Additional information from archival sources was used to analyse the composition of the trade flows of each residency, in particular those where the product selection gave little indication of the composition of total trade.

Table 19. Average annual share of selected products in the trade totals, 1900/1940 (as a percentage)

	Foreign exports 1900/40	Foreign imports 1900/40	Exports to Java 1923/37	Imports from Java 1923/37
Lampung	96	49	38	28
Aceh	95	59	8	14
East Sumatra	94	62	17	24
Bangka	94	70	88	35
Belitung	91	68	25	23
Southeast Kalimantan	91	66	49	40
Palembang	87	70	85	38
West Kalimantan	87	66	62	30
Jambi	85	70	22	23
Tapanuli	79	51	11	16
Manado	78	73	37	30
West Sumatra	73	63	66	33
Bengkulu	73	41	32	30
South Sulawesi	60	47	24	26
Riau	58	59	84	20
Bali and Lombok	55	43	47	47
Timor and Dep.	28	27	6	42
Maluku	27	74	12	36
Outer Islands total	85	62	61	32

APPENDIX C

Construction of an index for prices

To measure the performance of an economy in real as opposed to nominal terms, it is necessary to eliminate the effects of inflation on production (or export) figures. The growth rate of production figures expressed in current (nominal) prices needs to be deflated using a price index. Boomgaard has noted that it has escaped the attention of many historians that such an index must be used if we want to measure the performance of an economy in 'real' (as opposed to nominal) terms (Boomgaard 1991:58). Usually, aggregate production figures (in our case, export figures) constitute a sum total of all products for all sectors and are obtained by adding quantities in monetary units. Often, these quantities are given in value based on current prices. Theoretically, real values could be reconstructed by multiplying the underlying quantities with real prices, but that goes beyond the scope of this study. Data are lacking for the real price for each year for each commodity in each province. In the analysis of export production by residency in the Outer Islands, I have stuck to the aggregate export figures in the original, current (nominal) prices. When comparing regions, there is no need to deflate. Only when analysing time series does deflation become important.

Theoretically, creating an index for the export package without disassembling the data into separate products is not correct, because the composition of the export package changed over time. However, as a general indication of price movement, the Laspeyres indicator suggested by Van Ark can be used (Van Ark 1988; see also Maddison 1989a). Van Ark constructs his price index by weighting factors based on the volumes of a large group of export commodities, and he also discusses previous exercises. Based on the CKS index calculations, Korthals Altes has supplied another series of price index figures for imports and exports, the latter constructed by weighting factors on the basis of the volumes of five major export products. Korthals Altes changes the weights of the composition of the export index rigorously per decade, but, by using wholesale prices, does not include changes in average quality (Table 20 and Figure 19) (Korthals Altes 1994:158-65; Van der Eng 1995). I have used the indices constructed by Van Ark in several graphs to compare the development over time of interregional and foreign trade flows.

In order to compare the export behaviour of different provinces, the use of current prices is acceptable as long as we keep in mind that all provinces experienced the same underlying inflationary and deflationary movements of prices. For example, during the years 1919-1920, a price inflation (due to the rise in demand following the end of the First World War) inflated the value of foreign exports. Roughly a decade later, the dramatic fall of export production shortly after 1929 was to a large extent due to the price fall that followed the Great Depression. Since the price level collapsed for all goods, not only for export goods but also for import goods, the fall in export revenues in terms of real prices was not as bad as the decline in current prices suggests. Most export-producing provinces steadily increased their output during the Depression. The estates laid off workers and saved on production costs, while the indigenous producers, who had low production costs anyway, increased their output with family labour. By deflating per capita export revenues (from Figure 24a) it can be shown that exports displayed a steady increase in East Sumatra, while in Southeast Kalimantan exports remained on pretty much the same level. The true expander in such an exercise appears to be Palembang, where exports increased consistently over this period, and where the Depression does not seem to have caused any harm. The comparative advantage of Palembang, as explained above, was largely due to a combination of strong products (coffee, tea, oil). But again, it should be kept in mind that in such exercises any comparative advantages may be due to the weighting factors used in the aggregate price index, and trade flows ought to be deflated by commodity.

Table 20. Price indices for colonial Indonesia, 1913-1940

	Van Ark 1913 = 100	Korthals Altes 1913 = 100			Van Ark 1913 = 100	Korthals Altes 1913 = 100	
	Exports	Exports	Imports		Exports	Exports	Imports
1913	100	100	100	1927	132	202	157
1914	109	109	103	1928	111	149	152
1915	124	141	115	1929	98	136	151
1916	118	152	154	1930	82	91	142
1917	134	139	203	1931	57	57	112
1918	167	110	256	1932	37	40	90
1919	195	300	275	1933	35	37	78
1920	268	503	303	1934	37	45	74
1921	154	201	181	1935	36	45	72
1922	146	176	182	1936	42	59	74
1923	156	237	181	1937	59	82	98
1924	150	222	179	1938	48	58	94
1925	152	282	173	1939	–	75	95
1926	139	233	163	1940	–	76	113

Source: Van Ark 1988:120; Korthals Altes 1994:159-60.

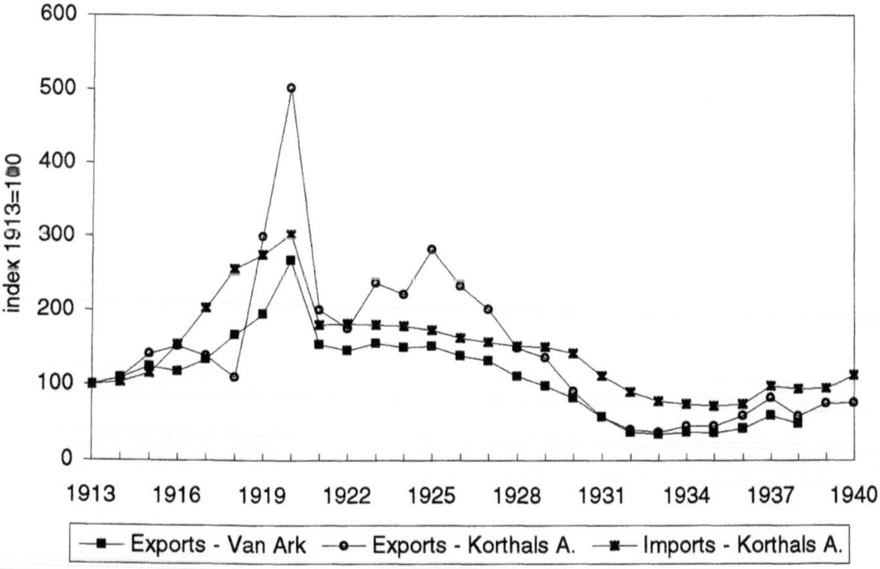

Figure 19. Price indices for the Netherlands Indies, 1913-1940 (Van Ark 1988, Korthals Altes 1994) (Table 20).

APPENDIX D

Statistics

Table 21. Foreign trade of the Outer Islands, 1900-1940 (in thousands of guilders)

Year	Foreign exports	Foreign imports	Year	Foreign exports	Foreign imports
1900	73,593	55,111	1920	752,411	304,613
1901	77,604	72,972	1921	538,957	300,897
1902	82,162	61,356	1922	620,324	200,416
1903	84,963	59,863	1923	548,531	181,485
1904	99,677	63,077	1924	630,020	211,742
1905	107,739	96,151	1925	947,639	287,399
1906	116,575	71,413	1926	851,161	330,167
1907	129,884	73,356	1927	818,166	324,940
1908	135,457	77,278	1928	736,849	338,890
1909	142,578	84,116	1929	734,741	378,624
1910	153,959	95,674	1930	592,977	305,540
1911	169,067	109,847	1931	397,101	172,137
1912	211,348	104,538	1932	289,303	115,996
1913	317,278	136,549	1933	276,118	100,716
1914	301,197	120,727	1934	296,114	96,794
1915	325,258	113,163	1935	275,311	96,514
1916	344,223	115,710	1936	344,502	102,194
1917	325,190	154,127	1937	662,421	179,377
1918	321,451	165,127	1938	442,235	166,331
1919	743,399	214,960	1939	474,007	158,726
			1940	588,526	137,527

Source: *Statistiek handel, scheepvaart* 1900-09, 1909-23; *Jaaroverzicht* 1925-42; *Statistiek intergewestelijke handel* 1922-42. Henceforth: Trade statistics.

Note: Trade values, unless separately specified, refer to value in current prices.

Indonesian exports formed a high percentage of GDP: they reached almost 30 per cent in 1925. The percentage fell during the Depression and rose again to about 25 per cent in 1937 (Booth 1992a:102-3, 1998:204).

Table 22.1. Composition of aggregate Outer Islands exports by destination, 1923-1938 (as a percentage and in millions of guilders)

	Exports to Java (%)	Exports to Outer Islands (%)	Foreign exports (%)	To Java	To Outer Islands	Foreign exportse	Total exports
				(million guilders)			
1923	16.2	9.7	74.1	120	72	549	741
1924	13.7	8.7	77.6	111	71	630	812
1925	9.9	6.5	83.6	112	74	948	1,134
1926	12.2	7.3	80.5	129	77	851	1,057
1927	13.2	7.2	79.6	136	74	818	1,028
1928	14.0	8.0	78.0	135	78	737	950
1929	14.1	9.4	76.6	135	90	735	960
1930	16.1	9.1	74.8	128	72	593	793
1931	17.6	9.1	73.4	95	49	397	541
1932	15.0	9.9	75.1	58	38	289	363
1933	14.6	9.6	75.8	53	35	276	364
1934	14.2	9.1	76.7	55	35	296	386
1935	13.9	9.7	76.4	50	35	275	360
1936	12.1	8.9	78.9	53	39	345	437
1937	8.1	9.8	82.1	65	79	662	806
1938	10.4	12.1	77.5	59	69	442	570

Source: Trade statistics.

Table 22.2. Composition of aggregate Outer Islands imports by origin, 1923-1938 (as a percentage and in millions of guilders)

	Imports from Java (%)	Foreign imports (%)	Imports from Java	Foreign imports	Total imports
			(million guilders)		
1923	33.0	67.0	89	181	270
1924	32.3	67.7	101	212	313
1925	29.8	70.2	122	287	409
1926	28.4	71.6	131	330	461
1927	32.6	67.4	157	325	482
1928	31.7	68.3	157	339	496
1929	31.6	68.4	175	379	554
1930	33.3	66.7	153	306	459
1931	39.0	61.0	110	172	282
1932	42.9	57.1	87	116	203
1933	42.6	57.4	75	101	176
1934	44.9	55.1	79	97	176
1935	44.3	55.7	77	97	174
1936	47.4	52.6	92	102	194
1937	45.3	54.7	148	179	327
1938	43.0	57.0	125	166	291

Source: Trade statistics.

Table 23. Major ports in colonial Indonesia in 1938 (in thousands of guilders)

	Exports in 1938	Imports in 1938
Outer Islands:		
Palembang	93,385	28,041
Belawan	86,323	35,096
Balikpapan	46,142	10,272
Macassar	22,991	16,833
Pontianak	13,375	6,076
Banjarmasin	13,071	2,409
Padang	8,202	8,671
Manado	2,288	2,520
Java:		
Tanjung Priok	90,945	134,674
Surabaya	45,717	100,160
Semarang	30,529	52,988

Source: *Statistisch Jaaroverzicht* 1938 (*Indisch Verslag* 1939), II:336.

Table 24. Foreign trade of the Outer Islands in selected years, 1900-1940 (in thousands of guilders; I = imports, X = exports)

	1900		1910		1920	
	I	X	I	X	I	X
East Sumatra	21,435	18,645	26,646	32,080	115,933	222,148
Palembang	4,374	8,038	7,294	19,714	20,523	62,173
Southeast Kalimantan	1,810	1,495	8,763	21,928	29,501	210,839
Aceh	4,643	4,475	11,824	10,093	10,584	9,284
West Sumatra	6,599	7,106	7,579	9,745	32,012	21,680
Jambi	516	653	1,074	2,098	3,587	11,726
Lampung	28	58	42	452	287	263
South Sulawesi	4,292	9,282	7,577	21,729	33,675	61,431
Manado	2,349	2,659	5,305	8,737	9,189	13,287
West Kalimantan	2,487	11,187	5,063	8,752	11,808	20,126
Riau	1,500	2,828	2,262	4,281	17,201	84,897
Bangka	742	65	3,181	352	6,075	2,900
Belitung	860	956	2,078	2,368	4,945	20,622
Tapanuli	–	–	1,003	1,244	3,427	3,508
Bengkulu	331	439	1,052	219	1,249	316
Maluku	975	3,081	2,572	5,203	2,031	3,428
Timor and Dep.	54	123	129	83	188	94
Bali and Lombok	2,116	2,600	2,230	4,880	2,396	3,690

Table 24 – continued

	1930		1940	
	I	X	I	X
East Sumatra	104,915	193,590	43,096	196,744
Palembang	46,517	78,148	31,457	137,461
Southeast Kalimantan	29,553	97,288	13,406	82,083
Aceh	10,567	9,675	2,273	8,401
West Sumatra	17,348	20,629	8,063	6,989
Jambi	5,228	10,925	3,051	22,326
Lampung	2,212	18,684	1,082	8,380
South Sulawesi	22,254	29,327	11,531	11,526
Manado	11,153	23,007	2,078	3,304
West Kalimantan	14,858	28,233	5,451	30,620
Riau	11,340	22,452	8,246	22,452
Bangka	10,491	17,841	5,738	41,544
Belitung	6,821	20,831	–	–
Tapanuli	2,716	6,465	757	8,810
Bengkulu	2,252	3,842	634	637
Maluku	3,910	5,403	436	552
Timor and Dep.	327	764	41	72
Bali and Lombok	3,078	5,872	187	3,014

Source: Trade statistics.

Table 25.1. Exports of the Outer Islands by region (including interregional exports),1924-1938 (as a percentage and in millions of guilders)

	1924/28 Interreg. exports (%)	Foreign exports (%)	Total exports (mill.)	1929/33 Interreg. exports (%)	Foreign exports (%)	Total exports (mill.)	1934/38 Interreg. exports (%)	Foreign exports (%)	Total exports (mill.)
East Sumatra	3.0	97.0	280	5.6	94.4	154	5.2	94.8	142
Palembang	18.6	81.4	100	27.2	72.8	86	21.6	78.4	91
SE Kalimantan	15.4	84.6	166	14.8	85.2	93	12.0	88.0	66
Aceh	11.3	88.8	18	20.3	79.7	9	24.6	75.4	8
West Sumatra	38.5	61.5	44	44.6	55.3	28	47.1	52.9	17
Jambi	2.5	97.5	28	11.1	88.9	9	12.1	87.9	10
Lampung	40.2	59.8	23	30.4	69.6	20	23.7	76.3	12
West Kalimantan	10.1	89.9	55	13.7	86.3	23	18.3	81.7	20
South Sulawesi	31.0	69.0	58	42.8	57.2	43	38.5	61.5	34
Manado	23.6	76.4	33	17.4	82.6	21	36.2	63.8	13
Riau	6.2	93.8	29	8.3	91.7	18	4.1	95.9	18
Bangka	81.0	19.0	50	67.8	32.2	41	45.6	54.4	47
Belitung	3.3	96.7	37	7.0	93.0	17	80.7	19.3	2
Tapanuli	36.0	64.0	19	47.6	52.4	10	37.8	62.2	8
Bengkulu	76.6	23.4	16	67.8	32.2	11	48.7	51.3	3
Maluku	66.3	33.7	15	58.7	41.3	9	78.5	21.5	7
Bali and Lombok	59.1	40.9	20	62.8	37.2	16	55.7	44.3	10
Timor and Dep.	98.4	1.6	5	94.7	5.3	3	97.1	2.9	2
Outer Islands	20.2	79.8	996	24.9	75.1	609	21.6	78.4	512

Source: Trade statistics.
Notes: Interregional exports are exports to Java and exports to (other) Outer Islands. The interregional exports of Timor, Bangka, Bengkulu, Maluku, and Bali were larger than the foreign exports of these provinces: on average, interregional exports of Timor (1924-1938) constituted more than 94% of its trade. Since Bangka's tin first went to Batavia, it is obvious that Bangka exported as much as, or even more than, Belitung during this period (see Table 41.1). This more complete picture of provincial exports can be used to determine per capita export figures that rehabilitate several provinces as important exporters: Tables 26.1 and 26.2.

Table 25.2. Imports of the Outer Islands by region (including interregional imports), 1924-1938 (as a percentage and in thousands of guilders)

	1924/28 Interreg. imports (%)	Foreign imports (%)	Total imports (mill.)	1929/33 Interreg. imports (%)	Foreign imports (%)	Total imports (mill.)	1934/38 Interreg. imports (%)	Foreign imports (%)	Total imports (mill.)
East Sumatra	13.9	86.1	105	19.1	80.9	89	30.8	69.2	61
Palembang	24.5	75.5	46	34.6	65.4	42	37.5	62.5	32
SE Kalimantan	38.3	61.7	53	53.3	46.7	39	62.3	37.7	31
Aceh	20.1	79.9	12	27.2	72.8	10	43.9	56.1	5
West Sumatra	42.8	57.2	36	47.4	52.6	26	47.8	52.2	15
Jambi	18.2	81.8	12	30.4	69.6	5	48.5	51.5	5
Lampung	91.8	8.3	12	88.2	11.8	12	84.8	15.2	7
West Kalimantan	24.1	75.9	28	33.8	66.2	16	47.9	52.1	13
South Sulawesi	27.3	72.7	35	34.8	65.2	27	34.5	65.5	21
Manado	30.4	69.6	17	31.3	68.7	12	50.5	49.5	7
Riau	4.5	95.5	15	11.1	88.9	9	18.3	81.7	7
Bangka	44.2	55.8	15	50.4	49.6	14	40.4	59.6	11
Belitung	41.2	58.8	11	52.3	47.7	7	10.8	9.2	1
Tapanuli	45.3	54.7	7	58.8	41.1	5	66.1	33.9	3
Bengkulu	70.5	29.5	8	67.1	32.9	6	67.7	32.3	3
Maluku	43.8	56.1	7	45.8	54.2	5	70.7	29.3	3
Bali and Lombok	77.5	22.5	13	82.9	17.1	9	92.3	7.7	6
Timor and Dep.	82.3	17.7	2	84.7	15.4	1	92.5	7.5	1
Outer Islands	30.9	69.1	432	37.9	62.1	335	45.0	55.0	233

Source: Trade statistics.
Note: Interregional imports are imports from Java.

Table 26.1. Per capita Outer Islands exports by region, 1926/30 and 1931/35 (in guilders)

	Average 1926/30			Average 1931/35	
	Only foreign	Including interregional		Only foreign	Including interregional
Belitung	441	458	Bangka	49	130
Bangka	81	308	Belitung	103	111
East Sumatra	150	155	East Sumatra	59	63
SE Kalimantan	97	113	Palembang	46	60
Palembang	74	99	SE Kalimantan	37	43
Riau	86	92	Riau	34	38
Jambi	88	91	Lampung	23	32
Lampung	51	80	Jambi	15	18
West Kalimantan	55	61	Bengkulu	6	18
Bengkulu	17	53	West Kalimantan	12	15
Manado	24	31	Maluku	4	9
Maluku	11	27	South Sulawesi	5	9
West Sumatra	15	23	West Sumatra	5	9
South Sulawesi	13	19	Manado	7	9
Tapanuli	11	18	Tapanuli	3	6
Aceh	15	17	Bali and Lombok	2	6
Bali and Lombok	5	12	Aceh	4	5
Timor and Dep.	0.1	3	Timor and Dep.	0.02	1
Outer Islands	40	52	Outer Islands	16	21

Source: Trade statistics; reconstructed population figures (Appendix A).

Table 26.2. Per capita Outer Islands imports by region, 1926/30 and 1931/35 (in guilders)

	Average 1926/30			Average 1931/35	
	Only foreign	Including Java		Only foreign	Including Java
Belitung	101	176	Belitung	20	44
Bangka	49	93	Bangka	21	44
East Sumatra	65	76	East Sumatra	24	32
Palembang	42	55	Palembang	12	20
Riau	50	54	Lampung	2	19
Jambi	36	45	SE Kalimantan	6	16
Lampung	5	45	Riau	13	16
SE Kalimantan	27	45	Jambi	8	13
West Kalimantan	27	36	West Kalimantan	7	12
Bengkulu	9	27	Bengkulu	3	10
West Sumatra	11	20	Manado	4	6
Manado	12	17	Aceh	4	6
Aceh	11	14	West Sumatra	4	8
South Sulawesi	8	12	South Sulawesi	4	6
Maluku	8	13	Maluku	2	5
Tapanuli	4	8	Tapanuli	1	3
Bali and Lombok	2	8	Bali and Lombok	0.3	3
Timor and Dep.	0.3	1	Timor and Dep.	0.07	0.6
AVG	25.9	41.3	AVG	7.6	14.6
STD	26.1	40.8	STD	7.2	12.8
Outer Islands		26			10

Note: STD = standard deviation; AVG = mean.
Source: Trade statistics; reconstructed population figures (Appendix A).

Table 27. Regional share in foreign exports leaving the Outer Islands (as a percentage)

	1900/40		1905/30	
	Years included	Average share in %	Years included	Average share in %
East Sumatra	41	31.1	26	30.6
Southeast Kalimantan	41	16.9	26	19.7
Palembang	41	12.2	26	10.2
South Sulawesi	41	6.9	26	6.8
West Kalimantan	41	5.3	26	4.8
Riau	41	4.7	26	5.9
West Sumatra	41	3.7	26	3.6
Manado	41	3.3	26	3.5
Aceh	41	2.9	26	3.2
Belitung	35	2.6	26	2.7
Bangka	41	1.9	26	0.8
Bali and Lombok	41	1.7	26	1.6
Jambi	41	1.7	26	1.7
Indragiri	40	1.6	25	1.4
Lampung	41	1.2	26	0.9
Ambon	41	1.0	26	0.9
Tapanuli	33	1.0	23	0.9
Ternate	23	0.8	18	0.7
Bengkulu	41	0.3	26	0.2
New Guinea	17	0.2	17	0.2
Timor and Dep.	41	0.1	26	0.1

Source: Trade statistics.

Table 28. Regional share in aggregate foreign export revenues and surplus on the balance of trade, 1900-1940 (in thousands of guilders and as a percentage of all Outer Islands)

	Total foreign exports (1900-1940)	%	Total foreign imports (1900-1940)	Trade surplus (1900-1940)	%
Cluster I					
East Sumatra	5,081,367	31.60	2,123,556	2,957,810	30.99
Southeast Kalimantan	3,059,743	19.03	628,067	2,431,676	25.48
Palembang	1,946,006	12.10	706,932	1,239,074	12.98
Clusters II and III					
Riau	1,032,616	6.42	331,468	701,147	7.35
South Sulawesi	937,027	5.83	572,511	364,516	3.82
West Kalimantan	770,086	4.79	356,934	413,151	4.33
West Sumatra	495,758	3.08	484,357	11,401	0.12
Manado	456,373	2.84	277,158	179,215	1.88
Belitung	435,377	2.71	111,810	323,567	3.39
Bangka	361,629	2.25	201,492	160,137	1.68
Aceh	360,071	2.24	315,743	44,328	0.46
Jambi	357,764	2.22	121,565	236,199	2.47
Cluster IV					
Lampung	228,668	1.42	24,012	204,655	2.14
Bali and Lombok	193,845	1.21	76,158	117,686	1.23
Tapanuli	163,706	1.02	64,347	99,358	1.04
Ambon	102,185	0.64	68,400	33,784	0.35
Bengkulu	55,753	0.35	49,101	6,652	0.07
Ternate	31,250	0.19	15,173	16,077	0.17
Timor and Dep.	6,522	0.04	6,443	79	0.00
New Guinea	4,257	0.03	901	3,355	0.04
Outer Islands	16,080	100.00	9,544		100.00

Source: Trade statistics.

Notes: The figures are arranged in order of the percentage share of total export earnings. Note that this comes close to yielding the four clusters used in this study, although Clusters II and III are mixed together. The only exception is Lampung; in this study it is put in Cluster II, but appears in this table in Cluster IV.

Table 29. Share by cluster in the total trade of the Outer Islands, 1924-1938 (average over the years stated, as a percentage of total trade)

Exports	1924/28	1929/33	1934/38
Cluster I	57.9%	57.8%	61.1%
Cluster II	24.7	23.0	20.2
Cluster III	11.9	12.8	14.5
Cluster IV	5.5	6.4	4.3
Imports	1924/28	1929/33	1934/38
Cluster I	46.9%	49.9%	52.6%
Cluster II	35.0	33.5	32.3
Cluster III	9.6	8.9	8.6
Cluster IV	8.5	7.7	6.5

Source: Trade statistics.
Notes: Cluster I: East Sumatra, Palembang, Southeast Kalimantan; Cluster II: Aceh, West Sumatra, Jambi, Lampung, West Kalimantan, South Sulawesi, Manado; Cluster III: Bangka, Belitung, Riau; Cluster IV: Tapanuli, Bengkulu, Maluku, Bali, Timor. Figures include the interregional trade with Java.

Table 30. Interregional trade of the Outer Islands by province, 1925 (in millions of guilders)

	Imports from Java	Exports to Java	Exports to other Outer Islands
East Sumatra	10.1	5.0	1.9
Southeast Kalimantan	22.3	19.3	9.1
Palembang	9.8	7.9	6.4
West Sumatra	14.3	9.9	8.0
West Kalimantan	6.8	4.7	0.4
South Sulawesi	8.0	2.6	14.0
Aceh	2.0	0.2	1.7
Jambi	2.3	0.1	0.3
Lampung	9.0	6.7	0.6
Manado	4.7	0.9	5.7
Bangka	6.4	30.9	0.4
Belitung	4.0	0.5	0.5
Riau	0.4	1.4	0.2
Maluku	3.2	1.0	10.9
Bali and Lombok	9.6	6.7	4.4
Bengkulu	4.8	9.2	3.9
Tapanuli	2.5	2.4	3.3
Timor and Dep.	1.6	2.4	2.7

Source: Trade statistics.
Note: The provinces in the left column are grouped into the four clusters.

Table 31. Foreign exports and export surplus of East Sumatra and its share in the total foreign exports of colonial Indonesia (in millions of guilders and as a percentage)

	Export value			Export surplus		
	East Sumatra	Colonial Indonesia	%	East Sumatra	Colonial Indonesia	%
1910	32	157	20.5	6	60	10.1
1925	316	964	32.8	239	671	35.6
1939	141	474	29.7	93	314	29.5

Source: Trade statistics.

Table 32. Surplus on the balance of trade as a percentage of total exports, 1923-1938

	E Sumatra	Palembang	SE Kalimantan	Bangka	Belitung	Riau	W Kalimantan	Jambi	Lampung
1923	65	72	81	77	79	29	45	71	59
1924	68	62	75	69	77	46	47	61	49
1925	73	61	73	64	76	61	62	71	52
1926	64	52	69	71	64	32	46	49	56
1927	58	53	63	63	71	45	47	55	34
1928	47	44	60	76	59	38	36	48	47
1929	40	29	52	70	59	46	35	51	40
1930	39	44	54	66	46	49	31	40	41
1931	43	63	67	61	60	53	23	26	33
1932	47	68	60	51	57	53	14	7	35
1933	49	73	62	57	75	60	24	29	46
1934	58	67	58	72	79	66	26	42	38
1935	56	63	55	79	-	61	9	23	46
1936	59	69	51	77	-	60	17	28	47
1937	62	64	54	79	-	69	46	59	52
1938	49	65	52	48	-	43	29	48	24

	W Sumatra	Aceh	S Sulawesi	Manado	Tapanuli	Bengkulu	Bali	Maluku	Timor
1923	21	23	43	48	58	61	54	52	57
1924	23	29	47	53	61	63	49	54	62
1925	28	53	37	49	73	57	35	57	65
1926	15	43	40	50	62	45	33	57	52
1927	18	25	36	49	58	51	35	57	61
1928	10	14	38	45	53	51	36	50	63
1929	11	4	42	44	48	46	35	48	61
1930	5	12	35	44	48	49	30	46	66
1931	6	31	32	44	49	47	51	49	49
1932	6	43	30	35	54	51	55	54	39
1933	9	30	43	33	56	48	47	57	43
1934	13	15	31	17	64	16	50	50	49
1935	7	24	35	10	62	26	35	48	54
1936	13	45	45	20	64	13	41	40	63
1937	2	61	44	60	75	30	43	69	72
1938	6	45	36	60	51	14	35	58	54

Source: Trade statistics.

Notes: These 'surplus proportions' include exports to Java and exports to the Outer

Islands, as well as imports from Java. The surplus on the balance of trade was calculated as follows: total exports (foreign plus interregional) minus total imports (foreign plus interregional). This figure was then divided by the total export value (again, foreign plus interregional) and multiplied by 100 to obtain a percentage. The period 1923-1938 was chosen because interregional trade statistics are available for these years. This period embraces the major business cycles of the time, including the boom in the 1920s (which started after the 1921-1923 recession), the Depression, and recovery from the Depression starting in 1936.

Table 33. Surplus on the balance of trade as a percentage of total exports, 1923-1938

	Average annual surplus in %	Standard deviation 1923-1938
Bangka	67.5	9.0
Belitung	66.8	10.1
Southeast Kalimantan	61.6	7.3
Palembang	59.3	11.1
Tapanuli	58.5	7.9
Timor and Dep.	56.9	8.6
East Sumatra	54.8	9.6
Maluku	52.9	6.4
Riau	50.7	10.0
Jambi	44.3	16.0
Lampung	43.7	8.1
Bengkulu	41.8	5.2
Bali and Lombok	41.5	7.4
Manado	40.1	17.3
South Sulawesi	38.4	4.9
West Kalimantan	33.6	13.8
Aceh	16.1	30.7
West Sumatra	12.1	6.7
Outer Islands (average)	46.7	

Source: Table 32.
Note: These figures include exports to Java and to the other Outer Islands, as well as imports from Java (Table 32).

Table 34. Price indicators of major agricultural products, 1927-1940 (in guilders per 100 kg; indices)

	Rubber	Coffee	Copra	Pepper	Index 1927 = 100: Rubber	Coffee	Copra	Pepper
1927	131	85	23	119	100	100	100	100
1928	85	68	24	172	64.9	80.0	104.3	144.5
1929	72	82	21	161	55.0	96.5	91.3	135.3
1930	54	53	17	112	41.2	62.4	73.9	94.1
1931	23	37	13	59	17.6	43.5	56.5	49.6
1932	12	28	9	37	9.2	32.9	39.1	31.1
1933	10	35	8	29	7.6	41.2	34.8	24.4
1934	17	29	4	31	13.0	34.1	17.4	26.1
1935	21	22	5	19	16.0	25.9	21.7	16.0
1936	24	15	8	13	18.3	17.6	34.8	10.9
1937	63	25	12	22	48.1	29.4	52.2	18.5
1938	41	28	7	15	31.3	32.9	30.4	12.6
1939	51	17	5	14	38.9	20.0	21.7	11.8
1940	60	19	4	11	45.8	22.4	17.4	9.2

Source: Calculated from trade statistics.
Notes: These prices are the prices used in the trade statistics (for foreign exports). No allowance is made for differences in quality. Dry equivalents are used for rubber. Coffee includes Arabica, Liberia, and Robusta; pepper includes black and white pepper. The prices do not differentiate between high or low quality and may differ from actual market prices (Table 35).

Table 35. Market price of coffee, copra, rubber, and pepper, 1920-1940 (in guilders per 100 kg)

	Robusta		Copra		Rubber		White Pepper	Black pepper
	TS	Rotterdam	Amsterdam	Java	London	Batavia	Batavia	Batavia
1920	74	97.3	60.0	48.3	113	105.0		
1921	45	61.3	35.4	28.8	56	51.5		
1922	57	67.3	28.6	25.0	50	48.0		
1923	68	81.8	32.8	28.5	84	82.0		
1924	85	108.8	34.1	29.7	76	72.5		
1925	102	122.0	36.0	30.7	126	174.0		
1926	50	108.3	34.1	29.2	132	123.0		
1927	81	94.0	32.8	28.4	102	99.0	129.8	206.5
1928	69	100.3	32.0	27.2	59	58.5	146.3	225.0
1929	84	93.7	27.5	23.3	57	54.0	132.0	230.0
1930	60	61.3	22.9	19.4	33	30.5	76.8	105.4
1931	37	52.0	15.4	12.7	16	15.0	45.4	71.2
1932	33	49.3	13.0	9.8	9	8.5	34.5	43.1
1933	35	40.0	9.4	7.2	12	11.0	23.0	35.9
1934	26	33.3	7.0	4.8	21	20.0	25.5	58.1
1935	21	29.0	9.3	7.0	20	18.5	15.1	35.8
1936	18	29.5	12.1	9.3	28	26.0	11.3	23.8
1937	-	32.0	15.4	11.7	39	36.0	16.8	29.3
1938	-	26.8	10.3	6.4	29	24.0	14.4	22.0
1939	-	29.0	10.8	6.1	34	31.5	10.5	20.0
1940	-	-	-	5.2	41	32.0	8.2	18.5

Source: Korthals Altes 1994:72-99.

Notes: Robusta TS: Coffee prices as used in the trade statistics. No other prices were available for this period. Prices derived from the trade statistics are 'to some extent fictitious', although less so than prices calculated from freight figures (Korthals Altes 1994:72). Copra: averages for 'Netherlands Indies fair merchantable sundried' (Korthals Altes 1994:75). Note that prices could vary considerably in different markets. For example, the rubber price in Singapore differed from the rubber price in the ports, which in turn differed from the rubber price in the interior. These prices are also used in the graph in Figure 11, where the pepper price is the average of white pepper and black pepper, even though these prices could fluctuate in separate directions.

Table 36.1. Selected foreign exports from East Sumatra by value, 1900-1940 (in millions of guilders)

	Tobacco	Petroleum	Rubber	Coffee	Tea	Palm oil	Fibres	Other
1900	13	2	–	0	–	–	–	3
1901	14	5	–	2	–	–	–	4
1902	16	6	–	2	–	–	–	2
1903	15	8	–	3	–	–	–	3
1904	16	10	–	1	–	–	–	4
1905	16	9	–	1	–	–	–	5
1906	15	11	–	1	–	–	–	5
1907	15	12	–	1	–	–	–	6
1908	18	18	–	2	–	–	–	7
1909	11	19	–	1	–	–	–	6
1910	7	16	–	2	–	–	–	9
1911	12	19	2	1	–	–	–	7
1912	37	15	10	0	–	–	–	6
1913	70	31	11	1	–	–	–	8
1914	44	32	13	3	–	–	–	8
1915	48	25	28	3	1	–	–	7
1916	48	25	44	2	2	–	–	7
1917	10	32	57	0	2	–	–	8
1918	25	35	32	0	1	–	–	7
1919	57	27	90	3	4	–	–	10
1920	123	13	70	1	4	–	1	10
1921	80	11	32	2	3	2	4	9
1922	56	15	35	0	6	2	4	10
1923	65	34	55	2	11	1	5	10
1924	92	21	71	2	12	2	8	15
1925	37	23	184	1	10	2	8	51
1926	52	21	167	1	10	4	9	15
1927	91	14	148	2	11	7	11	19
1928	76	11	102	0	12	8	10	23
1929	64	27	79	0	12	10	12	24
1930	46	29	55	0	10	13	15	25
1931	32	20	29	0	9	11	8	19
1932	32	15	14	0	5	11	5	14
1933	21	18	12	0	4	10	6	13
1934	27	20	30	0	7	8	4	10
1935	22	15	27	0	5	13	5	9
1936	31	12	35	2	7	21	5	12
1937	29	28	90	1	8	25	10	17
1938	27	28	45	1	9	16	5	11
1939	16	23	63	1	9	0	6	24
1940	32	24	111	1	6	0	6	16

Source: Trade statistics.

Notes: 'Other' products include exports of copra, pinang nuts, pepper, timber, rattan, gutta percha, fish, and some tin. Rubber includes both estate and indigenous production.

Table 36.2. Selected foreign exports from East Sumatra by volume, 1900–1940 (in thousands of kg; petroleum and palm oil in thousands of litres)

	Tobacco	Petroleum	Rubber	Coffee	Tea	Palm oil	Fibres
1900	21,612	51,798	–	806	–	–	–
1901	17,772	118,393	–	1,447	–	–	–
1902	20,082	136,201	–	4,077	–	–	–
1903	18,320	–	–	2,501	–	–	–
1904	20,201	–	–	2,206	–	–	–
1905	19,465	–	–	1,837	–	–	–
1906	19,082	201,631	–	1,895	–	–	–
1907	19,320	203,582	–	1,848	–	–	–
1908	22,793	280,673	–	1,517	–	–	–
1909	13,532	345,117	–	1,817	–	–	–
1910	13,205	368,145	–	1,123	–	–	–
1911	11,540	408,592	–	1,120	–	–	–
1912	14,987	325,189	1,784	531	–	–	–
1913	25,777	276,858	3,036	1,276	–	–	–
1914	16,873	207,460	4,760	2,895	195	–	–
1915	20,841	190,821	9,604	3,130	645	–	–
1916	20,750	166,068	15,014	2,195	1,533	–	–
1917	4,488	218,689	20,860	122	1,542	–	–
1918	3,953	188,032	19,431	106	2,222	–	–
1919	37,045	111,332	37,749	3,202	4,380	–	7
1920	20,544	65,603	32,572	1,441	5,008	298	718
1921	14,142	65,583	34,416	688	4,514	2,492	4,378
1922	15,186	69,458	41,473	446	6,022	2,544	7,754
1923	14,874	259,533	51,165	607	7,231	2,717	11,463
1924	18,081	183,973	54,342	886	7,277	5,030	16,202
1925	74,956	220,141	70,685	427	6,620	6,881	19,324
1926	15,188	95,205	71,416	301	7,975	12,743	21,839
1927	21,658	173,442	83,998	457	9,233	20,853	28,190
1928	17,693	159,753	87,054	177	9,988	26,003	28,008
1929	17,227	415,749	92,549	210	11,538	32,141	33,766
1930	18,421	660,016	75,579	309	10,158	45,920	60,938
1931	17,624	336,559	98,973	247	14,315	57,868	45,866
1932	14,942	493,131	92,419	752	14,322	80,244	58,287
1933	9,675	681,769	92,759	923	12,320	109,379	62,887
1934	11,378	877,815	139,091	1,069	11,969	115,950	41,583
1935	10,263	491,414	87,213	1,599	11,127	138,310	59,951
1936	11,748	400,256	102,052	2,790	12,329	167,593	43,604
1937	12,189	579,579	156,542	2,529	12,071	190,448	54,084
1938	11,928	702,456	105,088	2,492	12,567	211,467	53,022
1939	8,700	864,720	119,693	1,801	11,203	0	65,653
1940	11,584	941,492	181,378	1,404	9,734	0	55,037

Source: Trade statistics.
Notes: Volumes of tobacco, rubber, coffee, tea, and fibres in thousands of kilos. Palm oil and petroleum in thousands of litres. Rubber: dry equivalents of both estate and indigenous production.

Table 37. Share of oil and tin in foreign exports from the Outer Islands, 1900-1940 (in millions of guilders and as a percentage)

	Total exports	Oil	Tin	Percentage of oil	Percentage of tin
1900	73.59	4.59	0.60	6.2	0.8
1901	77.60	11.69	0.68	15.1	0.9
1902	82.16	11.16	0.78	13.6	1.0
1903	84.96	15.05	0.89	17.7	1.0
1904	99.68	21.17	0.84	21.2	0.8
1905	107.74	21.39	1.76	19.9	1.6
1906	116.57	23.78	1.81	20.4	1.6
1907	129.88	27.50	0.15	21.2	0.1
1908	135.46	33.56	1.51	24.8	1.1
1909	142.58	34.69	1.50	24.3	1.1
1910	153.96	36.60	1.69	23.8	1.1
1911	169.07	46.96	1.66	27.8	1.0
1912	211.35	51.48	1.78	24.4	0.8
1913	317.28	112.28	1.55	35.4	0.5
1914	301.20	136.27	2.16	45.2	0.7
1915	325.26	140.90	10.66	43.3	3.3
1916	344.22	151.72	6.15	44.1	1.8
1917	325.19	156.99	9.93	48.3	3.1
1918	321.45	186.01	11.04	57.9	3.4
1919	743.40	345.28	20.89	46.4	2.8
1920	752.41	302.77	21.11	40.2	2.8
1921	538.96	263.02	14.31	48.8	2.7
1922	620.32	330.54	23.43	53.3	3.8
1923	548.53	177.03	25.12	32.3	4.6
1924	630.02	132.91	35.18	21.1	5.6
1925	947.64	170.35	32.97	19.0	3.5
1926	851.16	155.61	33.43	18.3	3.9
1927	818.17	112.85	40.25	13.8	4.9
1928	736.85	128.33	49.63	17.4	6.7
1929	734.74	160.21	45.91	21.8	6.2
1930	592.98	169.34	29.91	28.6	5.0
1931	397.10	116.26	18.21	29.3	4.6
1932	289.30	88.74	7.86	30.7	2.7
1933	276.12	97.34	8.79	35.3	3.2
1934	296.11	90.97	15.19	30.7	5.1
1935	275.31	81.58	17.92	29.6	6.5
1936	344.50	91.39	26.65	26.5	7.7
1937	662.42	151.00	55.41	22.8	8.4
1938	442.24	156.19	21.57	35.3	4.9
1939	474.01	152.58	33.94	32.2	7.2
1940	588.53	158.50	39.76	26.9	6.8

Source: Trade statistics.
Notes: Tin from Bangka was shipped abroad through Tanjung Priok at Batavia. This table only gives figures for direct foreign trade. See Table 41.1 for interregional export figures for Bangka.

Table 38. Foreign oil exports from major oil-producing regions, 1900-1940 (in thousands of guilders)

	East Sumatra	Palembang	Riau	Southeast Kalimantan
1900	2,072	2,520	–	–
1901	4,739	4,012	–	2,934
1902	6,063	3,988	–	1,108
1903	8,015	6,310	–	0,710
1904	10,117	6,094	–	4,957
1905	9,341	7,111	–	4,934
1906	11,131	8,179	–	4,465
1907	11,738	10,046	–	5,713
1908	17,942	8,718	–	6,894
1909	18,925	5,905	–	9,860
1910	15,530	11,013	–	10,055
1911	19,362	8,445	2,110	17,044
1912	14,953	9,374	4,760	22,357
1913	30,695	13,450	21,625	46,463
1914	31,844	19,547	29,860	55,011
1915	25,079	19,896	29,595	66,335
1916	24,973	4,815	48,293	73,635
1917	31,789	19,460	46,314	59,428
1918	35,367	18,360	36,478	95,804
1919	26,825	39,834	82,760	195,117
1920	12,565	51,079	53,730	185,110
1921	10,774	47,608	59,049	144,726
1922	15,240	72,052	72,941	169,951
1923	34,202	43,113	–	99,231
1924	20,626	36,122	–	75,777
1925	23,492	40,006	–	106,834
1926	20,879	16,169	–	88,257
1927	14,284	44,212	–	54,343
1928	11,032	40,018	–	77,262
1929	25,862	46,676	–	87,652
1930	29,265	63,950	–	76,117
1931	19,755	47,499	–	48,997
1932	14,660	33,883	–	40,189
1933	17,933	39,910	–	39,493
1934	19,840	39,200	–	31,895
1935	14,802	37,340	–	29,442
1936	12,196	48,181	–	31,010
1937	27,717	69,995	–	53,260
1938	28,056	75,994	–	52,122
1939	22,509	82,176	–	47,887
1940	24,496	92,731	–	41,254

Source: Trade statistics.

Table 39. Share of oil-producing regions in total oil exports, 1900-1940

	Percentage of total Outer Islands oil exports
Southeast Kalimantan	46.61
Palembang	27.29
East Sumatra	15.99
Riau	10.04
South Sulawesi	0.03
Aceh	0.02

Source: Trade statistics.

Table 40. Bangka: tin production and labour force, 1911-1940

	Average production per year 1911-40 (in thousands of kg)	Average number of mine workers 1911-40 (in thousands)
1911-20	14,474	20,0
1921-30	18,942	19,7
1931-40	16,019	8,1

Source: Somers Heidhues 1992:129; *Jaarboek Mijnwezen* 1911-40.

Table 41.1. Tin exports (including interregional exports) from Bangka and Belitung, 1911-1940 (in metric tons)

	Exported abroad from Belitung	Exported abroad from Bangka	Exported from Bangka and Belitung to Java	Exported abroad from Java	Total volume of tin exported abroad
1911	2,740	5,111	n.a.	2,176	10,032
1912	2,910	4,762	n.a.	1,988	9,673
1913	2,512	3,508	n.a.	2,126	8,164
1914	3,580	2,319	n.a.	1,452	7,356
1915	6,063	2,285	n.a.	9,863	18,220
1916	5,970	4,512	n.a.	19,726	30,222
1917	7,050	2,536	n.a.	15,606	25,214
1918	4,578	334	n.a.	11,571	17,175
1919	9,181	954	n.a.	16,942	27,114
1920	8,790	1,367	10,265	13,549	24,385
1921	11,124	790	13,044	13,538	26,246
1922	17,657	0	10,473	15,457	34,028
1923	15,101	452	15,417	15,164	30,728
1924	16,899	1,517	10,854	15,728	34,151
1925	15,106	2,783	10,800	14,714	32,615
1926	14,475	0	14,979	16,641	31,177
1927	17,149	0	12,584	15,809	33,138
1928	17,433	9,199	14,404	14,178	42,602
1929	18,686	7,562	15,091	13,554	41,611
1930	17,291	8,029	13,760	14,589	39,909
1931	13,884	6,283	15,136	12,987	33,155
1932	7,256	2,412	6,213	8,220	17,890
1933	7,073	352	7,758	8,932	17,028
1934	9,476	1,868	10,152	10,674	23,445
1935		14,944	11,558	11,400	27,882
1936	–	22,888	12,704	13,060	39,236
1937	–	33,322	13,018	13,633	50,561
1938	–	16,998	n.a.	7,322	26,371
1939	–	24,588	n.a.	12,773	39,157
1940	–	30,339	n.a.	20,999	51,357

Source: Trade statistics; Clemens et al. 1992:74.

Notes: Belitung is included under Bangka from 1935. Interregional trade figures to Java from Bangka and Belitung for 1900-1919 and 1938-1940 are not available (n.a.).

Table 41.2. Source of foreign exports of tin, 1911-1940 (as a percentage of volume of total foreign tin exports from colonial Indonesia)

	Belitung	Bangka	Outer Islands	Java	Total volume*
1911	27.3	50.9	78.3	21.7	10,032
1912	30.1	49.2	79.4	20.6	9,673
1913	30.8	43.0	74.0	26.0	8,164
1914	48.7	31.5	80.3	19.7	7,356
1915	33.3	12.5	45.9	54.1	18,220
1916	19.8	14.9	34.7	65.3	30,222
1917	28.0	10.1	38.1	61.9	25,214
1918	26.7	1.9	32.6	67.4	17,175
1919	33.9	3.5	37.5	62.5	27,114
1920	36.0	5.6	44.4	55.6	24,385
1921	42.4	3.0	48.4	51.6	26,246
1922	51.9	0	54.6	45.4	34,028
1923	49.1	1.5	50.6	49.4	30,728
1924	49.5	4.4	53.9	46.1	34,151
1925	46.3	8.5	54.9	45.1	32,615
1926	46.4	0	46.6	53.4	31,177
1927	51.7	0	52.3	47.7	33,138
1928	40.9	21.6	66.7	33.3	42,602
1929	44.9	18.2	67.4	32.6	41,611
1930	43.3	20.1	63.4	36.6	39,909
1931	41.9	19.0	60.8	39.2	33,155
1932	40.6	13.5	54.1	45.9	17,890
1933	41.5	2.1	47.5	52.5	17,028
1934	40.4	8.0	54.5	45.5	23,445
1935	–	53.6	59.1	40.9	27,882
1936	–	58.3	66.7	33.3	39,236
1937	–	65.9	73.0	27.0	50,561
1938	–	64.5	72.2	27.8	26,371
1939	–	62.8	67.4	32.6	39,157
1940	–	59.1	59.1	40.9	51,357

* Volume in metric tons

Source: Clemens et al. 1992:74.

Table 42.1. Coal exports by volume, 1927-1934 (in thousands of tons)

	Palembang		West Sumatra		Southeast Kalimantan	
	Foreign exports	Exports to Java	Foreign exports	Exports to Java	Foreign exports	Exports to Java
1927	88	116	100	241	327	204
1928	80	121	110	186	389	220
1929	91	132	130	223	366	193
1930	111	132	120	251	357	198
1931	143	46	60	252	215	167
1932	86	27	23	224	162	103
1933	96	39	17	251	161	98
1934	102	42	17	213	123	109

Source: Trade statistics.

Table 42.2. Coal exports by value, 1927-1934 (in thousands of guilders)

	Palembang		West Sumatra		Southeast Kalimantan	
	Foreign exports	Exports to Java	Foreign exports	Exports to Java	Foreign exports	Exports to Java
1927	909	962	1,120	2,665	2,320	1,669
1928	912	1,016	1,336	2,262	3,336	2,070
1929	958	1,244	1,579	2,666	3,333	1,864
1930	1,054	1,259	1,402	2,949	3,159	1,904
1931	1,186	383	608	2,639	1,541	1,379
1932	592	152	179	1,751	778	544
1933	545	175	101	1,491	632	383
1934	480	159	85	1,072	421	371

Source: Trade statistics.

Table 43. Rubber exports from the Outer Islands, 1927-1938
(in millions of guilders; in millions of kg; as a percentage)

	Total value*	% indigenous	% estates	Total volume*	% indigenous	% estates
1927	304	49	51	228	65	35
1928	194	42	58	213	60	40
1930	112	38	60	208	57	42
1932	22	22	78	179	46	54
1934	63	48	50	298	62	36
1936	61	32	69	251	60	40
1938	106	56	44	244	60	40

* Includes exports from Riau with an unspecified value of indigenous rubber.
Source: Trade statistics.

Table 44.1. Indigenous rubber exports from major export regions by value, 1927-1938 (in thousands of guilders)

	Jambi	East Sumatra	Palembang	West Kalimantan
1927	29,697	18,342	21,777	29,916
1928	16,478	12,741	11,351	15,494
1930	9,230	5,320	5,104	9,795
1932	1,357	548	420	1,205
1934	4,030	4,999	5,343	5,772
1936	2,374	4,422	1,895	3,389
1938	8,854	8,289	9,725	12,272

	Southeast Kalimantan	West Sumatra	Riau
1927	28,740	1,395	–
1928	16,391	634	–
1930	8,907	251	–
1932	833	–	–
1934	6,144	353	–
1936	2,847	208	571
1938	11,021	1,556	1,761

Source: Trade statistics.

Table 44.2. Estate rubber exports from major export regions by value, 1927-1938 (in thousands of guilders)

	East Sumatra	Palembang	Southeast Kalimantan	West Kalimantan	Riau
1927	128,858	973	1,623	1,847	2,791
1928	89,285	688	1,403	1,276	2,228
1930	55,571	495	1,043	843	2,390*
1932	13,853	166	282	139	232
1934	25,857	331	630	244	1,112*
1936	32,481	789	974	342	385
1938	36,277	1,207	1,019	177	437

	South Sulawesi	Manado	West Sumatra	Jambi
1927	12	443	624	71
1928	55	291	544	122
1930	72	149	261	30
1932	30	25	6	7
1934	79	59	83	24
1936	144	73	164	9
1938	176	83	103	18

* Including an unknown value of indigenous rubber.
Source: Trade statistics.

Table 44.3. Indigenous rubber exports from major export regions by volume, 1927-1938 (dry-equivalent volume in tons)

	Jambi	East Sumatra	Palembang	West Kalimantan
1927	39,286	17,452	22,096	25,092
1928	33,241	19,415	17,917	21,034
1930	27,216	16,484	14,004	25,906
1932	24,793	9,343	6,866	20,637
1934	25,486	30,589	32,714	34,685
1936	25,972	17,290	21,380	37,163
1938	22,207	20,287	23,964	30,354

	Southeast Kalimantan	West Sumatra	Riau
1927	26,461	1,292	–
1928	24,007	681	–
1930	23,994	518	–
1932	13,683	–	–
1934	36,253	2,096	–
1936	30,325	2,194	4,560
1938	27,385	3,866	4,301

Source: Trade statistics.

Table 44.4. Estate rubber exports from major export regions by volume, 1927-1938 (dry-equivalent volume in tons)

	East Sumatra	Palembang	Southeast Kalimantan	Riau
1927	66,119	488	808	1,477
1928	67,642	509	981	2,447
1930	72,113	625	1,271	2,883*
1932	81,299	929	1,528	1,315
1934	89,562	1,103	2,076	5,213*
1936	79,357	1,883	2,357	950
1938	75,816	2,597	2,189	895

	West Sumatra	Jambi	West Kalimantan	South Sulawesi	Manado
1927	316	37	964	6	223
1928	396	94	967	38	203
1930	322	37	1,078	86	179
1932	24	41	845	165	140
1934	262	88	850	263	206
1936	386	20	797	342	174
1938	215	38	364	361	171

* Including an unknown quantity of indigenous rubber.
Source: Trade statistics.

Table 44.5. Reconstructed price of indigenous rubber by region, 1927-1938 (in guilders per kg)

	Jambi	East Sumatra	Palembang	West Kalimantan	Southeast Kalimantan	West Sumatra
1927	0.76	1.05	0.99	1.19	1.09	1.08
1928	0.50	0.66	0.63	0.74	0.68	0.93
1930	0.34	0.32	0.36	0.38	0.37	0.49
1932	0.05	0.06	0.06	0.06	0.06	–
1934	0.16	0.16	0.16	0.17	0.17	0.17
1936	0.09	0.26	0.09	0.09	0.09	0.09
1938	0.40	0.41	0.41	0.40	0.40	0.40

Source: Trade statistics.

Table 44.6. Reconstructed price of estate rubber by region, 1927-1938 (in guilders per kg)

	Jambi	East Sumatra	Palembang	West Kalimantan	Southeast Kalimantan	West Sumatra
1927	1.93	1.95	1.99	1.92	2.01	1.97
1928	1.30	1.32	1.35	1.32	1.43	1.38
1930	0.80	0.77	0.79	0.78	0.82	0.81
1932	0.17	0.17	0.18	0.16	0.18	0.24
1934	0.27	0.29	0.30	0.29	0.30	0.32
1936	0.42	0.41	0.42	0.43	0.41	0.42
1938	0.48	0.48	0.46	0.49	0.47	0.48

Source: Trade statistics.

Table 44.7. Regional share of indigenous rubber in total foreign rubber exports, by value, 1927-1938 (as a percentage)

	Jambi	East Sumatra	Palembang	West Kalimantan	Southeast Kalimantan	West Sumatra
1927	99.8	12.5	95.7	94.2	94.7	69.1
1928	99.3	12.5	94.3	92.4	92.1	53.8
1930	99.7	8.7	91.2	92.1	89.5	49.0
1932	99.5	3.8	71.6	89.7	74.7	0
1934	99.4	16.2	94.2	95.9	90.7	80.9
1936	99.6	12.0	70.6	90.8	74.5	55.9
1938	99.8	18.6	89.0	98.6	91.5	93.8
Average	99.6	12.0	86.7	93.4	86.8	57.5

Source: Trade statistics.

Table 44.8. Regional share of indigenous rubber in total foreign rubber exports, by dry-equivalent volume, 1927-1938 (as a percentage)

	Jambi	East Sumatra	Palembang	West Kalimantan	Southeast Kalimantan	West Sumatra
1927	99.9	20.9	97.8	96.3	97.0	80.3
1928	99.7	22.3	97.2	95.6	96.1	63.3
1930	99.9	18.6	95.7	96.0	95.0	61.7
1932	99.8	10.3	88.1	96.1	90.0	0
1934	99.7	25.5	96.7	97.6	94.6	88.9
1936	99.9	17.9	91.9	97.9	92.8	85.0
1938	99.8	21.1	90.2	98.8	92.6	94.7
Average	99.8	19.5	93.9	96.9	94.0	67.7

Source: Trade statistics.

Table 45. Total estate rubber production in 1932

	Production (in thousands of kg)	Number of estates
East Sumatra	71,197	185
Aceh	5,836	44
Tapanuli	3,929	25
Lampung	3,719	21
Riau (including Indragiri)	2,703	23
Southeast Kalimantan	1,570	54
West Kalimantan	1,091	102
Palembang	912	13
South Sulawesi	198	7
Manado	120	5
Jambi	58	34
Bengkulu	19	5
West Sumatra	7	20
Maluku	0	4
Outer Islands	91,360	544
Colonial Indonesia	150,900	1,072

Source: *Landbouwexportgewassen* 1933:90-5.

Table 46. Percentage of water and impurities in indigenous rubber as used in 1932

	Scrape	Slabs
East Sumatra	50	30
Aceh	30	15
Tapanuli	50	30
West Sumatra	30	20
Riau	30	10
Jambi	40	30
Palembang	50	30
Bangka, Belitung	50	25
West Kalimantan	50	30
Southeast Kalimantan	50	30

Source: *Landbouwexportgewassen* 1933:95.

Notes: After 1925, indigenous rubber was registered in three categories:

1. 'dry rubber through mangles' (blanket sheet, prepared, scrape-smoked, or non-smoked);
2. indigenous rubber: wet rubber; slabs ('koeken'), either wet or partly dry;
3. raw, unprocessed (unpurified) scraps (scrape rubber, usually mixed with bark) and 'earth rubber' (this was the dirtiest kind, also called 'inferior rubber').

In the trade statistics, dry equivalents were calculated by multiplying the volume by a standard moisture percentage for each category for each province. After 1 October 1934 a more detailed classification was introduced. Huff claims that all rubber exports from the Netherlands Indies between 1906 and 1932 should be reduced by 20 to 30% because of the undifferentiated export statistics. I chose not to do so, as it is repeatedly reported in the literature that rubber statistics were underrecorded in the early 1920s, which may compensate for the loss (ARA Kol, MvO 212, J. Tideman 1928:256; Huff 1994:196; Luytjes 1925b:15; Ozinga 1940:293-4, 297-8, 301).

Table 47. Difference between production and export of coffee in colonial Indonesia, 1928-1932 (in millions of kg and as a percentage)

	Estate production	Estate percentage	Smallholder production (estimates)	Smallholder percentage	Total production	Exported volume
1928	55.3	56.1	70.6	43.9	125.9	114.5
1929	55.3	51.4	58.6	48.6	113.8	81.8
1930	40.3	57.4	54.2	42.6	94.5	61.5
1931	48.7	52.8	54.5	47.2	103.2	68.6
1932	62.7	52.8	70.0	47.2	132.7	113.8

Source: *Landbouwexportgewassen* 1933:113. See for export figures for 1880-1941: Bulbeck et al. 1998:156-7.

Notes: Smallholder coffee cultivation was concentrated largely in the Outer Islands (see Table 48). Most estate coffee production was in Java (see Table 49).

Table 48. Export surplus of indigenous coffee exports from the Outer Islands in 1932 (in thousands of kg)

	Arabica	Robusta	Total
Palembang	80	28,436	28,516
Bengkulu	15	12,485	12,500
West Sumatra	498	12,026	12,524
Lampung	0	7,947	7,951
Tapanuli	1,179	3,670	4,849
South Sulawesi	1,485	0	1,485
Bali and Lombok	1,466	88	1,554
Manado	31	447	483
Timor and Dep.	33	0	33
East Sumatra	62	0	62
Outer Islands	4.850	65,099	69,958

Source: *Landbouwexportgewassen* 1933:111.

Table 49. Total estate coffee production in colonial Indonesia in 1932

	Production (in thousands of kg)	Number of estates
Lampung	2,751	14
Palembang	2,295	8
West Sumatra	1,491	21
Bengkulu	1,441	7
Manado	1,334	8
East Sumatra	1,061	5
Aceh	494	20
Sulawesi	270	11
Maluku	131	6
Tapanuli	6	3
Timor and Dep.	1	9
Bali and Lombok	1	1
Outer Islands	11,276	123
Java	51,439	303
Colonial Indonesia	62,715	426

Source: *Landbouwexportgewassen* 1933:108.

Table 50. Regional composition of coffee exports from the Outer Islands (including interregional exports), 1918-1937 (as a percentage and in millions of kg)

	West Sumatra	South Sulawesi	Palembang	Bengkulu	Lampung	Other	Total volume
1918	8.8	1.7	57.5	15.1	5.8	11.2	17
1919	16.7	5.0	37.7	8.9	5.3	26.5	45
1920	20.9	5.0	53.3	0.8	3.3	16.8	31
1921	12.8	0.1	54.6	14.6	3.0	15.0	22
1922	19.4	7.0	41.4	14.2	6.5	11.6	34
1923	14.2	0.5	53.5	15.6	5.3	11.0	26
1924	18.5	0.2	56.1	12.7	2.6	9.9	38
1925	19.4	0.1	56.8	12.3	4.2	7.2	39
1926	24.2	3.6	48.8	12.8	2.0	8.6	54
1927	27.3	3.6	39.7	17.7	2.4	9.3	62
1928	30.2	3.3	38.6	18.3	2.1	7.5	75
1929	32.5	4.2	31.6	17.9	4.4	9.3	63
1930	29.0	3.2	31.2	20.0	6.0	10.6	58
1931	30.4	4.6	40.4	5.5	6.7	12.4	46
1932	21.6	2.9	42.7	17.9	3.2	11.7	72
1933	24.2	3.8	38.6	14.1	6.2	13.1	52
1934	29.5	6.2	42.8	1.4	1.5	18.6	43
1935	23.2	3.6	36.8	17.0	4.1	15.3	56
1936	20.3	3.3	42.2	14.2	4.9	15.1	72
1937	20.0	2.8	40.6	15.5	4.7	16.5	64

Source: Trade statistics.
Note: Includes foreign exports and exports to Java.

Table 51. Regional composition of copra exports from the Outer Islands (including interregional exports), 1918-1937 (as a percentage and in millions of kg)

	South Sulawesi	Manado	Riau	West Kalimantan	West Sumatra	Other	Total volume
1918	19.9	25.7	10.9	23.3	1.9	18.3	120
1919	45.5	13.2	5.7	9.1	14.0	12.6	297
1920	35.4	13.8	4.9	19.0	10.5	16.4	166
1921	30.8	21.1	8.2	19.7	5.9	14.3	227
1922	23.9	24.5	7.3	18.5	7.3	18.5	298
1923	24.7	24.5	4.0	20.5	9.1	17.2	274
1924	25.1	22.1	8.2	19.9	7.9	16.9	290
1925	25.0	24.0	7.7	18.7	8.3	16.3	330
1926	26.4	25.2	4.2	20.6	8.7	14.9	349
1927	20.1	27.2	8.3	19.8	8.4	16.3	346
1928	24.1	25.8	5.8	18.1	7.1	19.2	426
1929	22.9	25.9	8.8	16.5	7.6	18.3	427
1930	27.3	26.5	0	20.0	8.3	17.9	360
1931	23.9	26.7	1.1	21.0	7.3	19.9	350
1932	17.2	25.9	11.6	18.6	6.5	20.2	414
1933	35.9	21.5	0	19.1	4.3	19.2	421
1934	39.3	21.2	0	17.9	4.8	16.8	378
1935	36.8	16.6	13.6	13.3	4.1	15.7	514
1936	35.0	17.7	13.6	13.7	4.2	15.8	549
1937	41.9	16.1	3.6	16.3	6.5	15.6	455

Source: Trade statistics.
Note: Includes foreign exports and exports to Java.

Table 52. Pepper exports from the Outer Islands (foreign exports only), 1901-1940 (annual average as a percentage and in thousands of kg)

	Aceh	East Sumatra	Palembang	Bangka	Lampung
1901/10	36.6	13.6	19.2	2.6	10.0
1911/20	30.4	7.9	13.8	15.8	8.5
1921/30	14.1	1.1	5.0	18.6	48.0
1931/40	2.5	0	1.9	24.9	63.4

	West Kalimantan	Southeast Kalimantan	Other Outer Islands	Total volume
1901/10	3.2	8.7	6.2	10
1911/20	11.7	10.3	1.6	13
1921/30	7.1	5.9	0.3	19
1931/40	2.2	4.7	0.2	45

Source: Trade statistics. See also Bulbeck et al. 1998:96, 100-1.

Table 53.1. Interregional coffee exports to Java as a share of total volume of coffee exports, 1918-1937 (average annual percentage)

	Palembang	West Sumatra	Lampung	Bengkulu	Manado	Other	Outer Islands
1918/22	71	29	37	57	23	40	50
1923/27	21	4	53	61	13	49	28
1928/32	28	1	34	18	7	14	20
1933/37	17	4	22	20	2	18	17

Source: Trade statistics.

Table 53.2. Interregional oil exports to Java as a share of total volume of oil exports, 1918-1937 (average annual percentage)

	Palembang	East Sumatra	Southeast Kalimantan	Outer Islands
1918/22	21	1	8	5
1923/27	12	0	8	9
1928/32	23	0	3	8
1933/37	9	0	1	4

Source: Trade statistics.

Table 53.3. Interregional rubber exports to Java as a share of total volume of rubber exports, 1918-1937 (average annual percentage)

	Palembang	East Sumatra	Southeast Kalimantan	Aceh	Jambi	West Kalimantan	Outer Islands
1918/22	8	1	8	12	0	8	4
1923/27	1	0	1	2	0	1	1
1928/32	0	0	1	0	0	1	1
1933/37	0	1	0	0	0	0	1

Source: Trade statistics.

Table 53.4. Interregional copra exports to Java as a share of total volume of copra exports, 1918-1937 (average annual percentage)

	South Sulawesi	Manado	West Kalimantan	Outer Islands
1918/22	12	14	35	19
1923/27	1	2	5	4
1928/32	4	3	1	5
1933/37	1	0	13	5

Source: Trade statistics.

Table 54.1. Share of imports of rice and selected foodstuffs by region (including imports from Java), 1924-1938 (as a percentage of total imports per province)

	Rice imports			Selected foodstuffs		
	1924/28	1929/33	1934/38	1924/28	1929/33	1934/38
East Sumatra	23.5	20.7	14.8	3.2	3.0	3.5
Palembang	10.8	7.2	2.1	3.0	2.2	2.8
Southeast Kalimantan	14.0	6.8	1.7	2.3	1.8	1.0
Aceh	11.0	13.2	4.8	4.9	3.7	3.6
West Sumatra	1.9	2.2	0.4	2.2	1.7	0.7
Jambi	36.4	40.6	15.2	5.1	5.2	4.4
Lampung	5.1	3.5	1.5	0.6	0.8	1.9
West Kalimantan	32.1	33.2	16.7	3.8	3.1	2.5
South Sulawesi	1.5	0.4	0.2	1.6	1.5	1.6
Manado	36.2	44.7	13.4	1.9	1.2	1.2
Riau	32.6	30.3	16.0	2.4	1.9	2.9
Bangka	44.6	37.7	19.3	2.1	1.2	1.1
Belitung	23.0	23.8	8.4	0.9	0.7	0.7
Tapanuli	5.9	3.3	0.3	2.9	1.6	1.2
Bengkulu	8.0	6.9	1.5	1.0	0.8	0.9
Maluku	36.3	34.7	17.3	2.1	1.4	1.3
Bali and Lombok	1.3	2.1	0.8	1.2	0.6	0.2
Timor and Dep.	8.9	5.4	1.4	2.5	2.4	1.9

Source: Trade statistics.
Notes: The selected imports are calculated as a percentage of the total imports per province, in five-year periods (based on value). Selected foodstuffs other than rice include flour, fresh fish, dried fish, coffee, and coconut oil. These figures cover both foreign imports and imports from Java; no distinction can be made between European and indigenous imports. Note that these figures merely give the proportion of total imports and tell us nothing about whether the absolute values increased or fell. See Table 25.2 for total average annual imports in these five-year periods, and for the percentage of this trade that was imported from Java (in thousands of guilders and as a percentage).

Table 54.2. Share of imports of selected consumer goods and selected capital goods by region (including imports from Java), 1924-1938 (as a percentage of total imports per province)

	Selected consumer goods			Selected capital goods		
	1924/28	1929/33	1934/38	1924/28	1929/33	1934/38
East Sumatra	18.0	11.6	11.5	16.1	14.0	16.2
Palembang	19.6	11.5	11.4	25.5	24.9	35.0
Southeast Kalimantan	15.5	9.7	11.0	28.1	18.7	12.7
Aceh	30.6	14.5	9.9	4.1	6.3	9.7
West Sumatra	36.0	22.4	25.4	11.9	12.0	12.0
Jambi	19.3	11.9	7.9	6.1	4.1	6.3
Lampung	10.8	8.5	9.0	13.6	11.4	6.2
West Kalimantan	18.9	12.1	11.5	4.7	3.8	4.7
South Sulawesi	30.0	23.3	22.7	6.1	7.6	7.3
Manado	27.4	17.9	20.4	6.3	6.2	5.6
Riau	11.7	8.6	11.0	21.4	12.1	23.1
Bangka	11.1	5.4	4.3	8.2	9.9	26.8
Belitung	6.6	4.0	5.6	19.5	18.6	10.3
Tapanuli	18.6	8.6	4.0	11.9	9.7	7.7
Bengkulu	10.7	8.4	10.4	15.0	13.0	11.3
Maluku	18.7	7.7	6.6	6.0	5.0	5.1
Bali and Lombok	36.8	25.0	26.2	8.4	9.5	6.1
Timor and Dep.	22.9	14.6	13.0	9.6	9.7	7.4

Source: Trade statistics.

Notes: Selected imports are calculated as a percentage of total imports per province, for five-year periods. Selected consumer goods include textiles, clothes, cigars, gambir, and motorcars, but no foodstuffs. Selected capital goods are machines, iron (such as nails, bars, pipes, rails), cement, and trucks. These figures include foreign imports and imports from Java. See Table 25.2 for total average annual imports in these five-year periods, and for the percentage of this trade that was imported from Java (in thousands of guilders and as a percentage).

Table 55. Per capita import value by region (including imports from Java), 1923-1938 (index 1923 = 100)

	East Sumatra	Palembang	Southeast Kalimantan	Bangka	Belitung	Riau	West Kalimantan	Jambi	Lampung
1923	100	100	100	100	100	100	100	100	100
1924	109	125	123	118	148	114	105	115	144
1925	130	196	171	163	145	154	161	228	172
1926	152	225	194	162	221	184	170	228	210
1927	189	228	175	199	206	144	154	228	244
1928	192	223	167	192	224	155	140	154	284
1929	205	330	217	222	224	151	130	154	348
1930	177	261	159	205	196	115	102	112	274
1931	109	125	84	146	91	67	65	69	159
1932	77	85	66	92	50	47	47	49	122
1933	65	73	61	70	35	36	41	42	99
1934	65	91	66	74	40	33	40	48	101
1935	63	94	57	81	0	38	40	45	104
1936	72	94	66	100	0	54	45	52	98
1937	110	192	130	163	0	88	93	152	106
1938	104	164	107	166	0	98	60	85	145

	West Sumatra	South Sulawesi	Manado	Aceh	Bengkulu	Bali	Maluku	Tapanuli	Timor
1923	100	100	100	100	100	100	100	100	100
1924	118	115	93	101	120	127	88	105	84
1925	129	139	118	122	170	149	92	159	90
1926	134	133	121	134	208	153	95	220	117
1927	132	132	108	140	218	161	80	230	98
1928	142	148	124	158	224	191	87	202	96
1929	148	137	109	168	220	187	89	198	103
1930	117	127	91	146	150	158	75	148	77
1931	82	95	56	100	116	94	50	97	66
1932	59	69	45	70	92	64	34	70	47
1933	49	64	37	55	64	54	24	61	43
1934	46	57	25	48	55	52	19	55	35
1935	42	59	32	45	53	57	22	48	37
1936	43	65	36	39	55	63	25	52	36
1937	72	90	47	55	67	84	36	76	49
1938	55	84	30	51	59	82	37	76	62

Source: Trade statistics.

Note: Includes foreign imports and imports from Java. It should be noted that these indices are based on current (nominal) prices, which ought to be deflated in order to analyse imports in 'real' or volume terms. See also Appendix C.

Table 56.1. Foreign rice imports and interregional rice trade, 1917-1926 (annual average in millions of kg)

	Foreign imports	+ Imports from Java	– Exports to Java	– Exports to Outer Islands	= Net imports*
East Sumatra	109	1	0	1	109
Southeast Kalimantan	33	3	0	0.1	36
West Kalimantan	35	0.08	0	0	35
Bangka	21	8	0	0	29
Palembang	27	2	0.2	2	26
Belitung	24	0	0	0	24
Riau	22	1	0.04	0.2	23
Manado	16	0.03	0	0	16
Jambi	13	2	0	0.1	15
Maluku	12	3	0	0.3	14
Aceh	6	0.1	0	1	5
Lampung	0.1	3	0.6	0	3
Bengkulu	0.01	2	0	0	2
Tapanuli	2	0.1	0	0.1	2
Timor and Dep.	0	1	0.5	0.4	0.1
West Sumatra	1	1	1	3	-2
South Sulawesi	6	0.4	0.1	9	-3
Bali and Lombok	1	1	9	6	-13
Outer Islands	326	30	12	23	321

* Calculated as foreign imports plus imports from Java minus exports to Java minus exports to other Outer Islands.

Source: Trade statistics.

Notes: Calculated over the years 1917, 1920, 1923, and 1926. Foreign rice exports are assumed to be negligible and were not included.

Table 56.2. Foreign rice imports and interregional rice trade, 1929-1937 (annual average in millions of kg)

	Foreign imports	+ Imports from Java	- Exports to Java	- Exports to Outer Islands	= Net imports*
East Sumatra	180	23	0	1	203
Bengkulu	0.4	97	0	0.1	98
Bangka	40	7	0	0	46
West Kalimantan	40	7	0	0	46
Manado	35	3	0	0.04	38
Riau	20	1	0	0.1	21
Southeast Kalimantan	13	7	0.09	0.2	19
Palembang	15	7	1	2	19
Jambi	16	3	0	0.4	19
Maluku	8	2	0	0	11
Belitung	9	2	0	0.09	11
Aceh	9	2	0	0.6	10
West Sumatra	3	1	0	0.6	3
Lampung	0.3	3	0.5	0.1	3
Tapanuli	1	0.02	0	1	0.5
Timor and Dep.	0.02	0.5	0.4	1	-1
Bali and Lombok	0.06	0.5	7	10	-17
South Sulawesi	0.3	0.4	0.8	30	-30
Outer Islands	389	167	10	46	500

* Calculated as foreign imports plus imports from Java minus exports to Java and exports to the other Outer Islands.
Source: Trade statistics.
Notes: Calculated over the years 1929, 1932, 1935, and 1937. Foreign rice exports are assumed to be negligible and were not included in this table.

Table 56.3. Rice trade in Java and the Outer Islands (annual average in millions of kg)

	1917, 1920, 1923, 1926	1929, 1932, 1935, 1938	1939, 1940*
Java:			
Foreign imports to Java	230	159	n.a.
Imports from Outer Islands	9	8	22
Exports to Outer Islands	30	22	150
Net interregional exports	21	14	128
Outer Islands:			
Foreign imports to Outer Islands	326	425	
Imports from Java	30	22	
Exports to Java	9	8	

* From Creutzberg 1978, table 6, quoted in Dick 1990:311.
Source: Trade statistics; Dick 1990:311.

Table 56.4. Domestic rice trade of Java, Bali, and South Sulawesi, 1917-1937 (in thousands of kg)

	Java		Bali		South Sulawesi			
	Exports to Outer Islands	Imports from Outer Islands	Exports to Java	Exports to Outer Islands	Imports from Java	Exports to Java	Exports to Outer Islands	Imports from Java
1917	32,762	20,562	15,171	3,071	1,438	255	12,596	432
1918	33,539	11,902	9,956	–	30	561	–	593
1919	50,453	6,687	6,084	–	6	21	–	–
1920	36,416	5,009	3,195	145	.	67	1,066	2
1921	–	–	10,315	–	536	45	–	1,130
1922	16,468	8,356	6,074	–	.	13	–	923
1923	18,608	15,706	12,513	13,672	101	41	10,234	471
1924	16,387	13,554	10,037	–	155	58	–	237
1925	33,797	4,999	4,784	–	1,418	179	–	227
1926	32,653	4,508	4,395	5,258	1,335	77	10,893	734
1927	38,724	9,567	9,120	–	980	367	–	489
1928	33,548	11,965	11,716	–	286	107	–	311
1929	30,135	9,824	9,495	9,178	678	95	20,661	142
1930	30,621	5,482	5,135	–	2,428	27	–	201
1931	29,837	7,359	6,973	–	3,462	174	–	273
1932	17,083	10,997	10,433	7,740	324	223	17,667	284
1933	27,053	7,136	4,662	–	323	301	–	90
1934	55,483	22,661	12,472	–	119	6514	–	61
1935	41,815	10,332	4,164	11,258	282	1116	36,339	27
1936	101,998	9,464	1,135	–	2,409	141	–	490
1937	197,143	10,251	5,640	10,457	690	1803	44,719	1,162

Source: Trade statistics.

Table 57. Pearson correlation coefficient between import and export values, 1900-1940

	M/X 1900-1940 (N = 41)	M/lag(X) 1904-1940 (N = 37)	M/lag2(X) 1904-1940 (N = 37)	M/X 1901-1940 First differences
Lampung	0.94	0.91	0.79	0.85
Jambi	0.91	0.85	0.78	0.78
West Kalimantan	0.89	0.86	0.74	0.74
West Sumatra	0.87	0.81	0.50	0.52
East Sumatra	0.84	0.88	0.80	0.51
Southeast Kalimantan	0.83	0.81	0.74	0.35
South Sulawesi	0.83	0.91	0.64	0.33
Bengkulu	0.81	0.72	0.53	0.40
Palembang	0.80	0.77	0.74	0.45
Belitung	0.79	0.82	0.77	-0.02
Riau	0.79	0.74	0.74	0.55
Maluku	0.76	0.74	0.61	0.37
Tapanuli	0.67	0.55	0.23	0.33
Bangka	0.65	0.67	0.59	0.27
Bali and Lombok	0.52	0.54	0.33	0.31
Manado	0.46	0.38	0.30	0.15
Aceh	0.40	0.45	0.44	0.31
Timor and Dep.	0.03	-0.08	-0.15	0.02
All Outer Islands	0.90	0.91	0.80	0.54

Source: Trade statistics.

Notes: Only foreign trade. Maluku includes Ternate, Ambon, and New Guinea. Belitung: 1900-1934, Tapanuli: 1908-1940. Riau includes Indragiri. For Riau *without* Indragiri (N = 41): R = 0.79. For Indragiri (N = 34): R = 0.93.

M/Lag(X) is the correlation coefficient between foreign imports and the foreign exports of the previous year. Similarly, M/Lag2(X) is the degree to which foreign imports correlate with the value of foreign exports two years earlier. Because the lag calculations could only be calculated over the period 1904-1940 (N = 37), the M/X correlation was also calculated over this shorter period. This yielded the same values as the M/X correlation over 1900-1940 (N = 41).

'First differences' calculates the correlation over the first differences of each time series, thus eliminating the effects of the common trend. All regions are based on 1901-1940 data, except Belitung 1901-1934 and Tapanuli 1909-1940. These results show that, in fact, only in Lampung, Jambi, and West Kalimantan do imports display a significant correlation with exports.

Table 58. Payments made by the tobacco industry in East Sumatra, 1926-1938 (in thousands of guilders)

	1926	1928	1930	1932	1934	1936	1938
Salaries of Europeans	4,750	4,750	4,750	3,475	2,305	2,254	2,453
Wages of non-Europeans	24,285	28,053	26,657	13,851	10,027	10,190	11,511
Indigenous suppliers to estates	3,168	4,753	2,795	765	690	704	943
Rentals etc. (*hasil tanah*)	4,896	544	556	489	457	460	470
Taxes	6,050	3,848	2,753	1,672	506	691	1,677
Medical care, rice, housing	3,580	3,393	2,368	1,755	1,108	1,035	794
Pensions	446	510	505	452	295	204	273
Immigration and repatriation costs	1,562	1,940	1,120	621	96	126	158
Contributions of a nonobligatory nature	39	62	41	61	54	21	10
Total	48,776	47,854	41,545	23,140	15,538	15,685	18,288
Area under tobacco (in 1000 ha)	19	21	20	17	11	12	13
Payments per planted hectare (in thousands of guilders)	2.5	2.3	2.1	1.4	1.4	1.3	1.4
Percentage paid in wages (to non-Europeans)	50%	59	64	60	65	65	63
Percentage paid as taxes	12%	8	7	7	3	4	9

Source: Pelzer 1978:110; De Ridder 1935:80-1.
Notes: I have added the share of taxes. The figures were originally derived from the annual reports of the DPV and the AVROS as collected by T. Volker (see De Ridder 1935:79-80; De Waard 1934:282 and Thee Kian Wie 1977:103).

Table 59. Percentage of Indonesians engaged in estate agriculture, indigenous agriculture, and non-agricultural sectors by region in Sumatra in 1930

	Estate agriculture	Indigenous agriculture	Total agriculture	Non-agricultural sector
East Sumatra	45.2	38.3	83.5	16.5
Lampung	13.3	64.8	78.1	21.9
Aceh	8.1	70.8	87.9	21.1
West Sumatra	2.2	81.0	83.2	16.8
Tapanuli	2.7	86.1	88.8	11.2
Jambi	1.1	88.3	89.4	10.6

Source: *Volkstelling* 1933, IV:92-93. Quoted in Thee Kian Wie 1977:110.
Note: This table refers to both indigenous Batak/Malay and Javanese inhabitants.

Table 60.1. Coolies in East Sumatra, 1919-1932

	Average total number of coolies	Number of laid-off coolies	Laid-off coolies in per cent
1919	288,428		
1920	301,998	22,705	7.5
1924	233,285	18,396	7.9
1928	318,672	24,778	7.8
1930	356,646	41,983	11.8
1932	214,174	53,993	25.2

Source: Figures from the Labour Inspectorate. ARA, Kol. 1901-63, MvO 188 H.E.K. Ezerman (East Sumatra 1933) appendix 41 G-H.

Table 60.2. Coolie immigration 1933-1938 and restitution by the Registration Office per coolie

	Number of immigrant workers	Restituted sum (in guilders)
1934	4,750	6.70
1935	12,917	2.95
1936	17,624	2.07
1937	53,898	0.38
1938	17,252	0.99

Source: ARA, Kol. 1901-63, NHM vol. 9127: VvS 509 (Agency Medan 1933), 6; VvS 513 (Agency Medan 1937) 11-2; VvS 514 (Agency Medan 1938) 9; VvS 515 (Agency Medan 1939) 4.

Table 60.3. Coolies in East Sumatra with contracts containing the penal clause, 1925-1938

	Total number of coolies	Under penal clause in per cent
1925	222,018	88.6
1929	302,703	86.5
1930	285,285	82.8
1932	167,837	16.3
1933	170,598	7.0
1934	166,776	3.6
1938	206,498	2.9

Source: Langeveld 1978:appendix III; ARA, Kol. 1901-63, NHM vol. 9127: VvS 505 (Agency Medan 1929); VvS 510 (Agency Medan 1934) 3; VvS 511 (Agency Medan 1935) 5; VvS 513 (Agency Medan 1937) 3; VvS 514 (Agency Medan 1938) 4.

Table 60.4. Total coolie population by province, 1922 and 1929

	1922	1929		1922	1929
East Sumatra	189,300	302,700	Tapanuli	3,700	7,300
Palembang	8,600	40,780	Maluku	2,100	3,800
Bangka + Belitung	37,600	39,700	Manado	1,900	2,000
(Belitung		19,000)	Jambi	0	1,400
Southeast Kalimantan	19,200	36,300	West Kalimantan	600	1,400
Aceh	9,000	29,940	South Sulawesi	0	100
West Sumatra	16,600	26,600	Bali and Timor	0	0
Bengkulu	8,700	16,500			
Lampung	10,800	16,000			
Riau	7,300	10,100	Total	315,500	534,200

Source: Tergast 1931-32:232; *Statistisch Jaaroverzicht* 1929 (*Indisch Verslag* 1930):226.
Note: Includes both contract coolies and so-called 'free' coolies. *Statistisch Jaaroverzicht* gives lower figures.

Table 60.5. Javanese coolies in East Sumatra, 1919-1939 (in thousands)

	1 Recruited in Java	2 Returned to Java	3 Deceased	4 Deceased Javanese	5 Net change	6 Total no. Javanese	7 Change	8 Settled
1919	43	13	19.24	4.2	25.8	216		
1920	35	16	13.50	3.0	16.0	222	6	10.0
1921	22	31	10.00	1.9	10.9	189	33	22.1
1922	7	24	7.91	1.3	18.3	159	30	11.7
1923	11	16	5.51	0.9	5.9	155	4	1.9
1924	22	15	5.95	1.0	6.0	171	16	10.0
1925	43	13	6.09	1.2	28.8	193	22	6.8
1926	50	16	8.38	1.8	32.2	218	25	7.2
1927	45	15	7.15	1.7	28.3	237	19	9.3
1928	39	17	7.81	2.0	20.0	252	15	5.0
1929	60	22	7.28	2.0	36.0	272	20	16.0
1930	25	25	7.23	1.9	1.9	260	12	10.1
1931	0.6	24	5.86	1.2	24.6	205	55	30.4
1932	0	21	4.63	0.7	21.7	151	54	32.3
1933	0	7	6.24	0.9	7.9	149	2	5.9
1934	0	4	7.96	1.1	5.1	143	6	0.9
1935	3	3	8.39	1.4	1.4	170	27	28.4
1936	5	1	6.71	1.2	2.8	178	8	5.2
1937	42	6	7.88	1.7	34.3	212	34	0.3
1938	15	6	7.71	1.6	7.4	207	5	12.4
1939	17	9	6.56	1.4	6.6	210	3	3.6

Source: Langeveld 1978:tables I-III and appendix III.
Notes: Total number of Javanese workers includes female workers (on average 30-40%). 'Net change', Column 5, is the result of subtracting the second and fourth columns of this table from the first column. This forms the annual increase, considering the number of recruited, returned, and deceased Javanese coolies. In Column 7,

'Change' represents the change in total number of coolies compared to the previous year. The difference between Columns 7 and 5 is the number of coolies that were either sent away to or recruited from the region surrounding the estates (Column 8). The average of all the figures in Column 8 is 6.3, which means that each year, an average of 6,300 coolies left the estates without returning to Java. This amounted to 126,700 coolies over the whole period.
In the decade preceding the Depression, the annual average was 7,800 coolies, amounting to 86,300 settlers in the 1920s.

Table 61: Bankruptcy among import traders in East Sumatra, 1919-1939

	Total Bankruptcies	European firms	Chinese firms	European Percentage	Chinese Percentage
1919	95	16	64	17	67
1920	112	26	67	23	60
1921	148	37	88	25	59
1922	208	28	127	13	61
1923	120	23	65	19	54
1924	104	12	68	12	65
1925	90	18	48	20	53
1926	52				
1927	77				
1928	78				
1929	103				
1930	171	34	108	20	63
1931	287	35	209	12	73
1932	262	30	180	11	69
1933	183	28	107	15	58
1934	137	13	88	9	64
1935	153	15	101	10	66
1936	96	15	68	16	71
1937	69	17	37	25	54
1938	105	11	75	10	71
1939	138	16	101	12	73

Source: ARA, Kol. 1901-63, NHM vol. 9127: VvS 495 (Agency Medan 1919); VvS 504 (Agency Medan 1928) 16; VvS 506 (Agency Medan 1930) 10; VvS 507 (Agency Medan 1931) 9; VvS 508 (Agency Medan 1932) 12; VvS 509 (Agency Medan 1933) 21; VvS 510 (Agency Medan 1934) 15; VvS 511 (Agency Medan 1935) 14-15; VvS 512 (Agency Medan 1936) 16; VvS 513 (Agency Medan 1937) 17; VvS 514 (Agency Medan 1938) 14; VvS 515 (Agency Medan 1939) 9.
Note: Includes only clients of the NHM.

Table 62. Government revenues and expenditure in colonial Indonesia, 1924-1929 (in thousands of guilders)

	Revenues	(Taxes)*	Expenditure	Budget surplus
1924	494,475	320,040	401,765	92,710
1925	523,591	341,559	415,088	108,503
1926	531,749	344,175	431,522	100,227
1927	511,735	322,238	465,957	45,778
1928	543,483	361,218	501,590	41,893
1929	516,539	344,772	502,320	14,219
Average	520,262	339,000 (= 65.2%)	453,040	67,222

* Taxes are also included in the figures for Revenues.
Source: *Statistisch Jaaroverzicht* 1929 (*Indisch Verslag* 1930), II:441.

Table 63.1. Government expenditure in the Outer Islands by province, 1929-1930 (in thousands of guilders)

	1929			1930		
	L	LS	T	L	LS	T
Aceh	13,812	3,179	16,991	12,963	3,055	16,018
Tapanuli	5,788		5,788	5,772		5,772
East Sumatra	14,222	7,021	21,243	15,705	7,222	22,927
West Sumatra	18,469		18,469	15,185		15,185
Bengkulu	3,615		3,615	3,048		3,048
Lampung	2,848		2,848	3,500		3,500
Jambi	2,891		2,891	3,486		3,486
Palembang	16,964		16,964	14,805		14,805
Riau	2,384	628	3,012	2,559	788	3,347
Bangka	6,770		6,770	2,608		2,608
Belitung	875		875	888		888
West Kalimantan	4,136	1,890	6,026	4,713	1,950	6,663
Southeast Kalimantan	8,555	2,599	11,154	8,990	2,664	11,654
South Sulawesi	9,494	4,920	14,414	9,860	4,754	14,614
Manado	6,562	2,325	8,887	7,014	2,418	9,432
Bali	4,820		4,820	4,722		4,722
Timor and Dep.	2,774	2,500	5,274	2,720	2,756	5,476
Maluku	7,809	1,185	8,994	8,198	1,317	9,515
Total Outer Islands			159,035 (= 30 %)			153,660 (= 30%)
Java			364,859			362,993

Source: *Statistisch Jaaroverzicht* 1929 (*Indisch Verslag* 1930):470-1; *Statistisch Jaaroverzicht* 1930 (*Indisch Verslag* 1931):460-1, 494-506.
Notes: L = *Landskassen* (residency treasuries); LS = *Landschapskassen* (district treasuries / indirectly administered territories); T = Total

Table 63.2. Government revenues in the Outer Islands by province, 1929-1930 (in thousands of guilders)

	1929			1930		
	L	LS	T	L	LS	T
Aceh	8,689	3,479	12,168	8,120	3,055	11,175
Tapanuli	5,959		5,959	5,798		5,798
East Sumatra	48,069	9,073	57,142	43,949	7,224	51,173
West Sumatra	14,215		14,215	14,073		14,073
Bengkulu	3,668		3,668	3,551		3,551
Lampung	5,558		5,558	5,533		5,533
Jambi	3,628		3,628	3,895		3,895
Palembang	18,712		18,712	20,044		20,044
Riau	6,953	623	7,576	5,407	788	6,195
Bangka	9,411		9,411	9,831		9,831
Belitung	6,065		6,065	5,074		5,074
West Kalimantan	8,763	2,030	10,793	7,315	1,951	9,266
Southeast Kalimantan	14,744	2,917	17,661	12,876	2,664	15,540
South Sulawesi	11,517	5,593	17,110	12,452	4,754	17,206
Manado	7,072	2,694	9,766	6,119	2,417	8,536
Bali	7,822		7,822	8,235		8,235
Timor and Dep.	2,097	2,781	4,878	2,211	2,756	4,967
Maluku	5,204	1,296	6,500	6,453	1,317	7,770
Total Outer Islands			218,632 (= 34%)			207,862 (= 38 %)
Java			416,227			342,220

Source: *Statistisch Jaaroverzicht* 1929 (*Indisch Verslag* 1930):470-1; *Statistisch Jaaroverzicht* 1930 (*Indisch Verslag* 1931):460-1, 494-506.

Table 64. Government budgets of the Outer Islands by province: per km², per capita, and as a percentage of total exports

	A	B	C	D	E	F	G	H	I
East Sumatra	1,674	94.6	280.2	242	541	14	31	8	18
Palembang	1,096	86.4	100.3	171	232	14	18	15	20
Southeast Kalimantan	1,367	392.7	166.4	30	40	9	11	7	9
Aceh	1,003	55.4	17.9	289	202	16	11	89	62
West Sumatra	1,919	49.8	44.1	305	283	8	7	34	32
Jambi	245	44.9	28.1	78	87	14	16	12	14
Lampung	360	28.8	22.9	122	192	10	15	15	24
West Kalimantan	828	146.8	54.7	45	63	8	11	12	17
South Sulawesi	3,087	100.5	57.8	145	171	5	6	25	30
Manado	1,139	88.6	33.0	106	96	8	7	29	26
Belitung	73	4.8	36.5	184	1,050	12	69	2	14
Bangka	205	11.9	49.5	218	823	13	48	5	20
Riau	298	31.7	28.5	106	195	11	21	12	22
Tapanuli	1,041	39.1	19.3	148	148	6	6	30	30
Bengkulu	323	26.2	16.4	116	135	9	11	19	22
Maluku	893	496.5	15.2	19	16	11	9	63	51
Bali and Lombok	1,802	10.3	20.5	459	800	3	5	23	40
Timor and Dep.	1,657	63.3	4.9	86	78	3	3	112	101
AVG per province			65.8	159	286	10	17	29.2	21.4
STD			55.3	108	297	4	17	28.4	30.7
VC (coefficient of variation)			1.2	0.7	1.0	0.4	1.0	1.0	0.7

Source: Tables 14, 25.1, 63.1, and 63.2.

Notes:

A : Total population 1930 (x 1000)

B : Area (1,000,000 km²)

C : Average annual exports (foreign plus interregional) in 1924-1928 (in millions of guilders)

D : Total expenditure 1930 per km² (in guilders per km²)

E : Total revenues 1930 per km² (in guilders per km²)

F : Total expenditures 1930 per 1000 inhabitants (guilders per 1000 inhabitants)

G : Total revenues 1930 per 1000 inhabitants (guilders per 1000 inhabitants)

H : Total expenditures 1930 as a percentage of the average annual export value 1924-1928 (foreign plus interregional)

I : Total revenues 1930 as a percentage of the average annual export value 1924-1928 (foreign plus interregional)

VC: Coefficient of variation, calculated as standard deviation (STD) divided by the mean (AVG).

Table 65. Per capita trade in 1926-1930 and per capita government expenditure and revenues in 1930 (index East Sumatra = 100)

	Expenditure 1930	Revenues 1930	Average exports per capita 1926/30	Average imports per capita 1926/30
East Sumatra	100	100	100	100
Palembang	100	58	63	72
Southeast Kalimantan	64	35	73	59
Aceh	114	35	11	18
West Sumatra	57	23	15	26
Jambi	100	52	59	60
Lampung	71	48	52	59
West Kalimantan	57	35	39	48
South Sulawesi	36	19	13	16
Manado	57	23	20	22
Belitung	86	223	295	233
Bangka	93	155	199	123
Riau	79	68	59	71
Tapanuli	43	19	11	10
Bengkulu	64	35	34	36
Maluku	79	29	18	17
Bali and Lombok	21	16	8	10
Timor and Dep.	21	10	2	2
Average	69	55	60	55
Standard deviation	27	53	73	54
Coefficient of variation	0.4	1.0	1.2	1.0

Source: Tables 26.1 and 26.2; Table 64, Columns F and G.
Note: In this table the provinces are grouped into the four clusters

Correlation coefficients:
- per capita expenditure in 1930 and per capita average exports in 1926-1930: $R = 0.44$ ($N = 18$, $R^2 = 0.19$).
- per capita expenditure in 1930 and per capita revenues in 1930: $R = 0.51$ ($N = 18$, $R^2 = 0.26$).
- average per capita imports in 1926-1930 and average per capita exports in 1926-1930: $R = 0.95$ ($N = 18$, $R^2 = 0.98$).

Figures

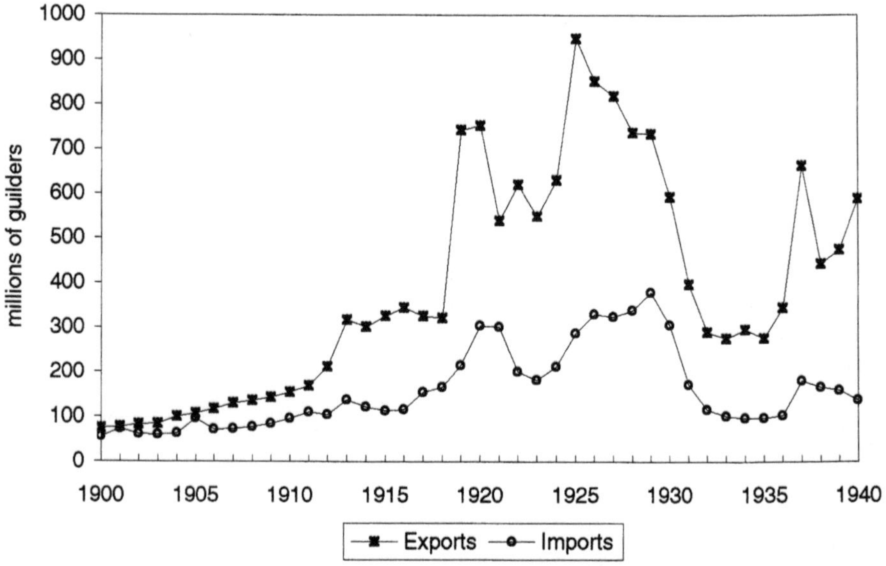

Figure 20. Foreign trade of the Outer Islands: exports and imports, 1900-1940 (Trade statistics).

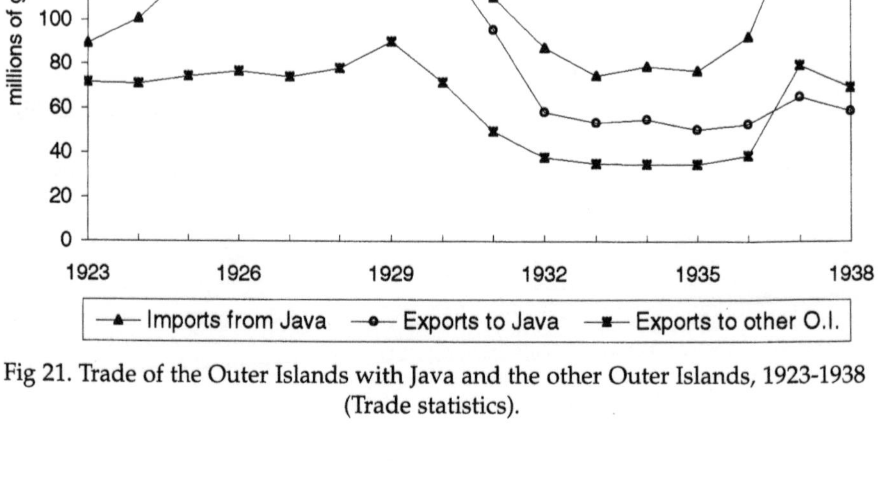

Fig 21. Trade of the Outer Islands with Java and the other Outer Islands, 1923-1938 (Trade statistics).

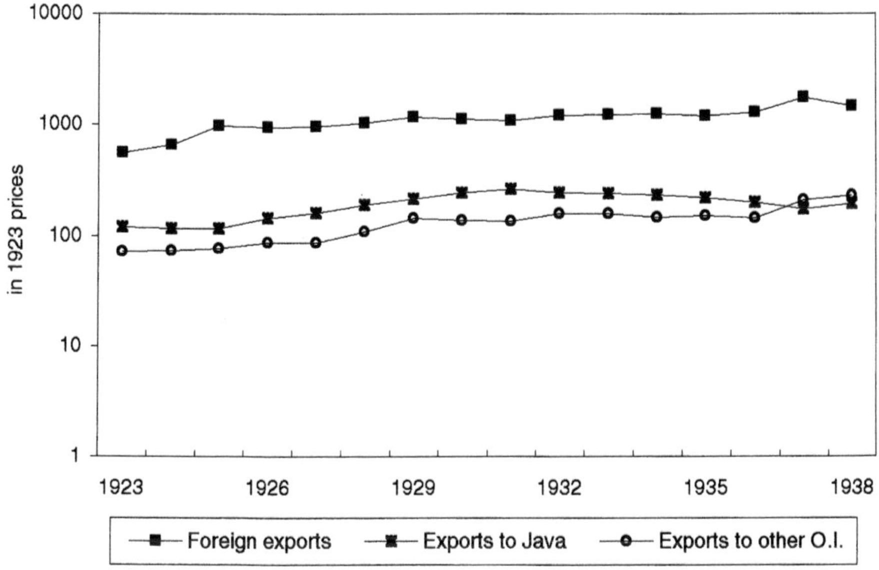

Figure 22. Growth of foreign and interregional exports from the Outer Islands deflated by Van Ark price index, 1923-1938 (Trade statistics).

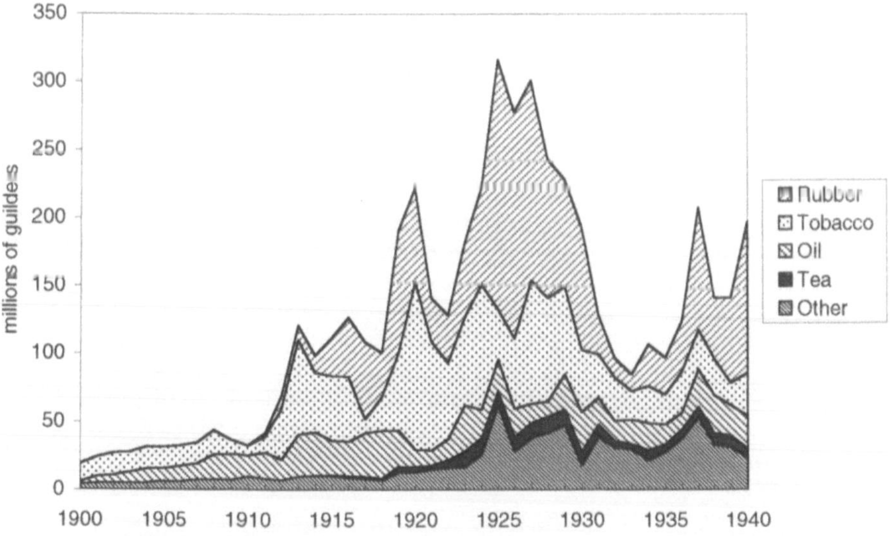

Figure 23a. Composition of foreign exports, 1900-1940: East Sumatra (Trade statistics).

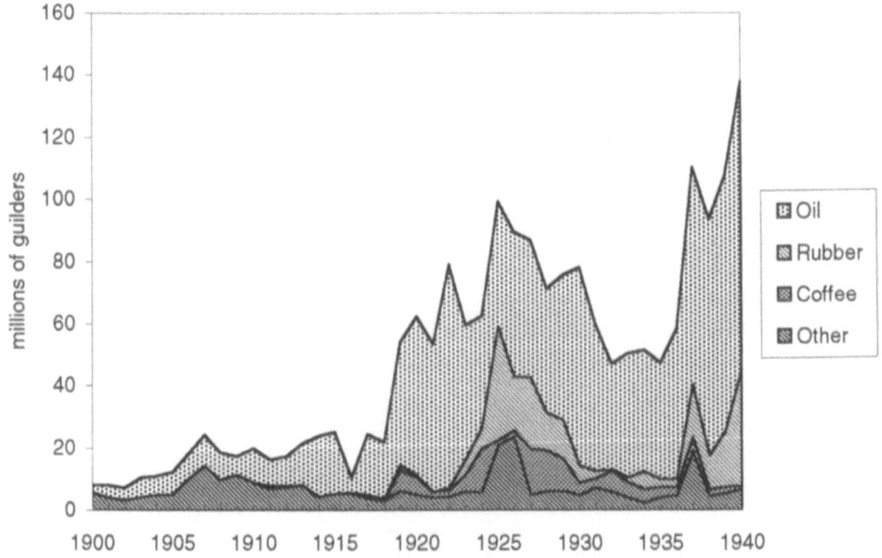

Figure 23b. Composition of foreign exports, 1900-1940: Palembang (Trade statistics).

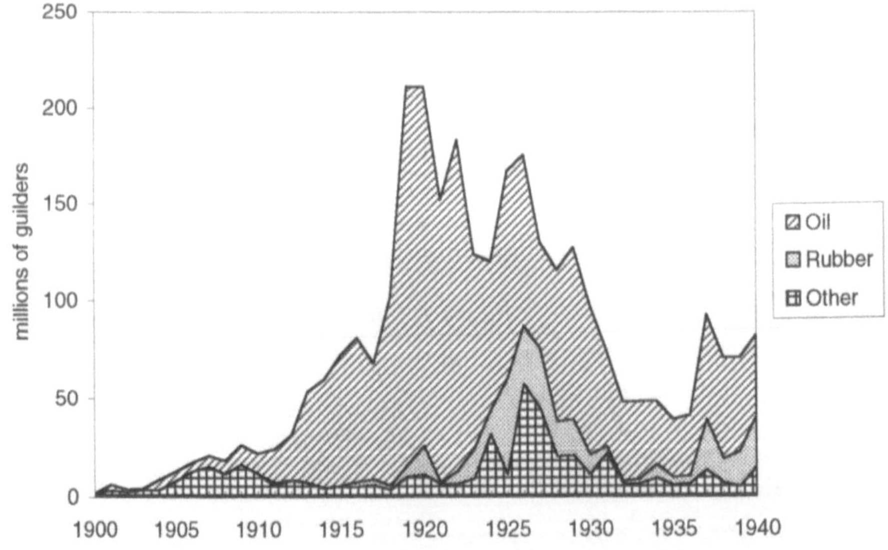

Figure 23c. Composition of foreign exports, 1900-1940: Southeast Kalimantan (Trade statistics).

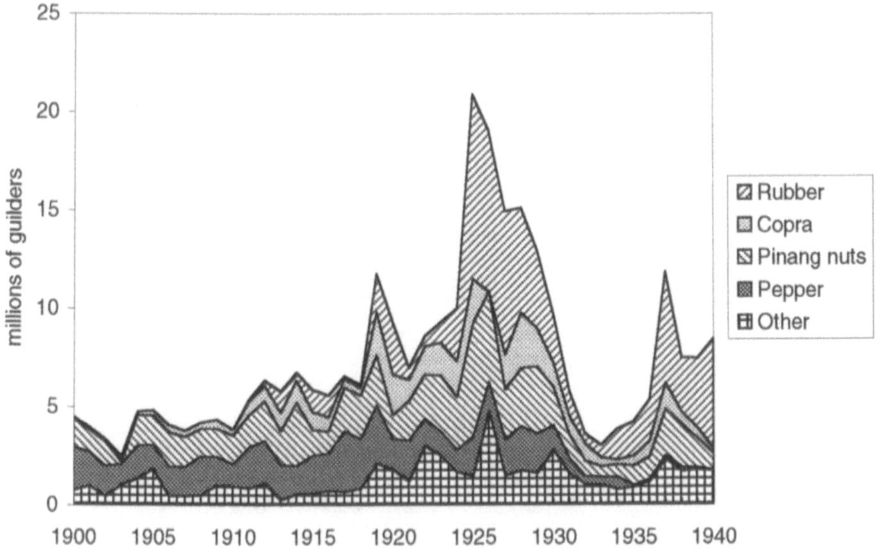

Figure 23d. Composition of foreign exports, 1900-1940: Aceh (Trade statistics).

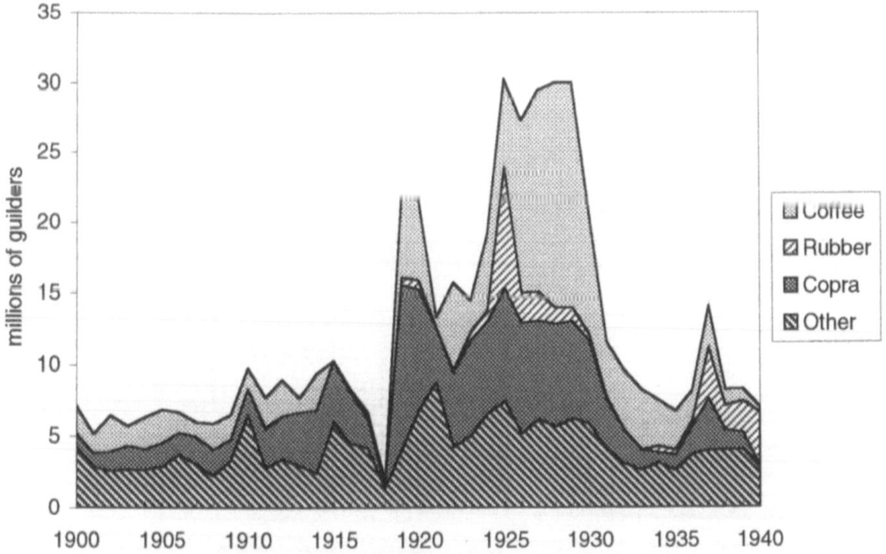

Figure 23e. Composition of foreign exports, 1900-1940: West Sumatra (Trade statistics).

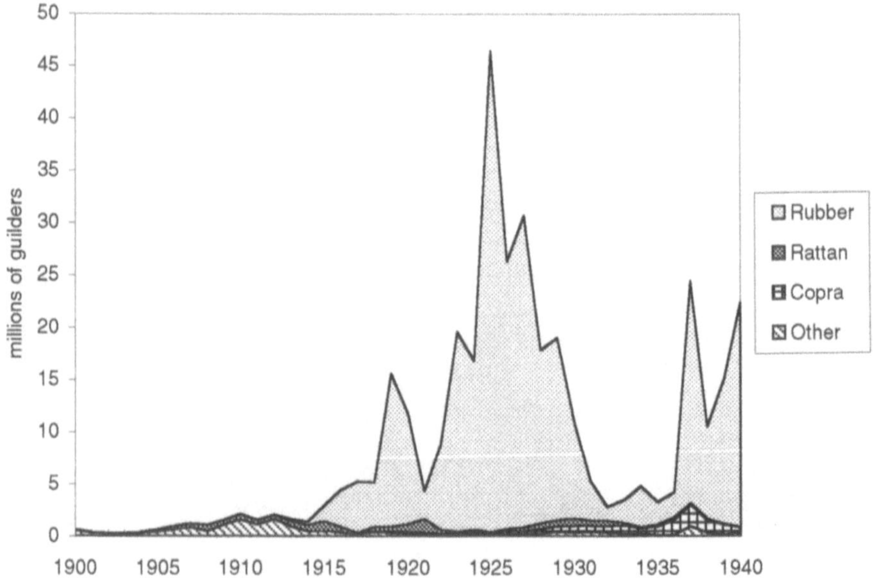

Figure 23f. Composition of foreign exports, 1900-1940: Jambi (Trade statistics).

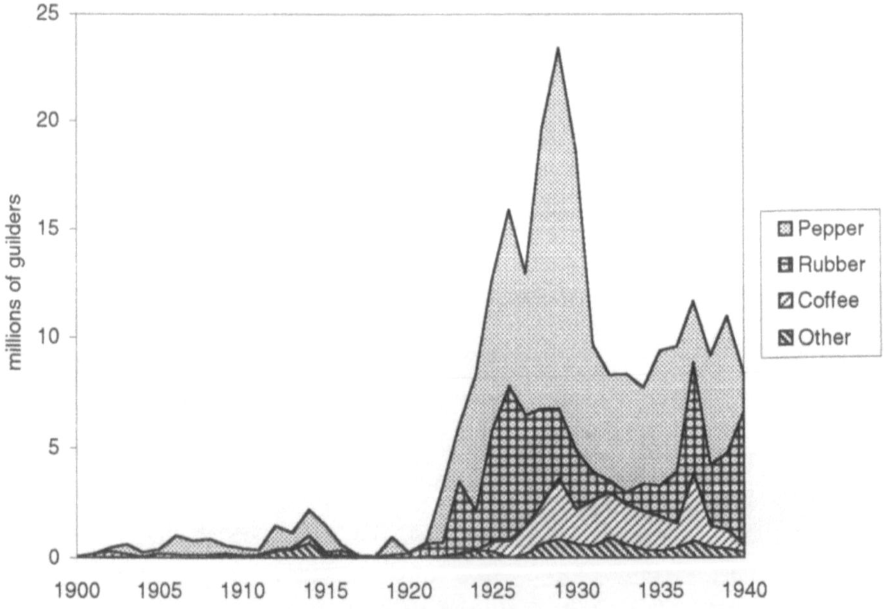

Figure 23g. Composition of foreign exports, 1900-1940: Lampung (Trade statistics).

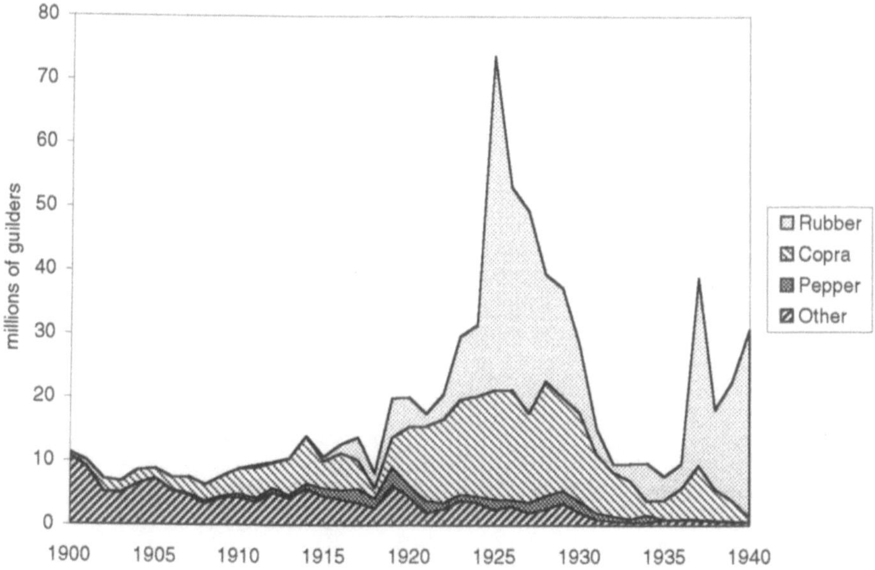

Figure 23h. Composition of foreign exports, 1900-1940: West Kalimantan (Trade statistics).

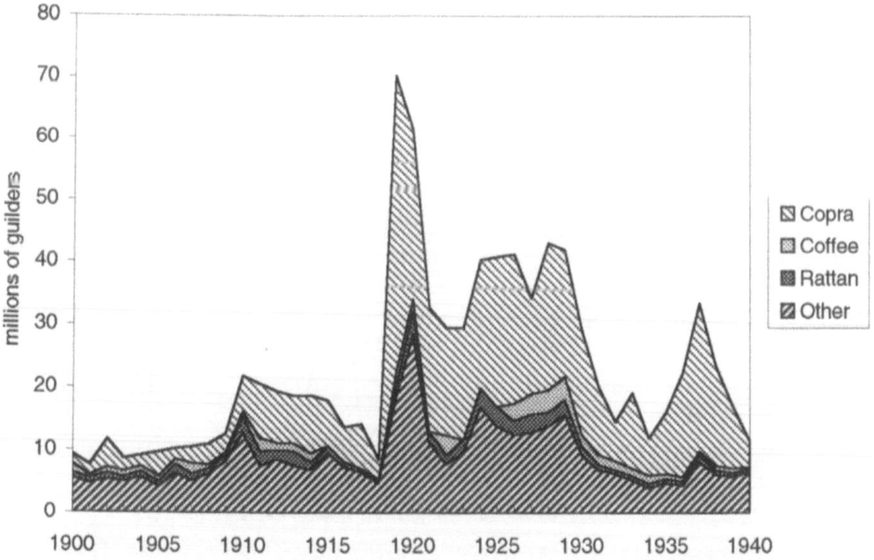

Figure 23i. Composition of foreign exports, 1900-1940: South Sulawesi (Trade statistics).

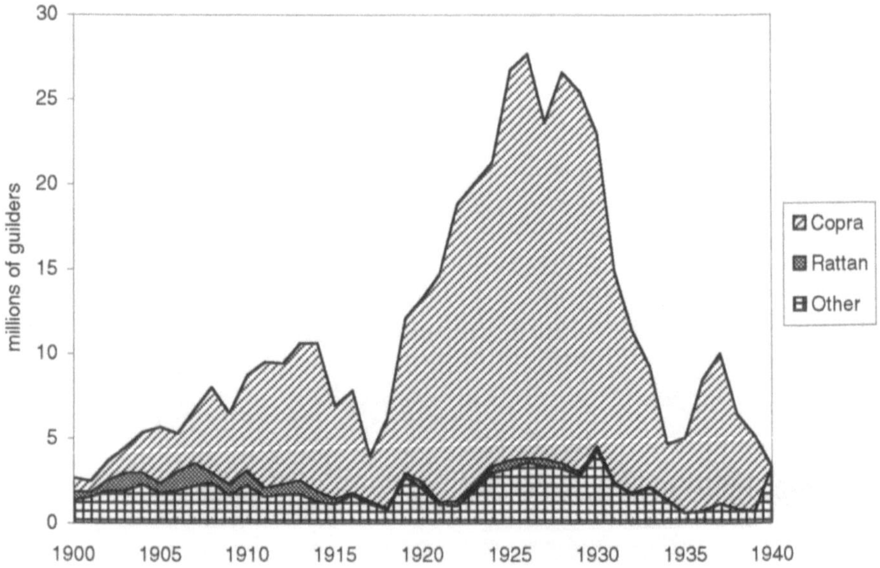

Figure 23j. Composition of foreign exports, 1900-1940: Manado (Trade statistics).

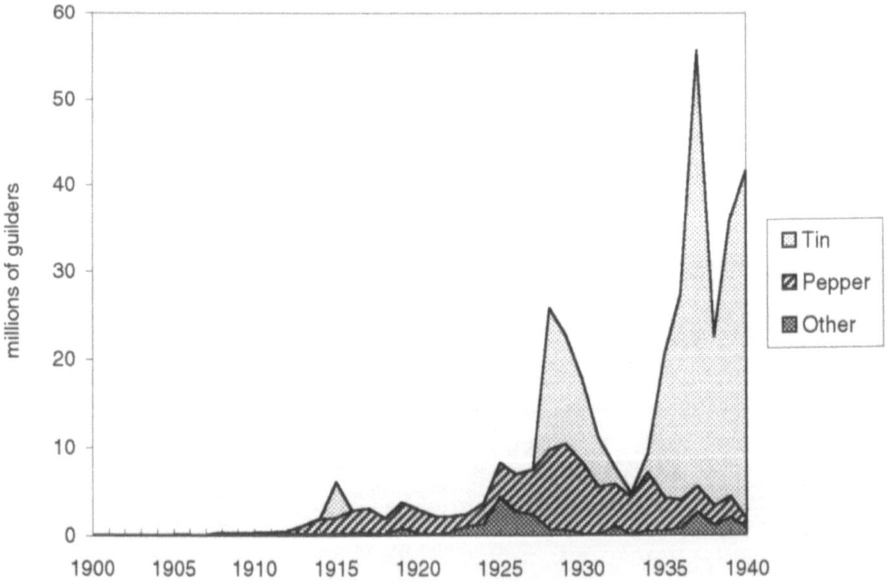

Figure 23k. Composition of foreign exports, 1900-1940: Bangka (Trade statistics).

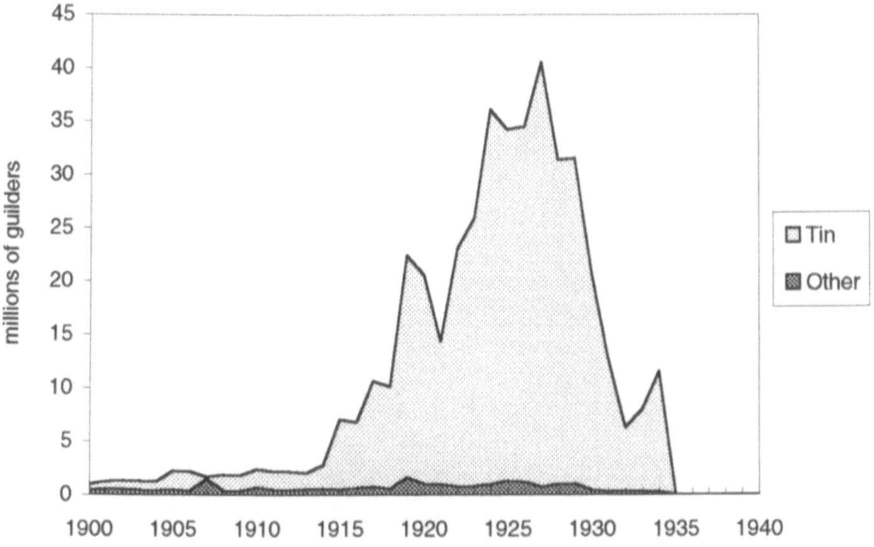

Figure 23l. Composition of foreign exports, 1900-1940: Belitung (Trade statistics).

Figure 23m. Composition of foreign exports, 1900-1940: Riau (Trade statistics).

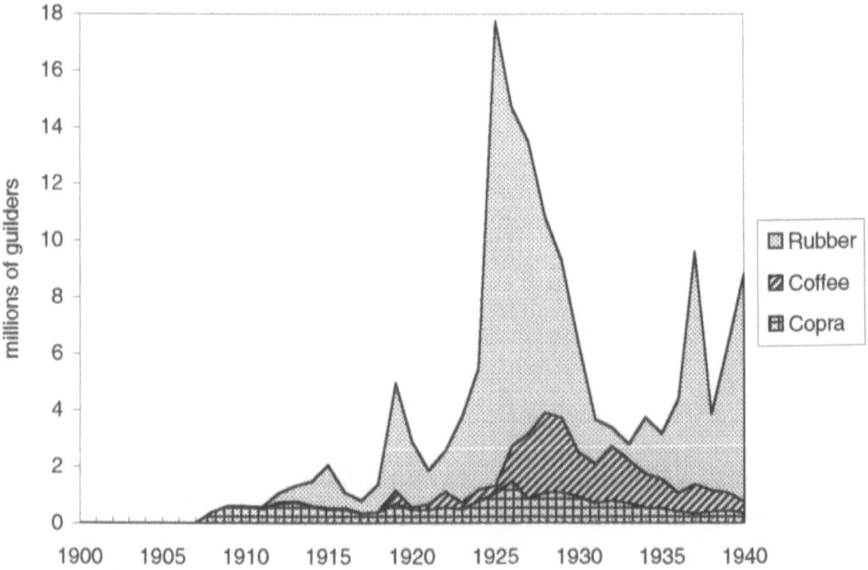

Figure 23n. Composition of foreign exports, 1900-1940: Tapanuli (Trade statistics).

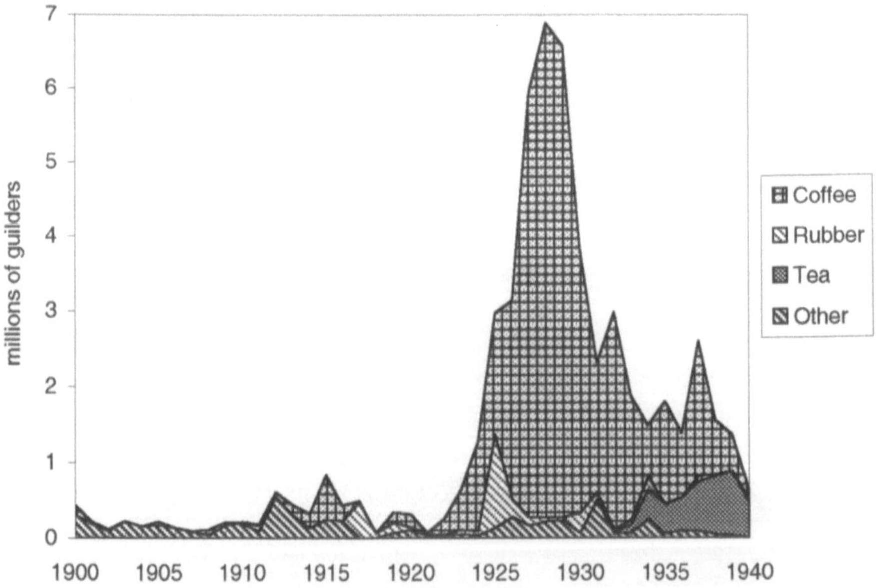

Figure 23o. Composition of foreign exports, 1900-1940: Bengkulu (Trade statistics).

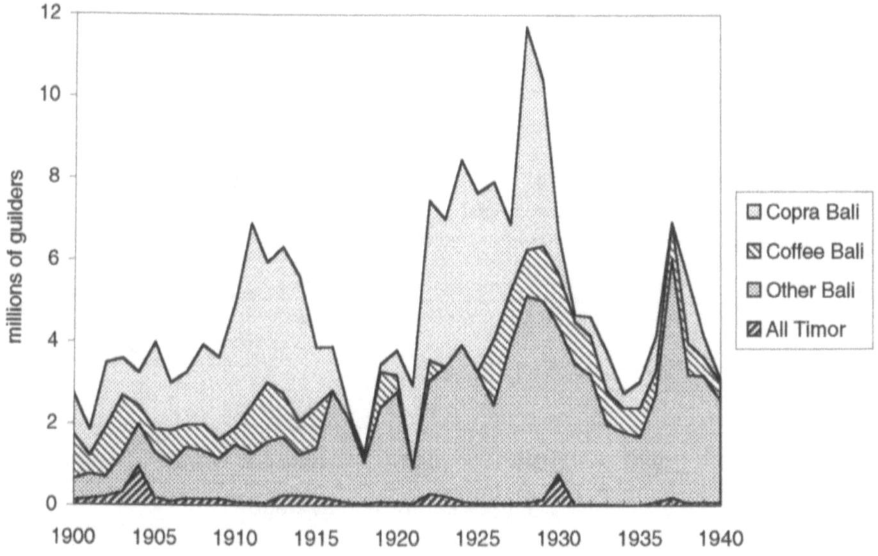

Figure 23p. Composition of foreign exports, 1900-1940: Bali and Lombok, Timor and Dependencies (Trade statistics).

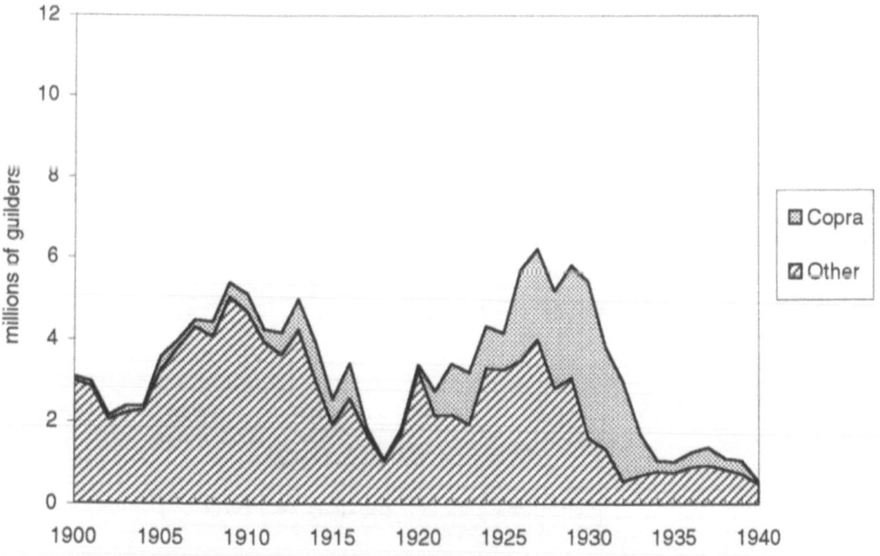

Figure 23q. Composition of foreign exports, 1900-1940: Maluku (Trade statistics).

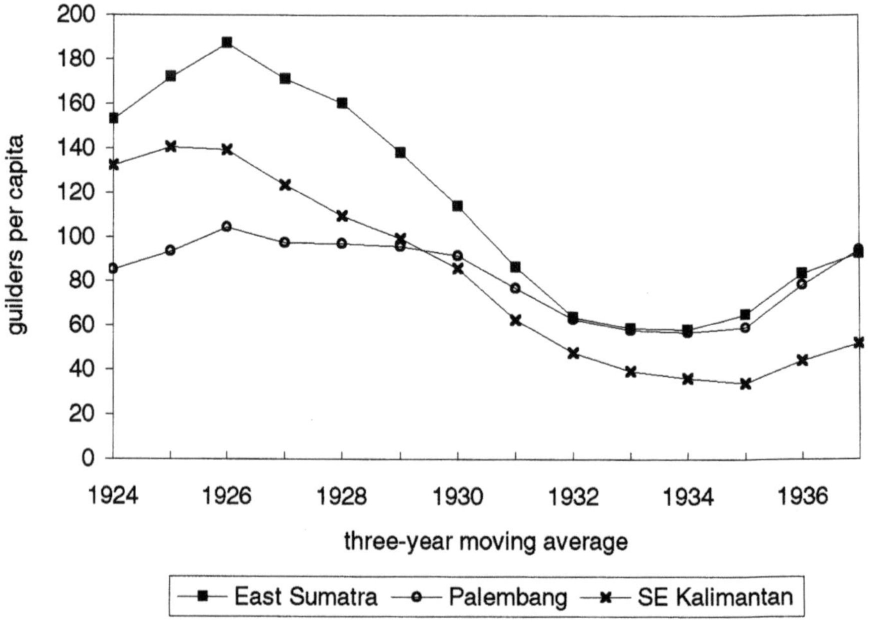

Figure 24a. Per capita exports (including interregional exports) of East Sumatra, Palembang, Southeast Kalimantan, 1924-1937 (Trade statistics and reconstructed population figures).

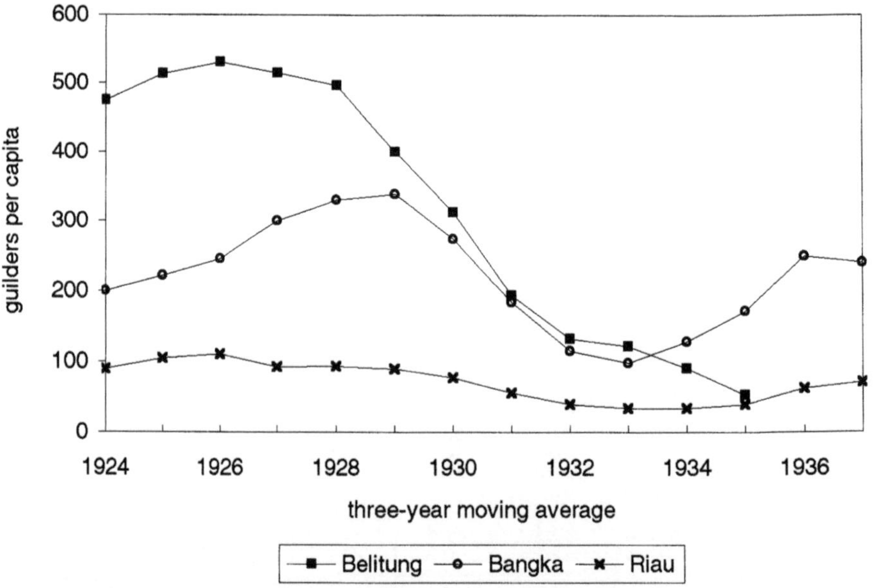

Figure 24b. Per capita exports (including interregional exports) of Bangka, Belitung, Riau, 1924-1937 (Trade statistics and reconstructed population figures).

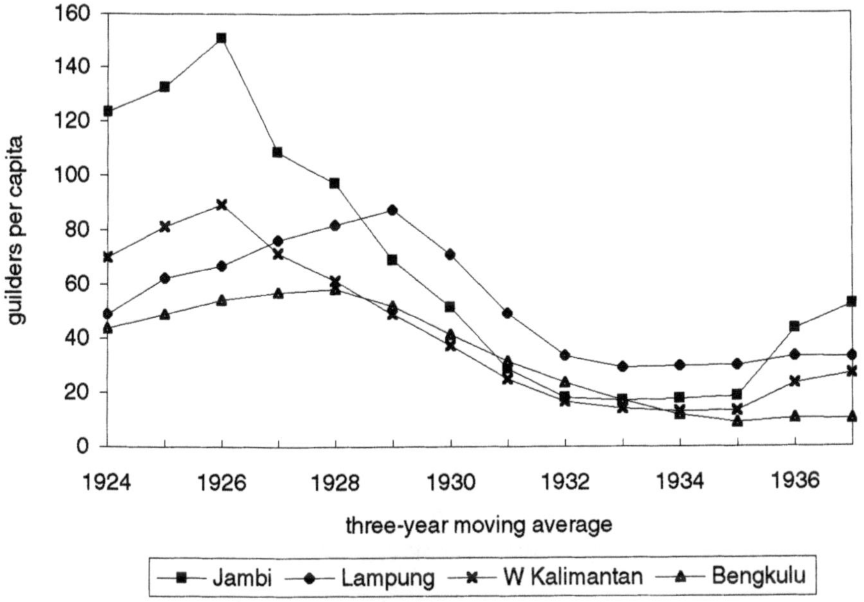

Figure 24c. Per capita exports (including interregional exports) of West Kalimantan, Jambi, Lampung, Bengkulu, 1924-1937 (Trade statistics and reconstructed population figures).

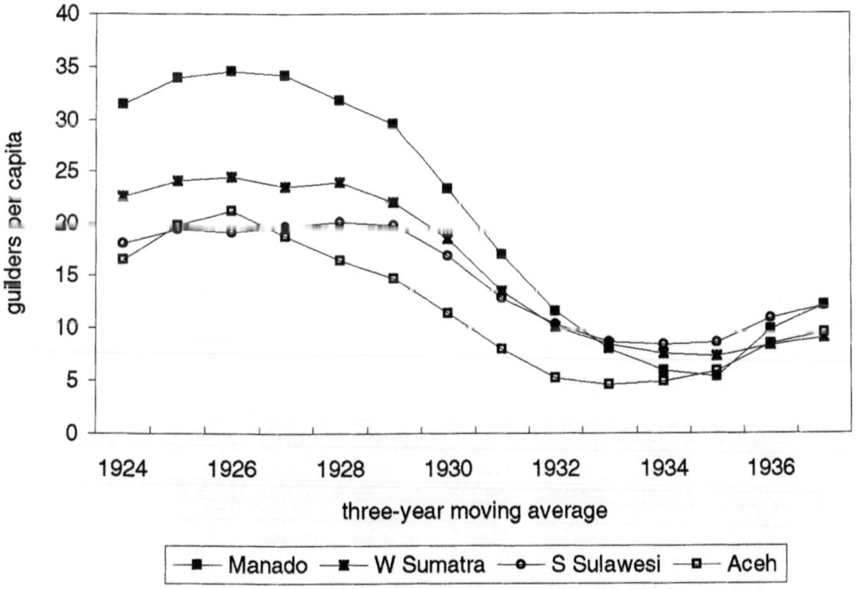

Figure 24d. Per capita exports (including interregional exports) of South Sulawesi, Manado, Aceh, West Sumatra, 1924-1937 (Trade statistics and reconstructed population figures).

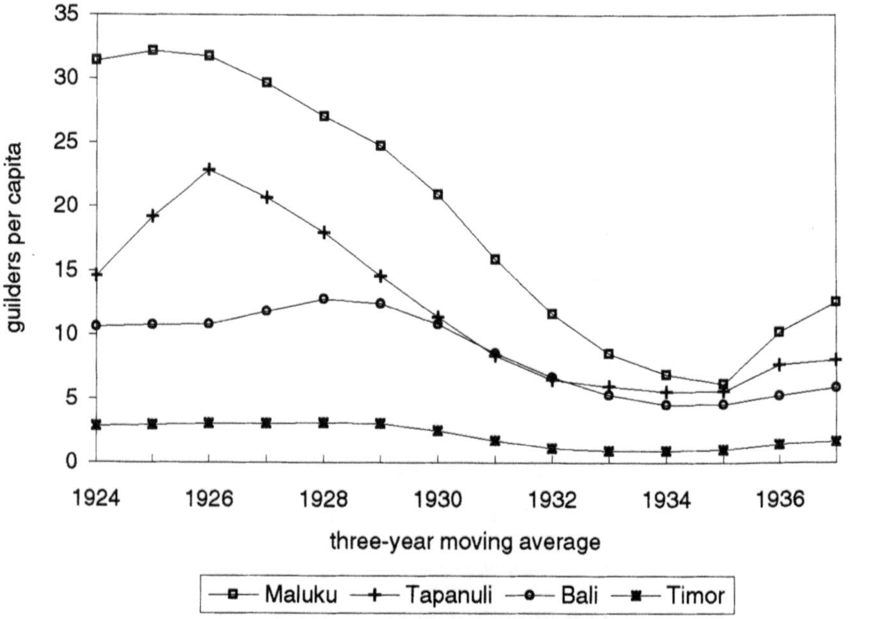

Figure 24e. Per capita exports (including interregional exports) of Bali, Maluku, Tapanuli, Timor and Dependencies, 1924-1937 (Trade statistics and reconstructed population figures).

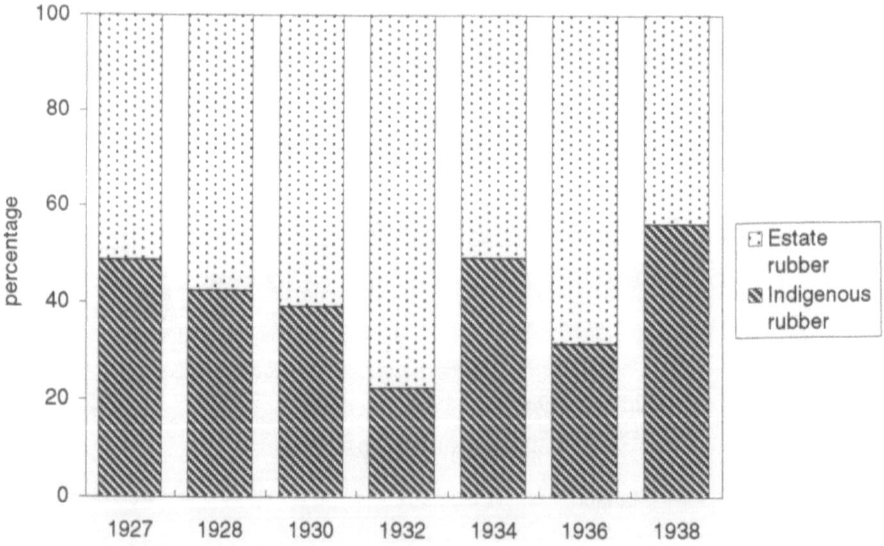

Figure 25a. Estate and indigenous rubber exports: percentage distribution by value, 1927-1938 (Trade statistics).

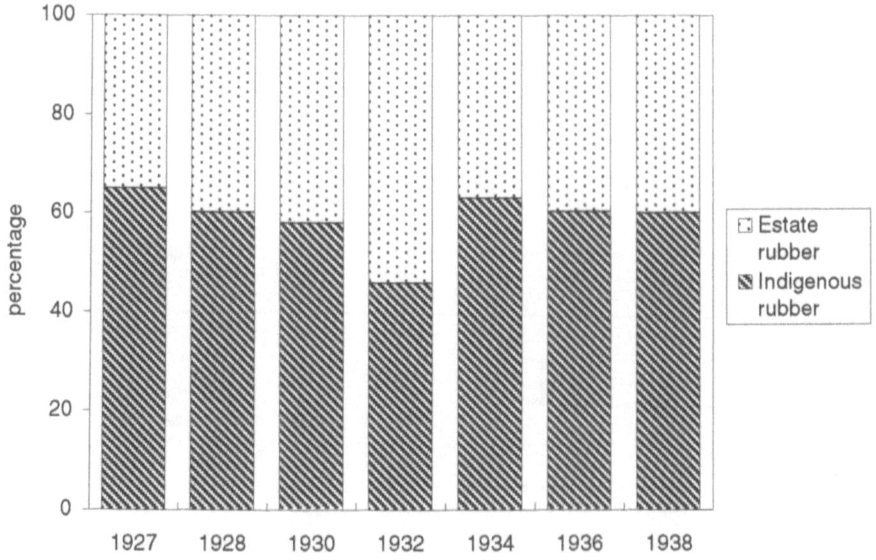

Figure 25b. Estate and indigenous rubber exports: percentage distribution by volume, 1927-1938 (Trade statistics).

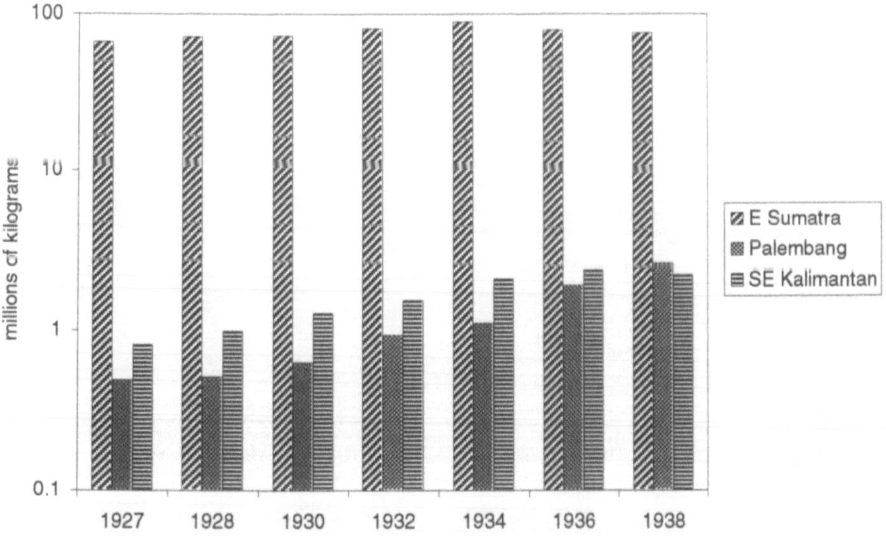

Figure 26. Estate rubber exports from major provinces, 1927-1938 (Trade statistics).

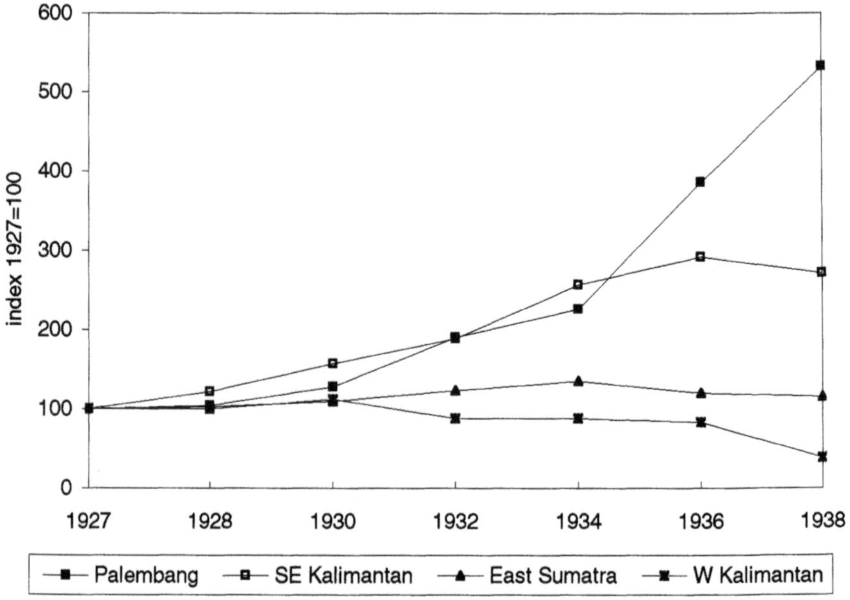

Figure 27. Volume index of estate rubber exports, 1927-1938 (Trade statistics).

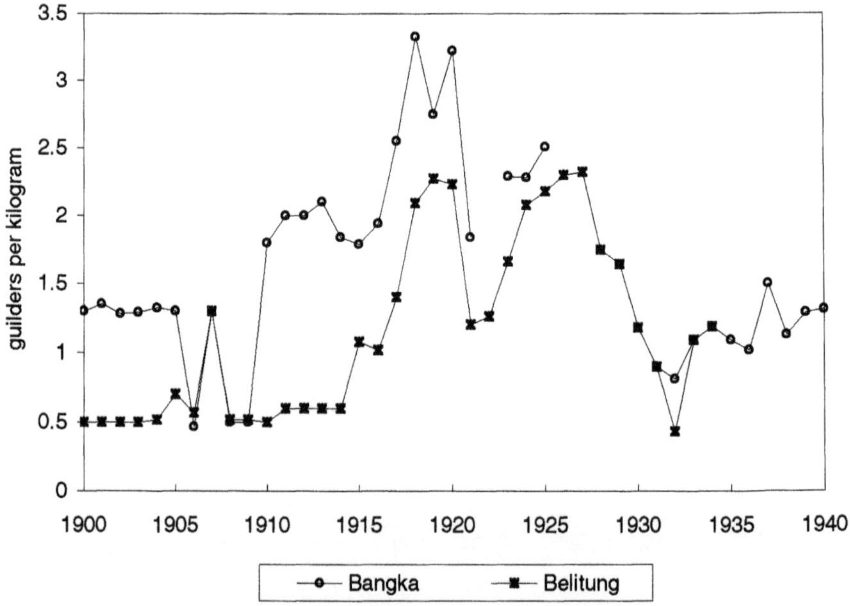

Figure 28. Reconstructed tin prices in Bangka and Belitung, 1900-1940 (Trade statistics).

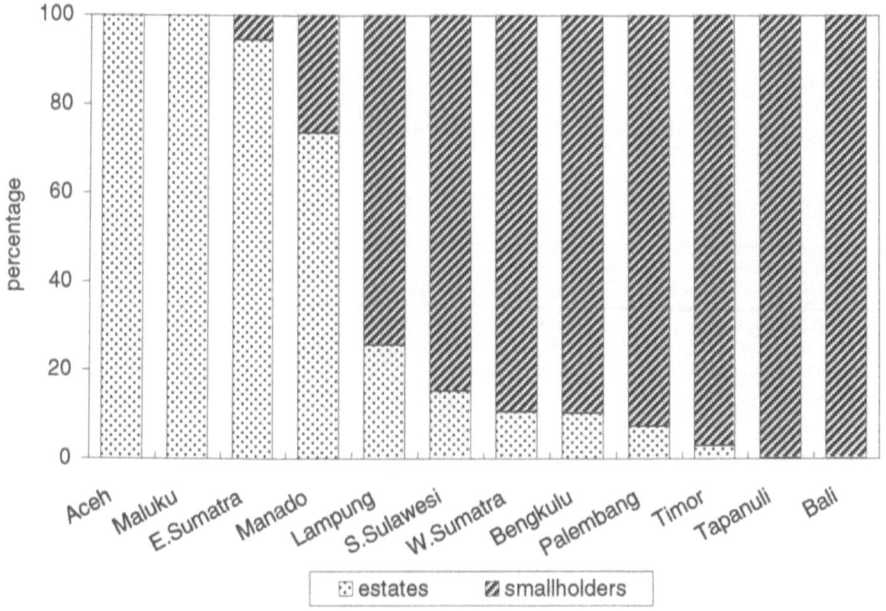

Figure 29. Coffee: estate versus indigenous production in 1932 (Trade statistics).

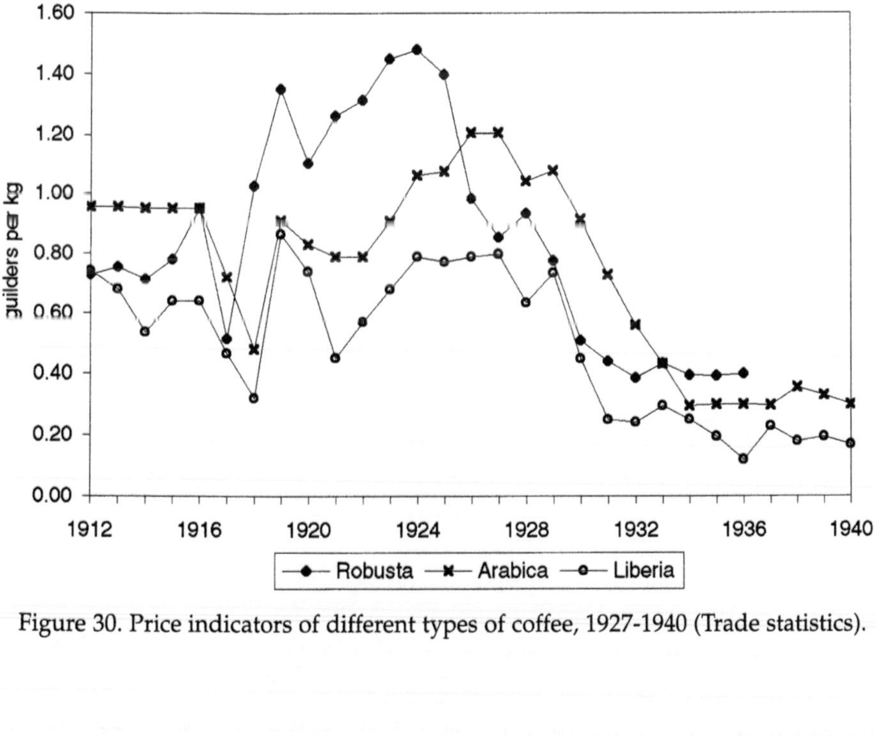

Figure 30. Price indicators of different types of coffee, 1927-1940 (Trade statistics).

Bibliography

Archival Sources

Algemeen Rijksarchief: Ministerie van Koloniën 1901-1963: Memories van Overgave (MvO).

MvO	*Residency*	*Years*
157-160	Aceh (Atjeh)	1918-1936
163-170	West Sumatra (Sumatra's Westkust)	1910-1937
171-178	Tapanuli (Tapanoeli)	1908-1936
181-193	East Sumatra (Oostkust van Sumatra)	1905-1938
195-205	Bengkulu (Benkoelen)	1906-1939
206-215	Palembang	1906-1936
216-226	Jambi (Djambi)	1908-1936
229-235	Lampung (Lampongsche Districten)	1900-1937
236-242	Riau (Riouw)	1908-1936
243-249	Bangka (Banka)	1906-1938
250-259	Belitung (Billiton)	1907-1932
260-265	West Kalimantan (Westerafdeling van Borneo)	1912-1938
270-279	Southeast Kalimantan (Zuider- en Oosterafdeling van Borneo)	1906-1937
280-298	South Sulawesi (Celebes)	1904-1933
302-309	Manado (Menado)	1906-1941
311-315	Amboina	1908-1930
321-328	Ternate	1909-1932
329-335	Maluku (Molukken)	1926-1937
339-352	Timor and Dependencies	1908-1938
355-370	Bali and Lombok	1905-1936
371	New Guinea	1924
732	Tapanuli	1920
1031	Hulu Sungai (Southeast Kalimantan)	1929
1110	South Sulawesi	1935
1175	Manado	1921
1176	Manado	1934

Algemeen Rijksarchief: Nederlandsche Handel-Maatschappij: Jaarverslagen van de vestigingen in het Oosten 1860-1940. Verslagen van de Subagenten (VvS).
NHM 9086-9240: Jaar- en reisverslagen van de vestigingen in Nederlands-Indië.

Vol.	No.	Agency	Residency	Years
9086-9089	3-46	Banjarmasin	SE Kalimantan	1877-1940
9101	184-186	Jambi	Jambi	1937-1939
9118-9120	398-425	Kotaraja	Aceh	1904-1931
9120	426-431	Langsa	Aceh	1917-1922
9120-9123	432-463	Macassar	S. Sulawesi	1910-1939
9124-9128	476-515	Medan	East Sumatra	1900-1939
9130-9132	543-574	Padang	West Sumatra	1900-1931
9132-9135	575-616	Palembang	Palembang	1900-1939
9145-9146	742-762	Pontianak	West Kalimantan	1914-1939
9164	936-941	Sibolga	Tapanuli	1926-1931
9188	1190-1193	Tanjungbalei	East Sumatra	1914-1917
9188	1194-1204	Tebingtinggi	East Sumatra	1912-1922
9193	1257-1268	Telukbetung	Lampung	1912-1922, 1939

Published works

Alberts, A.
1989 *Een kolonie is ook maar een mens*. Amsterdam: Van Oorschot.
1979 *In en uit het paradijs getild*. Amsterdam: Van Oorschot. [Also published as: *Namen noemen; Zo maar wat ongewone en openhartige herinneringen aan het leven in het verloren paradijs, dat Nederlands-Indië heette 1939-1947*, 1962.]
1992 *Twee jaargetijden minder*. Amsterdam: CPNB.

Aldcroft, D.H.
1993 *The European economy, 1914-1990*. London: Routledge.

Allen, G.C. and A.G. Donnithorne
1957 *Western enterprise in Indonesia and Malaya; A study in economic development*. London: Allen and Unwin.

Anderson, B.R. O'G.
1983 'Old state, new society; Indonesia's New Order in comparative historical perspective', *Journal of Asian Studies* 42:477-96.

Anrooij, F. van
1979 'Crisis en financieel beleid in Nederlands-Indië (1920-1925)', in: *Between people and statistics; Essays on modern Indonesian history*, pp. 119-32. The Hague: Nijhoff.

Arabieren
1917 'Arabieren', in: *Encyclopaedie van Nederlandsch-Indië* I, pp. 55-6. 's-Gravenhage: Nijhoff, Leiden: Brill.

Ark, B. van
1988 'The volume and price of Indonesian exports, 1823 to 1940; The long-term trend and its measurement', *Bulletin of Indonesian Economic Studies* 24-3:87-120.

Atmodipoerwo, Soenardjo
1934-35 'Ananascultuur en -handel in de residentie Palembang', *Landbouw* 10:465-85.

Azis, I.J.
1991 'Key issues in Indonesian regional development', in: H. Hill (ed.), *Unity and diversity; Regional economic development in Indonesia since 1970*, pp. 55-74. Singapore: Oxford University Press.

Baak, P.E.
1993 'Out of the shadow, into the spotlights; The indigenous aspects of plantation development; The case of the emergence of Syrian Christian planters in princely Travancore in the first half of the twentieth century', *Itinerario* 17-2:74-96.

Bailie, J.H.
1925 *De bevolkingsrubbercultuur in Nederlandsch-Indië, IIb: Bandjermasin*. Weltevreden: Landsdrukkerij.

Baks, J.
1989 'De Steenkolen-Maatschappij "Poeloe-Laoet" in Zuid-Oost Borneo, 1903-1913', in: A.H.P. Clemens and J.Th. Lindblad (eds), *Het belang van de Buitengewesten; Economische expansie en koloniale staatsvorming in de Buitengewesten van NederlandsIndië 1870-1942*, pp. 123-50. Amsterdam: NEHA.

Baldwin, R.E.
1963 'Export technology and development from a subsistence level', *Economic Journal* 73:80-92.
1966 *Economic development and export growth; A study of northern Rhodesia, 1920-1960*. New York: Wiley.

Barlow, C.
1978 *The natural rubber industry; Its development, technology, and economy in Malaysia*. Kuala Lumpur: Oxford University Press.
1989 'A comparison of factors influencing agricultural development in Malaya and Indonesia, 1870-1940', in: A. Maddison and G. Prince (eds), *Economic growth in Indonesia 1820-1940*, pp. 227-58. Dordrecht/Providence: Foris. [KITLV, Verhandelingen 137.]

Barlow, C. and J. Drabble
1990 'Government and the emerging rubber industries in Indonesia and Malaya 1900-1940', in: A. Booth, W.J. O'Malley and A. Weidemann (eds), *Indonesian economic history in the Dutch colonial era*, pp. 187-209. New Haven: Yale Center for International Area Studies.

Baudet, H.
1980 'Nederland en de rang van Denemarken', in: C. Fasseur (ed.), *Geld en geweten; Een bundel opstellen over anderhalve eeuw Nederlands bestuur in de Indonesische archipel*, Vol. II, pp. 241-56. Den Haag: Nijhoff.

Baudet, H. and M. Fennema et al.
1983 *Het Nederlands belang bij Indië*. Utrecht/Antwerpen: Spectrum.

Bauer, P.T.
1948 *The rubber industry; A study in competition and monopoly*. London: Longmans, Green.

Benkoelen
1917 'Benkoelen', in: *Encyclopaedie van Nederlandsch-Indië* I, pp. 269-273. 's-Gravenhage: Nijhoff; Leiden: Brill.

Benzoë
1917 'Benzoë', in: *Encyclopaedie van Nederlandsch-Indië* I, p. 274. 's-Gravenhage: Nijhoff; Leiden: Brill.

Bertling, C.T.
1925 'De Chineezen op de oostkust van Borneo', *Koloniale Studiën* 9-1:1-35.

Between people and statistics
1979 *Between people and statistics; Essays on Indonesian history, presented to P. Creutzberg*. The Hague: Nijhoff.

Birnberg, T.B. and S.A. Resnick
1975 *Colonial development; An econometric study*. New Haven: Yale University Press.

Bläsing, J.F.E
1978 'Handelsgeschiedenis', in: H. Baudet and H. van der Meulen (eds), *Kernproblemen der economische geschiedenis*, pp. 240-51. Groningen: Wolters-Noordhoff.

Blecker, R.A.
1997 'The "unnatural and retrograde order"; Adam Smith's theories of trade and development reconsidered', *Economica* 64:527-37.

Blink, H.
1918 'Sumatra's Oostkust in haar ontwikkeling als economisch gewest', *Tijdschrift voor Economische Geographie* 9:57-156.

Boeijinga, K.J.
1926 'De visscherij van Bagan Api Api', *Koloniaal Tijdschrift* 15:449-78.

Boeke, J.H.
1930 *Dualistische economie*. Leiden: Van Doesburg.
1946 *The evolution of the Netherlands Indies economy*. New York: Netherlands and the Netherlands Indies Council, Institute of Pacific Relations.
1953 *Economics and economic policies of dual societies – as exemplified by Indonesia*. Haarlem: Tjeenk Willink.
1955 *Economie van Indonesië*. Fifth edition. Haarlem: Tjeenk Willink. [First edition 1940.]

Boomgaard, P.
1986 'The welfare services in Indonesia 1900-1942', *Itinerario* 10-1:57-81.
1987 *Children of a colonial state; Population growth and economic development in Java, 1795-1880*. Amsterdam: Free University Press.
1991 (ed.) *The colonial past; Dutch sources on Indonesian history*. Amsterdam: Royal Tropical Insitute. [Bulletin of the Royal Tropical Institute 323].
1993 'Uplift down the drain? Effects of welfare measures in late colonial Indonesia', in: J.P. Dirkse, F. Hüsken and M. Rutten (eds), *Development*

and social welfare; Indonesia's experiences under the New Order, pp. 247-53. Leiden: KITLV Press. [Verhandelingen 156.]

Boomgaard, P. and A.J. Gooszen
1990 *Population trends 1795-1942*. Amsterdam: Royal Tropical Institute. [Changing economy in Indonesia; A selection of statistical source material from the early 19th century up to 1940, 11.]

Boomgaard, P. and J.L. van Zanden
1990 *Foodcrops and arable lands, Java 1815-1942*. Amsterdam: Royal Tropical Institute. [Changing economy in Indonesia; A selection of statistical source material from the early 19th century up to 1940, 10.]

Boomgaard, P. and R. de Bakker
1996 *Forests and forestry 1823-1941*. Amsterdam: Royal Tropical Institute. [Changing economy in Indonesia; A selection of statistical source material from the early 19th century up to 1940, 16.]

Booth, A.
1988 *Agricultural development in Indonesia*. Sydney: Allen and Unwin.
1989 'The state and economic development in Indonesia; The ethical and New Order eras compared', in: R.J. May and W.J. O'Malley (eds), *Observing change in Asia; Essays in honour of J.A.C. Mackie*, pp. 111-26. Bathurst: Crawford House Press.
1990a 'The evolution of fiscal policy and the role of government in the colonial economy', in: A. Booth, W.J. O'Malley and A. Weidemann (eds), *Indonesian economic history in the Dutch colonial era*, pp. 210-43. New Haven: Yale Center for International Area Studies.
1990b 'Foreign trade and domestic development in the colonial economy', in: A. Booth, W.J. O'Malley and A. Weidemann (eds), *Indonesian economic history in the Dutch colonial era*, pp. 267-95. New Haven: Yale Center for International Area Studies.
1991 'The economic development of Southeast Asia: 1870-1985', in: G.D. Snooks, A.J.S. Reid and J.J. Pincus (eds), *Exploring Southeast Asia's economic past*, pp. 20-52. Melbourne: Oxford University Press Australia. [*Australian Economic History Review* 31:1.]
1992a 'International trade and domestic economic development; An Indonesian case study', in: M. Arsjad Anwar, Thee Kian Wie and Iwan Jaya Azis (eds), *Pemikiran, pelaksanaan, dan perintisan pembangunan ekonomi*, pp. 99-152. Jakarta: Fakultas Ekonomi Universitas Indonesia (ISEI).
1992b (ed.) *The oil boom and after; Indonesian economic policy and performance in the Soeharto era*. Singapore: Oxford University Press.
1998 *The Indonesian economy in the nineteenth and twentieth centuries; A history of missed opportunities*. London: Macmillan.

Booth, A. and P. McCawley (eds)
1981 *The Indonesian economy during the Suharto era*. Kuala Lumpur/Oxford: Oxford University Press.

Booth, A., W.J. O'Malley and A. Weidemann (eds)
1990 *Indonesian economic history in the Dutch colonial era*. New Haven: Yale Center for International Area Studies. [Monograph Series, Yale University Southeast Asia Studies 35.]

Bor, R.C. van de
1906a 'Een en ander betreffende het ressort van de controleur te Sarolangoen, onderafdeling Boven-Tembesi der afdeling Djambi', *Tijdschrift voor het Binnenlandsch Bestuur* 30:1-13.
1906b 'Aanteekeningen betreffende het grondbezit in de Boven-Tembesi (Djambi)', *Tijdschrift voor het Binnenlandsch Bestuur* 30:179-90.

Bossenbroek, M.
1996 *Holland op zijn breedst; Indië en Zuid-Afrika in de Nederlandse cultuur omstreeks 1900*. Amsterdam: Bert Bakker.

Bottema, J.W.T.
1995 *Market formation and agriculture in Indonesia from the mid-nineteenth century to 1990*. Jakarta: Drukkerij Desa Putera. [PhD thesis, Catholic University Nijmegen.]

Bousquet, G.H.
1939 *La politique musulmane et coloniale des Pays-Bas*. Paris: Paul Hartmann. [Translated as: *A French view of the Netherlands Indies*, London: Oxford University Press, 1940.]

Brand, J. van den
1902 *De millioenen uit Deli*. Amsterdam: Hoeveker en Wormser.

Brandt, W.
1948 *De aarde van Deli*. 's Gravenhage: Van Hoeve.

Breman, J.
1983 *Control of land and labour in colonial Java; A case study of agrarian crisis and reform in the region of Cirebon during the first decades of the 20th century*. Dordrecht: Foris. [KITLV, Verhandelingen 101.]
1990 'The civilization of racism; Colonial and post-colonial development policies,' in: J. Breman (ed.), *Imperial monkey business; Racial supremacy in social Darwinist theory and colonial practice*, pp. 123-52. Amsterdam: VU University Press.
1992a 'Controversial views on writing colonial history', *Itinerario* 16-2:39-60.
1992b *Koelies, planters en koloniale politiek; Het arbeidsregime op de grootlandbouwondernemingen aan Sumatra's Oostkust in het begin van de twintigste eeuw*. Third edition. Leiden: KITLV Press. [Verhandelingen 123.] [First edition 1987.]

Broek, J.O.M.
1942 *Economic development of the Netherlands Indies*. New York: Institute of Pacific Relations.

Broersma, R.
1916 *De Lampongsche Districten*. Batavia/Rijswijk: Javasche Boekhandel en Drukkerij.
1920 *Palembangsche verkenningen*. Semarang: s.n. [Reprint from *De Locomotief*.]
1925 *Atjeh als land voor handel en bedrijf*. Utrecht: Cohen.
1926 'De Indiër met zijn rubber', *Koloniaal Tijdschrift* 15:146-65.
1927 *Handel en bedrijf in Zuid- en Oost Borneo*. The Hague: Naeff.

Brook, C.P., H.W.J. Doffegnies and C.G. Slotemaker
1926 *De bevolkingsrubbercultuur in Nederlandsch-Indië, V: Tapanoeli en Sumatra's Westkust*. Weltevreden: Landsdrukkerij.

Brookfield, H.
1975 *Interdependent development; Perspectives on development*. London: Methuen.
Brown, R.A.
1994 *Capital and entrepreneurship in South-East Asia*. London: Macmillan; New York: St. Martin's Press.
Bruin, A.G. de
1918 *De Chinezen ter Oostkust van Sumatra*. Leiden: Oostkust van Sumatra-Instituut.
Bruyn Kops, G.F. de
1919 *Overzicht van Zuid-Sumatra*. Amsterdam: Zuid-Sumatra Instituut.
Bulbeck, D., A. Reid, Lay Cheng Tan and Yiqi Wu
1998 *Southeast Asian exports since the 14th century; Cloves, pepper, coffee, and sugar*. Leiden: KITLV Press; Singapore: Institute of Southeast Asian Studies; Canberra: Research School of Pacific and Asian Studies.
Burger, D.H.
1954 'Boeke's dualisme', *Indonesië* 7:177-98.
1975 *Sociologisch-economische geschiedenis van Indonesia*. Wageningen: Landbouw Hogeschool Wageningen, Afdeling Agrarische Geschiedenis; Amsterdam: Koninklijk Instituut voor de Tropen; Leiden: KITLV. 2 vols.
Butcher, J. and H. Dick (eds)
1993 *The rise and fall of revenue farming; Business elites and the emergence of the modern state in Southeast Asia*. New York: St. Martin's Press.
Caldwell, J.A.M.
1964 'Indonesian export and production from the decline of the Culture System to the First World War', in: C.D. Cowan (ed.), *The economic development of Southeast Asia; Studies in economic history and political economy*, pp. 72-101. London: Allen and Unwin.
Campo, J.N.F.M. à
1986 'Een maritiem BB; De rol van de Koninklijke Paketvaart Maatschappij in de integratie van de koloniale staat', in: J. van Goor (ed.), *Imperialisme in de marge; De afronding van Nederlands-Indië*, pp. 123-78. Utrecht: Hes.
1992 *De Koninklijke Paketvaart Maatschappij; Stoomvaart en staatsvorming in de Indonesische Archipel 1888-1914*. Hilversum: Verloren.
1993 'Perahu shipping in Indonesia 1870-1914', *Review of Indonesian and Malaysian Affairs* 27-1/2:33-60.
Caoutchouc
1917 'Caoutchouc', in: *Encyclopaedie van Nederlandsch-Indië* I, pp. 436-9. 's-Gravenhage: Nijhoff; Leiden: Brill.
Cator, W.J.
1936 *The economic position of the Chinese in the Netherlands-Indies*. Oxford: Blackwell.
Chew, E.C.T. and E. Lee (eds)
1991 *A history of Singapore*. Singapore: Oxford University Press.
Chineezen
1917 'Chineezen', in: *Encyclopaedie van Nederlandsch-Indië* I, pp. 480-7. 's-Gravenhage: Nijhoff; Leiden: Brill.

Clarence-Smith, W.G.
1998 'The economic role of the Arab community in Maluku, 1816 to 1940', *Indonesia and the Malay World* 26-74:32-49.
Clemens, A.H.P.
1989 'De inheemse rubbercultuur in Jambi en Palembang tijdens het Interbellum', in: A.H.P. Clemens and J.Th. Lindblad (eds), *Het belang van de Buitengewesten; Economische expansie en koloniale staatsvorming in de Buitengewesten van NederlandsIndië 1870-1942*, pp.213-42. Amsterdam: NEHA.
1992 'Regional patterns in the foreign trade of the Outer Provinces 1911-1940', in: A.H.P. Clemens, J.Th. Lindblad and L.J. Touwen, *Regional patterns in foreign trade 1911-1940*, pp. 33-45. Amsterdam: Royal Tropical Institute.
Clemens, A.H.P. and J.Th. Lindblad (eds)
1989 *Het belang van de Buitengewesten; Economische expansie en koloniale staatsvorming in de Buitengewesten van Nederlands-Indië 1870-1942.* Amsterdam: NEHA.
Clemens, A.H.P., J.Th. Lindblad and L.J. Touwen
1992 *Regional patterns in foreign trade 1911-1940.* Amsterdam: Royal Tropical Institute. [Changing economy in Indonesia; A selection of statistical source material from the early 19th century up to 1940, 12B.]
Cohen, H.
1939 'De economische beteekenis der bosch-bijproducten van de buitengewesten', *Koloniale Studiën* 23:460-96.
Colijn, H. and D.G. Stibbe (eds)
1929 *Neerlands-Indië; Land en volk, geschiedenis en bestuur, bedrijf en samenleving.* Amsterdam: Elsevier. 2 vols. [First edition 1911-12.]
Colijn, H. and W. Verbeek
1907-14 *Politiek beleid en bestuurszorg in de Buitenbezittingen.* Batavia: Landsdrukkerij. 3 vols.
Colombijn, F.
1991 'Nostalgia for a better future; Organization of economic life in a colonial trading town: Padang (West Sumatra) 1906-1942', *Economic and Social History in the Netherlands* 3:155-83.
1992 'Uiteenlopende spoorrails; De verschillende ideeën over spoorwegaanleg en ontginning van het Umbilin-kolenveld in West-Sumatra, 1868-1891', *Bijdragen en Mededelingen betreffende de Geschiedenis der Nederlanden* 107:383-97.
1994 *Patches of Padang; The history of an Indonesian town in the twentieth century and the use of urban space.* Leiden: Research School CNWS. [PhD thesis, Leiden University.]
Coolhaas, W.Ph.
1943 *Insulinde; Mensch en maatschappij.* Deventer: Van Hoeve.
Cramer, J.C.W.
1934 'De rubberhandel in de Hoeloe Soengei', *Koloniale Studiën* 18:366-401.
Creutzberg, P.
1972-75 (ed.) *Het ekonomisch beleid in Nederlands-Indië; Capita selecta; Een bronnenpublikatie.* Groningen: Wolters-Noordhoff. 4 vols.

1975 *Indonesia's export crops 1816-1940*. The Hague: Nijhoff. [Changing economy in Indonesia; A selection of statistical source material from the early 19th century up to 1940, 1.]
1976 *Public finance 1816-1939*. The Hague: Nijhoff. [Changing economy in Indonesia; A selection of statistical source material from the early 19th century up to 1940, 2.]
1977 *Expenditure on fixed assets*. The Hague: Nijhoff. [Changing economy in Indonesia; A selection of statistical source material from the early 19th century up to 1940, 3.]
1978 *Rice prices*. Amsterdam: Royal Tropical Institute. [Changing economy in Indonesia; A selection of statistical source material from the early 19th century up to 1940, 4.]
1979 *National income*. Amsterdam: Royal Tropical Institute. [Changing economy in Indonesia; A selection of statistical source material from the early 19th century up to 1940, 5.]

Cribb, R.
1993 'Development policy in the early 20th century', in: J.P. Dirkse, F. Hüsken and M. Rutten (eds), *Development and social welfare; Indonesia's experiences under the New Order*, pp. 225-45. Leiden: KITLV Press. [Verhandelingen 156.]
1994a (ed.) *The late colonial state in Indonesia; Political and economic foundations of the Netherlands Indies 1880-1942*. Leiden: KITLV Press. [Verhandelingen 163.]
1994b 'Introduction; The late colonial state in Indonesia', in: R. Cribb (ed.), *The late colonial state in Indonesia; Political and economic foundations of the Netherlands Indies 1880-1942*, pp. 1-9. Leiden: KITLV Press. [Verhandelingen 163.]

Cubitt, G., T. Whitten and J. Whitten
1993 *Ongerept Indonesië; De biologische diversiteit van Indonesië*. Weert: M & P.

Cumming, T.J.
1924 *De bevolkingsrubbercultuur in Nederlandsch-Indië, Ia: Djambi*. Weltevreden: Landsdrukkerij.

Derksen, J.B.D. and J. Tinbergen
1980 'Berekeningen over de economische betekenis van Nederlands-Indië voor Nederland', in: C. Fasseur (ed.), *Geld en geweten; Een bundel opstellen over anderhalve eeuw Nederlands bestuur in de Indonesische archipel*, Vol. II, pp. 225-40. Den Haag: Nijhoff. [First published *Maandschrift Centraal Bureau voor de Statistiek* 40 (1945):210-6.]

Deventer, C.Th. van
1899 'Een eereschuld', *De Gids* 17:205-57.

Dick, H.W.
1986 *The Indonesian interisland shipping industry; An analysis of competition and regulation*. Singapore: Institute of Southeast Asian Studies, Asean Economic Research Unit.
1989 'Japan's economic expansion in the Netherlands Indies between the First and Second World Wars', *Journal of Southeast Asian Studies* 20:244-72.

1990 'Interisland trade, economic integration, and the emergence of a national economy', in: A. Booth, W.J. O'Malley and A. Weidemann (eds), *Indonesian economic history in the Dutch colonial era*, pp. 296-321. New Haven: Yale Center for International Area Studies.

1993a 'Indonesian economic history inside out', *Review of Indonesian and Malaysian Affairs* 27, I-II:1-12.

1993b 'Nineteenth-century industrialization; A missed opportunity?', in: J.Th. Lindblad (ed.), *New challenges in the modern economic history of Indonesia*, pp. 123-49. Leiden: Programme of Indonesian Studies.

1996 'The emergence of a national economy, 1808-1990s', in: J.Th. Lindblad (ed.), *Historical foundations of a national economy in Indonesia, 1890s-1990s*, pp. 21-51. Amsterdam: North Holland. [KNAW, Verhandelingen, Afd. Letterkunde, Nieuwe Reeks, 167.]

Dirks, N.B. (ed.)

1992 *Colonialism and culture*. Ann Arbor: University of Michigan Press.

Dirkse, J.P., F. Hüsken and M. Rutten (eds)

1993 *Development and social welfare; Indonesia's experiences under the New Order*. Leiden: KITLV Press. [Verhandelingen 156.]

Dobbin, C.

1983 *Islamic revivalism in a changing peasant economy; Central Sumatra, 1784-1874*. London: Curzon. [Scandinavian Institute of Asian Studies Monograph Series 47.]

1996 *Asian entrepreneurial minorities. Conjoint communities in the making of the world-economy 1570-1940*. Richmond: Curzon. [NIAS Monographs in Asian Studies 71.]

Doel, H.W. van den

1994 *De stille macht; Het Europese binnenlands bestuur op Java en Madoera, 1808-1942*. Amsterdam: Bert Bakker.

1996 *Het rijk van Insulinde; Opkomst en ondergang van een Nederlandse kolonie*. Amsterdam: Prometheus.

Doorman, W.H.C.

1910 'De tinontginningen in Nederlandsch Oost-Indië, in het bijzonder die op Billiton', *Indische Gids* 32:595-619.

Doorn, J.A.A. van

1985 'De Nederlandse samenleving in Indië', in: F.L. van Holthoon (ed.), *De Nederlandse samenleving sinds 1815; Wording en samenhang*, pp. 139-57. Assen: Van Gorcum.

1994 *De laatste eeuw van Indië; Ontwikkeling en ondergang van een koloniaal project*. Amsterdam: Bert Bakker.

Doorn, M. van and G.J. Telkamp

1977-79 *Bouwstoffen voor de sociaal-economische geschiedenis van Indonesië van ca. 1800 tot 1940; Een beschrijvende bibliografie – deel 2: de Indische Gids 1879-1941*. Amsterdam: Royal Tropical Institute.

Dros, N.

1992 *Wages 1820-1940*. Amsterdam: Royal Tropical Institute. [Changing economy in Indonesia; A selection of statistical source material from the early 19th century up to 1940, 13.]

East Asian miracle
1993 *The East Asian miracle; Economic growth and public policy; A World Bank policy research report*. New York: Oxford University Press for the World Bank.

Eiland Billiton
1918 'Het eiland Billiton als tineiland en de Billiton Maatschappij', *Tijdschrift voor Economische Geographie* 9:391-8.

Elson, R.E.
1984 *Javanese peasants and the colonial sugar industry; Impact and change in an East Java residency, 1830-1940*. Singapore: Oxford University Press.
1997 *The end of peasantry in Southeast Asia; A social and economic history of peasant livelihood, 1800-1990s*. London: Macmillan.

Eng, P. van der
1990 *Growth and productivity change in Indonesian agriculture, 1880-1985*. Groningen: Institute of Economic Research. [Institute of Economic Research Memorandum 348.]
1991 'An observer of 65 years of socio-economic change in Indonesia: Egbert de Vries', *Bulletin of Indonesian Economic Studies* 27-1:39-55.
1992 'The real domestic product of Indonesia 1880-1989', *Explorations in Economic History* 29:343-72.
1993a *Agricultural growth in Indonesia since 1880; Productivity change and the impact of government policy*. Groningen: Universiteitsdrukkerij. [PhD thesis, Groningen University.] [Also published as: *Agricultural growth in Indonesia; Productivity change and policy impact since 1880*. New York: St. Martin's Press, 1996.]
1993b *The 'colonial drain' from Indonesia, 1823-1990*. Canberra: Research School of Pacific Studies. [Economics Division Working Papers – Southeast Asia 93-2.]
1995 Review of W.L. Korthals Altes, *Prices (non-rice) 1814-1940*. Amsterdam 1994, *NEHA Bulletin* 9:163-5.
1996a 'A revolution in Indonesian agriculture? A long-term view on agricultural labour productivity', in: J.Th. Lindblad (ed.), *Historical foundations of a national economy in Indonesia, 1890s-1990s*, pp. 351-68. Amsterdam: North Holland. [KNAW, Verhandelingen, Afd. Letterkunde, Nieuwe Reeks, 167.]
1996b 'Challenging changes; Current themes in the economic history of Indonesia', *NEHA Bulletin* 10:89-113.
1996c *Agricultural growth in Indonesia; Productivity change and policy impact since 1880*. New York: St. Martin's Press.

Erman, E.
1994a 'Tauke, kuli dan penguasa; Eksploitasi hutan panglong di Riau', *Sejarah: pemikiran, rekonstruksi, persepsi* 5:20-33.
1994b 'Panglong; Lumber mills in Riau in colonial times', *Indonesian Environmental History Newsletter* 4:2-5.

Evans, P
1986 'Generalized linkages in industrial development; A re-examination of basic petrochemicals in Brazil', in: A. Foxley, M.S. McPherson and G.

O'Donnell (eds), *Development, democracy and the art of trespassing; Essays in honour of A.O. Hirschman*, pp. 7-27. Notre Dame: University of Notre Dame Press.

Fallows, J.
1994 *Looking at the sun; The rise of the new East Asian economic and political system*. New York: Vintage Books.

Fasseur, C.
1979 'Een koloniale paradox; De Nederlandse expansie in de Indonesische archipel in het midden van de negentiende eeuw (1830-1870)', *Tijdschrift voor Geschiedenis* 92:162-86.
1980 (ed.) *Geld en geweten; Een bundel opstellen over anderhalve eeuw Nederlands bestuur in de Indonesische archipel*. Den Haag: Nijhoff.
1990 'Clio and Clifford Geertz', *Itinerario* 14-2:71-80.
1993 *De Indologen; Ambtenaren voor de Oost 1825-1950*. Amsterdam: Bert Bakker.
1994 'Cornerstone and stumbling block; Racial classification and the late colonial state in Indonesia', in: R. Cribb (ed.), *The late colonial state in Indonesia; Political and economic foundations of the Netherlands Indies 1880-1942*, pp. 31-56. Leiden: KITLV Press. [Verhandelingen 163.]

Fernando, M.R. and D. Bulbeck (eds)
1992 *Chinese economic activity in Netherlands India; Selected translations from the Dutch*. Singapore: Institute of Southeast Asian Studies, Asean Economic Research Unit.

Feuilletau de Bruyn, W.K.H.
1924 'Onze petroleumindustrie en de internationale positie van Nederlandsch-Indië', *Koloniale Studiën* 8-1:247-99.

Fischer, E.J. (ed.)
1994 *Katoen voor Indië; Sociale ondernemers op het spoor naar vooruitgang 1825-1940*. Amsterdam: NEHA.

Fisher, C.A.
1964 'Some comments on population growth in Southeast Asia with special reference to the period since 1830', in: C.D. Cowan (ed.), *The economic development of South-East Asia; Studies in economic history and political economy*, pp. 48-71. London: Allen and Unwin.

Frank, A.G.
1973 'The development of underdevelopment', in: C.K. Wilber (ed.), *The political economy of development and underdevelopment*, pp. 94-104. New York: Random House.

Fukuyama, F.
1992 *The end of history and the last man*. New York: Free Press.
1995 *Trust; The social virtues and the creation of prosperity*. London: Hamish Hamilton.

Furnivall, J.S.
1944 *Netherlands India; A study of plural economy*. Cambridge/New York: Cambridge University Press. [Originally published 1939.]

Gade Ismail, M.
1994a *Seuneubok lada, uleëbalang, dan kumpeni; Perkembangan sosial ekonomi di daerah batas: Aceh Timur, 1840-1942*. [PhD thesis, Leiden University.]

1994b 'The economic position of the uleëbalang in the late colonial state; Eastern Aceh, 1900-1942', in: R. Cribb (ed.), *The late colonial state in Indonesia; Political and economic foundations of the Netherlands Indies 1880-1942*, pp. 79-91. Leiden: KITLV Press. [Verhandelingen 163.]

1996 'Aceh's dual economy during the late colonial period', in: J.Th. Lindblad (ed.), *Historical foundations of a national economy in Indonesia, 1890s-1990s*, pp. 229-48. Amsterdam: North Holland. [KNAW, Verhandelingen, Afd. Letterkunde, Nieuwe Reeks, 167.]

Garnaut, R.G. and P.T. McCauley (eds)

1980 *Indonesia; Dualism, growth and poverty*. Canberra: Research School of Pacific Studies, Australian National University.

Gautama, S. and R.N. Hornick

1972 *An introduction to Indonesian law; Unity in diversity*. Bandung: Alumni Print.

Gelder, A. van

1950 'Bevolkingsrubber', in: C.J.J. van Hall and C. van de Koppel (eds), *De landbouw in den Indischen Archipel*, Vol. III, pp. 427-75. 's-Gravenhage: Van Hoeve.

Gerretson, F.C.

1971-73 *Geschiedenis van de 'Koninklijke'*. Baarn: Bosch en Keuning. 3 vols. [First edition 1932-1941.] [Translated as: *History of the Royal Dutch*, Leiden: Brill, 1953-57. 5 vols.]

Gerritsen, D.J.

1935 'De tinfusie', *Koloniale Studiën* 19:135-75.

1938 'Nogmaals de tinfusie', *Koloniale Studiën* 22:417-54.

Getah pertja

1917 'Getah pertja', in: *Encyclopaedie van Nederlandsch-Indië* I, pp. 783-4. 's-Gravenhage: Nijhoff; Leiden: Brill.

Gevers, F.P.A.

1991 'Koloniale bedrijfsvoering in het Interbellum; De N.V. Deli-Maatschappij aan Sumatra's Oostkust, 1918-1940', *Jaarboek voor de Geschiedenis van Bedrijf en Techniek* 8:136-59.

Gillis, M., D.H. Perkins, M. Roemer and D.R. Snodgrass

1987 *Economics of development*. New York: Norton.

Gogh, F. van

1938 'Het ontstaan en de groei van de ondernemings- en bevolkingsrubbercultuur in Nederlandsch-Indië', *Economisch Weekblad van Nederlandsch-Indië* 7:125-9.

Golay, F.H.

1976 'The "colonial drain" revisited', in: C.D. Cowan and D.W. Wolters (eds), *Southeast Asian history and historiography; Essays presented to D.G.E. Hall*, pp. 268-387. London: Cornell University Press.

Gonggrijp, G.

1938 *Schets eener economische geschiedenis van Nederlandsch-Indië*. Second edition. Haarlem: Bohn. [First edition 1928.]

Goor, J. van
1986a (ed.) *Imperialisme in de marge; De afronding van Nederlands-Indië*. Utrecht: Hes.
1986b 'De Lombokexpeditie en het Nederlandse nationalisme', in: J. van Goor (ed.), *Imperialisme in de marge; De afronding van Nederlands-Indië*, pp. 19-70. Utrecht: Hes.
1994 *De Nederlandse koloniën; Geschiedenis van de Nederlandse expansie 1600-1975*. 's-Gravenhage: SDU.

Gooszen, A.J.
1994 *Een demografisch mozaïek; Indonesië 1880-1942*. [PhD thesis, Agricultural University of Wageningen.]

Graaff, B. de
1997 *'Kalm, temidden van woedende golven'; Het Ministerie van Koloniën en zijn taakomgeving, 1912-1940*. 's-Gravenhage: SDU.

Graaff, E.A. van de
1955 *De statistiek in Indonesië*. 's-Gravenhage: Van Hoeve.

Graaff, M.G.H.A de and A.M. Tempelaars
1991 *Inventaris van de Memories van Overgave 1849-1962 op microfiches*. Den Haag: Algemeen Rijksarchief.

Greene, M.
1987 *The Penguin business dictionary*. London: Penguin Books.

Habiboe, R.
1989 'De economische ontwikkeling van de Molukken 1900-1938', in: A.H.P. Clemens and J.Th. Lindblad (eds), *Het belang van de Buitengewesten; Economische expansie en koloniale staatsvorming in de Buitengewesten van NederlandsIndië 18701942*, pp. 243-80. Amsterdam: NEHA.

Haga, B.J.
1919 'De garnalenvisscherij van Bagan Api-Api', *Koloniale Studiën* 3-1:151-59.
1920 'De klappercultuur en coprahandel in de Poelau Toedjoe (Riouw)', *Koloniale Studiën* 4-2:314-42.

Hagreis, B.J. and H. Vonk
1927-28 'Beknopte beschrijving van de inheemse landbouw in Tapanoeli', *Landbouw* 3:681-706.

Hall, C.J.J. van
1942 *Insulinde; Werk en welvaart*. Naarden: In den Toren.
1943 *Insulinde; De inheemse landbouw*. Deventer: Van Hoeve.

Hall, C.J.J. van and C. van de Koppel (eds)
1946-50 *De landbouw in den Indischen Archipel*. 's-Gravenhage: Van Hoeve. 3 vols.

Handboek cultuur- en handels-ondernemingen
1888-1940 *Handboek voor cultuur- en handels-ondernemingen in Nederlandsch-Indië*. Amsterdam: De Bussy.

Heersink, C.G.
1999 *Dependence on green gold; A socio-economic history of the Indonesian coconut island Selayar*. Leiden: KITLV Press. [Verhandelingen 184.])

Henley, D.E.F.
1989 *The idea of Celebes in history*. Clayton: Centre of Southeast Asian Studies, Monash University. [Working Paper 59.]
1995 *Nationalism and regionalism in a colonial context; Minahasa in the Dutch East Indies*. Leiden: KITLV Press. [Verhandelingen 168.]

Higgins, B.
1955-56 'The dualistic theory of underdeveloped areas', *Economic Development and Cultural Change* 4:99-115. [Originally published in *Ekonomi dan Keuangan Indonesia* 8 (1955):58-78.]
1984 'Jan Boeke and the doctrine of "The little push"', *Bulletin of Indonesian Economic Studies* 20-3:55-69.

Hill, H.
1989 (ed.) *Unity and diversity; Regional economic development in Indonesia since 1970*. Singapore: Oxford University Press.
1992a 'Indonesia's foreign investment regime since 1986; Balancing economic imperative and political constraints', in: M. Arsjad Anwar, Thee Kian Wie and Iwan Jaya Azis (eds), *Pemikiran, pelaksanaan, dan perintisan pembangunan ekonomi*, pp. 591-615. Jakarta: Fakultas Ekonomi Universitas Indonesia (ISEI).
1992b 'Regional development in a boom and bust petroleum economy; Indonesia since 1970', *Economic Development and Cultural Change* 40:351-79.

Hill, H. and A. Weidemann
1989 'Regional development in Indonesia; Patterns and issues', in: H. Hill (ed.), *Unity and diversity; Regional economic development in Indonesia since 1970*, pp. 3-54. Singapore: Oxford University Press.

Hirschman, A.O
1977 'A generalized linkage approach to development, with special reference to staples', in: *Economic Development and Cultural Change* 25, Supplement:67-98.
1980 *National power and the structure of foreign trade*. Berkeley: University of California Press. [First edition 1945.]

Hoedt, Th.G.E.
1929 'Enige voorname verschilpunten bij de koffiecultuur in Oost-Java en in Zuid-Sumatra; Voordracht gehouden voor de kring Benkoelen der "Zusuma" te Kepahlang op 18-1-1929', *De Bergcultures* 3:887-99.
1930 *Indische bergcultuurondernemingen, voornamelijk in Zuid-Sumatra; Gegevens en beschouwingen*. Wageningen: Veenman. [PhD thesis, Agricultural University of Wageningen.]

Homan, G.D.
1987 'That "beautiful tobacco"; The Sumatra cigar wrapper and the American tariff, c. 1880-1941', *Economisch en Sociaal-Historisch Jaarboek* 50:145-56.

Hoogland, W.H. (ed.)
1927 'De ontwikkeling van Palembang', *Algemeen Landbouwweekblad voor Nederlandsch-Indië* 12:549-56.

Houben, V.J.H.
1987 'Native states in India and Indonesia; The nineteenth century', *Itinerario* 11-1:107-34.

1988 'History and morality; East Sumatran incidents as described by Jan Breman', *Itinerario* 12-2:97-100.

1993 '"Colonial history" revisited; A response to Breman', *Itinerario* 17-1:93-8.

1994 'Profit versus ethics; Government enterprises in the late colonial state', in: R. Cribb (ed.), *The late colonial state in Indonesia; Political and economic foundations of the Netherlands Indies 1880-1942*, pp. 191-211. Leiden: KITLV Press. [Verhandelingen 163.]

1995 'Labour conditions on Western firms in colonial Indonesia; Outline of an approach', *Jahrbuch für Wirtschaftsgeschichte* (1995):93-108.

1996 'The Labour Inspectorate and labour conditions in the Outer Islands and Java, 1900-1940', in: J.Th. Lindblad (ed.), *Historical foundations of a national economy in Indonesia, 1890s-1990s*, pp. 193-206. Amsterdam: North Holland. [KNAW, Verhandelingen, Afd. Letterkunde, Nieuwe Reeks, 167.]

Houben, V.J.H., J.Th. Lindblad et al. (eds)

1999 *Coolie labour in colonial Indonesia; A study of labour relatons in the Outer Islands, c. 1900-1940*. Wiesbaden: Harrassowitz.

Hövig, P.

1937 'De tinfusie', *Koloniale Studiën* 21:491-518.

Hovinga, H.

1996 *Eindstation Pakan Baru 1943-1945; Dodenspoorweg door het oerwoud*. Fourth edition. Amsterdam: Buijten en Schipperheijn. [First edition 1976.]

Hüsken, F.

1994 'Declining welfare in Java; Government and private inquiries, 1903-1914', in: R. Cribb (ed.), *The late colonial state in Indonesia; Political and economic foundations of the Netherlands Indies 1880-1942*, pp. 213-27. Leiden: KITLV Press. [Verhandelingen 163.]

Huff, D.

1973 *How to lie with statistics*. Harmondsworth: Penguin Books.

Huff, W.G.

1993 'The development of the rubber market in pre-World War II Singapore', *Journal of Southeast Asian Studies* 24:285-306.

1994 *The economic growth of Singapore; Trade and development in the twentieth century*. Cambridge: Cambridge University Press.

Indisch Staatsblad

1847-1939 *Indisch Staatsblad; Staatsblad voor Nederlandsch-Indië*. Batavia: Landsdrukkerij.

Indisch Verslag

1931-38 *Indisch Verslag*. 's-Gravenhage: Rijksuitgeverij.

Indonesian economics

1961 *Indonesian economics; The concept of dualism in theory and policy*. The Hague: Van Hoeve.

Jaarboek Mijnwezen

1880-1939 *Jaarboek van het Mijnwezen in Nederlandsch Oost-Indië*. Amsterdam: Stemler; Weltevreden: Landsdrukkerij.

Jaaroverzicht
1925-42 *Jaaroverzicht van den in- en uitvoer van Nederlandsch-Indië gedurende het jaar 1924-1940*. Weltevreden: Kolff; Batavia: Landsdrukkerij. [Mededeelingen van het Centraal Kantoor voor de Statistiek (Statistisch Kantoor) 20-176.]

Johan, J.
1934-35 'Bereiding van smoked sheets in de Chinese districten van West-Borneo', *Landbouw* 10:189-204.

Jong, J.J.P. de
1998 *De waaier van het fortuin; De Nederlanders in Azië en de Indonesische archipel 1595-1950*. Den Haag: SDU.

Jonge, J.A. de
1968 *De industrialisatie in Nederland tussen 1850 en 1914*. Amsterdam: Scheltema en Holkema.

Josselin de Jong, P.E. de (ed.)
1984 *Unity in diversity; Indonesia as a field of anthropological study*. Dordrecht: Foris. [KITLV, Verhandelingen 103.]

Kahin, A.R. (ed.)
1985 *Regional dynamics of the Indonesian revolution; Unity from diversity*. Honolulu: University of Hawaii Press.

Kahn, J.S.
1993 *Constituting the Minangkabau; Peasants, culture and modernity in colonial Indonesia*. Providence: Berg.

Kamerling, R.N.J.
1979 'De copra-olie industrie in Nederlands-Indië gedurende en kort na de Eerste Wereldoorlog (1914-1921)', in: *Between people and statistics; Essays on Indonesian history, presented to P. Creutzberg*, pp. 101-17. The Hague: Nijhoff.
1982 *De N.V. Oliefabrieken Insulinde in Nederlands-Indië; Bedrijfsvoering in het onbekende*. Franeker: Wever.

Kamphues, A.
1988 'Na Rhemrev; Arbeidsomstandigheden op de westerse ondernemingen in de Buitengewesten van Nederlands-Indië, 1904-1938', *Economisch en Sociaal-Historisch Jaarboek* 51:299-337.

Kindleberger, C.P.
1958 'The terms of trade and economic development', *Review of Economics and Statistics* 15, Supplement:72-85.
1990 *Historical economics, art or science?* Berkeley: University of California Press.

Kindleberger, C.P. and B. Herrick
1983 *Economic development*. New York: McGraw-Hill. [First edition 1958.]

Klein, P.W.
1989 'The China seas and the world economy between the sixteenth and nineteenth centuries; The changing structures of trade', in: C.-L. Holtfrerich (ed.), *Interactions in the world-economy; Perspectives from international economic history*, pp. 59-90. New York: Harvester Wheatsheaf. [Also published in: C.A. Davids, W. Fritschy and L.A. Valk (eds), *Kapitaal, ondernemerschap en beleid; Studies over economie en politiek in Nederland, Europa en Azië van 1500 tot heden*, pp. 385-408. Amsterdam: NEHA.]

Knaap, A.J.
1912 'Het katoenvraagstuk', *Koloniaal Tijdschrift* 1:13-75, 172-81.

Knaap, G.J.
1987 *Kruidnagelen en Christenen; De Verenigde Oost-Indische Compagnie en de bevolking van Ambon 1656-1696*. Dordrecht: Foris. [KITLV, Verhandelingen 125.]
1989 *Transport 1819-1940*. Amsterdam: Royal Tropical Institute. [Changing economy in Indonesia; A selection of statistical source material from the early 19th century up to 1940, 9.]

Kol, H. van
1903 *Uit onze koloniën; Uitvoerig reisverhaal*. Leiden: Sijthoff.

Kolff, G.H. van der
1929 'European influence on native agriculture', in: B. Schrieke (ed.), *The effect of Western influence on native civilisation in the Malay archipelago*, pp. 103-25. Batavia: Koninklijk Bataviaasch Genootschap van Kunsten en Wetenschappen.

Koloniaal Verslag
1900-30 *Koloniaal Verslag; Bijlage C van het verslag der handelingen van de Tweede Kamer der Staten-Generaal*. 's-Gravenhage: Algemeene Landsdrukkerij.

Kommer, A. van
1989 'De Deli-Maatschappij aan de Oostkust van Sumatra, 1900-1940', in: A.H.P. Clemens and J.Th. Lindblad (eds), *Het belang van de Buitengewesten; Economische expansie en koloniale staatsvorming in de Buitengewesten van Nederlands-Indië 1870-1942*, pp. 97-118. Amsterdam: NEHA.

Koppel, C. van de
1946 'Enige statistische gegevens over de landbouw in Nederlands-Indië', in: C.J.J. van Hall and C. van de Koppel (eds), *De landbouw in den Indischen Archipel*, Vol. I, pp. 301-423. 's-Gravenhage: Van Hoeve.

Korthals Altes, W.L.
1986 *De betalingsbalans van Nederlandsch-Indië 1822-1932*. [PhD thesis, Erasmus University, Rotterdam.]
1987 *Balance of payments 1822-1939*. Amsterdam: Royal Tropical Institute. [Changing economy in Indonesia; A selection of statistical source material from the early 19th century up to 1940, 7.]
1991 *General trade statistics 1822-1940*. Amsterdam: Royal Tropical Institute. [Changing economy in Indonesia; A selection of statistical source material from the early 19th century up to 1940, 12A.]
1994 *Prices (non-rice) 1814-1940*. Amsterdam: Royal Tropical Institute. [Changing economy in Indonesia; A selection of statistical source material from the early 19th century up to 1940, 15.]

Kousbroek, R.
1992 *Het Oost-Indisch kampsyndroom; Anathema's 6*. Amsterdam: Meulenhoff.

Krafft, A.J.C.
1929 *Coöperatie in Indië; Een sociaal-paedagogisch vraagstuk*. Groningen: n.n.

Kroon, A.H.J.
1928 'Landbouw in Palembang', *Algemeen Landbouwweekblad voor Nederlandsch-Indië* 13:2-3, 36-7.

Kuitenbrouwer, M.
1986 *Nederland en de opkomst van het moderne imperialisme; Koloniën en buitenlandse politiek, 1870-1902*. Amsterdam/Dieren: De Bataafsche Leeuw. [Translated as: *The Netherlands and the rise of modern imperialism; Colonies and foreign policy, 1870-1902*, Oxford: Berg, 1991.]
1994 'Drie omwentelingen in de historiografie van het imperialisme; Engeland en Nederland', *Tijdschrift voor Geschiedenis* 107:559-85.
Kuznets, S.
1966 *Modern economic growth; Rate, structure and spread*. New York/New Haven: Yale University Press.
Laanen, J.T.M. van
1980 *Money and banking 1816-1940*. Amsterdam: Royal Tropical Institute. [Changing economy in Indonesia; A selection of statistical source material from the early 19th century up to 1940, 6.]
1990 'Between the Java Bank and the Chinese moneylender; Banking and credit in colonial Indonesia', in: A. Booth, W.J. O'Malley and A. Weidemann (eds), *Indonesian economic history in the Dutch colonial era*, pp. 244-66. New Haven: Yale Center for International Area Studies.
Landbouwexportgewassen
1931 *De landbouwexportgewassen van Nederlandsch-Indië in 1930*. Weltevreden: Albrecht. [Mededeelingen van het Centraal Kantoor voor de Statistiek 97.]
1933 *De landbouwexportgewassen van Nederlandsch-Indië in 1932*. Weltevreden: Albrecht. [Mededeelingen van het Centraal Kantoor voor de Statistiek 115.]
Langeveld, H.J.
1978 'Arbeidstoestanden op de ondernemingen ter Oostkust van Sumatra tussen 1920 en 1940 in het licht van het verdwijnen van de poenale sanctie op de arbeidscontracten', *Economisch en Sociaal-Historisch Jaarboek* 41:294-368.
Legge, J.D.
1964 *Indonesia; Modern nations in historical perspective*. Sydney: Prentice Hall.
Leinbach, T.R.
1972 'The spread of modernization in Malaya: 1895-1969', *Tijdschrift voor Economische en Sociale Geographie* 63:262-75.
Leirissa, R.Z.
1993 'The structure of Makassar-Bugis trade in pre-modern Moluccas', *Review of Indonesian and Malaysian Affairs* 27, 1-2:77-90.
1996 '"Copracontracten"; An indication of economic development in Minahasa during the late colonial period', in: J.Th. Lindblad (ed.), *Historical foundations of a national economy in Indonesia, 1890s-1990s*, pp. 265-77. Amsterdam: North Holland. [KNAW, Verhandelingen, Afd. Letterkunde, Nieuwe Reeks, 167.]
Lenstra, R.
1986 'Jacob Theodoor Cremer, het koloniaal beheer en het Nederlands belang in Atjeh', *Economisch en Sociaal-Historisch Jaarboek* 49:165-216.

Leur, J.C. van

1955 *Indonesian trade and society; Essays in Asian social and economic history*. The Hague: Van Hoeve.

Lindblad, J.Th.

1985a 'Economic change in Southeast Kalimantan 1880-1940', *Bulletin of Indonesian Economic Studies* 21-3:69-103.

1985b 'Strak beleid en batig slot; De Oost-Borneo Maatschappij, 1999-1940', *Economisch en Sociaal-Historisch Jaarboek* 48:182-211.

1986 'Economische aspecten van de Nederlandse expansie in de Indonesische archipel, 1870-1914', in: J. van Goor (ed.), *Imperialisme in de marge; De afronding van Nederlands-Indië*, pp. 227-66. Utrecht: Hes.

1988a *Between Dayak and Dutch; The economic history of Southeast Kalimantan 1880-1940*. Dordrecht/Providence: Foris. [KITLV, Verhandelingen 134.]

1988b 'De handel tussen Nederland en Nederlands-Indië, 1874-1939', *Economisch en Sociaal-Historisch Jaarboek* 51:240-98.

1989a 'The petroleum industry in Indonesia before the Second World War', *Bulletin of Indonesian Economic Studies* 25-2:53-77.

1989b 'Economic aspects of the Dutch expansion in Indonesia, 1870-1914', *Modern Asian Studies* 23:1-23.

1989c 'De opkomst van de Buitengewesten', in: A.H.P. Clemens and J.Th. Lindblad (eds), *Het belang van de Buitengewesten; Economische expansie en koloniale staatsvorming in de Buitengewesten van Nederlands-Indië 1870-1942*, pp. 1-34. Amsterdam, NEHA.

1990a 'The economic history of colonial Indonesia; A historiographical survey', *Economic and Social History in the Netherlands* 1:31-49.

1990b 'The process of economic development in the Outer Provinces of the Dutch East-Indies', *Journal of the Japan-Netherlands Institute* 2:208-34.

1991 'Foreign investment in late-colonial and post-colonial Indonesia', *Economic and Social History in the Netherlands* 3:183-208.

1993a (ed.) *New challenges in the modern economic history of Indonesia*. Leiden: Programme of Indonesian Studies.

1993b 'Economic growth in the Outer Islands 1910-1940', in: J.Th. Lindblad (ed.), *New challenges in the modern economic history of Indonesia*, pp. 233-63. Leiden: Programme of Indonesian Studies.

1993c 'Ondernemen in Nederlands-Indië ca. 1900-1940', *Bijdragen en Mededelingen betreffende de Geschiedenis der Nederlanden* 108:699-710.

1994a 'The contribution of foreign trade to colonial state formation in Indonesia 1900-1930', in: R. Cribb (ed.), *The late colonial state in Indonesia; Political and economic foundations of the Netherlands Indies 1880-1942*, pp. 93-116. Leiden: KITLV Press. [Verhandelingen 163.]

1994b 'Trends en bedrijfsvoering in de koloniale landbouw; Voorbeelden uit Nederlands-Indië, c. 1915-1940', in: H.A. Diederiks, J.Th. Lindblad and B.M.A. de Vries (eds), *Het platteland in een veranderende wereld; Boeren en het proces van modernisering*, pp. 57-78. Hilversum: Verloren.

1995 'Colonial rule and economic development; A review of the recent historiography on Indonesia', *Jahrbuch für Wirtschaftsgeschichte* (1995):9-22.

1996a (ed.) *Historical foundations of a national economy in Indonesia, 1890s-1990s.* Amsterdam: North Holland. [KNAW, Verhandelingen, Afd. Letterkunde, Nieuwe Reeks, 167.]

1996b 'Business strategies in late colonial Indonesia', in: J.Th. Lindblad (ed.), *Historical foundations of a national economy in Indonesia, 1890s-1990s,* pp. 207-27. Amsterdam: North Holland. [KNAW, Verhandelingen, Afd. Letterkunde, Nieuwe Reeks, 167.]

1996c 'The economic history of colonial Indonesia in Southeast Asian perspective, c. 1850-1942.' Paper presented at the 14th Conference of the International Association of Historians of Asia, Bangkok, 20-24 May 1996.

1998 *Foreign investment in Southeast Asia in the twentieth century.* London: Macmillan.

Locher-Scholten, E.B.

1981 *Ethiek in fragmenten; Vijf studies over koloniaal denken en doen van Nederlanders in de Indonesische Archipel 1877-1942.* Utrecht: Hes.

1994a *Sumatraans sultanaat en koloniale staat; De relatie Djambi-Batavia (1830-1907) en het Nederlandse imperialisme.* Leiden: KITLV Uitgeverij. [Verhandelingen 161.]

1994b 'Dutch expansion in the Indonesian Archipelago around 1900 and the imperialism debate', *Journal of Southeast Asian Studies* 25:91-111.

Loos, H. and D. van Beusechem

1925 *De bevolkingsrubbercultuur in Nederlandsch-Indië; III: West Borneo.* Weltevreden: Landsdrukkerij.

Luytjes, A.

1925a *De bevolkingsrubbercultuur in Nederlandsch-Indië; IIa: Zuid- en Oost Borneo.* Weltevreden: Landsdrukkerij.

1925b *De bevolkingsrubbercultuur in Nederlandsch-Indië; VII: eindrapport.* Weltevreden: Landsdrukkerij.

Maas, J.G.J.A. and F.T. Bokma

1950 'Rubbercultuur der ondernemingen', in: C.J.J. van Hall and C. van de Koppel (ed.), *De landbouw in den Indischen Archipel,* Vol. III, pp. 237-426. 's-Gravenhage: Van Hoeve.

Mackie, J.A.C.

1971 'The Indonesian economy, 1950-1963', in: B. Glassburner (ed.), *The economy of Indonesia; Selected readings,* pp. 16-69. Ithaca/London: Cornell University Press.

1976 (ed.) *The Chinese in Indonesia; Five essays.* Melbourne: Nelson.

1980 'The concept of dualism and its application to Indonesian agriculture', in: R.G. Garnaut and P.T. McCauley (eds), *Indonesia; Dualism, growth and poverty,* pp. 295-306. Canberra: Research School of Pacific Studies, Australian National University.

1992 'Dualism and market segmentation in Indonesia', in: M. Arsjad Anwar, Thee Kian Wie and Iwan Jaya Azis (eds), *Pemikiran, pelaksanaan, dan perintisan pembangunan ekonomi,* pp. 49-68. Jakarta: Fakultas Ekonomi Universitas Indonesia (ISEI).

Maddison, A.

1989a 'Dutch income in and from Indonesia', *Modern Asian Studies* 23:645-70.

1989b 'Dutch income in and from Indonesia, 1700-1938', in: A. Maddison and G. Prince (eds), *Economic growth in Indonesia 1820-1940*, pp. 15-42. Dordrecht/Providence: Foris. [KITLV, Verhandelingen 137.]

Maddison, A. and G. Prince (eds)
1989 *Economic growth in Indonesia 1820-1940*. Dordrecht/Providence: Foris. [KITLV, Verhandelingen 137.]

Mansvelt, W.M.F.
1924-26 *Geschiedenis van de Nederlandsche Handel-Maatschappij 1824-1924*. Amsterdam: Nederlandsche Handel-Maatschappij. 2 vols.

Markt
1932 'De markt voor exportproducten te Banjermassin gedurende 1931', *Economisch Weekblad van Nederlandsch-Indië* 1:91-3.

McFadyean, A. (ed.)
1944 *The history of rubber regulation 1934-1943*. London: Allen and Unwin.

Meier, G.M.
1984 *Leading issues in economic development*. Fourth edition. New York: Oxford University Press. [First edition 1964.]

Meilink-Roelofsz, M.A.P.
1968 'Memories van Overgave van bestuursambtenaren in het voormalig Nederlands-Indië', *Nederlandsch Archievenblad* 72:14-8.

Mendelaar, J.J.
1925 'Djambi, de rubber en de Djambiër', *Koloniale Studiën* 9-2:325-61.

Muchie, M.
1989 'Colonialism and the development debate', in: M. Muchie, H.L. Wesseling and O. Prakash (eds), *North–South perspectives; Debates on colonialism and North–South relations*, pp. 9-50. Amsterdam: Royal Tropical Institute. [Bulletin of the Royal Tropical Institute 319.]

Multatuli
1988 *Max Havelaar of de koffieveilingen van de Nederlandsche HandelMaatschappij*. Rotterdam: Elsevier. [First edition 1860.]

Myint, H.
1958 'The "classical theory" of international trade and the underdeveloped countries', *Economic Journal* 68:317-37.
1971 *Economic theory and the underdeveloped countries*. London: Oxford University Press.
1980 *The economics of developing countries*. London: Hutchinson. [First edition 1964.]

Mijnbouw
1917 'Mijnbouw; Mijnontginning', in: *Encyclopaedie van Nederlandsch-Indië* I, pp. 837-47. 's-Gravenhage: Nijhoff; Leiden: Brill.

Myrdal, G.
1968 *Asian drama; An inquiry into the poverty of nations*. New York: Pantheon. 3 vols.

Neytzell de Wilde, A.
1935 *Welvaart en traditie*. Wageningen: Veenman.

Neytzell de Wilde, A. and J.Th.Moll
1936 *The Netherlands Indies during the Depression; A brief economic survey*. Amsterdam: Meulenhoff.
Nieuwenhuis, A.W.
1904-07 *Quer durch Borneo; Ergebnisse seiner reisen in den jahren 1894, 1896-97 und 1898-1900*. Leiden: Brill.
Nitisastro, Widjojo
1970 *Population trends in Indonesia*. Ithaca: Cornell University Press.
Ohler, N.
1980 *Quantitative Methoden für Historiker; Eine Einführung*. München: Beck.
O'Malley, W.J.
1977 *Indonesia in the Great Depression; A study of East-Sumatra and Yogyakarta in the 1930s*. [PhD thesis, Cornell University, Ithaca.]
1990 'Introduction', in: A. Booth, W.J. O'Malley and A. Weidemann (eds), *Indonesian economic history in the Dutch colonial era*, pp. 1-24. New Haven: Yale Center for International Area Studies.
Onderzoek mindere welvaart
1905-14 *Onderzoek naar de mindere welvaart der inlandsche bevolking op Java en Madoera*. Batavia: Kolff/Ruygrok. [12 parts in 45 vols.]
Ours, J.C. van
1995 'The price elasticity of hard drugs; The case of opium in the Dutch East Indies, 1923-1938', *Journal of Political Economy* 103:261-79.
Overzicht der geldmiddelen
1916 *Overzicht der geldmiddelen van Nederlandsch-Indië van 1867 af*. 's-Gravenhage: Nijhoff.
Ozinga, J.
1929 Palembang en de landbouw', *Algemeen Landbouwweekblad voor Nederlandsch-Indië* 13-45:1558-62.
1940 *De economische ontwikkeling der Westerafdeling van Borneo en de bevolkingsrubbercultuur*. Wageningen: Zomer en Keuning. [PhD thesis, Utrecht University.]
Parimartha, I Gde
1995 *Perdagangan dan politik di Nusa Tenggara 1815-1915*. [PhD thesis, Free University, Amsterdam.]
Peeters, J.C.M.
1994 *Kaum Mudo – Kaum Tuo; Sociaal-religieuze verandering in Palembang, 1821-1942*. [PhD thesis, Leiden University.]
Pekelharing, N.R.
1925 *De bevolkingsrubbercultuur in Nederlandsch-Indië; Ib: Djambi*. Weltevreden: Landsdrukkerij. [Translated as: *Native rubber cultivation in the Dutch East-Indies*. Vol. I, Djambi, 1925.]
Pelras, C.
1996 *The Bugis; The peoples of South-East Asia and the Pacific*. Cambridge: Blackwell.

Pelzer, K.J.

1978 *Planter and peasant; Colonial policy and the agrarian struggle in East Sumatra, 1863-1947*. 's-Gravenhage: Nijhoff. [KITLV, Verhandelingen 84.]

1982 *Planters against peasants; The agrarian struggle in East Sumatra 1947-1958*. 's-Gravenhage: Nijhoff. [KITLV, Verhandelingen 97.]

Phoa Liong Gie

1936 'De economische positie der Chineezen in Nederlandsch-Indië', *Koloniale Studiën* 20-5/6:97-119.

Ploeg, F.P.C.S. van der

1945 *Insulinde; Schatten van de bodem*. Deventer: Van Hoeve.

Poelinggomang, E.L.

1993 'The Dutch trade policy an its impact on Makassars trade', *Review of Indonesian and Malaysian Affairs* 27-1/2:61-76.

Poeze, H.A.

1982-95 *Politiek-Politioneele Overzichten van Nederlandsch-Indië; Bronnenpublikatie*. Vol. I. The Hague: Nijhoff. Vol. II-III. Dordrecht: Foris. Vol. IV. Leiden: KITLV Uitgeverij. 4 vols.

Polak, J.J.

1945 *The national income of the Netherlands Indies, 1921-1939*. Amsterdam: n.n.

Post, P.

1991 *Japanse bedrijvigheid in Indonesië 1868-1942; Structurele elementen van Japan's economische expansie in Zuidoost Azië*. [PhD thesis, Free University, Amsterdam.]

1993 'Japan and the integration of the Netherlands East Indies into the world economy, 1868-1942', *Review of Indonesian and Malaysian Affairs* 27-1/2: 134-65.

1996 'The formation of the pribumi business élite in Indonesia, 1930s-1940s', *Bijdragen tot de Taal-, Land- en Volkenkunde* 152:609-33. [Also published in: Peter Post and Elly Touwen Bouwsma (eds), *Japan, Indonesia and the war; Myths and realities*, pp. 87-100. Leiden: KITLV Press, 1997. [Verhandelingen 173.]]

Potter, L.

1993 'Banjarese in and beyond Hulu Sungai, South Kalimantan; A study of cultural independence, economic opportunity and mobility', in: J.Th. Lindblad (ed.), *New challenges in the modern economic history of Indonesia*, pp. 264-98. Leiden: Programme of Indonesian Studies.

Potting, C.J.M.

1987 'De muntvoorziening in Nederlands-Indië, 1877-1913', *Economisch en Sociaal-Historisch Jaarboek* 50:111-44.

1989 'De komst van Nederlandse banken naar Sumatra, 1877-1914', in: A.H.P. Clemens and J.Th. Lindblad (eds), *Het belang van de Buitengewesten; Economische expansie en koloniale staatsvorming in de Buitengewesten van Nederlands-Indië 1870-1942*, pp. 67-94. Amsterdam: NEHA.

1997 *De ontwikkeling van het geldverkeer in een koloniale samenleving; Oostkust van Sumatra 1875-1938*. [PhD thesis, Leiden University.]

Prince, G.H.A.
1978 'Theorieën over voorsprong en achterstand', in: H. Baudet and H. van der Meulen (eds), *Kernproblemen der economische geschiedenis*, pp. 263-95. Groningen: Wolters-Noordhoff.
1989 'Dutch economic policy in Indonesia, 1870-1942', in: A. Maddison and G. Prince (eds), *Economic growth in Indonesia 1820-1940*, pp. 203-27. Dordrecht/Providence: Foris. [KITLV, Verhandelingen 137.]
1993 'Economic policy in Indonesia 1900-1942', in: J.Th. Lindblad (ed.), *New challenges in the modern economic history of Indonesia*, pp. 161-81. Leiden: Programme of Indonesian Studies.
1995 'Dutch economic policy in colonial Indonesia 1900-1942; Some key topics', *Jahrbuch für Wirtschaftsgeschichte* (1995):23-44.
1996 'Monetary policy in colonial Indonesia and the position of the Java Bank', in: J.Th. Lindblad (ed.), *Historical foundations of a national economy in Indonesia, 1890s-1990s*, pp. 55-70. Amsterdam: North Holland. [KNAW, Verhandelingen, Afd. Letterkunde, Nieuwe Reeks, 167.]

Purwanto, Bambang
1992 *From dusun to the market; Native rubber cultivation in Southern Sumatra, 1890-1940*. [PhD thesis, University of London.]
1993 'The economy of the native population of Southern Sumatra between 1850 and 1910', *Review of Indonesian and Malaysian Affairs* 27-1/2:106-33.
1996 'The economy of Indonesian smallholder rubber, 1890s-1940', in: J.Th. Lindblad (ed.), *Historical foundations of a national economy in Indonesia, 1890s-1990s*, pp. 175-92. Amsterdam: North Holland. [KNAW, Verhandelingen, Afd. Letterkunde, Nieuwe Reeks, 167.]

Ranken, E.A.
1989 'De niet-Europese bijdrage tot de economische ontwikkeling van West-Borneo, 1900-1940', in: A.H.P. Clemens and J.Th. Lindblad (eds), *Het belang van de Buitengewesten; Economische expansie en koloniale staatsvorming in de Buitengewesten van Nederlands-Indië 1870-1942*, pp. 177-209. Amsterdam: NEHA.

Ray, R.K.
1995 'Asian capital in the age of European domination; The rise of the bazaar, 1800-1914', *Modern Asian Studies* 29:449-554.

Regeerings-Almanak
1900-40 *Regeerings-Almanak voor Nederlandsch-Indië*. Batavia: Landsdrukkerij.

Reid, A.
1979 *The blood of the people; Revolution and the end of traditional rule in northern Sumatra*. Oxford: Oxford University Press.
1988 *Southeast Asia in the age of commerce, 1450-1680*, Vol. I: *The lands below the winds*. New Haven/London: Yale University Press.
1993 *Southeast Asia in the age of commerce, 1450-1680*, Vol. II: *Expansion and crisis*. New Haven/London: Yale University Press.
1995 'Maluku revisited', *Bijdragen tot de Taal-, Land- en Volkenkunde* 151:132-5.

Reitsma, H.A. and J.M.G. Kleinpenning
1985 *The third world in perspective*. Assen/Maastricht: Van Gorcum.

Ricklefs, M.C.
1993 *A history of modern Indonesia since ca. 1300*. Basingstoke/London: Macmillan. [First edition 1981.]
Ridder, J. de
1935 *De invloed van de Westersche cultures op de autochtone bevolking ter Oostkust van Sumatra*. Wageningen: Veenman. [PhD thesis, Leiden University.]
Rohwer, J.
1995 *Asia rising; How history's biggest middle class will change the world*. Singapore: Butterworth-Heinemann Asia.
Rostow, W.W.
1956 'The takeoff into self-sustained growth', *Economic Journal* 66:25-48.
1960 *The stages of economic growth; A non-communist manifesto*. Cambridge: Cambridge University Press.
Rothe, C.
1950 'De arbeid in de Landbouw', in: C.J.J. van Hall and C. van de Koppel (eds), *De landbouw in den Indischen Archipel*, Vol. III, pp. 310-47. 's-Gravenhage: Van Hoeve.
Rudin, W.F.
1935-36 'De bevolkingskoffiecultuur in de Marga Ranau (residentie Palembang)', *Landbouw* 11:256-322.
Rutgers, A.A.L.
1925 *De toekomst van de bevolkingsrubber in Nederlandsch-Indië*. [Reprint from *De Indische Mercuur*, 27-11-1925.]
Said, E.W.
1978 *Orientalism*. New York: Pantheon Books.
Schefold, R. (ed.)
1995 *Minahasa past and present; Tradition and transition in an Outer Island region of Indonesia*. Leiden: Research School CNWS.
Scheltema, A.M.P.A.
1929 'Eenige gegevens betreffende den economischen toestand in de regentschappen, van waar in 1928 de meeste contractkoelies vertrokken', *Koloniale Studiën* 13-2:414-29.
Scholte, P.T.
1989 'De Mijnbouw-Maatschappij "Salida" in West-Sumatra, 1910-1933', in: A.H.P. Clemens and J.Th. Lindblad (eds), *Het belang van de Buitengewesten; Economische expansie en koloniale staatsvorming in de Buitengewesten van Nederlands-Indië 1870-1942*, pp. 151-73. Amsterdam: NEHA.
Schouten, M.J.C.
1998 *Leadership and social mobility in a Southeast Asian Society; Minahasa, 1677-1983*. Leiden: KITLV Press. [Verhandelingen 179.]
Schulte Nordholt, H.
1991 *State, village, and ritual in Bali; A historical perspective*. Amsterdam: VU University Press.
1996 *The spell of power; A history of Balinese politics 1650-1940*. Leiden: KITLV Press. [Verhandelingen 170.]

Scott, J.C.
1976 *The moral economy of the peasant; Rebellion and subsistence in Southeast Asia.* New Haven: Yale University Press.

Seagrave, S.
1995 *Lords of the rim; The invisible empire of the overseas Chinese.* New York: Putnam.

Seers, D. (ed.)
1981 *Dependency theory; A critical reassessment.* London: Pinter.

Segers, W.A.I.M.
1988 *Manufacturing industry 1870-1942.* Amsterdam: Royal Tropical Institute. [Changing economy in Indonesia; A selection of statistical source material from the early 19th century up to 1940, 8.]

Setten, D.J.G. van
1912 'Het katoenvraagstuk in Nederlandsch-Indië en in het bijzonder in betrekking tot de residentie Palembang', *Koloniaal Tijdschrift* 1:1103-15.

Sjahrir, S.
1987 *Indonesische overpeinzingen.* Fifth edition. Amsterdam: Bezige Bij. [First edition 1945.] [Translated as: *Out of exile,* New York: John Day, 1949.]

Slotemaker, C.G.
1926 *De bevolkingsrubbercultuur in Nederlandsch-Indië; VI: Riouw, Oost-Sumatra en Atjeh.* Weltevreden: Landsdrukkerij.

Smail, J.R.W.
1961 'On the possibility of an autonomous history of modern Southeast Asia', *Journal of Southeast Asian History* 2:72-102.

Smits, M.B.
1926 'Economische verschijnselen in een paar rubbergewesten', *Economisch-Statistische Berichten* 11:492-4.

Snooks, G.D., A.J.S. Reid and J.J. Pincus (eds)
1991 *Exploring Southeast Asia's economic past.* Melbourne: Oxford University Press. [*Australian Economic History Review* 31-1.]

Somers Heidhues, M.F.
1992 *Bangka tin and Mentok pepper; Chinese settlement on an Indonesian island.* Singapore: Institute of Southeast Asian Studies.

Spaans-van der Bijl, T. (ed.)
1991 *Tot betere tijden? Het levensverhaal van Willem van Pelt (1920-1959), rubberplanter op Sumatra.* Amsterdam: Veen.

Starink, L. and M. de Waard (eds)
1993 *Economen over de nieuwe revolutie in NRC Handelsblad.* Amsterdam: NRC Handelsblad.

Statistiek handel
1909-23 *Statistiek van den handel en de in- en uitvoerrechten in Nederlandsch-Indië over het jaar 1909-1923.* Batavia: Landsdrukkerij.

Statistiek handel, scheepvaart
1877-1909 *Statistiek van den handel, de scheepvaart en de in- en uitvoerregten in Nederlandsch-Indië over het jaar 1874-1908.* Batavia: Landsdrukkerij.

Statistiek handelsbeweging
1921 *Statistiek van de handelsbeweging der Buitenbezittingen gedurende de jaren 1917, 1918 en 1919*. Batavia: Departement van Landbouw, Nijverheid en Handel. [Mededeelingen van het Statistisch Kantoor 3.]

Statistiek intergewestelijke handel
1922-40 *Statistiek van de intergewestelijke handelsbeweging der Buitengewesten over het jaar 1921-1939*. Buitenzorg: Departement van Landbouw, Nijverheid en Handel. [Mededeelingen van het Centraal Kantoor voor de Statistiek 3-89.]

Statistisch Jaaroverzicht
1929-40 *Statistisch Jaaroverzicht van Nederlandsch-Indië*. Weltevreden: Statistisch Kantoor van het Departement van Landbouw, Nijverheid en Handel. [Also published as part of *Indisch Verslag*.]

Stoler, A.L.
1985 *Capitalism and confrontation in Sumatra's plantation belt, 1870-1979*. New Haven/London: Yale University Press.
1988 'Working and revolution; Plantation labourers and the people's militia in North Sumatra', *Journal of Asian Studies* 47:227-47.

Stroomberg, J.
1934 'De invloed van Japan op de handel van Nederland en Nederlandsch-Indië', *Tijdschrift voor Economische Geographie* 25:76-80.

Suchtelen, B.C.C.M.M. van
1939 *Neêrlands nieuwe eereschuld aan Indië*. Hilversum: Brand.

Sundrum, R.M.
1986 'Indonesia's rapid economic growth 1968-1981', *Bulletin of Indonesian Economic Studies* 22-3:33-44.

Suryadinata, L. (ed.)
1993 *Chinese adaptation and diversity; Essays on society and literature in Indonesia, Malaysia and Singapore*. Singapore: Singapore University Press.

Sutherland, H.A.
1985 'The identification of regions in colonial Southeast Asia', *Itinerario* 9-1:124-34.
1994 'Writing Indonesian history in the Netherlands', *Bijdragen tot de Taal-, Land- en Volkenkunde* 150:785-804.

Tammes, P.M.L.
1947 *De bevolkingscultuur van klapper, in het bijzonder in Oost Indonesië*. Batavia: Departement van Economische Zaken. [Mededelingen van het Departement van Economische Zaken in Nederlandsch-Indië 11.]

Taselaar, A.P.
1998 *De Nederlandse koloniale lobby; Ondernemers en de Indische politiek, 1914-1940*. Leiden: Research School CNWS. [PhD thesis, Leiden University.]

Tergast, G.C.W.C.
1931-32 'De invoer van rijst in de Buitengewesten', *Landbouw* 7:195-235.
1932 'Telling der rubberbomen in Palembang', *Economisch Weekblad van Nederlandsch-Indië* 1:769-73.

The Siauw Giap
1989 'Socio-economic role of the Chinese in Indonesia, 1820-1940', in: A. Maddison and G. Prince (eds), *Economic growth in Indonesia 1820-1940*, pp. 159-83. Dordrecht/Providence: Foris. [KITLV, Verhandelingen 137.]

Thee Kian Wie
1977 *Plantation agriculture and export growth; An economic history of East Sumatra, 1863-1942*. Jakarta: Indonesian Institute of Sciences (LIPI).
1980 'Historical research and economic development', in: L. Blussé, H.L. Wesseling and G. Winius (eds), *History and underdevelopment; Essays on underdevelopment and European expansion in Asia and Africa*, pp. 53-76. Leiden: Leiden University, Centre for the History of European Expansion.
1989a 'Industrialization in India and Indonesia', *Itinerario* 13-1:133-54.
1989b 'The development of Sumatra, 1820-1940', in: A. Maddison and G. Prince (eds), *Economic growth in Indonesia 1820-1940*, pp. 133-58. Dordrecht/Providence: Foris. [KITLV, Verhandelingen 137.]
1994 *Explorations in Indonesian economic history*. Jakarta: Lembaga Penerbit Fakultas Ekonomi, Universitas Indonesia.
1996 'Economic policies in Indonesia during the period 1950-1965, in particular with respect to foreign investment', in: J.Th. Lindblad (ed.), *Historical foundations of a national economy in Indonesia, 1890s-1990s*, pp. 315-329. Amsterdam: North Holland. [KNAW, Verhandelingen, Afd. Letterkunde, Nieuwe Reeks, 167.]

Thomas, K.D. and J. Panglaykim
1976 'The Chinese in the South Sumatran rubber industry; A case study in economic nationalism', in: J.A.C. Mackie (ed.), *The Chinese in Indonesia; Five essays*, pp. 139-98. Melbourne: Nelson.

Tideman, J.
1918 'De koelieordonnantie en hare toepassing', *Koloniale Studiën* 2-2:31-74.
1919 'De huisvesting der contractkoelies ter Oostkust van Sumatra', *Koloniale Studiën* 3-2:125-49.
1938 *Djambi*. Amsterdam: Koloniaal Instituut.

Todaro, M.P.
1989 *Economic development in the Third World*. New York: Longman. [First edition 1977.]
1992 *Economics for a developing world; An introduction to principles, problems and policies for development*. New York: Longman. [First edition 1977.]

Touwen, L.J.
1990a 'Experiences in data archiving; Developing the History of European Expansion Databank. A pilot project of the Netherlands Historical Data Archive', in: *L'Ordinateur et le métier d'historien; Volume des actes du IVe Congrès 'History and Computing'*, pp. 129-36. Bordeaux: Maison des Pays Iberiques.
1990b 'Statistics on Anglo-African trade 1699-1808', in: M. Johnson, J.Th. Lindblad and R. Ross (eds), *Anglo-African trade in the eighteenth century; English statistics on African trade, 1699-1808*, pp. 53-96. Leiden: Centre for the History of European Expansion.

1991 'Voordeel van veelzijdigheid; De economische ontwikkeling van Palembang en Djambi tussen 1900 en 1942', *Economisch en Sociaal-Historisch Jaarboek* 54:134-82.

1992 'Computerizing the foreign trade statistics of colonial Indonesia', in: A.H.P. Clemens, J.Th. Lindblad and L.J. Touwen, *Regional patterns in foreign trade 1911-1940*, pp. 13-16. Amsterdam: Royal Tropical Institute.

1993 'Electronic bookshelf or electronic library? An examination of the Medieval and Early Modern Data Bank', *Historical Social Research* 18-2:213-29.

1999 'Moving towards a national economy in late colonial Indonesia', *Itinerario* 23-3/4:145-61.

2000a 'Entrepreneurial strategies in indigenous export agriculture in the Outer Islands of colonial Indonesia, 1925-1938', in: P. Boomgaard and I. Brown (eds), *Weathering the storm; The economies of Southeast Asia in the 1930s depression*, pp. 143-70. Singapore: ISEAS, Leiden: KITLV Press.

2000b 'Regional inequalities in Indonesia in the late colonial period', *Lembaran Sejarah* 3-1:102-23.

2001 *Shipping and trade in the Java Sea region 1870-1940; A collection of statistics on the major Java Sea ports*. Leiden: KITLV Press.

Trebilcock, C.

1981 *The industrialization of the continental powers, 1780-1914*. London: Longman.

Turnbull, C.M.

1982 *A history of Singapore, 1819-1975*. Kuala Lumpur: Oxford University Press. [First edition 1977.]

Turpijn, J.

1933 'Boeginese handelsprauwen', *Economisch Weekblad van Nederlands-Indië* 2:118-20.

Van der Kraan, A.

1980a *Dutch rule on Lombok 1900-1940; The development of underdevelopment*. Townsville: James Cook University of North Queensland.

1980b *Lombok; Conquest, colonization and underdevelopment, 1870-1940*. Singapore: Heinemann.

1993 'Trade, rajas, and bandars in South Bali', in: J. Butcher and H. Dick (eds), *The rise and fall of revenue farming; Business elites and the emergence of the modern state in Southeast Asia*, pp. 103-24. New York: St. Martin's Press.

Van Niel, R.

1990 'Colonialism revisited; Recent historiography', *Journal of World History* 1:109-24.

Velde, J.J. van der

1982 *Brieven uit Sumatra, 1828-1949*. Franeker: Wever.

Velsing, M.T.

1925 'De bevolkings-rubber-cultuur in de afdeeling Oeloe-Soengei, residentie Zuider- en Oosterafdeling van Borneo', *Koloniale Studiën* 9-1:200-29.

Verslag belastingdruk

1929-30 *Verslag van den belastingdruk op de Inlandsche bevolking in de Buitengewesten*. Weltevreden: Landsdrukkerij. 2 vols.

Verslag economischen toestand
1924 *Verslag van den economischen toestand der inlandsche bevolking*. Weltevreden: n.n. 2 vols.
Verslag economischen toestand en belastingdruk
1929 *Verslag van den economischen toestand en den belastingdruk met betrekking tot de inlandsche bevolking van de gewesten Oostkust van Sumatra en Lampongsche districten*. Weltevreden: Landsdrukkerij.
Vink, G.J.
1946 'Bedrijfseconomie van de bevolkingslandbouw', in: C.J.J. van Hall and C. van de Koppel (eds), *De landbouw in den Indischen Archipel*, Vol. I, pp. 239-85. 's-Gravenhage: Van Hoeve.
Vleming, J.L. (ed.)
1926 *Het Chineesche zakenleven in Nederlandsch-Indië*. Weltevreden: Landsdrukkerij.
Vogel, J.
1992 *De opkomst van het Indocentrische geschiedbeeld; Leven en werken van B.J.O. Schrieke en J.C. van Leur*. Hilversum: Verloren.
Volkstelling
1933 *Volkstelling 1930; Deel IV: Inheemse bevolking van Sumatra; Deel VII: Chineezen en andere vreemde Oosterlingen in Nederlandsch-Indië; Deel VIII: Overzicht voor Nederlandsch-Indië*. Batavia: Landsdrukkerij.
Vuuren, L. van
1941 *Nederlandsch-Indië als producent van grondstoffen voor wereldbehoeften*. Utrecht: Kemink.
Waard, J. de
1934 'De Oostkust van Sumatra', *Tijdschrift voor Economische Geographie* 25:213-21, 255-74, 282-301.
Warren, C.N. and B. van Staalduinen
1925 *De bevolkingsrubbercultuur in Nederlandsch-Indië; IV: Palembang*. Weltevreden: Landsdrukkerij.
Weidenbaum, M. and S. Hughes
1995 *The bamboo network; How expatriate Chinese entrepreneurs are creating a new economic superpower in Asia*. New York: Free Press/Simon and Schuster.
Weisfelt, J.
1972 *De Deli Spoorweg Maatschappij als factor in de economische ontwikkeling van de Oostkust van Sumatra*. Rotterdam: Bronder. [PhD thesis, Erasmus University, Rotterdam.]
Wellan, J.W.J.
1932 *Zuid-Sumatra; Economisch overzicht van de gewesten Djambi, Palembang, de Lampoengsche districten en Benkoelen*. Wageningen: Veenman.
1935 'De stad Palembang in 1935, 275 jaar geleden, als een phoenix, uit haar asch herrezen', *Koloniaal Tijdschrift* 24:215-32.
Wellenstein, E.P.
1925 Het onderzoek naar den belastingdruk op de inheemsche bevolking van Nederlandsch-Indië. Weltevreden: Kolff. [Reprint from: *Koloniale Studiën* 9-4 (1925):23-46.]

1931 *Nederlandsch-Indië in de wereldcrisis*. Weltevreden: n.n. [Publicatie, Vereeniging voor studie van koloniaal-maatschappelijke vraagstukken 19.]

Wertheim, W.F.
1956 *Indonesian society in transition; A study of social change*. The Hague: Van Hoeve.

Wesseling, H.L.
1988a *Indië verloren, rampspoed geboren, en andere opstellen over de geschiedenis van de Europese expansie*. Amsterdam: Bert Bakker.
1988b 'The giant that was a dwarf, or the strange history of Dutch imperialism', *Journal of Imperial and Commonwealth History* 16-3:58-70.
1994 'Overseas history in the Netherlands after the Second World War; Historical backgrounds, modern developments, present-day situation', *Itinerario* 18-2:97-115.

Wiener, M.J.
1995 *Visible and invisible realms; Power, magic and colonial conquest in Bali*. Chicago: Chicago University Press.

Williamson, J.G.
1965 'Regional inequality and the process of national development; A description of the patterns', *Economic Development and Cultural Change* 13:3-45. [Reprinted in: L. Needleman (ed.), *Regional analysis*, pp. 99-158. Harmondsworth: Penguin Books, 1968.]

Wolff, H.W.
1910 *People's banks; A record of social and economic success*. London: King.

Wong Lin Ken
1978 'Singapore; Its growth as an entrepot port, 1819-1941, *Journal of Southeast Asian Studies* 9:50-84.

Woude, S.M. van der
1932 'Indische herinneringen; Zwerftochten door de Riouw Archipel; Koeliewerving', *Indische Gids* 54:1-57.

Wijnaendts van Resandt, W.
1928 'Het verkeersvraagstuk in Midden-Sumatra', *Koloniale Studiën* 12-2:69-88.

Young, K.R.
1990 'The cultivation system in West Sumatra; Economic stagnation and political stalemate', in: A. Booth, W.J. O'Malley and A. Weidemann (eds), *Indonesian economic history in the Dutch colonial era*, pp. 90-110. New Haven: Yale Center for International Area Studies.

Zanden, J.L. van
1985 *De economische ontwikkeling van de Nederlandse landbouw in de negentiende eeuw 1800-1914*. Wageningen: Afdeling Agrarische Geschiedenis, Landbouwhogeschool. [A.A.G. Bijdragen 25.]

Zed, Mestika
1996 'The dualistic economy of Palembang in the late colonial period', in: J.Th. Lindblad (ed.), *Historical foundations of a national economy in Indonesia, 1890s-1990s*, pp. 249-64. Amsterdam: North Holland. [KNAW, Verhandelingen, Afd. Letterkunde, Nieuwe Reeks, 167.]

Zwaag, J. van der
1991 *Verloren tropische zaken; De opkomst en ondergang van de Nederlandse handel- en cultuurmaatschappijen in het voormalige Nederlands-Indië*. Meppel: Feniks Pers.

Index

The index does not include the names of the individual Outer Provinces since these occur frequently throughout the book.

www.ingramcontent.com/pod-product-compliance
Ingram Content Group UK Ltd.
Pitfield, Milton Keynes, MK11 3LW, UK
UKHW041335110926
15112UKWH00015B/45

9 789067 181594